THE ARCHIVAL IMPERMANENCE PROJECT

Ross Lipman was born in Chicago in 1963 and began making 8mm films at age 13. After graduating from the University of Michigan in 1985, he spent the next several decades as a nomad, with stops in London, Santa Fe, Budapest, a coal mining town in Slovakia, and San Francisco, before settling in Los Angeles. In his capacity as Senior Film Restorationist at UCLA Film & Television Archive, where he served for 17 years, and since then with his own company, Corpus Fluxus, he has restored films from the dawn of cinema to the present era. He was a 2008 recipient of Anthology Film Archives' Preservation Honors, and is a three-time winner of the National Society of Film Critics' Heritage Award.

In parallel to his restoration work, Lipman's films have screened throughout the world and been collected by museums and institutions including the Academy Film Archive, Anthology Film Archives, Northeast Historic Film, the Oberhausen Kurzfilm Archive, Budapest's Balázs Béla Studios, and Munich's Sammlung Goetz. His feature documentary *Notfilm* was named one of the 10 best films of the year by *Artforum*, *Slate*, and many others. His writings on film history, technology, and aesthetics have been published in *Artforum*, *Sight and Sound*, and numerous academic books and journals.

For further information see www.corpusfluxus.org.

THE ARCHIVAL IMPERMANENCE PROJECT

FILM RESTORATION POETICS, CASE STUDIES, AND HISTORIES

Ross Lipman

Sticking Place Books
New York

© Sticking Place Books 2025
© Ross Lipman

www.stickingplacebooks.com

Cover image: photocollage by Charlotte Pryce and Ross Lipman, 2025.
Pacific Ocean, December 24, 2014 and microphotograph of cross-section of Kodachrome film emulsion.
Back cover image: photograph of Ross Lipman © Kris Cohen.

All rights reserved

No part of this book may be reproduced, stored in or introduced into a retrieval system, or transmitted, in any form or by any means (electronic, mechanical, photocopying, recording or otherwise) without the written permission of the publishers, except in the case of brief quotations embodied in critical articles or reviews.

ISBN 978-1-942782-91-9

Contents

Acknowledgements   xi

Introduction: The Persistence of Revision   xv

I. POETICS

On Restoration

    Technical Aesthetics in the Preservation of Film Art
        with particular reference to the small-format experimental film   3

    In Search of the Lacuna: The Elusive Art of Film Preservation   9

    The Gray Zone: A Restorationist's Travel Guide   13

On Viewing and the Cinematic Experience

    In Search of Sight-Specific Cinema   41

    Babel: The Remake   45

    A New Model for Moving Image Museums   47

    The Archival Impermanence Project
        or: Performing Cinema in the Age of the Death of Everything   57

II. CASE STUDIES

Essays and Lectures

    On Pre-cinema Moving Images
        Eadweard Muybridge, Zoopraxographer (Thom Andersen, 1975)   65

On Classical Film Restoration Models
    Tillie's Punctured Romance (Mack Sennett, 1914)   75

On Archival Documentaries and Compilation Films
    The Times of Harvey Milk (Rob Epstein, 1984)   95

On Digital Restoration's Relation to Film, and Multi-versioning
    CROSSROADS (Bruce Conner, 1976)   107

Short Takes

On Secondary Authors
    Faces (John Cassavetes, 1968)   121

On Disparities Between Artists' Intentions and the Historical Record
    Wanda (Barbara Loden, 1970)   127

On Parallel Digital and Analog Workflows
    The Juniper Tree (Nietzchka Keene, 1990)   133

On Analog Video Works
    Hoop Dreams (Steve James, 1994)   139

On Conceptual Factors in Restoration Strategy
    The Man Without a World (Eleanor Antin, 1991)   147

On Films Without Authoritative Versions I
    Fireworks (Kenneth Anger, 1947 / 195x / 196x / 198x, etc.)   153

On Films Without Authoritative Versions II
    The Innerview (Richard Beymer, 1973 / 1975, etc.)   163

On the Fading of Non-representational Color
    Time of the Heathen (by Peter Kass, 1961)   173

On Non-narrative Fiction
    Nightshift (by Robina Rose, 1981)   179

On Re-restoration
    Killer of Sheep (by Charles Burnett, 1977)   185

III. HISTORIES

Essays and Lectures

    On *Shadows* (1957/9)
        Mingus, Cassavetes, and the Birth of a Jazz Cinema   191

    On *The Exiles* (1961)
        The Savage Heart of Kent Mackenzie   229

    On Samuel Beckett's *Film* (1965)
        Reframing Berkeley: The Form of Non-being   255

    On Competing Histories of American Experimental Film
        My Art is Better Than Your Art, or:
        Skill and Dilettantism in Canon Formation   275

Short Takes

    American Neorealism 1948 — Present   295
    Series details, screening introductions, and program notes for:

        In the Street / The Quiet One   301
        The Savage Eye   304
        On the Bowery / Shadows   305
        The Cool World   307
        Spring Night Summer Night   308
        Bushman   312
        The Visitors   314
        Neorealist shorts   315
        Killer of Sheep / Bless Their Little Hearts   318
        Frownland   322
        The Other Side   323

    Short Takes — People
    Biographical texts and tributes to:

        Barbara Loden   325
        Stephen Lighthill   331
        Barney Rossett   333
        Tom Chomont   335
        Sid Laverents   337
        Bruce Baillie   339
        Artur Aristakisian   341

Short Takes—Films
Film screening introductions and program notes for:

Dawn to Dawn	346
The Connection	347
Gamperaliya	351
Sunday / Point of Order!	354
Come Back to the 5 & Dime, Jimmy Dean, Jimmy Dean	357
Ornette: Made in America	362
Matewan	366
The Sid Saga	370

APPENDICES

Teaching resources — 373

    Some Notes on Color — 374

    Some Notes on Close-up Photography — 385

Early publications

    Problems of Independent Film Preservation — 389

    A Brief Note on Dye Stability — 401

Sample Preservation Histories — 403

    Documents prepared for UCLA Film & Television Archive: films by Kenneth Anger — 404

Sample Production and Migration History

    Document prepared for the Bruce Conner Family Trust: A MOVIE — 413

A Note on Sound — 421

Bibliography: Complementary Video Works — 425

Index — 427

This book is dedicated, with all the affection of an inquisitive stray cat who showed up at the door and was met graciously, to the three mentors who most profoundly inspired it: Rudolf Arnheim, Dennis Couzin, and Robert Gitt.

Acknowledgements

I must begin with a thank you to Paul Cronin and the crazy utopian project that is his Sticking Place Books. In prior years I'd received a nice publication offer from a respected academic press, but struggled with their protocols, and found myself unable to bring my signature to contract. So I lingered, floating in this purgatory, until I met an outlier who could offer the flexibility I sought.

The result is a book with unusual structure. Some of its aspects are quite practical—intended for working archivists and teachers. Some of it is historical, of hopeful appeal to cinephiles and those seeking to learn more about the films they love. Other sections are meditative, for those who dream. Woven through these disparate threads is a notion I first heard marked by my colleague Rick Prelinger, who distinguished between The Archive, as discussed by theorists, and archives (small "a"), where living people work and research. This book, even when dreaming, is firmly grounded in the latter. It is in this spirit that I thank some of the many colleagues who also dwell there and helped in ways large and small.

Restorations tend to be collaborative, so I must first express my gratitude to a small handful of colleagues with whom I've established particularly close collaborations over the years: Vincent Paul-Boncour, Antonella Bonfanti, Jillian Borders, Dave Cetra, Peter Conheim, Daniela Currò, Kate Dollenmayer, Dennis Doros, Andrew Drapkin, Raymond Foye, Letizia Gatti, Elena Gorfinkel, Jere Guldin, Amy Heller, Shawn Jones, Doug Ledin, Jeff Lambert, Paul Malcolm, Denise Marques, Sabrina Negri, Joe Olivier, Jesse Pires, John Polito, Celine Ruivo, Jason Sanders, Jon Shibata, Amy Sloper, Walt Rose, Michelle Silva, and Steve Wiener.

Of course there are many others who could easily fit into the above category, but to keep things flowing, order is helpful, and so I'll follow this with some dear colleagues at institutions I've worked with over the years, enabling many of the projects discussed. I should begin with the two archives at which I worked.

At UCLA Film & Television Archive and Stanford Theatre Laboratory, in addition to those included above, I'd like to single out Jeff Bickel, Mimi Brody, Alejandra Espasande, Susan Etheridge, May Hong HaDuong, Steven Hill, Charles Hopkins, Lucy Laird, Sharol Olson, Mark Quigley, Amos Rothbaum, Cheng-Sim Lim, Dave Tucker, Todd Wiener, and Tim Wilson.

At the Pacific Film Archive, I'd also like to thank Kathy Geritz, Nancy Goldman, Edith Kramer, Kate McKay, and Susan Oxtoby.

An essential part of my work is made possible by the extraordinary skill and dedication of colleagues at the laboratories. Here, I should begin with my current teammates at Illuminate Hollywood: Sandy Crawford, Christopher Dusendschön, Jim Hardy, Jason Ruitenbach, Shane Strickland, Bill Tayman, and Steve Weiner (again).

In the sound department, joining John Polito at Audio Mechanics are Clay Dean and Oki Miyano. Meanwhile, Simon Daniel has been doing many wonderful transfers and shooting all my track negatives for decades.

At Fotokem, I should further single out Alistor Arnold, Mike Broderson, Andrew Oran, Angelique Perez, Josh Rushton, Scott Thompson, and Kim Young.

At Film Technology: Ralph Sargent, Roy Siriwattanakamol, and Alan Stark.

At Colorlab: Constance Critchlow, Scott Mueller, AJ Rohner, and Vinny Terlizzi.

Then there are the many fine organizations with which I've been able to partner over the years:

At the Academy Film Archive and Academy Museum: Cassie Blake, Tuni Chatterji, Brian Drischell, Hyesung ii, Joe Lindner, Taylor Morales, Mike Pogorzelski, K.J. Relth-Miller, Sean Savage, Teague Schneiter, Mark Toscano, Dan Wagner, and Mae Woods.

At Arbelos: David Marriott and Ei Toshinari.

At Anthology Film Archives, I should single out Evelyn Emile, John Klacsmann, Andrew Lampert, John Mhiripiri, and Jed Rapfogel.

At the British Film Institute: James Bell, Julie Pierce, Giulia Saccagna, Kieron Webb, and Doug Weir.

At Smithsonian NMAAHC: Walter Forsberg and Blake McDowell.

At Eye Filmmuseum: Anna Abrahams, Giovanna Fossati, and Simona Monizza.

At L'Immagine Ritrovata: Davide Pozzi and Elena Tammaccaro.

Of course, many other dear colleagues, at institutions or out in the wild, have all contributed in ways large and small to the body of work discussed here. Thanks go to Barry Allen, Brecht Andersch, Snowden Becker, Viviana García Besné, Bill Brand, Serge Bromberg, Kevin Brownlow, Suzanne Ceresko, Jean Conner, Grover Crisp, Aaron Cutler, Claire Didier, Stefan Drössler, Skip Elsheimer, Leo Enticknap, Dino Everett, Carolyn Faber, Paula Félix-Didier, Ally Field, Dave Filipi, Nick Fraccaro, Michael Friend, Gregg Garvin, Julia Gibbs, Marsha Gordon, Kim Gott, Kimberly Granholme, Ronald Grant, Oliver Hanley, Miriam Hansen, Esther Harris, Alex Horwath, Fabio Huerta, Martin Humphries, Bruce Jenkins, Malin Kan, Christopher King, Martin Koerber, Tim Lanza, Lumia Lightsmith, Regina Longo, Jeff Martin, Jeff Masino, Nicola Mazzanti, Don McMahon, Alice Moscoso, Tamao Nakahara, Gina Napolitan, Sungji Oh, Magnus Rosborn, Jonathan Rosenbaum, Sukhdev Sandhu, Isabella Scaffidi, Regina Schlagnitweit, Mariana Shellard, Anthony Slide, Jacqueline Stewart, Dan Streible, Amy Taubin, Kathy Thomson, Gary Vanisian, Timoleon Wilkins, and Elzbieta Wysocka.

On many occasions I've been fortunate to work personally with directors, cinematographers, estates, and families. Thanks here for the honor of working with Thom Andersen, Eleanor Antin, Bruce Baillie, Richard Beymer, Charles Burnett, Tom Chomont, Erik Daarstad, Nancy de Antonio, Julie Dash, Harry Dodge, Dan Drasin, Rob Epstein, Joanna Frank, Lelia Goldoni, Steak Haus, Silas Howard, Steve James, Sid and Charlotte Laverents, Ed Lachman, Diane and Kiki Mackenzie, Frederick Marx, John Morrill, Patrick Moyroud, Marva and Thomas Nabili, Gordon Quinn, Maggie Renzie, Barney and Astrid Rosset, Robina Rose, Nancy Savoca, John Sayles, Randolph Sellars, Dan Talbot, Haskell Wexler, and Billy Woodberry.

I also extend gratitude to those who in so many ways enable our work: the funders. Individual funding credits accompany the case studies, but for their exceptional commitment to the field I must single out The Film Foundation, National Film Preservation Foundation, and the Packard Humanities Institute.

Last but not least, I must thank my wife, Charlotte Pryce, and our son, Ish Lipman, for their ongoing support, insight and patience—not just through the course of this book's long genesis, but in all aspects of our lives. They know what I mean when I speak of patience.

As for the individuals to whom this book is dedicated, there is more to be said about them in the introduction.

Introduction
The Persistence of Revision

> The more a thing tends to be permanent, the more it tends to be lifeless.
> Alan Watts, *The Veil of Reality*

In 1957, Rudolf Arnheim, by then one of the world's most eminent art historians, returned to his early days as a film theorist and published his seminal *Film as Art* in English. The original German text was first published back in 1933, and in his new introduction, he wrote, "It frequently happens that a guiding theme, whose development will occupy a man's later life, takes shape around his twentieth year."[1] His early vision arose from his studies at that age with the celebrated psychologists Max Wertheimer and Wolfgang Köhler. Their development of Gestalt theory at the turn of the 20th century advanced the notion that the perceiving senses and brain actively seek pattern and structure amidst the flood of stimuli they receive—and in so doing, help create and define such structures themselves.

Their young student, in turn, sought to show that "artistic and scientific descriptions of reality are cast in molds that derive not so much from the subject matter, as from the properties of the medium employed."[2] In particular, Arnheim set out to test his mentors' ideas against the hard stone of cinema, recorded as it was by a mechanical, non-human vision. Being mechanical, it should in theory not hold the biases of human perception, and record things more clinically. Yet he found that in cinema's very limitations and imperfections—its failures at clinical representation—lay room for intervention, and hence its capacity as an artform. *Film as Art* arose from that effort, and stands today as one of the earliest instances we have of a fully developed theory of moving images.

So, too, I've found, can technical limitations play an essential part in the quixotic task of moving image restoration. Arnheim's comments about the origins of his visions struck me upon recently rereading them. When I turned twenty myself—in 1983—I was an undergraduate at the University of Michigan in Ann Arbor, where Arnheim had retired from Harvard, and was teaching occasional courses in an emeritus position. I was startled and honored that he allowed me, a wide-eyed undergrad, into his small graduate seminars over the next two years, and to this day wonder what he saw in me. He would cease teaching entirely around the time I left Ann Arbor, and I was one of his last students.

My goal in working with Arnheim back then was to further my pursuit of a non-existent major: studying film by way of its component arts, across different departments in the university. It would encompass visual, linguistic, and audio artforms, and of course, their interaction. The self-invented major never materialized, and while ideas did, I never imagined that, some forty years later, those ideas would grow into the book you're now holding.

The essays that follow will delineate the ways in which the intangible concept of an artwork dances with the physical world in the creation, and re-creation, of it. In these introductory thoughts, however, I hope to trace my own journey in more detail. One's ideas often have an odd interaction with the events of one's life, and so it was with me.

In parallel to my aesthetic interests, I was in the immediately following years a characteristically rebellious twentysomething. After collecting my undergraduate degree, I found myself living in a squat in East London, and working days in the bookshop of the Royal Academy. One morning, while standing on the landing of my squat, a somewhat nebulous but inspiring vision arose of a future wherein I'd earn my living by working on quality films—most likely documentaries—and find time on the side to make my own eccentric works, which stood little chance of financial success.

So it was that I eventually abandoned the squat, and by a circuitous route made my way to an eccentric private film school in New Mexico. There I learned many practical skills, as well as a lot of doggerel. Its patriarchal founder enforced, among other things, the notion that one should always exaggerate one's qualifications to command unearned respect. I suppose that fell in line with the old chestnut, "fake it 'till you make it." Despite having my own interests in the boundaries of fact and fiction, I quickly fell afoul of him, even being suspended for the crime of shooting my own camera exercise rather than directing others to do it, as industry protocols and the school mandated. I eventually dropped out.

Resurfacing in Chicago, I called Astro Labs on Erie Street, seeking advice on how to create some complex visual effects for a film I meant to make. The project was never begun, let alone completed, and I'm relieved that today I can't even recall what it was. But on the advice of the New Mexican patriarch, I falsified a production company name to legitimize myself, and got Astro's owner on the phone. It took about one minute for him to see through the bluff. He basically told me to cut the crap, and go take Dennis Couzin's course in optical printing at Columbia College. It was by this roundabout route that I eventually got precisely where I needed to be—which was in Dennis' classroom.

There is an adage that says "when the student is ready, the teacher will appear." Dennis Couzin, who was himself fond of Arnheim, took his principles to a cellular level: breaking down cinema to its most basic components, like the properties of light and the fundamentals of photochemistry. These natural principles were the microcosm that mirrored the macrocosm. As above, so below… Or is it vice versa?

Such questions might seem irrelevant to filmmaking but they're invaluable in restoration. It was Dennis who would help bridge the gap between Arnheim's theory and the practice into which I'd later descend. It's from him that I learned the techniques of film printing and processing, how to operate lab equipment, how to alter standard practices, and how to think about it all. He was the archetypal mad scientist and also an outlaw, at least in the academic sense—far too individualist to fit comfortably in any institution. It's for this reason that his relative anonymity is proportional to Arnheim's renown. To this day, Dennis argues tooth and nail against every proposition I put to him. I doubt I was the student he sought, but I was the one he got, and he's done a noble job of tolerating me through the years.

Having dropped out of the film school in New Mexico, I stayed in Chicago and on Dennis' advice, switched to his other class at the School of the Art Institute of Chicago (SAIC). There, for a single fee of $180, I spent a full year as a "student at large," working alongside the graduate students and meeting my future wife, the experimental filmmaker Charlotte Pryce. I never got my MFA, but I got a hell of an education. But all good things come to an end, and so Charlotte and I left the city in 1990.

After a few years abroad we returned to the U.S., and it was on a cross-country Amtrak train to San Francisco that another vision arose. Digital cinema was in its infancy then, and though it was of horrifically low quality, the writing was on the wall. During that train ride, I thought that analog film could survive another ten years or so, at which point it would likely live primarily in museums and other rarified contexts. There had to be professions ahead that would serve to keep it alive.

I was aware of film archives already, having been inspired by a brilliant film researcher named Ray Hemenez, who had visited the odd documentary school in New Mexico. Ray used to talk about "films of need"—those works produced by some vital force that compelled their existence—and it was his dedication and influence that led to my procuring a part-time job doing film research back in Chicago, during my SAIC days. So in that sense I was a primed canvas. I'd also frequented the cinematheques and seen some restorations, but never considered the process before.

Thus, in that train ride, I "invented" the idea of restoration in my head, utterly unaware of the fine tradition that was already established. Someone would need to preserve photochemical film culture: why not me? This was in 1993, three years before the founding of the National Film Preservation Foundation, so I was at least a bit ahead of the curve.

By 1995, I had managed to secure a position at the Pacific Film Archive (PFA) in Berkeley. I worked as their cataloger, and although I was too junior a staff member to be assigned preservation work, it was soon recognized that I had a deeper grounding in lab work than anyone on staff, and so I was allowed to shadow their preservation projects. As a result I wrote my first technical essay, "Problems of Independent Film Preservation," included here as an appendix. Edith Kramer, the PFA's brilliant curator, was a formidable presence and initially mortified that my text might prove embarrassing to the archive. (I was a bit of a wildcard, and it included some informal anecdotes.) Luckily no embarrassment arose, and she forgave me.

I say "luckily" because another key event happened at this time. In the mid-1990s, it's safe to say that UCLA Film & Television Archive set the bar for excellence in film restoration.

That's largely due to their preservation department's visionary founder, Robert Gitt. During my PFA years, Bob presented his celebrated "Century of Sound" illustrated lecture at the archive's theater, and upon seeing it, my slow-developing path to restoration became an obsession. In Bob I found someone who could help me bring the inspirational principles and fundamental techniques I'd learned from Rudolf Arnheim and Dennis Couzin fully into the practical world. In the wake of his presentation I got to know him, and some years later, when a position opened as his assistant, he hired me. This was in no small part thanks to Edith. My direct supervisor at the PFA was the wonderful Nancy Goldman, who was Head of Cataloging. Bob didn't know her, and unbeknownst to me, called Edith instead, to scope me out. Luckily, Edith gave me high marks, despite my guerilla authoring of that essay.

I should add that, were I to have applied for the same job today, I might not have been hired at all. At the time of the job posting, the graduate degree programs in film archiving were in their infancy. As such, their diplomas did not stand out, and Bob took a chance on me. In the intervening years the programs have become more well established, and most archival jobs now require applicants to have completed one of them. Bob had only completed an undergraduate course of study himself, at Dartmouth, and was, happily, open to the merits of one who'd created his own path to the archives. But times change, and just as I was one of Arnheim's last students, so was I also one of the last of that era of pre-degree archivists.

I cannot say enough about Bob's role in my development, and also his role in defining the larger field of restoration. Though he was a leading figure in his day, times recede fast, and not as many in the community know of him today. But it's not an exaggeration to say that, (alongside Kevin Brownlow and others), he took esoteric workflows from the underground world of film collectors and elevated them to a sophisticated practice that still underlies restoration principles in the contemporary digital world.[3] Above all, he sought to bring the highest standards of picture and sound quality to the screen—and to a startling degree, managed to succeed.

It was now 1999. Although I began my stint at UCLA in an assistant's role, it soon became clear that Bob's workload was far too big, and his greatest need was for me to direct my own projects. So within the year I was doing that, and from those projects came many of the case histories contained in this book. In turn, from those essays arose an increasing articulation of my views on restoration.

So what were, or are, those views? Unsurprisingly, they've changed over time. But I'm in good company in this regard. In her essential text, *From Grain To Pixel*, Giovanna Fossati notes the many paradigmatic shifts in cinema culture over the years, and observes that "ethics… need to be placed within the same transitional framing [as moving image culture itself]."[4] The same applies equally to aesthetics, methodology, and theory. The subtitle of her book, *The Archival Life of Film in Transition*, speaks directly to this. It's all moving. As in the Tao, the only constant is change itself.

The salient change of recent times is of course the transition from photochemical to digital imaging. While archival practice might still be focused on film, the work around it began integrating the new technologies. Just prior to the line I quoted above, Fossati wrote that "we are coming to the point where the choice between preserving film-born film as data rather than as film… will be legitimate and ethically defensible."[5] It's hence no surprise to find that questions relating to this issue run through the pages of this book. That said, the ways in which those questions are discussed has changed in notable ways over the years, and it's useful to trace their precise course of evolution.

On an unwittingly parallel track to Fossati, the present work grew from the ashes of an idea I had back in the 1990s for a book called *Grain*. Its premise was that the granular structure of silver halides in a film's emulsion represented a holistic, organic imaging system that's of a piece with our natural world. This holistic model would be contrasted with digital representation systems, which—being binary abstractions—are detached from the physical world they represent. A film's grain structure is random, whereas digital video is in essence a regulated grid of 1s and 0s. The uniform structure of pixels represented what I ultimately viewed as the gentrification of chaos.

    I sought to trace these tendencies back through time within the larger mimetic tradition of representational art: the analog centuries, when organic means of rendering the world were the only ones available to artists. At some point along the way, well before the age of digitization, these integrated models of representation began to bifurcate into a distinction between content and carrier. This separation would reach its apotheosis in the digital image's complete disembodiment of the things it encodes.

    It was a grandiose idea… and far above my own ability to execute it. The idea never materialized in that form, and when Fossati's far more developed book arose, with its resonant title and focus on archiving, I was freed from the task of writing something I was frankly, unqualified to write anyway. So I continued with the essays I'd been writing, aware that they danced around my underlying concerns, with no need of tying them together.

    Now, in grouping them here, their own internal story arises. *The Archival Impermanence Project* joins a diverse assembly of academic and non-academic texts, illustrated lecture adaptations, and archival documents. It's broken into three sections: Poetics, Case Studies, and Histories, along with attendant appendices. Though discrete, the essays talk to each other with constant cross-references, and, by accident, work cumulatively, despite slippage and outright contradiction. As a grouping, they mark the change from singular notions of organic authenticity to a multi-versioned world; one that is "beyond the physical body," or "post-medium"—at least temporarily.

    While constantly engaged with the strange interaction of the technical and the aesthetic, the early writings seem to dwell a bit more in the former, and the later writings, more in the latter. This no doubt reflects my own personal journey. In a journal entry as far back as 1987 I find myself writing, "I must come to terms with the technology that makes my life possible." When I wrote that, I was mid-air on a flight back to the US from a failed trip to Brazil, in my tumultuous mid-twenties. What the heck compelled me to think that, at that moment? It was just a few months before I'd arrive in New Mexico, where I'd begin addressing that very task, by learning how film worked. Somewhere, amidst the chaos of my youth, I knew what I needed. With hindsight, I see a traditional arc unfolding: my younger, sharper mind taking on things requiring a high level of processing, and the older mind bringing a wider, more nuanced perspective.

In 2017 my colleague Sabrina Negri invited Giovanna Fossati, myself, and some others to join an archival panel at the annual conference of the Society of Cinema and Media Studies, which was taking place in Chicago. I used the occasion to revisit some of the essays I'd written, and in so doing, noted points of development between them. In 1996, I had written:

> For a preservation to be considered authentic, *the method of duplication* should accurately reflect the nature of the work being duplicated.

And then:

> Benjamin's notions of "unique testimony" and "aura" may thus be interpreted as the expressive and powerful aspects of a work present in its original physical viewing form. Any material transformation of a work which does not preserve those qualities may be considered a transposition to another medium.[6]

At this point, I was firmly in an Arnheimian world in which aesthetics were organically tied to their plastic form, and an inseparable bond existed between them.

By 2009, the same year that *From Grain To Pixel* was published, I was writing,

> The choices made (by a preservationist) may make the difference between an effort that is faithful to the spirit of the work and one that is not.

I was speaking specifically of preserving works that have multiple past iterations (i.e., different imprints), and continued,

> You'll note that I've used the word *faithful* in describing a rendition, and carefully avoided *authentic*, a term I've used elsewhere in the past. There's a reason for this. When there is no definitive work to preserve, *authenticity* is impossible.[7]

The implications extend beyond the case in point. These quotations are pulled from "The Gray Zone," which remains to this day the most concise articulation of my approach to restoration. In comparing the propositions above with my thoughts of 1996 that preceded them, one finds notions of "authenticity" being supplanted by a different aim: that of "faithfulness."

This evolution was in no small part enabled by my increasing realization that good things were now possible in the digital realm; a notion I'd previously questioned. When digital video was first coming into use in the 1990s, the quality was remarkably low, and I felt it was an unsuitable medium for many audiovisual tasks, as it could not then create nuanced renditions of light, color, or detail. But things would soon change.

"The Gray Zone" anticipates that change. Its ideas were first presented in lecture form, but as noted, not published until 2009.[8] It's no accident that *From Grain To Pixel* came out concurrently, for we were all responding to the same events; situated precisely in the last fleeing moments of film's dominion over the archival field. Just a few years later, the archives and studios would begin slowly, then quickly, abandoning photochemical preservation in their workflows. The thoughts grew in parallel, and by 2012, I was beginning to question the nature of restoration itself:

> Under current conditions of relentless technological transformation, moving-image conservation, preservation, and restoration may no longer be seen as guarantors of timelessness but, increasingly, as dynamic functions of the present historical moment….

And,

> … What was formerly thought of as a singular work may now be seen as a constantly changing entity as it is repeatedly presented over time—here projected as a photochemical print; there digitally reconstituted for all manner of size and screen.[9]

The essay from which these quotes are taken, "Conservation at a Crossroads," notes the transformation of my practice from one that was primarily photochemical to one that resulted in multiple editions intended to exist alongside each other; a practice I called versioning, or multi-editioning. Would the photochemical print in a multi-edition of a film-originated work be inherently more "authentic" than its digital counterpart? Not necessarily.

As just one example, there is no laboratory I know of that currently makes 16mm "filmout" prints[10] by means of a laser recorder. Rather, a number of home-made devices that rephotograph a monitor tend to be used, and these invariably reduce sharpness considerably, while also affecting tonal range and color. One thus might have a blurry, low-quality 16mm preservation print of a sharp original, and a sharp, well-rendered video version. Neither might be "authentic" but both might be faithful, in their own way.

Similarly, my ideas on "digital restoration" changed over time. One of my earliest projects to integrate such tools was the Academy Award-winning documentary *The Times of Harvey Milk*. Its workflow is discussed in the 2003 case study presented here,[11] where I propose that the whole notion of "digital restoration" is an oxymoron for film-based works: "One can't restore something to a form in which it didn't originally exist."[12] In the ensuing years I would rail against the countless DVDs released that billed themselves as "restorations" when they weren't accompanied by photochemical workflows. To me, such efforts should more accurately be called *digital remastering*. But somewhere along the way, that hardline position became untenable, unless I was content to play the role of crank or troll for the rest of my life. The practice was too commonplace.

On pondering the matter further, I determined that for myself, the term "digital restoration" would have another meaning entirely; one that could still be used by the DVD-releasers, but which I understood in my own way. I took the term to suggest that the cinematic image, once organically embodied in the grains of silver halide in a film's emulsion, had been severed from its body and was now floating freely in a disembodied state. There, it could be "restored" before its eventual re-incarnation in some kind of a viewing system. Hence the term "digital restoration" referred not to the film, but to its severed image. The pros and cons of such a state were of course open to interpretation—but it did seem to describe the situation.

Nowadays we are in a different epoch that largely fulfills Fosatti's prophecy: few archives are able to maintain medium integrity in their restorations of film-originated works. The vast majority of projects on which I work are completed only in digital editions. This "loss of the physical" of course extends to many other aspects of our lives. Yet there is a deceptive aspect of this notion in cinema, for our digital files still need to be reconstituted as light and sound to be perceived by a viewer. The technologies that enact those reconstitutions have their own properties and limitations. It's no doubt for this reason that the most recent texts collected here tend to focus on presentation as much as restoration proper. We can create the most high-quality edition of a film imaginable, but it's a moot point if it's then viewed in sub-standard conditions.

For an approach to these dilemmas in both areas (restoration and exhibition), I turn back to "The Gray Zone" and this thought:

> It helps to hold in mind a model of the work that is at once physical, and transcends physicality. One needs an abstracted concept of the work at hand's essence.[13]

This might seem to some an impossible task, but that is by no means a reason to abandon it, or never to start. For those up for the effort, I won't say more here, but refer you to the essay itself. I will also cite the words of Andrei Tarkovsky. Speaking of artists, he writes that

> The subject grows within him like a fruit, and begins to demand expression. It is like childbirth… The poet is not master of the situation, but a servant.[14]

So it is with restoration: the film's essence seems to grow of its own accord in the process of working.

Long before reading Tarkovsky's remarks above, I'd come to a similar place. I could see the process unfolding in UCLA's Bob Gitt, whom I could watch closely, and felt the same things myself. I would say it's a calling. Over the years I've worked with many fine colleagues, but few were like Bob. Others, with the best of intentions, might place themselves at the service of the institution that employed them, and some had less noble motivations than that. Often, institutional needs of the moment seemed to be at odds with what was best for the film being restored. Hence Bob and I developed a shadow practice of "work-arounds" to make sure the best results possible arrived on the screen, whether institutionally mandated, or budgeted, or not. This is not to suggest subversion, unethical activity, or things less severe. I merely realized that my allegiance lay less with my employers, than to the films themselves.

So it is that we set out on our seemingly impossible task. Like climbing a mountain, it's often wise to focus primarily on the steps in front of you, lest it seem too daunting. When I look at the work of the three to whom this book is dedicated, I to this day strongly feel my own failings. So too might a novice, when imaging the restorationist's true work, wonder how they could presume to enter a dialogue with a masterwork. Nonetheless, we proceed.

I previously noted that Rudolf Arnheim's *Film as Art* found the core of the medium's potential lay precisely in its *imperfections*. The same might be said for restoration: as the technology of representation changes, so do the qualities of that representation. However, those changes simultaneously create new realms of interpretation, and it's here that the restorationist lives. One works with the limitations of the medium at hand. Some things may be lost, but perhaps others gained.

In direct analogy, my own limitations as a student have hopefully led to something new in my own work. I can't do what those who inspired me did, nor should I try. But I can do something else. And so too, to the next. In this movement and flux lies its own continuity.

Many of the ideas presented here first appeared in a lecture I've presented for decades, which has changed over time, as described. That lecture's title is the same as this introduction: "The Persistence of Revision." Its content has changed, while its name remains. The same principle underlies the name of my website, Corpus Fluxus. On that site, one finds a short text, which seems a fitting place to end this prelude, and begin our book proper:

> *The act of preservation is a quarrel with the conditions of time. Our efforts to stave off the inevitable in essence just hasten it. Preserving is by definition intervening in a native state of flux.*
>
> *To restore a work is to knowingly tamper and alter, to work responsively and correctively with natural and man-made ravages of time and chance. The struggle itself is where a work is renewed: the point at which the finite object meets the infinite world it represents, a continuous act of destruction and regeneration.*

Ross Lipman, Los Angeles, January 2025

Endnotes

1. Rudolf Arnheim, *Film as Art* (California, 1957).
2. Ibid.
3. For those seeking to know more about Bob Gitt, his career, and his methodology, I recommend seeking out an interview I conducted with him on behalf of the Academy of Motion Picture Arts and Sciences' Oral History Program. For a deep dive into his actual work, I recommend his "Century of Sound" documentary series, adapted from the earlier lectures, and his documentary film, *Charles Laughton Directs* The Night of the Hunter.
4. Giovanna Fossati, *From Grain to Pixel: The Archival Life of Film in Transition* (Amsterdam, 2009).
5. Ibid.
6. "Technical Aesthetics in the Preservation of Film Art" (1998) and its original publication details can be found in the Poetics section of this book. Prior to this I'd taken an even more extreme position, suggesting that film-to-film preservation efforts that don't closely match the film-to-film printing method originally used when the film was made might be called "translations." See "Problems of Independent Film Preservation" (1996), included here as an appendix.
7. "The Gray Zone" (2009) and its original publication details can be found in the Poetics section of this book.
8. "The Gray Zone" appeared in lecture form in 2005 and 2008.
9. "Conservation at a Crossroads" and its original publication details can be found in the Case Histories section of this book.
10. "Filmout prints" refers to a process whereby a film-originated work is digitized and then output back onto photochemical filmstock, allowing it to retain its medium integrity by way of a "Digital Intermediate" step in the middle. Laser recording has long been the best method for achieving a high quality result when undertaking this process.
11. The discussion of *The Times of Harvey Milk* restoration can be found in the Case Histories section.
12. I also discuss related issues in the short documentary "The Restoration of John Cassavetes' *Shadows*," which appeared as a bonus feature on the DVD release of the film and which can currently be viewed on the Criterion Channel.
13. "The Gray Zone," op cit.
14. Andrei Tarkovsky, *Sculpting in Time* (Bodley Head, 1986).

PART ONE

POETICS

This essay grew out of an earlier piece that took a focused look at photochemical film printing challenges, some of which are of diminished relevance today. The earlier piece is presented in Appendix 2, while its successor is presented here in full. While it precedes my complete immersion in restoration practice, it nonetheless serves as an effective entry point to the concerns of this compilation. Like many an initiate, I could not ignore the immense impact of Walter Benjamin's thoughts on mechanical reproduction, and with the brashness of youth felt I might have something to add to the volume of words following in his wake. While I can only claim to have read a fraction of those words, I still find something of relevance here; particularly on the inherent ambiguity that, for me, imbues Benjamin's essential essay with much of its power.

Originally published in Big As Life: An American History of 8mm Films *(a special edition of* Cinematograph*), Museum of Modern Art/San Francisco Cinematheque, 1998. Portions of the essay are excerpted from the longer article, "Problems of Independent Film Preservation," published in the* Journal of Film Preservation, *Vol. XXV, No. 53, 1996.*

Technical Aesthetics in the Preservation of Film Art

with particular reference to the small-format experimental film

The following discussion seeks to define principles for the successful preservation of film art in a context of changing modes of production. While individual works arise inseparably from the techniques with which they were made, their subsequent reproduction can lead to a Cartesian cleaving of content and form: their entire substance may in fact be materially transformed. To help understand the nature of this problem, Walter Benjamin's notions of artistic authenticity provide an invaluable starting point. Expanding on his basic arguments, I will describe some practical dilemmas in the preservation of small-format experimental films as well as some possible solutions to those problems. Moving from specific examples to their theoretical implications, we can begin to develop a working model of film preservation which more fully integrates technical and aesthetic concerns.

Duplication and Authenticity

In his profound and deeply ambivalent essay on "The Work of Art in the Age of Mechanical Reproduction," Walter Benjamin suggests that the technology which enables us to duplicate artworks, while in one sense preserving and disseminating them, in a very fundamental way also disables them. Stressing precisely those elements of a painting which are not duplicable (its physical character and unique historical testimony to time and place of exhibition; facets subsumed in the concept of the aura) as the essential elements of its power, Benjamin posits the mass-reproduced duplicate as a hollow shell of the original art object: a disembodied ghost of a once-alive entity. Tracing the act of reproduction from the woodcut through engraving to the modern era, he pinpoints the advent of lithography, photography, and film as the point at which the trajectory of reproduction takes its plummet, by means of the speed and volume with which these media can be duplicated and made available. What our era has gained in access and multiplicity, it has lost in authenticity and spirituality.

    In a fundamental way, I believe Benjamin is correct. An abundance of inferior duplicates injures or confuses the aesthetic value of an original work, and helps contribute to a general milieu of cheapness. However Benjamin stumbles over an essential aesthetic point in his essay, which is concerned foremost with broad movements and social implications.[1] The woodcut, engraving, and for that matter the scripted play or scored musical work—as well as the motion picture (in most instances) are intended to be viewed in duplication, not their "original" rendering. He states that the woodcut "may be said to have struck at the root of the quality of authenticity,"[2] thereby grounding his definition of the concept in a singular physical presence. But it would be folly to consider all these forms intrinsically inauthentic, and I suspect Benjamin himself would not wish to go that far.[3]

    This issue demands a precise analysis, especially insofar as Benjamin's evaluation of diminished authenticity and spiritual substance is so convincing. As technology develops quickly and our perceptual skills seem to regress accordingly, it's all too tempting to let such questions fall into obscurity. I would like to suggest, though, that our notions of authenticity need not be extinguished in the age of mechanical—or even electronic—reproduction. Rather, our notions of it must be substantially transformed.

Some Issues of Printing Fidelity

The small-format artist's film would not seem an ideal vehicle with which to discuss these concerns, in that small-gauge works are often intended to be viewed in their camera-original form. I will argue, however, that the first item of consideration in preserving any film is the nature of the individual work at hand, and that the "original-specific" work is a special instance, with its own considerations. In other regards, the small-format film, because of its non-industrial intent, is an ideal vehicle for discussing the duplication and preservation of film art.

Problems of film preservation, already heightened in experimental work, demand unique considerations in the case of the small-format piece. Foremost among these, surprisingly, is the fact that most small-format works exist only in "reversal" form, with a positive image. One would think that there would be a film printing stock intended to make high-quality copies from a positive, as opposed to negative image, but this is sadly not the case. Kodak's current "internegative" stock, 7272, from which positive viewing copies can be struck, is a historical relic which actually greatly increases the final image contrast of the film it is intended to reproduce. A low-contrast positive stock intended for "TV prints" (7385) is sometimes used in conjunction with it, but this produces a desaturated look inappropriate for many subjects. And 7399, the reversal printing stock intended for this purpose, can no longer be printed with a high-quality soundtrack.[4] To even begin considering the printing and/or preservation of a small-format film (or for that matter, any film which exists only as a positive image copy), one must first address this question. But wound up within this are the unique aspects of the individual work itself.

Early in the planning of the New York Museum of Modern Art/San Francisco Cinematheque's small format-preservation project, we conducted a short series of tests to find possible printing methods. While the tests were ultimately separate from the actual project, they nonetheless provide a convenient focus point for analyzing issues and techniques. Using the Canadian firm Optimage, which employs several methods of contrast reduction, we printed outtakes from the works of Joe Gibbons, Ellen Gaine, and Scott Stark. Each piece raised different aesthetic considerations, and hence suggested different printing paths.

Gaine's films, all black-and-white Super-8, feature delicate tones and spectacular swirling grain fields. The delineations of grey were lost entirely and the granularity increased to a state of blotchiness in the first test, which consisted of a traditional blow-up to 16mm internegative and a positive print. As there is no low-con stock for B/W material we requested that Optimage run a new test, in which they decreased the developing time/temperature combination, and increased exposure. This technique of over-exposing and "pull" processing is somewhat accepted with color internegatives, where it does not entirely eliminate the contrast boost, but rather gives it a good nudge in the right direction. With Gaine's work, it did just the trick, adding some fine detail in the greys, while reducing the clotting of grain.

Stark's piece was made by respooling Standard 8mm Kodachrome into a 35mm still camera and exposing still images of his garden across the film strip without regard to its perforations. Again Optimage's standard blow-up—which included a low-con 7385 print— did not do justice to the rich detail of the images. While their method did reduce contrast, the attendant decrease in saturation diminished both the color intensity of the Kodachrome and the flickering effect caused by the irregular frame line.[5] While a conventional 16mm optical internegative would have too much contrast, we found that we could thread the needle by using the special diffusion within Optimage's printer, and striking a standard 7386 positive release print.

It is worth noting that Stark's method of making this film renders notions of a standard 24 (or 18 or 16) frames-per-second projection speed somewhat meaningless. In fact, Stark would often present the piece as a projection performance on a variable speed projector, varying the playback rate from 24 fps all the way down to 6 fps. While this effect could be simulated by step-printing, it should be pointed out that the perceptual effect of watching a single frame repeated is different than that of watching that same frame once with an extended shutter-time.[6]

This also points out the inherent flaw in step-printing an 18 fps original to 24 fps for 16mm viewing: a subtle stutter is created every sixth second. One may mask this by varying which frame is repeated, so that the stutter is less rhythmic, but complicated sequencing or manual adjustment of this is not always a practical option, and the skill with which it is done can vary widely. Ideally, if a blow-up of an 18 fps original is attempted, it will be done frame-for frame, and projected at the 18 fps rate. But as 18 fps projectors are no longer standard, many small-format film artists forsake blow-up entirely.

Gibbons' *Punching Flowers* raised other considerations. Here the low-con 7385 stock's desaturation effectively rendered the muted tones in Gibbons' original work. While this stock, intended for video-transfer prints, has too little density and richness for most purposes; in this case the subject matter demanded exactly these qualities. In fact, however, this led to another question. A companion test on regular 7386 print stock, while boosting contrast, showed such an improvement in saturation that both project coordinator Steve Anker of the Cinematheque and myself agreed it in fact looked *better* than the original. The issue then became whether in fact our aim as preservationists were best served by faithfully rendering the qualities of the original work, or in fact enhancing them. Steve preferred the more saturated ("enhanced") version for its wonderful vibrancy and dynamism, while I myself found the muted 7385 more in keeping with the work's wry meditations on nature and beauty. This is not to say that I would always opt for "preservation" over enhancement; but simply that I preferred it in this case. Of course neither interpretation is right or wrong in absolute—they remain judgments. And it is just this sort of precise judgment which is demanded of the preserving archivist.

These two approaches highlight an intriguing dilemma in film preservation. In her essay "Principles of Film Restoration," Eileen Bowser describes several different types of restored films which one might encounter.[7] Among the varying types she distinguishes between those restoration efforts which come as close as possible to simulating an existing original, to the point of including imperfections, and those which attempt to best approximate the aesthetic effect *intended* by an original work. When a scenario arises wherein both these conditions cannot be met, Bowser concludes that the former approach is usually considered preferable from an archival perspective.

Punching Flowers also brought out an issue of great relevance to the small-format film, suggested briefly earlier. Shot in handheld Super 8, it is in many ways an archetypal amateur film. The physical conditions of screening in 16mm, as well as a variety of social constructs, create more of a sense of professionalism in 16mm work than in the small-format underground or basement-screening genres. While some home movies or "actualities" footage, viewed primarily for image content, may benefit from blow-up,[8] it is quite conceivable that other works would actually *suffer* in blow-up. In fact, one quickly runs into a philosophical impasse when pondering the preservation of works whose strengths lay in their rejection of traditional notions of the permanence of art; or, as Benjamin suggests, were grounded in their unique physical form and/or temporality. Both Steve Anker and I felt that this film would ideally be viewed in an intimate, less formal small-format projection, which led us to consider instead striking a Super-8 contact print — or even reducing from a 16mm internegative. Some purists might suggest the film's themes imply it should not be duplicated or preserved at all, even in Super-8, and should be projected only as camera-original. Yet as preservationists we ultimately opted to proceed, and to employ the more stable medium of 16mm for each stage of printing. This compromise should be seen as a subjective call, in which the losses of blow-up were outweighed by the attendant advantages. Others may fairly challenge that call. At this point, the act of preservation might be seen as entering into a formal dialogue with the original work.

Toward an Aesthetics of Authentic Reproduction

I hope these brief examples have provided an indication of the types of issues that may arise in preserving the small-format artist's film. My intent has not been to provide a comprehensive overview of the topic, but rather to illustrate how technical considerations in film printing are inseparable from the specific work being printed. Motion picture film is a medium which allows mass duplication, but the methods of duplication are variable, and should be adapted to specific projects. As a principle, the direction of effort must stem from the original work, and move toward a technical solution.

With this in mind, we may begin developing our transformed notions of authenticity within the world of mechanical reproduction. Our concept may apply to those media which inherently assume duplication, as does the motion picture. For a preservation to be considered authentic, the *method of duplication* should accurately reflect the nature of the work being duplicated. At a coarse level, a process which transforms the material nature of the work would inherently be inappropriate for the preservation of art. At a finer level, the material process should consider the properties of the piece being reproduced. For the film, these properties may include color, tone, granularity, contrast, light dispersion, aspect ratio, or hundreds of other components — each weighed in relation to the form, thematics, and content of the work itself.

Benjamin's notions of "unique testimony" and "aura" may thus be interpreted as the expressive and powerful aspects of a work present in its original physical viewing form. Any material transformation of a work which does not preserve those qualities may be considered a transposition to another medium. If an established film printing method is appropriate, solutions may be more easily implemented. But it may also be necessary to stretch the limits of existing tools. Experimental artists in particular have treated the medium in a non-industrial manner, and it is not reasonable to assume that industrial standards of reproduction will do them justice.

No doubt as new technologies develop and others fade, some works will be stripped of their power the way a painting is inherently stripped in the act of reproduction itself. Borderlines of authenticity may become grey. In cases when completely authentic reproduction is impossible, the principles outlined here may serve as a guide for developing the best reproduction methods available under existing conditions. To conserve the heritage of film art, we can ask for no less than such a careful consideration of methodology, however elusive it may prove. It is the task of a film's preservers to put themselves at the service of these flickering phantoms.

Endnotes

1. While Benjamin's oeuvre lies precisely in his bold linkage of aesthetic nuance to the sociological theater in which such nuances operate, it is arguable that within this context, the social analysis of particular artistic function is the essay's primary direction of emphasis. As a Marxist, Benjamin exalts the film's ability to celebrate and politicize social dynamics, to democratize the elite arts, and to depict the detail of physical reality. He suggests that these qualities can have a distancing effect—a very nearly Brechtian one—in that they deny a meditative relationship between viewer and film. This distance becomes manifest in an ability to receive artworks in the "state of distraction" so symptomatic of our times. Benjamin sees this state as hopeful insomuch as he finds it anathematic to fascism. But his discomfort at the attendant spiritual loss is unmistakable. Therein lies the heart of the essay's ambivalence.
2. Walter Benjamin, "The Work of Art in the Age of Mechanical Reproduction," reprinted in *Illuminations* (Schocken, 1985), 243.
3. Benjamin was aware of the limitations of his definition. In particular he acknowledges the capabilities of the photographic form when he writes that "for the last time the aura emanates from the early photographs in the fleeting expression of a human face." Ibid, 226. His subsequent argument, that later photographs function in a more literal manner and often demand specific explication, helps to illustrate again that his concerns lie primarily in a historical social critique and less with the medium's inherent formal properties.
4. One can find an analysis of the technical aspects of this problem in my essay, "Problems of Independent Film Preservation," from which the present work is in part adapted.
5. Kodachrome's unique color palette poses a problem in duplication, in that no printing method available can do justice to its richness. The 7399 reversal stock designed to print from all color projection-contrast materials, including Kodachrome, is a VNF-process film, whereas Kodachrome utilizes a singular 14-step process, unique to itself. This becomes especially problematic in small-format work, where one may encounter an abundance of Kodachrome originals.
6. Super-8 projector shutters are cut to show a frame three times. A single frame step-printed twice would therefore flash six times upon projection.
7. *Griffithiana*, Anno XIII, n.38/39, Oct. 1990.
8. From a purely visual standpoint, the crucial issues are reproduction method and projected image size. If 16mm and 8mm copies of an 8mm original are projected to the same dimensions, the 16mm will often be superior—depending on the optics of the blow-up system. When the 16mm print fills a larger screen, as is often the case, the effectively greater image dispersion can increase perceived graininess.

This piece serves as a missing link between my early Benjamin-inspired musings and the more fully developed "Gray Zone." It was originally presented as a lecture at the Harvard Film Archive in December 2006, and much of that discussion is omitted here. What remains is a basic vocabulary that informs the subsequent distillation, and a time-stamped commemoration of a zeitgeist already disappearing to the winds of time. At the time of presentation I could confidently single out Read and Meyer's Restoration of Motion Picture Film *as the essential reference of the field. While still vital, that text's impact has since been surpassed by Giovanna Fossati's excellent* From Grain To Pixel, *which pursues different aims. Fossati notes in her book's subtitle that moving images live in transition, and I find a particular detail in the following text nicely highlights her point: the discussion of the presence of dirt in restorations. Now, nearly two decades have passed since this lecture, and contemporary audiences of archival cinema have largely grown to expect an immaculately cleaned image. The piece also helps establish the almost mystical process of transformation that sometimes occurs in our work.*

In Search of the Lacuna
The Elusive Art of Film Preservation

It's no coincidence that film preservation has leapt into public consciousness at the precise historic moment that motion picture film faces its potential demise in the wake of digital technology. Moving image works are more accessible than ever, while the actual viewing of projected film is becoming a specialized experience. A major aspect of our visual culture stands at risk of being forgotten, just as new digital works are creating preservation challenges for future generations.

The poignancy of our transitional epoch highlights the role of the archivist: to conserve audiovisual art and documents with an understanding of both the physical properties of a specific work, and the cultural context of its production and reception. The endeavor demands a sharp eye and a firm commitment to the advancing art of cinema in its historical context.

I must confess I paused before calling our work "The Elusive Art," as it might imply that it's perpetually unattainable. I assure you that's not the case. What I mean to suggest is that film preservation is an endeavor undertaken on unfirm ground. If you were to ask ten archivists to define "film preservation," you'd be very likely to get ten outwardly similar but substantially different answers. Practices vary widely from country to country, from archive to archive, and from laboratory to laboratory. So I'd like to offer some working definitions and guiding principles upon which we can build a common understanding.

At the broadest level, most archivists agree, we need to distinguish between preservation and access. The former would broadly cover those activities related to saving audiovisual works from physical loss, and the latter would be enabling their viewing and study. Of course the two activities ideally work in tandem, but in archival practice it's often a useful dividing point, as each field has its distinct needs, which are not identical.

From this point on the water gets a bit murky. What exactly is moving image "preservation"? While it can be traced back to at least the 1930s, the field has transformed much over time, and in fact it's only recently that we've begun to accumulate a substantive amount of literature on the topic. The field is so new, that of many wonderful works, only one is generally acknowledged to serve as an indispensable, comprehensive reference. This would be *Restoration of Motion Picture Film* by Paul Read and Mark-Paul Meyer. While it is in many ways written as a textbook or laboratory guide, it does seek to place its content in a theoretical framework. I'd like to single out one quote in particular which cuts to the heart of all our efforts in the field:

> *Film restoration is essentially duplication.... Unlike in fine arts, in film restoration the original artifact can be repaired and cleaned, but the process of self-destruction cannot be stopped. The only way to preserve these films for later generations is to duplicate them onto modern film stock.*
>
> —Read and Meyer (1)

One should further point out that in the great majority of circumstances, films are intended to be viewed in the form of reproductions or duplicates. With digital media, the question of an "original" gets transformed yet further. And as archival-quality duplication can be extremely expensive, decisions need to be made in maintaining the longevity of a collection.

At UCLA we distinguish between three basic levels of activity. It's rare that I find a pre-prepared document to be of use in defining things, but on the counter in the archive's laboratory a while back I found an old handout that works surprisingly well. Please note that the terms bear some resemblance to—but also striking differences from—their usages in art conservation parlance. To quote just the beginning:

> *Conservation is the storage and maintenance of items in the collection according to accepted archival standards in order to ensure that they survive in good condition for the enjoyment of present and future generations.*

Conservation's focus is hence the maintenance of a physical object. This task includes maintaining archival temperature and humidity-controlled conditions in storage vaults, transfer of items to inert polypropylene containers, and basic hand-repairs. This stage of work starts and ends with the actual artifact.

The next level of work is *Preservation*, which UCLA defines as "unmodified" duplication. By "unmodified" we mean routine photochemical film printing, using a lab's standard practices. In this case the conserved artifact is printed directly onto a more stable medium, usually polyester-based motion picture film. Special hand-repairs (in a preceding conservation stage) are often needed to enable successful printing.

The third stage is *Restoration*, which UCLA defines as:

> *the process of combining picture and sound elements from different sources in order to restore a work that has been significantly altered back to its original form. Alterations can occur for many reasons: prints of an early film may have lost key scenes or whole reels to damage or deterioration; a film may have been censored due to political or social pressure. The Archive staff checks with archives all over the world, with the studios and broadcast networks, and with private collectors to find missing reels and bits of film and video. The staff must then compare all the material they have collected in order to select the best and most complete parts to assemble the restored work.*

I would place special emphasis on the word "best." Sources that are identical in content may vary widely in image and sound quality.

And the definition of "best" is highly subjective. To cite just one striking example, those who are used to watching DVDs more than film often have very low tolerance for dirt particles, which are easily removed digitally, whereas film preservationists often place a premium on image sharpness and color rendition.

An integral part of the process is manipulating the duplication techniques to adjust, modify, and improve image quality of sub-standard source materials, or to better represent the characteristics of an obsolete film stock or other medium. Unlike preservation, this might involve the use of non-standard lab practices, such as forced processing to manipulate image contrast: it's potentially a complicated business. If I were to fine-tune these definitions I'd go so far as to say "manipulation of process" is as essential to the act of restoration as content modification.

What one finds in all three levels of engagement—conservation, preservation, and restoration—is a separation of the film-viewing experience from the original production artifact. Even conservation copies fit this bill. If a project's original source is negative film, it's not projected, and if it's a print, it's by definition a copy already.

Read and Meyer describe the ultimately indescribable difference between an original and a copy as the *lacuna*, a term commonly used by art conservators to describe a place in a painting where paint has fallen off the canvas. Its precise definition is "a space where something has been omitted or has come out; gap; hiatus." A lovely word… but I do have one quarrel with it, which is that it doesn't speak to the magical act of transformation that can also happen in the restoration process. When a work is replicated, qualities of the receiving medium add their own unique characteristics, and when carefully applied, these characteristics can work harmoniously with the source to create a copy that miraculously carries a large portion of the actual work. The result is in essence something that never existed in physical form—but that is a working condition of duplication. In many ways our interventions all seek to bridge the lacuna.

While one can argue about the *nature* of intervention, the intervention occurs whether one acknowledges it or not, through the mere act of duplication. It's the task of film restorationists to understand the properties of both the source medium and receiving medium, as well as, ultimately, the specific work at hand, to complete the act of preservation.

A key aspect of the process is knowing exactly where you stand within it. Any of the three levels of engagement we've discussed—conservation, preservation, or restoration—can be appropriate under the right circumstances. When managing a film collection, one needs to carefully evaluate what the collection consists of, and then vary one's approach accordingly, treating each component of the collection in a manner suited to it.

As technologies advance, digital tools will obviously play an increasingly significant part in our efforts. Digital media will in turn need its own digital preservation. It offers unparalleled benefits in the area of access, and will continue to aid in the restoration of analog works.

Already the studios, as well as some of the European archives, are doing restorations utilizing digital intermediates for the complete length of a work. In these cases the digital component is, as its name indicates, an *intermediate*—the end output is back to film. This is appropriate, as unlike electronic imaging technologies, wherein the content is in essence an encoded signal, photochemical images have distinct physical properties which are intrinsically a part of their makeup, and need to be retained in any true preservation. When well-executed, the intermediate process enables the integration of digital image repair into an archivally legitimate workflow.

Yet as the film viewing experience becomes increasingly rare, and commercial and economic imperatives dictate industry changes, there will be increasing pressure to *keep* things digital. Our cultural memory stands at risk of being lost. Just as we wouldn't mistake a photograph of a painting for the painting itself, we will need to maintain our ability to articulate distinctions between different audiovisual media.

It's the job of moving image archivists to understand the unique aspects of each medium they collect, and preserve those aspects. When tough choices need to be made, and something is sacrificed for economic reasons, those choices need to be made from a perspective of such understanding. It's only through a careful consideration of an artwork's relation to its source medium and receiving medium that we can create the magical space in which it comes to life. The preservationist's art is that of bridging the lacuna—of bringing audiovisual works of another era into the present—looking closely at the work's original context and qualities, using the best of currently available tools, with an eye to the future.

This 2009 essay remains the most articulated expression of my views on the field. Although its focus is photochemical restoration, the underlying principles hold true in my current practice, however transformed.

"The Gray Zone" was originally published in The Moving Image, *Vol. 9, No. 2, Fall 2009. Early versions were presented at the UCLA Film & Television Archive's James Bridges Theater on May 3, 2005, and at the Korean Film Archive on May 23, 2008.*

The Gray Zone
A Restorationist's Travel Guide

> The production of a perfect picture by means of photography is an art; the production of a technically perfect negative is a science.
>
> —Ferdinand Hurter and Vero Charles Driffield, at a meeting of the Society of Chemical Industry, May 7, 1890

With a simple gesture the world divides.

Hurter and Driffield's declaration of a new method of determining the sensitivity of glass plates was nothing less than a call for the reconceptualizing of all photographic practice. By "picture" they meant the image one saw, and by "negative," the photographic material itself.[1]

Photographers were at that time concluding the transition from wet and homemade supplies to dry and store-bought ones. The initial need was for plates that had more consistent properties and were transportable. Hurter and Driffield's contribution, coming on the heels of their invention of the light meter, was to mathematically relate a plate's exposure to image density; to precisely measure the response of any given emulsion to light.[2] Their "characteristic curve," which charted this, marked the transformation of photography from an individualized, artisanal practice into an industrialized process. It symbolically sealed the moment at which photographers, in essence, stopped making their own supplies and handed that task to private manufacturers.[3]

Whereas before practitioners integrated both artistry and science, now one could choose. And choose they did. After abandoning the manufacture of materials, photographers gradually surrendered other aspects of their craft, making manifest George Eastman's legendary Kodak slogan, "You Press the Button, We Do the Rest." There were exceptions of course—but the push-button culture had arrived.

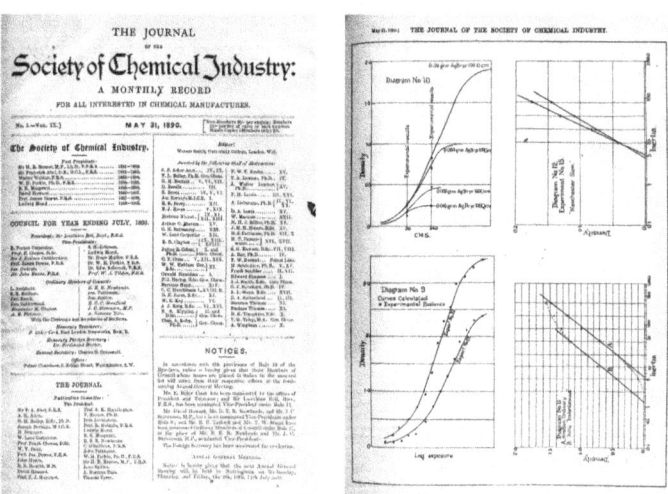

Figure 1. Ferdinand Hurter and Vero Charles Driffield and the 1890 presentation of the characteristic curve. Graphs, lower left: a simple plot of density versus log exposure. As the exposure increases, so does the density. The slightly steeper curve at left implies a higher contrast image, in that it takes less of a change in exposure to result in a greater difference in density or opaqueness. Note the small irregularities, as indicated by the dots from which the curve is deduced.

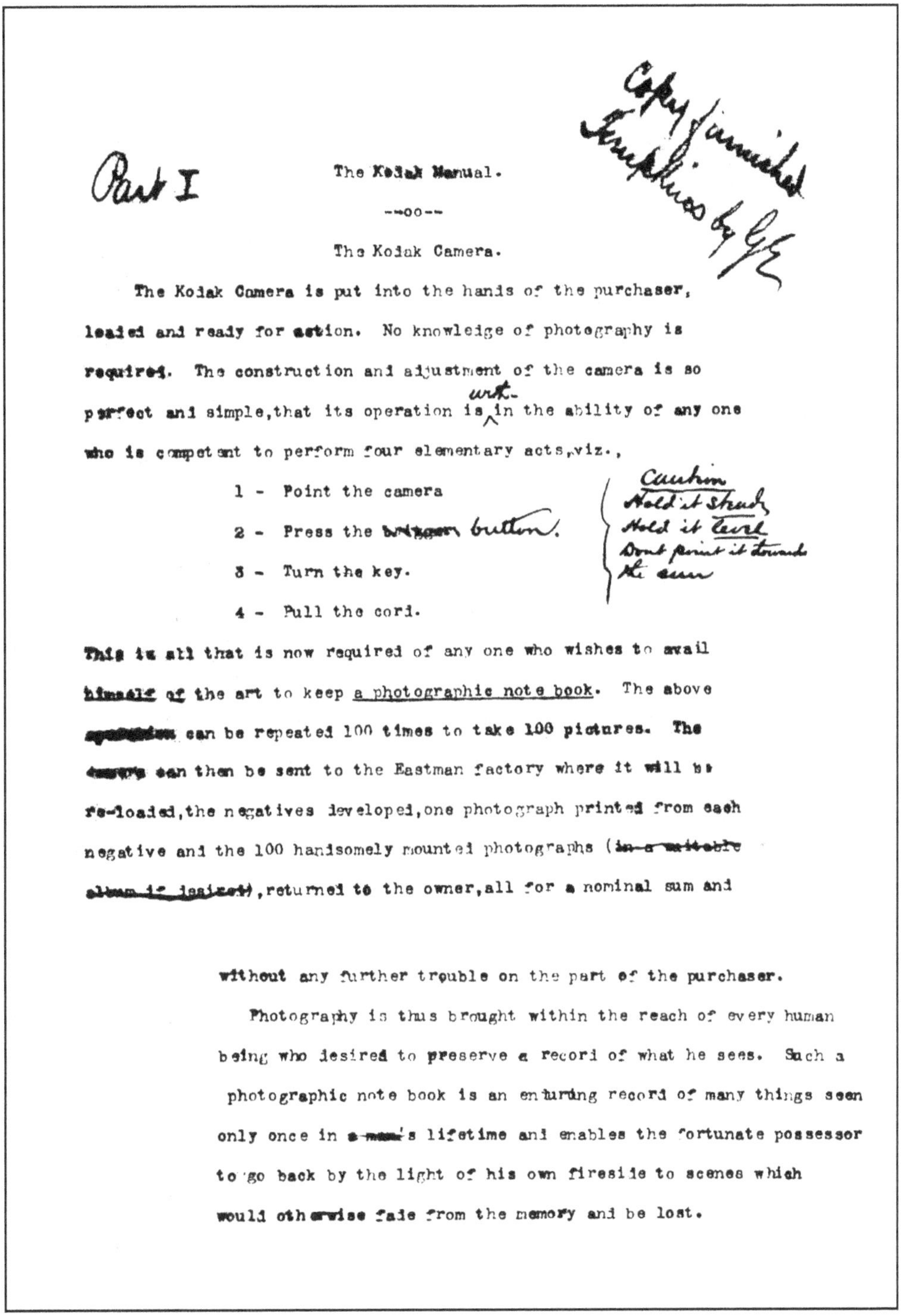

> Part I   The Kodak Manual.
> --oo--
> The Kodak Camera.
>
> *Copy furnished Humphries by GE*
>
> The Kodak Camera is put into the hands of the purchaser, loaded and ready for action. No knowledge of photography is required. The construction and adjustment of the camera is so perfect and simple, that its operation is *with-* in the ability of any one who is competent to perform four elementary acts, viz.,
>
> 1 - Point the camera
> 2 - Press the ~~trigger~~ *button.*
> 3 - Turn the key.
> 4 - Pull the cord.
>
> *Caution / Hold it steady / Hold it level / Don't point it towards the sun*
>
> ~~This is~~ all that is now required of any one who wishes to avail ~~himself~~ of the art to keep <u>a photographic note book</u>. The above ~~operation~~ can be repeated 100 times to take 100 pictures. The ~~camera~~ can then be sent to the Eastman factory where it will be re-loaded, the negatives developed, one photograph printed from each negative and the 100 handsomely mounted photographs (~~in a suitable album if desired~~), returned to the owner, all for a nominal sum and
>
> without any further trouble on the part of the purchaser.
> Photography is thus brought within the reach of every human being who desired to preserve a record of what he sees. Such a photographic note book is an enduring record of many things seen only once in ~~a man~~'s lifetime and enables the fortunate possessor to go back by the light of his own fireside to scenes which would otherwise fade from the memory and be lost.

Figure 2. Excerpts from George Eastman's notebooks for the first Kodak manual.

While celebrating Hurter and Driffield's invaluable role as enablers of modern photography, I would like to call into question some of the side effects of this vision—for while it was truly visionary, it came at a cost. At the core of their work is the practice of quantification: creating a working system for the transfer of a fluid, mobile world into measurable units. A space that was continuous was now marked, drawing a line in the sand between art and science.[4] C. P. Snow formally announced the divorce decades later in his classic 1959 lecture, "The Two Cultures."[5] For Snow, it was nothing to celebrate. It pointed to the loss of something fundamental in our lives.

The loss is of a unified view of the world.[6] This line mapped an undivided land, carving a whole into sections. The markings can at first aid the visitor, but they are deceptive, leading to false turns and artificial crossroads. Today we face another such pivotal moment in that traditional photochemical techniques are being replaced by digital ones. On a daily basis methods are being devised—and just as quickly revised—to facilitate the translation of images into binary units.

Digitization is however not so much a revolution as the crystallization of social currents generated much earlier. The end user is more reliant on manufactured tools, the manufacturer, on quantification. While an analysis of the digital manifestations of the dilemma lies beyond the scope of the present study, the digital era's ghostly presence lingers in waiting throughout. The world spins before us, more marked than ever, and more confusing because of the markings. How can one navigate?

As one intimately involved with both the technical and aesthetic dimensions of image reproduction, the moving image restorationist is in an ideal position to assess the terrain, and so I offer this small travel guide in hopes that it might aid our transit. To mitigate our loss we need to move into the future with an understanding of the past. I shall not always address these concerns directly, but rather present a generalized field map filtered through their prism— and a model for how to traverse the field. In so doing I'll indirectly address both Hurter and Driffield's mathematicization and C. P. Snow's two-culture divide. Appropriately, the discussion shall be at times decidedly non-technical. At other times it will dive into minutia of photographic theory. Examples will come from both personal experience and the work of others. Our queries will loom in the background. The exploration will focus on our fast-disappearing photochemical heritage, as it is only with this physical grounding that we can set course successfully into a perilously disembodied digital world.

Before we set out, please note that the crossing of the terrain follows no logical order; or at least not a conventionally recognizable one. It is precisely in a circuitous navigation that we can preserve not only individual works but also, perhaps, something larger in our culture.

Introduction

By definition, moving image restoration is undertaken on constantly shifting ground, taking a work from the past and bringing it to an ever-evolving present. This elusive task requires a judicious, carefully wielded mixture of science, artistry, and scholarship. At its heart, however, is choice. What is often unacknowledged is the extent of the process' subjectivity.

Restoration is not a precise science, and the standards for which we strive are at a fundamental level not truly standardized—nor even standardizable. When I say this, I by no means decry such things as photographic aim densities, process control, or theatrical audio levels—measurable benchmarks that enable our work. Nor do I renounce, even figuratively, the many excellent texts on restoration theory or practice in the fields of both fine art and cinema. All such texts are of use. However, one must be prepared to abandon standards of any kind, even as one uses and respects them. The final text on any work is the work itself. Carefully honed standards and theoretical recommendations are essential tools, but they must be understood as means and not ends, one component of a larger social project. That project integrates aspects of mechanical and electronic duplication, historical research, and aesthetic judgment, in continual interplay with each other. That interplay gives a work its new existence and yet is beyond prescription or measurability.

It's this interplay I'd like to examine. In encountering it, we'll enter the space I like to call "the Gray Zone," in playful allusion to both the photographer's density charts and Ansel Adams and Fred Archer's unique method of controlling film exposure. The Gray Zone is that uncharted territory where a preservationist needs to make decisions when there is no definitive guide left by the filmmakers. The choices made may make the difference between an effort that is faithful to the spirit of the work and one that is not. And they very much determine the ultimate experience one undergoes when viewing it. If poor judgment is used, a film can, ironically, be lost in the very act of preservation.

This loss can occur through a creeping dissipation; one which may in fact go entirely unnoticed. To achieve a faithful rendition, a restorationist will ideally operate in an artisanal mode, using subjective vision to integrate both sides of Hurter and Driffield's duality in a mysterious alchemy beyond art or science. It is here that we can find the elusive qualities of a cultural work, even as the world around it changes.

You'll note that I've used the word *faithful* in describing a rendition, and carefully avoided *authentic*, a term I've used elsewhere in the past.[7] There's a reason for this. When there is no definitive work to preserve, *authenticity* is impossible.

The Outer Zone

I'd like to begin by examining a commonly stated goal of film restoration—that we seek to "recreate a film's original viewing experience." The levels at which this concept crumbles are multitude. Not only is it impossible, it is not truly the goal.[8]

From a purely objective standpoint, the ability to technically recreate original conditions is always beyond reach. The physical materials and methods of duplication and exhibition available today differ from those of the past. Different technologies lead to different experiences. To cite just one obvious example, early silent films were hand-cranked and projected at a variety of running speeds. While one can theoretically recreate a hand-cranked experience, there is no definitive speed at which to crank. An interpretive act is needed to realize the presentation. It is in essence a performance, nonrepeatable.[9] A contemporary constant-speed projector denies the possibility by definition.[10]

Put this aside, however. Let's try to duplicate the film. It's a silent film, and it's tinted and toned. How do we emulate the actual colors? Even if we use the actual dye formulae of the period, the chances of precise emulation are near zero, due to process and procedural variations, and the dyes' different interaction with modern film stocks. I mention this all quite briefly, just to note the ground at our first footfall. In both cited instances we're in the Gray Zone. To address these issues one must venture into subjective space. Our choices will determine the viewing experience.

The dilemma has echoes in photographic history. At a glance, the preservationist regards the *artwork* as the early photographer did nature, in a desire to duplicate the subject. In the case of the preservationist, the subject is simply film itself. Yet while many theorists considered the aim of photography to be accurate rendition (of the world), others soon found that notion to be an impediment. Henry Peach Robinson, one of the great proponents of photography as an artform, declared,

> In the early days we were surprised and delighted with a photograph, as a photograph… just because we had not hitherto conceived possible any definition or finish that approached Nature so closely… But we soon wanted something more… The photograph told us everything about the facts of nature and left out the mystery.[11]

So too, a mechanized reproduction of an artwork, in an accumulation of detail, stands at risk of missing the essence of its source. Neither photographer nor preservationist can truly emulate their subject in total, and both risk a qualitative loss endemic in rote duplication. Each needs to conceive an *idea* of their physical subject, as the subject is guided into a new physical incarnation.

But what is this mysterious idea? Be the subject a film or reality itself—how can one manage such a transformation, when both referent and product are in a concrete sense ultimately indefinable? Robinson, not surprisingly, called precisely for subjectivity on the part of the photographer who aspired to art. I reconcile the seeming paradox in practice with a conceptual model for the indefinable itself.

In black-and-white film, there are an infinite variety of tones between pure black, the absence of color, and pure white, the composite of the visual spectrum. In between are shades of gray. The photographer breaks them down to twenty-one units in a standard step chart for reference, a chart known as the "gray scale." Each step is given one-fourth the light exposure of the previous step; a log density difference of .15. But this breakdown is arbitrary. In fact there are any number of potential gray scales out there. The numbers don't matter in themselves, they're only tools. My interest is in the shades *between* the gradations.

The gray scale is itself analogous to cinema. Just as the step chart breaks up a continuum of tones into discrete units, so does cinema break up the continuum of time into twenty-four still photographs per second. The magic occurs only when the units are resynthesized into a unified percept.

○   ○   ○

I've provided some introductory examples from silent films to establish the dilemma of duplication, but similar problems occur with sound films. I'll return to technical aspects of the question in detail later. Let's now resume our examination of the cinematic viewing experience. Even if one were to imagine a case where all the physical tools of replication and presentation were identical, the social conditions of a previous era cannot be repeated. Suppose, in the mid-1990s, a studio releases a film with a specific marketing plan. The perceptual constructs surrounding and emanating from just the publicity will in either large or small ways affect our perception of the film's viewing. Now take a re-release of the same film only a decade later. Even if our marketing strategists were to use a "Recapture the Magic!" theme, the act of *re*capturing something is different than the initial capture. By definition, the passage of time implies change.

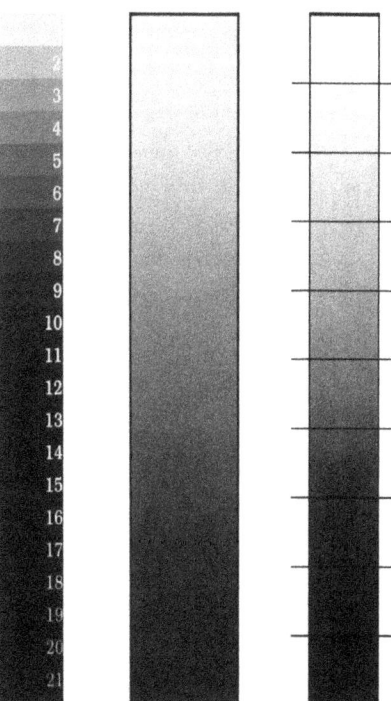

Figure 3. Left: traditional twenty-one step gray scale. Center: continuous toned gray scale. Right: zoned continuous gray scale.

Beyond intentional marketing, the social conditions affecting each viewer will have transformed with time. For example, a film from the 1940s might seem slow-paced to a viewer in the 1980s, and a film considered extremely violent in the 1980s might be deemed suitable for even young children in our current era.

This is just the beginning. I could try to enumerate the levels at which the notion of "re-creation" falls apart at the philosophical level, but shall leave that project to other travelers. My aim here is merely to establish a fundamental paradox in preservation. The paradox is that "preservation" of a temporal experience, even a mechanized one, is impossible. Only once one has accepted this, and embraced the paradox of preservation, can one begin to approach the individual work.

○ ○ ○

Moving on from the viewing experience, the first question one must ask in a restoration project is *what* exactly one should be restoring. An initial step in answering this is sorting through a work's physical iterations. Until this point we have been presupposing that a specific work existed in one unique historical edition regarding content. Yet in recent years we've seen an increased interest in alternate versions of films. This is in part due to the "menu" structure of the DVD format (as well as its marketing), but it extends to archival cinema exhibition and even the occasional theatrical release. The interest in differing versions of a work perhaps culminated in the 2007 release of the "Ultimate" DVD edition of Ridley Scott's *Blade Runner*, which included no fewer than five distinct versions of the film, each of which is quite different. The DVD set itself may even be deemed a version.

The question does not, however, end with mere duplication of the existing editions of a work. As exemplified by the *Blade Runner* set's inclusion of a "2nd" director's cut, new editions can be made and not all of them spurious. "Reconstruction" is the task of creating alternate versions of established works that never previously existed in that form. One of the most celebrated and, I feel, successful instances of this is the 1998 edition of Orson Welles' *Touch of Evil*, which based its decisions on a 58-page document Welles sent to Universal chief Edward Muhl after his shock at seeing the studio's initial edit. The result cannot truly be deemed Welles' work, and its creators would not presume it to be—it was hardly an objective process. However, it demonstrably contains strong traces of Welles' vision and can certainly claim at least as much validity as the original studio release of 1958.

In addition to encountering versions created over time, a preservationist may also on occasion find simultaneous editions of a single initial release. These include domestic and foreign versions of silent films, road show prints that may differ from other copies, or, today, specialty format editions that allow different experiences from conventional film prints. The possibilities are myriad. Archivists thus need to know something of the historical arc of a work's life, but we can see that the idea of a single authoritative version starts proving evasive— if it ever indeed truly existed. In wading through multiple versions of a work, the archivist must consider the relative merits of each iteration, and make specific decisions about *what* to preserve.

This work occurs on the outer boundary of the Gray Zone. While research is essential, the nature of research is not fixed. It's a world of alternate edits, rough cuts, fragments, and offhand conversation: an indefinite process. And it remains just the outer edge of the Zone. I've in part lingered here to allow the idea to sink in, to establish the basic principle of subjectivity in restoration. As one ventures further in and gets familiar with the broad characteristics of the Gray Zone's landscape, one begins to discern a finer degree of topological detail. If you will, of climates and microclimates, of different areas to distinguish. It's here that I'd now like to take us.

The Inner Zone

Ansel Adams and Fred Archer developed the Zone System of photographic exposure while teaching at the Art Center School in Los Angeles in the late 1930s. They broke the gray scale down not into twenty-one discrete steps but into ten graduated and shifting Zones. Or eleven… or perhaps nine. Depending on the photographer. To quote Adams,

> A gray scale of 10 steps seems to be most convenient. With solid black and pure white as the extremes, there are eight discrete shades of gray in between—not too many to visualize, and yet enough to symbolize various values in the subject.

Further emphasizing the system's subjectivity, he continues,

> The term "middle gray" as I use it is more an emotional value than a quantitative physical value. If we spin a disk surfaced with equal areas of black and white, we get a 50% gray tone which would not be "middle gray" at all, but a value lying between Zones VII and VIII of the exposure scale.[12]

Kodak's standard gray card—which has only an 18 percent reflectance—falls into the middle zone, number V.[13] The location of the mix of pure black and white not in Zone V but in Zone VII or VIII shows the human side of not just the Zone System but the larger human experience, as suggested by Kodak's and Adams' choice of a centering point. Why is 18 percent gray considered the middle? It is a subjective quantification of our perception.[14]

The zones of Adams' system are not discrete like the step scale. They're graduated, and require further subjectivity in their reading.[15] The zones of the scale are only meaningful in relation to actual photographic situations. And the definition of a "zone" has itself shifted over the years, sometimes including the photographic subject, sometimes speaking strictly of a negative. In such an elusive system, only the act of *looking* is essential. For this reason I see Adams' and Archer's zones as part of a larger single Zone—the terrain in which we're now walking.

Orientation tips are offered by one of the Zone System's main practitioners, the photographer Minor White. The classic *New Zone System Manual* by White, Richard Zakia, and Peter Lorenz states, "After grasping an intellectual meaning of some one zone, let the heart inform you about its emotional meaning."[16] Cognition works in concert with intuition. The *Manual* uses the term "interface" to describe "the time and space between subject values and print values, where man and medium meet, [where] techniques and sensibilities interact."[17] White's interface is key. The Zone System was conceived primarily for artists seeking to learn the mysteries of the science behind their art. But as a way of thinking, it's equally important for the technician seeking the artistry behind one's science. It's both precise and vague, cutting and loose. And in this regard it's extremely appropriate to the discipline of film preservation.

When I say this, I'm not suggesting actual use of Adams and Archer's system in archival practice. Rather I suggest it as metaphor and model for the integration of art and science; for a critical part of our work occurs in the space of the Gray Zone.

○ ○ ○

Having established the impossibility of recreating an original viewing experience, and having also raised the question of version authenticity, I would now at last like to concentrate on the technical and aesthetic issues of duplication that arise when one *does* have a specific version of a historical work to restore, and illustrate how in even these cases the restorationists' work is often entirely subjective.

We here encounter a variation of the goal of recreating an "original viewing experience"—the notion that our job is to allow a film to be presented "in the way it was intended to be seen." This variant phrasing of the question moves away from the historical aspects of a viewing experience and toward the issue of authorial intent. But as we all know, clear traces of the filmmaker's intent don't always exist, and the interpretation of what does exist can be highly idiosyncratic.

A question we must thus ask after "What are we preserving?" is "Who is the author?" Again, it's not as straightforward as one may think. In almost all cases, film is a collaborative medium. Beyond the obvious artistic cooperation between crew members in a production, in cases of editorial conflict between a director and studio, the released product can in fact be seen as the work of a noncorporeal, composite author.

Let's proceed further. We know that questions begin when a filmmaker has not had editorial control, but a film's authorship extends well beyond editing. A copy of a film can be a shot-for-shot match of the original and still be unfaithful. An easy example of this is colorization. A colorized work's duration and overall form remain intact, but it's been aesthetically transformed. Another, only slightly more elusive area of authorship is image composition. If an artist makes a choice to paint—or film—on a rectangular canvas, subsequent reframings by others clearly alter it. Yet this is common practice in nontheatrical release.

Figure 4. Zone System models (photographers unknown).

We all understand that at a basic level there's a difference between home video and theatrical viewing, but you'll notice an increasing level of acceptance as one goes through even these few examples. Who hasn't watched a cropped video?[18] It's like reading a reductive newspaper story or listening to a political speech and telling ourselves, "I don't know the truth, but I know this is a lie, so it's ok." We acknowledge there's a distortion, and with a slight nod, let it pass. There's nothing we can do about it. Yet when we consider these altered works, we are clearly losing something. We must consider that the producers and technicians who created those iterations of a work have become part of its "composite author"—*without changing the editorial content*.

In the process of restoring John Cassavetes' *Faces*, I came across a 35mm magnetic track produced by a major studio that distributed the film at one time. In an effort to boost dialogue clarity, they had equalized out the soundtrack's low frequencies, with the result that in one sequence, the background traffic noise was entirely removed. The technicians who did this likely never knew it was missing, but they were most certainly in the Gray Zone. The decision—even if passive—affects the work. They are participating in the film's authorship.

And so our original question returns, transformed: "*What* should we preserve?" The answer lies beyond common notions of authorship. I would like to suggest a model of director as agent: an agent in service of a film. The director's vision can be seen as both part of, and external to, the person who conceives it. The vision can guide the creative process, but in a collaborative medium a work takes on a life of its own, a life that in most cases evades final ownership by a single *auteur*. The work becomes a nebulous, indeterminate concept, which all its authors—from director to production team to restorationist—serve. The restorationist and labs join their predecessors in an act of interpretation, whether aware of it or not.

○ ○ ○

Now let's go still deeper into this murky territory, and take some examples from independent cinema, which is often produced with extremely low budgets and limited resources. In the case of the American West Coast movement of the 1950s and '60s, filmmakers such as Jordan Belson and the Whitney brothers were highly skilled technicians. They got around budget difficulties by becoming laboratories in themselves. At the other extreme, East Coast artists Jack Smith and the Kuchar brothers created an underground aesthetic, using low-budget production qualities as an essential component of their work. They focused their energies on what happened in front of the camera rather than at the lab. Post-production work was literally, an afterthought.

Thus a question arises. While it might make sense to emulate the release print of a carefully honed Jordan Belson film, is it inherently desirable to mimic all aspects of an underground work? The original printing of these movies may have fallen outside the direct control of the filmmaker; the look of a particular title determined by circumstance as much as choice. Yes, one could reasonably say a filmmaker's allowing circumstance into the process is a choice in itself. But does that imply a restorationist should always duplicate that circumstance?

Let's look at a specific case. Charles Burnett's *Killer of Sheep*, an extraordinary portrait of life in South Central LA, was shot in the streets with non-actors and location sound recording.[19] Burnett spent years getting the film made—concentrating on the characters, the scenes, and getting the film shot. Then more years editing. Lab work was not a key component of the finished piece. At the time I restored the film, he told me that as a result of creating a "found film" effect in the camera, on contrasty 16mm high-speed black-and-white stocks, printing problems were created in post-production that were never satisfactorily resolved. These involved picture tonality—the renditions of white, black, and gray. Indeed, when I printed a series of tests, I found there was much more picture information in the original negative than was ever realized. So my question is: which is Charles' "real" work? The camera original, or an old release print?

The conventional answer is, strangely, the release print. However this should be understood as an ideological answer arising from longstanding traditions of preserving Hollywood cinema; films made with a high degree of control at the laboratory. A countering argument, a very strong one, could say that in this case, emulating an old release print is preserving the work not of the filmmaker but whoever worked the night shift at Deluxe Labs on a given night in 1975. And while the shift worker participated in the authoring of one iteration of *Killer of Sheep*, I would suggest *Killer of Sheep* is in the end an elusive entity, beyond iteration.

By carefully controlling all of the printing stages in our lab work at Film Technology Company, we were able to retain much more information from the film's original negative than had ever been seen before—without reducing the number of printing generations. The primary method used for this was simply lowering contrast in a contact-printed 16mm fine grain master positive, from a standard gamma 1.4 to 1.2.[20] However to arrive at this, an entire second set of tests was conducted, printing both the masterpositive and subsequent duplicate negative at a variety of gammas to best prise out the detail we now knew was there in the original.

While this is fairly straightforward in concept—a "mere" reduction of contrast—I've in fact worked on projects where contrast has been reduced at one printing stage only to be reintroduced later.[21] An example of this was our restoration of *Multiple Sidosis*, a legendary amateur film shot by former vaudeville performer Sid Laverents. In this case, the film's reversal camera rolls were lost, so our only source was a pristine Kodachrome print.[22] Here we encountered a problem: because no existing film stock is ideally suited for printing from Kodachrome, one often has to go to great lengths to successfully duplicate it.[23] For *Multiple Sidosis*, Walt Rose of Fotokem Laboratories and I initially reduced the inevitable contrast build-up by the somewhat standard method of overexposing the internegative stock and then "pull-processing" two stops.[24]

A conventional print from the new negative showed the desired tonal range, however Sid Laverents had used strong colors in shooting portions of the film, and the initial test prints failed to match the lovely color saturation of the old Kodachrome copies. Furthermore, if we tried pulling even one stop less, we suffered from unwanted contrast build-up.

Happily, we found that by printing onto Kodak's higher contrast Premiere positive stock, we were able to retain the vital mid-range detail, while allowing the color saturation to resemble the original. The prints were striking—but it should be noted that this method clearly defies conventional wisdom. There should really be no need to reintroduce contrast that previously needed reduction.[25]

A possible explanation for our successful result lies in the inherent folly of a high-gamma intermediate. Building in lower contrast at an earlier stage retains more pictorial information through that generation, some of which might be retained even through later contrast boosts. When the information is lost earlier, it's most definitely gone forever.[26] While this is just a speculative explanation, the result in this instance was a "restored" print of *Multiple Sidosis* that was quite faithful to the original look of the film.[27]

In the case of *Killer of Sheep*, on the other hand, our prints looked different than any previously seen. In a logical paradox, I feel our restoration was "faithful" in that it better corresponded to the camera negative, and hence Charles' vision, than the old release copies had. Here we created a physical rendering not of the old *Killer of Sheep*, but rather an abstracted idea of the essence of it.

○   ○   ○

I've offered a case where my contact with a filmmaker directly confirmed his dissatisfaction with "original" prints. Yet even a filmmaker's approval of an old print doesn't always imply that the print is definitive. A filmmaker as rigorous as Stan Brakhage approved dozens of inferior prints in the 1990s to maintain good relations with his lab, which was undergoing difficulties at the time.

So we see that we need to revisit another common notion: that an old print is by definition authoritative. An artwork is often fluid, beyond embodiment in one physical form. When comparing existing prints of independent films, one is as likely to encounter a field of snowflakes as identical copies. The strength of a restoration thus lies in its process. When it comes time to duplicate a film, be it to intermediate or print, the nuances become vital, and can transcend the source material.

One should note that even studio work—which usually experiences much tighter regulation than independent cinema—is still variable in that it's subject to the whims of the laboratory's chemical control. The top labs in Los Angeles will not generally reprint if their control is within two "light points" of aim on a standard fifty-point printing scale. Thus any given print of a film can have a startling five-point swing and be deemed acceptable.[28] Much of my dialogue with graders, however, is over questions of a single point, a degree not easily

 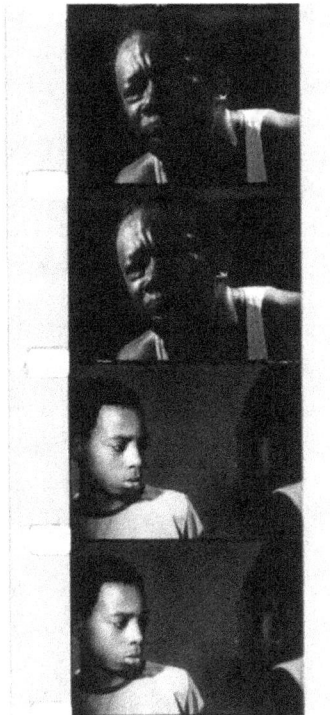

Figure 5. Charles Burnett's *Killer of Sheep*, 16mm print tests. Courtesy Milestone Films.
Left: release print from old distribution negative. Right: test print from original camera negative.

distinguishable even when control is on aim. When one's playing field is finer than the scale of measurement, one is in the heart of the Gray Zone.

The Outer Zone Revisited

Having now passed through the heart—a discussion of the nuance of technical reproduction—let's carry on and exit through the far side. We'll return to our earlier discussion of editorial content and reconstruction, but with a different twist. The generalized examples offered on our entry will be reexamined through the lens of a personal encounter with the issues they raised.

Some years ago I worked on the restoration of the early films of John Sayles. I recently came across an interview I did with David Chute at the time of their release by IFC. Speaking of the project, I said, "We're not in the business of doing new versions for commercial release."[29] While I love the youthful idealism I expressed in this interview, I later came to confront a situation in which I was forced to eat my words. Not surprisingly, it occurred in the Gray Zone.

When Dennis Doros and Amy Heller of Milestone Films picked up the restored *Killer of Sheep* for distribution, they soon found out why this undisputed masterpiece of American cinema had never received wide release. Charles Burnett, not dreaming his radical vision would be so widely acclaimed, used a "needledrop" soundtrack consisting of a range of blues records and other works—all under copyright. Doros and Heller took on the daunting task of clearing the music rights. It took seven years and a vast amount of money, but their efforts were largely successful. There was one notable exception. The film's penultimate cue, Dinah Washington's "Unforgettable," which plays as Stan, the protagonist, is seen leading sheep to their death in the slaughterhouse, was unavailable. Despite everyone's best intentions, a substitute would need to be made for release.

Burnett's original cut was now fully preserved in the vaults of the UCLA Film & Television Archive, so from an archival standpoint the film was safe. But knowing that changes would occur in its public release whether any of us liked it or not, I chose to participate in the process, and help create a new version of a work that I felt was already perfect in itself. Remembering the careful sound restoration work previously conducted with John Polito at his Audio Mechanics studio, my feeling was that the new cue would be integrated more smoothly if the technical work was conducted with our involvement.

The question was, what would the replacement be? At some point in the proceedings, Doros made an amazing discovery: Burnett had originally intended another song to be used for the film. Luis Russell's "Sad Lover Blues" was initially slated for inclusion, but the record had, quite literally, broken. What's more, "Sad Lover Blues" was apparently intended for the precise spot of the Dinah Washington song. The switch would be perfect, and in effect emulate the original concept. Doros spoke with Burnett, and cleared the rights to "Sad Lover Blues."

Yet something felt wrong. Despite, or because of the symmetry, the story was almost *too* perfect—which turned out to be the case. Amy Sloper, my preservation intern at the time, was about to conduct an interview with Burnett, and so I had her ask him more about it. Revisiting the broken record story, Burnett recalled that "Sad Lover Blues" was actually replaced not by "Unforgettable" but by *another* Dinah Washington song, "This Bitter Earth." The latter song plays during Stan's dance with his wife, and, as brilliantly acted by Henry Sanders and Kaycee Moore, is one of the film's most emblematic moments. Today the scene seems so vital I felt the original record was almost destined to break, to make way for "This Bitter Earth." The story had resonance, and stuck with me.

Flash forward two years. In early 2007 we were doing the video mastering for the Milestone DVD release. Not knowing what to substitute for "Unforgettable," we still thought we'd try "Sad Lover Blues," as it was at least in the general spirit of the film. Doros, Kathy Thomson of Modern VideoFilm, and I were setting up the picture and sound reels for transfer, preparing them for Burnett's arrival. Yet looking at a rough sync of "Sad Lover Blues" with the film's end, the effect was all wrong. The lyrics brought a literalism inappropriate to the scene, and the tone seemed markedly too light.

To Doros' quite understandable consternation, I suggested we also prepare a draft of the ending reusing "This Bitter Earth," the other Dinah Washington song. Milestone had only cleared the rights to that song *once*, and using it twice would double the already considerable cost. But he and Heller more than sportingly encouraged the test.

When Burnett arrived shortly after and was told today we'd master the film's end, he said he'd in fact meant to talk about that. He'd been thinking it over and was worried that "Sad Lover Blues" wasn't right for the ending. Might it be possible to try "This Bitter Earth" instead? And so the cards fell. We told Charles yes, a rough cut was in fact already prepared.

In previewing the two options, it became clear that "This Bitter Earth" integrated much better, functioning as a kind of reprise. Doros and Heller, who would be hit hard in the pocketbook, showed true dedication to the art of cinema in their support, and the choice was unanimous.[30] Fate had revealed itself: we'd all worked to serve a noncorporeal concept of what *Killer of Sheep* might be. We were all in the same Zone.

○　○　○

I'd like to conclude our journey with another story from the lab work on *Killer of Sheep*.

After completing the video transfer at Modern, Burnett and I went to Audio Mechanics to master the revised soundtrack. That sound session showed me a new side of Burnett, and a recounting of how the session unfolded returns us to an earlier touchstone.

I'd had the pleasure of working with Burnett for many years, yet in all the time I'd known him, had never seen him take a close interest in the restoration process. Like most filmmakers, his main focus was on his current work. Having seen his films, I understood his genius full well but had not experienced it firsthand. Even in the video sessions, he'd lingered in the background, letting Kathy Thomson and myself handle most of the details. But the sound mastering of the new ending was different entirely. He became intensely involved. And the point at which he came alive is revealing. It was not at the textural level of the equalization and mix but, fittingly, at the editorial level of the song's placement.

An engineer mixing the sound in Burnett's absence might think, for example, that one should begin the cue at the same moment "Unforgettable" had begun. But that decision is actually in the Gray Zone. Even if matching an insertion point were to work in a given case, one would still need to determine entry and exit points *within* the replacement song itself, which would likely differ in total length from the original. Any synchronization or relationship between image and music, be it sound or lyric, would depend on this choice. Furthermore, the entry and exit spots in the preexisting film are nonspecific guides at best. The mood, flow, and sonic texture of a song are dynamic elements, and cause emotional and sensual responses not just in relation to the images shown under them but in the sound and image that precede and follow. Editorial pacing is dependent on all these factors. Indeed, in *Killer of Sheep,* even slight variations of cue entry and cue selection created vastly different viewing experiences. Observing these slight differences was integral to the process of placement.

Earlier I gave the example of filmmakers being more closely invested in particular areas of the complex art of cinema. Here at last I had the chance to see Burnett operate in one of his vested areas. Leaving technical issues to John Polito and myself, he artfully guided all the editorial work on the new song's insertion. Not only did we shift the entry point, but we also (nearly subliminally) modified the subsequent closing cue, Paul Robeson's "Going Home," to flow smoothly from "This Bitter Earth." It was here, in these editorial choices, that Burnett was indeed, going home. And our role as restorationists was to recede in accordance.

The Restorationist as Stalker

I've told these stories to illustrate that the Gray Zone has no clear map. One must proceed with eyes and ears open, responding to the work, its history, and one's personal vision. I never thought I'd participate in a definitive work's alteration, but I've learned there are times when even that may be appropriate, depending on what's done. There are principles, but no rules. Tools, but no assembly kits. Markers remain fluid.

The question ultimately becomes, how does one navigate this Zone? I can only humbly offer a few basic suggestions, because in practice their application is so varied as to defy systemization.

My basic principle is to allow the subject to help determine its own method of preservation. One must find an interface with the work one is preserving. Such questioning involves both materiality and concept. It demands sympathy with the spirit of the work. If a filmmaker was invested in lab techniques, such as the West Coast artists mentioned earlier, then an unfaded print may be an invaluable reference. Ironically, if poor lab work helped define a piece, then indeed one might preserve *that*—the rough lab work.

To articulate this further, I would ask if a particular aesthetic characteristic of an old print of a film was a *conscious artistic choice* on the part of the maker. Barring that, I'd ask—was it an *un*conscious artistic choice? And lastly, if none of the above, was it a happy accident? If yes, by all means—preserve that quality. If none of the above, we remain in the Gray Zone.

Here we can start to look further back than the print. In films where a documentary aspect was important, or the recording of action was essential, one might consider preserving those qualities latent in the photographic original—even if they were absent in viewing copies. Then aspects of those qualities can be emphasized or deemphasized in future generations.

These are only examples. In all cases, it helps to hold in mind a model of the work that is at once physical and transcends physicality. One needs an abstracted concept of the work at hand's essence.

○ ○ ○

While an idealized notion of an artwork would seem elusive, it is not as elusive as one would think. To help appreciate this, I'd like to return at last to our discussion of early photographic history. We need look no further than the antique stereoscope. As we know, the stereoscope creates its image of three-dimensionality by the use of two discrete images that are synthesized in our brain to a single perception, through the mechanism of our binocular vision.

Figure 6. A stereograph. When viewed through a stereoscope the two images are synthesized into a single image. Together they offer a model for the perceptual linking of multiple components of an artwork into a unified whole. Analog cinema, filmed and projected as discrete frames, is of course another such model.

The stereoscope is an ideal model for a dualistic concept of artworks. Just as its true existence lies somewhere between its multiple physical components and the unified percept our mind creates from them, so too can we create a holistic restoration through a unification of two discrete views of an artwork—the physical and the conceptual.[31] Our task is to explore those links. A work's physical properties may not be able to be reproduced identically, but with an understanding of both the piece and its formal properties, it may nonetheless be successfully rendered.

To achieve this understanding, one cannot rely on either an artistic or scientific background in isolation. They need to be integrated. Even Hurter and Driffield were ultimately forced to acknowledge a need for the linking of the disciplines. While their personal work was decidedly technical, they recognized an absence in their efforts, and so sought the help of an artist. The tale is a parable of the Gray Zone.

Echoing questions we raised earlier, they informed photographer Peter Henry Emerson that

> The difficulty we hope to be able to overcome is the decision of the right moment at which to stop development so that the resulting print will be true to nature. At the present the experienced eye can alone decide the point.
> The particular problem, in the solution of which we should highly esteem your kind assistance, is to decide when a print *is* true to nature.[32]

A telling problem indeed.

In 1889, shortly before Hurter and Driffield unveiled their curve, Emerson had published *Naturalistic Photography for Students of the Art*. Emerson's book laid out a complex and rigorous methodology for the creation of photographic artworks. The crux of his interest lay in the truthful depiction of human perception.[33] In his zealous pursuit of the rendition of nature as seen by the eye, he seemed an ideal complement to the two researchers and the perfect soul to address their dilemma.

Yet the proposed dialogue backfired. Emerson was devastated by Hurter and Driffield's revelation that photosensitive materials could behave in a regularized pattern. He felt the regularity denied any meaningful human intervention and hence prevented photography being truly deemed an art. By 1891 he had written *The Death of Naturalistic Photography*, a renunciation of his original ideas.

The point of his departure is revealing. Stating "the limitations of photography are so great that… the medium must always rank the lowest of all arts," he then specifies, "the all-vital powers of selection and rejection are fatally limited, bound in by fixed and narrow barriers."[34] For Emerson, the predictable patterns of photographic response did not allow sufficient room for manipulation. He saw no value in an aesthetics of the infinitesimal and, in a twist of fate, shut off any possibilities therein.[35]

It was precisely Hurter and Driffield's regimented study of photographic properties that led to Emerson's renunciation of many years' labor in developing his theory of a new art. And yet, Hurter and Driffield were no better off themselves—for of course no one could ever truly decide when a photograph *was* true to nature.[36] For all their study, the enigma of reality and its depiction remained, laughing at all those who tried to pin it down.

○   ○   ○

So where does that leave us?

In my description of the Gray Zone to this point, I've focused on its allusion to the density scale, and Adams and Archer. But cineastes will of course recognize one other nod of the head. I refer of course, to Andrei Tarkovsky's *Stalker*, which takes place in a mythical territory called "the Zone."[37] It's a space that defies description; at once precise and imprecise, concrete and changing, with its own indescribable order. It's a place in which magic is possible.

The film centers on two men's journey through the Zone. The two are known archetypically by their profession. One is a Writer, the other a Scientist. Both are leaders in their fields. They've trained extensively for their journey, yet individually they are each lost in the Zone—they need a third party to help them through it. Their guide is the Stalker, a mysterious figure lurking on the outskirts of civilization; at once a part of it and entirely removed. Both Writer and Scientist need him to complete their journey, yet he remains forever outside their recognized disciplines. It is precisely this remove that lets him operate within the mystery of the Zone.[38]

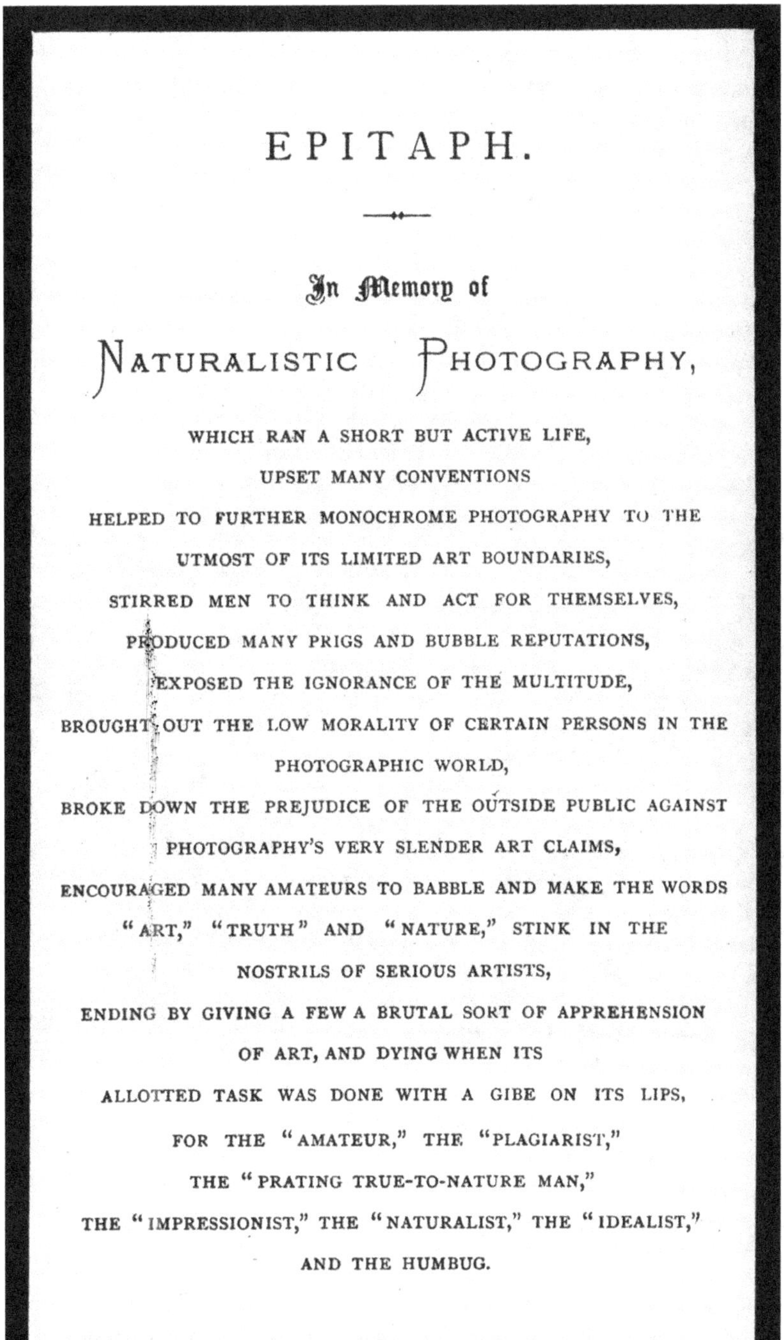

EPITAPH.

In Memory of

NATURALISTIC PHOTOGRAPHY,

WHICH RAN A SHORT BUT ACTIVE LIFE,

UPSET MANY CONVENTIONS

HELPED TO FURTHER MONOCHROME PHOTOGRAPHY TO THE
UTMOST OF ITS LIMITED ART BOUNDARIES,

STIRRED MEN TO THINK AND ACT FOR THEMSELVES,

PRODUCED MANY PRIGS AND BUBBLE REPUTATIONS,

EXPOSED THE IGNORANCE OF THE MULTITUDE,

BROUGHT OUT THE LOW MORALITY OF CERTAIN PERSONS IN THE
PHOTOGRAPHIC WORLD,

BROKE DOWN THE PREJUDICE OF THE OUTSIDE PUBLIC AGAINST
PHOTOGRAPHY'S VERY SLENDER ART CLAIMS,

ENCOURAGED MANY AMATEURS TO BABBLE AND MAKE THE WORDS
"ART," "TRUTH" AND "NATURE," STINK IN THE
NOSTRILS OF SERIOUS ARTISTS,

ENDING BY GIVING A FEW A BRUTAL SORT OF APPREHENSION
OF ART, AND DYING WHEN ITS
ALLOTTED TASK WAS DONE WITH A GIBE ON ITS LIPS,

FOR THE "AMATEUR," THE "PLAGIARIST,"
THE "PRATING TRUE-TO-NATURE MAN,"
THE "IMPRESSIONIST," THE "NATURALIST," THE "IDEALIST,"
AND THE HUMBUG.

Figure 7. The concluding page of Peter Henry Emerson's *The Death of Naturalistic Photography* (1891).

I propose a model of the restorationist as Stalker—bridging the gap between C. P. Snow's "two cultures" of art and science—in an alchemical process of cultural continuation. The Restorationist uses standards but is not slave to them, seeing the work at hand as both a physical and abstract entity. The Restorationist uses both visions in rendering a work, and in the rendering *re-members* an abstraction, sundered from its original physical embodiment by time.

Figure 8. In the Zone: Andrei Tarkovsky's *Stalker* (1979). The Stalker (Aleksandr Kajdanovsky) pictured center, between Scientist (Nikolai Grinko) and Writer (Anatoli Solonitsyn). Courtesy Kino International Corp.

The Restorationist re-members the work in a newly ephemeral corporeality. In thus re-membering a work, we re-member the larger split in our culture, exemplified in photographic history by the profound mathematicization of Hurter and Driffield, which severed the picture from the film. Just as Hurter and Driffield revolutionized photography through their implementation of measured systems, so now must we use their system as one tool in another stage of revitalization, one beyond systematization itself. We need to bring our systems back to earth.

The present epoch of digitization—in some ways the epitome of mathematicization—ironically, takes us further from the realm of science. It severs the digitizer from the physical world. In a world comprised of data, the natural sciences retreat. Yet we need to recall the obvious: that all digital media works, including translations of photochemical media, must be temporally reconstituted in a physical embodiment to enable perception by a viewer.

At play are both process and form. Herein lies our challenge. Although we can't return to an Edenic paradise, we can still strive to rejoin a severed whole. Restorationists don't stop the mill of time—it moves ever on. Technology advances; the world changes. Our goal is simply to move forward while remembering the past.

Our hope lies in choice. That is our art, our discipline. Our choices determine which aspects of a work survive, and which do not. Scales must be fluid rather than fixed. They should be used in our work but only as tools. *Choice* is our guide through the Gray Zone—a place beyond clear demarcation, beyond zeros and ones: an infinite scale of changing tones, navigated by subjective will in a continual dance with chance.

Endnotes

1. Ferdinand Hurter and Vero Charles Driffield, "Photochemical Investigations and a New Method of Determination of the Sensitiveness of Photographic Plates," *The Journal of the Society of Chemical Industry*, May 31, 1890, 455.
2. The light sensitivity of the film is related in terms of log exposure to the resulting density (or opaqueness) of the metallic silver in the developed negative. The classic presentation of the method for still photographers can be found in M. J. Langford, *Basic Photography* (Amphoto/Focal Press, 1973), 217–41. For its historical cinematic counterpart, see Raymond Spottiswoode, *Film and Its Techniques* (California, 1951), 174–89. (It should be noted that, like the present study, Spottiswoode's seminal book employs a geographic metaphor of mapping to establish its approach.)
3. Hurter and Driffield's work, though iconic, was of course only one of many factors in this larger social change, which arguably traces back to Richard Leach Maddox's introduction of the gelatin emulsion in 1871. For an overview of the progress toward an industrialized photography, see Beaumont Newhall, *The History of Photography* (Museum of Modern Art and Little, Brown and Company, 1982), 123–29.
4. If their union arguably culminated in Leonardo, they began to separate thereafter. It is not the aim of this guide to chronicle the vast history of this complex relationship. However, it is worth noting that early photographers often referred to their practice by the hybrid term "art-science," with discomfort in the fact that it was fully recognized as neither.
5. Snow concentrates on the scientific revolution—which he dates to the twentieth century, while admitting the date is subjective. C. P. Snow, *The Two Cultures and the Scientific Revolution* (Cambridge, 1959) and *The Two Cultures: And A Second Look* (New American Library, 1964). The lecture was based on ideas originally presented in "The Two Cultures," *New Statesman*, October 6, 1956.
6. In this sense, I am inverting some of Snow's sentiments. While arguing in general for increased intermingling of the disciplines, the bulk of his lecture calls for a greater understanding of the scientific revolution on the part of literary intellectuals, who too easily dismiss the positive aspects of technological progress. In comparing the twentieth century's crisis to the earlier industrial revolution, Snow amusingly notes that massive benefits of any particular technological leap are inevitably accompanied by deleterious side effects, observing, "there must have been similar losses—spread over a much longer period—when men changed from the hunting and food-gathering life to agriculture.

For some, it must have seemed a genuine spiritual impoverishment." (Snow, *The Two Cultures and the Scientific Revolution*, 32)

7. Ross Lipman, "Technical Aesthetics in the Preservation of Film Art," in *Big As Life: An American History of 8mm Films* (a special edition of *Cinematograph*) (Museum of Modern Art/San Francisco Cinematheque, 1998). Questions of authenticity quickly get complicated in art forms whose defining characteristics usually presuppose multiple articulations, such as a movie's viewing copies. This earlier essay analyzes cinematic authenticity in light of issues raised in Walter Benjamin's "The Work of Art in the Age of Mechanical Reproduction." The present work advances and in some ways reinterprets my earlier arguments.

8. One of the most articulate and sensible arguments for this strategy is Eileen Bowser's "Principles of Film Restoration," *Griffithiana*, 13, no. 38/39 (October 1990), 172–73. Bowser wisely couches the notion as one of several viable options an archive might take in approaching a preservation project. Portions of "The Gray Zone" may in part read as a response to, or continuation of, Bowser's work. A key difference would be that her primary interests are ethical and her aims concrete, whereas the present study is concerned with aesthetics and its aims abstract.

   Some background is instructive, for while the history of film archiving is well documented, the history of restoration techniques and strategies is largely not. At a broad stroke what's now known as "restoration" is in no small regard traceable to private film collectors, who began reassembling complete works from incomplete prints and fragments they acquired. The collector's market likewise figured in early efforts to create duplicate and reduction negatives at laboratories, with the Museum of Modern Art's Circulating Library representing a formative institutional parallel. At the intersection of these two methodological arcs—assembly and printing—one finds the birth of modern film restoration practice.

   Robert Gitt, who began as a collector in the 1950s and eventually went on to establish new quality standards for restoration as an art form in itself, recalls very consciously striving for Bowser's goal in his pioneering work—while simultaneously stating he does not recall the idea's having a particular source. It seems to have developed organically as laboratory techniques advanced and the historical moment of older films' creation receded, addressing a cultural need. Now that the artistic precision of Robert Gitt, Kevin Brownlow, and others has become established precedent, younger practitioners find themselves revisiting the same questions in terms appropriate to their own era. In this sense the present work, while in some ways polemical, represents more truly the continued refining of a cultural project that spans generations. The history of this larger project remains a topic ripe for future investigation.

9. The best projectionists of the silent era in fact considered interpretation to be a part of their craft, for both good and bad. F. H. Richardson wrote, "The operator 'renders' a film, if he is a real operator, exactly as does the musician render a piece of music... In the *Passion Play* he can make Peter act the part of a jumping jack and he can turn a horse race into a howling farce, by over-speeding and under-speeding... [He] must be guided by if he wishes to produce artistic projection... Only the application of brains to the matter of speed can properly rend a film." F. H. Richardson, "The Projection Department," *The Moving Picture World*, December 2, 1911, 721, 722; reprinted in David Pierce (ed.), Silent Film Bookshelf, http://www.cinemaweb.com/silentfilm/bookshelf/18_11_11.htm.

10. At a fundamental level, even the light passing through the projectors has changed, as modern 35mm projectors use xenon bulbs with different characteristics than traditional carbon arcs. Distinctions include both color temperature and intensity, varying over the long life of bulbs and the short life of carbon rods, and hence even during individual screenings. Carbon arc enthusiasts in fact represent a highly specialized subgroup within the extended archival film community.

11. Henry Peach Robinson, "Idealism, Realism, Expressionism," chap. 9 of *The Elements of a Pictorial Photograph* (n.p., 1896), reprinted in Alan Trachtenberg, ed, *Classic Essays on Photography* (Leete's Island Books, 1980), 96.

12. Ansel Adams, *The Negative: Exposure and Development* (Morgan & Morgan, 1968), 16.

13. Some claim that although the cards indeed have an 18 percent reflectance, light meters built to ANSI standards are calibrated for 12 percent, a discussion that only highlights the variability at play.

14. Some have speculated that it suggests a bias toward the rendering of Caucasian skin tones. Indeed, exposing one's film at a centered light reading from 18 percent gray will frequently result in underexposure of black skin. One of my early photography teachers, in an attempt at humor, referred to this problem with a call for "race attenuation filters." Adams notes that Caucasian skin tones tend

to fall in Zone VI, with an average reflectivity of 30–40 percent. He explains that "a surface of average tonality—such as the middle step of tone of a full-scale glossy print—would have a reflectance of about 18% and relates to Zone V of the exposure scale... . 'Middle Gray' [herein] represents the *geometrical mean* of the extremes of useful values" (Adams, *The Negative*, 16). An operative phrase is "useful values," which can presumably vary. A standard twenty-one-step scale has a maximum density (or D-max) of 3.05. Other scales utilize entirely different D-maxes.

15. In practice it is much easier to both make and accurately reproduce a stepped gray scale. For this reason it is common to see stepped scales, even in a zoned presentation. The Zone System practitioner understands that the stepped scale is a stand-in for the continuous scale, and remembers that each marked step falls near the middle of the range of that particular zone.
16. Minor White, Richard Zakia, and Peter Lorenz, *The New Zone System Manual* (Morgan Press, 1976), 4.
17. White, Zakia, and Lorenz, *New Zone System Manual*, 8.
18. As this article goes to press, the term "video" already carries an archaic ring, in its colloquial usage referring to an analog VHS tape. While contemporary media is largely digital, similar issues occur nonetheless. In a perverse inversion of the dilemma, it is now common to see "stretched" images, in which material originally in the 1.37:1 or 1.33:1 aspect ratios are expanded to fit a 1.77:1 high-definition format, without attendant masking. Even in screenings at academic conferences devoted to cinema scholarship it is quite common to see abnormally short, wide actors marching through a flattened landscape, without the slightest acknowledgment from presenters or viewers.
19. Although the lead roles were played by trained actors Henry Sanders and Kaycee Moore, most of the incidental roles were played by Burnett's friends and acquaintances.
20. The term "gamma," used as shorthand for "contrast," technically refers to the straight-line portion of the characteristic curve, or the portion of the curve wherein a particular film responds to light in a consistent manner.
21. In point of fact most printing systems used throughout film history have involved low-contrast negatives and intermediates in combination with high-contrast prints. In still film printing, the combination of negatives and positives ideally results in a gamma of 1.0—which is known as the Goldberg condition—wherein the final contrast matches the initial source. While the aim gamma is higher for motion pictures, which are projected in darkness, the basic principle still holds. In this instance, however, I refer to the process of altering standardized procedures to selectively control image rendition.
22. There is a phenomenon archivists call Shepard's Law (after the restorationist David Shepard), which states, "The moment a project is completed, better source materials will be found." The phrase "Shepard's Law," as it's been handed down, is in fact a bastardization of "Shepard's Second Principle of Film Restoration." For the amusing original explication of both Shepard's Principles, see David Shepard, "The Restoration of *Nanook*," *Blackhawk Bulletin*, February 1975, 50. Indeed, this principle proved apt in the case of *Multiple Sidosis*. Shortly after completion of our project Sid Laverents found his original 16mm A-B-C-D rolls. With luck we will be able to "re-restore" *Multiple Sidosis* some time in the future.
23. A detailed discussion of these issues can be found in my essay "Problems of Independent Film Preservation," in *Journal of Film Preservation* 25, no. 53 (1996), 49-58.
24. We also took the somewhat unusual step of printing onto a camera stock rather than Kodak's 72 internegative stock, which often suffers from a displeasing green-magenta shift when printing from materials other than the ECO stock it was designed to complement.
25. By this I mean to say that, in theory, it's unnecessary to add more contrast after the basic reduction needed to approximate Goldberg conditions has been attained.
26. By the math a master positive of gamma 1.2 printed to a duplicate negative at gamma .7 would identically match a gamma 1.4 masterpositive printed to a gamma .6 duplicate negative. Yet in actuality, will it? A test of this would occur in the Gray Zone.
27. Another potential factor in such scenarios is the respective shapes of the masterpositive and negative films' characteristic curves, and how they align with each other. By targeting a printing exposure for a specific portion of a film stock's curve, detail may be preserved in specific parts of the image and sacrificed in others. While this technique is rarely customized on a project basis, it is not unlike the standard practice of overexposing printing elements to help distinguish an image's D-min (density minimum) from its base density.

28. Practice in this regard varies, particularly with color film. As an example, one major Los Angeles laboratory tends to accept prints two points too red or magenta but reject prints that are two points too green, on the grounds that in their view cooler colors generally produce less pleasing Caucasian skin tones.
29. Ross Lipman, in David Chute, "About the Restorations," http://www.johnsaylesretro.com/body-brother-restor.html
30. Doros additionally made certain not to mention the rights clearance issues to Charles once he arrived, so that his preference wouldn't be influenced by financial considerations.
31. Technically speaking one needs to remember that the commonly used term "stereoscope" refers specifically to the viewer with which one sees the dual images. The images themselves are referred to jointly as a stereograph.
32. Ferdinand Hurter and Vero Driffield, in Peter Henry Emerson, *Naturalistic Photography for Students of the Art and the Death of Naturalistic Photography* (1899; rprt. Arno Press, 1973), book 2, 103. Emerson had initially contacted Hurter and Driffield, and quotes their reply at great length.
33. Emerson's notions of truthful depiction were quite specific and to a large extent based on Helmholtz's *Physiological Optics* of 1867. Helmholtz had demonstrated that human vision was only truly sharp in a small area of our field of sight, focused on the center of the retina. Outside of this central area vision quickly blurs. One of Emerson's primary arguments was that photographers should emulate this condition, to the point of focusing only a composition's main subject and intentionally defocusing other portions of the image. In this sense his definition of truth indeed takes on an anthropocentric cast, if perhaps an idiosyncratic one.
34. Emerson, *Naturalistic Photography.*
35. Emerson's own theories, in seeking definition, arguably led him into a corner. He writes: "Since all mental process… consists for the most part in differentiation—that is in the analysis of an unknown complex into known components—surely it were a Folly to confuse any longer the aims of Science and Art. Rather should we endeavor to draw an indelible line of demarcation between them, for in this way we make mental progress, and Science and Art at the same time begin to gather together their scattered forces, each one taking under its standard those powers that belong to it, and thus becoming … stronger and more permanent; for evolution is integration and differentiation passing into a coherent heterogeneity." "Science and Art," in Emerson, *Naturalistic Photography*, book 3, 67.

    For more on the mutual influences of Emerson and Hurter and Driffield, as well as a historical analysis of the limitations inherent in attempts to disassociate the art and science of photography, see Nancy Newhall, *P. H. Emerson: The Fight for Photography as a Fine Art* (Aperture, 1975), and John Richardson's web essay, "Double Vision Is but Perfect Vision: Stereography, Photography, and Cinema," http://wwwmcc.murdoch.edu.au/ReadingRoom/stereo/pres/index.htm.
36. In a telling remark that echoes Hurter and Driffield's dilemma and anticipates this essay, Raymond Spottiswoode's classic early text observed that "the theory of sensitometry oversimplifies the facts. Straight-line sensitometry exists only in textbooks, and while perfectly well adapted to control, fails when applied to interpretation." Although Spottiswoode's intent here is specific and practical, the implications can be read more broadly. Indeed, the observation appears in a section whose heading is "Practice and Theory Diverge." Spottiswoode, *Film and Its Techniques*, 185–86.
37. The film is loosely based on the novel *Roadside Picnic* by Boris and Arkady Strugatsky.
38. Both Emerson and Henry Peach Robinson (who feuded bitterly) evinced similar notions at points within their photographic theory, if to different degrees. Emerson described a "seer" who could pierce the veil of reality and then transfer it to a photograph (see Emerson, *Naturalistic Photography*, book 1, 183). Robinson was decidedly more democratic and strongly believed that the art of photography was accessible to anyone. He nonetheless notes that "only the educated eye of one familiar with the laws upon which pictorial effect depends… can discover these accidental beauties, and ascertain in what they consist." Henry Peach Robinson, *Pictorial Effect in Photography: Being Hints on Composition and Chiaroscuro Effects for Photographers* (Piper and Carter, 1869), 12.

    The two rivals here parallel each other in a celebration of the artist, and Emerson in particular reveals a shade of elitism. I would posit the Stalker as an alternative position from which one can approach these questions, while noting that, like anything of value, the position requires a certain discipline to attain. Perhaps this is merely another form of idealism. Tarkovsky himself decries the spiritual dearth of modern society and deifies the artist: "The beautiful is hidden from the eyes of those who are not searching for the truth, for whom it is contraindicated… those people who see art and condemn it… are neither willing nor ready to consider the meaning or aim of their existence in any higher sense." Tarkovsky continues, "the artist cannot be deaf to the call of truth; it alone defines his creative will, organizes it… An artist who has no faith is like a painter who has been born blind" Tarkovsky, *Sculpting in Time: Reflections on the Cinema*, trans. Kitty Hunter Blair (The Bodley Head, 1986), 42–43. He herein points to a contemporary crisis of faith that can be symptomatic of a scientific view of the world, but simultaneously permeates contemporary art. Both disciplines are linked. Faith is the characteristic that distinguishes the Stalker, and the tool that lets him organize a sense of truth within the Zone.

This short rumination marks a shift in my theoretical work's focus from restoration practice itself to cinematic perception. Although they're closely interlinked, the former is ultimately dependent on viewing conditions, and so the practical focus on specific artworks becomes moot in absence of their reception. This essay also points toward differing, if not conflicting, notions of media literacy operating in today's culture. We're surrounded by an abundance of images and hence everyone might lay claim to fluency in them. My take is that an unrecognized and fluid language of perception underlies the common forms people feel they know well. The lack of awareness of these underlying principles amidst the ongoing image explosion points to a collective void; our cultural loss as lamented by Benjamin.

Originally published in The Moving Image, *Vol. 12, No. 1, Spring 2012.*

In Search of Sight-Specific Cinema

The conundrum that shadows me is, somewhat absurdly, the place of medium integrity in the age of the "post-medium artist." I enjoy the irony, but it's an all too real question. Canadian filmmaker Michael Snow spoke to this quite eloquently at the Experimental Media Congress in Toronto last year.[1] Looking at differences between the newer and older work presented, he singled out an attention to "qualities" in the latter, largely absent in the former. By "qualities," I understood him to mean a sensuality dependent on physiological perception, and also on an elusive essence somehow interwoven with a work's physical form. The newer work, in contrast, relied largely upon an image's representational and associative properties.

This broad characterization is, if true, in no small part tied to the technologies that produced the work, and should by no means be viewed as bad in itself. It's merely change. The crudity of available video equipment simply may have led artists to abandon formal subtleties.[2] But as the focus of the present issue is "experimental cinema and the archive," we as archivists need to be concerned with them. The question is exceptionally pressing in the case of experimental cinema, where so many of the artists' primary interests were embedded in those elusive "qualities." Of course there are distinct qualities in electronic imaging as well as photochemical works, if one is looking. So in principle, it's not a digital/analog question.

In point of fact we've been vexed by a digital/analog dichotomy put forth all too frequently. Historically two camps have arisen, and like factional politicians, each depends on strong passions, or rejection (of the old or new) to further sectarian agendas. As Václav Havel said, hatred seeks its lightning rod.[3] We need to move past that, toward an appreciation of forms in themselves, allowing each to live with its unique character celebrated.

As part of that we need to be cognizant of the challenges of digital media, correcting the myth of its easy replication. Not only is digital replication as challenging as anything in the photochemical realm, it can be more so. Tracing the electronic image back to its analog roots, one finds Stan Brakhage noting that video was an impractical form for anyone interested in color (for example), because the actual hues seen by a viewer were usually dependent on a subjective "knob-twiddling," on an unknown monitor.[4] While things have certainly improved since Brakhage's observations, it's not by as much as one would think. We might successfully use current tools to preserve a work, but without appropriate viewing conditions the enterprise's value is compromised. A focused discussion of electronic image presentation standards is well beyond the scope of these informal thoughts, but I will say that anyone who has presented work at a variety of contemporary venues knows that actual video projection conditions vary tremendously in practice.

So we return to the notion of increasing appreciation of "qualities"—whatever they may be, and of working to present them appropriately. The scope of this problem can't be overstated, and it's misunderstood at even the professional level. Programmers, scholars and critics understandably seek DVD "screeners" or data streams for home preview, while only the best fully realize that some works will not survive such a translation. All too often I'll encounter those who say, "I'm a professional. I can imagine the difference." When I hear that I usually think (not vindictively, but observationally) that their professionalism resides in other areas. As Duke Ellington said when asked what jazz was, "If you have to ask, you'll never know." Some things need to be experienced, not imagined or visualized. As someone who works closely with these issues on a daily basis, I know from experience that I myself can't always appreciate the differences until I perceive them directly. I can recall situations in which I was ready to dismiss works as inconsequential on small-monitor viewing, only to realize my error upon seeing them in their appropriate context. Now I know better—or at least enough to appreciate what I *don't* know.

One thing I do know is that there is no easy answer. We can hope that photochemical cinema lingers in some form for many a year, but there's no denying that among experimental media artists it already stands at a remove from common practice, and the further one goes into digital production, the more confusing it all gets. Contemporary productions freely mingle multiple formats within a single work, leveled out. That's all well and good, but troubles arise when the memory of physical form itself is lost. A medium is viewed as a carrier of content, apart from it—whereas in older works, as Michael Snow suggested, they might be indivisible.

The rate of technological change is part of the challenge. Things come and go so quickly that the phrase "post-medium" becomes less ironic, and more and more relevant. If artists make work that is medium-independent, what does preservation (and presentation) mean exactly? The continual transcoding of digital images across platforms, even within a single production, calls into question the very idea of an "original" or master source to emulate.

We thus need to look at each work individually, and understand both its internal nature and presentation context. Many curators and archivists already understand this, and make every effort to preserve and present works in a way that's formally appropriate, even if that appropriateness is ambiguous. Once we've established the work and its methods of presentation, with the formal properties of each piece distinct or at least considered, a chance arises for future viewers to see those differences. The project is at once technical, educational, and aesthetic.

This isn't to say works can't be "preserved" as technology shifts, but simply that as archivists and/or artists, we need to keep an eye on the shifts. The challenge of digital media for artists is to reclaim "qualities" as viable working materials. As our tools develop, what's now a challenge will be recognized as opportunity.

Archivists and curators can't fully address cultural change, but there's at least a fighting chance with technology. One can reproduce artworks and create physical conditions in which they're seen, even as the apparatus changes. Perhaps most vitally, we can increase understanding of—and sensitivity to—the potentials of differing media. In so doing, we can help future viewers and creators to See more fully.

Endnotes

1. April 7-11, 2010. The first Congress, also in Toronto, had taken place in October 1989, so the recent event inevitably invited a historical perspective.
2. My generalization here should not be mistaken for polemic. Clearly, early video art practitioners such as Nam June Paik were deeply invested in formal questions, which were very much in the air at the time of video art's inception. What's interesting to note is that video's progress over the ensuing decades largely coincided with a move away from this line of thought.
3. Václav Havel, address at "The Anatomy of Hate" Conference, Oslo, August 28, 1990. http://vaclavhavel.cz/showtrans.php?cat=projevy&val=299_aj_projevy.html&typ=HTML
4. While I just decried dichotomization—and hate speech aside—one can't help but enjoy the occasional good rant. Brakhage declared, "Where video is an art it is like sand painting—now you see it, now you don't. It has no permanence, there is no way you can preserve it. What makes it even harder to accept as an art is that the medium for looking at it is intrinsically hypnotic, which is perfect for advertising but lousy if not impossible for an aesthetic ecology. And its luminescent lighting actually sickens people. Then for a colorist like me it cannot hold any interest because it doesn't have any color—it's whatever color the set is when you twiddle the knobs." From Suranjan Ganguly, "Stan Brakhage: The 60th Birthday Interview," in *Experimental Cinema: The Film Reader*, eds. Wheeler W. Dixon and Gwendolyn Audrey Foster (Routledge, 2002), 160.

This short musing is all that emerged from thoughts once intended for a book-length work on the nature of film grain. Originally published in Incite #6, *Fall 2015.*

Babel: The Remake

> "Now the whole earth had one language and few words.
>
> Then they said, "Come, let us build ourselves a tower with its top in the heavens."
>
> And the LORD said, "Behold, they are one people, and they have all one language; and this is only the beginning of what they will do; and nothing that they propose to do will now be impossible for them."
>
> So the LORD scattered them abroad from there over the face of all the earth.
>
> Therefore its name was called Ba'bel,* because there the LORD confused the language of all the earth."
>
> — Genesis 11

The Digital Revolution is Babel renewed. In 35mm film, visible to the naked eye, one finds a universal language of sparse beauty and elegance. But humanity's great project of Conquest does not end with the physical world, and so the infinite spectrum of light and sound is turned to a Tower of Zeros and Ones, and therein presumed mastered.

The Tower stretches to the heavens in that all is converted, or seen to be. In the course of conversion the common tongue stutters amidst scattered formats. One compressed this way, one that. Each replaced by the next, in its time.

---

* In Hebrew, "balal" or "lebalbel" means to jumble.

You may say, this binary state of things is as old as the stars, always flickering, always burning.

An ongoing Tao of presence and absence.

So how do things differ now? What's lost in translation?

Once upon a time, impermanence — in its continuum — proved the nature of permanence. It alone was eternal. Whereas the new impermanence masquerades in eternity's garb.

A digital Babel confounds the nature of things living in time.
The bond between light and material is severed, and confusion permeates the image.

Copper engraving by L. A. Corvinus in J. J. Scheuchzer's *Sacred Physics*, 1735.

A rant, but not a manifesto. The original version, written in 2013, was far more harsh. As I wrote, I constantly heard my old high school English teacher Mrs. Burrow's formidable voice calling for evidence supporting my claims, and hence dug into the dirty business of naming names guilty of the faults described. But it's not my aim to distract from ideas by getting into the mud on this artist or that, which is after all just my own predilection. Far better to leave it to the reader to try the ideas presented against their own experience, and accept or argue the claims by their own measure. I myself found the original draft petty, and never attempted to publish it. I've since revised and truncated it, focusing more purely on idea than example. But a hint of the original diatribe remains… and for a more lighthearted suggestion of the excised material one can see "My Art is Better Than Your Art" in the Histories section of this volume.

A New Model for Moving Image Museums

It's one of our culture's great ironies that museums and galleries devoted to the visual arts face backbreaking challenges when presenting cinematic works. Coming from traditions of painting and sculpture, gallery spaces can invite viewers to wander through fully lit rooms at their own pace, with sounds in abundance. This contradicts the needs of a time-based medium, which often requires an enclosed environment with focused reception. While some institutions and artists have sought solutions to these problems, the fact is that many artists have responded in reverse, by creating works that require neither darkness nor silence, commencement nor conclusion. They make works that exist in time, but don't articulate it as a property. This is of course a potentially valid strategy, but what of works that don't follow those conventions?

    This essay is at once a re-consideration of conservation strategies and a call for a new kind of cinematic museum. It addresses methods of duplication, restoration, and presentation. It asks how institutions can preserve the cinematic experience in all its forms, including both photochemical and digital technologies.

I. The Problem of The Museum

The term "moving image art" suggests different things to different ears, ranging from high to low culture. In recent years fine art museums have absorbed it as a sub-category of time-based media, which can also include sound-specific works, installations, and sculptural works that incorporate moving images. Experimental film and art cinema are largely distinct from gallery-based "TBM," and all three would distinguish themselves from popular cinema, which can lay its own legitimate claim to the "moving image art" label. In my own use of the term "moving image art" I would like to envision not so much an improved museum that contains TBM, as a museum specifically devoted to the moving image in its multiplicity of forms. To realize our museum, it's instructive to examine not just individual works, but the interconnected practices of their restoration and presentation.

Elsewhere I've argued for subjectivity in restoration,[1] a controversial approach within traditional art conservation practice.[2] Alongside this, I advocate the use of *non*-subjective standards in exhibition design; an approach one might think equally heretical if one were to base one's judgment on a survey of contemporary exhibition practice.

Cinema as a single-channel medium is historically a form intended for controlled environments. From shortly after its inception, the collective wisdom of its creators was directed at an experience in a darkened room, with a set beginning and end.[3] In commercial cinemas and art cinemas alike, light and sound levels are now standardized, and, in general, presented with established and measurable qualities. Museums and galleries, originally conceived for the presentation of non-time-based works in light-flooded and sound-flooded environments to ambulatory audiences, are misfit for moving image presentation in their very concept. To use them for this purpose is an unconscious act of misguided habit, akin to scratching a phantom limb.

In recent years curators and scholars have begun recognizing the problem, although solutions remain elusive. Fault lines lay along technical, aesthetic, and socio-economic axes. How can we begin addressing the proper presentation of moving image works in museums and galleries? To begin to answer these questions, let's first isolate two of the major praxes on which the answers may lie.

The White Cube and the Black Box

The term "white cube" was adopted to describe modern gallery spaces designed primarily for two and three-dimensional works intended for viewing with some form of direct or incidental light. The "black box" on the other hand, can accommodate darkness, and as generally understood in the museum context is conceived specifically for flexibility; to adapt to the needs of any work.[4] Some artists have effectively worked with lit or partially lit rooms as effective components of their moving image work, while others distinctly call for darkness. We should be able to agree that certain pieces have unique properties that demand presentation in one or the other environment. Surely the broad range of our available terms can accommodate anything. Why then, has it so frequently proven difficult to implement ideal conditions?

In the well-established world of mainstream cinematic exhibition we already find the tools one needs to begin creating controlled conditions within a darkened room. Yet these excellent tools—allowing precise measurement of light and sound levels—are rarely found in museum black boxes. The problem may lie in the very versatility of the black box model. In seeking to allow anything, many museums understandably avoid the physical limitations that come with long-term installation of heavy equipment.

One can argue that the lack of implementation of these already-standardized presentation models is merely a symptom of the galleries' need to accommodate a multiplicity of works, but on examination the problems are more complex. The nearly systemic avoidance of such tools and standards is not merely a practical and financial issue, but also cultural.

Medium Integrity

Art conservation, emerging from the tradition of painting, is historically based on the notion of a unique *ur* artifact which demands a concrete retention of its physical properties. In moving image archive parlance this takes the form of a preservation of *medium integrity*. This good impulse remains at odds with the common museum and gallery practice of presenting moving image works in uncontrolled white cube, or at best, compromised black box conditions. Such conditions in effect sabotage the best efforts at retention of medium integrity by eliminating the conditions of a work's subsequent reception, even as they hold steadfast to the physical artifact. So one finds a fundamental contradiction at the heart of many institutions' goals and practices.

To fully understand this, traditional art conservation must be distinguished from motion picture preservation, which is historically based on the creation of new duplicate copies, as is appropriate for a medium whose existence is in fact predicated on replication. In an alignment of disparate practices, conservators in both motion picture archives and art museums alike have sensibly argued for the maintenance of integrity of physical form within duplication as a fundamental principle of the preservation of moving image artworks. This line of thinking acknowledges that an *ur*-artifact might not be presentable, but its viewing copies should retain its most essential formal properties.

However an additional crisis has emerged in our era that begs—in fact demands—a practical re-evaluation of all these questions. This is of course the transition to digital technology, which has threatened the very existence of photochemical media. While it seems likely that photochemical imaging systems shall continue to exist in some form, the existence of an economic social structure enabling the maintenance of standardized industrial production of a variety of film stocks and their subsequent presentation seems far less secure. What is certain is that digital presentation of images shall proliferate, and conservators and curators will need to wade in the muddy ethical and philosophical waters it presents.

Vitally parallel to the technical-digital revolution is a socio-political sea change in the nature of art itself, identified by Rosalind Krauss as the post-medium condition. While this term originates in its description of conceptual art, which did away with physical objects as a primary site of human expression, the term is of extreme value in describing the digital crisis, which encompasses the wholesale de-physicalization of moving images. The de-physicalization of artworks and de-physicalization of images are linked in their crystallization of a centuries-in-the-making Cartesian split of spirit from body. When properties of light, color, and sound—or for that matter anything—are transformed to value-free binary placeholders—one needs to accept on faith that those numbers will effectively embody their original source when reconstituted—or, heretically, one must re-evaluate the very notion of historic artistic presentation and the attendant meaning of physicality.

The Artists' Response

Artists have understandably responded to the situation in a variety of ways. Tacita Dean has nobly championed the singular properties of photochemical film, culminating in the self-reflexive statement *Film* presented in large-screen vertical projection in the Tate's Turbine Hall, accompanied by an in-depth catalog featuring discussions of the subject. For decades, Bill Viola led the field of artists actively exploring the formal properties of electronic imaging systems.

But for every Dean or Viola, there are dozens of artists who have moved in precisely the opposite direction, creating works that do not rely on formal properties as key components of their work. Consciously or unconsciously responding to the practical reality of white cube presentation, they create works in which some or all of the following general characteristics may be found:

> Compositionally, there is a tendency to emphasize graphic design and the representational/cognitive aspects of imagery, while de-emphasizing nuances of light and color, which are less easily duplicated and which may be compromised in a lit room.
>
> Audio may function as an environmental stimulant, but does not rely heavily on syntactical or time-based structures. It presumes that noise bleed from nearby galleries may be present and overlapping with its own sound. For these reasons, focused listening is not essential.
>
> Time-based works tend to avoid a reliance on sequential viewing, but rather assume that most viewers (being ambulatory) might walk in and out, not experiencing the totality of a work. Duration may be present, but is not essential.

Cumulatively, these factors describe an acceptance of conditions wherein artworks may be received in a state of distraction as opposed to focused attention.[5] A useful formulation in regard to the above is that one should be prepared to distinguish between works that are black-box specific, white-box specific, or presentation-agnostic.[6] The latter term describes works which do not have specific demands for successful exhibition; an increasingly common phenomenon.

In such a climate, outward rebellion against mainstream culture is seen as the artist's default response to mainstream cinema, even as they mirror it in method. Benjamin Buchloh has eloquently stated that this takes the form of a deskilling, in which artists disregard or openly scorn "outdated" notions of form, structure, and craftsmanship.[7]

This needs to be understood as ironic in a context wherein this very deskilling — accompanied by a digital democratization of access to professional production tools — blurs distinctions between professional and amateur artists. The artists' rebellion, as witnessed in the formal characteristics described, rejects the skilled "middle brow" art cinema while aping a less articulated popular culture (such as the common YouTube video[8]) in an eschewing of aesthetic rigor. Galleries in turn sell the rebellion against formal skill to collectors at premium prices, in a classic Situationist instance of recuperation, commodifying rebellion itself.

These are, unfortunately, restrictive conditions for both artists and museums, in that notable sectors of meaningful work are denied access to appropriate presentation by both practical exhibition factors and cultural momentum. As Buchloh points out, not all art need be oppositional to or supportive of power or structure in the abstract.[9]

Conversely, cultural authority need not be corrupted in practice. One merely needs to envision a healthy society, in which the structures of power recall the reasons for their creation, and in responsive action to change, find appropriate balance.

The museum as currently configured currently has little to offer the moving image artist outside of capital and prestige. It does not offer sufficient ways to effectively share the artistic encounter. While I wouldn't go so far as to say white cube conditions preclude the possibility of aesthetic experience, I will say they make it very, very difficult for the black box artist. So we are faced with the challenge of creating better black boxes within a museum context.

II. Against Authenticity—for the moment!

The decline of focused reception is one of the most profound cultural losses of recent decades. It can be witnessed at every level of society, from the multiple windows open on the nation's laptops, to the overcrowded public spaces of the world's cities. The mind's baseline setting is "multi-task," and seclusion itself has become an antiquarian concept.[10] Amidst this, our generation has witnessed an explosion of contexts in which moving images are received. The days when commercial cinemas dominated disappeared long ago with the advent of television, a form which now itself fades as works are displayed on personal devices including laptops, tablets, and smartphones.

Moving image art has split into distinguishable (if semi-overlapping) categories of experimental film, world cinema, underground works, web works, and gallery-based media art.

The challenge facing museums with a broad interest in the range of moving image expression is to create spaces that allow all these forms to exist, and be seen in ways appropriate to each. As a cultural corrective, cinema art practitioners need to envision environments allowing focused reception, as well as the works that demand them, amidst the normative pressures of distraction.

The goal is no less than the re-creation an aesthetic consciousness in a de-aestheticized digital era. While it is ultimately up to artists to, in Buchloh's formulation, re-skill themselves, art professionals can help engender that awakening by creating the experiences that inspire future generations. This can be enabled with a new concept of moving image museums; one that embraces wider definitions of cinematic art, and—in acknowledging the relation between media and its presentation—offer better spaces for the work to be shown.

To realize these conditions, it's instructive to reconsider the ways conservators and exhibitors alike approach the handling of moving image works. In contrast with prior notions of both art conservation and moving image preservation, one needs to address the radical notion that artworks in many cases no longer demand a singular physical form. As Kraus' post-medium model indicates, cinema has been de-physicalized in the move away from photochemical imaging systems. Frequently, no one iteration of a particular piece can be acknowledged as definitive. Makers ranging from the commercial to fine art world alike anticipate that their works will undergo numerous mutations allowing presentation in different contexts.

Art professionals need to address this dynamic. In a post-medium age, rather than holding in mind a singular physical presence as authentic, one needs to consider multi-versioning for specific exhibition contexts. In this framework, the very concept of preservation is fundamentally transformed. Authoring and editioning for different viewing conditions become considerations, transforming notions of the fundamental nature of authenticity. A museum or gallery restoring a single work may need to create a multiplicity of distinct iterations of it, anticipating the points at which its digitized identity is physically reconstituted in the world.

This process can be viewed from the vantage of a traditional restoration / access split, in which—inverting much contemporary thought and practice—restoration work emphasizes the subjective, and museum presentation emphasizes the standardized. These two components—restoration and access—work in tandem with each other in the "realization" of a work.

From Lab to Gallery: Restoration

Pip Laurenson has succinctly described the state of affairs in writing, "a notion of authenticity based in material evidence that something is real, genuine or unique is no longer relevant to a significant portion of contemporary art."[11] While some works negate the need for medium integrity intrinsically, others are faced with its unattainability due to technological obsolescence. These conditions are all the more difficult to acknowledge, in that "conservative" is built into very word "conservation": scientific distance and objectivity have been fundamental working assumptions. Yet to approach the restoration of many contemporary works, interpretation is intrinsic to the process by both definition and practical limits. Authenticity becomes an elusive if not absurd pursuit, in that:

> a) it's physically impossible to recreate identical light and color values in a different physical medium than the one of origin, and
>
> b) it's potentially detrimental to try too literally, in that efforts to do so can fool one into thinking one's achieved an ontologically impossible success, precluding other effective results.

This was well-evidenced in a presentation I recently saw at a film archiving conference, in which a leading institution exhibited the digital rendition of a film originally shot on long-discontinued Kodachrome stock. Kodachrome remains legendary to the present day for its vivid, unfading colors, and many archivists including myself have spent many hours trying to faithfully render its unique "look" using today's non-Kodachrome film stocks. The presenters at hand had an excellent understanding of the importance of color palette to the work, explaining how they had diligently used their computers to recreate the distinctive feel of the stock. The only problem was that to this viewer's eye the resulting work did not successfully evoke Kodachrome. In fact it looked nothing like it—in my personal view. This is entirely subjective, but no more subjective than the presenters' suggestion that their work had objectively achieved its aim. The point is that subjectivity is built into the process, whether acknowledged or not. For this reason, I mischievously come out here "Against Authenticity" in restoration, words I surely never thought I'd type.[12] Of course, I can praise interpretation, but to engage in it well is a far from easy task.

From Lab to Gallery: Access

At the same time that the place of subjectivity in restoration needs to be considered, we can conversely seek greater control in establishing viewing conditions. As indicated, it's easy to create white cubes for works that don't need focused reception or are presentation-agnostic; the trick is rather, to effectively integrate the black box into museum experiences.

To this end, perhaps our greatest asset is ironically the commercial cinema, which has acknowledged the importance of standards for decades. We can look to commercial cinemas in the creation of light and sound-proofed rooms. Sound levels can be accurately measured from pink noise played through loudspeakers and read on SPL meters. Screen brightness can be accurately measured in footlamberts. Also, greater effort can be placed in employing pre-determined start times and announced durations—perhaps even using ticket-based systems for selected works—to allow museum goers to maximize their viewing experience.

III. A New Model for Moving Image Museums

As one who generally finds rules confining and limiting, I am often uncomfortable with such well-intended enterprises as "codes of ethics" and "best practices" documents, which upon creation, tend to quickly bump up against real-world situations that indicate the limits of their terms. Rather, I tend to encourage fluid principles to which one can look, and then adapt to specific circumstances. Many of the things I suggest have been implemented in variation at numerous institutions globally. With these things in mind, I can encourage the following components of our hypothetical museum:

> a) More active partnerships not just between museums and artists, but also between curators and conservators. In particular I believe museums and galleries should seek to create more detailed restoration and presentation agreements to help determine which factors might be crucial in later re-visitations of a work. These essential documents vary considerably in content and form, from gallery to gallery, from artist to artist, and even work to work. They might additionally contain such information as guidelines for transcoding and re-mastering existing pieces in not-yet-developed media forms, and for control of exhibition conditions as they arise.[13]
>
> b) A three-faceted museum, including:
>> 1) dedicated large black boxes with calibrated projection and sound systems, as well as planned programming, on the model of traditional cinematheques
>> 2) white cubes/open gallery spaces for light-based artworks that call for lit rooms, or that do not require focused reception
>> 3) dedicated small black boxes, for temporary exhibitions as well as small-party viewing by selection. By this latter phrase I mean to suggest small rooms in which limited groups of viewers can enter and select works for viewing from a menu or even catalog.
>
> c) Alongside the above efforts, moving image professionals can include "medium studies" education as part of their public missions. Museum-goers should be aware that context of viewing can be an integral part of the moving image experience, in much the same way that seeing a reproduction of a painting is not the same thing as seeing the original painting. Some works simply can't be properly experienced on an iPhone. Artists should likewise be advised that creation of viewing and/or reproduction instructions may become a vital part of their practice.

While one would hardly want to police these things, one can certainly try to improve conditions and minimize damage. To mitigate the increasing loss of focused reception in our culture, I advocate a two-fold principle. In the restoration and re-mastering of moving image works, I suggest we prepare a move away from the notion of singular physical presence determining medium integrity, even as we acknowledge its importance. If only by necessity, we must ask how to adapt an existing work for differing contexts when appropriate, while somehow retaining its essential character. To do so we will likely need to beware of slavish replication, and acknowledge the role of active interpretation on the part of conservators. In parallel to this, we need to encourage the use of measurable standards in presentation venues. This will allow artists and restorationists to work on the honing of their projects with reasonable confidence that their efforts will be successfully represented in the world.

In so doing—by allowing the multiple forms of moving image art to exist side-by-side in appropriate presentations—we can begin to address some of the cultural problems that exist in today's media landscape, including the class divide as represented in high, low, and middle-targeted works, and expressed in different technologies and practices. It would appear today's artists need to re-skill themselves, while museums and galleries need to re-examine their core focus on the ambulatory viewer. Re-skilling artists and re-aestheticizing viewers are investments in establishing tradition and cultural continuity, at a time of rapid cultural change.

All this might seem absurdly daunting in a world of technological obsolescence, where one's life experiences may not even speak to the next generation, let alone subsequent ones. But it's precisely our challenge.

Endnotes

1. Ross Lipman, "The Gray Zone," *The Moving Image*, Vol. 9, No. 2, Fall 2009, 1-29.
2. I will primarily use the term "conservation" in association with art museum practice, and "restoration" in association with film archiving practice, although the terms are used in both contexts. In brief, "conservation" will refer to the physical maintenance of a prime artifact; "restoration" will refer to a process whereby the potentially abstract essence of a work is recreated in a duplicate copy by a variety of means.
3. Somewhat apart from this particular dynamic lies early cinema's history as a fairground attraction, as noted in extensive scholarship by Tom Gunning and others. The present essay, while fully acknowledging the artistic potential of "pure entertainment," is primarily concerned with moving images as art regardless of social strata, and hence focuses on the consideration of works made with more overtly conscious artistic intent.
4. The use of the term "black box" in museums and galleries is pre-dated by its use in the theater where it generally refers to an unadorned, dark four-walled room in which performances occur.
5. As with so many things, much of our thinking on these issues can trace to Walter Benjamin's "The Work of Art in the Age of Mechanical Reproduction" (reprinted in *Illuminations* (Schocken, 1985).
6. Certainly other formulations exist (web-based works, small-screen works, etc.), but they need not be a core issue of the present discussion.
7. Benjamin H.D. Buchloh, "Farewell to an Identity," *Artforum*, December 2012, 252-261.

8. At the same time I would be remiss to ignore the existence of many skilled YouTube video makers. It's interesting to look for distinctions between the best of these, and institutionally-endorsed artists who on occasion explore similar themes or forms. But that's for another time… the present discussion's reference is to the millions of lay-practioners.
9. Buchloh, ibid. The Duchamps and the Warhols, in their de-aestheticization, are only meaningful in a context of skilled artistry that's calcified. When everyone is deskilled, such work loses its meaning. In this light, the subsequent Koonses and Hirsts may be seen as far more decadent and removed from life than anything a skilled artist could produce. To carry de-skilling into today's fine art world is as indulgent as the patriarchy Duchamp and Warhol challenged; self-reflexivity doing nothing to redeem it. Whatever the implied critique, if we're blind to this dynamic we replicate it.
10. To take a rather immediate example, as I've tried to write this paragraph I've been interrupted by no less than a phone call, a rambunctious teenager, an oversensitive smoke alarm, a neighbor's car alarm, and a family of skunks that lives behind our Los Angeles home.
11. Pip Laurenson, "Authenticity, Change and Loss in the Conservation of Time-Based Media Installations," *Tate Papers*, October 2006, 9, http://www.tate.org.uk/research/publications/tate-papers/authenticity-change-and-loss-conservation-time-based-media.
12. I've previously called for transformed notions of authenticity. The present tongue-in-cheek formulation simply carries the notion a bit further. See: Ross Lipman, "Technical Aesthetics in the Preservation of Film Art," in *Big As Life: An American History of 8mm Films* (a special edition of *Cinematograph*) (Museum of Modern Art/San Francisco Cinematheque, 1998), an earlier essay which examines moving image forms in light of Walter Benjamin's specific notions of the meaning of authenticity.
13. An excellent model for such documents is likely the multi-page instruction manual for presentation of Christian Marclay's *The Clock*, although at the time of writing this essay I have yet to be able to view a copy to verify this.

If "The Gray Zone" is the clearest distillation of my thoughts on restoration proper, this more informal companion piece synthesizes an approach to restoration's sister, exhibition, at its most fundamental level. It follows a direct line of thought from "A New Model."

Written amidst the pandemic's height, "The Archival Impermanence Project" transposes my thoughts on viewing from the gallery to the home. While its immediate inspiration was the conditions of lockdown, the pandemic's impact on our field was but a part of larger cultural forces which preceded and follow that moment. The essay's underlying principles hold true for theatrical presentation as well as the home: while cinema is largely seen as a fixed art, each presentation of a film is a discrete instance whose variables depend on the context of viewing. In this light, one might find a resolution of some paradoxes latent in Benjamin's pioneering vision.

Originally published as a web-piece in Caligari *#4, Spring 2022. https://caligaripress.com/The-Archival-Impermanence-Project-or-Performing-Cinema-in-the-Age-of*

The Archival Impermanence Project
or:
Performing Cinema in the Age of the Death of Everything

Amidst all the other crises facing us today, lies cinema's. What does that mean? Who even cares? Some friends of mine recoil at the word cinema itself, which for them suggests pretension and snobbery. Others don't mind the word, but think such worries are inconsequential in the scheme of things. It's hard to argue with that when the world is burning. But in such times it's more important than ever to find moments of reprieve, and that's something the cinema can give in welcome abundance. So what do I mean when I say the cinema is in crisis?

Obviously the theaters are challenged by pandemic-induced restrictions of all kinds. But what of home viewing, which offers at least glimmers of hope? It's both a blessing and a curse. As a film restorationist by trade and filmmaker by night, I've been looking at such questions for a few decades now, and it's interesting to see how my views have developed over the years.

Back in the early 1990s, when digital was just a blip on the horizon, I was among the film purists who looked ahead to preserving the organic aesthetics of photochemical film. At that time digital quality was more or less terrible, and I focused on sustaining the analog experience for as long as possible. I was fortunate to find work at the UCLA Film & Television Archive under the tutelage of preservation visionary Robert Gitt, where we strived to create the best possible photochemical renditions of works ranging from Hollywood classics to experimental film and beyond. But somewhere along the years things began to change. Digital quality improved, and Bob and I diverged on one small practical axis. He considered his job complete when the film print was made, whereas I began a parallel practice in digital remastering.[1] Today it's the digital versions of my restorations that are seen in the great bulk of instances, and Bob concedes wishing he'd done more back in the day.

Nowadays digital quality has risen to such levels that it's almost a non-issue—at least one I don't need to discuss in this context—because much larger problems exist. Those problems arise when one reinvestigates the nature of the cinematic experience itself. When I say the "cinematic experience" I use the term in the broadest sense—to encompass everything from theatrical viewing to the museum and gallery to the home. Uniting these disparate environments, I'd like to take one point of departure that defines our term. The cinematic experience is one that requires *focused viewing*, as distinct from distracted engagement— a phenomenon noted by Walter Benjamin decades ago that now defines our times.

Let's first look at distraction in the home, which has increasingly become the main battlefront on which the unconscious war on cinema unfolds. The war is unintentional, and entirely understandable. We're all exhausted and stressed out by the demands of everyday life. When one connects to a screen, it's precisely distraction that's usually sought—a way to forget our troubles. But let's distinguish between *escape* and *transportation*; two modes of leaving those troubles. The first being flight from a bad place; the second being a means of reaching another, hopefully better one. Our quotidian screen engagements offer the former; cinema offers the latter. The trick is that to experience it, one intrinsically needs to bypass distraction, which is no easy task.

The movie theater, developed upon centuries of change in traditional theaters, is perfect for the task. But in the present moment it's not as readily accessible. We're more frequently watching at home. So let's take a look at some of the forms distraction takes in a home viewing environment. I herewith present:

A Home Viewer's Guide to Distraction

Light Pollution

Until recent times most moving image works were designed for viewing in a darkened room, yet are now most frequently viewed with incidental light that affects the tones and colors of the images. This can be further exacerbated by reflections on a glass screen.

Sound Pollution

Noise unconnected to a work by definition distracts from it.

Picture and Sound Quality

Moving toward the device itself, a number of factors beyond reasonable viewer control offer further distraction:

> small screen size
> buffering or freezing of video streams
> compression artifacts
> picture and sound out of sync in video stream
> watermarking

Display Context and Viewer Engagement

The above presupposes a viewer at least aspires to a concentrated viewing state. But that's a presumption. Let's list a few other factors that come into play through passive or active choice:

passive choice
viewing on small screens when better options are available in the home
not optimizing screen brightness or sound level[2]

active choice
using multiple devices at once (e.g., phone and laptop)
having multiple windows open on a single screen

Our active choices speak to a multi-tasking mode of engagement at a polar end from the dedicated viewing experience. Many viewers quite understandably enjoy chat rooms or monitoring social media while a work is in progress. This practice extends to theaters and museums, as seen in the frequent checking of phones during a movie or amidst an exhibition. An analysis of the social ramifications of this phenomenon is only peripheral to this discussion, so let's just say it serves a function outside the domain of the artist—which remains my present point of concern.[3]

Even when one optimizes the surrounding conditions, another challenge arises. The comfort of home viewing invites an impatience that the theater discourages. If a work doesn't engage immediately, it's easy to switch off. Switching off can be a welcome option amidst an onslaught of dross calling for eyeballs, but that's again not my concern here. Rather, I want to facilitate an active engagement with those works that merit it. Some works don't make their strengths known until time has elapsed, and they face severe challenges in the present reception climate. We live in a world where more people are viewing more content than ever, but poorly and in fragments.

Although my main focus is home viewing, these conditions are by no means unique to it. A surprising amount of the same problems arise in supposed bastions of art: the museums and galleries. As a matter of practice our institutions have historically relied on models designed for static, non-time-based artworks. While painting and sculpture can be challenged by similar issues, it needs to be noted that some of the very things *required* for their viewing become problems in themselves for moving image works. As just one example, painting and sculpture require an ambulatory viewer. The moment one of those ambulatory viewers ambulates, they become a distraction themself, for other nearby viewers engaged with a time-based work.[4] This small example speaks to a much larger dynamic embedded in the construct of museum-based viewing. Just go through the list above. There's an inherent conflict between traditional museum and gallery exhibition and the moving image that our institutions have yet to successfully address, and only begun to acknowledge.

Connected to this is an unrecognized issue of social class, hinted at earlier. While on the one hand some lovers of popular movies deem "cinema" a realm of rarified snobbery, on the other, parts of the art world are also averse to it. For them, cinema is not rarified, but coarse and populist. Here high and low culture join in rejection of a middle road. In formal practice, the museums' bias takes the form of distinction between the white cube of the gallery and the black box of the theater. While countless dollars are available to the museums for display practices compatible with commodifiable (or sellable) art forms like painting, it's much harder to arrange an allocation of those deep resources for the creation of "theaters within museums" which hint at the populist. In this way the distracted viewing of the fine art world serves as mirror to the distraction of escapist entertainment.[5]

But let's for a moment forget the richest of institutions and look at smaller arts organizations that, with limited resources, would like to address the attention deficit with tools available. Here they can join the motivated home viewer—as well as the theaters—in considering what conditions are needed for the presentation of "cinema" in its myriad forms. And to reiterate my very subjective definition, I use the word *cinema* to describe works that need dedicated attention.

I've first delineated a host of problems, obstacles, and barriers to cinema's ideal reception. Let's now start looking at some practical things one can do to address the problem, in the form of three simple principles:

THE FOCUSED SPACE

> in which one attempts to create an environment for viewing that minimizes distractions like light and sound pollution

THE FOCUSED TIME

> in which one attempts to carve out an unbroken time to experience a work in completion, as the film's makers intended.

THE CINEMA PERFORMANCE

> in which one works with the available equipment to present the work in the best way possible in a given environment

Through these principles we arrive at a place wherein the presentation of a recorded work becomes in essence an ephemeral experience: at once fixed and variable. While seemingly oxymoronic, such a concept in fact can be traced to cinema's early days of hand-cranked projectors, when projectionists adjusted a film's speed of movement through the varying pace of their cranking. Each screening was different. The tradition has continued in one form or another throughout the decades—in forms as diverse as Benshi narration, live musical accompaniment, special format works, expanded cinema, moving image-based performance works, and more recently, live documentary.

From a preservation and restoration perspective, this shift of emphasis from the artwork itself (be it filmic material, or its more recent cousin the digital file) to one encompassing both the work and its presentation, would seem to be common sense. Nonetheless it marks a radical shift in our understanding of archival practice. Our entire notion of what's considered "archival" is challenged if the work is understood to be ephemeral in its very essence.

And so we find ourselves seeking a condition of *archival impermanence*: in which the act of preservation acknowledges that—like the philosopher's tree falling in the forest—an artwork exists only in its moment of presentation. If the conditions of presentation aren't suitable to its perception, the work in its truest sense cannot be experienced. Herein Bishop Berkeley's celebrated notion that "*to be is to be perceived*" cannot be brought into focus, let alone challenged.

At the professional worker and creator's end the act of production now, in essence, asks for the creation of multiple editions of a work calibrated for different environments. The home, the theater, and the gallery each have different conditions one can target in a work's editioning, with further divisions within each. For the archivist, this means expanding our notions beyond the singular work toward rather, a transmutable essence; one that becomes embodied in unique presentations adapted to the environment in which they take place.[6]

But if we seek to truly preserve our moving image culture, we need to expand our notions of the work further—to include its enactment as part of its being. The home viewer, the theater, and the gallery alike can all join in this project in their own way—by exploring the perceptual variables of their unique spaces in a spirit of cinematic performance.

Having done these things, there is a last barrier in our path — and alas it's a formidable part of our epoch, beyond control. I speak of our common cultural exhaustion. In times such as ours, when everyday life is overwhelming in itself and the future seems so dark many dare not even think of it, it's hard to waste energy on any of this. Who has bandwidth left for pursuits of aesthetics? In a modern spin on Bertolt Brecht's dictum that "food comes first and then morality,"[7] we can say that rest comes first and then the world of dreams. But without the dream there is no respite, even in rest. So paradoxically, in the end we need both.

To resolve this conundrum, my reply is that our pursuit of focused attention can be selective. Distracted viewing serves its purposes, while art serves its own, and they are not in conflict. So let's agree it's okay to indulge in simple pleasures, and hope that amidst them we still find a voice that yearns for something more… something that isn't escape, but which transports.

To achieve that, we need to understand the conditions in which such transportation is possible, and work to cultivate those conditions. It may grant only a moment's transcendence, but in the end the moment is what we have, and for it we can be grateful. Like the monk's sand mandala, raked over upon its completion, the cinema performance is an experience that takes place in time and is gone. Like a dream, it disintegrates upon contact with consciousness. Yet in its very ephemerality lie the spores of renewal, waiting to grow wildly amidst the ashes of a burning world.

Endnotes

1. This would refer to the creation of digital editions of works created in analog media.
2. At the most rudimentary level, one can adjust brightness and volume to taste, or set a desired viewing mode on one's television. At a more ambitious level, one could aspire to standards desired by a work's creators; for example by selecting the recently implemented "Filmmaker Mode" on their viewing device.
3. One could reasonably ask what it says about our cultural epoch that "distraction" is the reigning paradigm. At present I'm simply choosing to ask how to remedy the situation in selected circumstances.
4. Among museums and galleries, *time-based media* is a term commonly used to describe works that exist in time with a fixed duration, and can include films, videos, audio recordings, digital works, etc..
5. Elsewhere I've discussed how moving image creators respond in turn by creating works intended to be viewed in distracted conditions. "In Search of Sight-Specific Cinema," in *The Moving Image*, Vol. 12, No. 1, Spring 2012.
6. I've previously discussed this notion in "Conservation at a Crossroads," in *Artforum*, October 2013.
7. "Food is the first thing, morals follow on."—Bertolt Brecht, *Threepenny Opera*, 1928.

PART TWO

CASE STUDIES

On Pre-Cinema Moving Images

Eadweard Muybridge, Zoopraxographer

Directed by Thom Andersen with Fay Andersen and Morgan Fisher.

Text: Thom Andersen. Music: Michael Cohen. Featuring: Dean Stockwell (narrator).

Original release: 16mm, color, 59 min., 1975.

Restored in 35mm and digitally remastered in 2013 by UCLA Film & Television with funding from The Packard Humanities Institute and Thom Andersen.

Restored from the original 16mm color reversal A/B rolls and the original 16mm fullcoat magnetic soundtrack. Digitally remastered from the restored 35mm internegative and digital audio files.

Restoration conformed and supervised by Ross Lipman in consultation with Thom Andersen. Laboratory services by The Stanford Theatre Film Laboratory, Audio Mechanics, Endpoint Audio Labs, NT Picture & Sound, Modern VideoFilm, Inc. Photochemical color grading by Sharol Olson. 35mm blow-up by Dave Tucker. Audio restoration by John Polito. Digital color restoration and grading by Gregg Garvin. Special Thanks: Vincent Pirozzi. Distributed by Cinema Guild.

This opening text in our collection of case studies offers a glimpse at some of the issues raised in the restoration of "pre-cinematic" (or proto-cinematic) moving image media.

It was originally published in the booklet accompanying Cinema Guild's 2016 DVD release of Eadweard Muybridge, Zoopraxographer.

The accompanying color illustrations were originally presented in an illustrated lecture entitled "Interpreting Pre-Cinematic Color," delivered at the UCLA Film & Television Archive's Festival of Preservation in 2013, The Association of Moving Image Archivist's "Reel Thing" Technical Symposium in 2014, and the Cinémathèque française's "Toute la mémoire du monde" Festival in 2018.

Thom Andersen, Re-Zoopraxographer

Eadweard Muybridge, Zoopraxographer (1975) marked not just an auspicious beginning to Thom Andersen's career in feature films, but the culmination of a multi-year exploration of Muybridge's work across multiple platforms. He initially approached the subject in the mid-1960s in a short 16mm film that re-interpreted aspects of Muybridge's time experiments,[1] and soon thereafter in the pages of *Film Culture* with a prose essay. Like Muybridge's initial struggles to document motion at Leland Stanford's behest in 1872, these early efforts were promising but in a larger sense unfulfilled. It wasn't until 1878 that Muybridge's efforts came to full fruition with the publication of *The Horse in Motion*. Andersen, for his part, would join his filmic and literary voices in *Eadweard Muybridge*: a collision of re-animated photographs and spoken narration. In this collision he arrived at his true authorial vision, a vision that transcended his earlier work and which would soon define the essay film itself for the next generation of American cineastes.

In 2013, while employed at the UCLA Film & Television Archive, I undertook the restoration and remastering of *Eadweard Muybridge*, in direct collaboration with Andersen. We discovered that not only were there no good viewing prints extant, but the film's original camera a/b rolls were suffering from severe color fading. To address this, we found ourselves in essence "breaking apart" the original shooting sequence before reconstituting it. This process in many ways paralleled Andersen's original re-photography methods, which in their turn had figuratively paralleled Muybridge's own techniques for reconstituting motion. As Muybridge broke motion apart with serial photographs and re-assembled it with the zoopraxiscope, Andersen broke apart Muybridge's accomplishments and re-assembled them in his film, transformed. Decades later, in breaking apart the decaying 16mm elements of *Eadweard Muybridge*, we sought to bring the work into the present. In reconstituting the film, we found that we had at once preserved it and transformed its implications on the nature of time.

One can view the capture and reception of motion in Muybridge's era, Andersen's early career, and the present day as discreet snapshots that reveal different perceptions of time itself. By tracking Andersen's production methods and the methods employed in the film's restoration, one finds a locus for understanding how the receptive apparatus of the cinematic illusion itself has changed over the years. Whether these discrete snapshots point to a larger unity is in the mind of the beholder.

The Making of *Eadweard Muybridge, Zoopraxographer*

Andersen notes that Muybridge's zoopraxiscope was a device without a future, and that Muybridge was the first and last zoopraxographer. Yet his images themselves, divorced from their apparatus, have enjoyed a tremendous longevity. Efforts to re-animate Muybridge's motion studies using conventional cinematic technology trace back to at least J. Stuart

Blackton, an early movie pioneer who in his later years documented the history of cinematic illusion across a series of works beginning with *The Film Parade* (1933).

Figure 1A. Thom Andersen at the time of making *Eadweard Muybridge, Zoopraxographer*.

Figure 1B. The Monkees' Michael Nesmith at the mixing console during the recording of Mike Cohen's score for the film, which took place in Nesmith's studio. Filmmaker Morgan Fisher, who worked with Andersen on the film is seen rear left. Andersen is rear center with back to camera, and composer Cohen is far right.

Andersen cites among his personal motivations a double-edged homage and friendly rebuttal to a USC colleague who had re-animated Muybridge's images for a class project,[2] and more importantly, to the works of documentarian Louis Clyde Stoumen.[3] Stoumen's *The Naked Eye* (1956) recounted aspects of the history of photography by use of still photographs; a technique he advanced further in *The True Story of the Civil War* (1957). *Eadweard Muybridge* took these techniques and advanced them yet again; its celebrated 1975 release perhaps joined with Stoumen's 1957 Civil War documentary in inspiring a young Ken Burns, who made his first explorations of the technique just a few years later.

To create *Muybridge*'s re-animations, Andersen and his wife Fay photographed over 3,000 source images, many of them Muybridge originals in special collections libraries, onto BW negative film. Andersen printed all the resulting positives himself, working in the UCLA art department darkroom from midnight to 8am. Then the pictures were cut and pasted by hand onto animation cells for their photography onto 16mm film. When the laborious re-animation process exceeded time limits in UCLA's workrooms, the production moved shop to the Dickson/Vasu studio, where it was completed on any downshooting stand not occupied by the 1970s Peanuts cartoons, which were shot there simultaneously.[4]

Figure 2. *The Steamer "Golden City" on the California Dry Dock*, 1868. Albumen silver print, gold chloride tone.

Importantly, Andersen meticulously noted the exposure intervals, which the notoriously detailed Muybridge had himself documented when shooting the original serial photographs. To the extent possible Andersen used the film industry's standard 24 frames-per-second cadence of image and darkness—a byproduct of a film projector's rotating shutter and intermittent movement—as a vehicle to carry and emulate Muybridge's original intervals; even inserting black frames when needed to represent Muybridge's exposure times.

Muybridge, in this work, had shot BW negatives using a variety of early photographic techniques including wet plate collodion and dry plate bromide processes. These were in turn printed to positive, at which point they were usually imbued with a monochrome color inherent to the method of printing. In capturing his Muybridge animation cells, Andersen re-photographed his BW still prints onto 16mm color reversal film stock, and color tone emulation was applied to the resulting projection prints. Thus Andersen followed in Muybridge's footsteps in using a BW source to generate a color end product.

Figure 3. *Pigeon Point Lighthouse*, 1873. Albumen silver print, unverified tone.

The Re-making of *Eadweard Muybridge, Zoopraxographer*

In restoring and remastering the film, we undertook the creation of motion picture copies—as is required for the archival retention of medium integrity—and a parallel digital remastering, as is largely essential for presentation in today's exhibition environments.

The fundamental problem we encountered, as mentioned earlier, was color-fading. Andersen had shot primarily on Eastman Commercial Original (ECO) reversal film 7252, which characteristically fades to a disturbing lilac hue, completely out of keeping with the demands of the project.[5] This particular lilac should be distinguished from the magenta color commonly seen in faded positive projection prints of theatrical release movies and also from the subtler yellow-dye fading common to negative stocks. It's a problem that archivists who work with 16mm independent films know well, and a vexing one, as restoration methods are both costly and inconsistent. In similar cases many preservationists hope to find an unfaded viewing print as an alternate source, but in this case there were no better alternatives.

Figure 4. *General View of Experimental Track, Background, and Cameras.*
Plate F, 1879, from *The Attitudes of Animals in Motion*, 1881. Collodion printing-out paper, selenium tone.

    To solve our problem we turned to the pictures themselves. As the bulk of the film was comprised of Muybridge's own images, we realized that for those portions of the movie we could simply print to a panchromatic BW negative stock, bypassing the color fading entirely. Then, in parallel to both Muybridge and Andersen's original working methods, we could re-inject monochrome color when making positive viewing copies by simply using colored light to expose the prints. To help compensate for the lack of contrast in the faded original (a result of dye fading to the blue end of the color spectrum), we closed the optical printer's blue light vane, so that only yellow light would expose the film. After careful testing, the BW film was additionally push-processed as a further contrast boost.

    However for those shots that utilized a full spectrum of color this method would be insufficient, as it results in a monochrome negative image. Thus the remaining images in the film were exposed onto color negative stock, in hopes of retaining what little color information still lurked beneath the lilac. These shots were then assembled onto a "B-roll," to enable easy scanning for digital color correction as well as more effective color printing in our photochemical copies.

Figure 5A-5B. Samples of Andersen's faded 16mm Eastman Commercial Original color reversal film stock. Note the lilac color even extends to the frameline/sprocket area which should in fact be a true black.

Most notably, we used digital color restoration tools on the crucial end shot of two women kissing, and of Muybridge's stereograph cards, which in their original iterations featured a monochrome photographic print applied onto cardboard of a different color. For these images, we carefully emulated the color palette of the original cards, as documented in numerous books. The digital file was printed back out to color negative film and inserted into the B-roll.

The two resulting 35mm rolls (BW A-roll and color B-roll) were then printed to 35mm viewing copies as well as a fully restored 35mm color interpositive.

The Re-making of Time, and the Un-making of Eadweard Muybridge

The technique of matching the color of the stereographs to photographic references points in some ways to a departure from standard archival practice, in that it suggests we were aiming to emulate not so much the 1975 film *Eadweard Muybridge, Zoopraxographer*, but rather Muybridge's original images themselves. This was admittedly the case. Andersen had long lamented the 1975 version's shortcomings in rendering the color quality of Muybridge's

72 The Archival Impermanence Project

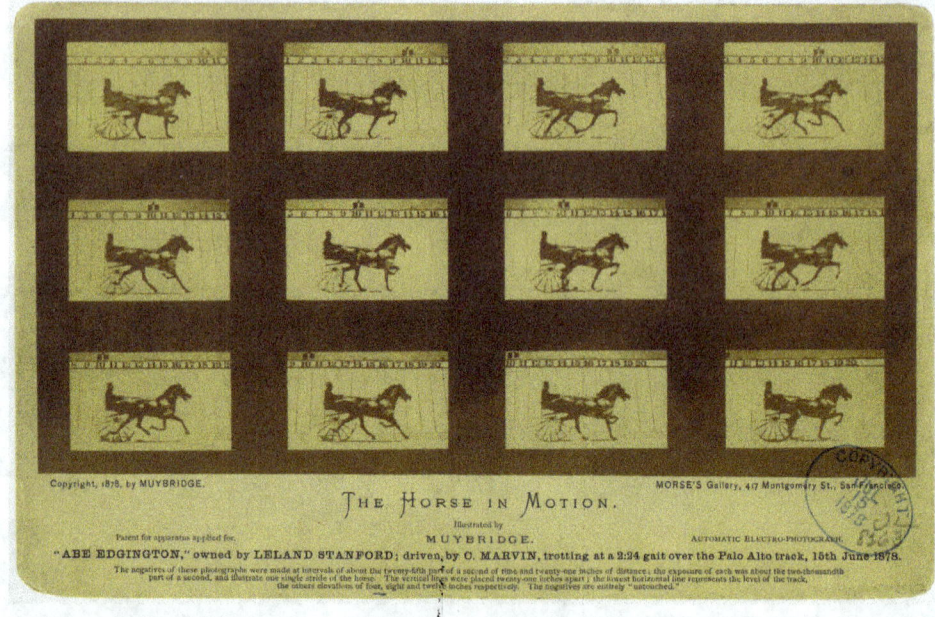

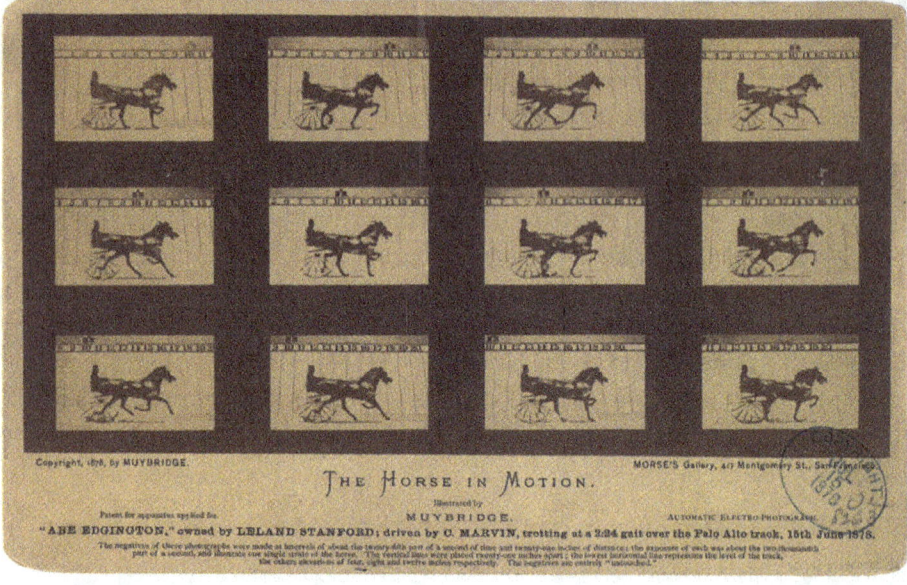

Figure 6A and 6B. *The Horse in Motion. "Abe Edgington," owned by Leland Stanford, driven by C. Marvin, trotting at a 2:24 gait over the Palo Alto Track*, 1878. The same original card in collection of Library of Congress, as reproduced in two different sources. The color difference is solely the result of re-photography and subsequent printing.

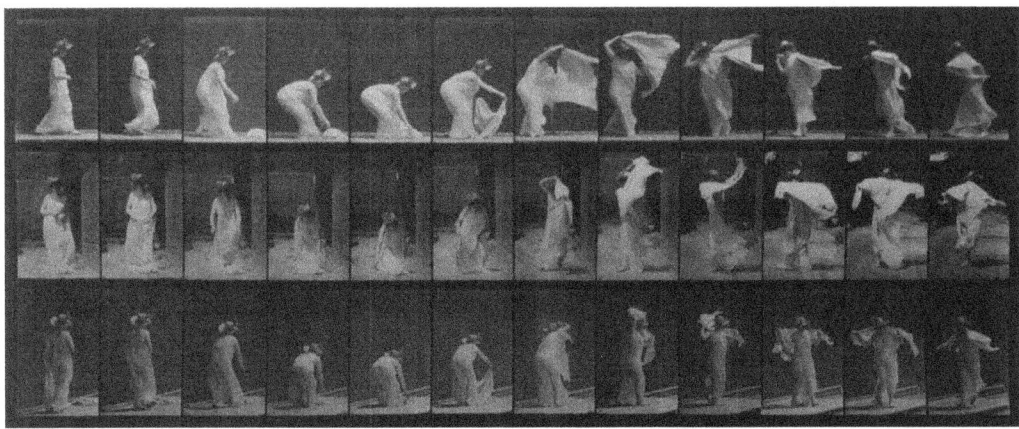

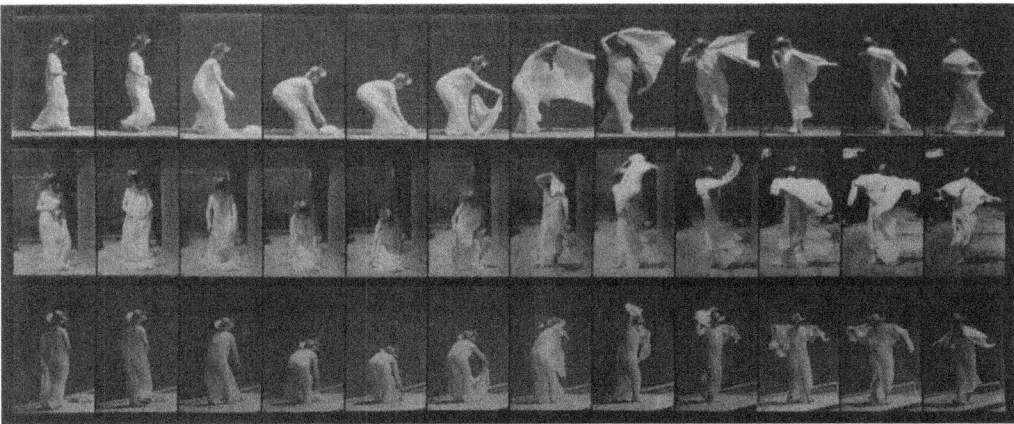

Figure 7A and 7B. *The Human Figure in Motion.* Eadweard Muybridge original collotype ca. 1883-1887, from collection of Thom Andersen. The top image captures the subtle color found in the aging original. The lower image removes the chroma, yielding a pure black-and-white rendition..

actual works. Workflow issues at the time had further prevented the initial 16mm viewing prints from doing justice to the diversity of Muybridge's practice, which encompassed a multiplicity of techniques employed across a long career that began well before his famed motion studies, and is fully documented in the film. In our restoration we thus applied a variety of monochrome hues emulating the range of methods employed by Muybridge over the course of the years, including collodion printing-out paper and silver albumen prints with differing tones applied, as well as photogravure and collotype printing.

In some cases we had Muybridge originals as references; in other cases we relied on reproductions in books. Further complicating our task was the fact that many of the reproductions themselves varied greatly in quality, even when emanating from a single source. One can additionally surmise that the originals we viewed exhibited different color properties than they did in Muybridge's day, due to simple aging effects, even when the medium in question was relatively stable. The colors we arrived at were in a sense research-based "imaginary composites" that sought to emulate a hypothetical version of Muybridge's work that in fact does not exist today. They reflect a series of choices made when no single reference can serve as a reliable guide, a territory I call "the Gray Zone." This workflow, while on the one hand exceedingly meticulous, points to larger questions of subjectivity in a process of restoration that for many years was considered an objective science-based practice.

Finally, in the stage of digital remastering, our method points to a transformation of the nature of Muybridge's work itself. In parallel to the photochemical work documented in the body of this essay, we simultaneously created a version for digital exhibition. While these copies retain the 24 frames-per-second cadence of digital cinema and Andersen's 16mm original, they have a qualitative difference in time base that is particularly crucial to this project. The interval of black between discrete frames is absent in conventional digital cinema, and hence is only present in those shots where Andersen himself intentionally inserted blackness.

As Andersen's narration brilliantly notes at the end of the film, in Muybridge's projection of single frames interspersed with darkness, he

> *transformed photography from the Zenonian reverie on movement it had been into the modern instrument that recovers the unity of human motion, the motion by which Zeno's Paradoxes are refuted in a single step.*

The cinematic illusion of Muybridge and photochemical cinema refutes Zeno in the human brain's joining of those intermittent flashes of light. The absence of darkness in contemporary digital cinema, as industrially configured, constitutes a different representation of time in motion.

Endnotes

1. In *Parallaxis* (ca. 1965), Andersen photographed quotidian actions in time. He felt the experiment a failure that was more successfully realized in the closing images of *Eadweard Muybridge, Zoopraxographer*.
2. Dave Hanson. This effort was notable for accompanying the re-animations with ragtime music.
3. More direct inspirations included contemporary artists working with serial imagery. In particular, Andersen admired the curatorial efforts of John Coplans, whose 1968 exhibition "Serial Imagery" at the Pasadena Art Museum traced the practice from Monet to Warhol, inspiring not just Andersen but notable figures including Roy Lichtenstein. Andersen also cites his interest in artists working with grids, including Sol LeWitt, Carl Andre, and Donald Judd. (Thom Andersen interview, August 28, 2016.)
4. Animating the still images was problematic at UCLA due to the facility's lack of polarizing filters, which sometimes resulted in reflective glare that necessitated re-shooting at Vasu. Nick Vasu allowed Andersen to personally use the Acme animation cameras. Vasu technicians conducted the more complex camera movements on an Oxberry stand.
5. The film's concluding sequence was shot at a speed of 256 frames per second. To accommodate the shortened exposure times, a higher-speed Ektachrome reversal stock was used, with different fading properties.

On Classical Film Restoration Models

Tillie's Punctured Romance

Directed by Mack Sennett.

Featuring: Marie Dressler, Charlie Chaplin, Mabel Normand.

Original release: 35mm, B&W, 1914. (RT indeterminate)

Restored in 35mm in 2004 by UCLA Film & Television Archive and the British Film Institute with funding from UK Film Council, The Film Foundation and the National Film Preservation Foundation. Subsequent digitization by Lobster Films.

Restored from an original nitrate print, numerous nitrate print and safety duplicate negative fragments, a 35mm acetate print, a 16mm master positive, and 16mm print fragments. Digitally remastered from the restored 35mm internegative.

Restoration conformed and supervised by Ross Lipman with the assistance of Nancy Mysel. Laboratory Services by Triage Motion Picture Services: Tony Munroe, Paul Rutan, Jr., Dave Tucker, and Title House Digital. B&W grading by Sharol Olson. Historical Consultant, Bo Berglund. Special Thanks to David Pierce. Institutional assistance from Academy Film Archive, Film and Photo, Ltd., Film Preservation Associates, Library of Congress, Norsk Filminstitutt. Additional thanks to Vrej Allahveredian, Kevin Brownlow, Carl Davis, Robert Gitt, Jere Guldin, John Hampton, Mike Mashon, Thierry Mathieu, Tom E. Murray, David W. Packard, Mike Pogorzelski, Richard Roberts, Tony Scott, David Shepard, Anthony Slide, Rob Stone, Brent Walker, Serge Bromberg. Distributed by Lobster Films.

Although somewhat elaborate in approach, the following study delineates classical restoration methodology as defined in the texts joined in the Poetics section, and practiced by the major film archives. It functions as a baseline from which the other studies expand. Originally published in The Journal of Early Popular Visual Culture, *Vol. 2, No. 7, July 2009.*

Tillie's Punctured Legacy

Observations on the Restoration of Chaplin's First Feature

Abstract

Tillie's Punctured Romance, the 1914 Keystone feature starring Marie Dressler and Charles Chaplin, has been widely acclaimed as a cinematic touchstone and dismissed as a minor work, largely ignored by Chaplin himself. This essay is at once a restoration case study and an analysis of how the restoration process shed light on differing historical responses to the film. The restoration team, perhaps ironically, can be seen as the latest in a long string of "secondary authors" interpreting the work, even as they seek to return it to its original form. The work strategy, described in detail, speaks to *Tillie*'s initial version while at the same time dating itself to the present epoch—suggesting both a contemporary interest in historical veracity and the potential limits of that pursuit.

Overview

Film preservation methodology is something like quicksilver: slippery, evasive, constantly changing its shape. To try to define immutable principles is futile, as the moment they're defined they tend to lose their efficacy. In truth the only tenet I've found to be continually effective in my work as a restorationist is that each project must determine its own methodology and techniques.

Tillie's Punctured Romance, produced in 1914 by Mack Sennett's Keystone, is something of an oddity—a film everyone has heard about, but relatively few have seen. *Tillie* is on the one hand celebrated as a landmark film that helped catapult Charlie Chaplin to his worldwide fame—arguably the first feature-length slapstick comedy; and simultaneously considered a mediocrity, a mere footnote in film history.

Is there a historical reason for these two diverging yet concurrent views? Can the film's restoration illuminate the way in which this state of affairs may have arisen? I would argue yes, and yes. *Tillie's Punctured Romance*'s singular position in cinema's development, coupled with its own internal formal properties, suggested a preservation strategy uniquely suited to the film. What's more, the resulting work reveals a path by which the diverging interpretations of *Tillie* in fact converge, around a historical process of cinema reception.

Preservation Pre-History

Despite *Tillie*'s legendary status—or perhaps because of it—we were unable to find any existing original printing elements. Even before the film's release in December 1914, it became entangled in a snare of legal disputes and distribution struggles that were largely to characterize the film's fate,[1] and in turn, its restoration process. The company that released *Tillie*, the Alco Film Corporation, was dissolved within several months of the film's launch. Since that time, the film passed through a successive string of releasers and owners, ultimately passing into the public domain; and in the process experienced a bewildering process of reissues and revisions.

The film was shortened, re-edited, duped, cropped, re-duped, its speed was changed, sound effects were added, etc. Each new version was an attempt to update the film, repackaging the magic into something more palatable to modern audiences. And each version was further from the original. If *Tillie*'s status has declined in recent years, it's at least in part due to these impositions, or the work of what one may call "secondary authors."

As just one example, many of the initial cuts and changes eliminated scenes and evidence of the musical theater tradition from which the film emerged. In point of fact *Tillie* was part of a much larger movement adapting theatrical conventions to the cinema at the advent of the feature film.² Such tropes were largely seen as irrelevant distractions in later versions, integral though they may have been to the original.

In a related effort, key scenes involving the stage star Dressler were frequently excised, and her name was removed from the main title.³ Another common target for revision (and one by no means unique to *Tillie*) was the film's intertitles, which were regularly adapted to reflect the language of the day, as shall be discussed later.

It's alas beyond the scope of this essay to provide a comprehensive chronicle and analysis of the film's reissue history, but suffice to say that it graphically maps the industry's shifting notions of audience interests, aesthetic sensibilities, and attitudes toward early cinema. This is evident in both content and form, subject, and the sensual perception of that subject. Sometimes the film would be renamed, sometimes not, but in all cases the film's original identity was obscured. Each releaser placed a unique time-dated stamp on the film. What comes down to us today are thus an abundance of bastard fragments, low quality dupes, and spurious reissue copies.

Figure 1. Keystone's ad before the sale to Alco. *Motion Picture News*, November 14, 1914.

Preservation Strategy

How is one to make sense of this in an attempt to authentically restore *Tillie*? The best existing single source we could locate was an original six-reel nitrate print, in the hands of a private collector. That print, which was direct from the camera negative of 1914, was very sharp, and would hence serve as an excellent starting point in terms of both image quality and content. However, the print had an average of about 40 splices *per reel*, or approximately 240 sections where footage was missing. At some point, only a few frames were missing, at others, entire scenes.

In this regard, it bore similarities to the best version of *Tillie* commercially available when we began the project.[4] This is part of a paradox of image quality, wherein—in the absence of the original—the sharpest sources are the earliest projection prints, which have accumulated decades worth of wear and tear.

The usual tactic, and most practical one in such cases, would be to try to fill in the largest gaps and leave the smaller ones alone, as was done with the high quality commercially available version. We had the advantage of an even better image source: the original nitrate print, and then adopted another strategy, which arose from a close look at the film. The comedy in *Tillie* is in many ways pure Keystone—based in essence on a rapid-fire stream of physical actions and sight gags. What's more, given Marie Dressler's extremely gestural acting—encompassing both broad and subtle movements and constantly shifting facial expressions—as well as Chaplin's well-known physical and emotional dexterity, we found that much of the comedy was lost when even a few frames were gone.

Thus we set out on the task of trying to insert as much of the missing footage as possible, even if the gap was only a few frames. It is in effect taking the essence of classical film restoration methodology, and then simply applying it at an extremely painstaking and detailed level. But seeing as many of the gaps were minutes long, we also had to determine how to reconstruct the narrative itself.

Preservation in Practice

To solve these parallel tasks, we set out to view as many copies of the film as possible. In total, upwards of thirty copies or fragments were examined. Not only did these differ greatly in content, but also in image quality. It emerged that the film had in fact made use of very careful continuity match cutting, despite its often anarchic staging—something completely unclear in most existing versions of the film. Thus by careful analysis of the action, combined with a technical evaluation of the source elements' origins and provenance, it was in fact possible to reconstruct the film's original narrative to a surprising degree.

Perhaps less surprising was the fact that once the narrative flow was reinstated, the film's coherence and entertainment value improved concurrently. While certainly not a four-star picture by contemporary standards, it's much better than was previously realized, and indications emerge as to why *Tillie* caused such a sensation at the time. One sees the slapstick chaos of the early Keystone shorts mixed with contemporary theatrical traditions, played out on an epic canvas. One can see Marie Dressler, as it were, symbolically handing the torch of American popular culture to her co-star, Chaplin.[5] And while the new medium's growth pains are apparent, so is the excitement.

Figure 2. Alco's two-page spread. *Motion Picture News*, December 12, 1914.

At a technical level, inserting the hundreds of sections described was an ornate balancing act. Having as they did, varying croppings, contrast ratios, and framelines, matching them to each other would normally be in practice an insurmountable task. This major obstacle was overcome by matching everything—all sources—as closely as possible to the original nitrate print. Obviously where the image was degraded there were severe limitations to what could be done. But within those perimeters exceedingly painstaking work was undertaken by Triage Motion Picture Services to try to attain seamlessness.

A central part of achieving this was our decision to optically reduce the film, without cropping the image, from full-frame silent 1.33: 1 aperture to sound Academy aspect ratio, a process referred to as "FA to RA" printing (full aperture to reduced aperture). The high quality of the optical printer lenses allowed this to be accomplished with no visible image degradation when compared with contact printing, and was in fact essential to attaining image alignment. Sources with errant framelines in any direction from the perforations could then be inserted perfectly, with no cropping or misalignments at edit points. This technique would further allow all of our splices, of which there would be hundreds, to be completely invisible on screen, falling as they would in the extended Academy frameline area.

As far as source selection, a premium was clearly image quality and lack of prior cropping. Extensive contrast testing was done on all elements inserted. While low-grade material is evident at many points throughout the film due to necessity, I believe less than thirty seconds worth comes from sound-aperture cropped sources. And to our delight, for much of the film we were able to locate very sharp sources indeed.[6]

Alternate Versions

Among those sources were, needless to say, several of the reissue versions that I mentioned earlier. In many cases we were able to successfully print the desired frames from the reissues while leaving the reels intact. However in two instances it became necessary to temporarily excise the needed scenes for printing. One of these sources was arguably of historical interest, being a classic representation of a "hodgepodge" *Tillie*—a crazy quilt of previous reissues slapped together with a few new intertitles thrown in.[7] While most of it was useless for our restoration, the temporary removal of a few shots for printing would constitute (slight) damage to a print that some scholars could conceivably wish to view. Yet to leave it intact would prevent the successful restoration of the original.

This points to a common but rarely discussed paradox of film preservation. From a purist and completist standpoint, *all* versions of a film would be preserved, no matter their artistic or historical merit. However film archives usually operate with financial and material limitations, making this perfect goal unattainable.

To solve this dilemma I made a Betacam SP telecine transfer of the print, taking the somewhat unusual tact of recording beyond the picture area's borders. In this manner the entire film image was included in the transfer, allowing the shifting framelines and aspect ratios of the version's multiple sources to be visible on an underscanned monitor. Thus interested scholars would be able to access the version, such as it is, for study. At the conclusion of printing, the printing rolls were isolated for eventual re-insertion into the print.

The other "version" which needed to be disassembled was not a true reissue, but rather an early—and to large extent successful—attempt to restore the film to its original form. This 16mm print was assembled from five distinct 16mm reduction prints in the collection of John Hampton, founder of Los Angeles' famous Silent Movie Theater. The only known public exhibitions of the print were on its premises.[8]

While the visual quality of its sources was for the most part very poor (as one would expect given the limited lab resources of the era), Hampton had done an excellent job of reconstructing the film's original narrative, and this print proved helpful to my own efforts on a number of occasions. What's more, it also contained some unique footage, and three of Hampton's source prints eventually made their way into our own restoration. In each specific case of course, they had to be contrast-tested and repositioned to match the appropriate insert spot in our original nitrate print. Again, at the conclusion of the work, the rolls were placed aside for future reinsertion, although in this case the fragile condition of the print would render it unprojectable. Its historical relevance would be primarily as an artifact, in so much as its uniqueness—a reconstruction of the continuity and not a re-edit—would be superseded by our own, more complete, work.

Titles

A critical component of any silent film restoration is its intertitles. It goes without saying that we wanted to use the original, sparsely worded Keystone titles and not later impositions, be they additions, embellishments, or explanatory text. We were fortunate to have what proved to be a complete list of the originals[9] provided by Bo Berglund, whose consultation proved particularly invaluable in this area. We were also extremely lucky to find actual frames for all of them, and thus avoid the problem of determining layout and which Keystone format to emulate in any recreation. In fact the original intertitles, while clearly Keystone's in design, had trademark signs such as the Keystone "K"s removed, presumably to facilitate the film's sale on the state-rights market.

Figure 3. Post-Alco publicity from the Bert Levey theater circuit. Left: May 1915. Right: December 1915. Note that by December, Dressler still receives top billing (perhaps for legal reasons), however her picture is in fact below Chaplin's. Later releases and publicity would of course highlight Chaplin.

In addition to the main title, original credits, and intertitles, we decided to include the original "part titles" as an integral component of the restoration. It is often forgotten that early features were generally presented in discreet reels on a single projector, often with each reel functioning as a structural unit.

Such was the case—at least to a degree—with *Tillie*. This was most apparent at the transition from Reel One to Reel Two. Reel One ends with Charlie and Marie Dressler leaving

Marie's farmhouse in the country. Reel Two opens with them amidst the heavy traffic of a city street. While a stark contrast may have been intended, when executed as a straight cut in a double-mounted reel it instead creates a logical gap; particularly given the film's previously mentioned highly developed continuity. And in most instances there would have been a pause at that point for the reel change.

Reissues of the film invariably inserted an explanatory card to smooth the transition. One early example read, "From the pure breath of the open spaces to the fetid atmosphere of the wicked city is but a step—and what a step!"[10] But as Bo Berglund has observed,[11] the elaborate language is out of keeping with the understated brevity of the Keystone originals.

In reality, the cards reading "End of Part One" and "Marie Dressler in Tillie's Punctured Romance Part Two" were the original punctuation to the reels. By re-inserting these and the other part titles for the first time since the film's original release, we were able to help elucidate the film's native six-reel structure.

Digital tools were also applied to this end. While we had the original part titles in all but one case, the artwork in some instances was blurred by multiple printing generations. On a digital workstation we were able to composite sharp portions of alternate reels' cards with blurred portions of a problematic one, to create sharp renditions of each.[12]

Figure 4. Left: a typical Keystone intertitle at the time of *Tillie*'s release
Right: An intertitle from *Tillie*. Note the missing Keystone "K"s.

Running Speed

Another critical issue in the presentation of restored silent films is projection speed. Volumes have been written on this topic, dating back to the silent era itself.[13]

Scholars and presenters often rely on loose guidelines, such as using the end digits of year of production, so that a 1919 film might be projected at 19 frames per second, while a 1921 film would screen at 21 frames per second.[14] Obviously there are extreme limitations as to how rigidly one can take this. Other generalizations of debatable value include the notion that slapstick comedies intrinsically have to be projected at fast speeds. This position, for example, was put forth by several members of a silent film internet discussion group who were speculating on the restoration of *Tillie*.[15]

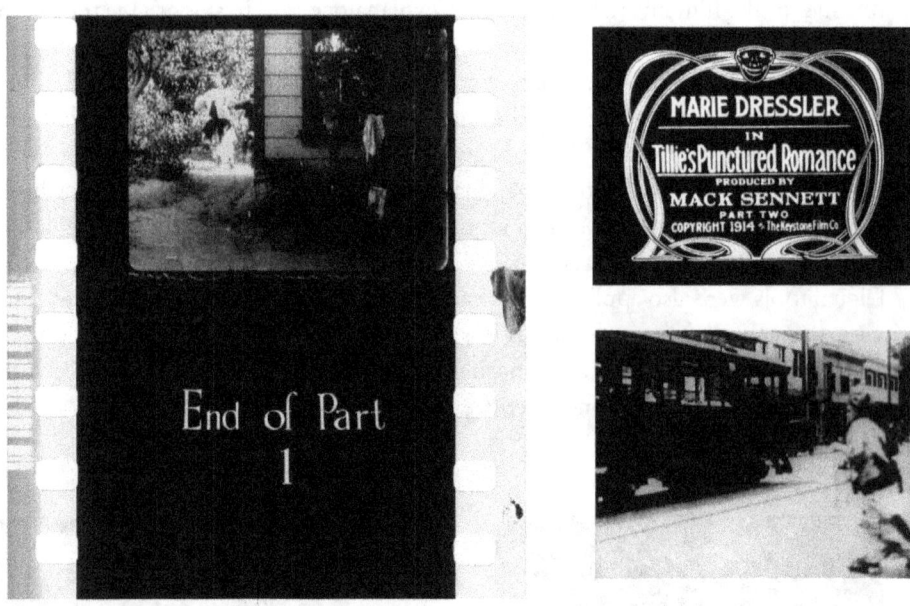

Figure 5. The transition from reel one to reel two as it originally appeared. On left, the last frame shows Dressler and Chaplin running away from the farm, followed by the reel end card. In a single projector theater, there would be a pause for rethreading before the appearance of the title card for reel two. As reel two's action begins, Dressler and Chaplin are in the midst of city traffic. Note that each of the film's reel title cards matched; thus the film's main title is identical to this card for reel two, save for the listing of the part number.

If one considers that early silent films were hand-cranked in both filming and projection, often at variable rates within the same film, it quickly becomes apparent that no one projection speed can be considered truly authoritative for any given film of the era.[16] Such was the case with *Tillie*. When one watches the film projected at a constant speed—any speed—one can see variations from scene to scene, and also within scenes. For example the film's climactic chase sequence had been (not surprisingly) shot undercranked in relation to the rest of the film, and would hence appear sped-up if the movie were projected at a constant rate.

So the question arises, what is appropriate for the film? While its comedy is indeed often lightning quick, it was strikingly apparent that much of the physical humor was in fact lost when the entire film was projected fast. The work's sheer length became a factor. Watching the slapstick sped up for the duration of a full-length feature was perceptually exhausting.

What about approximating a sense of "natural" movement? Even if one were to aim for this, which is of course subject for debate in any situation, to achieve it would be extremely difficult. The projectionist would need to in effect "perform" with the film by changing the speed of a variable speed projector spontaneously to keep up with the action. In point of fact many projectionists of the silent era did precisely this, making each presentation unique.[17] However modern projection conditions make this difficult under the best of circumstances, and it was also not clear that this approach was appropriate for *Tillie*.

After extensive testing of each reel, 18 frames per second arose as a nearly ideal all-around rate. Some movement appeared slow, much natural, and some fast. The whole film seemed to come alive at 18 frames per second, and so that is the speed we selected for our presentations. However the print of course exists as a discreet entity, and those with differing opinions can screen the restored print at a speed of their own choosing.

Color

Just as no one speed can usually be considered authentic for a given silent film, so too can accurate color recreation be an elusive goal. For in truth, no two tinted or toned prints are truly identical, in so far as dye concentration and absorption rates were likely to vary as each print was in turn immersed in the baths. Film and dye deterioration often fluctuate throughout a shot, and frequently within the area of a single frame. It's thus virtually impossible to declare the color simulation of any early film authoritative. Preservationists need to combine research, extensive lab testing, guesswork, and ultimately, subjective judgments to recreate tints by either dye immersion/chemical baths, or colored light exposures.

In the case of *Tillie*, historical research proved the decisive factor. All the tinted fragments we found dated from reissues. In the absence of evidence of any tinted original prints, we decided to print in black-and-white. It was arguably the easiest decision of the process.

Music

More interesting was the question of what to do about musical accompaniment. Just as an early film's color could differ in physical iterations of a single title, and running speed fluctuate with presentation, so too would a film's musical accompaniment vary with performance. When musical documentation exists at all, it's often in the form of cue sheets—a notation of suggested themes, or types of themes—to accompany specific scenes or sequences. Individual interpretations, often literal, sometimes not, were then developed from the suggestions. In cases where an original score was known to exist its execution would likely vary in instrumentation and arrangement, so that a single film might be accompanied by a full orchestra in New York, and a solo piano in South Dakota. Even in instances where an original score or cue sheet exists, one must ask to what extent its authorship is an integral part of the film, produced in consultation and collaboration with the same production team responsible for the work's visual content.

While the film *Tillie's Punctured Romance* was ostensibly based on the musical comedy *Tillie's Nightmare*, it in fact bore little resemblance to the stage version. It was known that a "Professor Winkler" had been hired to create scores for Alco's releases,[18] however we were unable to locate any such score for *Tillie*, nor a document of one. It seemed likely that this "Professor Winkler" was none other than the composer Max Winkler. In his memoir/essay "The Origin of Film Music,"[19] Winkler speaks of working with Mabel Normand, but makes no mention of Chaplin, Dressler, or *Tillie*, which suggests that it's highly unlikely he ever wrote, arranged, or cued such a score. While one would expect that a high-profile title like *Tillie* would certainly have been chosen by Alco for scoring, it is unknown today whether it in fact came to pass.

Given a lack of evidence of an original score, we deemed the accompaniment distinct from the restoration; and rather tied to specific presentations of the film.[20] Our decision was in part tied to issues of running speed, as noted above. Not all venues would have the capacity to accurately synchronize a picture rate of 18 fps with a recorded track during projection.[21] Options for doing this increase in video and electronic media; however such steps would represent a translation of the original work to a different medium, and would hence be distinguished from archival restoration (which by definition retains integrity of medium).

Ultimately we felt that even should we create a score quite appropriate to the film, it would be necessary to recognize its contemporary origins. This speaks to the larger issue of "secondary authors" raised earlier—the composer and musicians would join the preservation team in the process of interpreting the work.

A nearly complete preview of the restored *Tillie* took place at the London Film Festival on November 2, 2003, with solo piano accompaniment by Stephen Horne, who had been able to review the edition's content on a video copy created just prior to the screening. At the UCLA Film and Television Archive's Festival of Preservation U.S. premiere at the Academy of Motion Picture Arts and Sciences on July 31, 2004, Ken Winokur presented an original small ensemble score based in part on the stage play's songs and in part on research of other period music.

While the inclusion of themes from the stage play no doubt lends an air of authenticity to this interpretation,[22] the result must be understood as only one, arguably strong, possibility.

Cinematic Perception

The sensual perception of a film is a complex phenomenon, encompassing both the physical print itself, the technical perimeters and theatrical environment of screening, and presentational variables such as the music accompaniment of "silents," as discussed above. Arguably the most unique factor in the restored *Tillie* was the extreme length to which insertion of missing frames was carried out. The shortest insert length, determined by the ability of Triage's film printers

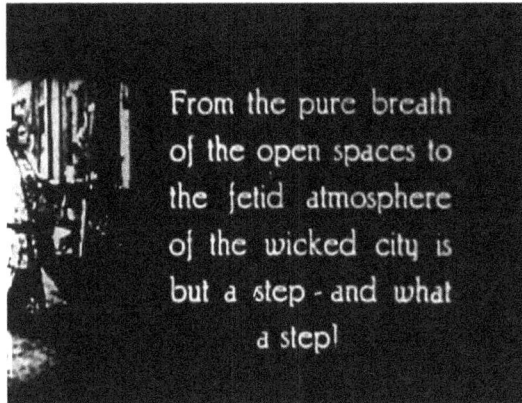 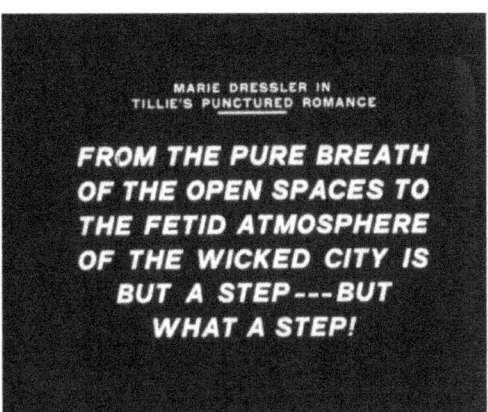

Figure 6. Left: an early reissue intertitle that attempts to bridge the narrative gap between the reels. Note that the tone is decidedly more verbose than the sparse Keystone originals, as shown in Figure 4. Right: The Blackhawk version, also needing to bridge the narrative gap, adapted the reissue text and transposed it into a visual format similar to the Keystone originals. There are numerous differences however, which again can be seen by a close comparison with the authentic sample card in Figure 4.

to change grading lights while exposing raw stock, was four frames. At our chosen speed of 18 frames per second, some inserts thus appear on screen for less than one third of a second.[23] As stated, every effort was made to match the differing sources for contrast, gradation, and alignment. However with substandard materials, there are inherent constraints as to what is possible via analog methods.

The question then arises: how will such inserts or flashes be perceived? Heading into the restoration's first screening,[24] I had some trepidation about this very issue. My own analysis, gathered first through observation of the audience, and verified afterwards by comments (both solicited and unsolicited) was that while an adjustment period was felt by many attendees, it was brief and the flashes were soon assimilated into the viewing experience. A clear consensus seemed to arise that—given the nature of the film's physical acting styles—insertions of even fleeting missing image sequences greatly enhanced the viewer's perception of the film's content.

I would not argue that such methodology is always advisable; rather that this particular picture called for it. In particular the fluidity of Dressler's and Chaplin's physical performances is highlighted. In other cases, for example slightly less kinetic performance-based films, the technique could potentially prove distracting.

This restoration strategy pointedly illuminated our role as the latest in *Tillie*'s succession of secondary authors. Our edition at once spoke to the film's original 1914 release, and a contemporary appreciation of "authenticity" that distinguishes it from past re-releases. Our restoration, while likely quite close to the original in content, varied from it formally, in that the qualitative differences of the multiple sources evoke a different physiological perception of the image than did the single-source original.

The work speaks to an increased appreciation of historical accuracy, and a philosophical irony inherent in preservation itself. As imaging technology advances, the ability to improve the rendition quality of the worst sources of *Tillie* will likely increase accordingly. Should that occur, future restoration efforts might bring us closer to the original—while the very technologies that enable it speak to a widening cultural gap from the time of the film's production.

The Future of the Past

It should thus be noted that, with the exception of the intertitles, many of which were scanned, digitally retouched, and output back to film, the restoration was implemented completely with conventional analog technology. The strategy enabled the project to take full advantage of the superior image quality and archival stability of motion picture film, while retaining the integrity of the work's original physical form.

Since the restoration's completion in 2004, high-resolution digital intermediates which would allow similar benefits have become increasingly prevalent in restoration work. In such systems, the film—like the titles—would be scanned, digitally aligned, graded, cleaned up, and recorded back to motion picture film. However this work is exceedingly costly, and were the project undertaken today (in 2009) with an inflation-adjusted budget, it would nonetheless have remained prohibitive.

Having said this, the laborious analog procedure described was conceived and conducted precisely in anticipation of potential future work in the digital domain. The careful insertion of the missing frames, even those of very low quality, facilitates the creation of an extremely sharp version of the complete film in the future. Computerized frame interpolation (such as the method already employed by John Lowry) could potentially sharpen blurred images using accurate picture detail from adjacent frames, without having to interpolate any motion. Thus an essentially analog restoration anticipates further work, as new technological tools become available and affordable. Digital dirt and scratch removal could—at that time—additionally enhance the result.

The Curtain Call

I've tried to illustrate how a film's preservation strategy needs to develop organically from the work at hand, rather than following a preset concatenation of principles or prescription of methods. *Tillie's Punctured Romance*, standing as a true landmark in the early days of the feature film, with its carefully staged continuity and gestural physical comedy, demanded a grueling strategy of piece-by-piece restoration. The reestablishment of the film's original dramatic structure helps to illustrate some of the long-forgotten reasons for the film's

Figure 7. An example of a mid-shot edit between two sources in the restoration. Note that not only is there a significant drop in image quality between the two sources, but a completely different framing. Chaplin's feet, for example, are missing in the bottom source. The black band down the left side of the sequence, to the right of the perforations, is the unused soundtrack portion of the film stock; a result of the "FA to RA" (full aperture to reduced aperture) optical printing. By printing the film in this manner one can perfectly align the two sources, despite their different framings, while retaining the original's aspect ratio. At times, as few as four frames were used for mid-shot inserts. (Four frames was the minimum needed to allow for a light grading shift at Triage Motion Picture Services, the lab printing the film.)

popularity. It also points to its lasting significance as a work on the cusp of musical theater in the Dressler style, and the celluloid slapstick oeuvre embodied in the acting of its all-star cast.

The diverging critical analyses of *Tillie* that developed over the years can in some ways be seen as responses to diverging Tillies. In the absence of an authoritative cinematic "text," reviewers potentially fall prey to the work of secondary authors. Only by analyzing reissues in relation to the original can a clearer picture arise.

The film concludes with its stars taking a last curtain call, in the theatrical tradition. But in a final bit of cinema magic, in footage not seen since the film's original release, Charlie and Mabel suddenly disappear from the frame via a bit of Méliès-ian stop-motion cinematography. The stage star Dressler, incredulous, is left behind to shrug whimsically at the new medium's tricks.

As the shot progresses, our restoration source elements get progressively worse and worse, so that by the end we see a high-contrast Dressler bidding farewell. And as a colleague of mine observed, the progressively deteriorating footage reminds us that the old film stocks are taking their last bow as well.

Figure 8. The lost curtain call. Dressler—as was somewhat common at the time—also appears on stage at the film's beginning. The opening sequence commences with her as herself in a gown; dissolves to her in costume, and then to Tillie on location in the film proper.

Frame enlargements of *Tillie's Punctured Romance* courtesy UCLA Film & Television Archive and the British Film Institute.

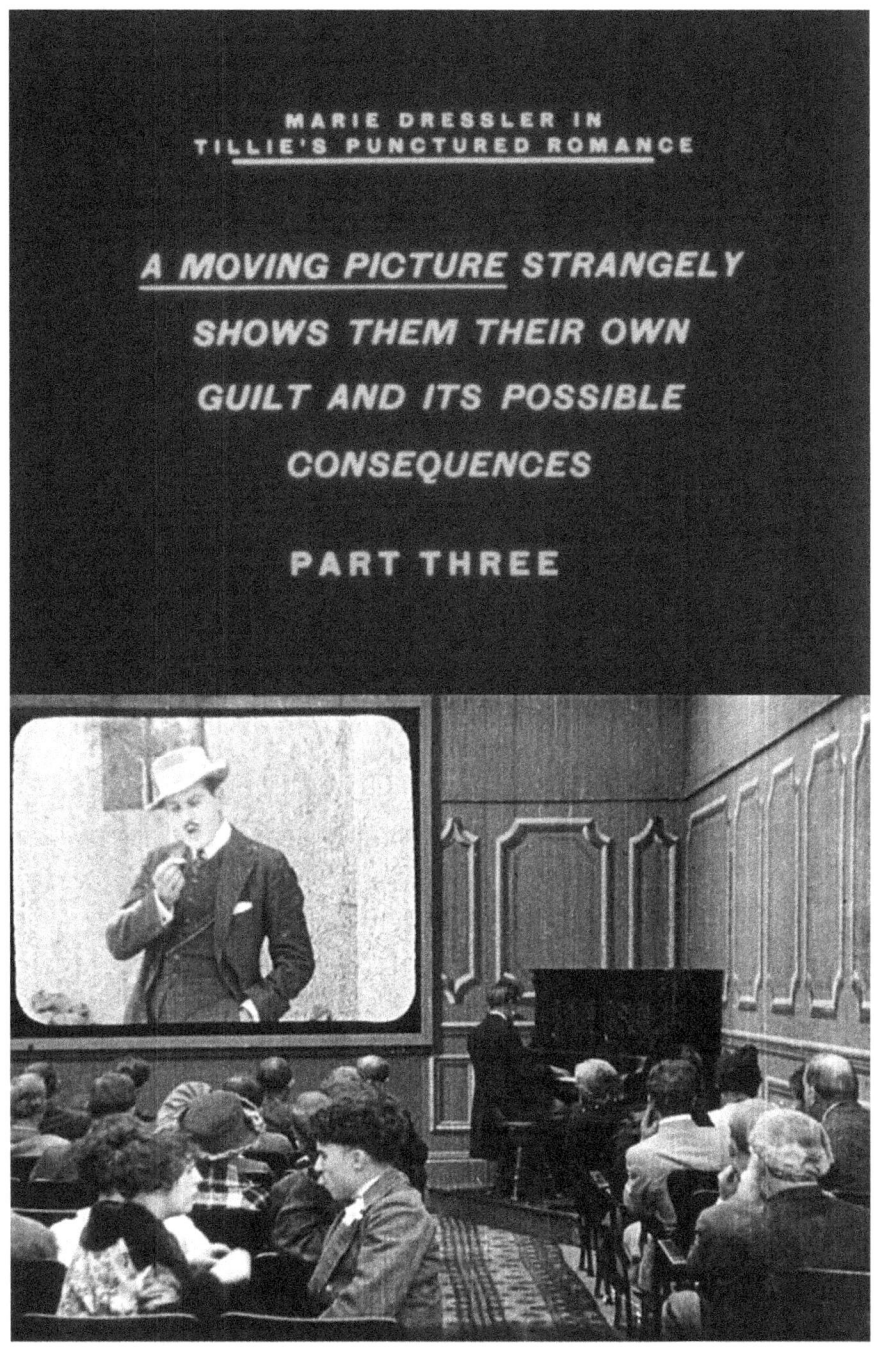

Figure 9. Chaplin and Normand watch a film-within-a-film that mirrors their own scheming. This early example of self-reflexive cinema, along with the opening and closing curtain calls, suggest a growing awareness of the transitional moment at which the film arose.

Endnotes

1. For an account of *Tillie's* early legal history, see Kalton C. Lahue and Terry Brewer, *Kops and Custards: The Legend of Keystone Films* (Oklahoma, 1968), and Bo Berglund, "The Making of *Tillie's Punctured Romance*," http://www.cinetecadelfriuli.org/gcm/previous_editions/edizione2004_frameset.html. Bo Berglund served as historical consultant for our restoration efforts, and was an invaluable aid to the project.
2. The film would likely not even exist apart from this tradition. Sennett originally conceived of it as a vehicle for the theatrical star Marie Dressler, and it is loosely adapted from one of her plays. It's likewise fitting that Alco was the company to release *Tillie*, as the company specialized in filmed adaptations of successful stage works, in keeping with the "Famous Players in Famous Plays" concept of Adoph Zukor. For more information on Alco, see Steven Phipps, "The Nightingale and the Beginnings of the Alco Film Corporation," *Film History*, Vol. 4, No. 4, 1990, 323-335.
3. The film's original complete title was *Marie Dressler in Tillie's Punctured Romance*, wording which appeared not just in the main title sequence but on every intertitle and part title. That it is today considered a Chaplin film is at least in part revisionist history, even more so considering Chaplin didn't direct the film and makes few references to it in his autobiographical works.
4. This was the Image Entertainment DVD. The primary source for both the DVD and the previous Blackhawk reissues was a 16mm reduction negative, now owned by David Shepard, which had been struck from a 1920 reissue nitrate print (off the original negative) that had subsequently been lost to fire after being loaned to Paul Killiam. While quite sharp overall, this version has a high quantity of splices, which result in a sense of jerky, irregular motion. The large number of cuts, while perhaps the result of ordinary damage, suggests it may also have been prepared with a preservation strategy somewhat common in the pre-digital era, wherein dirty or marred frames would be intentionally removed to create a cleaner image.
5. Dressler of course enjoyed a resurgence late in her career, in films including *Anna Christie* (1930), *Min and Bill* (1930), *Emma* (1932), and *Dinner at Eight* (1933).
6. In addition to the six-reel original nitrate print we found numerous fragments of original nitrate prints, as well as high quality acetate duplicate negative sections printed directly from discarded original print fragments in the collection of our collaborator, the British Film Institute. We additionally had access to the David Shepard/Blackhawk reduction negative, which as noted, was the best commercially available source.
7. The Burwood Pictures Corporation reissue of 1950.
8. *Los Angeles Examiner*, September 6, 1957, announces a weeklong screening run of the film and briefly describes Hampton's work on it. A second clipping dated June 7, 1962 announces another screening. It seems likely that Hampton may have shown it on a few other occasions before closing the theater in 1981.
9. A Swedish censorship list, which proved to be a direct literal translation when compared with existing examples of the original title cards.
10. A variation of this (sample) text later resurfaced in the Blackhawk reissues, with the design changed from the "original" reissue art cards to a facsimile of the genuine Keystone layout, giving the somewhat misleading impression that it may have been authentic. In fact all the cards in that version are well-intentioned facsimiles, which a close examination will reveal.
11. Berglund, op. cit.
12. This same method was used to fill in the needed characters for the one missing part title. It should be noted that the part titles heading each reel are identical in layout to the film's main title.
13. Many of these, including Kevin Brownlow's excellent survey of the issue ("Silent Films: What Was the Right Speed?" *Sight and Sound*, Summer 1980), are collected on David Pierce's "Silent Film Bookshelf" webpage: http://www.cinemaweb.com/silentfilm/bookshelf/.
14. While 16 fps stood as an informal (and frequently varied-upon) norm for many years, projection speeds began to inch upwards in the early 1920s, at least in the United States. This is in part because of the increased prevalence of the new movie palaces then being created, which had much larger screens. The increased projection throw and attendant screen size required greater illumination, with the result that

the typical circular projector shutter was frequently reduced from three blades to two, allowing more light to pass with every rotation. As a result, the intermittent light flashes on the screen occurred at a slower rate, creating a visible pulsing on the screen at lower speeds. Increasing both camera and projection speeds helped to eliminate or minimize the problem. True standardization was not to take place until the advent of sound films. For an excellent discussion of the technological and cultural factors in this transformation, see Leo Enticknap, *Moving Image Technology* (Wallflower, 2005), 138-144.
15. Alt.movies.silent internet group, March 10–12, 2004. *Tillie's Punctured Romance*—Restoration & new score. http://groups.google.com/groups?hl=en&lr=&ie=UTF-8&group=alt.movies.silent. The ensuing dialogue, including the oft-repeated myth of a missing scene where Charlie falls off a balcony as in *His Favorite Pastime*, can perhaps be seen as an example of how internet discussion groups—with their spontaneity and immediate response system—can on occasion create a "snowball effect" of misinformation based on opinion or memory.
16. As the silent era progressed, some studios or distributors would try to suggest guidelines for specific titles to varying degrees of success. See: Enticknap, op cit., 143.
17. Kevin Brownlow and Patrick Stanbury frequently use a variation of this method today. Alternately, one archive where I worked would on occasion vary speed from reel to reel, depending on the film. But these are somewhat rare cases.
18. *Motion Picture News*, October 17, 1914, 2. I am once again indebted to Bo Berglund for calling my attention to this.
19. Max Winkler, "The Origin of Film Music: An Employee of Fischer's Music Store Invented the Musical Cue Sheet," *Films in Review*, December 1951, 38. This essay is in fact an excerpt of Winkler's 1951 autobiography, *A Penny From Heaven*.
20. This is not to suggest that there is an intrinsic problem with "marrying" a contemporary score to a film's restoration. In point of fact a well-prepared recorded track is frequently preferable to live performance by an unprepared accompanist, as varying venue logistics frequently prevent accompanists from even a single viewing of a title in advance of a screening.
21. Brownlow and Stanbury use video as a tool in this regard. At a characteristic screening of their restorations (frequently created in collaboration with composer Carl Davis), Stanbury is stationed in the booth, watching a video or DVD of the film that was produced in perfect sync with the score, which is played back over the cinema's sound system. He simultaneously watches the actual film projection through the booth window, and adjusts the projector speed to keep pace with the image on the video monitor. The results of this method are typically outstanding, yet the extremely specialized playback conditions greatly limit the number of venues that can accommodate it.
22. Winokur, in an ironic but affectionate homage, chose the play's title, *Tillie's Nightmare*, as the name for his ensemble.
23. In reality it's indeed even less, as this number does not account for the projector's shutter movement, which would further reduce the amount of time each frame is seen.
24. The 2003 London Film Festival work-in-progress screening described previously.

On Archival Documentaries and Compilation Films

The Times of Harvey Milk

Director: Robert Epstein. Producers: Richard Schmiechen, Robert Epstein.

Cinematographer: Frances Reid. Composer: Mark Isham.

Featuring: Harvey Fierstein (narrator).

Original release: 16mm, color, 87 mins., 1984.

Restored in 35mm in 2000 by UCLA Film & Television Archive in cooperation with Telling Pictures, the James C. Hormel Gay and Lesbian Center and Earle-Tones Music, Inc. with funding provided by The Ahmanson Foundation in association with the Sundance Institute. Subsequent digital remastering funded by Criterion.

Restored and remastered from the original 16mm color negative A/B rolls, 16mm reversal and 1" video elements, the original Sound One 35mm 6-track master sound mix and Mark Isham's original PCE-F1 stereo music masters.

35mm restoration and digitally remastering supervised by Ross Lipman in consultation with Robert Epstein. Laboratory services by Monaco Film Labs and Video Services. Photochemical color grading by Kip Hansen. Digitally restored sequences by Dust Restauration S.a. Video-to-film transfers by Swiss Effects. Video remastering by 4 Media Company, Dolby LT/RT stereo mix by Lora Hirschberg, Rob Epstein, Ross Lipman, at Skywalker Sound. Audio restoration services, transfers, and remastering by John Polito, Audio Mechanics, Peter Oreckinto, DJ Audio, Lora Hirschberg, Mark Isham, Skywalker Sound. Special thanks to: Scott Smerdon, Whitney Saik, New Yorker Films, OUTFEST. Distributed by Janus Films and Criterion.

Following on our model of "classical film restoration"—historically developed for fiction films—this text looks at some of the ways these principles are transformed when restoring documentaries; particularly those employing extensive use of archival footage. As the project discussed took place in 1999-2000, the piece also serves as a time capsule of my early views on digital restoration, which were to transform substantially in subsequent years, as documented in later texts. My early views are left in situ here, as it seems valuable to track the process of change. Cumulatively, the examples cited point to an under-discussed dimension of the craft: when not *to do something.*

The text was adapted from an illustrated lecture initially presented at UCLA's James Bridges Theater on February 27, 2003, and reprised in later iterations at the Billy Wilder Theater in Los Angeles and the Instituto Moreira Salles in Rio de Janeiro, in collaboration with Mutual Films. Additional sections were integrated from catalog notes written for UCLA's Festival of Preservation in 2000, and a text essay published in the booklet accompanying Criterion's 2009 DVD release of the film.

The Times of Harvey Milk

A Case Study in the Preservation of Independent Documentary Film

Independent film restoration is becoming more and more prevalent, if not quite viewed as a distinct branch within the larger field of archiving. But that day may soon come, as archivists begin to recognize the ways in which a work's formal qualities and production aspects affect methodologies of restoration. It is at this meeting point—of technique and form—that I'll focus my remarks tonight. I'll be arguing that an archivist's methodology of preservation should grow outwards from the unique properties of the work at hand, and not originate from any pre-ordained ethics or one-size-fits-all philosophy.

To begin, I'd like to present a model of what I'll call "classical" film restoration, as practiced by such institutions as UCLA, the Academy, and many others. When restoring a film, the "classical" preservationist begins by thoroughly searching out the existing physical elements of the title, and then conducting a thorough analysis and comparison to determine which are the earliest, most complete and/or authentic copies, and which are in the best physical condition. Then there is the often exhausting job of assembling the film, using the best of the source elements to weave, if you will, a complete negative—authoritative in content and unsurpassable in quality. Along the way extensive knowledge of film history and technology is employed, as current laboratory techniques are used to replicate a look appropriate to the time of the film's original release.

With independent cinema these general principles still hold, but their application is substantially transformed. *The Times of Harvey Milk* is a compilation documentary, utilizing sources including 16mm color negative interviews, 16mm reversal news footage, Super 8 home movies, still photographs, audio cassettes, and a variety of video news formats.[1] Each one of these presents its own problems if one needs to trace a shot back to its source. I say "if." It took director Rob Epstein and producer Richard Schmiechen's team took over six years of in-depth research and editing to assemble their story, and it's far beyond the purview of an archivist's job description to replicate each step of that work. One might well call it absurd, as it's in essence re-making the film. But there are instances *within* workflows when such considerations become appropriate, and so it was here. In such instances, it's ultimately the work at hand that should dictate those decisions.

The Times of Harvey Milk had its beginnings in 1978, shortly after Rob Epstein and the other members of a collective which came to be known as the Mariposa Group released the groundbreaking documentary, *Word Is Out: Stories of Some of Our Lives* (1977). This earlier film celebrated the lives of a wide range of figures within the Bay area gay and lesbian communities, and was comprised primarily of interviews. Epstein had joined the project after seeing a newspaper ad, and was subsequently asked by Peter Adair (*Word Is Out*'s producer and to a large degree its inspirational force), to seek out younger members of the community to be interviewed for the film.[2] So it was that Rob, at age 21, went on to become one of its five directors as well.

Adair and Epstein soon planned to collaborate on another project, but in the wake of the terrible murders of Harvey Milk and San Francisco Mayor George Moscone by San Francisco Board of Supervisors member Dan White, the canvas suddenly largened.[3] Rob Epstein wanted to use the charismatic Milk as a new focal point for the developing film. Adair disagreed on this point, and ultimately bowed out, but he encouraged the young director to press on with his vision. Epstein's vision entailed extensive use of archival footage, alongside powerful interviews that followed in the style of those in *Word Is Out*. Thus began the aforementioned years of research and editing; the results of which we now needed to restore.

The film was completed and released in 16mm in 1984. At the time our restoration effort commenced in 1999, there were already early warning signs that the days of quality presentation of 16mm might be numbered, and given the film's importance, we opted to blow it up to 35mm in our restoration.[4] But what issues might be raised by the myriad sources compiled within the film? Could they all be dismissed with a sweep of that hand, arguing "that's how the film had always been seen?

As one example, Rob informed me that he'd never been happy with the quality of the video-to-film transfers made in the early 1980s, which comprise a large component of the finished work.[5] He wanted to redo the transfers with a company called Swiss Effects, which I knew was being lauded in the independent film scene as the best in the business at that time.

There were indeed many problems with the video footage, and so I asked myself a question which might seem odd, but is one I frequently ask myself when restoring an independent film. Do those flaws in some way contribute to the overall effect of the work? Are they actually an integral part of the complete piece, and in fact something that should be left alone? The answer to this million-dollar question is: yes and no. Some help, some hurt. It depends… largely, I'm afraid, on the preservationist's judgment.

The simple fact is that a preservationist makes thousands of such decisions on each project, whether acknowledged or not. For to do nothing is still a decision. Such instances (of doing nothing) fall into a broader category of what one might call "invisible subjectivity"—flashpoints in the workflow that go unmarked but contribute to the audiovisual properties of the end result. So I went through the film from start to finish, studying the problems and pondering how to approach each; also considering by practical necessity the high costs of re-transfer. Ultimately I pared it down to a list of shots I deemed of highest priority, and then planned a series of tests.

The first question was, naturally, how to locate sources for the shots in question. Unlike Hollywood features which are archived by their producing studio, independent films have no central home where one can begin to search for *ur* elements. Each film is its own story, and trying to track down the camera original or printing elements for any particular independent film can be an unending series of dead ends, ranging from moldy garages to long-closed labs, defunct distributors, and eccentric relatives of dead directors.

In the case of *Harvey Milk*, we were very lucky. Not only had Rob Epstein retained control of his original negative and other pre-print elements, but even the *outtakes* were available. This is highly unusual, but due to the large quantities of oral history interviews and rare footage compiled, their importance had been recognized, and the elements stored at the James C. Hormel Gay and Lesbian Center of the San Francisco Public Library.[6]

By going through the Hormel material I was eventually able to locate Epstein's 1-inch compilation master videotape, which served as the source for all original video-to-film transfers.[7] Here I was able to get a close look at his working methods. Not only were there a number of shots which didn't make it into the finished film, but it was clear that most of the image degradation was built into his master.

If one traces a news shot's history-from video news footage in the street, to a possible studio submaster, then an edited story, and perhaps a studio master or dubbing copy, one finds four or five generations before it gets to the filmmaker. The film's editor receives hundreds of shots from these different sources, dubs "selects" to submasters, and finally, dubs again, to the transfer master. Needless to say, the generational loss in *Harvey Milk*'s source transfer master was profound, but to hunt down each shot's *ur* source individually would be setting out on the absurd road of remaking the film from scratch. We contented ourself with the good fortune of finding the original compilation master, and used that as the source for our work.

The first test was a new transfer by Swiss Effects, followed by a kind of control. The latter was a new transfer from the same master tape, but done by 4MC, the lab that did the original transfers in the early 1980s, and who—somewhat miraculously—were still offering the same service they had offered at the time of *Harvey Milk*'s original production.[8]

The results were surprisingly different, yet in other ways quite similar. The most notable difference was the color, and in fact a byproduct of the grading of the film print, not the transfer to negative. This perfectly illustrated my notion of the "invisible subjectivity" of lab work, in that it merely reflected the choice of the graders—but it did little to highlight the qualitative difference of the two film-out methods. Neither method addressed the fundamental problem of image sharpness. In fact the main difficulty here was not a matter of transfer technology, but simple generational loss.

That said, a closer glance revealed there were indeed some differences between the two methods. Some of the varied video sources had an inherent image fringing that was heightened in the Swiss Effects, accompanied by a richer and stronger degree of color saturation than was found in the 4MC result, which was lower in contrast. Herein I think lay much of the reason for Swiss Effect's success. Contemporary tastes leant more heavily to bright, high contrast images, which can increase a sense of sharpness when dealing with the low-resolution digital video that was also common to the cultural moment, by default of the technology available to filmmakers at the time. So I would argue that Swiss Effects' moment in the sun might be better understood as the result of contemporary factors than true technical superiority.

In any event the contrast change was not marked enough to justify the cost of re-transferring most of the video-to-film material.[9] More frequently, the original transfers were superior in that the lower contrast and saturation of the 4MC system offered a degree of warmth well suited to the humanity of the subject material. For example we retained the 4MC transfers for most close-ups of human faces. There were, however, a few shots for which the Swiss Effects process was well matched, an example being dramatic scenes of the "White Night" street riots that rocked San Francisco following the lenient sentencing of Dan White in 1979. In this instance, the bolder contrast worked in harmony with the starkness of the horrific events. In each case, it was a question of matching form to content. When considering the long and crazy road to filmout, 4MC's early method got the job done surprisingly well in most instances, and the Swiss Effects transfers filled in the gaps.

○ ○ ○

Similar discretion was employed in our use of digital restoration tools. When *The Times of Harvey Milk* was restored, digital restoration was in its infancy, and its high cost was rarely an option for independent films, which suffered from funding challenges. Fortunately UCLA had received a generous grant from the Sundance Foundation to restore such films, and we were able to conduct experiments with it. Please be aware that the term *digital restoration* can often be an oxymoron. One cannot "restore" something to a form in which it never existed. The term *restoration* inherently presupposes a physical integrity of media. So when one sees a DVD labeled "newly restored" one can in a fundamental way often dismiss the claim.[10] However, digital tools can be an important part of preservation work when carefully applied, and when the results are successfully rendered back to archivally stable motion picture film. Those conditions aren't always easy to realize. I won't be going into an in-depth analysis of digital restoration today, but I will provide a brief glimpse into its use in *The Times of Harvey Milk*.

At a broad level, digital picture restoration can be broken down into "hand-painting" techniques, where specific problems are repaired on a frame-by-frame basis, and automated techniques, where formulae are devised to mathematically guess what the picture was *supposed* to look like, and recreate it synthetically. An early instance of the latter was the Lowry system, but that required a vast array of hard drives with their attendant costs, which was beyond our means in this instance.[11] Hand-painting was even more expensive, but was in use by the studios on classic features at the time of our work. As *The Times of Harvey Milk* was an Academy Award-winning film of vast cultural importance, we were fortunate to experiment with some mid-level automated picture restoration. But far from helping us, our tests instead served as an example of the pitfalls that sometimes arise with this approach.

One of the tests explored an early digital sharpening tool, here applied to some of the video-originated images that suffered severe generational loss in the aforementioned dubbing process. Alas the technology we tested generated substantial strobing artifacts, while doing little to restore the sharpness that might have been present in a first generation original. Needless to say the processed footage was not used in the restoration.

Another test involved the repair of a badly scratched Super 8 home movie—in this case some extraordinary footage of Harvey Milk's appearance at the Pride march in Los Angeles on July 2, 1978, shot by gay underground film pioneer Pat Rocco. Would future historians consider the home movie's scratches a patina of authenticity that should be retained? Or would they be deemed a troublesome distraction that should be removed? As luck would have it, I knew a lab technician who had been involved in the original blow-up to 16mm, and to my surprise he revealed that the film's production team had originally tried to eliminate the scratches by optically printing the shot with a Super 8 "wet gate"; a very rare piece of equipment in those days.[12] Part of the reason for their rarity is their cost, but also their fragility in use. It's very difficult to get the wetgate perchlorethelene solution to distribute evenly over such a small area as a Super 8 frame. So the lab's efforts failed, and they printed dry. But what this told me was that the original *intention* was indeed to eliminate those scratches, which gave me enough justification to experiment with digital scratch removal.

For better or for worse, the specific problem with the footage was vertical "tramline" scratches, which is one of the more difficult things to address via automated techniques. Our test significantly reduced the scratches, but did not eliminate them entirely. What's worse, a careful comparison with the original revealed image distortion that was notable enough to impact on the expressiveness of Harvey Milk's gestures.

While we didn't wind up using either of the two Super 8 shots' repairs, we did find a few others in the film that benefitted from treatment. But I cite the failures, rather than successes, as an example of the attention demanded with digital work. One cannot take it on faith that "changed" means "improved," let alone "restored." In hindsight, these tests offered a fascinating snapshot of one moment in the relentless march of our culture toward digital everything.[13]

o o o

Just as discretion proved valuable in our picture work, restraint proved helpful in our work on the sound restoration.

The original 6-track mix for *The Times of Harvey Milk* suffered from an advanced case of what's called "sticky shed." Magnetic recording tape is comprised of iron oxide particles held onto a polyester or acetate film base by a binder. Archivists have another way to describe it: rust glued on plastic. In "sticky shed," the metal oxide begins flaking off the film base.

After playing a single test reel of *Harvey Milk*, the heads on our playback unit were a dark brown. To recover this track, we had to bake each reel in an oven for 36 hours; an act which temporarily stabilizes the iron oxide.

Once the transfer was completed we could move on to the sound embedded in the oxide, and the real questions began. Rob Epstein revealed that the film's original score by Mark Isham had in fact been composed and recorded in stereo. However it had never been heard that way because the film had only been released in 16mm, a mono format.

Although audio reformatting is common in the studios, who face commercial imperatives to "keep things new," it's less common among archives, who have a historical obligation to a given film's history. It can indeed be ethically questionable for historically-minded restorationists to create stereo versions of mono films. To quote critic Jonathan Rosenbaum, "You might as well reshoot *Citizen Kane* in 3-D or Cinerama on the theory that if those technologies had been available to Welles in 1940 he surely would have used them."[14]

The devil, however, lies in the details of the given history. For example, stereo technology was in some instances available to directors who actively chose not to use it. A case in point was Hitchcock's decision to release *Vertigo* in mono, despite recording Bernard Herrmann's score in stereo. In this instance, Hitchcock's directorial choice might suggest a mono restoration strategy.

Here we faced a different situation. We were working closely with a living director, from a source that was intended for stereo from its conception. Nonetheless, I felt we still had a historical obligation to the film as it's been known to us for years. In the end we created two distinct versions—one direct preservation of the mono track, and another of our new stereo edition.[15]

First however, we needed to consider overall sound quality. Just as the picture was comprised of a variety of different video and film elements, the sound came from a range of sources including everything from raw TV news footage to homemade cassette tapes, each with their own problems. Mark Isham's original stereo stems were in fact a complete oddity—an early digital format called PCM-F1, which is a complicated way of saying they were recorded on an old Betamax videotape.[16]

Now it's worth pointing out that in independent film in particular, sound is traditionally the poor cousin of picture. Many of us have seen low-budget films with professional-level picture quality, but a nearly incomprehensible soundtrack. Indeed, a number of the sources for *Harvey Milk* had a high degree of noise: hiss, rumble, distortion; you name it.

A lot of this can be cleaned up today with digital audio tools, which were integrated into restoration workflows prior to picture. In the old days, pops and clicks in an audio track might be reduced in a magnetic element by literally scraping the oxide off with a razor. Such analog practices have long-since been replaced by digital equivalents that are far more nuanced and versatile. And whereas only the highest budget shows can afford quality digital picture restoration, sound work is much more accessible. So it's both ironic and appropriate that today we can do extensive clean-up work on independent film sound. Ironic… in that the films *themselves* might not have had such resources; and appropriate, in that in many cases it's much needed.

But such powerful tools risk over-inspiring: they can engender a sense of power that develops its own momentum, and for that reason they're fraught with peril. One can sometimes go too far. When one removes noise, something is in essence taken away from the film. In many cases the omitted thing is incidental or distracting, but for films that have a rough edge to them—such as many independent films—one runs the risk of squeezing the life out of them. They might become clean, but bloodless.

For *Harvey Milk*, there were sections where this would clearly be the case, and others that would obviously benefit from the new technology. In general, the sequences we cleaned up most thoroughly were interviews staged specifically for the film, and in-studio news footage—sections wherein the noise artifacts were not markedly a factor in conveying the mood of the scene. This work was done by the highly skilled John Polito of Audio Mechanics in Burbank.

Once we completed the sound clean-up, our master file was given to Lora Hirschberg, Rob's mixer, who then edited the original stereo stems into the cleaned-up master. But the work didn't stop there. Unlike conventional two-channel stereo, analog theatrical stereo is in fact four channels, matrix-encoded through the Dolby Lt/Rt system. To make an Lt/Rt properly one needs to do a full mix in a studio.

Rob and Lora wanted to do the mix at Skywalker Sound in the Bay area, where Lora was currently working. This terrified me, as I envisioned the film suddenly acquiring the sound of an exploding Death Star or thundering dinosaur. Picking up on my trepidation, Rob assured me, "Don't worry Ross. It won't sound like *Star Wars*." So we went to Skywalker and in two days completed the Lt/Rt mix. As with the picture, our goal was always to let our technical decisions develop organically from the film itself. My voice was by definition one of conservatism, and Rob and Lora also had a great appreciation of the original mono version, which had been mixed by the legendary Lee Dichter of Sound One. In the end, the stereo effects are usually so subtle they're virtually unnoticed.

o o o

Cumulatively, the choices made in our restoration point to a philosophy of both experimentation and judicious restraint. While new technologies were available, tests revealed that they weren't yet fully developed, and so they were only employed selectively. In all cases, the moments of use were determined by the form and content of the film itself.

The Times of Harvey Milk premiered at the Telluride Film Festival in August 1984, six months after Dan White was released from prison for the terrible events chronicled in the picture. While there is an irony in this, it's one the film fully understands. Early on, we hear Milk's voice read a pre-recorded will which was to be played back only in the event of his death by assassination. "I have never considered myself a candidate," says Milk, "I have always considered myself part of a movement; part of a *candidacy*." There is a palpable rawness to Milk's voice, which had been captured on an old cassette player. That rawness would not benefit from being restored to the polished luster of a studio recording.

In the spirit of Milk's words, Epstein and his colleagues had larger issues on their minds than a particular miscarriage of justice, as horrifying as this one was. The film seeks to speak to the fundamental human issues that underlie political events, not just the events themselves. It's hence not accidental that the title is *not* "The Life and Times of...," but simply *The Times of Harvey Milk*.[17] The finished film speaks to that wave of social change of which Harvey Milk is a notable part—a leader and a martyr, but still just a part—a tide of which he is ultimately one component.

That tide grew into a wave that encompassed both politics and cinema. Epstein assembled a team on both sides of the camera that from historical vantage, reads as a veritable "Who's Who" in independent documentary and Bay Area progressive politics.[18] What began as a small grassroots project in the late 1970s swelled to a large team of contributors by project's end, and parallels the political rise of the gay rights movement, which the film chronicles.

This specific trajectory of the film, its participants, and its political message, is finally mirrored by the overall rise to prominence of independent cinema in general, which has now become a vital player in our common culture. *The Times of Harvey Milk* was awarded the Oscar for Best Documentary of 1984. And just as mainstream America was at last ready for a gay-themed Oscar winner, the archival community is now beginning to devote more of its focus to alternative, independent voices such as this. It's my hope that in the coming years we'll be able to continue this work.[19]

Endnotes

1. In his classic book *Films Beget Films*, filmmaker and historian Jay Leyda describes "compilation films" as works whose substance is history itself: movies made of other movies. Jay Leyda, *Films Beget Films: A Study of the Compilation Film* (Hill & Wang, 1964).
2. While much of the film's history is well documented, some of the lesser-known details presented here were provided in a series of phone conversations between Robert Epstein and the author. *Word Is Out* and the Mariposa Group's history were discussed on April 25, 2000.
3. The film was originally intended to deal with Proposition 6, a piece of legislation on the 1978 California ballot being promoted by State Senator John Briggs. Proposition 6 controversially aimed to ban any openly gay person from working in the California public school system.
4. Surprisingly, the film had never been blown up to 35mm at the time of release. While some archivists prefer to keep 16mm works in their original format, the choice is debatable, and actual practice is diverse.

My own view is that some small-format works are indeed best left that way, but not all, and *The Times of Harvey Milk* is not one of them. The film is inarguably, history writ on a large canvas, and the ability to retain the film's original 1.37 aspect ratio and photochemical qualities is a simple matter in blowup. The higher resolution and decrease in relative grain are in fact an improvement—a refinement of what already resided there, rather than a formal change of properties.

5. Unlike contemporary documentaries, which routinely transfer old film to digital video, *The Times of Harvey Milk*, conversely, took old Electronic News Gathering ("ENG") video footage and transferred it to motion picture film.
6. While the collection was much too large and cumbersome for an archive to successfully itemize and catalog, the SFPL's team acknowledged the collection's value and simplified matters by accessioning it at the "collection" rather than "item" level, meaning they took the boxes from Epstein's company, Telling Pictures, as they were and just put them on the shelf. The UCLA Film & Television Archive was later able to acquire the collection from SFPL, where it currently resides. We're indebted to SFPL librarian Susan Goldstein and her colleagues for their foresight and excellent work with the collection in the early years.
7. With the help of an excellent finding aid prepared by a Telling Pictures intern, I was able to effectively sort through 50 large boxes, creating a small stack of master tapes and original film elements. These items, along with Epstein's own holdings, would prove vital to the restoration of the film.
8. 4MC's early video-to-film service was initially developed by a lab called Image Transform back in 1972, working closely with the US government. Image Transform was subsequently absorbed by 4MC, and the process was discontinued shortly after our project was completed in 2000. At a broad level the method involved making 16mm fine grain master positive color separation masters from a video source with an electron beam recorder, which might be seen as a predecessor of contemporary laser recorders, as distinct from telecines. The three 16mm color separations were then reconstituted as a composite color internegative, usually in 35mm. When our preservation work was done in 2000 (16 years after the original production) 4MC's method was basically the same, although improvements in film stocks might yield a somewhat sharper result. Subtle improvements to the system might have effectually arisen over the years as a result of adjacent changes in video workflow prior to transfer, such as noise reduction and sharpening tools that were not available in previous decades. I'm indebted to video engineer Robert Jung, who worked with the system through the duration of its existence, for his insights into its nuances. Swiss Effects' proprietary method, in contrast, was apparently closer to an updated version of a kinescope.
9. Further complicating matters was the fact that any video-to-film transfer would need to match the original transfer frame-for-frame to be successfully integrated with the original negative. Easier said than done, when one considers that not only is there the issue of frame rate (24 frames-per-second in film, 29.97 in NTSC video), but also the issue of field dominance, in which each video frame is broken into distinct subfields, with the dominant field possibly altering with each of the myriad sources appearing in the film. A number of shots simply didn't match, despite the lab's best efforts.
10. A more appropriate term for the work conducted in a video-only release of a film-originated work would be "digital remastering."
11. Lowry Digital Image was founded in June 1998. John Lowry coincidentally founded the aforementioned Image Transform company in 1971, working with NASA to process live images from Apollo 16 the following year.
12. Most of the original lab work for *Harvey Milk* was done at Monaco Labs in San Francisco. UCLA, in agreement with Telling Pictures, decided to do the preservation work for the film at Monaco as well. The Super 8 to 16mm blow-up in question, however, was originally performed at W.A. Palmer Labs, which had subsequently gone out of business. While other labs subsequently installed Super 8 wet gates, none was in fact available in the U.S. when we preserved *Harvey Milk* in 2000.
13. The digitally treated sections (as well as the new Swiss Effects transfers) were cut into UCLA's 35mm printing negative. To ensure preservation of the film in its original form and format, an additional 16mm color interpositive was made directly from the original 16mm negative, which stands as a "pure," high quality archival record without digital or electronic modification. Records of all shots that were replaced in the 35mm version are maintained in an internal UCLA database.

14. Jonathan Rosenbaum, *Placing Movies: The Practice of Film Criticism* (California, 1995), 131 (originally published in *The Chicago Reader*, April 10, 1992).
15. A similar-but-different approach might work for films like *Vertigo*. One might duplicate the initial recording session's stereo stems and archive them for historical posterity, while releasing the restored film for exhibition in its original mono.
16. All we had to do was locate the original stereo tape, which didn't prove easy. After reviewing the contents of nearly 50 boxes in the Hormel Collection, a lab's printing elements, and the personal archives of both Rob Epstein and Mark Isham, the supposed stereo music master was not to be found. As we were preparing to abandon the effort, Isham at last found it in an unmarked box in a back room of his studio. As *Harvey Milk* was to a large extent the film that helped launch Isham's incredibly successfully career, he had kept the tapes. For a less famous film it seems likely we might not have been as successful in our search.
17. A few friends of Milk's were actually quite relieved by this. Andrew J. Epstein, in a web memoir of Richard Schmiechen, affectionately writes, "I was expecting to see a movie called the 'life' of Harvey Milk, which I was not so sure the world really needed. The Harvey Milk I knew was a lunatic, a madman who drank and drugged as much as me." (http://www.ajepstein.com/photo%20gallery/richardbody2.html).
18. Practically everyone associated with the film went on to make a lasting contribution to the cause of social justice or the art of cinema. From narrator Harvey Fierstein to cinematographer Francis Reid and co-editor Deborah Hoffmann (*Complaints of a Dutiful Daughter*), to supplemental photography by Jon Else (*The Day After Trinity*) and legendary gay filmmaker Rosa Von Prauheim, to composer Mark Isham and sound editor Lee Dichter, one sees in nascent form—like a snapshot of youth from the vantage of age—the base of the groundswell that independent film enjoys today. Last but not least was the film's producer, Richard Schmiechen, who unfortunately had his career cut short by AIDS at age 45 in 1993. On the political front, the most notable contributor is Tom Ammiano, interviewed in the film as a gay schoolteacher. Ammiano later became a two-time president of the same San Francisco Board of Supervisors on which Harvey Milk once sat as the first openly gay elected public official in California. In 1999, Ammiano ran a stunning write-in campaign for mayor, nearly defeating the famed Willie Brown.
19. When it came time to produce the Criterion high-definition master in 2009, we had the advantage of upgraded digital tools, and the Criterion DVD release hence contains numerous repairs and improvements upon the initial analog stages of work. We were also able to considerably improve the color by using the extended grading range of the digital arsenal. The restoration project—beginning in 1999 and continuing through to the Criterion edition—ultimately integrates old and new technologies in the archival preservation and presentation of a now-classic documentary that is, in itself, a compilation of material made by technologies both old and new.

On Digital Restoration's Relation to Film, and Multi-versioning

CROSSROADS

A film by Bruce Conner.

Original release: 35mm and 16mm, B&W, 36 min., 1976.

Restored in 35mm and 4K digital in 2013 by the Conner Family Trust and the Michael Kohn Gallery in collaboration with UCLA Film & Television Archive.

Restored from the original 35mm picture negative and 35mm Dolby A mono track negative, the original ¼" audio music recordings made at Different Fur Studios (Patrick Gleeson mono; Terry Riley stereo), and a DAT made directly from the ¼" master in 2002.

Restoration supervised by Michelle Silva and Ross Lipman and conformed by Ross Lipman. Laboratory Services by NT Picture & Sound, and Audio Mechanics. Digital grading by Shawn Jones. Audio restoration by John Polito. Additional photochemical printing at Cinetech. Special thanks: Dave Cetra, Jean Conner, Michael Kohn, Shawn Jones, Joe Olivier, and the staff of Cinetech. Distributed by the Conner Family Trust.

This text marks a transformation in my thoughts on cinematic authenticity, and how to approach such questions in practice amidst a rapidly changing world. Originally published in Artforum, *October 2013.*

Conservation at a Crossroads

Introduction

In 1996, I was working at the Pacific Film Archive in Berkeley. Although I was the cataloger, their visionary curator Edith Kramer knew I had a background in film printing and processing, and she let me hang around the screening room when the archive preserved CROSSROADS, Bruce Conner's profound reworking of the Bikini Atoll atomic bomb test footage.[1] The film, featuring a transcendent dual score by Patrick Gleeson and Terry Riley, is today considered Conner's masterpiece and one of the most provocative and compelling works on the atomic era extant. Having newly joined the PFA, I was honored to be a fly on the wall as they worked.

At various stages along the way Conner would come by the theater with Michael Friend of the Academy Film Archive, who was overseeing the project. Witnessing their extreme dedication and the brilliant results of their efforts, it was with both excitement and curiosity that, seventeen years later, I received the opportunity to revisit CROSSROADS. What had changed in the archival field since the excellent, author-approved 1996 work?[2] The short answer is everything.

The long answer requires discussion. If the fundamental goal of moving image preservation is saving works for posterity, why was new work needed so soon? Clearly, technological change creates necessity of action. However in so doing, it also quietly requests a reconsideration of the fundamental nature of the permanence of art. One can certainly aim for posterity, but such aims must realistically be tempered with the understanding that all best efforts will fall short in practice as well as theory. Under such conditions, moving image conservation, preservation and restoration[3] become less an exercise in timelessness, and increasingly, a dynamic function of the present historical moment.

Let's then, describe that present. The most fundamental sea change I've witnessed in my practice over the years is the loss of the singular work. Art conservation is traditionally based on the tactile maintenance of a unique physical object. In a parallel concept, moving image works—which are mechanically reproduced in multiple copies—have demanded maintenance of their own medium integrity. Both notions are now if not obsolete, in danger of becoming so. Rosalind Krauss' pioneering declaration of a new post-medium condition implicitly predicted our contemporary digital culture, in that the digitization process translates physical properties to disembodied abstract/numeric values.[4] Moving image works are, in practice, subsequently reconstituted in a variety of physical forms, but what is the meaning of medium integrity in such a context?

Stated clearly, a singular work may now be seen as a constantly changing entity as it is repeatedly presented over time. This challenges prior notions of authenticity, even those used for mass-reproduced works. The reality is that moving image restorationists must envision multi-tiered strategies that address conventional notions of archival procedure, and simultaneously consider the limitations of current exhibition contexts, even as we seek to improve them.[5] Our work on CROSSROADS offered a unique opportunity to address these issues in both theory and practice.

Figure 1. Still image from the 2013 digital remastering of Bruce Conner's CROSSROADS (1976).

Bruce Conner and CROSSROADS

The works of Bruce Conner are particularly salient, in that his oeuvre spanned both black box and white cube environments, even though neither term was commonly used when the works were created.[6] Conner, as filmmaker and artist, adeptly bridged the worlds of international cinematheques and art galleries. Accordingly, his work must be addressed from both film archive and museum perspectives. His deep investment in formal and presentational qualities only increases the relevance of CROSSROADS to the above concerns.

The present project was conceived as a new working model for moving image museum mastering, to exist as a limited edition of six copies with production overseen by the Michael

Kohn Gallery and the Conner Family Trust in collaboration with the UCLA Film & Television Archive. Our goal was to at once attain the highest standards in archival film preservation, and simultaneously ensure the maintenance of CROSSROADS' unique aesthetic character in translation to new media forms needed for contemporary exhibition, through careful control of the digital remastering process.[7]

Figure 2. Two still images from Bruce Conner's CROSSROADS (1976), before and after the film's restoration.

If these two parallel aims might seem contradictory to some, the contradiction is not as great as one might think. At every step, we held two well-established principles[8] firmly in mind:
    1) Never do anything irreversible
    2) Document our intentions and methodology so as to not falsely represent the nature of our work

The realization of our efforts can be seen as an intentional attempt at *versioning*, with distinct iterations created in both photochemical and digital media. These iterations targeted both cinematheque and gallery spaces in a variety of ways. To help elucidate our strategies, it's instructive to begin with a short recap of CROSSROADS' unique production history.

In 1974, Conner contacted the U.S. National Archives with a request to access the government's nuclear test footage. As Conner described the project for the Pentagon's perusal, "there would not be any commentary or dialogue involved. Music and sound effects would accompany the images in a proper and natural and manner. The spectacle of the underwater detonation would be the substance of the film production."[9] To Conner's pleasant surprise he was granted approval, and in characteristically subversive manner, completed the film to coincide with the American Bicentennial.

The recording of both halves of the dual soundtrack occurred at Patrick Gleeson's studio, Different Fur Music in San Francisco. Although Riley's score was mixed in stereo[10] and Dolby Stereo was publicly introduced in 1976, it was not yet readily available at the time.[11] The film was thus released in 35mm standard mono sound, as well as 16mm, which is inherently mono.

The 1996 joint preservation by PFA and the Academy was also conducted in 35mm with mono sound, and served as an excellent record of the original 1976 release. However in 2003, Conner himself went back to the original stereo Riley recordings and released a new version—in standard definition *video*. At this time he also re-framed many of the pictorial compositions to eliminate or reduce visible scratches in the source footage, and made a slight editorial change in the pacing of the end credits while leaving their text unchanged.

When we approached the project anew we thus confronted a work which had itself metamorphosized under the artist's guidance over the years, from conception to initial realization to subsequent revision, at key points responding to the practical limitations and production climate of the moment. We too would continue that process, even as we sought to preserve the film's essence in the translation to digital media.

From Film to Digital and Back Again

Our practical work began with a careful replication of the authorized 1996 photochemical preservation. This effort had been conducted at the Cinetech laboratory in Los Angeles, which, like many photochemical labs, was in the process of closing its doors due to paradigmatic changes unfolding in the industry as the new project commenced. We created a single new checkprint which emulated the 1996 print, and it was completed and viewed on the very last day of Cinetech's operation, October 10, 2012. This print would serve as a starting point for our subsequent labors.

The primary preservation elements of the earlier project were 35mm fine grain master positives, still in perfect condition in the vaults of the Pacific Film Archive and UCLA.[12] Given the thoroughness of the prior endeavor, no further work was needed to ensure archival preservation of the 1976 version with full medium integrity retained. But what of Conner's revisions, and particularly, the demands of current exhibition? While museum conservators are well aware of the importance of medium integrity, we were not surprised to learn that many of the purchasing institutions had no viable way to properly present 35mm film.[13]

In immediate terms I can say that the museums acknowledged the ethical need for 35mm elements, but simultaneously needed a high quality digital edition to effectively exhibit the work. This practical imperative intersected with our studies of CROSSROADS' production history to enable a strategy that supplemented and ultimately complemented the 1996 archival work. The following is an overview of the praxes on which our efforts unfolded, which cumulatively provide a snapshot of both the promise and technological limits of the present historical moment.

Versioning

To complement our photochemical film print, we began our digital work by scanning and archiving the original 35mm negative to 4K resolution files.[14] All digital picture work was conducted at NT Picture & Sound in Los Angeles under the supervision of Shawn Jones, an Academy Award-winning engineer and brilliant technical innovator. After scanning, Bruce Conner's long-time assistant Michelle Silva of the Conner Family Trust and I conducted a close review of the differing content in the 1976 photochemical and 2003 standard definition video versions. We ultimately determined that, while fully preserving both versions, our primary exhibition edition would be one that in essence never existed before: a high resolution re-interpretation of the final 2003 low-resolution Conner cut. This would be re-mastered for appropriate presentation in a variety of contemporary exhibition conditions including both 35mm film and digital media. Motion picture archivists generally refer to this type of "new" version as a *reconstruction*. In this case the reconstruction represents the primary public component of what is in reality a multi-tiered strategy that at once acknowledges an archival imperative to respect the artist's original vision, and self-consciously exhibits a subjectivity which is becoming increasingly acknowledged in restoration work.[15]

Grain Management

Early digital restorations were frequently conducted by laboratory technicians who were accustomed to working on new Hollywood films, with the result that many exhibited a degree of polish and, if one will, sterility, that was not characteristic of certain historical titles. As our collective understanding of the process has progressed, archives and laboratories alike have become increasingly aware of photochemical image characteristics that should ideally be retained in translation to digital media. Primary among these is film grain, which fundamentally differs from the regularized structure of pixels. Whereas early efforts frequently removed grain as undesirable, newer productions have made efforts to retain it.

As this concept has gained credence, it's become increasingly common to remove grain for a variety of reasons, and then later generate *digital* grain to replace it. Dirt removal software tends to work much better on a de-grained image. However not all grain is alike. Even when

Figures 3— 6. Still images from the 2013 digital remastering of Bruce Conner's CROSSROADS (1976).

one's "replacement grain" is specifically modeled on the original grain removed from the source, transformations occur. For CROSSROADS it was determined that retention of grain character was a high priority, to be place above digital cleanup when conflict between the two arose.[16] This decision would set the table for the remainder of our work.

Dirt and Scratch Removal

Just as human subjectivity plays a greater role in the restoration process than many care to admit, so too does "digital subjectivity." If a computer is going to assess an image to distinguish intended content from incidental damage, a degree of interpretation is built into the computation process by definition. As the above suggests, it's easy for a computer to mistake grain for dirt. Continuous vertical "tramline" scratches present even more difficult challenges for digital software, which can't easily distinguish the tramlines from naturally occurring vertical lines in a composition. In such cases digital hand-painting is usually preferable, in that it directs the subjectivity to human discretion. However hand-painting is extremely expensive.

The question then becomes, in what area should a project compromise? For CROSSROADS, we used automated cleanup just to the point where grain patterns would become noticeably affected upon continuation, and then applied extensive hand-painting. Certain production "problems" were intentionally retained as part of the work.[17] The result is a new version which is substantially cleaner than the original copies, but far from pristine. While future tools could enable a more thorough cleanup, the current work embodies an engaged dance between the film's content and the limits of technology—as did the original.

Stabilization

A common selling point of digital cinema is that it's more stable than motion picture film, which when projected, often exhibits a subtle jitter that the human brain steadies in the act of perception. In my experience stabilization can be overrated. When the jitter is not pronounced, the brain's internal regulating process works just fine, and an over-stabilized image can lose a sense of dynamism. In the case of CROSSROADS, selected shots exhibited a jitter that traced to environmental conditions at the time of filming the atomic explosion, and hence inherently demanded retention. Others exhibited a jitter that traced to camera problems that

Conner was known to dislike, and could be improved upon. Still others traced to undesirable camera problems that, when addressed with digital stabilization, exhibited artifacts including image softening and blurring. In such cases the stabilization was dialed back, retaining both image sharpness and problematic jitter.

Flicker and Pulsing

Conner's meticulous production notes expressly state a desire to retain exposure variations within selected shots. Where indicated, these exposure variations were retained. Elsewhere, digital color and density correction tools enabled a degree of pulse elimination not easily obtained with photochemical film grading.[18] In some cases this process resulted in a flattening of image that drained it of character, so again the process was dialed back to resemble the original, flaws included.

Framing and Repositioning

When a work is translated from one medium to another its image composition is frequently cropped, often broadly and sometimes subtly. As an example of the latter, Bruce Conner had intentionally magnified selected shots in CROSSROADS to eliminate visible scratches when remastering it to standard definition video. The 2003 edition thus had different framings than the 1976 initial film release. When it came time to conduct our principal work, we found we could indeed eliminate selected tramline scratches by this method, reducing the need for digital cleanup. We further found that the tightly controlled framelines of digital cinema allowed us to be more conservative in our cropping than Conner had in 2003. We thus created a version with framings that perfectly emulated neither the 1976 or 2003 versions, but sat somewhere between the two.[19] Such re-positionings may sound heretical to armchair notions of ethical purity, but are completely commonplace, and here acknowledged, if slight.

Contrast and Color Correction

The change described above is but part of a larger phenomenon. I've previously remarked that it's a misnomer to think that "perfect emulation" of a static original is the consensus aim of restorationists, or in fact even possible.[20] The perceptual experience of photochemical film is different than that of digital images when viewed on monitors, and yet again in projection. We thus utilized available color correction tools to moderate density and contrast, optimizing the image for presentation in its contemporary digital environments, while simultaneously retaining its general "film" character in grain structure, flicker, and image stability.

While this might concern theorists not versed in technology, such variances are again a commonplace reality, if oft misunderstood. I would suggest that it's ontologically impossible to

replicate one medium in another. In medium translations, interpretation is intrinsically part of the work process, whether acknowledged or not. Its key challenge is skillful execution.

Digital Film-out

Upon completion of the digital version, we conducted extensive testing to ensure the highest possible quality in digital-to-film recording and subsequent 35mm film prints.[21] As we had already interpreted the tonal character of the image, it did not make sense to base this work on side-by-side comparisons with older prints, which would by its very definition yield a mismatch. We conducted such studies only upon completion of the work, for research purposes exclusively. Similarly, we retained our working premise that the new 35mm prints constitute a different medium than the digital version. Our decisions were ultimately based on a rigorous procedure that is best described as LUT-wedging, wherein Shawn Jones at NT Picture & Sound created eighteen custom-modified LUTS to enable the most satisfying 35mm black and white film rendition of the digital work.[22] Upon project completion, we had thus created a total of three distinct versions of CROSSROADS: 35mm analog/photochemical, digital, and 35mm digital film out; each with distinct image characteristics acknowledged.

Re-imagining the Space of Sound

Just as the picture of CROSSROADS was subjectively rendered, so too was the sound. As mentioned, Conner had not initially released the film in stereo because of practical industrial limitations at the time of completion. As archivists we intrinsically and ethically sought to ensure preservation of the work as released. However, having thoroughly secured that,[23] we then, as with the picture, evaluated the source material to determine strategy for our primary exhibition versions. Again we modeled our work on Conner's final 2003 re-mastering, and again, subtly re-envisioned it for contemporary technology. In so doing we similarly transgressed borders that normative thinking had heretofore considered firm. The primary axis on which this occurred was, by default and intent alike, the adapting of acoustical dimensioning to current exhibition conditions.

As discussed, Terry Riley's score was initially mixed in two-channel stereo. After ensuring archival preservation of the un-retouched 1976 mono optical track, we then digitally restored the sound. Audio Mechanics studio founder John Polito, in close dialogue with Michelle Silva and I, conformed the original ¼" mix master to the final edit. He then carefully removed system-induced noise from re-recording while retaining sound anomalies tracing to the original recordings. The cleaned up files were archived in both mono and stereo.

The next step was to format the two-channel stereo version for exhibition. This was much less straightforward than one would think. Although 35mm prints with 5.1 Dolby Digital tracks can accommodate a straight rendition of two-channel sound within it, this practice is prohibitively expensive for virtually all but studio releases. The more viable option for independent artworks intrinsically spreads two stereo channels to four: left, center, right, and surround.[24] For our 35mm stereo prints we utilized this process of necessity, and the resulting track inherently features a slightly different acoustical dimensioning than either prior version, if only through the system's default encoding process.

For our digital version we needed to anticipate a multiplicity of playback environments, encompassing traditional cinematheque, museum, and gallery spaces. Crucially, we had to consider the many factors that go into white cube reception, and/or semi-controlled black box environments within museums. For this crucial stage of the work, we again did not adhere to strict literalist notions of reproduction. At this juncture, Michelle Silva's direct collaboration with the artist proved vital. In joining Silva's intimate knowledge of Conner's working methodology with the material evidence of his subsequent revision of it, we witnessed not a desire to freeze the picture and sound quality in exhibition technology of one era, but rather a clear effort to move and adapt. We thus, in dialogue with both composers, decided to carefully dimension the film's two scores within the 5.1 stereo format.

When I say this I should stress that we did nothing resembling the effects-based sound spreading sometimes undertaken for commercial films, whereby non-surround audio is expanded to 5.1 to create an illusion that different noises are happening in specific places around the theater. Rather, John Polito employed different techniques for each score to distribute the overall sound environmentally.[25] While doing the above work, we also ensured that our 5.1 version was 100% mono-compatible, meaning that if played back in a mono system, the output would emulate the mono original, and not a corrupted version of it. Not all methods of spreading retain this property.

Duration, Content, and Environmental Considerations in Moving Image Presentation

By the time one has gotten this far, it should be apparent that our reconstruction actively interpreted CROSSROADS in its rendition of it. The last aspect of our work which should be mentioned in this regard is the film's editorial content. Conner's 2003 video re-mastering featured only one notable change from the 1976 original: he ever so slightly re-adjusted the timing of the film's end credits. The original release—upon the idea of Terry Riley—featured an extended section of black screen while the music continued after the last image's fadeout, before the end credits at last commenced in silence. In 2003, Conner truncated the black ever so slightly, so that the credits began near the music's conclusion and ended in silence. While I know at least one purist who feels that the full black duration makes a crucial difference, both Michelle Silva and I agreed that Conner's 2003 choice, which retained a very lengthy black / music section, does full justice to the metaphysical meditation suggested by Riley's desired delay, while reducing the arguably unnecessary durational challenge posed by holding all credits until the music's conclusion. Having made this value judgment, I should specify that it describes only our thinking in selecting the 2003 edition as the model for our primary viewing version. As stated, we fully preserved both in the archives of UCLA.

The issue of duration itself should also be raised in the context of larger problems of gallery exhibition. CROSSROADS is relatively well suited to museum presentation in that, utilizing repetition of the bomb's explosion from multiple angles, its reception is not completely dependent on sequential viewing. Ambulatory viewers experiencing only a portion of the work can at least glimpse and sense aspects of the larger ideas behind it. Having said that, crucial things are missed in such a context. One of Conner's major structuring devices is his placement of Gleeson's score—which used recreations of representational and quotidian sounds including explosions, countdowns, and birds—prior to the transcendence of Riley's non-representational music. In gallery exhibition, not only will passing viewers largely miss this dynamic, but continual looping without interruption would make the piece cyclical; an interesting strategy in its own right but not Conner's intent. It would furthermore create the probability that some viewers might experience the Gleeson/Riley sequencing *in reverse*—and have to reconstruct Conner's design in their imagination, if they so desired.

Likewise, the film's last shot, which lingers over the sea for an extended time after the bomb's blast, can be hinted at but not fully experienced with mere glimpses. In this way CROSSROADS is not unique: key aspects of many moving image works cannot be fully conveyed in the context of ambulatory, non-sequential gallery viewing. This troublesome condition is only one of many that point to systemic dilemmas posed by the traditional nature of museums themselves, which are ill-adapted for audiovisual works, even though such works comprise the core expressive form of contemporary life.

Ironically, much of the careful effort that has gone into our work on CROSSROADS can be undone in practice if viewing conditions in the displaying institution are not well established. To address this, the Conner Trust and Michael Kohn Gallery negotiated detailed agreements with purchasers that consider both archival and presentational issues, assuring at least a degree of control over both exhibition and future remastering, to maintain the work as needed for posterity within the scope of the limited edition of six being generated.[26]

In this sense, our work on CROSSROADS is aimed firmly at the present, while remembering the past and anticipating the future. By creating and archiving multiple versions across a variety of platforms, I wish to suggest that neither these, nor re-mastering efforts to come, nor even Conner's own multiple reworkings of the piece can be practically understood as *singularly* definitive. That notion of authenticity is in transformation as we move further into the post-medium epoch. CROSSROADS now exists as a work out of time that resurfaces within it. Our multi-tiered iteration strives to be the best possible in its own historical moment, respecting the prior, and enabling the next.

Endnotes

1. The title is not in italics because Conner "hated letters that looked like they were falling over," and hence capitalized the names of all his film works. — Bruce Conner, as quoted in e-mail from Michelle Silva to Ross Lipman (July 25, 2013).
2. I briefly discussed the project in an earlier essay, "Problems of Independent Film Preservation," *Journal of Film Preservation*, Vol. XXV, No. 53 (1996), 50-51.
3. It's important to note that these terms have slightly different meanings in the museum and film archiving communities. To generalize definitions that will hopefully work for both of these two constituencies: *conservation* can be understood as the physical maintenance of a prime artifact; *preservation* as straightforward duplication in a single medium, and *restoration* as an interactive process whereby the potentially abstract essence of a work is recreated in a duplicate copy by a variety of means.
4. Krauss' formulation distinguishes between modernist notions of medium specificity and "technical support," which she describes as the underlying principles which help define a medium. The term itself is of great value in describing a digital crisis which encompasses the wholesale de-physicalization of artworks across multiple media forms, and Krauss' distinction is of particular use in considering the digital remastering process.
5. The situation is endemic to many contemporary media forms, so that discussion of it has even reached the mainstream media. See Melina Ryzik, "Why Artworks Crash," *The New York Times*, June 9, 2013, http://www.nytimes.com/2013/06/10/arts/design/whitney-saves-douglas-daviss-first-collaborative-sentence.html?pagewanted=all
6. The use of the term "black box" in museums is pre-dated by its use in the theater. I here use both terms as commonly understood in museum parlance, but also to distinguish between controlled spaces in cinematheques and uncontrolled or semi-controlled gallery spaces.
7. It should be noted that the six editions were supplemented by copies for the Conner Trust and UCLA, termed by the Trust as artist's proofs. The edition of six included both archival 35mm copies and digital media, as shall be described.
8. In considering methodological ethics I continually refer back to Eileen Bowser's classic short essay, "Some Principles of Film Restoration," *Griffithiana*, Anno XIII, n.38/39, October 1990.
9. Bruce Conner, letter to Russell Wagner, Directorate for Defense Information, March 28, 1974.
10. Via the use of tape delays at differing speeds, Riley expanded two separate Yamaha organ tracks to sixteen channels, then folded it down to a two-channel stereo mix. For his score, Gleeson carefully generated naturalistic sound effects on a Moog synthesizer.
11. The first Dolby Stereo release was Hollywood's 1976 remake of *A Star is Born*.

12. The Conner Family Trust transferred their film holdings to UCLA in 2008. In addition to the Academy's preservation materials, UCLA additionally houses all of CROSSROADS' original edited production elements.
13. The larger implications of these cultural conditions are best saved for a later discussion.
14. More specifically, we generated 4096 X 3112 10-Bit log DPX files on an Arriscan and archived them on LTO 5 tape.
15. See Pip Laurenson, "Authenticity, Change and Loss in the Conservation of Time-Based Media Installations," Tate Papers, October 2006, http://www.tate.org.uk/research/publications/tate-papers/authenticity-change-and-loss-conservation-time-based-media. It is also the central premise of my essay "The Gray Zone," *The Moving Image*, vol. 9, no. 2 (Fall 2009), 1-29.
16. Additional efforts were made to retain the original's film grain character in black background titles and white screen sections, which might otherwise be replaced by video blacks and pure whites.
17. Whereas one could strongly argue that printed-in scratches and blemishes are part of a given found-footage work, our research on CROSSROADS clearly indicated that Conner liked some of the "problems" present in the film's source footage, but wished others to be corrected.
18. This pulsing is often called "density breathing" by film restorationists. Video engineers sometimes use the term "shading error." I tend to dislike the latter, as its pejorative connotations are misleading when the characteristic is not problematic.
19. Our initial scans encompassed the entirety of the source negative's image area, ensuring all photographed content was retained and archived, before creating our final reconstruction.
20. "The Gray Zone," ibid.
21. We conducted our restoration work in 3K (3072 X 2334) to control costs with maximized efficiency, and then uprezzed for 4K filmout. Given that the NARA source footage was itself a duplicate, the downrez/uprez process involved a truly minimal compromise. As another point of reference, the projected 4K digital cinema resolution of a 1.37 Academy aperture image is 2960 X 2160, less than our working resolution.
22. LUT stands for Lookup Table, and broadly refers to the process whereby a digital image is translated from one platform to another, in this case from log color space for digital workstations to Fuji 35mm black-and-white digital separation film 4791. Not surprisingly in such instances, a straight application of math will not generally do the trick, especially when dealing with black-and-white stock. In my experience contrast problems are common, and some photochemical density grading is frequently needed even when the source file is a fully graded program. Shawn's extensive testing yielded one of the best black-and-white film outs that I've seen to date.
23. The original version was preserved to 35mm film, DVD-R data discs, and LTO tape.
24. The common alternative to Dolby Digital is Dolby Stereo, which uses Lt/Rt (Left total/Right total) matrixing to derive the four tracks.
25. For Riley's stereo tracks he employed careful channel separation to isolate discrete center audio and send de-correlated audio to the surround speakers. For Gleeson's mono score, he used frequency splitting to a similarly controlled purpose, with the express aim of avoiding affect or the creation of specific effects. It should be noted that if one sent identical signals to different speakers, our hearing process would perceptually create its own front/center emphasis, depending on where one was seated. The ear uses delays to help determine directionality, and when identical sounds arrive at both ears at once, we tend to center them. Frequency splitting helps create a sense of surround in this context. For this reason I jokingly refer to the Gleeson section of the film as being "mono surround," although the usage doesn't precisely match the term's technical definition.
26. Detailed exhibition and duplication agreements between museums and artists are becoming increasingly essential as the technologies that enabled the creation and display of specific works become obsolete.

On Secondary Authors

Faces

Director, Screenwriter: John Cassavetes. Cinematographers: Al Ruban, George Sims. Featuring: Gena Rowlands, John Marley, Lynn Carlin, Seymour Cassel. Producer: Maurice McEndree. Original release: 35mm, B&W, 130 min., 1968.

Restored in 35mm in 2006 by UCLA Film & Television Archive in cooperation with Faces Distribution Corp, with funding from The Film Foundation and The Hollywood Foreign Press Association.

Restored from the surviving 16mm original negative and reversal A/B rolls, a 35mm acetate dupe negative, the surviving 35mm original fullcoat magnetic recordings, and a 35mm acetate track negative.

Restoration supervised by Ross Lipman. Laboratory Services by Triage Motion Picture Services, Audio Mechanics, DJ Audio, NT Audio. B&W grading by Sharol Olson. Audio restoration by John Polito. Special thanks: Tony Munroe, Gena Rowlands, Al Ruban, Paul Rutan, Jr., Dave Tucker. Restoration print not in distribution; available from UCLA.

This text was adapted from a screening introduction originally presented upon the restoration's premiere at the James Bridges Theater in Los Angeles on August 19, 2006, and at the Chicago International Film Festival on October 26, 2008. It presents another perspective on the idea of "secondary authors" introduced in the earlier discussion of Tillie's Punctured Romance. *While that essay's use of the term focused primarily on editorial content, the discussion in this instance focuses on more elusive questions of interpretation and formal properties that can arise within content that is already fixed. Further information on the original production of* Faces *can be found in "Mingus, Cassavetes, and the Birth of a Jazz Cinema" elsewhere in this volume. Those interested in more information on the Cassavetes restoration project can find a short documentary on the restoration of* Shadows *on the Criterion Channel.*

Faces Behind *Faces*

John Cassavetes' *Faces*, his first film in 16mm after the 1959 *Shadows*, emerged after a gap of almost nine years, in which he tried to work within the confines of the Hollywood system. The films made in between were compromised, and the results were disastrous to his psyche. *Faces* was an attempt to return to his filmmaking roots, to take control of his career, and to regain his vision. However he realized he had changed in the years since *Shadows*—he was no longer in his twenties, and wanted to make a movie that was closer to what he was experiencing at that point in his life. He said:

> I wrote *Faces* out of a lot of anger and dismay with society... I wanted to show the inability of people to communicate; what small things will do to people...; and how, when they're not prepared to think with their own minds and to feel, how all this can become tragic....
> The result was a barrage of attacks on contemporary middle-class America, an expression of horror at our society in general.[1]

Yet, he goes on to say:

> I wrote this very bitter piece and the actors took it and couldn't make it bitter. That was their insight, their discovery, their feeling for people.... I couldn't erase a certain... humanness from these actors, to make them as hard as the characters they played might have been. They were so much better than the original concept that they made the picture quite wonderful.

These dual impulses of anger and compassion paralleled a formal tension between discord and harmony in the film itself, and were linked to the challenges faced in restoring it.
   Cassavetes' salute to his actors points to a dynamic common to both film production and restoration—in which a variety of people beyond a single auteur help give it shape. I've come to call these contributors "secondary authors."[2] In the following remarks I'll be looking at the initial production of *Faces*, as well as its afterlife in reprints and then restoration, to illustrate the profound impact secondary authors can have on a work, for both bad and—hopefully—for good.

○   ○   ○

Perhaps ironically, our discussion begins with Cassavetes' search for autonomy after his bad experiences in the Hollywood system. To ensure he had total control this time, *Faces* was entirely self-funded. As with *Shadows*, this meant a low-budget shoot with widely celebrated stripped-back production values. But to allow his actors an unprecedented freedom to fully create and develop their roles, he shot an extremely large amount of footage in this minimalist mode. Some accounts place the shooting ratio at a staggering fifty to one. This was by necessity followed by an extended and difficult editing process, involving resyncing virtually the entire film—in the process cutting it down from an initial assembly of over eight hours to a final running time of 129 minutes. Different structures were explored along the way.

Of the final edited version, much of the camera original is now lost. The surviving 16mm A/B rolls are incomplete, and much that remains is in terrible condition. The original footage that survives is a mixture of both negative and reversal stocks, making it challenging to print. Like *Shadows*, the film has a number of different looks within it—but here the different looks tended to break down by scene, as different sections of the film were deliberately shot with different stocks.

In the end we were able to duplicate nearly two thirds of the original film to 35mm in an extremely sharp blow up that retains the highest amount of picture detail possible… and also a lot of dirt. This resulted in a fine grain master positive that is part of a long-term strategy intended to enable future digital restorations to be made from the highest quality picture record possible. From that master positive, to my pleasant surprise, we were able to salvage over half the film in UCLA's final (complete) preservation elements.

To replace sections that were damaged, lost, or deteriorated, we went back to an old 35mm duplicate negative that was printed directly from the original blow-up by Adrian Mosher of Cine Services, made in 1968. Speaking of this initial lab work, Cassavetes said, "Mosher did the blow-up with as much love as we put into making the film. He was an artist; he cared about each frame." And indeed he did an excellent job, much of which was by necessity happily utilized in our restoration.

However I mention this not just to salute Adrian Mosher, but also to help illuminate one of the film's tensions I spoke of earlier. In this case it's the tension between Cassavetes' aesthetics and his… well, *non*-aesthetics in production. This contrarian impulse is apparent in the film's dramatic structure, which allows scenes to develop in extended "real" time that completely defies artistic convention, but yields an incredibly strong payoff. It's also embedded in the film's very appearance.

In an essay written for the recent Criterion Collection DVD of *Faces*, Stuart Klawans of *The Nation* intriguingly writes:

> The disc of *Faces* that you now hold is the most beautiful copy possible of a film that was meant to look lousy. Digital technology painstakingly reproduces John Cassavetes' lighting, which allowed his actors to move freely, and so lent his average interior the aura of a dentist's office; preserves the integrity of his compositions, which often had a lamp or table setting deliberately stuck in the foreground to block your view of the actions; registers with exquisite sensitivity each vagary of his camera as it chased after the actors and lost focus.[3]

Klawans points to an attempt to almost deliberately de-aestheticize aspects of the film, as part of Cassavetes' celebrated actor-based methodology. Said Cassavetes of the film's pictorial qualities:

> We didn't allow ourselves to polish up the image, or to use expressive lighting and fancy camera angles. I don't want it to look like a movie. If it's too perfect you don't believe it. I want it a little out of focus. I don't want you to admire the image. You never stop to look—so you *feel*.

Yet despite this provocative agenda, the film still has an extraordinary beauty to it, and that's not an accident. Cassavetes is if nothing else a director who embraced contradictions. Director of Photography Al Ruban's choice to use different film stocks to achieve varying effects for individual scenes, and Cassavetes' own comments praising the blow-up indicate a concern with pictorial quality that runs parallel with the important but sometimes overly celebrated disregard for it.

○ ○ ○

Let's now return to our production history. *Faces* was originally shot in 16mm's camera-native aspect ratio of 1.37:1, or a nearly square screen space,[4] and it's believed that it was originally presented that way in its 35mm release. However a number of problems occurred in the years that followed. In particular a laboratory fire some time after Cassavetes' death resulted in damage to a 35mm duplicate negative that his company, Faces Distribution, had been using to strike new distribution prints. To replace the damaged material, a new negative was made, but hairs in the printer gate were not sufficiently addressed, and made their way into the projected image.[5] For this reason, Al Ruban (who at that time ran Faces Distribution, and as noted had been one of the original cinematographers) determined after the fact that the film should be projected at 1.66 aspect ratio. The wider and narrower format would sufficiently crop the gate hairs in projection.

This meant, however, that the compositional balance of the photography by main camera operator George Sims and the numerous others involved in the shooting was thrown off, creating an unsettling viewing experience. To a degree, that's in keeping with Cassavetes' "non-aesthetic" side—but it also represented an instance of secondary authors—including the lab technicians who allowed the gate hairs into the new negative—to influence the form of the film.

When it came time to commence our restoration, we took a different approach, and employed the same technique we used with *Shadows*: including all of the picture information in the preservation elements, but magnifying the image ever so slightly, to place most source-related gate problems off-screen when projected with the correct 1.37 Academy aperture plate in place. This method would retain an authentic record of any *camera* gate hairs in Cassavetes original version in case historians felt them of importance, but minimize their scale on screen for viewers—all while retaining the correct/original aspect ratio. And by careful printing, we would avoid adding printer gate hairs of the kind found in the work of printer operators who came after Mosher.

At our premiere screening in Los Angeles, we still projected the film in the rectangular 1.66, per the request of Al Ruban, who had kindly green-lighted our project. But after the screening Al approached me and informed me that he'd changed his mind: if the problems were indeed off-screen, we should project it in its original 1.37 format. In my mind this is the correct decision, as it returns the work to its intended form, re-establishing the composition of the cinematographers.

In keeping with this quest for authenticity, our copy restores not just the film's original composition, but also the intentionally distinct look of the varying film stocks originally employed. That said, in some cases, the resulting aesthetics differ in subtle ways from the original Adrian Mosher blow-up, as well as from the later replacement dupe negative. For example, our blow-up is ever so slightly sharper than Mosher's and retains more of the original camera grain. Mosher's blow-up, in turn, might be described as somewhat creamier, and more glossy. The fact that our assembled new restoration incorporates parts of Mosher's work, as well as our own blown-up sections, is another subtle point of difference from its predecessors.

The result is a print of *Faces* that is at once identical to the commonly released version, and one that has, in essence, never been seen before.[6] But all of the post-production technicians—from Mosher to the replacement-negative team, to the restoration team—have in effect contributed as secondary authors, at least in so far as the film's pictorial properties are concerned.

○   ○   ○

While this is on the one hand *a priori*, it's on the other a bit controversial. The practice of restoration is often considered to be neutral; a point I've disputed in the past. I would offer, rather, that a film is actually altered by definition every time it's printed. It's more a question of degree, and of qualities. I would add further, that in some instances these changes are made unconsciously.

To illustrate this point I'll now relate some historical details concerning the film's soundtrack. In the course of my research I inspected numerous other past iterations of *Faces*, generated at various times over the years as its distributor changed. One of those prints was produced by a major Hollywood studio who temporarily held the rights. When the studio version was created, the sound engineers boosted the entire film's high frequency range to increase dialogue audibility, and rolled off a large portion of the low end. An unintentional byproduct of this was the elimination of some of the film's sound effects. For example, in the scenes where Gena Rowlands, John Marley and Fred Draper exit the Loser's Club, all sound save their voices drops out once the car doors are closed. Yet in the film's original soundtrack, traffic could still be heard faintly around them, lending atmosphere to the scene.

I cannot imagine that the technicians listened to that scene and decided they were going to get rid of those cars. Rather, they likely set their EQ for dialogue—perhaps elsewhere in the film—and had no idea they'd eliminated anything. By going back to Cassavetes' original sound mix and re-equalizing, we were able to create a more authentic and much higher fidelity soundtrack in our restoration; one that retains the traffic noise and other similar omissions in the studio print.

The very careful sound work is by John Polito of Audio Mechanics, and the high quality sound transfers are by DJ Audio and NT Audio. I'd like to thank Triage Motion Picture Services for their excellent printing of the film. As for picture, I'd particularly like to thank Dave Tucker for his meticulous blow-up work, Sharol Olson for her careful grading, and Tony Munroe, for putting up with me.[7] Lastly, I'd like to thank the Film Foundation and Hollywood Foreign Press Association, who quite simply, make our work possible. In our own small way, we might all be seen as joining a long line of secondary authors who helped bring *Faces* to the screen.

Endnotes

1. Quotes from John Cassavetes in this essay can be found in Ray Carney, *Cassavetes on Cassavetes* (Faber and Faber, 2001). Though it is an invaluable reference, Ray Carney's compilation does not specify original quote sources.
2. I should note that this designation does not intrinsically mean "collaborators" in the same sense as Cassavetes' actors and crew, who worked with him directly. My use of the term "secondary authors" does include original participants, but also speaks to those who came later.
3. The Criterion DVD was made prior to completion of UCLA's restoration.
4. While 1.37:1 is considered the standard, the fact is that in practice, 16mm camera apertures vary widely—if in small increments—around this figure, as do 16mm projector aperture plates, which are in theory, intended to crop the image slightly to a 1.33:1 aspect ratio. I use 1.37:1 here more as a matter of convenience than to suggest a precise measurement.
5. This statement includes some interpretation of Al Ruban's comments to me. It's not clear to me whether the hairs were aperture plate hairs from the production, or printer gate hairs from the blow-up. If the former, Adrian Mosher had apparently compensated by magnifying and/or cropping appropriately when doing his blow-up, while the later technicians did not. If the latter, the hairs could have been introduced by sloppy printing.
6. Manohla Dargis of *The New York Times* was in the audience at UCLA's restoration premiere screening, and told me afterwards that she was particularly stunned by the beautiful grain quality in the print, and that it was one of the most visually inspiring experiences she'd had in a theater.
7. The restoration was printed at Triage Motion Picture Services in Los Angeles, which was owned by Munroe and Paul Rutan Jr.. On a note of historical resonance, *Faces* was originally printed in 1968 at Perfect Films, which was at that time run by Paul Rutan, Sr. Rutan, Jr. was working there at the time, when he was only 15, and in his own words, "locked in the basement."

On Disparities Between Artists' Intentions and the Historical Record

Wanda

Director, Screenwriter: Barbara Loden. Cinematographer: Nicholas, T. Proferes.

Featuring: Barbara Loden, Michael Higgins.

Original release: 35mm, color, 102 mins., 1970.

Restored in 35mm in 2010 and subsequently digitally remastered by UCLA Film & Television Archive in cooperation with Televentures Corp and Parlour Pictures, with funding from The Film Foundation and GUCCI.

Restored from the original 16mm A/B rolls, a 35mm print, and the original 35mm and 16mm optical tracks. Digitally remastered from the restored 35mm internegative and digital audio files.

Restoration conformed and supervised by Ross Lipman in consultation with Nicholas Proferes. Laboratory services by Cinetech, Ascent Media, Audio Mechanics, and NT Picture & Sound. Photochemical film grading by Dave Cetra. Audio restoration by John Polito. Special thanks to: David Block, Mimi Brody, James Gott, Marco and Larry Joachim, Shawn Jones, Leo Kazan, Dave Osterkamp, Nicholas Proferes. Restored in cooperation with Televentures Corp and Parlour Pictures. Distributed by Janus Films and Criterion.

Partially adapted from an illustrated lecture originally presented at the Reel Thing Technical Symposium, Academy of Motion Picture Arts and Sciences in Los Angeles, 2010, and as a Keynote at the ZdC Conference at USC in 2011. First published in the present form as a web-piece in Criterion's The Current, 2019. https://www.criterion.com/current/posts/6237-defogging-wanda

Defogging *Wanda*

In early 2007 the UCLA Film & Television Archive received a call from Hollywood Film and Video announcing that the lab was, sadly, closing—and clearing their vaults in two days' time. Anything left was doomed to the dumpster. The next morning a group of us arrived to see what we could salvage.

Walking through the musty basement, dank stairwells, and narrow aisles was like walking through a shuffled deck of cards: artifacts from the 1950s to the present lay atop each other, in seemingly unknowable order. The only light came from a few incandescent bulbs hanging irregularly amid the dark corridors of shelves, casting a yellow glow that dropped quickly into shadow. Aging equipment was everywhere, some still functional, some showing years of rust, dust, and corrosion. Puddles of oily water lurked underfoot reflecting sickly rainbows, and the smell of old chemicals and mold hung in the air.

The films lay about in differing arrays, long forgotten by their makers: B, C, and D movies, industrial films, commercials, printing tests, and the stray experimental short. We began making piles to save in our collection.

In one aisle, buried in a large stack on the floor, I found some 16mm reels labeled "WANDA. Harry Shuster." Who on earth was he? Surely this couldn't be the classic independent film by Barbara Loden? Her name was nowhere to be found on either the boxes or the leaders. Taking no chances, I kept the oddity apart from my other discoveries; in fact, I took it back to our lab in my own car.

Immediately unspooling the reels on my workbench upon arriving, I realized we'd uncovered a piece of history. It was that *Wanda*—and no less than its original camera rolls. Harry Shuster, as I'd guessed, was the film's producer. One more day and it would have gone to landfill.

But how to fund a restoration? Enter the Film Foundation, which has saved so many classic works over the years. In coincidental great timing, they'd recently begun a partnership with Gucci, whose express aim was preserving works by women visionaries. And so our work commenced.

At that time digital restoration was advancing rapidly but had not yet overtaken photochemical printing in archival practice. Thus our work would be on good old-fashioned film, at least initially. We began as Loden had herself, with a blow-up to 35mm. But our route quickly began to vary. The exact stocks she used no longer existed, and their "official" replacements were problematic, increasing contrast and distorting color.

A crucial component of *Wanda*'s production, as I found in the camera rolls, was its Kodak Ektachrome ECB (7242) film stock, which has a unique color palette completely unlike Eastmancolor negative, Eastman Commercial film (ECO), or Kodachrome. In a stroke of luck, the bulk of the film was on this, and unfaded.

After extensive testing at Cinetech Laboratory, we decided to avoid Kodak's designated internegative, a holdover from a previous era that was not optimized for printing from projection-contrast film. We instead printed the reversal camera rolls to a low-speed negative camera stock and pull-processed to reduce contrast—as I'd successfully done on a number of past titles. It's interesting to note that in the intervening years, Kodak abandoned the interneg I nixed in favor of the camera stock. But this was years before that took place, and the result was stunning color.

Ironically, this led to what might strike some as an archival quandary. While the new color closely matched the original rolls, it was in fact much *better* than the old distribution prints, which apparently looked awful. To quote an early review in the British journal *Films and Filming* by Gordon Gow:

> *For the first couple of minutes, I thought it was all a ghastly mistake, this terrible muzz-colour... But soon it became obvious that Barbara Loden meant it to look messy, as if real life had been recorded perchance by an amateur photographer with cheap film and poor laboratory facilities.*

It's a nice interpretation. But was it valid? In *Film Journal*'s Summer 1971 interview with Loden, I found this:

> *Ruby Melton: The color in the film often has a washed-out, grainy effect and the lighting is sometimes very dim. Were these effects intentional?*
>
> *Barbara Loden: Unless you have your own laboratory, it's difficult to control the quality of the color. In our original print the color looked extremely good, but later prints made by different labs were not such good quality.*

Gow thought the poor quality of the release prints was Loden's aim, but her own comments belie this. He was responding to an innate quality in the movie that spoke through the poor printing, and in the process cast his sense of authenticity on what was in fact just a poor rendering. Our role as restorationists, in turn, involved deciding which aspects of the film's original "roughness" were intrinsic to production, and which came later.

Another question that arose was aspect ratio. 1.85 was clearly written on the leaders of an old 1970 distribution print in UCLA's collection, as was common with 35mm features at the time. Yet others disagreed. A pre-restoration French DVD release by Isabelle Huppert, Ronald Chammah, and Gemini Films chose the 16mm native aspect ratio of 1.37:1,[1] while the US pre-restoration Parlour Pictures DVD release chose 1.66:1, in dialogue with the film's cinematographer, Nick Proferes.

To get to the bottom of the matter, I consulted Proferes directly. He told me that *Wanda* had been shot on a 16mm Auricon hand-modified by none other than D.A. Pennebaker, to a wider aspect ratio. In those days Super 16 was coming into popularity as a low-budget option that offered a wider aspect ratio, 1.66, when blown up to 35mm for theatrical exhibition. Rather than re-outfit his company with Super 16 gear, Pennebaker literally hand-filed his camera's aperture plates to something near 1.66 for the shooting of his concert film, *Sweet Toronto*.

Yet I had the original camera rolls in my hands, and it was clearly 1.37, on double perf stock that would have precluded a 1.66 or Super-16 shoot. To be sure I wasn't delusional I also checked with Pennebaker himself, who said quite certainly that Proferes hadn't used one of his modified Auricons on *Wanda*. My guess is Nick used it on another, later film.

The question returns then: how should one frame it? In looking closely at *Wanda*, it became apparent that all ratios worked well. My ultimate assessment was that Proferes shot *Wanda* with both Academy format and widescreen exhibition in mind, as was sometimes done at the time. But none of the ratios worked for the whole movie. Virtually all shots had plenty of headroom and are most pleasing at 1.66, suggesting widescreen intentions—but there were moments of exception where both 1.85 and 1.66 proved problematic. To do the highest quality widescreen release in either of those formats would have required numerous framing "repos," or re-positionings—something Loden hadn't done at the time. In its native 1.37, many shots had copious headroom, but also a kind of classicism, with no invasive boom mikes. Further, Nick told me he had no widescreen guides in his viewfinder, so the camera's 1.37 frame was his only visible guide while shooting.

At the time of the restoration, our workflow itself dictated which ratio we would choose. The project mandated true archival preservation to 35mm film, and to save all picture information. We thus opted for a 1.37 preservation negative to make sure nothing was lost. That method prohibited repos, so our "safe" recommended projection aspect ratio was also the classic 35mm 1.37/Academy format. Projectionists and venues could, of course, opt to vary from that if they so chose, by simply changing their projector plates. (See illustrations.)

The restoration premiered at the Museum of Modern Art in 2010. Nick was one of the guests and confirmed he thought the Academy ratio worked wonderfully. Our choice was in a sense validated years after the restoration was completed, when I came across an earlier interview with Nick. In the 1991 documentary *Ich Bin Wanda*, he clearly states, "we had no idea of blowing it up." Was this prior memory more accurate than his later one? It seems likely, but in the end the images tell their own story… and with so many conflicting accounts, I like to think the jury will always be out.

The MoMA screening was a huge success, with lines around the block, Sofia Coppola introducing, and—so I heard—Madonna incognito in the audience. Years later, we digitized the film for TCM at Modern VideoFilm with ace colorist Gregg Garvin, and I was delighted when Criterion picked it up for distribution in 2018.

Nowadays its common to digitize, and rarer to complete photochemical stages of restoration. *Wanda*'s restoration journey was hence fortunate to encompass both analog and digital editions. The Criterion release retains the Academy aspect ratio and color grading, but has, happily, applied further digital cleanup, eliminating excess dirt and scratches we'd been unable to address in our earlier work.

On Disparities Between Artists' Intentions and the Historical Record

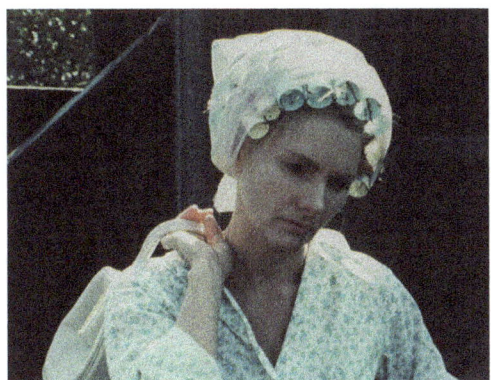
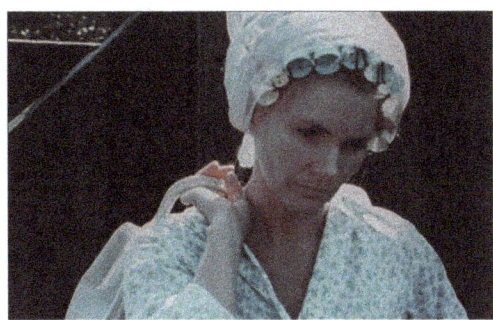
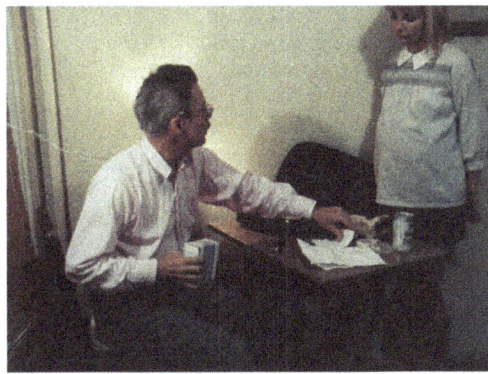

Wanda *restoration samples: Aspect Ratio and Image Quality*

The 1.37:1 samples are scanned from the restoration blow-up internegative

The 1.66:1 samples are from a prior DVD release, which was transferred from an old internegative

The samples illustrate how Wanda *was shot safely for both aspect ratios. While the majority of the film has headroom suggesting widescreen intent, problematic moments arise.*

Note, too, the qualitative difference between the sources. Both are only one printing generation away from the original 16mm reversal camera rolls, but the restoration negative has substantially finer tonal detail. The old internegative also exhibits color pollution in its grain pattern.

Example 1
a) 1.37:1 — classical composition with Barbara Loden's head vertically centered and fully depicted.
b) 1.66:1 — cropped. 1.66 framing likely intended (and successful) due to vertical frame level of Loden's eyes and her position frame right, but less balanced than 1.37.

Example 2
a) 1.37:1 — Loden is fully framed within the shot.
b) 1.66:1 — cropped; with Loden's head cut off. This shot features extensive motion which the camera tracks, but due to the unpredictability of action, it occasionally loses track of important compositional details. It's still successful at 1.66, as the pillow in Loden's shirt and Michael Higgins are the intended points of emphasis, but results in a slightly distracting awkwardness.

Images courtesy: Criterion Co., Marco Joachim, UCLA Film & Television Archive, Film Foundation / Gucci.

Today the film looks better than ever. It belies the oversimplified maxim that a restoration must look like the old viewing prints, rather than its source—a notion that in general holds better for Hollywood titles than independent works. The film is now recognized as an American classic. Tracing *Wanda*'s trajectory, from its original release in shoddy prints, to the 2010 35mm restoration that brought it back, to the Criterion digital release today, is to see a lost masterpiece arise from a fog.

Endnotes

1. I've noted elsewhere that while 1.37:1 is considered the standard, the fact is that in practice, 16mm camera apertures vary widely—if in small increments—around this figure, as do 16mm projector aperture plates, which in theory are intended to crop the image slightly to a ratio of 1.33:1. For a discussion of the actual standards, one can refer to "Some Notes on Close-up Photography" found in the appendices of this volume. I use 1.37:1 here more as a matter of convenience than to suggest a precise measurement.

On Parallel Digital and Analog Workflows

The Juniper Tree

Director, Screenwriter: Nietzchka Keene. Cinematographer: Randolph Sellars.

Featuring: Björk Guðmundsdóttir. Bryndis Petra Bragadóttir, Guðrún Gísladóttir, Valdimar Örn Flygenring, Geirlaug Sunna Þormar. Producer: Patrick Moyroud.

Original release: 35mm, BW, 78 mins., 1990.

Restored in 35mm and 4K digital in 2018 by the Wisconsin Center for Film and Theater Research and the Film Foundation, with funding provided by the George Lucas Family Foundation.

Restored and digitally remastered from the original 35mm BW picture negative A/B rolls and the original 35mm magnetic soundtrack.

Restoration supervised by Ross Lipman in collaboration with Amy Sloper, and in consultation with Patrick Moyroud and Randolph Sellars. Digital picture restoration services by Illuminate Hollywood. Photochemical printing by Fotokem. Photochemical color grading by Doug Ledin. Digital grading by Andrew Drapkin. Audio restoration by John Polito, Audio Mechanics. Special thanks to Simon Daniel, David Marriott, Andrew Oran, Jason Ruitenbach, Bill Tayman, Ei Toshinari, Steve Wiener. Distributed by Arbelos.

The following joins a text written for Arbelos' press kit for the film with introductory remarks made at the restoration's world premiere screening at the Egyptian Theater in Los Angeles, as part of AFI Fest 2018.

The Juniper Tree: A Study in Dual Workflows

I first learned of *The Juniper Tree* when my colleague Amy Sloper, then Director of the Wisconsin Center for Film and Theater Research, asked if I could sort through the holdings for a mysterious film in a Los Angeles vault prior to their shipment to Madison. Amy had studied with the film's director Nietzchka Keene as an undergraduate, and esteemed her highly. Indeed, the images I saw were both striking and intriguing; invoking an almost mystical quality, and as I learned more about the film I began to wonder why no one knew about it. Was it a mere curiosity? Like any archivist, I hoped for a lost jewel, but was nonetheless unprepared for just *how* good it was.

On the surface, *The Juniper Tree* is an ethereal horror film, loosely adapted from the Grimm Brothers fairy tale, but on closer examination it reveals itself as a visionary work that stands confidently in the art film canon. Diving in deeper, I learned that Nietzchka Keene was born in 1952 and completed her master's in film production at UCLA.[1] While there, in 1985, she'd been awarded a Fullbright Fellowship and used it to shoot *The Juniper Tree* on location in Iceland amidst a stunning volcanic ash landscape.

In its lead role she cast a young Icelandic singer named Björk Guðmundsdóttir, who was then just over 20 years old and, during the shoot, gave birth to a daughter.[2] When principal photography was completed, Keene returned home to the US to edit the film, and in the years that followed, Guðmundsdóttir shot to fame as Björk, lead singer of the Sugarcubes.

The film premiered at Sundance 1990, and went on to screen at more than 23 festivals, winning the Prix du Public at the Festival des Films des Femmes de Montreal, and the Prize for First Film at the Troia International Film Festival in Portugal. But since then it had largely dropped out of sight.

The film's original reviews were excellent, if frequently in that mainstream media way of placing an asterisk on anything that's challenging. The *Christian Science Monitor* deemed it "Demanding but impressive." The *St. Louis Post Dispatch* called it "ambitious and disturbing." The *Toronto Star* was, thankfully, less reserved, and acknowledged it as "Fascinating … absorbing, and stately." Perhaps the most glowing response was from the *Chicago Sun*, which said it "possesses all the formal grace of a Japanese No tragedy."

Given its good reception, I returned to my question of why it was almost unknown. I can only presume the film's quietly meditative and mystical quality was out of keeping with industry expectations for a "horror" film, and, as Björk's star had not yet fully risen, it was soon forgotten. Björk, for her part, continued her stunning ascent to fame but her next leading role in a film was not until *Dancer in the Dark* in 2000, for which she won the best actress award at Cannes. Alas her experience with director Lars von Trier was so dreadful that she said she'd never make another movie.[3]

Despite her aversion to cinema Björk's performance in *The Juniper Tree* is simply stunning, and in this sense alone the film is a true discovery. Not to be lost alongside her is an excellent turn by Bryndis Petra Bragadóttir as her sister. One could argue there is still a third notable performance: the Icelandic landscape itself, as depicted by cinematographer Randolph Sellars, is so palpable it almost functions as a character.

Nietzchka Keene's *The Juniper Tree* (1990).

Amy and her team at the Wisconsin Center for Film and Theater Research were far ahead of me and already realized the film's value, so together we set out to restore it. If others agreed with our assessment that it was indeed that rare lost jewel, we'd have a chance to correct the historical record and bring long overdue recognition to Nietzchka Keene and her absorbing vision. To our immense good fortune, The Film Foundation generously stepped in with funding, and we were off.

I should point out at this juncture—as I move on to a discussion of the work conducted—that in recent years it's become increasingly common to use the term "film restoration" when a project is only completed in digital form. Whereas historically film archives had sought to retain "medium integrity" by printing film-originated works back to film, their *ur* medium—that practice was now on the wane. A movie would begin on film, and end as digital-only, shedding its analog roots. In the case of *The Juniper Tree*, we were able to work both digitally *and* photochemically, completing the project to the highest archival standards in both 35mm and 4K digital editions.

This is not entirely unusual in itself, but our workflow was somewhat non-standard. When dual-format projects are undertaken, they almost always tend to do so via what's known as a "digital intermediate"—in which a film is scanned, cleaned up digitally, and then output back to film. In the case of color film, it's easy to attain a high quality filmout to 35mm film from a digital file, allowing the integration of the digital cleanup. In theory, black-and-white should be equally easy, but in practice it's not. Black-and-white filmouts are done less regularly than color, and my observation is that most labs are not as consistent in maintaining image quality when conducting them as they are with color films.[4]

The labs of course take pride in their work, and will understandably deny this, but my admittedly subjective study of the situation has been born out over many years of close viewing. For this reason, when conducting a photochemical restoration in black-and-white, one must in essence choose between a cleaned-up image that doesn't accurately replicate the tonal qualities of the film source, or a purely analog film print made photochemically that retains the tonality, but bypasses the digital intermediate—and with it, the cleanup.

Fortunately, *The Juniper Tree* had relatively little dirt, so the choice was easy. We chose to have two *separate* workflows: one analog-only; the other digital. Both workflows originated from the original 35mm black-and-white negative. The digital version scanned the negative, and cleaned up and graded the resulting file as is custom. But the photochemical version bypassed the digital image work. In so doing, our 35mm prints and preservation elements could be struck directly from the *ur* source—the original negative. The result is a stunning rendition of Randolph Sellars' exquisite black-and-white cinematography, as would not have been possible in a digital filmout that utilized available lab services.

The caveat, as noted, is that our 35mm print retained its film dirt even after multiple cleanings of the negative. This becomes a relevant discussion point in that audiences have now grown accustomed to seeing pristine digital restorations that are virtually or entirely dirt-free. As a result of this cultural acclimatization, dirt can be startling to some contemporary audiences. It's easy to assume the restorationists simply did a poor job of their work. Yet the truth of the matter is that historically, dirt was always a part of the film experience. So in cases where such workflows are undertaken, it becomes part of our job to fill in the knowledge gaps, and help manage expectations.

This might take the form of a technical note in the restoration credits that precede a film, or even a spoken introduction to a screening announcing the presence of that archaic phenomenon, *dirt*. On occasion I've offered friendly "trigger warnings" that some viewers might be startled to find, dare it be said, imperfections on the screen, and include contextualizing information that this is in fact how original audiences saw the movie.

As it turned out, with careful handling and wetgate printing, our photochemical prints of *The Juniper Tree* suffered only minimally from dirt. Just small particles appeared here and there, as they did upon the film's original release. The trade-off in terms of superior image rendition was more than worthwhile. It should be added however, that in this regard our photochemical work itself was not standard. Nietzchka Keene's original 35mm black-and-white negative was extremely low contrast, and required its own plan of attack. Intriguingly, the vintage prints struck from the negative were *not* low contrast, despite their low-con source.

As our goal was to print directly from the camera negative for maximum sharpness, we'd need to photochemically compensate for contrast to match the original look of the film.

Reverse-engineering the problem, my theory was that the negative got fogged in the process of flying the exposed raw stock back from Iceland, but cinematographer Randolph Sellars believes he packed the film in UV-protected bags before transport, and had no memory of using forced (or "push") processing to increase contrast at the time of the original production. So the vintage prints' production methodology remains a mystery.

Nietzchka Keene's *The Juniper Tree* (1990).

Regardless, standard printing wouldn't do the trick this time: To match the original release, we'd need to switch things up. We did this via high-gamma printing, or "pushing" Fotokem's chemistry to the degree needed to match the source prints. I've utilized this technique many times but to this day *The Juniper Tree* remains the only project in which I literally pushed the chemistry to its limits; the maximum possible contrast within Fotokem's system.

Our dual workflow method picked its poison so to speak, and in bypassing the conventional digital intermediate, prioritized image tonality over dirt removal. Today one can thus choose between two viewing experiences of the film with their own unique pleasures: a beautiful 35mm print that retains an analog patina of dirt, or an equally lovely—and immaculate—4K DCP.

I like to think that our careful attention to visual detail, illuminating Sellars' cinematography, helps make *The Juniper Tree*'s artistic accomplishments more fully apparent. Through its subsequent release by Arbelos Films, it's now been rediscovered, and stands today as a reclaimed masterpiece. But work remains to be done. Much of the film's power lies in its devastating evocation of the cultural isolation of visionary women in the middle ages. This theme still resonates today in the omission of Nietzchka Keene (who died tragically of pancreatic cancer aged just 52 in 2004) from most major film histories—an error we hope that *The Juniper Tree*'s new restoration may also help to remedy.

Endnotes

1. Keene graduated in 1989.
2. Some sources say the film was shot in 1987, but cinematographer Randolph Sellars says it was definitely 1986, before his child was born. Björk's baby son was born on set in June 1986.
3. She did at last returned to the screen in Robert Eggers' Viking epic *The Northman* in 2022.
4. I should add that while color filmouts are (in practice if not theory) generally superior to those in black-and-white, it's incorrect to assume that they're lossless. The loss might not be readily apparent in theatrical viewing, but a bench analysis of the resulting negative can serve as a gauge. One need not even conduct densitometric readings to establish it: the differences between an original color negative and a filmout negative made from it via a DI are often clear to the naked eye at fadeouts. When the two negatives are aligned on an optical bench, the fades will often appear to be of slightly different lengths and densities.

On Analog Video Works

Hoop Dreams

Director: Steve James. Cinematographer: Peter Gilbert.

Producer: Peter Gilbert, Steve James, Frederick Marx.

Featuring: William Gates, Arthur Agee.

Original release: 35mm, color, 171 mins., 1994.

Digitally restored and remastered in 2013 by the Academy Film Archive and UCLA Film & Television Archive in collaboration with the Sundance Institute, with funding from the Academy of Motion Picture Arts and Sciences and the Sundance Institute. Additional support provided by the Estate of Ronald Terry Shedlo.

Digitally restored and remastered from an assortment of Kartemquin Films D1 and D2 master videotapes ca. 1994 and 1995, and from a 35mm release print (logos).

Restoration Supervised by Ross Lipman and Mike Pogorzelski in consultation with Steve James and Kartemquin Films. Laboratory services provided by Modern VideoFilm and Audio Mechanics. Digital color grading by Gregg Garvin. Audio restoration by John Polito. Special thanks to the Academy Film Archive, Carolyn Faber, Nora Gully, Tim Horsburgh, Steve James, Kartemquin Films, John Nein, Vincent Pirozzi, Gordon Quinn, Todd Weiner, Warner Bros.. Distributed by Janus Films and Criterion.

Independent works from the mid 1980s to early 2000s present unique challenges from a restoration perspective, in that many were produced in video before low-cost video looked good. How does one help a work look its best, while retaining fidelity to its original form? I hope to eventually draft a sister piece to the following, discussing issues arising in works of the era shot in digital video formats. The present text was adapted from an illustrated lecture originally presented at the International Documentary Association's "Getting Real" Conference in the Academy of Motion Picture Arts and Sciences' Linwood Dunn Theater on September 25, 2018.

Restoring *Hoop Dreams*

From Tape to Screen

In this same Linwood Dunn Theater a month ago, Andy Maltz from the Academy's Science and Technology Council and Dr. Wolfgang Ruppel presented a talk on digital archiving in which they mentioned that a contemporary standard feature from a major studio had 35,000 deliverables. When hearing that, it's hard not to think: how does one *archive* such a thing? No, you don't need to archive all 35,000 items. But how do you even make sense of it? And how do you maintain quality?

While the not-for-profit archives don't face problems of that scale, the ones they do face are notable enough, and on their own scale, parallel the nightmare scenario I mentioned. As a way into the question, I'll be looking at the case of *Hoop Dreams*, which was named by no less than our own IDA as the greatest documentary of all time. That's a heady honor, but my task is merely to discuss the restoration, which is particularly interesting, and more than enough for today.

Our work transported many principles of classical film restoration to the 1980s and early 1990s — the twilight years between film and digital, when doc makers were working in analog video. Many of the issues I'll discuss have not just film, but pure digital counterparts, again transformed. But today we'll look at the no-man's land that divides them.

Hoop Dreams chronicled the lives and aspirations of two young basketball players from their days on the streets of Chicago, through their respective high school careers. It was produced by the extraordinary Chicago-based collective, Kartemquin Films, and shot between 1987 and 1991 primarily in Beta SP, by director Steve James, cinematographer Peter Gilbert, and lead editor Fred Marx. Several more years were devoted to editing, during which time they culled over 250 hours of footage.

It premiered at the Sundance Film Festival in January, 1994, where it won the Audience Award for best documentary, and when noted critic Roger Ebert immediately declared it "one of the best films on American life that I have ever seen" (*Siskel & Ebert*), it began its journey into history.

The film's complex back story led to a surprisingly challenging and ultimately rewarding restoration effort. Its extraordinary popularity and chronological tale naturally lent itself to a bewildering trail of alternative release versions and updates, as well as an evidence trail that was on the one hand overwhelming, and simultaneously filled with gaps and mysteries. The trick was to sift through mountains of data, vast quantities of tapes with the ever-ambiguous term "master" (which all archivists should studiously avoid using in absence of further detail), and recollections of living witnesses to narrow down the pool of most-likely sources for restoration.

Our project was a partnership between Kartemquin Films, the UCLA Film & Television Archive, the Academy Film Archive, and the Sundance Institute, who initiated the whole enterprise. I co-directed the restoration project in collaboration with Mike Pogorzelski, Director of the Academy Film Archive, in consultation with Steve James and Kartemquin archivists Nora Gully and Carolyn Faber. Our partner labs were Modern VideoFilm and Audio Mechanics.

At this point I should issue a warning: if you're number-phobic or data-sensitive, you may want to leave the room, or pending your vices, take a smoking break. On the other hand, I can reassure you that it's brief, and *intended to* be cautionary. When untying Gordian knots it's helpful to have some tools. This presentation illustrates our process, and offers an overview of our work. As such, it's in some ways an archive itself, of restoration-related documents.

Unlike the studio title I mentioned, Kartemquin had "only" 71 master elements archived on site. But due to the film's tremendous success, it had been released many times over the intervening decades, often with small changes or format variations in different markets. These later releases resulted in key sources being stored elsewhere. To make sense of all the surviving elements was an overwhelming prospect, but thankfully Kartemquin kept excellent records—and thank goodness we were only working with the edited "master" tapes, as that limited the documentation of relevant on-site materials to twenty pages. Had we needed the original production elements—which Kartemquin also kept—it would have been unfathomable.

The Kartemquin collection was supplemented by another 53 items at Warner Bros. The studio records were so detailed that to consider them in birds' eye view I had to print out hard copies and paste three sheets of paper together to reveal the off-screen fields. (See Figure 1.)

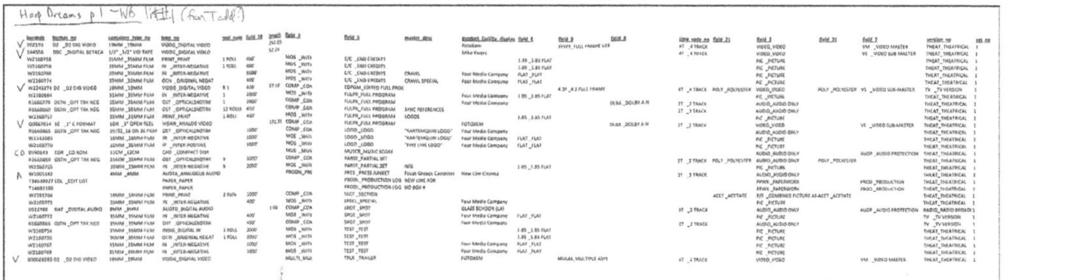

Figure 1. Sample of printout assembly of studio list; courtesy Warner Bros.

Then we had to reconcile the data in the lists with the actual tapes, which often had further information on their labels. From our research, a production and release history of the film began to arise. A key document in our efforts proved to be a 1995 memo from the production team that chronicled some of the changes after the Sundance premiere, including an important alteration of the on-screen text at the film's end, adapted to prevent legal trouble with St. Joseph's High School, as depicted in the movie. The memo also contained very important information on the original workflow and technical problems that occurred at the time of video mastering, which were baked into some—but not all—of the master elements. From this document we gleaned vital details about items in the collections that weren't included in the inventory records, or on the tapes themselves. (See Figure 2.)

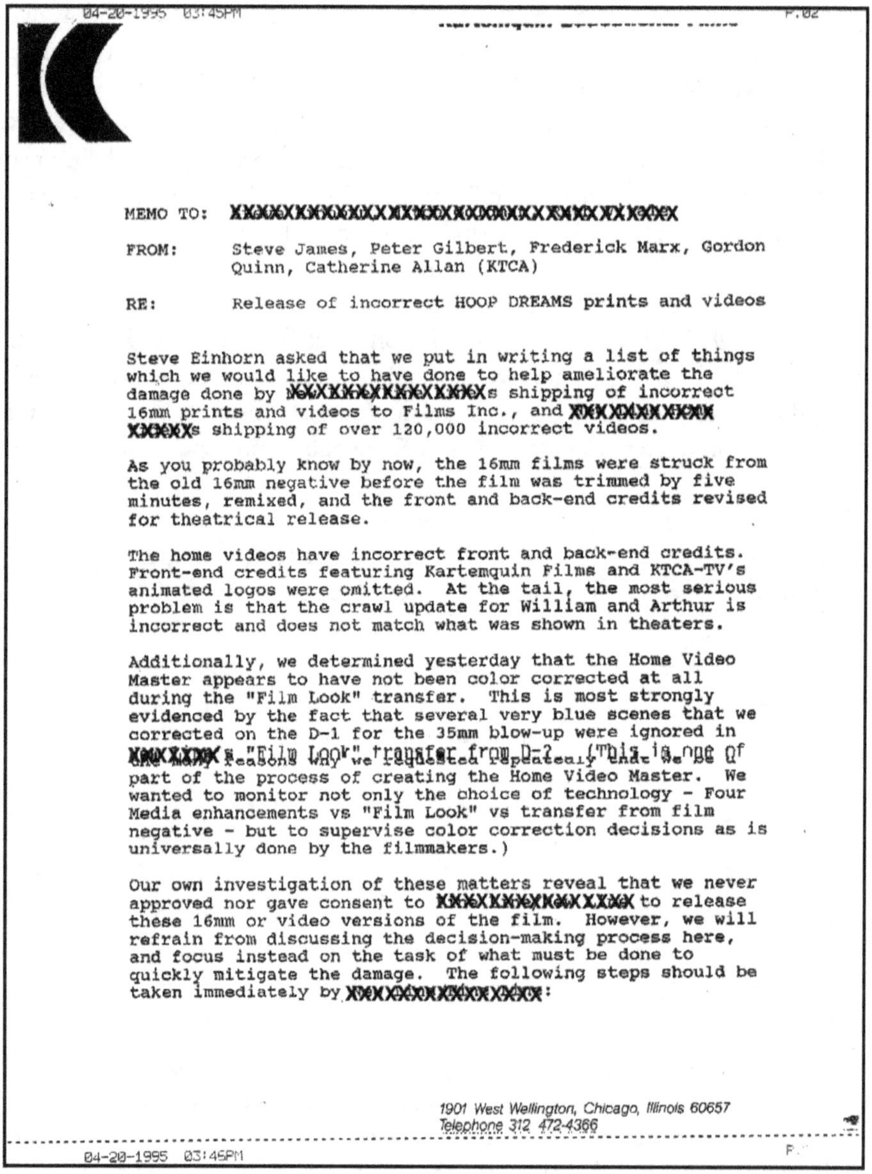

Figure 2. Redacted sample page of memo from Kartemquin to distributor, Apr. 20 1995.

To further sing the praises of Kartemquin's good practices, they even had their own version history. This is an extremely important thing to document, but very few independent producers do so. Their chronicle contained a few small errors I detected, but was an invaluable addition to our understanding of the complex history that preceded it. (See Figure 3.)

>
> HOOP DREAMS ONLINE & DISTRIBUTION HISTORY   _by Liz, October 2010
>
> Hoop Dreams was onlined twice:
>
> 1st online: at IPA
> - Was mastered to D2 (composite).
> - Was blown up to 16mm for Sundance screening.
> - This version was always 4x3.
> - everything went thru DVE
>
> The same D2 tape was then blown up to 35mm for the theatrical print master, but looked terrible (couldn't see a thing), had to re-online program.
>
> 2nd online: at Cutters
> - The film was re-onlined to D1 (component) to yield a higher quality tape master.
> - The tape master was 4x3. It was re-framed to fit into a 1.85 mask, and that picture was used to create the 35mm master.
> - Distributed by New Line/Fine Line
>
> This theatrical version is 6 minutes shorter than the Sundance version. The filmmakers were urged to shorten it, and they took out the 6 minutes in the second online.
>
> VHS/CRITERION:
> - Used the D1 component tape (that was used for 35mm blow-up) for home video master.
> - The D1 is texted.
>
> CAPITOL FILMS:
>   -Was out international distributor for a 15-year contract. It is believed that they were sent our only textless master. They went into administration, and potentially were bought by Think Films. As of Oct. 2010, we have not been able to get our masters back, they potentially are lost....
>
> Re-do of textless in Oct 2010
> To Ro*co films
>
> Digitized digibeta texted masters 4x3 @ DV50 and then digitized camera master betacam tapes to replace texted shots (Used paper EDL to track down tapes- these files are in hall boxes). NOTE: Bryan Mcknight shot had to be reconstructed in after effects (the camera master betacam was damaged at spot of shot).
>
> Laid off 2 digibeta texted and 2 digibeta textless for ro*co. at global -- files of these are on HDs @ KTQ. Still need to layoff to tape.
>
> Liz looked at D2s

Figure 3. Kartemquin production chronology notes.

Having all this in hand, we were at last ready to get our feet a little dirty. I began by making a shortlist of elements I wanted to inspect as part of our search for the most appropriate to our task. After completing inspection we drafted our own updated production chronology, linked to inventoried elements, using the data we'd found before, filling in holes and correcting known errors. This new list provided the precise information needed to secure the best elements for restoration. (See Figure 4.)

HOOP DREAMS						SELECT HOLDINGS NOTES		2013/07	
DATE	FORMAT	VERSION	RT	AR	LOGOS/CREDITS	QUALITY	NOTES		INV
12/19/93	D2	Sundance		4X3	original end credits	excellent	Sundance edit master.		Kartem
5/26/94	D2	release	169:34:00	4X3	no head logos	very good	"NTSC revised edit master" Originally marked as NG, w/ flaws marked in log. compare w/ Sundance for quality.		WB list 2, box 1
6/2/94	D2	release		1.85		not checked closely	letterbox		Kartem
8/2/94	D1	release		1.85		not checked closely but presumed best letterbox source	component edit master. Letterbox		Kartem
Aug-94	D1	release		1.85		sharp when viewed from tape; soft / sawtooth when viewed as 29.97 to 23.98 conversion	clone + extra part 3 (1st pt. 3 was in-progress).		Kartem
1/10/95	D2	release		4X3		fuzzy; processed	"Revised NTSC master"		WB list 2, Box 1
2/2/95	D1	release		1.85	no end credits	sweetening including sharpening & contrast boost	sweetened. Presumably from D1 edit master or clone. "Final stereo mix 1,2"		Kartem
6/1/95	D2	release		4X3	logos/credits only	probable best source for logos, credits	NTSC Original Transfer master logos (Fineline, Kar, KTCA), end credits only. No audio.		WB list 2, Box 1
6/14/95	D2	release		4X3		decent color correction applied. Slightly less sharp than 5/26/1994	clone, but R1 has different RT listed. Why?		WB list 2, Box 2
12/4/01	DB	release		4X3		slightly soft but good "film look" color correction	Full Frame TV version. New Line. possibly transferred from 6/14/1995 D2.		WB list 2, Box 2
11/19/03	DB	release		4X3		slightly soft, not as good color correct. bad credits.	4X3 Full Frame submaster, w/ Lt/Rt & ME		WB list 2, Box 8
2005	DVD	release	171	4X3		good.	Criterion edition. Believed to be transferred from a Digibeta source, but not verified.		
Oct-10	DVC Pro 50	release		4X3		not viewed in comparison setting	TEXTLESS, w/ re-transfer from original Beta SP tapes. Several shots digitally reconstructed, per Kartemquin notes. 720 X 480 (640 X 480).		

Figure 4. Selected and updated production chronology.

Having compiled this data, I then prepared a technical report for our colleagues, outlining a preservation strategy. Having conferred closely with Steve James and the Kartemquin team, we knew our definitive version should match not the 178-minute Sundance premiere version, but rather, the 171-minute final release version—albeit with numerous modifications to titles and credits that had arisen for very practical reasons in subsequent years. The problem (as noted in the fine print of the documents reproduced here) was that the theatrical release version was in 35mm film, and had been generated from a D1 tape master that had itself been *pre-cropped* to 1.85 aspect ratio from the 4X3 original. Luckily, our in-depth inspections had found an accurate D2 record of the correct cut that proved to be the highest quality source. This contradicted not just common sense (D1 generally being higher quality than D2), but also contradicted some of our earliest historical records—yet the proof was in the tapes.

In the end we used four different videotapes as our picture sources, along with a vintage 1995 film print that contained the original release logo. Still more sources were used for the sound. In addition to our full restoration of the definitive version, we also archived a protection copy of the longer Sundance "pre-release" version.

HOOP DREAMS   technical report – 09/04/2013

General goals: It's been generally determined that the primary goal is to preserve the original 4:3 aspect ratio of the original production, and NOT the cropped widescreen ratio of the theatrical release edition. Simultaneously, it's determined that the first priority is to preserve the content of the release version, rather than the Sundance pre-release version. These decisions would match those of the Criterion edition of 2005.

Best sources for multiple purposes above are likely the following:

- **12/19/1993 - D2**: Sundance version. Not first priority for preservation, but w/ excellent pictorial quality.
- **5/26/1994 - D2**: Release version. Best 4X3 pictorial quality of release version. In parts it may be equal to the Sundance D2, but its QC log lists it as NG, citing specific problems in certain places.
- **2/2/1995 - D1**: Cropped/1.85, but earliest record of "final stereo mix."
- **6/1/1995 - D2**: logos and credits only. Likely best source for these. (credit version discussion pending.)
- **12/4/2001 - DB**: Full frame TV version. Lower quality picture but very good "film look" color correction applied. Perhaps useful as a reference. Probable Criterion source.
- **10/2010 – files**: Best compiled source for textless, if needed.

General Strategy: It's still too early to determine with certainty, but in an ideal world with complete funding a workflow would look something like the following. Pending discussion, a deliverables list can be determined.

1A) Transfer audio (and picture reference) from:
    5/26/1994 - D2   (best picture source/reference)
    2/2/1995 - D1   (likely best sound source)

1B) Restore audio at Audio Mechanics from above.

2A) Conform best picture edit from the following sources, in 4X3, matched to EDL of release version:
    5/26/1994 - D2   (primary picture source)
    6/1/1995 - D2   (logos, titles, credits)
    12/19/1993 - D2   (alternate source, if needed (this is the Sundance version)

2B) Color correction. As a starting point, the following can be used for reference:
    12/4/2001 - DB
    Criterion DVD

2C) Digital clean-up as needed, including dropout, TBC issues, other TBD.

3) OPTIONAL: Make preservation transfer of Sundance version, and/or additional alternate credit sequences.

4) OPTIONAL: Make 35mm filmout version.

Figure 5. Excerpt of technical report prepared for restoration partners.

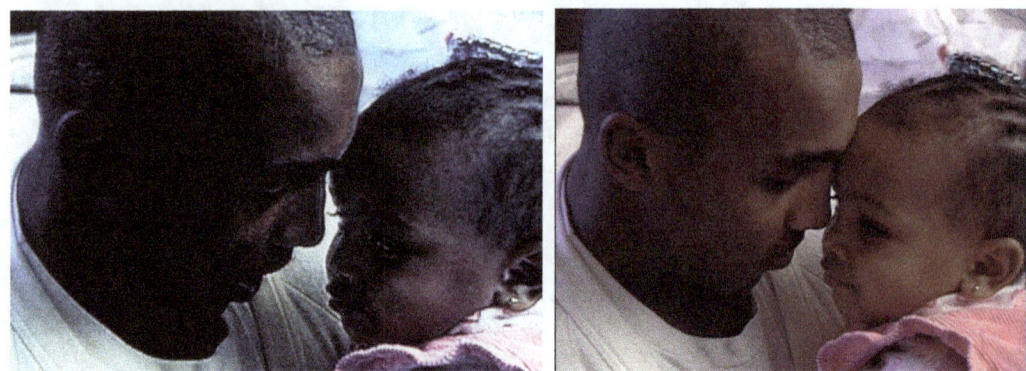

Figure 6A. William Gates and his daughter, as the image appears in a random source.
Figure 6B. The same image, as it appears in the final restored version.

Left aside in our discussion thus far is my usual investment in aesthetic issues, which most assuredly did take place amidst all the review work. Normally I try to avoid "apples and oranges" demonstrations, but here one seems appropriate, and hence I'll indulge. *Hoop Dreams* has been presented in many contexts and so I'll offer a traditional "before and after" comparison, with the caveat that the "before" sample is quite random, and something I'd under different circumstances consider a kind of cheat: it's pulled from the internet. However it more than adequately represents many of the lower grade actual samples I encountered, and hence the way thousands of viewers have experienced the film. The "after" image depicts our final restored version of the same image. (See Figures 6A and 6B.)

The difference is stunning, and a direct result of the extensive research conducted. It's both odd and telling that our source choices were different than any of the many preceding re-masterings of the film, which had perhaps not delved as deeply into the overwhelming cache of existing records. Our project's strategy grew from traditional models of film restoration, in which a work's authoritative version is traced back to its highest quality source, but these principles were adapted to the wild west of 1980s and '90s video formats. In the end it demonstrated the extreme importance of archiving not just the physical copies of a film, but also the records of its history. We're hence immensely grateful to our colleagues who compiled this important data over the decades. It was their pioneering work that proved the sword to sever the Gordian knot of overabundant options, or what's now known as "TMI"—Too Much Information. The results are now archived in the vaults and servers of both the Academy Film Archive and the UCLA Film & Television Archive, and we're delighted to report that the restored *Hoop Dreams* is now available from Criterion.

On Conceptual Factors in Restoration Strategy

The Man Without a World

Director, Screenwriter: Eleanor Antin. Cinematographer: Richard Wango.

Featuring: Pier Marton, Christine Berry, Eleanor Antin, Anna Henriques.

Original release: 16mm, B&W, 95 mins., 1991.

Digitally restored and remastered in 2020 by Milestone Films with funding from the Sunrise Foundation for Education and the Arts.

Digitally restored and remastered from the original 16mm camera negative black-and-white A/B/C rolls, and from the original ¼" audio music recording master.

Restoration supervised by Ross Lipman in consultation with Eleanor Antin. Digital picture restoration by Illuminate Hollywood. Color grading by Andrew Drapkin. 2020 score composed and performed by Alicia Svigals (violin) and Donald Sosin (piano). Original 1991 score by Lee Erwin restored by Peter Conheim, Cinema Preservation Associates. Special thanks: Dennis Doros, Amy Heller, Jason Ruitenbach, Bill Tayman, Cynthia Walk, Steve Weiner, and the Association of Moving Image Archivists. Distributed by Milestone Films / Kino Lorber.

The following documents one of my first notable projects that originated in film but was completed only in digital form. Now such practice is commonplace, but as detailed in the introductory "Persistence of Revision," back in the day it would have been considered questionable practice, and deemed "digital remastering" rather than "restoration." The following, somewhat playful text was originally written for Milestone's press kit for the film in 2020.

A Film Without a World

Restoring the lost masterpiece of Yevgeny Antinov

Yevgeny Antinov's *The Man Without a World* comes to us by way of Eleanor Antin, as his representative and alter ego. Or is it vice versa? She tells us, via a title card at the beginning, that it was shot in Poland in the late 1920s and was lost until its fortuitous early 1990s discovery in an archive in Odessa. The film was released at that time but has only now, decades later, been restored.

Strangely for a work from the late 1920s, the film's original camera negative has all the markings of an early '90s work. Its 16mm camera footage is even cut into A-B-C rolls, with the C roll demarcated for English intertitles. One can only assume the original Yiddish roll was lost in the intervening years!

When Milestone released the film in 1993, a duplicate negative was struck at Cinema Arts laboratory, which remains in physically pristine condition. So in *that* sense the film was already preserved. But archivists note the distinction between preservation and restoration. A film can be in great physical condition but still have problematically distracting dirt embedded or printed into the film material itself. Such was the case with *The Man Without a World*, and further work was needed.

Thus Milestone set out to restore it in 2020, with the generous help of the Sunrise Foundation (aptly named after Murnau's 1927 feature). The question immediately arose as to how "clean" a work like this should actually be. On the one hand, one might expect a film with such a checkered history as Mr. Antinov's to be filthy; a veritable blizzard of dirt particles. On the contrary, the film was only moderately dirty, and the original negative (that had been used to print the Cinema Arts dupe) was in quite good shape for something purportedly from the 1920s. Indeed one even finds interviews with Eleanor Antin herself, claiming (dubiously, no doubt) that it was not made in the shtetl, and that she shot it herself in San Diego years later.

How then, could one make sense of the matter? It's a humorous fact that viewers associate film dirt and scratches with authenticity. One could thus say, "leave the dirt in!" On the other hand, trained archivists know it's quite normal to remove dirt, safe in the knowledge that most films were reasonably clean at their time of creation. In the case of *The Man Without a World*, there was enough dirt to merit about 80 hours of cleanup—which would be far less than is commonly needed for a major silent feature such as Mr. Antinov's, but notably more than is commonly budgeted for say, an independent film shot mere decades ago in San Diego. Through our Sunrise grant and the generous help of the team at Illuminate Hollywood, we were able to clean up the most distracting dirt, while leaving at least a bit for those who like its patina of authenticity.

On Conceptual Factors in Restoration Strategy 149

The work itself was revealing. To clarify, some images will help. In Figure 1A, one sees a downrezzed reference copy (with time code window) of our new scan from the original negative, before cleanup was completed.

In Figure 1B, one sees the same image from an old 1990s transfer conducted by a now-defunct laboratory. Note that frame left in Figure A, there is visible cement/glue residue, which is absent in the older transfer. Its earlier absence establishes that the damage occurred after the film's initial printing, and could not be mistaken as part of Mr. Antinov's production.

In Figure 1C, one sees the final result, after cleanup by Illuminate, yielding a clean image that nicely renders the sharp detail in the original photography.

Figure 1A. A downrezzed reference copy (ca. 2020) of Milestone's new scan from the original negative, including visible cement / glue residue before cleanup was completed. (The glue residue is visible along the left edge of the frame.)

Figure 1B. The same image from an old 1990s transfer, when glue was not present.

Figure 1C. The restored final image. Note the finer resolution, as evident in the signage.

One other example merits a close look. In Figures 2A and 2B, one sees a traditional "before and after" sample illustrating repair of a vertical scratch. Such scratches are among the most difficult things to fix digitally, because their regularity from frame to frame defies most automated repair tools. The software tends to think they're intended, and they're hence usually best cleaned up manually, which can be very time intensive and hence costly. Luckily Illuminate's Jason Ruitenbach stepped to the plate and did a bravura job, completely eliminating a scratch that ran for many minutes of screen time.

The same images also offer a glimpse of a phenomenon of digital cleanup in which the removal of a large problem suddenly makes visible a smaller problem heretofore unseen. Look closely at the area to the right of the cleaned up scratch in Figure 2B. One sees the hint of another, smaller one emerging. Now look back at 2A. There, the larger scratch pulls the eye to it so strongly that the smaller one to its right is imperceptible. The lingering smaller one in our final result might be seen as another "patina of authenticity" for our friends who appreciate that. Special thanks go to Illuminate's Andrew Drapkin for his excellent work on the black-and-white grading.

Figures 2A and 2B. Traditional "before and after" images illustrating repair of a vertical scratch. The scratch can be seen bottom center in the left-hand image, running vertically up actress Christine Berry's arm.

One would be remiss to not discuss the accompanying music. At the time of the film's 1991 discovery premiere, Ms Antin added a score by organist Lee Erwin, which by all means had its merits but was arguably not an integral part of the original vision of Mr. Antinov. For the current edition Milestone hired the extraordinary duo of Alicia Svigals and Donald Sosin to compose a new score, and that is what accompanies the film today. Peter Conheim of Cinema Preservation Alliance was brought in to preserve Lee Erwin's score, so that is archived for posterity and available as well.

In regard to the new score, I hope Alicia and Donald won't mind my revealing that the first cue heard—over the opening restoration credits—is a new recording with vinyl record crackle added to evoke the feeling of age. I love Donald's assessment: "It sounds reasonably vintage, as much as the film looks vintage… which is to say… 60%?"

Now, as the release of the restored version approaches, we have the opportunity to address the biggest mystery of all. When first discovered in the 1990s the film was not widely recognized. It had its champions, but was more often overlooked. Like its hero Zevi, who was trapped between his conventional roots and his avant-garde art, the film was too experimental for some, while too traditional for others. It was too risqué, too political, too *much*—and literally, a film without a world. Today Yevgeny Antinov and his visionary representative Eleanor Antin both seem decades ahead of their time. The film's swirling, kaleidoscopic mix of poetry, politics, and humanity is the perfect blend for our present moment, and one that's ripe to at last be truly discovered.

On Films Without Authoritative Versions I

Fireworks (ca. 1947 / 195x / 196x / 198x, etc.)

Director: Kenneth Anger. Cinematographers: Kenneth Anger, Chester Kessler. Featuring: Kenneth Anger, Bill Seltzer, Gordon Gray.

Original release: 16mm, B&W, ca. 1947 (original 1947 preview version RT unknown)

Restored in 35mm and digitally remastered in 2006 by UCLA Film & Television with funding from The Film Foundation.

Restored from three original 16mm prints and Kenneth Anger's reconstructed duplicate A/B rolls.

Digitally remastered from the restored 35mm duplicate negative and digital audio files.

Restoration conformed to the ca. 1953 / 1963 / 1980 versions (15 minutes).

Restoration conformed and supervised by Ross Lipman, with the assistance of Nancy Mysel, in consultation with Kenneth Anger. Laboratory services by Triage Motion Picture Services, Audio Mechanics, DJ Audio, NT Audio, Post Logic. Photochemical grading by Sharol Olson. 35mm blow-up by Dave Tucker. Audio restoration by John Polito. Digital grading by Lou Levinson. Special Thanks to Anthology Film Archives, Canyon Cinema, Michael Friend, The Kinsey Institute for Research in Sex, Gender, and Reproduction, and Andrew Lampert. DVD/BRD released by Fantoma. Restored 35mm and 16mm prints not in distribution; available from UCLA.

The following text was adapted from a longer lecture on the restoration of films by Kenneth Anger which was initially presented at the Pacific Film Archive on April 17, 2007, and subsequently at a meeting of SMPTE (Society of Motion Picture and Television Engineers) at the Academy of Motion Picture Arts & Sciences' Linwood Dunn Theater in Los Angeles, at the Reel Thing Technical Symposium in Rochester, and the Images Festival in Toronto. For a synopsized version of the rest of the lecture (discussing Scorpio Rising, Kustom Kar Kommandos *and* Rabbit's Moon*), see Appendix #3: Sample Preservation Notes.*

Figure 1. Kenneth Anger and Gordon Gray in *Fireworks*.

Chasing *Fireworks*

In *Fireworks*, I released all the explosive pyrotechnics of a dream. The inflammable desires dampened by day under the cold water of consciousness are ignited at night by the libertarian matches of sleep, and burst forth in showers of shimmering incandescence. These imaginary displays provide a temporary release.

—Kenneth Anger

Today I'll be discussing UCLA's restoration of the films of Kenneth Anger. At the core of our work is the notion that a restoration strategy should be informed by both the aesthetic qualities of a work and an understanding of its historical context. This simple principle can of course become quite nuanced in its technical implementation.

The works of Kenneth Anger are especially challenging in that he's heavily invested in both avant-garde and Hollywood cinema, and simultaneously celebrated in the elite fine art world and the low-budget underground. As visual artworks, they present many unique challenges in restoration—from exquisite color to hand-modification of his original elements. The films also show a fascination with the extremes of human experience, taking an unflinching look at things most people would rather avoid. When preserving his films, one needs to address all these distinct issues and legacies. To study his life and works is to travel through cinema history.

Our project consisted of four films: *Fireworks*, *Rabbit's Moon*, *Scorpio Rising* and *Kustom Kar Kommandos*. This opening portion of the lecture will give an overview of our work on *Fireworks*.

Anger's quotation cited at the head of this presentation appeared as a spoken prologue to the film that appears in a 16mm print of the film dated to 1963. When I asked him about it, he told me that it was the original title sequence. This puzzled me. Listening to it, one already hears a reframing of the work in his discussion of it, past tense. And yet, as I'll explain, his statement proved grounded in truth.

Kenneth Anger

With the glamourous looks of a movie star, Kenneth Anglemyer took his celebrated chosen name at age 20 in homage to gay erotica images in magazines like *Physique Pictorial*, where bodybuilders would pose under names like "Ed Fury." Yet Anger was never simply a pretty face. He's universally acknowledged as one of the essential founders of the American avant-garde, beginning in the 1940s. Along with Maya Deren and Stan Brakhage, he's considered one of the three greatest artists in the movement's history, and the only one of these early greats still alive and working to the present day.

Anger is a historian himself, or at least a mythologist of the highest order. One of the central myths of his own life is his role as the androgenous Changeling Prince in Max Reinhardt and William Dieterle's 1935 film of *A Midsummer Night's Dream*. There are many who dispute Anger's account, and evidence supports their competing notion that it was in fact Sheila Brown. His birthdate—which is also controversial—is not in his claim's favor. The evidence would place it in 1927, making him about seven at the time of the film's production, and a bit older than the Prince appears to be. But the salient point here is not so much the fact as the myth itself, which Anger successfully purveyed to the point that people associate him with the role.

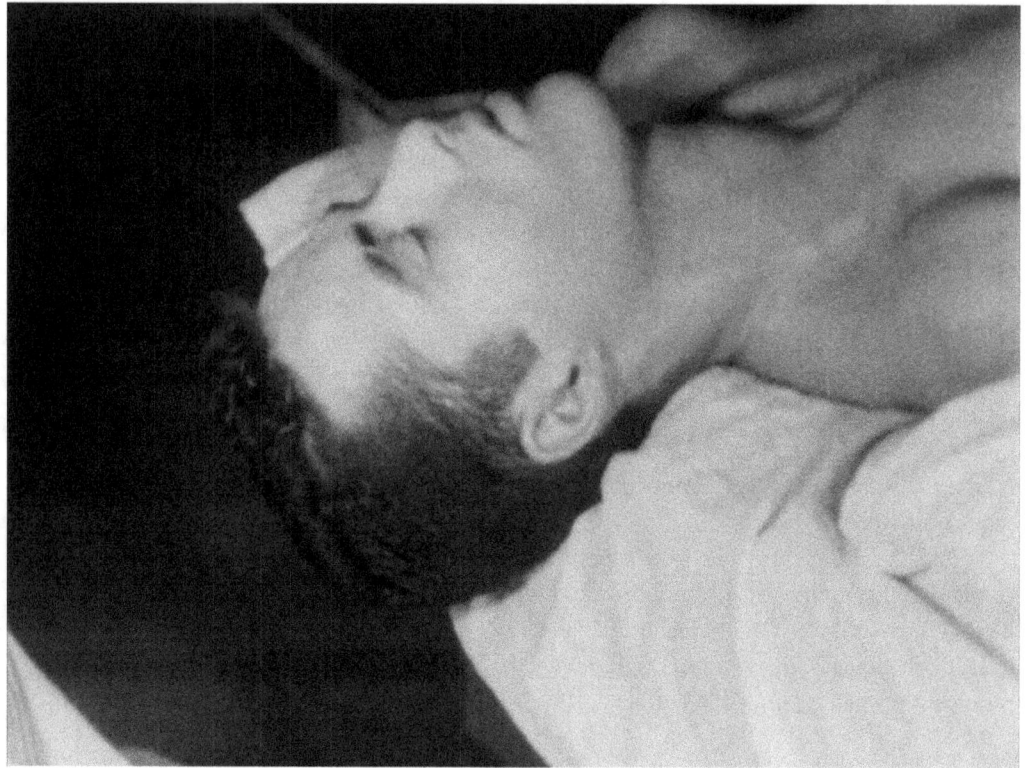

Figure 2. Kenneth Anger in *Fireworks*.

      The parable points to his fascination with Hollywood, which reached its apotheosis in his infamous *Hollywood Babylon* books, chronicling a litany of Tinseltown scandals over the course of decades. Unlike most avant-garde filmmakers, Anger courted both the glitter and dark underbelly of celebrity. Along the way he became a celebrity and icon in his own right, befriending the likes of Alfred Kinsey, Anaïs Nin, Mick Jagger, and Jimmy Page, while simultaneously living a life in the streets, among bikers, drifters, and punks. It's not ironic, but rather fitting, that the author of scandalous histories is himself a kind of legend, living a life at once extreme and the stuff of myth. While I've cited some stretchers, many of the legends are true, or contain a grain of truth. And each myth, whether true or not, contains a key to understanding his work and its place in history.

Fireworks

It's untrue that Anger has only made a few films. He's had a mercurial career, but a long one. In addition to his completed titles, there's an extensive history of revisions, alternate versions, aborted projects, and fragments that are now themselves considered complete works.

Fireworks, his earliest surviving film, had its public premiere at the Coronet Theater in Los Angeles in 1948. It later famously screened at the Festival du Film Maudit—the Festival of Damned Films—in Biarritz, France, in 1949, where Jean Cocteau awarded it the Poetic Film prize, and described it as "coming from that beautiful night from which all true works emerge."

Anger himself described the film in many ways over the years. The most celebrated of these accounts is that

> This flick is all I have to say about being seventeen, the United States Navy, American Christmas, and the Fourth of July.

Questions arise immediately, as those who disputed his birthdate say he wasn't really seventeen when he made it in 1947. But even if his birthdate is indeed 1927, making him all of 20 at the time, the film can very much still be *about* being 17.

Anger apparently made an early version that is now lost; even more incendiary than the one eventually released. It was initially screened in private groups which one attendee, Ed Earle, described.

> It was one of those things you sneak out of a brown paper bag, you know, the *Lady Chatterly's Lover* syndrome or a *Playboy* under the mattress. He really took delight in the fact that he had done something naughty. And when he first showed it to you, it was like flashing a centerfold at an adolescent.[1]

But there is of course more to it than that. The aspects of dream are essential. *Fireworks* shows the strong influence of LA local Maya Deren, and places the film firmly in the context of what P. Adams Sitney later labelled psychodrama—works depicting a search for self, or "quest for sexual identity," usually enacted in a trance state.[2] Gay erotica and psychodrama are in fact just two of the contexts from which Anger's early vision emerged.

Like many of Anger's films, *Fireworks* exists in different versions. The earliest surviving print we could locate was housed at the Kinsey Institute, and was struck in the mid-1950s.[3] It had no opening titles and in fact had no physical splices at the head leader's end, which from a technical perspective strongly suggested that no title sequence was missing. Had it been removed, a splice would be present. This would in fact verify Kenneth's claim that the titles I asked him about were, in effect, "original": no main title sequence seemingly *existed* prior to the prologue version, which was made some years after the original prints and Kinsey print.

And yet strangely—while absent a main title sequence, the Kinsey print did contain an "end" title, which makes one wonder about that opening. Could Anger really have made a film that had an end title, but no beginning? He has always been an innovator, and I believe the answer is yes. The definitive answer of course, seems lost to history.⁴

 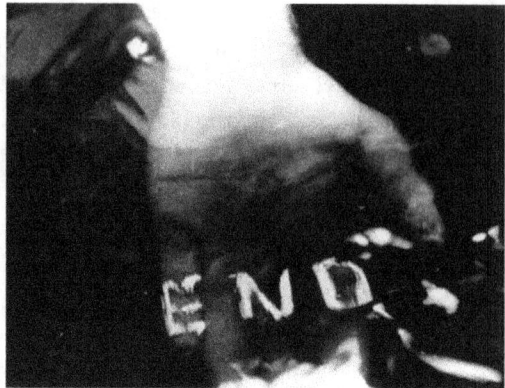

Figure 3A. The original opening image of *Fireworks*, of a torch being doused in water. Research suggests that the film's main title cards (white letters on solid black) were added at the time Anger created his spoken prologue to the film, years later.

Figure 3B. The original ending of the film, with the "end" title appearing atop a hand under water, reinforces the film's circular structure. Anger's final color edition, created decades later, omits this shot. The water's refraction of the text seen here creates a rippling effect that further amplifies its difference from the opening titles in later versions, which were remade over time, but all of which appear as conventional title cards of varying form.

Anger later created at least one hand-painted copy, which was destroyed in a fire at the Cinémathèque française. The likelihood is that other such painted "versions" existed, as he was legendary for showing up in projection booths around the world and hand-coloring the evening's prints prior to screening. But none of these iterations represent the film as it came to be known by the time we commenced the restoration. That claim falls to yet another version, created some time around 1980. This is the version that was then in distribution, and the final edit prior to our restoration work.

The 1980 version's prints were struck from a 16mm color internegative made off of Kenneth Anger's 16mm black-and-white positive A/B rolls. Yet despite its tracing to what was in theory the earliest generation source possible—the A/B rolls—notable differences could be found from the earlier versions. A blue color cast had been added to the film, and lightning bolts were interjected into the opening sequence. The film's main title, apparently first introduced in the "prologue" version, was replaced by a new title card in color. And the differences did not stop there. A close comparison with the earlier prints revealed that *every single shot* in the film had been truncated in the new edition. The final "end" title card, which appears superimposed on a hand underwater, is missing entirely in this version.

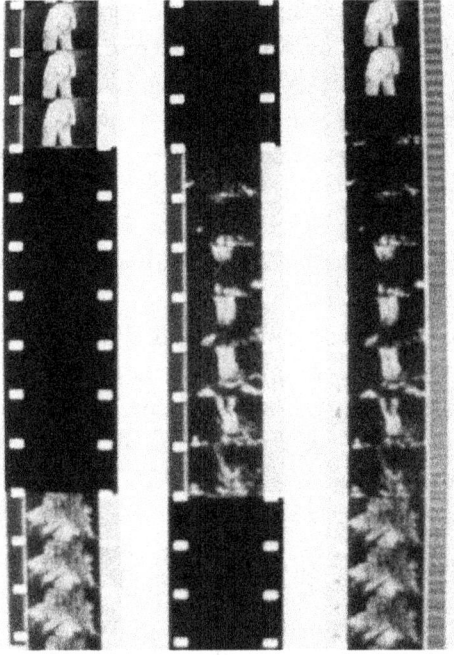

Figure 4. An example of the truncation of Anger's final edit of the film (Roman candle sequence).

Left and Center: Anger's simulated / re-edited 16mm a/b rolls of *Fireworks*. The a/b rolls are truncated positive copies of the original.

Right: An older 16mm exhibition print of *Fireworks*, from the Creative Film Society collection at UCLA Film & Television Archive.

Note how the earlier edition (on right) features an extra frame of the central water image near the top of the strip. Each shot in the film was truncated at either head, tail, or both.

The shot truncations ranged from a single frame to several seconds. The surprising technical explanation for these variations is that Anger's "A/B rolls" were not in fact original, but downstream duplicates made from earlier editions. The true originals had been lost at some point during the fifty-odd years between the film's production and its restoration. He had rebuilt them, and changed the work in the process.

While the editorial changes to the picture were substantial, the soundtrack—featuring Respighi's "Pines of Rome"[5]—had somehow not been changed at all. Rather, the truncation of every shot had shortened the picture enough to allow the old "original" audio track to be pushed up, now extending over the aforementioned main title sequence, replacing Anger's spoken prologue. This further supports the idea that the title had been absent in the original, and only added later, where it was accompanied by Anger's spoken introduction, rather than the sound of thunderclaps that had historically commenced the film in its earliest versions. What changed at a profound level was hence the *relation* of soundtrack to picture. At no moment in the film was the linkage of picture and sound the same as the earlier editions, despite the retention of the original audio and the same sequence of shots.

Restoration

We were thus faced with three surviving versions of the film, all of them authorized. With a limited budget, which were we to preserve? I ultimately developed a strategy whereby we printed the prologue version and the original release version to a single 35mm negative, compiled from three early prints. Each of the three source prints was damaged or truncated to some degree, but together they enabled a frame-for-frame recreation of the original in a form in which it hadn't been seen for many decades, including the re-insertion of the previously lost original end title. The "original" (pre-prologue) version preservation prints are derived simply by cutting off the prologue in the composite positive.

In addition to these 35mm copies, we also preserved the final, revised version in 16mm. But the challenges didn't stop there. Beyond the version issues and age-related damage, each of the early prints we inspected had completely different image grading, contrast, and sound quality. As is common with independent films, this meant that a large degree of subjectivity intermingled with the quest for authenticity in our restoration work in these areas.

To offer an example, the film's soundtrack featuring a "needledrop" recording of the music by Respighi, had reasonably high fidelity but a high degree of background noise in the earliest surviving print. Anger later re-recorded the soundtrack in a version with less background noise, but also lower fidelity. This begged the question of why his later recording was not clearly superior. Kenneth had no recollection of it. Our solution in this case was to make a preservation record of the original, noisy production for archival purposes (to document the film "as it was heard originally"), and simultaneously produce a new track negative using digital noise reduction tools to yield a version that contained slightly less noise, but retained the needledrop sensibility and high fidelity of the original.

In a parallel but not identical strategy, UCLA's 35mm picture restoration was done entirely through photochemical printing, which means it retained embedded dirt and other "problems" that had always been part of how the film was historically experienced by audiences. The recent DVD release by Fantoma contained a version of *Fireworks* that was based on our restoration and eliminated these picture artifacts digitally. From my perspective, that's OK, in so far as 1) the DVD medium already represents a significant formal transformation of the work, and more importantly, 2) the restored version exists on film at UCLA. The DVD is simply another version. But it's of course a great subject for debate.[6]

With all these versions, which one should be shown? Which is the best, or most authoritative? In some senses the answer is "all of them," but of course opinions arise. Upon the restoration's completion, most venues seeking to screen it opted for the version with Anger's spoken prologue. I understand that choice: it's nice to hear his voice, and it evokes his alternate lives as a historian and mythologize. But in that same respect it also veers a bit toward novelty. My own take is that by placing the film in a retrospective perspective through Anger's recollection, the prologue puts the work itself at a state of remove, and hence dampens its impact in subtle ways. There is a direct immediacy to the earlier version, which—in absence of titles or voice—immediately launches one into a piercing vision that grabs you by the shoulders and shakes without relenting until the very end.

But that's of course merely my opinion; another case of subjectivity.

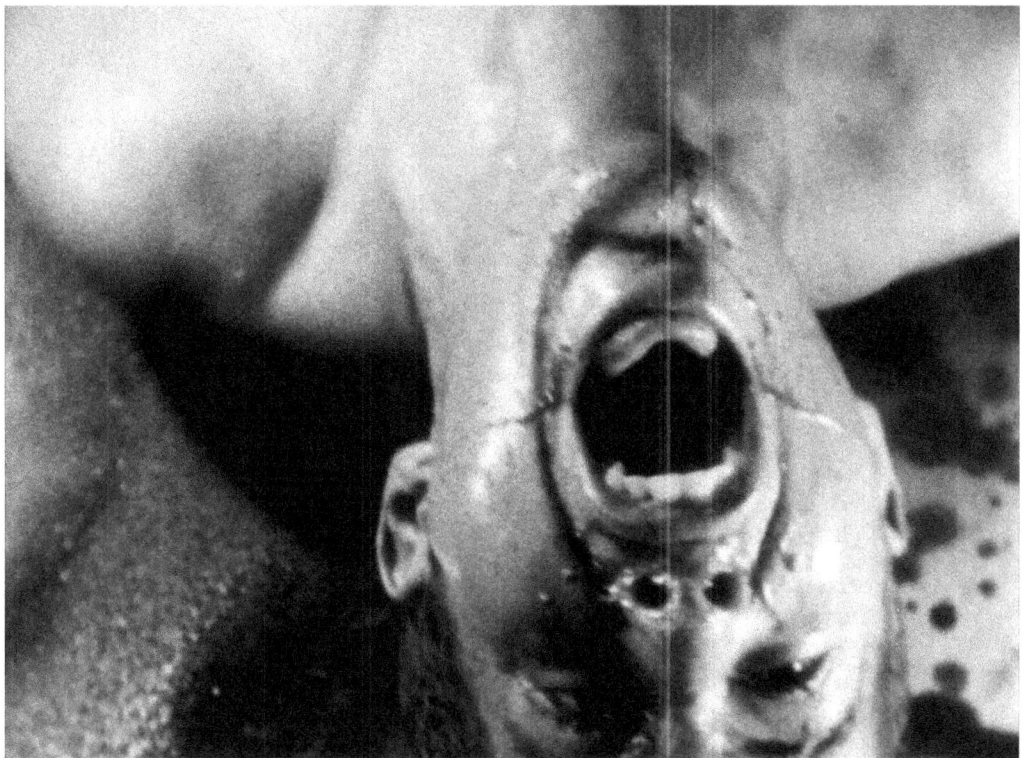

Figure 5. Kenneth Anger in *Fireworks*.

Before concluding, I'd like to offer one last quote by Anger. Just as the film transformed over the years, so did his description of it. I'd now like to go back to the earliest description I can find in Anger's own words. This is from a note to Frank Stauffacher of the Art in Cinema series in San Francisco, and is dated July 25, 1947:

> Formally this film is an investigation of the shock-image… It concerns that love which is at once beyond society and with which no compromise is possible — the subject of all great tragedy. The young man is an 'outcast'—the 'wild beast' who is tracked down through the night. His vision precludes his acceptance even by his own minority group.

The "wild beast" he mentions is not just his homosexuality, but his artistic vision, and his pain. *Fireworks* is an agonizing portrait of a mind tormented by demons it can't control; demons Anger will spend a lifetime wrestling.

Endnotes

1. This version is supposed to have substantially extended the sequence in which Anger writhes naked on the bathroom floor, has his genitals scratched out on the film, and is beaten in a urinal by the sailors.
2. In Sitney's pantheon, the prototype of the psychodrama is Deren and Alexander Hammid's classic *Meshes of the Afternoon*.
3. Soon after the film was made, Alfred Kinsey viewed it and subsequently purchased a copy for his pioneering studies in human sexuality.
4. For further historical context, one can look to Sitney's *Visionary Film*, first published in 1974. His detailed synopsis of the film therein makes clear that he's viewed the "prologue" version, which included the original "end" card, retained from the prior editions, as well as the main title added at the time the prologue was recorded. From this one can surmise that it was the primary version available at that time, but had been supplanted by the color version a decade later, without fanfare.
5. Intriguingly, this same piece of music also features prominently in Bruce Conner's A MOVIE(1958). Was Conner's later work, itself a series of filmic quotations, quoting Anger's earlier usage? Or was it coincidence? This is another question whose answer is lost to the caprices of history.
6. At the time this book is going to press (2025), many years after the original presentation of the lecture from which the present text was adapted, I'm struck by the fact that I mention embedded dirt as something one might want to keep. Nowadays it's *de rigueur* that such things would be cleaned in ideal circumstances. Elsewhere in this book there is discussion of retaining a film's *production* artifacts, but that's distinct from wear and tear to an exhibition print. I suspect I carried this lecture's discussion of dirt a bit further as a means of emphasizing distinctions between the Fantoma DVD and the UCLA print. Similar situations are described in other essays presented here, but with somewhat different emphases, most notably in the case study of *The Juniper Tree*.

POSTSCRIPT Aug. 25, 2025: In a variation of Shepard's Law (cited elsewhere in this volume), recent findings have shed light on some of the questions presented in this text, while raising new ones. Nearly twenty years after the restoration project described here was completed, I learned of a single-strand spliced "workprint" for *Fireworks* that confirmed Anger had indeed shot a main title sequence for the film at the time of production. Initial inspection reveals that it's similar in form to the end title described in the text, but the "F" in *Fireworks* is partially cropped, with a hand-painted F floating around the word, to compensate for the half-missing letter. As another point of difference, the title shot in the workprint (unlike the rest of the opening sequence, and end title) is in negative. My working theory is that Anger opted to use the negative because the inverted tones of the word's letters would be opaque, matching the India ink used to inscribe the missing F. The incomplete evidence available suggests he ultimately deemed this effort to compensate for the cropped letter unsuccessful, and so opted to omit the original main title entirely in publicly released versions of the film. The workprint contains other small differences from the established version, but does not contain the scenes described by Ed Earle in the text and is otherwise slightly truncated. So its place in Anger's ongoing development of the work remains unknown at present.

On Films Without Authoritative Versions II

The Innerview (ca. 1973 / 1975 / 198x / 199x / 200x / 201x / 202x, etc.)

Director: Richard Beymer.

Featuring: Joanna Frank (as Joanna Bochco), Richard Beymer.

Original release: 16mm, color, 1973. (original 1973 version RT unknown)

Digitally restored and remastered in 2023 by Lightbox Film Center at University of the Arts (Philadelphia) and Northeast Historic Film, with funding from the National Film Preservation Foundation, Ron and Suzanne Naples, and Richard Beymer.

Restored from the original 16mm A/B/C rolls, the original 16mm magnetic mix master, and 16mm print fragments. Restoration conformed to the 1975 version (89 minutes).

Restoration supervised by Ross Lipman in consultation with Richard Beymer. Digital picture restoration services by Illuminate Hollywood and Corpus Fluxus. Digital grading by Andrew Drapkin. Audio transfers and restoration by John Polito, Audio Mechanics. Special thanks: Dennis Bartok, Joanna Rachins (Frank/Bochco), David Marriott, Jesse Pires, Jason Ruitenbach, Bill Tayman, Steve Weiner, David Weiss. Distributed by Lightbox Film Center.

The text below joins two pieces; the first being a program note for the restoration's screening at Il Cinema Ritrovato in Bologna in June 2024; the second being an essay written for publication by Lightbox Film Center, Philadelphia, which never reached print as Lightbox's host, the Philadelphia University of the Arts, was sadly forced to close.
The Innerview has been in constant revision for over fifty years, but my research indicates that the now-lost original 1973 version centered on a metaphorical "self-interview" by Beymer, taking multiple forms. The second half of the entry below carries on from this, in a light-hearted tribute.

The Innerview (Richard Beymer, 1975 version)

Richard Beymer began one of the most surprising careers in the history of cinema as a child actor in De Sica's *Terminal Station* in 1953, appearing alongside Montgomery Clift and Jennifer Jones. He's of course best known for his unforgettable roles in *West Side Story* and *Twin Peaks*. But what did he do between these two milestones? He largely dropped out of Hollywood and became an independent filmmaker. What's even more unexpected is that the films are revelations. He began with an acclaimed 16mm civil rights documentary called *A Regular Bouquet* (1964) and then dropped entirely off the grid. His greatest achievement remains *The Innerview*, a feature length experimental film that he ostensibly completed in 1973 and has been revising ever since.

Figure 1. Richard Beymer and assistant in *The Innerview*.

A kaleidoscopic tour de force through the process of filmmaking, it's also a journey through an inner landscape that resonates with the best of 60s era psychedelia. Featuring a stunning performance by lead actress Joanna Bochco, as well as the ever-charismatic Beymer himself, *The Innerview* offers a parallel vision to the classic American underground of the era. In one of its few public screenings it caught the attention of the *Los Angeles Times*' Kevin Thomas, who wrote, "*The Innerview* is a thoroughly remarkable, dazzlingly complex achievement that must surely rank among the major works of the American avant-garde cinema… Moving beyond the mystery of love to the mystery of life itself, *The Innerview*'s flood of sometimes frightening, sometimes reassuring and always sensual images evokes a gamut of emotions—overpowering feelings of terror, despair and death mingling with a wonderous sense of oneness with nature and the universe."

The original 1973 version is lost beyond recovery, as Richard re-cut not just his original negative but all existing prints, in his on-going attempts at perfection. He's currently nearing completion of a new cut—fifty years in the making—that integrates substantially different sound and picture. This new project by Lightbox Film Center in collaboration with Northeast Historic Film and the National Film Preservation Foundation restores the 1975 version of the film—the last he completed on film, and in many ways the culmination of his early vision of the work.

As Beymer said, "I never left the movies. I just made other *kinds* of movies."

An Innerview with the Restorationist

Q. [Ross Lipman]: What can you say about the restoration of *The Innerview*?

A. [Ross Lipman]: How can one "restore" something that was never fixed to begin with?

Q. You're answering questions with questions.

A. I suppose the film dictates the reply.

Q. The film talks to you?

A. Let's not get too literal! But in its way, sure.

Q. What else did *The Innerview* tell you?

A. It's always changing, so the best we can hope for is a snapshot of one of its moments. As an archivist, it's easy to focus on the 1973 release version, since it's seemingly concrete. But even that proved elusive.

Figure 2. Original 16mm C-roll, reel four of *The Innerview*.

Q. Can I ask for some details?

A. After their initial screenings, Richard re-cut the 16mm A/B/C rolls. The original 16mm C-roll of reel 4 was so badly deteriorating that we had to remove all the opaque black leader between shots just to allow a scan that would salvage the images on the roll. The actual film was intact, but the leader was a mess. Richard, for his part, maintains to this day there were no C-rolls in the first place—but I prepped and repaired them myself, so we have a friendly disagreement there. In any event I could tell from inspection that the C-roll shots were superimpositions. We could rescue the images in isolation, but in absence of the spacing, we'd need a reference for their placement. Unfortunately, Richard had also cut up all the film's original showprints in making later versions. In the end I used the reel 4 C-roll's FCC (Frame Count Cuing) cards to get close. I say "close," because ironically in this case, the cards did not count actual frames but only rough footage placements: the superimposition fades were triggered by RF (Radio Frequency) silver-foil cueing on the film in printing, which was an imprecise method common at the time. That at least got me in the ballpark… then I hunted through old cut-up print fragments, and various old video transfers Richard had made to find out exactly where they went.

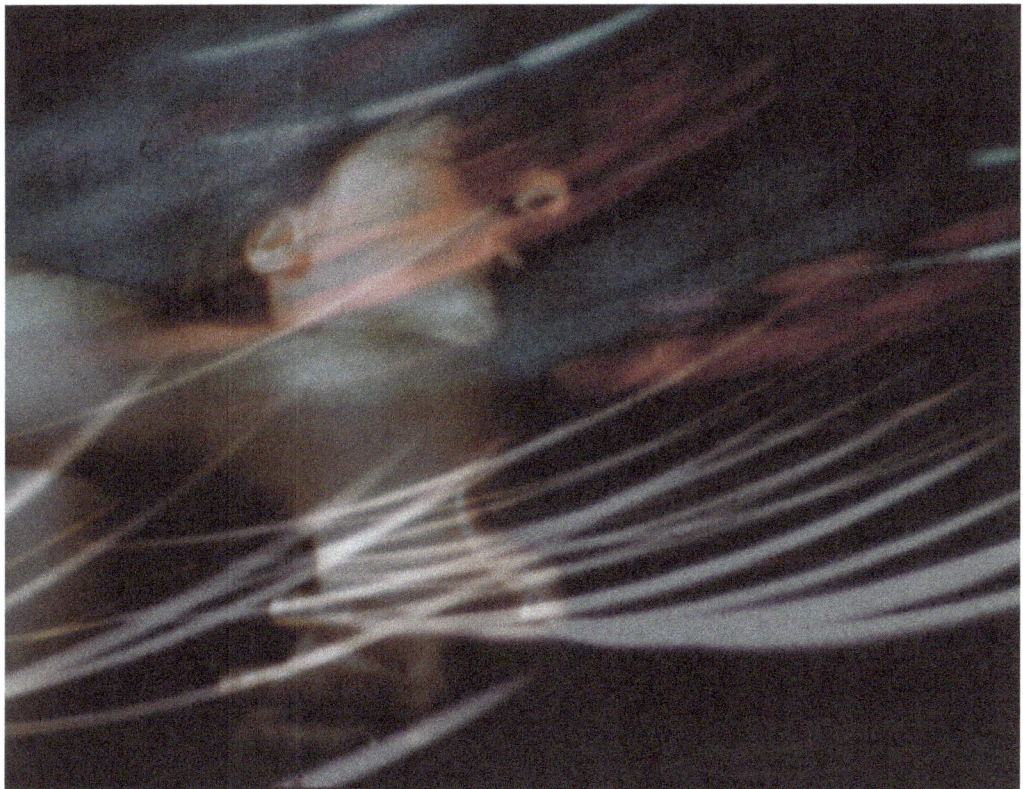

Figure 3. Sample of superimpositions in *The Innerview*.

Q. What about the sound?

A. It was just as confusing. In reviewing the new digitization of the audio I realized some lines of dialogue were missing. Yet our source was the original magnetic track! How could that be? I wound through the badly deteriorating mag mix on an inspection bench and found that sure enough, there was a splice at the exact point of the omission. Yet the film was otherwise in sync with picture: you see Richard on screen mouthing words silently. At some point after completing the initial print run, Richard had apparently decided to cut the spoken lines and leave only a visual impression of absent speech. When? It stumped both Richard and me—but in at least one of his many later revisions, he changed his mind and re-inserted the sound.

Q. What are the lines?

A. Not to be mysterious, but I'll tell you the lines later. He's still revising the film… only time will tell if they're in his new version. The key thing is: those lines were no longer in the supposedly "definitive" original elements, so to reconstitute the dialogue you're asking about, I had to again hunt through his later iterations and fragments. In the end, we restored the 1975 version, which reflected the final edit of the 16mm A/B/C rolls, and from what my research indicates, is the best distillation of his early ideas for the film.

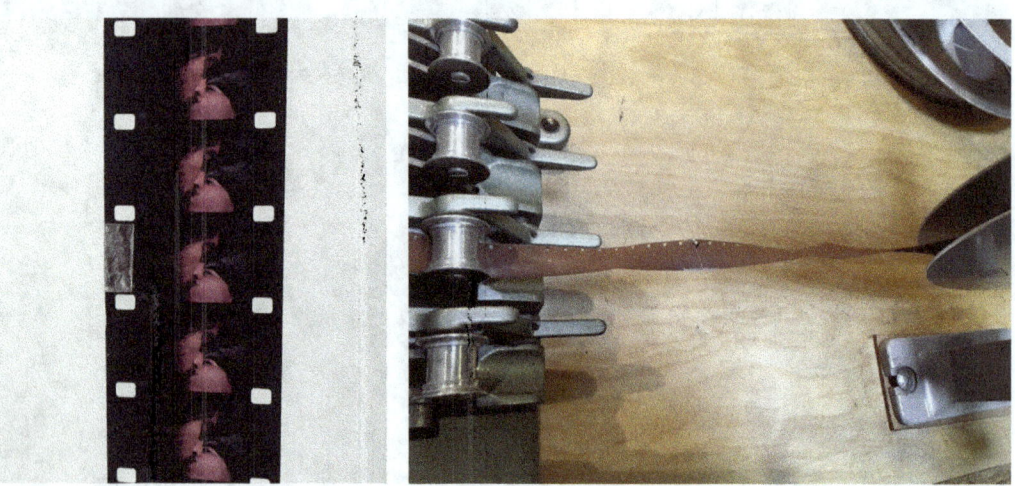

Figure 4 (left). Sample of RF cues in *The Innerview*.
Figure 5 (right). Original 16mm mag mix of *The Innerview*, with visible warpage and edits.

Q. Let's get less technical. How did you find the film in the first place?

A. Credit there goes to David Marriott of Arbelos Films, who came across a listing for it in the AFI Catalogue. His colleague Dennis Bartok was intrigued and tracked down Richard, who sent Arbelos a copy. When Dennis and David determined it was too eccentric for even their visionary label to restore, they asked, "Well, who *is* crazy enough to work on this thing?"

Q. The answer, apparently, is you. Or should I say, me.

A. My sanity aside, we had a number of extraordinary partners who made it possible, beginning with Lightbox in Philadelphia. Lightbox's curator Jesse Pires in essence enabled the whole project. Soon David Weiss and Northeast Historic Film came in, along with the National Film Preservation Foundation. So a lot of people saw the brilliance of the work.

Q. How did you meet Richard?

A. By phone. It was only in talking to him that I realized the version we'd all initially seen was not the original. Richard can't stand the original, and sent Arbelos his latest draft, from around 2019. But that's of course now long gone too.

Q. How so?

A. Simply put, it's *always* changing. If Covid hadn't gotten in the way, Richard said he'd have come out to LA to film me working, and put that in the film to mix it up still further.

Q. If Richard doesn't like the original, what does he like?

A. The one he's currently working on.

Q. Will we see it?

A. Impossible. It's like Heraclitus said, you can't step in the same river twice. We have to be content with the version he had yesterday.

Q. And tomorrow we can see today's?

A. Exactly.

Q. I'm a slow learner… but what can we say has definitely changed along the way?

A. Since the 2019 version, Richard stumbled across some old audio cassettes he'd recorded with his lead actress Johanna Bochco, and I believe he's currently mixing those in.

Q. The archivist in me shudders.

A. Richard would love that. He'd be the first to tell you he has no concern for archival protocols. But to return to the subject, he's been recording every aspect of his life for something like fifty years now, in every imaginable media format, and has a vast personal archive. One might describe it as glorious chaos.

Q. Raw footage?

A. Yes, but also quite a few completed works that are both singular and astonishingly good. Someone should really be looking at this material.

Figure 6. Joanna Frank in *The Innerview*.

Q. I hope Someone is reading this... But how can a work as good as *The Innerview*, made as it is, by a noted movie star, go unnoticed for nearly fifty years?

A. Richard won't trade on his celebrity backstory, and disregards the rules of the game. As we speak, Steven Spielberg is about to release his *West Side Story* remake, but Richard declined his invitation to the opening gala. His reason? "They'd want me to do promo photos with the new cast and all that garbage."

Q. So he's a bit of a recluse?

A. It depends on the context. For example he'll happily strip naked with a bunch of strangers and paint his body blue as part of an Ayahuasca ritual in South America.

Q. So there are two parallel forces at work: a vision pursued, and a refusal of niceties.

A. I imagine Richard's Hollywood pedigree doesn't help his being taken seriously. How could a glamorous star make anything of substance? "He's gone off the deep end," they say. "Poor guy."

Q. So what is it about *The Innerview* that stands out to you?

A. The ease with which it transports one to places other films don't even reach for. It's hard to think of a work that better conveys the ecstatic state, in both its darkness and its light. In some ways it aligns with the best aspects of the avant-garde, at moments evoking Bruce Baillie or Bruce Conner; at others Jack Smith or some of the Zanzibar films. But in the end it's completely its own thing. Be ready for hippie excess in all its glory… we're looking at the work of someone who let his imagination run freely. And it's exactly that freedom that lets him arrive at places other films can't, or rarely find.

Q. So it's—like his studio—a chaotic explosion?

A. Yes, but Richard is also surprisingly disciplined. A lot of *labor* went into this thing. Between the chaos and labor, one finds a sensitivity to the needs of the film. He always manages to find the right juxtaposition of sound and image to convey these ephemeral states of being.

In the end it falls outside our expectations or ability to classify. Paradoxically, the "Inner" view reveals a lot about the external world. Why has it been excluded from history? Our inability to place it reveals just how dependent on the game we actually are. Those who don't play nicely are exiled from the Republic, and that's been the case with Richard's work.

Q. Hmmm. Can I ask you about those lines now; the ones that are sometimes in and sometimes out?

A. It's the scene in the film where Richard's asked, "What are your films about?"

He replies, "The belief in illusion."

That part is in all versions; at least those that I've seen. But in the original prints, the interviewer follows up with, "Whose illusion?"

Richard answers: "Mine."

So then, let's experience his illusion. Let's get *The Innerview* out, and into light of day.

On the Fading of Non-representational Color

Time of the Heathen

Director: Peter Kass. Cinematographer: Ed Emshwiller. Music: Lejaren Hiller.

Featuring: John Heffernan, Barry Collins, Ethel Ayler.

Original release: 35mm and 16mm, B&W and color, 76 mins., 1961.

Digitally restored and remastered in 2023 by UCLA Film & Television Archive and Lightbox Film Center at University of the Arts (Philadelphia), with funding from Ron and Suzanne Naples.

Restored from the original 35mm picture and soundtrack negatives on loan from the British Film Institute, and from the original ¼" master recordings of Lejaren Hiller's score, provided by the Sousa Archives and University of Illinois Library. An additional 35mm reference print was provided by the Swedish Film Institute.

Restoration supervised by Jillian Borders (UCLA Film & Television Archive) and Ross Lipman (Corpus Fluxus). Digital picture restoration services by Illuminate Hollywood and Corpus Fluxus. Digital grading by Andrew Drapkin. Audio transfers and restoration by John Polito, Audio Mechanics. Special thanks: Espen Bale, May Haduong, David Marriott, Lynn McVeigh, Jesse Pires, Magnus Rosborn, Jason Ruitenbach, Bill Tayman, Ei Toshinari, Steve Wiener, Todd Wiener, Kieron Webb. Distributed by Arbelos.

This text was adapted from a lecture entitled "New Directions in Independent Film Restoration," originally presented at Il Cinema Ritrovato in Bologna in June 2023, and from a screening introduction by UCLA Head of Preservation Jillian Borders and myself on the occasion of the film's US restoration premiere at the UCLA Film & Television Archive's Festival of Preservation in April 2024.

The Restoration of *Time of the Heathen*

by Jillian Borders and Ross Lipman

Time of the Heathen was the only feature directed by Peter Kass, a legendary acting teacher at Julliard. Among his students were Olympia Dukakis, Faye Dunaway, John Cazale, and Val Kilmer. Kass was known as brilliant but severe: a colleague once described him as "a holy madman of the theater." He can be seen in his full glory instructing a young Kilmer in the autobiographical documentary *Val*. In *Time of the Heathen* he certainly drew outstanding performances from lead actors John Heffernan and young Barry Collins. While Barry Collins did not act again, one may recall John Heffernan from his supporting role in *The Sting*. Another notable performance in the film is that of Ethel Ayler, who plays the young woman—Ayler worked consistently in television, and appeared in Charles Burnett's *To Sleep with Anger*.

In discussing the film, we must however single out Kass' primary collaborator, Ed Emshwiller, who served as both cinematographer and de facto designer and art director. Emshwiller would go on to become a noted experimental filmmaker, a pioneer in video art, and Dean of the Filmmaking Department at California Institute of the Arts in Los Angeles. Back in 1961, he was primarily a science fiction artist. Emshwiller's cinematography and design work in *Heathen* are stunning, and particularly shine in a sequence near the end. The majority of the film is black-and-white, but at a certain point it shifts to color. We won't give anything away, but let's just say this is not *The Wizard of Oz*.

There were other important contributors. In the film's opening title sequence, one sees a triangle logo with the names Kass, Santvoord, and Emshwiller. The middle name belongs to Peggy Santvoord, a young art and film enthusiast who's credited as assistant director, and had previously worked with Kass on several stage plays. Santvoord came from a wealthy New York family, and after her tragic death in a plane crash in the Virgin Islands in 1965, the family established a foundation in her name that to this day supports the arts with financial grants.

Lastly, the film features an astounding score… but more of that later. The impetus for our restoration came from Jesse Pires, director and curator of Lightbox Film Center at the University of the Arts in Philadelphia. In 2019 Jesse curated an Emshwiller retrospective, entitled "Dream Dance," and in his research, happened upon the film and traced the original picture and track negatives to the British Film Institute. Through generous funding from Ron and Suzanne Naples, a restoration project was set in motion in collaboration with the UCLA Film & Television Archive.

The original picture and track negatives were sent to Los Angeles for inspection and cleaning. The BFI also had a vintage 35mm print, but it was sadly faded, and could not be used as a reference for the restoration's color sequences. Knowing what the black- and-white sections of the film should look like was straightforward, but as the lone color

Figure 1. John Heffernan in Peter Kass' *Time of the Heathen* (1961).

reel depicts hallucinations featuring multiple exposures in psychedelic color, it was hard to determine what the color had originally looked like. The Kass and Emshwiller families' personal 16mm prints were also faded, and the film itself was in essence a lost work, so we had no visual reference. How to approach it?

To get started, Andrew Drapkin—the excellent colorist at Illuminate Labs in Los Angeles—carefully read the color scopes, and by viewing the sequence as a whole, we were able to determine that certain shots were intended as a mix of black-and-white and color. Andrew then neutralized the black-and-white tonality of those shots, and we examined where the remaining colors in the frame fell with those settings. From that, we could work backward, and determine reference points for quite a few of the other shots. The sequence was now looking good, but for such experimental imagery, it was still niggling at us that we couldn't confirm the accuracy of what we'd achieved.

At this juncture, we began further research and discovered a cinephiliac blog post whose author mentioned seeing the film at the Finnish Film Archive years ago, and in the comments sections, a reader noted that it also screened on Swedish TV in the 1970s. We reached out to our FIAF partners and located an old print at the Swedish Film Institute. This was a stroke of

Figure 2. Barry Collins in Peter Kass' *Time of the Heathen* (1961).

tremendous luck, as the Swedes were pioneers of cold storage, and to our delight their print had indeed been frozen solid all the way back in 1970. We're immensely grateful to our forward-looking colleagues in Sweden. It had been unfrozen in 1991, but remained in climate-controlled vaults, and proved to be in excellent condition. Not completely unfaded perhaps — it was veering *slightly* red/magenta — but it still had excellent dye retention and could serve as our guide. Using the print as a reference, we were able to confirm the vast majority of our previous choices as quite accurate, as well as steer ourselves in the right direction for the remainder of the shots. Our thanks go to Magnus Rosborn and the staff at the Swedish Film Institute for their generous help.

As mentioned, the film also featured an extraordinary score. Its composer was Lejaren Hiller, who was trained in chemistry and was an early student of the experimental composer Milton Babbitt. Hiller is not well known today, but at the time of the making of *Heathen*, was somewhat infamous. In 1956, he was working as a chemist at the University of Illinois in Champaign, Urbana. Back then the university was home to Illiac 1, the first supercomputer housed at an academic institution. As a scientist, Hiller was able to access the computer, and programmed it to compose what he called the *Illiac Suite for String Quartet*. It was performed on August 9, 1956, and is now recognized as the first instance of computer-written

Figure 3. Ed Emshwiller's psychedelic sequence: a sample frame enlargement from the Swedish Film Institute's vintage 35mm reference print.

music. The event was every bit as controversial as you might expect. One listener likened the music "to a barnyard" (*The Guardian*), and many people were outraged at the mere idea of computers composing music. But in a precursor to issues arising in the present era, the art is in the programming—and the piece holds up extremely well, very worthy of revisitation by contemporary audiences.

Hiller made full use of all his knowledge and resources in the score of *Time of the Heathen*, integrating complete sequences of what the film's credits describe as "electronic sound" amidst an otherwise acoustic composition. As one can happily guess, the electronic sequences appear most prominently in Ed Emshwiller's color reel, providing a perfect complement to the extraordinary visuals.

The problem is that the low fidelity of the surviving original optical soundtrack did not do justice to Hiller's work. When we began the project we had no knowledge of Hiller, but upon hearing the score we recognized something special was going on, in both its acoustic and electronic sections. So we began research, and were surprised and delighted to find that the original magnetic recordings still survived, in the University of Illinois archives. We then listened to them along with John Polito at Audio Mechanics, and immediately confirmed that they were vastly superior to the old optical track.

We realized however, that they were in stereo. This presented another dilemma. Due to format limitations of the era, the film itself had of course been released in mono: so its pioneering score had never been fully presented. And we knew from *Illiac Suite* that stereo was an active component of Hiller's experimentation.

To address this, while simultaneously honoring the film's historical release format, we opted to make multiple versions of the film, including the original mono, as well as a new stereo edition. But from a technical standpoint, the challenge lay in completing our new stereo version in a manner faithful to the film's spirit and character. To do that, we worked with John Polito, who applied careful use of AI tools to isolate effects and dialogue from the mono optical, in absence of true D-M-E stems. We could then mix the new stems appropriately, effectively matching the relationships between sound components of the original mono in a stereo environment. This is now our preferred showcopy, but the original mono remains available in UCLA's preservation vaults. The restored film premiered at Il Cinema Ritrovato in Bologna in July 2023, and we're delighted that Arbelos Films has taken it on for distribution, so hopefully future audiences can now discover this once-lost work.

On Non-narrative Fiction

Nightshift

Director: Robina Rose. Cinematographer: Jon Jost. Music: Simon Jeffes.

Featuring: Jordan Mooney, Heathcote Williams, Anne Reese-Mogg, Jon Jost.

Original release: 16mm, color, 68 mins., 1981.

Digitally restored and remastered in 2024 by Lightbox Film Center at University of the Arts (Philadelphia) in collaboration with The British Film Institute & Cinenova, with funding from Ron and Suzanne Naples.

Restored from the original 16mm reversal A/B rolls and 16mm optical track on loan from the British Film Institute.

Restoration supervised by Ross Lipman in consultation with Robina Rose. Digital picture restoration services by Illuminate Hollywood and Corpus Fluxus. Digital grading by Andrew Drapkin. Audio transfers and restoration by John Polito, Audio Mechanics. Special thanks: David Marriott, Lynn McVeigh, Jesse Pires, Charlotte Procter, Robina Rose, Jason Ruitenbach, Bill Tayman, Ei Toshinari, Steve Wiener, Kieron Webb. Distributed by Arbelos in US, and by Cinenova in UK.

As with the text on The Innerview, *the following was written for publication by Lightbox Film Center, Philadelphia, and never reached print due to the closure of University of the Arts in Philadelphia, who hosted Lightbox at the time.*

Beyond the Initial Release

Restoring *Nightshift*

Robina Rose's *Nightshift* takes the ostensible form of a fiction film, but its narrative is elusive at best, and the ways in which it varies from traditional drama informed its restoration strategy. The film chronicles the events that transpire in the course of a single night at London's Portobello Hotel in 1981, as witnessed by artist and punk icon Jordan Mooney (aka Jordan), who plays the desk clerk. But as Jordan doesn't speak—save for the occasional greeting of "Reception"—the core of the film lies rather, in the events depicted themselves. These exist primarily as sensual experiences, in the interaction of sound and light; their dramatic value deceptively serving as just one component of their substance.

Indeed, inspection of the original film elements quickly reveals the stunning cinematography by independent film *enfant terrible* Jon Jost, which is characterized by a deep texture of image that evokes a Dutch painting. These qualities were in part enabled by the production's use of now-obsolete Fuji 16mm color reversal film stock, with lush warm colors and thick swimming film grain. Our job as restorationists was to preserve its evocative richness in the new digital edition. (See Figure 1.)

Figure 1. Robina Rose's *Nightshift* (1981).

While this might seem glaringly obvious, it was perhaps not as clear to previous technicians who had worked on the film, and—in earlier efforts—misrepresented its character with ill-fated attempts to make it look more like a "normal movie." This can be graphically illustrated in a comparison between photographs of two older sources. In our first example, one sees a section of the original 16mm color reversal stock with its warm color palette, displayed alongside a section of an original exhibition print, which sadly neutralized the original's native qualities. (See Figures 2A and 2B.)

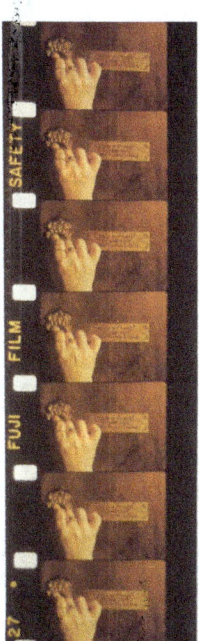 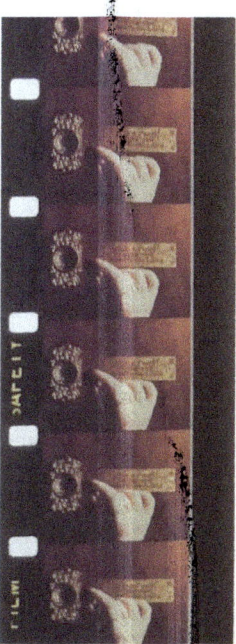

Figures 2A and 2B. Left: 16mm camera-original reversal. Right: 16mm original reversal exhibition print. (Note: images are different scale as source frames are not identical.)

In our second example, one finds a screen grab of an old video transfer, which matches the washed-out character of the print, displayed alongside the new restoration, which conversely, closely resembles Jon Jost's original photography. Director Robina Rose confirmed the warmer color was intended, and was delighted to see the result. The two examples, joined together give lie to the misconception that it's always the restorationist's job to recreate a film's viewing experience "as it was first seen in theaters." (See Figures 3A and 3B.)

In parallel to our work on picture, the film's sound underwent a similar journey. In Rose's vision of the hotel, the spoken words of the inhabitants are absorbed into an auditory field that's more truly sensual than linguistic. Even the sounds of Jordan operating the vacuum cleaner are composed—in a sequence that extends for three full real-time minutes—with an

Figures 3A and 3B. Top: old video transfer (Jordan Mooney). Bottom: Final restoration (Jordan Mooney).

end credit for "hoover music" going to Simon Jeffes. (Jeffes' Penguin Café Orchestra music also features throughout the film.) In point of fact, *Nightshift*'s audioscape can be heard as an extended instance of musique concrète, with the sound of a penny dropping in a music box carrying as much weight as the characters' dialogue. Here again, our effort was to preserve an elusive quality of sonic texture, as much as a literal record. And whereas again this would seem obvious, practical limitations of our source elements provided serious stumbling blocks.

The film's original magnetic track or mix master would be our ideal source, but if it existed, it was nowhere to be found. The film's original 16mm picture a/b rolls were accompanied, rather, by a 16mm optical track, with its severely limited audio range peaking at about 6,000 Hz. Intriguingly, old cataloging records indicated the vintage viewing print mentioned earlier had a magnetic soundtrack, which might have extended that range. This type of track would have been surprising to find, but at least the prospect held some intrigue. Upon receipt of the materials I eagerly unspooled the print on my workbench, and realized alas that it had been misidentified. It was a standard optical track, but printed so darkly that the contours of its variable area pattern had been invisible to the eyes of its previous inspectors. Under the circumstances, they'd mistaken it for the iron oxide of a mag track. I can only imagine what the thing sounded like, but it couldn't be good.

Stuck as we were with the surviving track negative, we took it to John Polito at Audio Mechanics, who transferred it utilizing special tools for cross-modulation cancellation to properly render the limited range of the optical source with minimal distortion. From there we carefully applied noise reduction and equalization to eliminate unintended hiss, crackle, and optical degradation, prising out the audioscape's contours.

In past years, the work would have stopped there—but new tools allowed us to go a step further. The biggest problem we faced was a murkiness in the optical track source, which worked against our attempts to articulate the nuance in the carefully constructed sound mix. This problem arose most prominently in some of the rare sections where the dialogue of the hotel's inhabitants was prominent. While their words were all just part of a *gestalt*, they were nonetheless meant to be intelligible in most cases, yet were buried in the optical track's baseline of noise. Using artificial intelligence tools—let's call them a somewhat poorer cousin of the expensive proprietary tools used by Peter Jackson on his Beatles documentary *Get Back*—we were able to isolate the dialogue from the sound effects amidst which they were embedded. Once isolated, we were then able to successfully apply targeted equalization and digital cleanup to the split tracks, before re-integrating them in a sharper, crisper audio track that would more closely approximate the clarity of the lost magnetic source.

Through these careful efforts with both picture and sound, we hope we've restored the exquisite audiovisual texturing that makes *Nightshift* come alive, evoking the long-lost ghosts that haunted the Portobello Hotel back in 1981.

On Re-restoration

Killer of Sheep

Director, Screenwriter, Cinematographer: Charles Burnett.

Featuring: Henry Sanders, Kaycee Moore, Charles Bracy, Eugene Cherry.

Original release: 16mm, BW, 83 mins., 1977.

Initially restored in 35mm in 2000 by UCLA Film & Television Archive, with funding from the Ahmanson Foundation in association with the Sundance Institute, and subsequently digitally remastered in HD in 2007 in cooperation with Milestone Films.

The restoration was digitally remastered and cleaned up in 4K / 16 bit digital video in 2025 by UCLA Film & Television Archive, Milestone Films, and the Criterion Collection.

Restored from the original 16mm A/B rolls, the original 35mm magnetic DM&E, and the original 16mm fullcoat magnetic mix. Digitally remastered from the restored 16mm fine grain master positive and the restored digital audio files.

Restoration conformed and supervised by Ross Lipman in collaboration with UCLA Film & Television Archive Head of Preservation Jillian Borders (in 2025), and in consultation with Charles Burnett. Photochemical laboratory services provided by Film Technology Company and DJ Audio. Digital laboratory services by Modern VideoFilm (2007) and Illuminate Hollywood (2025). 35mm film grading by Roy Siriwattanakamol. HD video grading by Kathy Thomson. 4K digital grading by Andrew Drapkin. Audio Restoration by John Polito (2000, 2007, 2025); 2025 Re-mix and editorial by Larry Blake. Additional transfers: Nick Bergh, Endpoint Audio. Special thanks to: Peter Becker, Maya S. Cade, Dennis Doros, Chris Dusendschön, May Hong HaDuong, Amy Heller, Zna Houston, Jonathan Burnett, Elizabeth Pauker, Giles Sherwood, Jason Ruitenbach, Shane Strickland, Fumiko Takagi, Bill Tayman, Steve Wiener, Todd Wiener. Distributed in BRD and streaming by Criterion, and theatrically by Milestone / Kino-Lorber.

———————

The following was adapted from a text written for Milestone's press kit accompanying the 2025 re-release of Killer of Sheep.

Re-Restoring *Killer of Sheep*

In my early days at the UCLA Film & Television Archive, I remember my surprise when Bob Gitt, the visionary founder of their preservation department, would re-visit titles he'd restored long ago, such as *Becky Sharp*. But what goes around comes around, and so when my friends at Milestone offered the opportunity to re-restore *Killer of Sheep*, I leapt at the opportunity. As Bob well knew, technological advances offered new opportunities to do things better, and in this sense, a film might never be considered "fully restored."

Now, some twenty-five years after our initial project commenced, I operate as a freelancer, but was happy to join forces with my good colleague Jillian Borders, now head of UCLA's preservation program. We naturally began by re-visiting the old work conducted. A description of that can be found in Milestone's press kit for the previous restoration:

> At a technical level *Killer of Sheep* demanded immediate attention, as it was already deteriorating when we received the material in 2000. The original 16mm A/B rolls as well as the magnetic soundtrack master suffered from vinegar syndrome, putting the film on a ticking clock. [Note: Vinegar syndrome is a degenerative "disease" that attacks the film, giving off an acetic acid odor in the process.]
>
> *Killer of Sheep* had previously existed only in rough 16mm copies, and the 35mm blow-up restoration better renders the beautiful quality of Charles' lovely in-the-street cinematography. One of the genuine privileges of doing this work at UCLA is that we're able to apply the best technical resources in LA to a small, low-budget production that would never otherwise benefit from such treatment. But despite the access to high-end resources, we made great efforts to preserve exactly the rough quality of the original, so as not to alter the work. Especially careful attention was given to image contrast and tonality, to carefully bring out the best aspects of the original negative. We're indebted to Film Technology Company for their excellent lab work. We also, with the help of John Polito of Audio Mechanics, conducted close and judicious work on the "*vérité*-like" soundtrack, which was often recorded by the many kids who appear in the film.

One of the things that stands out in the text above is my noting the rare chance to bring the best resources to a low-budget independent film. In the years since our initial work, the restoration of independent film has become common practice. What else has changed? Of course, our new work would be digital.

Although UCLA had kept the original 16mm a/b rolls of the film, they were—as already noted—badly deteriorated when the previous work had been done decades earlier. They were far worse now, despite having benefitted from climate-controlled storage since UCLA's move to the PHI Stoa in 2013. We conducted scanning tests, but the film was too brittle and warped for effective use. Luckily, the preservation elements we had created in the previous restoration were particularly well-suited for scanning. Our previous workflow, at Film Technology, had not only included full black-and-white grading of the original negative that was built into the resulting fine-grain master positive, but also extensive contrast adjustment, achieved by varying printing exposure and processing chemistry to extend the film's native latitude. The result was a low-contrast (and hence finer-grained) element that proved very effective for scanning and further digital grading. I'm indebted to my colleagues at Illuminate Hollywood for their excellent work; and would like to single out colorist Andrew Drapkin for his characteristic dedication as well as his patience with my many requests, while completing the project to highest standards. We're also especially grateful to Charles Burnett for his insights and advice throughout the process.

One of the key points of distinction between the current effort and the prior one is that we now have the advantage of digital cleanup. The prior transfer by Modern VideoFilm had excellent grading, but was only HD, and featured no cleanup whatsoever. The new work is in 4K 16-bit, and the many dirt particles and small exhibition artifacts that appeared in the old version have now been addressed.

Another area of interest is the soundtrack. The original audio restoration, conducted by John Polito, represented one of the most careful and productive jobs on which I'd worked. Prior to the initial restoration, as noted, the film had only been distributed in 16mm, and featured an often murky soundtrack. Our work at the time retained the "in the street" feel, but notably improved the intelligibility of the dialogue. Among other things, we had conducted extensive editing between the badly warped 35mm master magnetic track and the accompanying 16mm mag, which was needed as well, when the 35mm was too deteriorated for usage. As with picture, the surviving sound elements were now too deteriorated for effective use when we revisited the project in late 2024. (We're indebted to Nick Bergh for testing these materials!) But now we could do much more with the previous audio captures, using new tools.

As just one example, technology of the era had severe limitations in how it could address the "wow" and "flutter" that had by default arisen when the badly deteriorated magnetic tracks, with their severely warped edges, had irregularly made their way over the magnetic recording heads. That could now be corrected. Beginning with our old restored track, John Polito carefully went through the whole film and removed the wow. He additionally applied AI tools to further enhance the dialogue which we'd so carefully restored in previous years. The result is an excellent track that improves on the old edition, while simultaneously retaining the feel of authenticity and warmth in the original recordings, made as they were, by the kids who appear in the film.

In parallel to our work with Audio Mechanics, Larry Blake has made a new version of the soundtrack. Using John's freshly upgraded restoration as his source, Larry worked with Charles Burnett to slightly adjust some dialogue levels to match what Charles had sought on set back during the original shooting but hadn't achieved at the time. As part of the process, they also cleaned up some small irregularities of the original production. For example, in a scene where cricket sounds were heard inconsistently in the background, they're now consistent. In Larry's words, they've created "a more smooth experience." This collaboration between Audio Mechanics and Larry Blake is the version that will hit the theaters and be available on streaming platforms; meanwhile the restoration of the original version (as well as the unrestored sources) are safely stored in UCLA's vaults. We're deeply grateful to Charles Burnett, John Polito and Larry Blake for their generous contributions to the project.

A final but important historical footnote concerns the film's excellent use of music. At the time of the 2007 restoration's release by Milestone, clearance rights were unavailable for the film's final scene, which included Dinah Washington's searing rendition of "Unforgettable." An account of how we addressed that problem back in the day can be found in my essay, "The Gray Zone." Happily, in the intervening years, the rights issue was resolved, and the new release restores the original Dinah Washington ending of the film.

Cumulatively, the results you'll see and hear on screen offer the best current technology can offer… until the next new thing comes around. I imagine by then it'll be someone else's turn, but I'm glad to have been a part of this extraordinary film's history.

PART THREE

HISTORIES

On *Shadows*
(1957/9)

Shadows was restored by UCLA Film & Television Archive in association with Faces Distribution, with funding from The Film Foundation, the Hollywood Foreign Press Association, and the Ahmanson Foundation in association with the Sundance Institute. The restoration was subsequently digitally remastered by UCLA in collaboration with Criterion Corporation at Modern Film and Video. Laboratory services provided by Triage Motion Picture Services, Audio Mechanics, DJ Audio, Monaco Film and Video, and IVC, Inc.. Restoration and remastering supervised by Ross Lipman in collaboration with colleagues including audio restorationist John Polito, film grader Sharol Olson, optical printing technician Dave Tucker, and digital colorist Gregg Garvin. Distributed by Criterion.

This offering on Cassavetes' Shadows *opens our concluding section; of texts not so much discussing my work practice, as arising from it. Along the path of restoration, in analysis of a film's pre-production elements and documentation, I frequently encounter traces of a work's history that were previously unknown and in some cases of great relevance to an understanding of it. (In film scholarship parlance, these discoveries might be referred to as "evidence.") Such was the case with* Shadows, *where my research into the lost outtakes of Charles Mingus' celebrated score—in part motivated by my love for Mingus' music—led me down rabbit-hole after rabbit-hole, until I discovered not only a lost archive of photos of the film's entire production, including the score's recording, but the actual recordings themselves. As few of the audio tracks appear in the film, and as the first version of* Shadows *remains unavailable for viewing, I've only been able to present the recordings in excerpt form in an illustrated lecture derived from the far longer text presented here. That lecture was initially presented at the EMP Pop Conference in Seattle in April, 2008, and then on numerous occasions thereafter. The essay itself was first published in* The Journal of Film Music, *Volume 2, Nos. 2-4, Winter 2009, then in a revised edition in the online journal* Rouge. *The present version greatly expands on that, and has not been published in this form previously.*

Reading it now, I'm struck by themes that arise frequently in my personal work. A fascination with doppelgangers, and with (arguably) mis-matched collaborators is introduced here, returning again in Notfilm's *examination of Samuel Beckett and Buster Keaton, as well as in my notes for a never-completed exploration of the creative cross-talk between Barbara Loden and Elia Kazan.*

Throughout most of the essays that follow in this section, one also finds a recurring fascination with the creative process and its mysteries.

For their insight, generous help, and support in various aspects of the following essay, I'd like to thank Brecht Andersch, Helen Bandis, Nicole Brenez, Ray Carney, William Claxton, Fred Cohen, Lelia Goldoni, Ronald Grant, Jan-Christopher Horak, Martin Humphries, Adam Hyman, Marvin Lichtner, Adrian Martin, Grant McDonald, Sue Mingus, Mark Quigley, Jonathan Rosenbaum, William Rosar, Al Ruban, Bud Shank, John Shaw, Joseph Tepperman, Uwe Weiler, Pete Williams and Timothy Wilson.

Photos of Shadows *recording sessions courtesy of Marvin Lichtner and the Cinema Museum. Photo of Ben Carruthers courtesy of William Claxton.*

1st recording session: Charles Mingus, double bass; Phineas Newborn Jr. and Horace Parlan, piano; Jimmy Knepper, trombone; Dannie Richmond, drums; Shafi Hadi (Curtis Porter), tenor saxophone, Anthony Ortega, reeds; two other unverified musicians who are believed to be Clarence Gene Shaw (trumpet), and Seymour Barab (cello). Also present: Jack Ackerman, Seymour Cassel, Nica de Koenigswarter.

2nd recording session: Shafi Hadi, Dannie Richmond.

Mingus, Cassavetes, and the Birth of a Jazz Cinema

Introduction

In November 1958, John Cassavetes premiered his revolutionary independent film *Shadows* in a series of midnight screenings at the Paris Theater in New York City. *The Village Voice* critic Jonas Mekas immediately proclaimed it a work of genius, calling it "the most frontier-breaking American feature in at least a decade."[1] Most audience members, including Cassavetes, hated it.[2] Cassavetes reassembled his cast and crew and shot extensive new footage, modifying old scenes and adding new ones. The final version premiered at Amos Vogel's legendary Cinema 16 on November 11, 1959, and was an overnight critical sensation.

Shadows chronicled the lives of a mixed race family in which two light-skinned siblings (Lelia Goldoni and Ben Carruthers) and their darker-skinned brother (Hugh Hurd) live day to day in 1950s New York bohemia. The program notes from the 1959 screening (billed with Alfred Leslie and Robert Frank's *Pull My Daisy* as "The Cinema of Improvisation") described the film as "John Cassavetes' pulsating revelation of the demi-world of the night people; floaters, chicks, jazz musicians and hipsters in the neon-lit desert of Times Square." They continued, "Overpowering in its immediacy, this brilliant return to improvisation in the cinema etches a compassionate, violent portrayal of pick-ups and brawls, loneliness, casual affairs and search for identity."[3] These insightful early notes by Vogel go to the film's very core, yet simultaneously set the tone for many years of misconceptions.

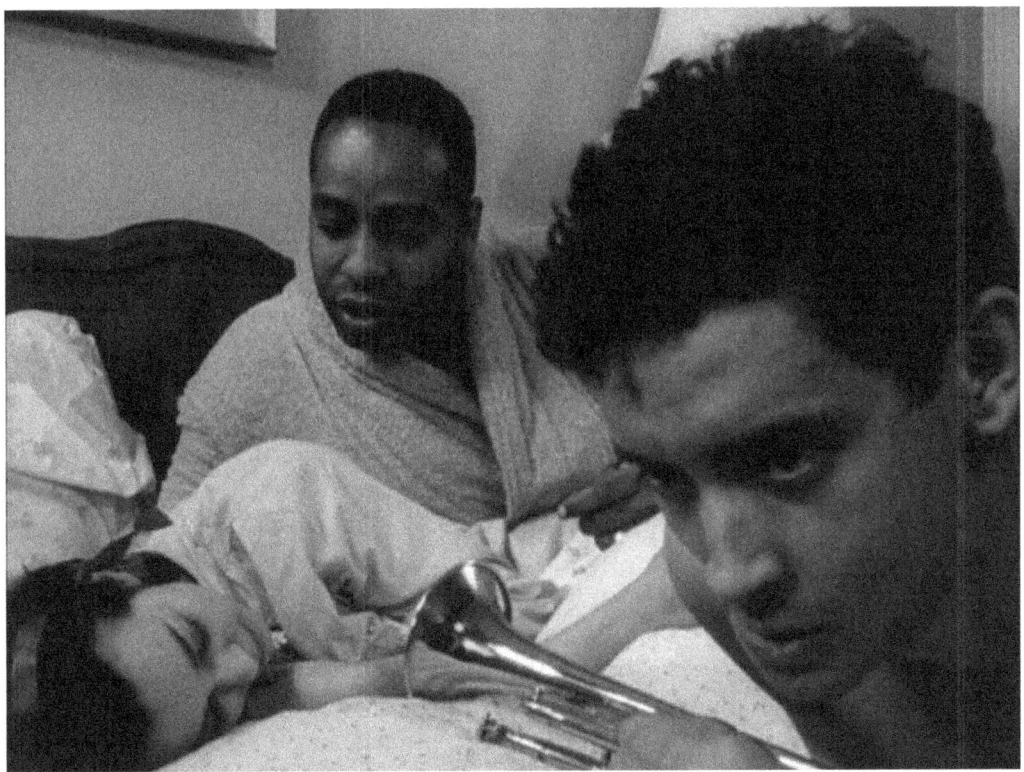

Figure 1. the three siblings (still frame)

One of the myths that propelled *Shadows* to instant notoriety was its improvisational origins. It's considered by many to be the first "true" cinematic jazz narrative, both for its racially charged subject and its unconventional, unscripted making in the streets of Manhattan.[4]

It's been further celebrated for an original score by one of the all-time jazz greats, Charles Mingus.

However much of the legend is deceptive. Little of Mingus' music appears in the final film. Actual jazz scenes are conspicuously absent. And recent writings by Ray Carney, Tom Charity and others have attempted to debunk or clarify much of the improvisation myth.

Carney reveals that when Cassavetes essentially reshot half the film in 1959 and formed the work's eventual release version, he used a script.[5] Even the supposedly improvised scenes from the first shoot were in essence "scored" by Cassavetes, who gave his actors not just notes but sequential scenarios and specific guidelines right from the start. They then developed the film's first draft through rehearsals in the Variety Arts building studio where Cassavetes ran acting workshops with a partner, Burt Lane.

The final work, which integrates footage from two distinct shooting periods, with gaping continuity mismatches and diverse acting and shooting styles, is in many ways a collage, and an excellent example of how our minds can synthesize and selectively process contradictions into a unified whole, creating both story and myth.

Like the splintered story and film footage, the final soundtrack is in essence a collage. The score by Mingus, the most authentic link to the New York jazz scene in the film, and a key to some of its most powerful moments, is not wholly improvised, and is actually just one of several musical components. The exact question of the score's provenance, and Mingus' role within it, leads further to the film's heart, and provides a central insight into its genuinely radical nature.

Shadows did develop a unique jazz cinema, but a quite different one than has been understood until now. Cassavetes' investment in jazz will be seen to permeate every level of his filmmaking throughout his career, at the same time that the jazz connection's outer trappings are questionable. Charles Mingus, conversely, embodied the jazz experience, while his surface involvement in the film was minimal. His contributions to the project, ironically, are central to it in their very limitations, and speak to both the development of Cassavetes' jazz cinema and Mingus' own subsequent work. Mingus was both the worst and best possible choice for Cassavetes' musical partner.

Sorting through the deceptive surfaces and deeper substance of *Shadows* is essential to understanding both the work itself and its truly revolutionary making. The film's most potent achievements are reflected in the odd collaboration of Mingus and Cassavetes, two of the century's most riveting American artists; a surprisingly unchronicled collision of dynamic forces that was outwardly a fiasco, yet nonetheless yielded a masterpiece.

Shadows and Masks

Despite his early association with jazz and the Beat movement, John Cassavetes was more truly a product of the theater world than anything else. *Shadows* had an incendiary dramatic agenda that's hard to fully understand today. The Cassavetes/Lane acting workshops were in part a direct response to and negation of Lee Strasberg's Actors Studio strand of Stanislavski's Method acting, which was then taking the nation by storm. Cassavetes and Lane particularly disliked the group critiques advocated by Strasberg. Cassavetes specifically pushed the actors to go beyond the "effective memory" technique (the most publicized component of the Method), and personally *create* their characters, primarily through improvisation—often using their own names. The participants then refined their parts in continued workshop development under his guidance.

The film's content was of course also transgressive for the time: an intensely earnest exploration of race relations. The twin rebellions of dramatic method and social content were to synthesize in what Cassavetes saw as the first "off-Broadway" film.

Yet his rebellion was ultimately his own, and quite distinct from the theatrical, cinematic or jazz avant-gardes as they're understood today. Tom Charity has noted that many filmmakers in the experimental tradition better fit the "beat" billing than Cassavetes, and his relationship to jazz was more aspirational than immediate. His actual concerns were more personal. The strength of *Shadows* lies not in the documentary accuracy of its portrayal of the bohemian jazz scene, but in the depth of its characters.

A brief glance at the role of the performing arts in Cassavetes' later films illuminates the dynamic. The white jazz musicians' problems in *Too Late Blues* (1961) serve as stand-in for the director's own artistic battles at the time of its making.[6] *Faces* (1968) is ostensibly set in a film production milieu that's absent after the first scene, and is ultimately a critique of the middle class. By *The Killing of a Chinese Bookie* (1976), the performance backdrop has transformed to the seedy underbelly of burlesque nightclubs. With *Opening Night* (1977), he at last openly explored his years in the theater with Gena Rowlands. Jazz was neither a life commitment nor portrait subject, but more arguably, a loved model for his own creative and social struggles.[7]

Cassavetes had claimed that at the time of making *Shadows*, he "wanted to be a black man, because it would be something so definite and the challenge would be greater than being a white man."[8] This impulse manifested most clearly in the character played by Ben Carruthers. In his own life Carruthers romanticized the jazz life, perhaps in part because he played no instrument. There's a famous photo of him in front of Birdland by photographer William Claxton. While very striking, the image reveals his discomfort with the saxophone he's holding; a discomfort also evidenced with the trumpet he carries in the film.[9] Carruthers genuinely reflects both his and Cassavetes' fascination with African-American life more than jazz itself.

In an ironic twist that's gone virtually unnoticed, the story's literal subject of blacks passing for whites is in fact mirrored in the film's making, wherein white actors actually passed for black. While Ben Carruthers was one eighth black, Lelia Goldoni was Sicilian, with no black heritage. In a modern echo of blackface, Carruthers used a sunlamp at the time of the initial shoot. To quote Carney, "when Hugh said that nobody would believe Lelia was his sister, (Cassavetes) replied, 'We'll let the audience worry about the mother and father.'" To a later query by Goldoni he said, "if they can believe it even for a second, maybe they'll start asking what being Negro means and start thinking about the whole concept."[10]

Figure 2. Ben Carruthers, "Birdland, 4 am, New York City, 1960," by William Claxton.

In fact he was right, as the very fact of its pretense embodied the theme of the film. *Shadows* is more accurately a portrait of confused identity than of the jazz/beat underground of 1950s New York. Blacks want to be white and whites want to be black; shadows are sibling to light.

While at a textual level the film speaks to a black desire for social acceptance, at a subtextual level it speaks of white envy for precisely that desire: the black American's life-affirming struggles of the era.[11] In this sense, *Shadows* is the filmic embodiment of Norman Mailer's controversial essay "The White Negro," written the very year of *Shadows*' initial shooting. Mailer famously romanticized the black American experience, and specifically jazz, as the cultural model for the hipster and Beat generation.[12]

It is this characteristic tension between the film's text and subtext that fuels the film. Race inversion and its attendant identity issues are both literally and formally a theme. The film's original negative editing leaders are inscribed with the now-forgotten working title *Screen-Shadows*, reminding one that cinema itself is a shadow-play, wherein the film stock's dark areas shadow the screen from the light of the projector's beam.[13] The racially ironic casting adds a further level.

In an odd testament to the strategy's success, Goldoni, who gives one of the film's most electrifying performances, had difficulties getting parts in subsequent years. She couldn't get white roles because she was believed to be black, and couldn't get black roles because she was too light-skinned.

The film's naturalist spin on blackface represents a significant transformation from the days of minstrelsy, in that the odd mix of envy and fear many whites held for blacks no longer needed to be masked in parody or stereotype. Masked, yes, in that the plot inverts the race/class aspirations that underline it, but a deeply humanist masking—as the film's title suggests. (Cassavetes said the name initially came from a charcoal sketch by one of the actors.)

Masks are themselves a theme, appearing in the crucial bedroom scene between Tony Ray and Lelia Goldoni as well as the scene at the Met or "the Margarine." The theme is carried further in Cassavetes' second, and only other 16mm production, *Faces*, which is in many ways a bourgeois companion piece to *Shadows*.

Cassavetes' studio partner Burt Lane believed that "personality masks" and their attendant unveiling were central to dramatic conflict, and this is apparent in both the race/identity questioning of *Shadows*, and the sexual/power struggles in *Faces*. Ray Carney points out that much of Cassavetes' dramaturgy in this area is directly indebted to Lane. In this sense, Cassavetes' very ideology is itself a mask or front, as much as the jazz trappings of his first film.

○   ○   ○

Charles Mingus was spearheading his own musical revolution at the precise moment of *Shadows*' making. An innovator in multiple forms like Duke Ellington, he was then leading a rotating ensemble called the Charles Mingus Jazz Workshop. Like Cassavetes, Mingus took mostly unknown artists and crafted an environment that gave extraordinary freedom to the participants, encouraging them to explore their own impulses and vision to an unprecedented degree. The similarities between the respective workshops of Mingus and Cassavetes are unmistakable.

In a representative description of his methodology, an anonymous Duke University website author claims that Mingus' unique approach to the bass—to be described more fully later—"by nature, leads to improvisation which, at the time, was frowned upon by many critics." Claiming that improvisation was nothing more than "spontaneous composition," Mingus refused to allow the critics to detract from his art and often encouraged instinctual playing."[14] Some of the biggest names in 1960s avant-garde jazz, including both Eric Dolphy and Rahsaan Roland Kirk, cut their teeth in Mingus' Workshops, which were jokingly called "sweatshops."

In other respects, Cassavetes and Mingus were complementary rather than similar. While *Shadows*' great emotional and personal authenticity does not quite extend to its outward depiction of the jazz/beat milieu, and Cassavetes' relation to the race issue was one of aspiration—Charles Mingus' connection was more than immediate. Mingus was a seething mixture of genius and fury, outspoken on issues of ethnicity and racism. In his autobiography, written in a unique form of third person (as both narrator and subject, part of a tripartite literary persona), he writes of his teen years:

Watts had its own pecking order like any average American community of working Negroes still too busy slaving as free men to evaluate themselves and their true position in society. Some of the fellows, three, four, five years older, selected Charles as the underdog because, well, he was kind of a mongrel, lighter than some but not light enough to belong to the almost-white elite and not dark enough to belong to the beautiful elegant blacks, the kind that make a man like Bud Powell say to Miles Davis, "I wish I was blacker than you." There really was no skin color exactly like his.

and:

Whenever he looked in the mirror and asked, "What am I?" he thought he could see any number of strains—Indian, African, Mexican, Asian and a certain amount of white from a source his father had boasted of. He wanted to be one or the other but he was a little of everything, wholly nothing, of no race, country, flag, or friend.[15]

This unique blend was to simmer inside Mingus his whole life. His music directly confronted race issues, as reflected in the titles of such works as "Prayer For Passive Resistance," "Free Cell Block F, 'Tis Nazi USA," and most famously, in the classic "Fables of Faubus."

He was legendary for his anger and prone to violent incidents; even known to punch out his fellow musicians. But his emotional range was far wider than his fiery reputation. Gary Giddins notes that "Mingus *was* the black-music experience in the United States—in its hybridization, its questing after form, its improvisation, competitiveness, impertinence, outrage, intellectualization, joy, emotionalism, bitterness, comedy, parody, and frustration."[16] *Shadows* would present a chance for him to vent his rage and vision in a new medium.

The Recording

As with all things Cassavetes, the stories surrounding the collaboration with Mingus on the film's score aren't completely consistent. It's best pieced together from several different accounts.

In 1957, Cassavetes, a rising young actor, appeared on New York radio host Jean Shepherd's program, *Night People*. Cassavetes described the acting workshops he was leading, which included a riveting improvisation on an interracial romance. He then launched into an impassioned plea for a new American cinema art; one based on actual life rather than Hollywood artifice. The next morning—so the legend goes—the program's listeners began showing up at the workshop, bringing money and volunteering to help. *Shadows* was born, and with it, the modern independent cinema movement.

Figure 3. from the opening credit sequence (still frame)

According to Mingus,[17] Jean Shepherd held a poll of his *Night People* listeners to see who they'd like to score the film, and he was picked. Shepherd had worked on Mingus' 1957 album *The Clown*, in which he improvised a story over Mingus' music for the record's title track. It wasn't Mingus' only spoken word piece of the era. He'd worked with several poets including both Langston Hughes and Kenneth Patchen around the time of the *Shadows* session.

Marshall Fine cites photographer Sam Shaw as the literal link between Mingus and Cassavetes,[18] but Shepherd was clearly a vital factor in that he also represented an aesthetic bridge between their improvisational and rebellious worlds. Shepherd was (not unaffectionately) described in Nat Hentoff's liner notes to *The Clown* as "a New York radio bard whose free-association stands on WOR have enlisted behind him a growing legion of 'night people' who profess vehement non-conformism with 'day people' but manage to be quite conformist within their rebelliousness."[19] Well before *Shadows*, he was improvising stories of unchronicled aspects of American life, often accompanied by cackles, kazoo, and percussion rapped out with his knuckles.

While coming from completely different places, both Cassavetes and Mingus were Night People, and their collaboration is ultimately a direct manifestation of not just their vision, but in a sense, Shepherd's. The film's opening titles read, in a symbolic gesture to the world from which it arose, "Presented by Jean Shepherd's Night People."

Cassavetes, for his part, said he'd originally wanted Miles Davis to score the film, but had decided against it when Davis signed with Columbia Records.[20] As a novice director, Cassavetes would be in for a challenge with either one of these two legendary personalities — but one has to give him credit for trying. He takes up the story here:

> Someone said there was this great improvisational artist down in the Village who'd cut a few records, so I listened to a couple and *oh!*—this guy was wonderful! Charlie Mingus. So Charlie said, "Listen, man, would you do me a favor? I'll do it for you, but you have got to do something for me."
> "Sure, sure," I say.
> "Listen, I've got these cats that are shitting all over the floor. Can you have a couple of your people come up and clean the cat shit? I can't work; they shit all over my music."
> So we went up with scrubbing brushes and cleaned up the thing. Now he says, "I can't work in this place. It's so clean. I've got to wait for the cats to shit."[21]

Whether Mingus was just playing games with him isn't clear. For at the same time, Mingus was taking the score quite seriously.[22]

At the time of the Workshops and *Shadows*' conception, in 1957, Mingus was at the center of the New York jazz/beat underground. A bridge between the bebop of Charlie Parker and the experimental jazz to emerge more fully in the next decade, his ensembles were among the most influential of the era.

If Mingus had unmet aspirations, they would only seem to be toward more "established" music and large-scale works approaching the classical tradition.[23] Alongside his intense involvement in pushing the limits of jazz improv, he had studied double bass and composition for years with the esteemed Herman Rheinshagen and Lloyd Reese.[24] As Mingus told *Down Beat* magazine:

> I have a melody in my head. I know what I'm going to do before I do it. I hear all the voicings: trumpet, saxes, all of them... If there's a trombone next to the baritone half a step away, I hear it. I have a symphony in my head all the time.[25]

Yet he had practical difficulties fully realizing his compositional vision during his lifetime. His most ambitious foray into this area was the ill-fated Town Hall Concert of 1962. Mingus feuded bitterly with the event's producer, George Wein, who planned the evening as a traditional performance. Mingus was writing the music up until the last moment, and pictured a recording session with frequent stops and starts. The resulting event was in many ways a debacle, with Mingus working hard to seemingly sabotage his own success.[26] It was only after his death that its accomplishment was truly realized.[27]

It is from this context—aspiration toward acceptance in the classical canon—that Mingus was to approach *Shadows*. His biographer, Brian Priestley, indeed describes Mingus' attraction toward working on such a "prestigious venture."[28] Cassavetes notes that "When Charlie looked at part of the film on the Moviola, he said, 'It's going to take me a long time, you know. I went to Julliard.'"[29] But in this case as well, there were cross-impulses at work.

Cassavetes, in love with the idea of a jazz improvised score, booked what he apparently thought was a lot of time to record—a double session, "three hours, with a projectionist."[30] The date was set for May 20, 1958, when they were in post-production on the first version of the film.

Mingus had other ideas. In an act of supreme irony, he chose to carefully compose every note of Cassavetes' off-the-cuff score. The irony is only heightened by Cassavetes' violent opposition to the controlling Hollywood studios, who were threatened precisely by the improvisational aspects of jazz. Whereas Cassavetes' race and class aspirations led to his attraction to jazz as a spontaneous "outsider" form, the composer he hired was conversely aspiring directly toward a fixed structure he rebelled against.

Both artists might here be seen contributing to what Erving Goffman called "deminstrelization," wherein an individual—of any race—concertedly aims to "show that the set of behavioral expectations held for him are the very ones which do not apply to him."[31] This should by no means be seen as defining or limiting—it's part of what drove their respective geniuses.

Yet Giddins notes that Cassavetes didn't appreciate the irony,[32] with good reason. As with the Town Hall concert, Mingus never finished the score, or for that matter even came close. To resume the story, Mingus showed up at the session with what Cassavetes said was about fourteen seconds' worth of music. Brian Case reveals that in their 1984 *Wire* interview, a seemingly snide Cassavetes "grinned at the recollection of Mingus and his retinue (arriving)—the jazz patroness Baroness Nica de Koenigswarter on one arm, a string of foxes on the other, the confused and brow-beaten members of the Mingus Workshop trailing reluctantly behind. And there were the standard Mingus death threats and tears." In the same interview, however, he notes, "(Mingus)… did all the copying and carried all the instruments there."[33]

The session eventually began, with the score that existed. Said Cassavetes:

> Everybody's saying, 'Why don't you just tell Charlie to improvise?' Then all the advice starts. So I said, "Come on, Charlie. You guys can improvise, you're wonderful, you can do that off the themes that you have." "No, man—can't do it! Can't do it! We're artists. It's gotta be written."[34]

According to trombonist Jimmy Knepper:

> It came out very stiff 'cause it was written so precisely—it was all eighth-note triplets and sixteenth-note triplets—and they wanted to record all the music in one date. But we took so long over this one tune that it never did get finished.[35]

Figures 4—5. the recording. Photos by Marvin Lichtner

Echoing the reviled Hollywood studios' arguments against jazz players, Cassavetes claimed the musicians couldn't read the music anyway, and described saxist Shafi Hadi blowing his instrument in frustration, casting furtive glances at Mingus.[35]

The question arises as to how exactly Mingus *could* have written such an intricate score as he envisioned, as even for the initial sequences he would have been without a film reference while writing. Video of course didn't exist, and Cassavetes would have had the only film workprint. At most, Mingus could have occasionally visited Cassavetes and producer/editor Maurice McEndree as they were cutting, and seen excerpts on the Moviola.

According to Gene Santoro, Mingus had "visited the set, talked with the director and actors, and composed motifs. Cassavetes left him to do what he wanted."[37] Cassavetes described Mingus' comprehensive vision during production and noted, "The minute he saw the film, he could see the rhythms of the city… pick them up and play Ben Carruthers on the street."[38]

Figures 6—8. Center: Mingus with Phineas Newborn Jr. Photos by Marvin Lichtner.

Figure 9. Dannie Richmond and Mingus. Photo by Marvin Lichtner.

But irrespective of what Mingus saw or how he saw it, there would be no practical way to sync music and picture until recording, so it's little wonder the result was incomplete. The low-budget nature and limited resources of the independent shoot distinguish it sharply from studio-produced jazz scores of the era, and in effect, led directly to a *need* to improvise.[39]

According to Cassavetes, when push came to shove, they played a part of what Mingus had written and improvised the rest. "Charlie was the conductor from the bass… In the end, everybody was doing everything. Charlie sang… played some piano, and Phineas Newborn, Jr. took over the bass."[40] Santoro adds that Mingus and drummer Dannie Richmond recorded effects separately.[41] They somehow got through the session. The musicians were paid about twenty dollars apiece for their work.[42]

The session's progression from fiasco to completion was in effect an exercise in disaster salvation, and ultimately typical of both artists. Its very failure led to spontaneous solutions. Summarizing the dynamic at play in Mingus' working process, Cassavetes said, "He was always torn between the two—the mathematical beauty of the composition and the freedom of improvisation."[43] What Cassavetes saw so clearly in the score to *Shadows* was to in fact describe much of Mingus' larger oeuvre. And in describing it thusly, Cassavetes perhaps also spoke unconsciously of himself.

Figures 10–11. Cassavetes and Mingus. Photos by Marvin Lichtner.
Courtesy of Marvin Lichtner and the Cinema Museum.

The First Cut

That the two men indeed reached a compromise is clear, as there are several Mingus cues in the film's final version, and apparently many more in the first. It has only recently become possible to get even a sense of the results. Ray Carney discovered a copy of Cassavetes' long-lost original edit of *Shadows*, and presented it publicly at the Rotterdam Film Festival in January 2004. After just two public screenings it's now unavailable once again due to legal disputes.[44] Fortunately Jonathan Rosenbaum was at the Rotterdam screening and has written a detailed account, claiming the Mingus score is one of the version's most experimental aspects.[45]

What was the initial collaboration like? Both Carney and Rosenbaum mention a muted trumpet mimicking speech sounds over Tony Ray's phone call scene, which appears quite differently in the later work. Rosenbaum cites Mingus' singing "Leaning on the Everlasting Arms" at one point, which corroborates Cassavetes' own account.[46] In another piece, for FIPRESCI, Rosenbaum further mentions "a highly fragmented approach that mixes brief, selected passages from a wide range of instruments, musicians, and arrangements."[47]

The description indeed bears resemblance to much of Mingus' music, particularly from the mid-to-late 1950s, and is instructive in understanding the affinity of his oeuvre to dramatic works. The previously mentioned Duke University website nicely summarizes this, saying Mingus "deliberately incorporated a variety of different styles into his unique sound. His approach to his instrument (pioneered by Duke Ellington and bassist Jimmy Blanton) was centered around the idea that the bass deserved equal footing with the other lead instruments. This idea led to a single-line vocalic sense of attack which is often referred to as the 'conversational approach.'"[48] Rosenbaum correctly notes this reached its peak in Mingus' collaborations with Eric Dolphy. Said Mingus:

> See, in bebop... aside from chord changes and patterns and lines... there was another expression on the bandstand that was called "conversation." That is the only thing that developed with Eric *past* (not *better* than) Bird... We used to really talk and say words with our instruments... We had different "conversations," we'd discuss our fear, our life, our views of God—which is still the main subject today.[49]

Rosenbaum's account of the use of varied styles is borne out in several fragments of the first version which Ray Carney has posted on his website, www.cassavetes.com. One excerpt is from the film's opening title sequence and features a short montage of music cues, ranging from a lush arrangement with cello and flute, to a romantic piano solo, to a dynamic excerpt of "Nostalgia in Times Square" which remains in the film's final version. The cues, which appear here over scenes of the characters wandering around the city, comprise a kind of overture. The use of varied styles is also evident in the brief segments appearing in the film's trailer.[50]

Carney's site also posts an unexpected clip: a scene of David Pokotilow meeting Benny and his friends after Lelia and Tony Ray abandon him in Central Park. The underlying music is in fact Mingus' later classic "Wednesday Night Prayer Meeting." Its appearance in *Shadows* before any released recordings of the song does not necessarily suggest it was written for the film.[51] Rather, its inclusion seems more likely to have been an on-the-spot decision. Mingus would have then pulled from existing or in-development material and improvised as appropriate. The mere act of choice involved can be seen as its own form of improv.

"Wednesday Night Prayer Meeting" in particular doesn't seem to have a specific connection to the scene it plays under, raising the question of whether its actual placement was an in-the-moment decision by Mingus or a subsequent editorial decision by Cassavetes. A close listen to the cue suggests the latter, as there appears to be a fade-out in the middle of a drum solo and then an abrupt edit as the main theme re-enters at the scene's conclusion. Both scenarios have their own implications toward improvisational methodology—performative in the case of Mingus, and editorially in the case of Cassavetes.

Intriguingly, it appears that both forces were at play. The answers lie in the session's recording tapes, which still exist in varying forms but are not easily accessible.[52] The tapes reveal that despite the legend of Mingus' "fourteen seconds" of music, significantly more was recorded. A close analysis of the tapes, in juxtaposition with the edited versions of the film, shows that both artists were ultimately navigating a hybrid space between composition and improvisation. The main title "overture" was in fact created entirely in the editing, and the "Wednesday Night Prayer Meeting" usage was also edited by Cassavetes. Both appeared quite differently in the first version than they did when the music was actually recorded.[53]

Throughout the tapes, one hears intense negotiation of specific cue recordings, mixed up occasionally with more extended takes that appear to be improvisational. The tapes, in all their roughness, reveal in microcosm a template for creation that was to color not only subsequent work on the film, but in fact much of Cassavetes' and Mingus' later oeuvres.

Visions and Versions

Regardless of how the film's recording session unfolded, and its arguable practical success (in that the music was at least recorded), both Mingus and Cassavetes seemed disgruntled with the experience, and subsequently moved in other directions. Both spoke relatively little of the collaboration. Mingus' initial *Shadows* experiments, including those with both mimicked speech and shifting ensemble methodologies, will be seen to be one step in the continuing evolution of his art. Cassavetes also refined his vision substantially after the initial cut of the film.

What happened between the two versions? Just as Mingus, a consummate improviser, had found improv not suited to his conception of the score; so did the disastrous Paris Theater screenings cause Cassavetes to further clarify his own improvisatory vision and working methods. He went back and reshot much of the story, according to Ray Carney, with carefully scripted new sequences.

He also omitted and recontextualized scenes from the original, modifying the film to such an extent that essential plot points and their effective meanings were entirely transformed. Both the act of scripting and the process of editorial revision were to become crucial components of Cassavetes' later methodological development.

In the process of revising *Shadows*, much of Mingus' music was apparently omitted from the film. When Cassavetes wanted to rescore the new cut, he said, Mingus was in Tijuana. Cassavetes instead approached the original session's tenor sax player, Shafi Hadi, who was more than happy to improv sax solos for the soundtrack.[54] Drummer Dannie Richmond accompanied Hadi on a number of takes. There are some wonderful photos by Marvin Lichtner of an ecstatic Cassavetes gesticulating like a madman, guiding and almost conducting Hadi through the recording.

In striking contrast, Lichtner's photos of Cassavetes and Mingus on the earlier date suggest the tension of their quite different relationship. The two men are sizing each other up, almost like boxers squaring off in a prizefight. Mingus stated, "Cassavetes thought you did a score in one day. He used my name but couldn't play my music."[55]

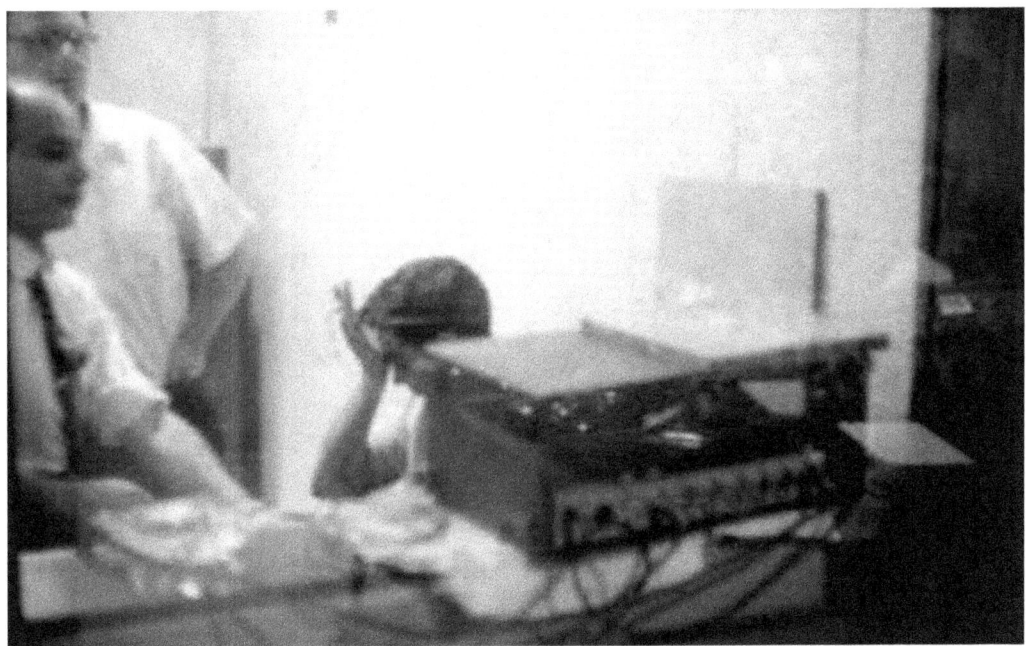

Figure 12. the mix. Photo by Marvin Lichtner.

What one hears in the finished film are in effect three scores alternating: one of Mingus fragments, one of Hadi sax solos, and a third by Cassavetes' friend Jack Ackerman, who wrote the nightclub and dancehall music one hears repeated in the film—including "A Real Mad Chick (is like an ice cream cone)," dropped over Irving Berlin's "A Pretty Girl is Like a Melody." The resulting assemblage is a key component of the "collage" nature of the film, which also encompasses the previously mentioned narrative and continuity gaps arising from the two shooting periods. Without a doubt the Mingus fragments are the most effective and powerful component of the film's soundtrack.[56]

The question arises however, as to which have been recontextualized from their initial recording. A scene featuring both artists at their best illuminates the question and is worthy of extended analysis. The party in the siblings' flat appears in each of the two versions, runs approximately five minutes, and uses music continuously throughout: the longest stretch of music in the film. Although it appears to be one extended cue, there are brief moments where it drops out, and other subtleties appear in the mix that reveal a true integration of sound and image.

Figure 13. the second recording: Dannie Richmond, Cassavetes, Shafi Hadi. Photo by Marvin Lichtner.

Figure 14. the second recording: Cassavetes and Hadi. Photo by Marvin Lichtner.

The scene commences with Lelia's introduction to Davey Jones. The underlying cue is classic ebullient Mingus: a chaotic mix of catcalls, shouts, percussive effects, bells, and a variety of whistles—but without a driving bass line to provide continuity. It almost suggests an informal band is goofing around at the party, as Mingus' screams sound like a partygoer's. Yet amidst the chaos, a flute solo evokes a more personal and intimate tone, in sympathy with the drama of Lelia's encounter.

An abrupt sound edit occurs at David Pokotilow's entrance to the room, when a burst of party noise indicates a shift of direction. The music cue seems to be edited as well, perhaps to a different portion of the same take. Underneath the party noise the drums kick in more prominently, heightening the celebratory hubbub as the viewer is broken out of Lelia's corner of the apartment. Then the din recedes as Pokotilow reaches Lelia and the interlude concludes. The flute, which had continued quietly throughout, now rises back to prominence, returning the film's focus to one of personal interchange. The drums in turn withdraw to the background.

Upon Pokotilow's exit there is another glimpse of the party, accompanied by a brief fade-out of the score which prefigures the next significant tonal change in the scene. The percussion almost immediately resumes, accompanied by an occasional swirling flute. Cassavetes cuts to Carruthers sulking in isolation. The levels of the tense yet oddly drifting cue subtly rise and fall, in and out, perfectly drawing the moment as Ben sits in an alienated funk, observing Hugh's African-American friends, and ultimately, rudely rejecting the advances of a young woman.

At the scene's pivotal moment the music drops out entirely, allowing the viewer—for the first time in the entire sequence—to focus solely on the dialogue. The woman tells Ben, "You're not kidding anyone but yourself... Your sense of values are all mixed up." Ben's response—a hostile shove—is accompanied by a piercing scream from Mingus, breaking the tension. An anarchic, raging crescendo occurs as the woman throws her drink at Ben, and a fight with Hugh explodes. The music raises the siblings' quarrel to one of the film's most dramatic moments; the only in which the contained emotions of the race issue are allowed to burst out fully.

In analyzing the extended scene, several things emerge. Unlike the previously mentioned "Wednesday Night Prayer Meeting," this cue was very clearly intended by Mingus to accompany the action with which it appears. Yet the resulting emotional and dynamic range of the music is so symbiotic with the picture that it's entirely impossible to determine how much is a result of sound editing and mixing, and how much occurred in the initial recording. Herein is seen the vast potential of what *Shadows* might have been, in more ideal circumstances. The moment the cue ends, the heightened emotions of the actors lose a level of depth as the scene continues, though still effectively. In fact the abrupt closure of the score allows an enraged scream to place a small exclamation point on the fight.

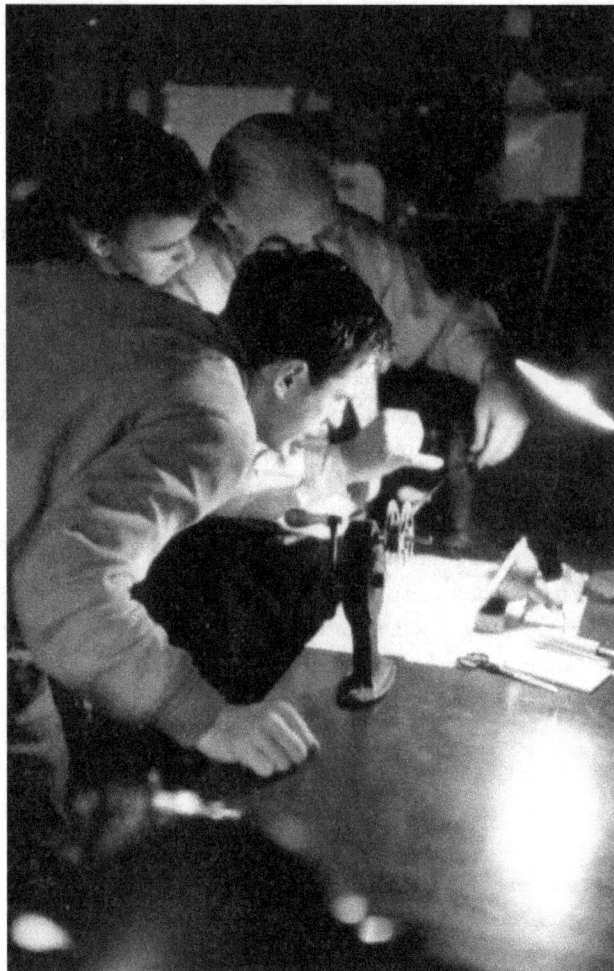

Figure 15. at the editing bench. Photo by Marvin Lichtner.

Another key cue has been overtly recontextualized—to a subtle and startling effect. It's a sparse drum rhythm that extends for just a few seconds. The first time it appears is in the scene between Lelia and Tony, just before they enter his apartment. It's the moment at which Lelia decides to sleep with him, and the rhythm, in its underscored urgency, suggests a quickening heartbeat as the stakes of their relationship suddenly rise drastically. The scene was filmed in the 1959 reshoot, and Cassavetes' brilliant placement of the cue sets up the fall in which Tony realizes his girlfriend is partially black.

The connection is made apparent by the second, later use of the cue, when the scene is reversed, and Tony enters Lelia's apartment to "apologize" for his racist response to his discovery. This scene used footage from both 1957 and 1959. In each of the two scenes, the music echoes a confrontation of one's greatest fears, yet in a way that's so understated it's barely noticed. Cassavetes' after-the-fact reuse of the cue (paralleled in his recycling of Ackerman's "Beautiful" in other parts of the film) is at once a maximization of limited materials and a structural device, unplanned by either artist at the time of the recording. It illustrates Cassavetes' particular genius for salvaging gold from scraps.

○ ○ ○

While Cassavetes continued developing the film well after the 1958 recording session, so did Mingus continue developing his score. A few songs in Mingus' repertoire grew out of it. A fragment of "Nostalgia in Times Square" is heard briefly before the fight in the alley, near the film's end in the final version. "Nostalgia" was eventually revised yet further, into "Strollin," with lyrics by Nat Gordon apparently influenced by the film.[57]

Another song associated with *Shadows* is "Alice's Wonderland." Both "Nostalgia" and "Alice's" were recorded in full on January 16, 1959. "Alice's," however, appears in neither version of the film. Nat Hentoff notes that "Mingus wanted to write for the love scene under which the music would have been played, and so he wrote a continuation of the score for himself."[58] The only scene in the final film that "Alice's Wonderland" would seem to fit is Lelia's dance with Davey Jones.[59] When synchronized, the effect is surprisingly stunning—adding a depth absent in the actual film (one of the aforementioned uses of Ackerman's "Beautiful"[60]).

As the scene in question may have been part of the reshoot, the synchronization exercise is academic; however it's instructive to read Mingus' own description of the piece and learn just how apropos it is. Saying the song "may be the prettiest thing I ever wrote," he goes on to describe it as a portrait of

> a girl trying to make it in this big, rough world, like I am. I try to show her sadness (the alto on top) but also her strength in her art and in her conviction in what she believes in (the tenor on the bottom) even if there are still harsh, unresolved parts of her life.[61]

Ray Carney has noted Cassavetes' attempt to have each character in the film have an epiphany, and the scene with Davey, Lelia's last, is clearly that. Mingus' unused cue draws the character perfectly.

Mingus later modified "Alice" as well. He renamed it "Diane," after Diane Dorr-Dorynek, his then-girlfriend and assistant, who perhaps also inspired his interpretation of Lelia Goldoni's screen character.[62] "Diane" additionally integrated aspects of "Self-Portrait in Three Colors," from *Ah Um*, Mingus' classic first Columbia album (performed by many of the same Workshop members present at the *Shadows* sessions), and which Dorr-Dorynek described as *Shadows*' "theme song."[63] Mingus' renaming of both *Shadows* songs, while consistent with a life of reinvention and revision, nonetheless suggests a distancing from an aborted collaboration.

The Cinema of Improvisation

Shafi Hadi's solos may be the only "traditional" improvs in the final version of *Shadows*, wholly made in the moment. But on closer analysis, they accompany primarily minor scenes.[64] In point of fact it's quite another dimension of the film that illuminates its revolutionary character, as well as ultimately, its connection to jazz. *Shadows* is not a film about jazz, it embodies it.

Even the supposedly improvised scenes from the initial workshops were clearly rehearsed by the time of filming. Their iteration changed, but their essence was established. Much of the dialogue was later redubbed. Revealingly, Cassavetes left in the famous end card which read, "The film you have just seen was an improvisation. " It *was* an improvisation—past tense.

This is most clear in the crucial confrontation between Tony Ray and Hugh Hurd in the door of the siblings' apartment, which clearly has the actors repeating lines developed through a rehearsal process. This was the exact workshop scene highlighted in Shepherd's radio broadcast. Despite the reworking, it remains a powerful scene and suggests the dynamism and rawness of the original concept. This dynamic of vital revision is at the core of Cassavetes' later work.

His great art was more truthfully that of finding the *spontaneity* of improv within a rehearsed or scripted form. Tom Charity, for example, has emphasized the improvisation of movement rather than text as being a central aspect of Cassavetes' art.[65] To quote Lelia Goldoni, the goal of their acting was to "respond to the given circumstances in the present moment of time."[66]

But Cassavetes was also a master of myth. The title card, which helped create the *Shadows* legend, stands as a testament to our love of that mythology more than truth itself. It created a legend, and in so doing threw many critics off the mark in their understanding of the film's artistry and its connection to jazz.

The collaboration of Mingus and Cassavetes on what's arguably the most famous beat or jazz film illuminates a fine point about the nature of improvisation. Theatrical improv is by common definition unscripted, with the performers determining the course of action as they go. Musical improvisation, at least pre-free jazz, tends to operate within some predetermined guidelines—like an existing song's harmonic structure, to pick an example in the western tradition.

That's ultimately much closer to Cassavetes' working methodology. He would give his actors actions, a story arc, or words, and then let them go. Cassavetes famously told his actors that they had to "own" their parts. But although the performances may have belonged to the cast, the scenarios were largely his.

Cassavetes, describing his eventual refinement of the process in *Faces*, said,

> The *emotion* was improvised. The lines were written. The *attitudes* were improvised. I give somebody some lines, and the interpretation must be their own.... Improvisation came into the film by permitting each actor to

interpret his role, rather than me interpreting the role as a director… As a technique, improvisation is useless. As a way to achieve an individuality in characterization, it's very, very constructive.[67]

This in turn points to Cassavetes' quarrels with the nature of authorship. Like jazz players taking a solo, Cassavetes' actors were highly individuated in the context of the work as a whole. He said:

[The performers] are like authors, because they create a character through their knowledge of people and their understanding of people…. I feel I'm gaining for the picture. There are more points of view than I could express.[68]

This is indeed the case. Cassavetes had originally conceived *Faces* as a bitter exposé of the empty lives of the middle class, yet he was first to observe that it was his cast who humanized his anger, through their love for their characters.

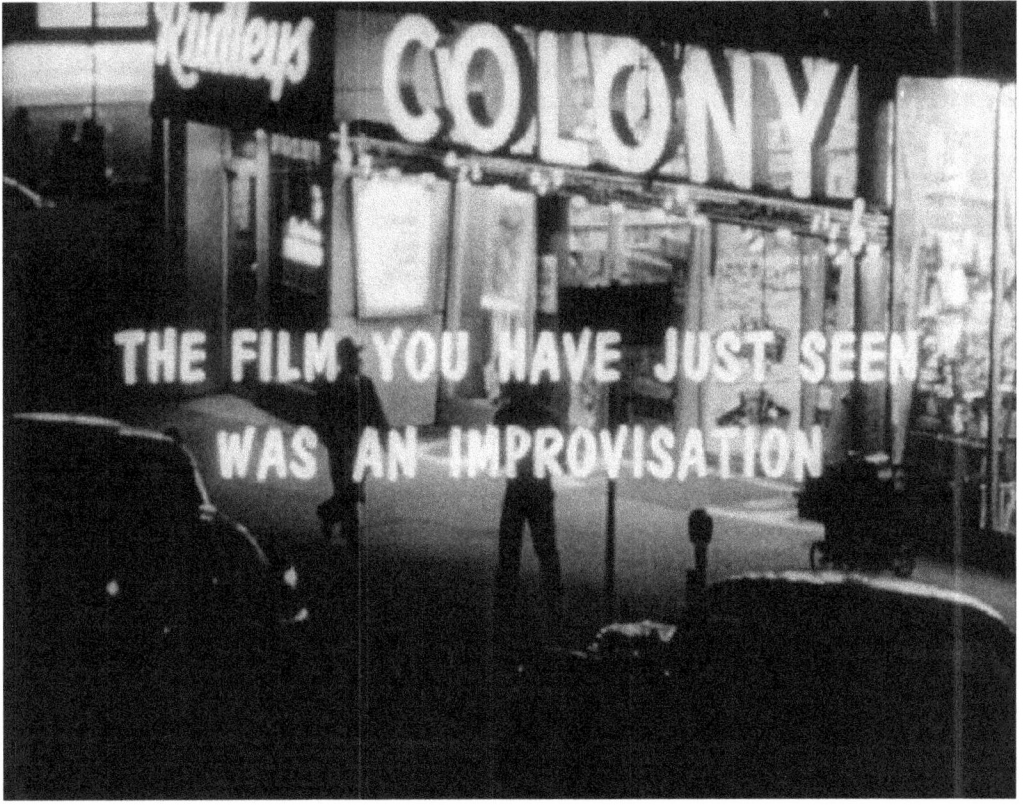

Figure 16. the end title card (still frame).

The technique reached its apotheosis in *Opening Night*, when he at last explored his life in the theater directly. *Opening Night* culminates in an extended play-within-a-film that at once destroys and revitalizes the script being performed. In what can be seen as the ultimate distillation of his dramaturgy, Cassavetes and Gena Rowlands very literally enact his methods and theories before a live audience and camera. The scene feels nothing like jazz, but is enabled precisely through an improvisatory ensemble method that echoes it.

Cassavetes' highly specific technique is ultimately reflective of a lifelong attempt to reconcile his theatrical experience with his cinematic vision. He remained a great innovator in working methods throughout his career, but the implicit conditions of improvisation—spontaneous creation—inherently argue with the nature of film, a recorded medium. Music of course can be recorded, and tape can "capture" a performance—but our very choice of verbs describing the task reveals much about the dynamic of recording an action. Once an improv has been recorded, its nature has been in essence transformed.

While much has been made of Cassavetes' work with directorial and performance methodology, it should be made clear that he was ultimately wrestling with the limitations of a "frozen" medium. He was notorious for recutting his films in multiple versions—not just *Shadows* but virtually all of his works. In the case of *Faces*, he initially intended each scene to be cut by a different editor. The sole existing print of a pre-release version of the film would seem to bear this out, with clear stylistic differences appearing between scenes.[69] The film's cinematographer, Al Ruban, eventually convinced Cassavetes that a single editorial voice was needed, and assembled the final version. The story is a clear example of Cassavetes' struggles with fixing a narrative down, and points to a quarrel with the limits of recorded media and authorship that extend beyond a film's performative aspect.

His arguments with the medium can ultimately be traced to his beginnings as a stage actor. The fluidity of live drama, with each performance of a work differing in iteration, is quite contrary to the fixed and lasting aspects of cinema. Yet he was to eventually bring an improvisatory performance-based spirit to the very process of editing.

One must specifically note the nature of Cassavetes' revision process. According to myth, the first version of *Shadows* was impressionistic, a free-floating artistic mood piece—and the subsequent release version was more coherent, more mainstream. Much of the myth is traceable in rough form to Jonas Mekas, who famously wrote of the first version's "breaks with made-up faces, with written scripts, with plot continuities," and described the final edit as "a bad commercial film, with everything that I was praising completely destroyed."[70] In point of fact, however, Cassavetes' final collage jumbled the narrative structure between the two drafts, disrupting a more-or-less coherent chronology in the 1957 version, creating numerous continuity lapses at both the scene and sequence levels in the 1959 version. Some of the many ruptured continuities include the rock club, money-borrowing, and fight scenes. A complete breakdown of the versions, allowing further analysis, appears as an appendix in Ray Carney's BFI Film Classics monograph on the film. Jonathan Rosenbaum also noted a "dogged obeisance to certain narrative conventions" in the initial cut.[71]

Faces is a further instance in which Cassavetes modified his initial chronology, from its form in the pre-release copy to a finished work that is a somewhat non-linear patchwork.[72] It should be noted that even the existing pre-release version of this film (there were in fact several others, which don't survive) was just another step in Cassavetes' revision process. *Faces* had originally been conceived as a two-act play, in which the first act was comprised of groups of men competing for the favor of a single woman, and the second act featured the reverse scenario. Hints of this structure still exist in the completed piece. In the case of both *Faces* and *Shadows* the project's evolution was from a coherent or defined structure to a more enigmatic one.

Cumulatively Cassavetes had an "improvisational" involvement throughout the creative process, extending well beyond the performative aspects of a work to encompass post-production, editing, and ultimately, the forming of "living" artworks. He would try to bring that freshness to all his films, by any means available to him, through a continuous struggle between twin poles of structure and spontaneity. And the elliptical narrative enigmas introduced in the editing often worked in balance with his gradual movement toward more tightly defined improvisations with his cast.

The final collaged score of *Shadows*, integrating the work of Hadi, Ackerman and Mingus, and the recontextualizing of numerous music cues as described, is an unheralded instance of Cassavetes' spontaneous methodology. In this sense, the act of editorial collage takes on an authentic jazz sensibility; an authenticity that is arguably absent in the film's outer fabric.

○   ○   ○

Mingus' own ambivalent relationship to improv has already been mentioned. But it went further. While he has on the one hand been celebrated exactly for his ability to inspire his collaborators into some of their most dynamic and memorable performances, even that aspect of his work isn't straightforward. Brian Priestley quotes saxist Jackie McLean describing Mingus as a controlling monster: "[he] was in the way so much, you couldn't play for it. The man'd stop your solos—he was totally tyrannical."[73]

In actuality Mingus' involvement with improvisation was, like Cassavetes', continually developing. By 1959—just shortly after the period described by McLean—Priestley notes that

> [his albums] with larger forces represent not only a major breakthrough in Mingus' own development but a complete break from the currently accepted methods of handling a seven-to-nine piece group. As in his attempted compositions for *Shadows*, it was axiomatic that such a group was really a miniature big band, and therefore had to be carefully structured and shrewdly orchestrated, but Mingus' method was now the trusted one of dictating lines for each player, and leaving structure and orchestration to arise spontaneously.[74]

For Mingus, the relationship between writing and performing was symbiotic. The anonymous website author writes that "even his style of composition favored improvisations for, after the mid-1950s, he rarely wrote down fully developed scores. Rather, he would sit at the piano and sing/hum melody lines and then allow his band members to expand on the line and contribute melodically, technically and perhaps most important to Mingus, personally."[75]

Mingus himself described the process in detail as it stood by 1959: "My present working methods use very little written material. I "write" compositions on mental score paper, then I lay out the composition part by part to the musicians. I play them the 'framework" on piano so that they are all familiar with my interpretation and feeling and with the scale and chord progressions to be used. Each man's particular style is taken into consideration. They are given different rows of notes to use against each chord but they choose their own notes and play them in their own style."[76]

The parallel to Cassavetes' unique brand of personalized yet guided theatrical improv is once again unmistakable. It's instructive to note that the key moment in his change of working method is exactly that of *Shadows*' making: 1957-1959. Conceivably, his frustrations with the film in part informed his shift at that time. His methodology was then shifting away from formal composition toward a process that gave him formal control within an improvisational context.[77]

Like Cassavetes, poles of freedom and structure were at the crux of Mingus' art, and his place between the poles was comparable. Paralleling Cassavetes' retreat from freeform improv, Mingus was initially resistant to free jazz and its apparent formlessness. In a legendary, perhaps apocryphal, encounter, he once sarcastically asked Ornette Coleman in what key he was playing, clearly expecting a non-answer. Coleman replied, "I think it's obvious it was C sharp, Charles." The conversation went downhill from there.[78]

Yet despite these examples of his favoring controlled form, it was none other than Mingus who helped lay the groundwork for free jazz. He was an early innovator of modal jazz, suspending traditional chord movement in his 1954 *Jazz Composer's Workshop* album, and developing the idiom further in his classic 1956 LP *Pithecanthropus Erectus*, which featured a section entirely without structure or theme.[79] The later *Charles Mingus Presents Charles Mingus* (1960) was in many ways a direct response to Ornette Coleman and the challenges of his music.

The connection of all this to *Shadows* is of no small importance, as it's this pivotal moment in jazz history which stands as backdrop to the film's making and release. Many consider the true emergence of free jazz to be November 1959, when Coleman began his legendary New York residency at the Five Spot in Greenwich Village—within days of the Cinema 16 premiere of the second version of Cassavetes' film on 24th Street, a few blocks away. It was during this residency that Mingus encountered Coleman.

The conflux of events was telling not just for Mingus and Cassavetes personally, but for their respective art forms. At the very same time, Jack Gelber's play *The Connection*, which featured jazz musicians playing on stage in character, was running at Julian Beck and Judith Malina's Living Theatre.[80] As Tom Charity observed, "improvisation was in the air."[81]

It was not simply in the air, but transforming rapidly. Just as Coleman and Mingus were wrestling with the limits of jazz, Cassavetes was in a completely different sense, doing the same with theatrical improvisation. In both cases formal structure was the axis, but the movements were in opposite directions. Jazz improv was loosening up, while Cassavetes' experiments with actors were in the process of tightening.

Tellingly, the 1960s saw theatrical performance move markedly toward the greater freedom allowed in its exercises, in the work of numerous groups including the Living Theatre. Their work in turn echoed a flourishing of the cinematic avant-garde, from which Cassavetes became increasingly disassociated. P. Adams Sitney's canonic *Visionary Film* chronicles the development of experimental cinema at this time as a movement away from experimental drama (or psychodrama) toward structuralism.[82] Cassavetes' innovations, while extremely daring, were conservative in comparison—revealing that his concerns lay more in the human theater and storytelling than experimentation itself. And Charles Mingus' deeply personal music was to follow a parallel path.

Mirrors

Some Cassavetes enthusiasts have felt threatened by factual challenges to the myth of his improvisations. They're merely following the wrong model. He did use improv, extensively, to create a breathtaking sense of spontaneity in film. His contribution, however, lay not in the making of improvised movies. It was to develop a uniquely jazz-inspired methodology.

His revolutionary contribution, as noted, was in fact a move toward a dramatic model that paralleled mid-50s jazz. Mingus was an ideal counterpart to Cassavetes in that he directly confronted the boundaries that Coleman extended, and consciously chose to retreat. As Brian Priestley noted, "Mingus' 1959-60 work had enabled him to discover that, for all he may have influenced the new avant-garde and enjoyed flirting with it, his allegiance to an overriding compositional form was far stronger."[83] Both Cassavetes and Mingus therein fit Nat Hentoff's dualistic description of Shepherd's Night People: "conformist within their rebelliousness."

Their genius flourished not so much in pure rebellion, as in disaster salvation. In the making of *Shadows*, their collaboration was itself just such a disaster: a case of two singularly minded artists vying for control. Mingus' arrival with an unfinished score, while infuriating Cassavetes, put him into the precise zone he needed to flourish: a zone of desperation that led to the brilliant music eventually recorded. Likewise Cassavetes, when faced with a catastrophic unveiling of the first version, essentially reinvented the movie and in the process, his subsequent methodology.

In this quite unexpected sense, the two did give birth to a unique jazz cinema. Cassavetes' later films, while mostly scripted, honed the basic techniques he originated in his first film, letting the actors improvisationally develop the scenes with a furious spontaneity steered by structures or texts. This improvisational approach extended even into post-production, through a collaged edit of *Shadows* that repurposed both dramatic scenes and music cues, and was paralleled by Mingus' continued revision of his own score.

Cassavetes' emphasis on the performer's personal contribution was also immediately analogous to jazz; particularly Mingus' brand of it. The ideology of the individual, which they both advocated, extended from the aesthetic to the political. Cassavetes claimed:

> All my pictures… are about individuals. That's the only thing I believe in… Groups can go fuck themselves. All of them. You know, a black to me is a black… when he's a person, he's a person… I don't care what title [they put] on—to me there's a name for each person.[84]

With its emphasis on solos, jazz, perhaps more than any other art form is an ensemble practice specifically integrating expression of the individual. This dynamic arguably peaked in the radical agenda and ensemble work of Charles Mingus. In the case of both Cassavetes and Mingus, the result of their methodology was a powerful ensemble exploration of the emotions of the players.[85]

Beyond its formal aspects, *Shadows* was consciously placed in a jazz milieu. This helped hide its true nature, for the film's New York jazz scene setting was in reality a working context for the more crucial exploration of race identity issues. Though Cassavetes' personal investment in those questions was fundamentally aspirational, the film succeeded on another level. For underneath its pretense, Mingus' participation lent the film a deep authenticity.

In the years after making *Shadows*, Cassavetes largely moved away from discussions of race, which he no longer felt to be as pressing. He said, reflecting on his earlier desire to be negro:

> Now, American black men are white men, so there's no challenge and I don't really wish to be that anymore. I don't know about other men's desires, but it is my desire to be an underdog, to win on a long shot, to gamble, to take chances.[86]

While both attitudes are distanced by the safety of his whiteness, they articulate the sentiment that made Cassavetes romanticize the black American's place in society. And they parallel Mingus' own very real struggles.[87] Beneath the mask of the film's plot—in Mingus' parts of the final "collaged" score—is a direct connection to Cassavetes' aspirational race and identity questioning. Mingus' life struggles, including his "upward" battle for the acceptance of large-scale jazz composition, are immediate reflections of the larger black experience of the era. They at once echo the film's story and invert the "downward" or "White Negro" impulses of Cassavetes.

Both men embody the era's fight for life, self-individuation, and identity. By a reductive analogy, they comprise two flip sides of Goffman's deminstrelization model. In the case of Cassavetes, the desire was escape from a stultifying white experience, in the case of Mingus, it was for a respect beyond any notions of race whatsoever. Their twin aspirations, mirrored in each other, lie at the heart of *Shadows*.

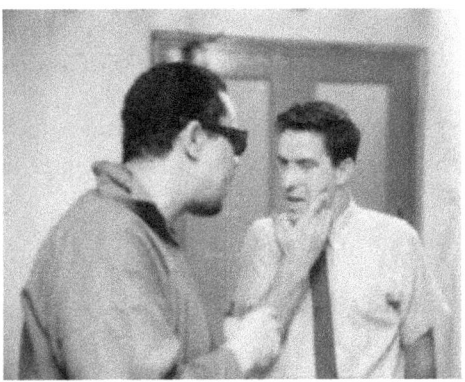

Figures 17–19. Cassavetes and Mingus. Photos by Marvin Lichtner.

For Mingus the challenges never disappeared. His autobiography describes his life's progress—again in third person:

> He fell in love with himself. 'Fuck all you pathetic prejudiced cocksuckers... I dig minds, inside and out. No race, no color, no sex. Don't show me no kind of skin 'cause I can see right through to the hate in your little undeveloped souls.'[88]

The book's title is, appropriately, a step further than Cassavetes: *Beneath the Underdog*. The collaboration, or non-collaboration, of Cassavetes and Mingus, is a study in alchemy. The two men couldn't work together, but along with a dynamic cast created a collage-like work that was far greater than the sum of its parts. If Mingus' technical role in the production was small, he's nonetheless at its core, for he bore in his life and music the validation of Cassavetes' themes.

Summarizing their collaboration, Cassavetes said:

> We had the same kind of artistic fury. We pretend we're loose and in the end we're dictators… I do think Charles was more of a structured person than I am. He lived in a very structured way even though he was a wild man… In other circumstances, and different times, I think he'd have been a classical musician and formal composer.[89]

In this light, their personal battles reflect a shared inner conflict that combusted on impact. The two in fact were like half-siblings in their disparate work within jazz and cinema. The self-claimed mongrel Mingus was Cassavetes' mirror—and his internal struggles between twin demons of spontaneous rage and formal control stoked the burning furnace of *Shadows*.

Endnotes

1. Jonas Mekas, *The Village Voice*, January 27, 1960, in *Movie Journal: The Rise of a New American Cinema* (Macmillan, 1972), 10.
2. Much of the audience walked out on the film. Cassavetes later described the evening as "absolutely disastrous," and amusingly added that "no one tried to phony up their reaction to it; one friend of mine patted me on the shoulder and said, "That's OK, John, you're still a good actor." Cassavetes, interview, *Playboy*, July, 1971, 70.
3. Amos Vogel, "The Cinema of Improvisation," Cinema 16 program notes, November 11, 1959, in Scott McDonald, *Cinema 16: Documents Toward a History of the Film Society* (Temple, 2002), 364.
4. Jazz, improv, and movies have of course been intertwined since cinema's inception, initially through improvised accompaniment to silent film, and an immediate transition to the sound era in the early Vitaphone programs. Yet while jazz-themed movies were prevalent, and original jazz-scored films date at least to the early 1950s, their level of authenticity is variable. Bud Shank, who played on Leith Stevens' score to *The Wild One* (1951)—considered by many to be the first completely jazz-scored film—felt that Stevens didn't have a true jazz background, and noted Shorty Rogers was brought in for the arrangements. In Shank's view, the studios opposed the use of actual jazz musicians, whom they thought couldn't read music, and insisted on studio orchestras. In the case of *The Wild One*, Rogers expanded the instrumentation and supplemented the studio musicians with ringers, including Shank. Shank felt in this case, and always, it was about control: the studios would say, "You'll play *this*," and were inherently threatened by improvisational forms. Conversation with Bud Shank, November 14, 2007.
5. Ray Carney, *Shadows* (BFI, 2001).
6. Although ostensibly a jazz film, *Too Late Blues* is at its core a love story. The jazz aspects revolve around a generalized depiction of an artist's struggle for integrity, and his sellout in the form of his work

for a wealthy countess. This paralleled Cassavetes' own ambivalence about working for Hollywood at that early point in his career, with the jazz milieu as an affectionate proxy. Ironically, Cassavetes may have initially intended the film as a return to more meaningful work after *Johnny Staccato*, a television series in which Cassavetes starred as a jazz-playing private eye.

The film's title enters when Ghost Wakefield (Bobby Darin) is told his attempts to reunite his group are "too late." Yet it proves untrue—they indeed reunite. In the original shoot, however, his lover then leaves. It's too late for her, but not the music. Paramount subsequently intervened and in the final version all are reunited. It's not "too late" for either.

In an early review of *Too Late Blues* in *Film Quarterly* (Winter 1961), the African-American critic Albert Johnson intriguingly celebrates the film's authenticity, distinguishing it from other quality studio jazz pictures: "In each of (the other) films, white musicians formed the center of the dramas," and in each appeared "such familiar stereotypes as the seductive femme fatale; the jazz-impelled neurotic hero; and the Negro jazz-philosopher, imparting the spirit of his music to an eager white youth. A further study of these… films reveals that the standard pattern of approach to the problems of jazz musicians has always been on a purely mythological level. The very fact that Negroes figure very minimally in these works indicates the limited awarenesses of the directors, writers, and actors concerning the milieu in which they were supposed to be involved."

Yet many of these characteristics still figure in some form in *Too Late Blues*, and even Johnson, one of the few to like the film, qualified his praise; "It is therefore, quite interesting to discover in John Cassavetes' new film, *Too Late Blues*, a truly challenging Hollywood film."

While characteristically brilliant at moments, the film was inherently compromised through its studio production, as Cassavetes himself was quick to acknowledge. The film is in effect, a compromised film about compromise. It stands as a fascinating if flawed hybrid of Cassavetes' work as an auteur and more formulaic Hollywood fare, and as an intriguing self-portrait of the artist at a moment before he leapt completely into the uncharted waters of a full-blown independent directing career.

7. Cassavetes also claimed a practical reason for his move away from jazz-scored films: "If I can't have a musician from the beginning of a picture, I'm dissatisfied. I want them every day for six months. Also, (film is) a bastardized form for serious musicians." Cassavetes, in Brian Case, "Nostalgia in Times Square," *The Wire*, Summer, 1984, 24. Indeed, for many of his subsequent films Cassavetes worked with musician Bo Harwood, who also did sound recording and editing, and was hence around the projects from start to finish.
8. John Cassavetes, in Ray Carney, *Cassavetes on Cassavetes* (Faber, 2001), 59. Though they provide an invaluable reference, Carney's works cited here do not designate their original quote sources. It should be noted that in the introduction to *Cassavetes on Cassavetes*, Carney acknowledges that he "took shorter statements that Cassavetes made on different occasions and placed them back to back to form one longer, more comprehensive statement." He also acknowledges that he "cleaned up' the text in several other small ways."
9. Lelia Goldoni told me that during production Carruthers developed a fascination with Miles Davis, which likely influenced his eventual choice of a trumpet. In some of the earliest shot scenes he carries drumsticks in his back pocket.
10. John Cassavetes, in Carney, *Shadows*, 16.
11. The dynamic persists to our current epoch, where the equivalent would be a white desire for "street cred," mirrored by the "successful" black's need to "keep it real." In both cases, material success is equated with whiteness and vitality with blackness.
12. Norman Mailer, "The White Negro," *Dissent*, Fall, 1957. Mailer's definition of the "hipster" as an elite vanguard is particularly idiosyncratic, and itself arguably quite stereotyped. He writes that its model, the Negro, "discovered and elaborated a morality of the bottom, an ethical differentiation between the good and the bad in every human activity from the go-getter pimp (as opposed to the lazy one) to the relatively dependable pusher or prostitute." Gene Santoro rightly notes that in his modern elegizing of the negative, Mailer falls directly in line with the post-Enlightenment notion of the Noble Savage. Gene Santoro, *Myself When I Am Real: The Life and Music of Charles Mingus* (Oxford, 2000) 132.

The term "White Negro" in fact originated centuries earlier, in the West Indies. It is not within the scope of this essay to provide a synopsis of the extensive literature on race identity or Whiteness in either cinema or American social history, but it is worth noting that by 1967, Gary T. Marx observed Mailer's views differed from the pejorative stereotypes used by social critics "only on the emotive dimension of prejudice; [Mailer and the Beat writers] like super-sexed, narcotics-using, primitive, easy-going, spontaneous, irresponsible, violent Negroes, while racists dislike them. Their conception of what it means to be Negro probably differs greatly from the experience of most Black people." Marx goes on to describe the upward social aspirations of a black bourgeoisie, in contrast with the downward aspirations of the hipsters and Beats. "The White Negro and the Negro White," *Phylon*, Summer 1967, 168-177.

    A recently rediscovered and more overlooked alternative to Mailer's romanticism can be found in Seymour Krim's 1959 essay "Anti-Jazz: Unless the Implications Are Faced," in *Views of a Nearsighted Cannoneer* (Excelsior Press, 1961), reprinted in Krim, *Missing A Beat: The Rants and Regrets of Seymour Krim* (Syracuse, 2010), 94-99. Krim's harsher assessment of the daily reality of black life at the time was completely out of step with his white peers, and lauded by James Baldwin, who himself condemned Mailer's views in Baldwin, "The Black Boy Looks at the White Boy," *Esquire*, May 1961; collected in *Nobody Knows My Name* (Dial, 1961).

13. Cassavetes recut his original negative after the re-shoot. The labeling was discovered in my inspection and repair of the negative while restoring the final version for the UCLA Film & Television Archive in 2002. The removal of the word "screen" from the film's final title eliminates the formal reference, situating the finished work more firmly in the realm of its characters.
14. "Charles Mingus: History," http://duke.edu/~rdk1.history.htm.
15. Charles Mingus, *Beneath the Underdog* (Vintage, 1971), 65-66. The book's working titles were *Half Yaller Nigger* and *Half Yaller Schitt-Colored Nigger*, but Mingus knew it could never be published under either of those names.
16. Gary Giddins, "Charles Mingus (Bigger Than Death)," in *Visions of Jazz: The First Century* (Oxford, 1998), 446.
17. Arnold Jay Smith, interview with Charles Mingus, "Charles Mingus: Developmental Changes," *Down Beat*, January 12, 1978, 22.
18. Marshall Fine, *Accidental Genius: How John Cassavetes Invented American Independent Film* (Miramax, 2005).
19. Nat Hentoff, in *Charles Mingus, The Clown* (liner notes), Atlantic, 1957; Rhino/Atlantic 1999 reissue.
20. Cassavetes apparently thought this was a form of selling out. Of the decision not to go with Davis he said, "We were a little bit crazy in those days. Very pure. [When Davis signed with Columbia] I got so angry I didn't want to use him. I saw Miles years later, and he said, 'What happened?' I felt really bad!" (John Cassavetes, in Case, 24). It should be noted that George Avakian had actually signed Davis to Columbia two years earlier, in 1955, shortly after the formation of Davis' legendary quintet with John Coltrane, Red Garland, Paul Chambers, and Philly Joe Jones.
    Perhaps ironically, Davis disbanded the quintet in 1957 and went to Paris, where he would eventually record the soundtrack to Louis Malle's *Ascenseur pour l'échafaud* (*Elevator to the Gallows*). Although the score was recorded on December 4, 1957, just a few months before the *Shadows* session, it's conceivable Cassavetes knew of the film. The convergences and divergences between *Shadows* and *Elevator to the Gallows* are illuminating, and will be discussed in a series of footnotes following.
21. John Cassavetes, in Carney, *Cassavetes on Cassavetes*, 77. As observed in footnote 7, Carney has combined comments made on several occasions. See also: Case, 24.
22. Characteristically, he took his jokes with cats seriously as well. See the "Charles Mingus Cat Toilet Training Program," on Sue Mingus' official Mingus website, www.mingusmingusmingus.com. The text was originally published in booklet form as a subscription bonus for her *Changes* magazine.
23. Many consider Charles Mingus to be the only legitimate heir to Duke Ellington in this regard. Mingus himself was not shy to acknowledge the debt, and indeed early in his career went under the name "Baron" Mingus.
24. Rheinshagen was the principal bassist of the New York Philharmonic. Reese was an extremely influential music and composition teacher in Los Angeles, and a key figure in the vital Central Avenue music scene. His many other students included Eric Dolphy and Buddy Collette.
25. Charles Mingus, in *Down Beat*, op. cit., 22.
26. It was during the crazed preparations that Mingus, in a stressed rage, broke trombonist Jimmy Knepper's jaw. The charts were still being copied as the concert began. All the musicians were in tuxedos except for Mingus, who was wearing a short-sleeved shirt, vest, sandals, and no socks. Bob Coss describes Mingus'

celebrated grabbing of the microphone in the middle of the event: "The microphone (he) grabbed had no amplification, but what he said, more or less, was: "Get your money back. I couldn't stop you from coming here. The press agents lied to you. You've been taken advantage of. Go out now and get your money back. I don't want you to think I've done this to you. It was supposed to be a recording session, but Mr. George Wein... changed it into a concert. So get your money back. The company has lots of money. It would take years to rehearse this music." Coss, "A Report of a Most Remarkable Event," *Down Beat*, December 6, 1962. At midnight, the venue owner shut off the power.

Gary Giddins (*Visions of Jazz*, 445) notes that "the disastrous Town Hall concert... eventually came to be reckoned as a defining moment (in Mingus' career), impenetrable, yet decisive." For a fascinating and extended account of the concert, see "Central Avenue Sounds: Buddy Collette," an oral history interview between Mingus' childhood friend and noted musician Collette, and Steven Louis Isoardi in 1989 and 1990. The entire interview is available at http://content.cdlib.org/xtf/view?docId=hb6g5010zj&brand=calisphere&doc.view=entire_text.

There is an indelible sequence in Thomas Reichman's 1968 documentary film *Mingus* that also bears relevance to the discussion—the final scene, in which Mingus is evicted from his New York studio. As Mingus is forcibly escorted away by the police, we hear his wife Sue's voice stating that they are trampling on his music. The film's penultimate image of Mingus' abandoned bass sitting unattended amidst his belongings in the street resonates as speaking archetypally of his lifelong struggles. Mingus' rage and regret are viscerally palpable in his interviews that pepper the scene.

27. Portions of the music were recycled into the subsequent triumphs of *The Black Saint and the Sinner Lady* and *Ah Um*, but that was not the end of it. Mingus was to spend the rest of his life continuing to develop the Town Hall music, into *Epitaph*, the mammoth 4,000-plus measure composition that was discovered posthumously.

Epitaph premiered with a 30-piece orchestra in 1988 (nine years after his death), at Lincoln Center under the baton of Gunther Schuller, and was an unqualified success. *The New Yorker* went so far as to call it the first advance in jazz composition since Ellington's *Black, Brown and Beige*. However, the event's staging was not without parallel to the original performance. While the charts were all prepared well in advance of the Lincoln Center premiere, they had been digitized, and computer glitches prevented their printing until the last minute, so that once again they needed to be sight-read by the musicians.

28. Brian Priestley, *Mingus: A Critical Biography* (Quartet, 1982), 90.
29. John Cassavetes, in Case, 24.
30. John Cassavetes, in Carney, *Cassavetes on Cassavetes*, 77-78. According to Louis Malle, the recording of the *Elevator to the Gallows* score took about seven hours: "We rented a sound studio in Paris, on the Champs-Élysées, and started working, as jazz musicians do, very slowly. We worked from something like ten or eleven that night until five in the morning. In one night, the whole score was recorded." Louis Malle, excerpted from *Malle on Malle*, ed. Philip French (Faber, 1993), in *Elevator to the Gallows* DVD (booklet), The Criterion Collection, 2007, 18.
31. Marx, op. cit. See: Erving Goffman, *Stigma: Notes on the Management of Spoiled Identity* (Prentice-Hall, 1963), 110. Goffman casts the term within a prescriptive orthodoxy whereby individuals "stigmatized" by a physical or social constraint may accept or not accept those limitations. He contrasts it with the notion of minstrelization as conceived by Anatole Broyard, and also labels this opposition "normification." For Goffman, a more middle road is often desired.
32. Gary Giddins, "Eternal Times Square," in *John Cassavetes: Five Films* DVD (booklet), The Criterion Collection, 2004.
33. Case, 24. Cassavetes' somewhat patronizing description of the scene strongly suggests that de Koenigswarter may have been a model for the countess in *Too Late Blues*.
34. John Cassavetes, in Carney, *Cassavetes on Cassavetes*, 78. See also: Case, 24.
35. Jimmy Knepper, in Priestley, 90.
36. Case, 24.
37. Santoro, 131. A comparison with *Elevator to the Gallows* is apropos. As Malle tells it, "I showed [Davis] the film twice, only twice. We agreed on the parts where we felt music was needed. And we took advantage of the one night off he had from the club.... I think that makes the score of *Elevator to the Gallows* unique. It's one of the very few films that is completely improvised; I don't think Miles

Davis had had time to prepare anything. We would run those segments that we had chosen for music, and he would start rehearsing with his musicians." Malle, op. cit., 18-19.

René Urtreger, the French pianist who worked with Davis on the film, said that Davis played them themes a few days before on the piano, but they didn't know what scenes they went with. Despite its improvisational nature and a magical atmosphere that permeated the session, the recording was in ways frustrating for Urtreger, as each cue need to be a very precise length, i.e. 39 seconds. "On Piano, René Urtreger," interview for *Ascenseur pour l'échafaud* DVD, Arte, 2005, in *Elevator to the Gallows* DVD, The Criterion Collection, 2006.

38. John Cassavetes, in Case, 24.
39. By way of contrast, a CD of the Ellington/Strayhorn score of *Anatomy of a Murder* contains fourteen alternate takes alone, suggesting the greater preparation enabled by professional production.
40. Cassavetes, in Case, 24.
41. Santoro, 131.
42. In comparison, Diane Dorr-Dorynek was paid $40.00 per week for doing the correspondence for Mingus' Jazz Workshop at that time.
43. John Cassavetes, in Case, 24.
44. Shortly after the release of the final cut, a public debate broke out in the pages of *The Village Voice* as to which version was better. Amos Vogel encouraged Cassavetes to take a stance resolving the issue, and the director came out strongly for the second. Some time after these disputes the initial cut was lost, and subsequently became a legend among film historians. The Cassavetes estate has taken the position that per his views at the time, the final cut is definitive and the first should not be shown. Ray Carney cites evidence that Cassavetes later backed off his hard-line statements and claimed he was not opposed to exhibition of the original. While Carney holds the rediscovered physical print, the Cassavetes estate has made claims to the intellectual content, and the film remains in limbo, unavailable for public viewing.
45. Jonathan Rosenbaum, "The Shadow of Shadows: First Thoughts on the First Version," *Cinema Scope*, Spring 2004, 58-61.
46. Case, 24.
47. Jonathan Rosenbaum, International Federation of Film Critics, Festival Reports, Rotterdam, 2004: "Simon Field and the Original Shadows," http://www.fipresci.org/festivals/archive/2004/rotterdam/jrosenbaum.htm
48. Duke University website, op. cit. A parallel to the phone booth scene appears in *Elevator to the Gallows*, when Jeanne Moreau wanders the streets in search of Maurice Ronet. Davis engages in a duet with tenor saxist Barney Wilen which suggests the hubbub of background conversation.
49. Charles Mingus, in Priestley, 114.
50. The trailer also contains what appears to be an outtake of a cue by Shafi Hadi and Dannie Richmond.
51. It's intriguing to note that "Wednesday Night Prayer Meeting" was included in the Jan. 16, 1959 Charles Mingus Jazz Workshop gig at the Nonagon Gallery in which Mingus later recorded his other *Shadows*-inspired works, the aforementioned "Nostalgia," and "Alice's Wonderland." Mingus may have retained some association of the song with the film for a time, although it does not appear on the album resulting from that session, released in turn as "Jazz Portraits," "Mingus in Wonderland" and "Wonderland." An early version of "Wednesday Night Prayer Meeting" in fact appeared in a collaboration with Langston Hughes on March 18th 1958, very close to the time of the original Shadows scoring session. However its record debut is primarily associated with the famous studio recording on the *Blues and Roots* album, which took place on February 4, 1959, shortly after the Nonagon live performance.
52. A number of tapes survive and the relationship between them remains unclear. Sue Mingus informs me she has at least one master tape buried deep in her archives, but said it is not easily located, and described it as "…only short fragments of a few seconds, nothing worth listening to." Sue Mingus, e-mail correspondence, June 29, 2010. Her description is largely confirmed by jazz historian Fred Cohen (phone conversation, October 20, 2010), who told me that they listened to a single 10" tape reel which consisted of short fragments, likely totaling less than ten minutes of material.

Four reels of *Shadows* tapes can also be found in the Library of Congress' Mingus collection, donated by Sue Mingus. It seems possible that she was unaware of the existence of the tapes when she donated her materials to the Library, and it is unknown whether any tapes still remaining among Sue Mingus' personal holdings duplicate the Library's. LOC Senior Studio engineer Larry Appelbaum said (phone conversation, November 18, 2010) that he believes the LOC tapes to in fact be the original, unedited masters. (However, in listening to them, one hears high-speed/high frequency sections that suggest a dub from another player being fast-forwarded or rewound.)

Still another tape apparently exists in the Debut collection in the vaults of Fantasy Records. Mingus discographer Uwe Weiler has created a detailed log of the latter (Uwe Weiler, "Charles Mingus Group—*Shadows* Film Soundtrack Recording," Revised Edition January 3, 2011). This document updates his 1995 book, *The Debut Label: A Discography*.) The Fantasy tape most likely traces directly from Mingus himself and the deposit of the Debut archive, in about 1961. Weiler reports that the *Shadows* outtakes were discovered by Ed Michel in a survey of the Debut holdings in 1995. However he qualified that this is a purely speculative history. Given the existence of many tapes, and the fact that no one source in itself is complete, many questions still exist regarding both content and provenance. Weiler, Cohen, and I hope to pursue this history further in the future.

53. Photographer Marvin Lichtner relates that he was at the infamous Paris Theater screening of the initial cut, and was standing in the back of the theater as the film ended. Immediately, during the expectant applause that followed, a lone figure stalked quickly up the aisle toward the exit. It was Mingus. Lichtner approached him, to congratulate him on his work. Mingus stopped in his tracks, looked him dead in the eye and said, "Go fuck yourself." Mingus was furious at Cassavetes' re-editing of the score. Marvin Lichtner, phone conversation, February 13, 2008.

54. See Carney, *Cassavetes on Cassavetes*, 78. In this telling, Hadi was paid $100.00 for the session. In his *Wire* interview, Cassavetes gives a slightly different account of the process, saying he saw Hadi on the street: "He was having a hard time and I said come on up and play something. He said, 'Can I just play what I feel? Sure. Let's go.'" Cassavetes, in Case, 24.

While it's possibly true that Mingus was away on the actual recording date, it's worth noting that around that very time, in the spring of 1959, Mingus was in fact in New York working on a semi-improvised teleplay, *A Song With Orange In It*, which also never fully incorporated his music. Along with his spoken word experiments, Mingus' *Shadows* score can be seen as part of a concerted investment in the integration of jazz with the literary and dramatic arts, even if the productions were often star-crossed.

55. Charles Mingus, in *Down Beat*, op. cit., 22.

56. Elements of collage may have appeared in the first version's soundtrack as well. David Meeker cites the inclusion of Jelly Roll Morton's "Jelly Roll Blues" in the initial cut. See Meeker, *Jazz on the Screen: A Jazz and Blues Filmography*, Washington, Library of Congress, 2007, 962.

57. At one point Mingus claimed "Strollin'" preceded "Nostalgia." See www.mingusmingusmingus.com. The chronology cited in this essay is based on Brian Priestley's account.

58. Nat Hentoff, *Jazz Portraits: Mingus in Wonderland* (liner notes), United Artists, 1959; Blue Note 1994 reissue.

59. Carney's BFI *Shadows* monograph posits that this scene was filmed in the reshoot, around the same time the recording was made. However, Jonathan Rosenbaum's *Cinema Scope* essay mentions an additional scene of Lelia Goldoni dancing in the first version (apart from the scene with Tony Ray, which is verifiably in both). If Rosenbaum's account is correct, Mingus would likely have seen it, although in the original cut the scene is accompanied by a Frank Sinatra record.

60. I assembled this clip purely as an experiment while completing the UCLA Film & Television Archive restoration of the film's release version.

61. Mingus, in Hentoff, *Jazz Portraits*.

62. Gene Santoro writes that "Diane was very smart and very beautiful. At times she had a self-possessed air, although others found her vulnerable, delicate, nervous, uncomfortable around people." Santoro, 132.

63. Diane Dorr-Dorynek (original liner notes), Charles Mingus, *Ah Um*, Columbia CK 65512, 1959; Sony/Columbia Legacy 1998 reissue. Brian Priestley notes that the title "Self-Portrait in Three Colors" anticipates the tripartite autobiographical voice assumed in Mingus' *Beneath the Underdog*. Brian Priestley (re-issue liner notes), *Ah Um*. This interpretation resonates with Mingus' own description of the personal aspects of "Alice's Wonderland," above.

64. In general his takes are easily distinguishable by their distinctly lighter tone, although they do on occasion echo aspects of the original Mingus approach. An example would be Hadi's use of

representational sounds, such as the sax's emulating the pulsating echo of a clock to suggest Hugh's chronic lateness in the train station scenes.
65. Tom Charity, *John Cassavetes: Lifeworks* (Omnibus, 2001), 22.
66. Lelia Goldoni, phone conversation, May 22, 2006.
67. John Cassavetes, in Carney, *Cassavetes on Cassavetes*, 161.
68. Ibid.
69. This is perhaps most marked in the extended episode when two businessmen visit Gena Rowland's house, which in the pre-release version includes incongruous background music that completely distinguishes it from the rest of the film.
70. Mekas, 10.
71. Jonathan Rosenbaum, *Cinema Scope*, op. cit., 59.
72. To cite one example, the film's early version opens with the sequence of John Marley and Lynn Carlin telling jokes in bed, then going unromantically and sadly to sleep, thus setting up his subsequent encounter with Gena Rowlands. The final version inserts the bedroom scene in the middle of a later sequence; what was initially a single shot of John Marley playing pool, requiring the viewer to deduce that the bedroom scene is a memory or flashback. The brevity of the pool shot contributes to the lack of clarity.
73. Priestley, 99. The quote would also appear attributable to John Handy. Gary Giddins (*Visions of Jazz*, 448) further notes that "Shafi Hadi said that he didn't feel free to express himself." Yet Giddins nonetheless observes Mingus incited some of Hadi's most inspired playing.
    It seems appropriate that Hadi, who had issues with Mingus, would leap at the chance to work with Cassavetes on his own in the second recording session. Cassavetes' descriptions of Hadi are notably more glowing than his descriptions of Mingus: "He comes in with his saxophone and behind him is his life, you know…. He played. He was terrific. He played the story of his life to music." (Cassavetes, in Carney, *Cassavetes on Cassavetes*, 78. See also Case, 25.) Carney adds that Cassavetes was so pleased he helped Hadi record an unreleased album of music based on the film. Conversely, Gene Santoro relates that when Mingus learned about Hadi's solos for the film, he immediately fired him (Santoro, 131).
74. Priestley, 99.
75. Duke University website, op. cit. For an extended explication of his views on the relationship between spontaneity and composition, see: Charles Mingus, "What is a Jazz Composer?," Let My Children Hear the Music (liner notes), Columbia Records, 1971; reprinted in *Charles Mingus, More Than a Fake Book* (Jazz Workshop, 1991), 155-157.
76. Charles Mingus in Dorr-Dorynek (liner notes), *Ah Um*.
77. Mingus was keenly aware of the resonant concerns of musical and dramatic improvisation, based not only on his *Shadows* work, but his previously cited experiences with *Song With Orange*, Shepherd, and numerous poets. Dorr-Dorynek links these efforts in noting "music and poetry (or acting) does seem to have a definite future." Describing his teleplay work specifically, she writes, "The acting methods used were peculiarly akin to jazz. The script formed the skeleton around which the actors might change or ad lib lines according to their response to the situation at that moment." Dorr-Dorynek (liner notes), *Ah Um*.
78. The story was told to me a by a musician in the experimental group Killsonic, one of whose members heard it from trumpeter Bobby Bradford, who in turn had played with Coleman. It should be noted that C sharp is an extremely rare key in jazz. Mingus, in the May 26, 1960 issue of *Down Beat*, said of Ornette: "It doesn't matter what key he's playing in…. It's like not having anything to do with what's around you, and being right in your own world. You can't put your finger on what he's doing." And in the same article: "It's like organized disorganization, or playing wrong right…. It gets to you emotionally, like a drummer. That's what Coleman means to me."
79. Although George Russell was the early proponent of modality, it is popularly associated with Miles Davis, and Gary Giddins notes that the first hints of it in his work appear in the *Elevator to the Gallows* score, when he more or less instructed his musicians to "play this for four bars, then this for four bars, and I'll make it up." "Miles Goes Modal," featurette in *Elevator to the Gallows* DVD, The Criterion Collection, 2006. While Davis was aware of Russell, it seems quite possible that the time-constrained conditions of the recording sessions, combined with no prior rehearsals, led Miles to experiment

with modality as an effective way of improvising a film score. If so, cinema can here be seen in effect influencing jazz history, in Davis' subsequent *Milestones* and *Kind of Blue*, the epitome of his modal work.
80. Shirley Clarke's subsequent film adaptation of *The Connection* in 1961 stands as an intriguing counterpoint to Cassavetes' *Too Late Blues*, made the same year. The overt traces of *The Connection*'s theatrical origins stand out prominently in some of the trained actors' performances, adding an air of artifice at odds with the groundbreaking pseudo-*vérité* style, and parallel Cassavetes' concurrent use of actors to portray musicians. However the actual musicians in *The Connection* (including Jackie McLean and composer/pianist Freddie Redd) are completely at ease and natural in performance, offering a commanding filmic presence and genuine jazz sensibility distinct from the actor-musicians in either film. Interestingly, actor Carl Lee's powerful lead role as a non-musician also stands out, suggesting it is not necessarily the staged dialogue of *The Connection* that engenders its occasional lapse into artifice.
81. Charity, 24.
82., P. Adams Sitney, *Visionary Film: The American Avant-Garde* (Oxford, 1974).
84. Priestley, 120. Gary Giddins (*Visions of Jazz*, 450) agrees: "[Mingus] extended the emotional and technical scope of jazz within its essential idiomatic constraints." One can in fact argue that both Cassavetes' and Mingus' innovations are at least as bold as their avant-garde counterparts, but their willingness to simultaneously embrace traditional forms denies their categorization as pure avant-gardists (if one is indeed compelled to categorize). See also: Charles Mingus, "An Open Letter to the Avant-Garde," *Changes*, June, 1973; reprinted in *Mingus, More Than a Fake Book*, 119.
84. John Cassavetes, in Carney, *Shadows*, 34.
85. Giddins writes that Mingus, "more than any other jazz composer of his generation… was willing—determined—to confront his fears and force his musicians to confront theirs. He was dogmatic, pensive, demagogic, irreverent, furious, nostalgic: a far cry from the cool and collected brainy music rife in jazz in the '50s." Giddins, *Visions of Jazz*, 455.

   This is perhaps the final irony—and blind fate—of Cassavetes not pursuing his first choice for the film, Miles Davis. The score for *Elevator to the Gallows*, improvised in precisely the way Cassavetes imagined, is monumentally beautiful, but austere and removed. As Malle notes, "It was not like a lot of film music, emphasizing or trying to add the emotion that is implicit in the images and the rest of the soundtrack. It was a counterpoint, it was elegiac—and it was somewhat detached. But it also created a certain mood for the film." (Malle, op. cit., 19) It was pure Davis; the embodiment of cool. Mingus, like Cassavetes, was pure fire, and *Shadows* (unlike *Elevator to the Gallows*) is a film of personal fire. Each film found the music perfectly suited to it.
86. John Cassavetes, in Carney, *Cassavetes on Cassavetes*, 59.
87. Mingus, reflecting on having to wait thirty years to have a particular composition played, noted that "When people are born free—I can't imagine it, but I've got a feeling that if it's so easy for you, the struggle and the initiative are not as strong as they are for a person who has to struggle and therefore has more to say." Mingus, "What is a Jazz Composer?," op. cit.
88. Mingus, *Beneath the Underdog*, 66.
89. John Cassavetes, in Case, 24.

On *The Exiles*
(1961)

The Exiles was restored by UCLA Film & Television Archive in association with the USC Moving Image Archive with funding from the National Film Preservation Foundation. The restoration was subsequently digitally remastered by UCLA in collaboration with Milestone Films at Modern Film and Video. Laboratory services provided by Fotokem, Audio Mechanics, and NT Audio. Restoration and remastering supervised by Ross Lipman in consultation with cinematographers John Morrill and Erik Daarstad, and in collaboration with colleagues including audio restorationist John Polito, film grader Walt Rose, digital colorist Gregg Garvin, sound engineer Shawn Jones, archivist Valerie Schwan, and Diane and Kiki Mackenzie. Distributed by Milestone.

> *This essay continues my investigations of the creative process, and the interweaving of a film's production methods with its form, content, and themes.*
>
> *"The Savage Ear of Kent Mackenzie" was originally prepared for Injerto, the experimental film symposium of the Ambulante Documentary Film Festival in Mexico City, February 2009, and later expanded for presentation at Los Angeles Film Forum's "Alternative Projections" conference at USC in 2010. A revised version was published under the title, "Kent Mackenzie's* The Exiles: Reinventing the Real of Cinema" *in Adam Hyman and David James'* Alternative Projections: Experimental Film in Los Angeles, 1945-1980 *(Indiana, 2015). The following text expands on past iterations and has not been previously presented in this form. Special thanks to Dennis Doros, Amy Heller, and Diane Mackenzie. Production photos courtesy Milestone Films.*

Figure 1: Hill X at night.

The Savage Heart of Kent Mackenzie

Introduction

> *"He became intrigued with photographing and recording outer reality in great detail, not for its own sake, but to express the inner emotional patterns of human beings."*

Thus begins Kent Mackenzie's master's thesis on the production of *The Exiles*.[1] The thesis is as revealing a text on filmmaking practice as I've encountered, as essential to cinematic literature as *The Exiles* itself is to American film history.[2] In those pages, Mackenzie reveals not only the techniques that enabled the film's making, but their strange interaction with the events depicted—and with the inner emotional patterns that lay beneath the production itself.

The quote I've presented is written in the third person, although Mackenzie was speaking of himself: "*He* became intrigued." This device is used only in the text's introduction, to assume an appropriately distanced tone for a scholarly work. He concludes the section by unapologetically noting that the remaining chapters comprise a highly personal account, and that he'll thereafter forego the third person for the first: be it the collective

> we rejected the... precious and sterile concepts of art,[3]

or the singular

> I wanted to smash the stereotypes.[4]

In reality this duality of first and third person mirrors the dualism of Mackenzie's own role in the production—as both insider and outsider, as participant and author.

The Exiles is a portrait of Exile, drawn by a man who is himself exiled, from both the native community he lovingly depicts and the scholars to whom he respectfully reports. He is at once among them and apart from them. This dynamic in turns fuels the film; a searing vision that simultaneously burns and freezes, making fiction from truth and truth from fiction.

This dualism is even embodied in the film's own cinematic encoding. *The Exiles* features an unsettling interaction of sound and image, which were separated in their original capture by the very equipment Mackenzie used, and was unique to a transitional moment in film history. Mackenzie's thesis ultimately shines light on these dualities of production and, in so doing, on the film's vital place in the development of cinema's elusive interaction with the world it depicts.

Inside / Outside

Kent Mackenzie's initial inspiration for *The Exiles* came from a story in *Harper's* in March 1956 by Dorothy Van de Mark, "The Raid on the Reservations," which he described as "a discussion of the continuing shenanigans on the part of the white man to obtain Indian land."[5] He goes on: "I was shocked and immediately wanted to go to war via the film medium."[6] On the encouragement of his employer, Charles Palmer, president of Parthenon Pictures, he made a research trip to the San Carlos reservation near Gobe, Arizona. He soon discovered, however, that his interests lay more in the plight of the young Native Americans who were moving *away* from the reservations to larger cities, and he ultimately wound up focusing his interests on a group living in Bunker Hill in downtown Los Angeles.[7] His depiction of that milieu now stands as a unique record of a lost moment in time.

The film's crew members claim they viewed the film as a documentary of that community and cultural moment.[8] Yet the movie we encounter belies this, or stated more temperately, stretches standard notions of the term. Mackenzie, for his part, suggests in his thesis that he viewed the film as neither document nor story, but something in-between. From today's vantage it's indeed best understood as a hybrid, of not just fact and fiction, but disparate views of an unfixed world.[9] As shall be seen, Mackenzie's cinema is infused with both his own vision and his subjects', not so much recording reality as creating its own. The film speaks directly back to the world of physical truth while remaining distinct from it, in a cinema of Exile.

To fully appreciate this, one must begin with Mackenzie himself. The director spent years integrating himself in the Bunker Hill Indian scene, and notes,

> *I enjoyed it so much that I began to spend my own recreational time on Main Street and often passed the whole night sitting talking in the parking lot opposite the Ritz Cafe. I started to walk like them, to drink what they drank, to try their language, to think in their terms, and to have some of their desires.*[10]

Yet he goes on,

> *I became so close to the situation that after the shooting was over I had a great deal of trouble deciding what the film was about… I made the early mistake of trying to be "one of the gang"…. I think I could have preserved my own outlook and identity much more clearly had I understood that you can seldom really become part of an unfamiliar group.*[11]

As Mackenzie went through this process he produced numerous cuts of the film, varying widely in content, before returning to something akin to his original vision.

The film's final version begins with a conventionally narrated prologue accompanied by the iconic photographs of Edward Curtis—another sympathetic recorder of Native American culture. The Curtis images are romanticized yet also speak to archetype in their searing close-ups of chiseled faces, and in his subjects' traditional dress that already spoke of a disappearing past. The aged photos, in tandem with the narration, place the film in a historical context which is sharply contrasted by the immediacy of what follows, as Mackenzie embarks on a more personalized tale in the film proper.

This perspective-shifting structure is echoed in the distanced third-person prologue of Mackenzie's thesis giving way to a first-person account, and again reinforces the notion of dualism. Although the Curtis sequence opens the film, it was in fact the last thing added, shortly prior to the film's release. At the very end of production Mackenzie thus reverted to his original role of outsider to the story, and placed his authorial distancing at the work's beginning, as a framing device.

In contrast, the film's haunting final shot—of Homer and his friends walking down the alley—is presented from the tragic perspective of Yvonne viewing her husband's life from a window. This image fuses the perspective of Yvonne and the audience. Both are exiled: Yvonne from her husband, and the audience with her, through the shot's empathetic point-of-view photography, as well as by the "window" of the film itself. Mackenzie herein shows that there is a role for impassioned observers. Their unique vantage allows insight precisely because it's both integral and peripheral. In this case it eschews the painterly romanticization of Curtis, lingering instead on the grit under the fingernails, as revealed in the many difficulties Yvonne faces.¹²

Between these two bookends of prologue and the conclusion, *The Exiles* immerses itself in the harsh beauty of its character's splintered lives. The city's squalor is exquisitely rendered. That squalor is put in relief, in turn, by a brief glimpse of reservation life. The reservation life is presented through the construct of a letter from home, read by Homer in front of a liquor store. The reservation is of course a place of internal exile; so the urban Indians who leave it are in essence exiled twice—first from mainstream America, then from their allotted lane within it. Originally conceived as a possible beginning for the film, the reservation sequence's reconception as a "cutaway" in the form of a letter is tellingly situated. Alcohol is omnipresent as the letter is read, lurking behind every streetlight, an opiate obliviating the life left behind, even as its omnipresence in so many scenes renders it nearly invisible, like the air.

Figure 2: Edward Curtis, *Iron Breast* (ca. 1900). Courtesy Library of Congress.

In light of this bleakness, it comes as no surprise that some reviewers have scorned *The Exiles* for a less-than-ennobling depiction of Native life; desiring instead images that might be viewed as more empowering.[13] This response aligns with a Western view that harkens back to notions of the "noble savage"—a valorization of authenticity in life deemed possible only Elsewhere. This elevation of the Other; arising from projected guilt, is arguably a flipside of the same racism it decries, denying the darker aspects of a society it would rather not see.

Mackenzie's urban exiles challenge the double-edged sword of romanticization by rejecting the initial Exile forced upon them and moving forward, for better or for worse; immersing themselves in the midst of the very order that brought about their banishment. They deny the confines of the reservation, and any kind of box one seeks to place them in.[14]

Mackenzie, in turn, stands on neither side, brutally revealing a multi-faceted view of a specific Indian subculture he loves for what it is. This vantage is the only one he can authentically achieve himself in his role as both friend and filmmaker, and is thus a subjective truth—a genuine blend of the real and imagined.

Reinventing the Wheel

Let's look, then, at the specific nature of Mackenzie's "subjective truth." Where is fiction simulating fact, and where the reverse? To unravel this question, one needs to look at Mackenzie's methodologies. In reading Mackenzie's account of *The Exiles*' production, one sees the filmmakers arriving at their aims only through an intensive period of experimentation. While they knew they wanted to reject the artifice of a sterile industry, it was another thing entirely to invent a new cinema from scratch.

In some ways such a task would seem unnecessary, in that the realist impulse had been at work in film since the days of the Lumières. In other ways, it was essential, in that reinventing the wheel was precisely what Mackenzie needed to do to find his unique cinematic vision. Said Mackenzie,

> *Although many of [the] films to which we were drawn were often classified by critics or historians as 'realistic,' 'neo-realistic,' or 'naturalistic,' we felt that the concern with physical reality was not for its own sake but to create living and vital images and symbols from recognizable elements of everyday life.*[15]

Mackenzie's quarrel is hence not so much with the films that are described this way, but rather the words themselves, which he saw as limiting. But he ultimately concludes that despite his admiration,

> *none of these films seemed to be really the films of our time. Even the best of them often made use of theatrical conventions and methods... We felt that we had to reject all the old methods and structures and study our subjects so intensely that we could develop new methods and structures of our own.*[16]

In the end, Mackenzie integrated aspects of many of his forbears' work, while rejecting others. Yet critically, he did this not from a polemical position, but rather a practical one. To reinvent his art, Mackenzie became strongly "content-oriented" and decided to "take his camera to life itself,"[17] letting what he saw before him dictate its own forms and structures. If something worked, it remained in the film.

This process can be seen unfolding at almost every stage of development, from conception to exhibition. For example, the cinematography—despite certain myths—was not an exact, clear recording of life's events, but rather a recreation of its experience. The film's lighting provides a useful analogue. The cinematographers did not exclusively use existing location light, but rather supplemented it with their own sources, and in some cases simply re-created its effects. Mackenzie notes,

> *In most circumstances what could be photographed with natural light did not simulate what the eye perceived… All the bar sequences and other night interiors had to be lit from scratch, and even the night street exteriors were usually augmented… In the shot where Homer and Rico walk away from Rico's apartment, for instance, there were lights set all the way down the alley.[18] Our approach to the lighting was always the same, however, not to introduce unnatural effects but to light the location to photograph the way the eye perceived it.[19]*

As copiously detailed in the thesis, *The Exiles*' purportedly realistic cinematography was in fact carefully crafted—and is ultimately an interaction between true incidental light and the skill, ingeniousness, and sometimes sheer desperation of its brilliant young crew.

In reading through the document, one realizes that Mackenzie was in fact developing and in turn applying a rigorous aesthetic and philosophical agenda at every level of production, encompassing both abstract concept and physical detail.[20] This is perhaps nowhere more evident than in the creation of the film's soundtrack, so it is here that I'll focus my most detailed discussion. The soundtrack's successes, and in some respects even failures, ultimately help illuminate the nature of the work's "subjective truth."

Diegetics in Exile pt. 1: Dialogue

The foremost factor in a consideration of *The Exiles*' soundtrack is its post-dubbing, or "looping."[21] The film was shot on location in downtown Los Angeles, primarily with a 35mm Arriflex camera. Significantly, sound was usually recorded simultaneously, if not truly synchronously. Given the film's low budget, Mackenzie could not afford a blimp to reduce the camera noise, or a synchronous motor.[22] The attendant camera noise and lack of sync rendered the original recordings unusable in the final film. Mackenzie was thus forced into re-recording the soundtrack later, exiling the images from the sounds with which they were originally embodied.

Figure 3: Right to left: Kent Mackenzie, Robert Kaufman, Erik Daarstad, unknown cast member.

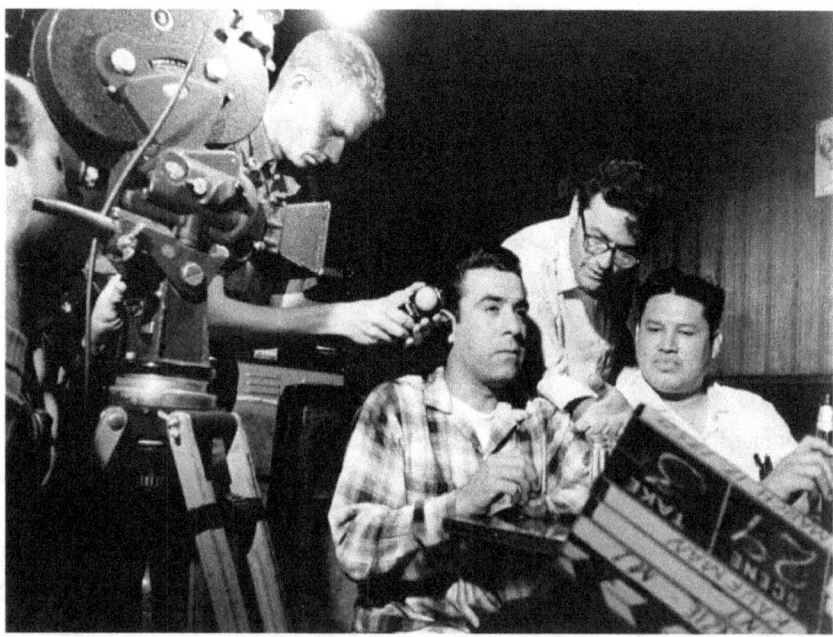

Figure 4: Cinematographer Eric Daarstad taking a light reading for Tommy, with Kent Mackenzie overlooking.

This estrangement has an eerie effect, creating a sensation of alienation in the viewer, even as it depicts alienation in it characters. Conversely, the film's narration—which one would normally think might have a near-Brechtian distancing effect—draws the listener precisely into the minds of the characters. These tendencies can be traced directly back to their methods of recording.

In the case of the dialogue, there was no written script, and Mackenzie used the original location recordings as a guide track for his cast as much as possible. Every effort was made to get the studio recordings to match the feel of the guide tracks. Mackenzie always brought several Indians to the studio, and they'd drink beer and kid each other throughout the session to stay relaxed, even as they recorded. When there was no guide track they would screen the film silently, and Mackenzie was astonished to find that the Indians frequently remembered their lines verbatim. It was particularly astonishing in that the original dialogue was largely improvised. Furthermore, Mackenzie had been careful while on the set to avoid lines that sounded too pat, or scripted, even when a scene's content was suggested in advance of the improv to advance a plot point.

While these efforts represented a strong desire to get the dialogue right, they were complemented by another important, if seemingly conflicting, element of Mackenzie's aesthetics. His interest in emotional rather than literal truth led him to in fact consciously forego accurate dubbing. He wrote:

> *Although we were concerned about "sync," we tended to pick the best and most natural rendition of the line in preference to the one that matched the lip movements most closely.*[23]

Furthermore:

> *We would make use of all the stutterings, overlaps, and other normal elements of the Indians' speech patterns, and we would treat this dialog [sic], not as the most important element of communication in the film, but merely as another sound effect in the environment.*[24]

In one of his most radical gestures as a realist, he ultimately utilized the spoken word not so much for its signifying code of language, but rather treated it as pure sound. To this end:

> *We purposely intended to obscure dialog at times with music or other background noises. The dialog as Homer and Rico walk through the Third Street Tunnel, for instance, was intentionally swallowed in the sounds and echoes of the cars rushing through the tunnel.*[25]

Not surprisingly, this led to trouble. He continues:

Figure 5: On location at the Morongo reservation.

Figure 6: Kent Mackenzie on location at the Morongo reservation, looking through viewfinder of the Mitchell camera without its sound blanket.

Figure 7: Cinematographer John Morrill on location at the Morongo reservation with Mitchell Camera under sound blanket. The sound blanket's availability allowed the original true-sync audio to be used for the reservation scenes.

> *When we dubbed the picture this was difficult to explain to the professional and more orthodox mixers, because they were used to clarity of speech above most other considerations.*[26]

Further problems arose beyond clarity; again tied to the methodology. He noted that the re-recorded lines "did not carry the excitement of the original production tracks."[27] This becomes most apparent in the way the dialogue is spoken, which despite all efforts, on occasion sounds slightly unnatural. An excellent example of this would the scene in which Tommy enters the Ritz Cafe. This extended tracking shot's complexity would have made the recording of good location sound virtually impossible, being filmed as it was prior to the availability of more portable equipment. Its most awkward moment occurs midway through the shot, when the actor walking behind Tommy speaks. At a quick glance it appears that Tommy's lines are poorly done, resulting in a slippage in the "suspension of disbelief." Only upon close viewing does it become apparent that the line is actually well dubbed—but for the actor standing behind Tommy. Even without that confusion, the scene's original spontaneity would be nearly impossible to emulate perfectly in a studio post-dub, under any conditions.

This sense of unease goes beyond the spoken lines to the actual quality of the sound—or precisely what Mackenzie considered his true material. He notes, "We could never achieve an outdoor presence no matter how many background tracks we added, and we could not effectively vary the perspective on the [sound] stage."[28]

This is no doubt linked to the conceptual contradiction of aiming to emulate reality via a method that, by unfortunate technical necessity, prevented its original capture. The split filming and looping ensure something that's neither fact nor fiction, but something between. In this light, however, one can use the film's "failures" in verisimilitude to pinpoint what it has in fact *succeeded* in creating. Mackenzie notes:

> *One odd problem which surprised everybody… was the tremendous rapidity of the Main Street patter on the original dialog tracks. Sometimes six or eight words would have been said in the space of ten frames. The Indians tried to duplicate this in the looping, but it was very difficult for them to talk that fast when they thought about it, although they did it all day without thinking about it.*[29]

The operative phrase here is "without thinking about it." The process of post-dubbing the dialogue by definition forced the actors not into an act of spontaneous creation, but conscious *re*-creation. This consciousness, or self-awareness, represents a fall from an Edenic condition of innocence, a banishment from self and home that is tantamount to Exile. The film's new reality, or subjective reality, is in fact Exile itself. This tension between reality and its alienated representation underlies the film and drives the unique sensation of cold fire that infuses it.

Diegetics in Exile pt. 2: Narration

Whereas dubbing dialogue, in the abstract, can be considered ill-suited to a work with a realist agenda, no such contradiction arises with the dubbing of narration, which has no inherent on-screen motivation or diegetic antecedent. A split of recording and filming are called for by definition. In the case of *The Exiles*, the separation is particularly fitting, and points to another aspect of the film. The tendency of the looped *dialogue* to create an experience of alienation in the viewer is inversely mirrored in its counterpart, the non-synchronous narration. The narrated sequences in fact draw the viewer directly into the minds of the film's subjects.

While this was precisely Mackenzie's aim, its success is nonetheless tied up in the means by which it was recorded. Ironically, here Mackenzie had to take his subjects away from a place of comfort to achieve the effect. He at first tried to record the narration in the Indians' homes. But he noted that the background noise from the streets was overpowering, and more critically:

> *The Indians were embarrassed to reveal their feelings because there was always someone dropping around. They would grandstand for their buddies, giving us self-conscious jokes about their life. They were seldom alone on Main Street and only reflected or revealed their inner thoughts on rare occasions.*[30]

The studio, which one might think would be cold and off-putting, was a better alternative in that it offered an anonymity the Indians needed to open up. However, there were still problems to solve. Mackenzie observed that "once they were at all removed from Main Street they felt ill at ease."[31] To remedy this, Mackenzie tried a number of techniques, which in fact varied with each subject:

> *I often spent several hours talking with Yvonne before she would be ready to record. Tommy usually took some drinks, and he was quite high when he gave the narration which comes over the drunk scene in the gas station. Homer was often left alone on the stage to think about his past for as much as hour before recording.*[32]

This illustrates not just Mackenzie's methodological fluidity, but his intimate knowledge of the cast and their respective roles in the film. Each method is suited to the character—from Tommy's representation of pure id (which drunkenness encouraged) to Homer's self-destructive brooding, to Yvonne's quiet resignation; bearing silent witness to the events around her.

And yet there's another key to the narration's success. While the recordings give the impression of being spontaneous speech, they're in fact highly edited. Mackenzie describes some of his strategies:

Figure 8: Hill X, daytime.

Figure 9: Cinematographer Eric Daarstad (right) on location at Hill X.

Figure 10: Cinematographer Eric Daarstad (bottom) on location at Hill X with Arriflex camera.

242　The Archival Impermanence Project

Figure 11: Sam Farnsworth on Hill X set with Magnerecorder.

In fitting the narration to the picture, we tried to match recording quality by cutting together material only from the same evening, or preferably the same tape... Great care was taken to preserve the meaning and pacing of the original statement...

Breaths and mumbles and phrases such as "man" and "you know" were eliminated whenever they interfered with intelligibility. However, in the gas station sequence these phrases, breaths, and mumbles were retained or even inserted to build the drunken mood.

In a few cases we had to go so far as to actually construct words out of consonants and sounds drawn from other words—not to insert words that had not been spoken but to clarify words which were badly slurred or mumbled. There were whole sections of narration track which consisted of one to four frame cuts.[33]

This would at first seem to contradict Mackenzie's earlier statement about trying to portray the vagaries of daily speech, and to treat speech as pure sound, yet a contradiction is not so straightforward. Whereas obscuring on-screen dialogue, or masking it with other diegetically motivated noises makes fundamental sense from a realist perspective, obscuring voiceover narration does not. However, even here Mackenzie carefully re-envisions his task.

He states that in contrast with conventional film narration, he was "not after information, but an emotional quality and general attitudes and feelings."[34] The implication, in light of his detailed account of the resulting methods, is that he had to work quite hard to achieve the suggestion of randomness.

Mackenzie's editing of actual speech to create, rather, the likeness of it, cuts to the heart of his methodology. As one reads through his thesis, one finds instance after instance where he needed to alter content-as-recorded to create the *semblance* of a more literal truth.[35]

Figure 12: Laying dolly track at Hill X.

Shadows of Forgotten Ancestors

In this sense, Mackenzie arrived by trial-and-error at a conclusion that bears some resemblance to the forbears he initially rebelled against, while simultaneously reinventing the rules in his own unique manner. To better understand this, an abbreviated glance at some historical precursors is instructive.

Through the course of his thesis Mackenzie himself cites many films he viewed, illustrating a respectable knowledge of his territory. He cites at once an admiration for his predecessors, and an attempt to create something distinct from them.[36] It is not the aim of this brief summary to provide an in-depth analysis of either Mackenzie's specific references or the larger canon—a topic to which volumes could be devoted—but merely to isolate some broad touchstones that enable a better understanding of Mackenzie's unique place within realist traditions.[37]

An early pinnacle of the attempt to integrate realism within a narrative construct would certainly be Stroheim, who according to legend, went so far as to insist the extras playing the Austrian troops in *Foolish Wives* wear the proper underwear beneath their uniforms. It is instructive to in turn contextualize Stroheim's rigor with the "realism" of his predecessor, stage director David Belasco, who famously added such literal flourishes as working laundromats to his productions.

Too frequently, however, the terms "realism" and "naturalism" are used interchangeably. Belasco's literalism helps distinguish him from his counterparts, the theatrical naturalists, who evoked the *sense* of reality rather than reality itself: the chamber drama's tragedy-in-an-afternoon, wherein the chaotic ebb and flow of actual events is highly sculpted and abbreviated, to seemingly occur within the two-to-three hour span of a play. This has a definite parallel in Mackenzie's structuring *The Exiles* around a twelve-hour span in the lives of his subjects. Mackenzie's twelve hours is not a true twelve hours, but rather its condensation into an eighty-two minute running time. Both Mackenzie and the naturalists in this sense utilize a neoclassical unity of time (abstracted from Aristotle), which asks that the action of a tragedy should encompass events which occur in no more than a twenty-four hour time span.

Mackenzie himself tends to use both terms—naturalist and realist—within his thesis. Yet intriguingly, he chose to distance himself from both terms, even as he embraced some of their tactics. In a characteristic comment he notes that "we felt from the beginning that expressing an inner reality was not merely a matter of more and more naturalist recording of outer reality, but a question of careful selection and emphasis."[38]

Mackenzie's film could indeed hardly be called naturalist in its aesthetics, yet in this crucial area he is arguable closer to the naturalists than the realists. A critical difference would be Mackenzie's particular *type* of selection and emphasis; his personal structuring (or at a surface level, "non-structuring") of the condensed time he presents. He carefully avoids the Aristotelian catharsis preserved by the naturalists, creating instead the appearance of a true "slice of life." *The Exiles* offers not the "dramatic reality" of Ibsen, but rather, a uniquely cinematic language that realistically renders the inner lives of its characters through an apparently unstructured time. Said one viewer at an early pre-screening of the work-in-progress, "This is a masterpiece. You have succeeded in finding the form of formlessness."[39]

To achieve this "effect," Mackenzie in fact held rehearsals for almost every scene in the film. Improvisation played a key role, in that the cast was largely allowed to ad-lib their own lines within a specific context. However the improvisations were then adapted and sculpted to fit the needs of the film.

Here we see again a blending of the literal impulse in the improvisations' authenticity, and the fictive impulse, in their subsequent shaping. This methodology bears surface similarity to Mackenzie's east coast contemporary, John Cassavetes, who also used forms of improvisation as a lens into the psyche of his characters. But there the similarities end—for the documentary aspect and attention to physical detail in Mackenzie's work bears greater resemblance to the seemingly distant Stroheim than Cassavetes. Mackenzie shot solely on location with non-actors playing themselves. Cassavetes' *Shadows*, despite the many legends surrounding it, was largely shot in Cassavetes' acting studio—and although the actors played versions of themselves, they were indeed actors. Cassavetes thus falls far more directly within a fiction tradition than Mackenzie.

What then, of the crew's documentary claims, and *The Exiles'* documentary counterparts? An obvious point of reference lies in the US portion of the Direct Cinema movement and the French *cinema vérité*. Certainly a kindred spirit can be found in their shared interest in taking cameras into previously unfilmable sites, with ostensible "fly on the wall" motives. And although some early reviewers may have deemed the Direct Cinema "objective," the editing and arguably subjective photographing of the best of these works structurally established a viewpoint even as the films textually withheld one. In this sense they truly share a common sensibility with *The Exiles*.

But to appreciate their difference it is critical to note the precise historical moment of *The Exiles'* production. Mackenzie and his crew began shooting in January 1958 and one hence needs to recognize the film's fantastic location cinematography[40] not as a contemporary, but as a pre-cursor to Direct Cinema. In fact Mackenzie, in a characteristically detailed note, delineates the history of technological developments that followed his production, including the portable Nagra sound recorders which were so crucial to his near-contemporaries.[41] It was the Nagra that enabled these latter movements to record synchronous sound on location.[42]

Figure 13: Nagra III sound recording unit.

Hence, *The Exiles*' groundbreaking use of location shooting and the outer *form* of sync sound is distinct from the "veritistas" in that the sound one hears in 99% of the film was not actually recorded at the time of production. Its unique creation dates mark it as an overlooked moment in cinema history, a missing link or stray evolutionary strand between the largely asynchronous social documentaries of the 1940s, and the in-the-street works of the 1960s. Indeed, Mackenzie's efforts to attain a location veracity that would only truly become attainable with technological innovations arising a few short years later led directly to the formulation of a unique aesthetic, perfectly suited to the film's theme.

Another key point of distinction is that Mackenzie's film clearly utilizes a fictional construct. To attempt to dub apparently synchronized dialogue (as *The Exiles* did) in a true documentary that aspired to authenticity would contradict its starting premise. And while *simulation* of reality in documentary dates at least to Flaherty (one of Mackenzie's self-professed influences), literal verisimilitude was a defining point of the Direct Cinema. Thus *The Exiles* use of non-synchronous sound not only helps distinguish it from that movement, but points back to the tenuous relationship between fact and fiction.

In the end a better—if still imprecise—point of reference would be the Italian neorealists, for both content and methodology. Not only were these works shot on location, sometimes with non-actors, but critically, they were post-dubbed. As was the case with *The Exiles*, this was by circumstance: Rossellini's *Rome, Open City* (1945) was shot in the streets because Cinecittà studios were heavily damaged in World War II, and were in fact being used largely to house refugees. Cumbersome sound equipment was impractical to use in the streets, and thus the key neorealist films were shot silently. Dialogue and sound effects were post-dubbed, and Cinecittà became so skilled in this that in future years it became famous for its post-dubbing.

Likewise, the Italian neorealist films are remarkable in both their class-consciousness and their compassionate view of humanity. In his thesis, Mackenzie acknowledges the work of De Sica (as well as Castellani) but he doesn't stop to linger over it. Perhaps he was too busy inventing his own version, creating a uniquely North American strain.[43]

There is one other touchstone worth examining. Shortly prior to *The Exiles*' production, Joseph Strick, Sidney Meyers and Ben Maddow's *The Savage Eye* attempted to weave a narrative around largely candid street footage shot in the Los Angeles area. To this end, loose fiction scenarios were constructed to be enacted in public spaces, and numerous potential plots and framing devices were conceived to accommodate the resulting footage. In the end, an excellent script (primarily by Maddow) was utilized to thread the disparate footage into a whole. The film sought to show a glimpse of humanity that was at once brutal and compassionate. Like *The Exiles*, it ultimately relied on spoken narration, and featured exquisite urban cinematography.[44]

Yet there the overlaps end. While both films are compelling historical documents, *The Savage Eye* today seems far harsher, its vision more brutal, its eye indeed more savage. Mackenzie's view is ultimately gentler even as it dives into hardship, finding a dignity in his characters' struggles that persists in spite of their often less than noble behavior.

The Savage Heart of Kent Mackenzie

One thus comes to a seeming contradiction in Mackenzie's portrayal of his subjects. Said Mackenzie early in his thesis, "We sought to avoid the romance of poverty."[45] Yet despite his well-established agenda, at a later point in the text he acknowledges, "to someone like myself who has spent a lot of time on Main Street, it is a very glossy, cleaned up, and possibly somewhat romanticized version of what takes place down there."[46]

Mackenzie perhaps refers here to the beauty of the film's cinematography, perhaps to views of the characters which he thinks he imposed upon them. Yet without a certain tenderness or compassion, Mackenzie's vantage would indeed be much more brutal, his eye and ear more savage. It is precisely this ability to transcend any one description that suggests the film's true strength, while avoiding "noble savage" tropes.

Its transcendence is no accident. Though Mackenzie repeatedly refers to the inexperience of himself and his crew in his thesis, he simultaneously delineates in astonishing detail a methodology imbued with respect for his subject and task. The methods he developed along with his crew are as intricate as anything in the professional film industry. What he lacks in experience, he makes up for in patience, discipline, and ingenuity.

By reinventing the wheel of cinematic language, he places *himself* in the position of savage or ingénu; encountering his new craft with an openness that escapes the brutality of convention or stereotype. This naïve outsider's vantage allowed an empathy that helped him hear his subjects and render their tale. In parallel to the Native Americans starring in the film, who lived as a distinct community in the heart of downtown Los Angeles, he and his colleagues created their own unique cinema in the heart of America's cinema production capital, while standing apart from it.[47]

The Release(s)

Even the film itself was in effect exiled for decades. To understand this, one needs to look at its release history. The initial composite print of *The Exiles* was completed in April 1961, and premiered shortly thereafter at the San Francisco and Venice International Film Festivals. Upon these prestigious screenings, it received some initial acclaim, being featured on the cover of *Film Quarterly*.[48] But then it disappeared, at least from public view.

In the years that followed, as Thom Andersen notes, "It was always there, hiding in plain sight." Yet it didn't receive widespread recognition until many decades later, when Andersen's *Los Angeles Plays Itself* championed it, leading to its restoration by the UCLA Film & Television Archive and distribution by Milestone Films in 2008, fifty years after shooting began.

When it was at last released, it was perhaps its very absence from the public eye, and attendant lack of critical context, that allowed an exceptionally varied range of responses to arise. The restoration's reviews touched on a surprising multiplicity of themes, both specific and general. The subjects discussed span from the film's portrayal of Native American life,[49] to its documentation of the downtown Bunker Hill neighborhood and a lost moment in Los Angeles history,[50] to its example of a non-Hollywood cinema focused on human interaction (a cousin of Cassavetes and the French New Wave),[51] to its music, including that of the Revels, and Native American chants.[52]

The diversity and enthusiasm of response speaks directly to the layered depth in Mackenzie's enterprise, and ultimately to its success in hitting viewers at both social and personal levels. By relentlessly showing the world in which his characters live, then tempering it with the internal revelations of the confessional narration, Mackenzie struck a chord of carefully observed pathos—a unique variant of the "noble savage" that is devoid of caricature and hence open to interpretation.

Figure 14: *Film Quarterly*, Spring 1962.

The Paradox of Realism

Toward the end of his thesis, Mackenzie asks, "Is there any such thing as 'objective reality'?"[53] He notes that our lives are experienced through the window of the senses, from each person's point of view—and yet a distinct physical world to all extents and purposes still seems to exist. We know this, or feel it, but it's indefinable.

And if reality itself was indefinable, how was one to depict it? He ultimately looked at his own methodology for answers. Acknowledging that one had to select and emphasize certain aspects of the world, he then went further and determined that active "control and manipulation of elements" was needed.⁵⁴ As justification for this viewpoint he proceeded to delineate the impact the camera can have on the events it records; in essence changing the flow of reality's fabric. This is well understood today, but Mackenzie, critically, arrived at his conclusion not through theoretical exercises, but rather through careful observation of his own working process—as evidenced for example, in the efforts required to relax his subjects enough to record the narration.

He then pinpoints another fundamental justification for artistic control of conditions: the technical means of recording image and sound have their own inherent physical limitations, and do not in fact replicate what the human eye perceives. Different photographic films, lenses, recording devices, etc., each "alter" physical reality even as they capture it, according to their distinct mechanical properties.⁵⁵

From these two factors—the camera's effect on what it records, and its technologically limited means of recording—Mackenzie arrived at a radical conclusion: artistic intervention is in fact *required* as a fundamental corrective for the act of filming's own inherent limits.

> *It seems to me that to minimize the intrusion of the crew and to adjust the technical means of reproduction so that they will represent with accuracy, much control is required on the part of the filmmaker. He has to use every method and trick at his disposal to reconstruct what was there before he came or to construct completely anew the elements he needs to express what he perceives.*⁵⁶

Thus we see cinematic reality as an exchange between the world and the filmmaker. The filmmakers' interventions in this view act as counterbalance to the mitigating effects of filmmaking's own impact on "external" reality.

Herein, Mackenzie again unknowingly arrives at a conclusion not dissimilar to the more classical cinema he sought to reinvent. In 1960—concurrent with *The Exiles*' post-production—Siegfried Kracauer published his *Theory of Film*, the seminal work on the nature of photographic reality. In it, Kracauer traces the twin impulses of realism and formalism in cinema to the Lumière brothers and Méliès, citing them as dialectical, and announcing room for the true art of cinema in the interplay of their polar tendencies, in the space between document and fiction. He saw cinema as the tool by which modern man, through this interaction, might redeem a lost sense of the physical world. In Los Angeles, Mackenzie was at that same moment developing through direct practice his own unique variant of this equation: concluding that the essence of the filmmaker's art was in fact nothing less than the careful shaping of a *subjective* reality.

Through the Window

To fully understand the personal nature of Mackenzie's subjective reality, one finally needs look no further than his work itself. *The Exiles* contains structures within structures, all of which ultimately intermingle with the world they depict. From the prologue's initial framing, at a distanced perspective that sets up the story before descending deep inside its then-contemporary narrative, to a conclusion that fuses its distanced and intimate vantages, a multitude of views are expressed which, cumulatively, shape their own totality.

At the heart of the film is a split consciousness, embodied in its split creation process of filming and sound recording. Its tactile Exile of sound from image parallels Mackenzie's intrinsic inability as a white filmmaker to truly become an insider to the Indian community. To go further in—if even possible—would represent a loss of his own self, the very thing needed to step back and make the film.

At a broad level, the "failure" of the audio to seem natural in some sequences is in this way a fitting reminder of Mackenzie's vantage. At a finer level, it also points to the issue of self-awareness, the existential crisis depicted in the film. In the difficulties the Indians faced in their studio sessions trying to re-create the speed of their original, ad-libbed dialogue, and in their parallel difficulties creating more intimate narration in the presence of their friends, one sees problems by no means unique to Native Americans, but rather common to the modern condition. They speak to the pain of being self-aware, the loss of a whole self from a state of unconscious being. They speak to modern man's displacement from himself to an exile from Edenic innocence.

This is reflected in the very sound of the occasionally awkward line readings. In this sense, the film's main apparent "failing" in fact furthers its meanings at a subliminal level.

And yet it is not the entire story. As noted, the film's prologue—completed last—reveals Mackenzie's authorial retreat to a more distanced perspective after an immersion in Indian life as he is exiting the project. But by placing it at the beginning of the film, Mackenzie allows a largely non-Indian audience to enter its world gradually. He segues from the Curtis photos to the film's story via a series of still photographs of the actors, frozen frame enlargements from the film itself.

The film's story, despite its contained "twelve hours in the life" surface, contains its own revealing form. Mackenzie claimed, no doubt accurately, that all three of the film's main characters—Homer, Tommy and Yvonne—exhibited aspects of himself. Yet it seems revealing that the film's chronology both begins and ends with Yvonne, from her initial appearance walking dreamily and longingly through the Grand Central Market to the film's conclusion, described earlier.

By bookending the story with Yvonne, Mackenzie ultimately gives privilege to her vantage, and a clue to where his role as filmmaker lies—even if part of him would still like to be carousing with Tommy and Homer. As noted, the film's concluding image is a classic point-of-view shot that fuses Yvonne's perspective with the viewer's as she looks through the window. At this juncture the only sound is muted street noise and the incidental dialogue of her husband and his friends wandering down the street to their next destination. What one hears is what Yvonne hears—or doesn't hear—as an overwhelming quiet pervades both sound and image.

At this point we descend into Yvonne's inner world without the device of narration. The image-through-window and muted sound unite in an overriding sense of pathos: Yvonne as excluded from her own life as Mackenzie from his subject, or the viewer from the film. The near absence of sound allows us to hear our thoughts fused with the sounds of the world, and they are Mackenzie's thoughts, as well as Yvonne's, and our own. They speak of the pain of Exile.

Mackenzie wrote, "I hoped that perhaps in some way we could bridge the gap between informational and theatrical films and involve audiences more deeply in the lives of our characters."[57] In this image one experience the summation of his aesthetic: a view of Exile that lies beyond fact or fiction—one that calls for a radical new terminology and cinematic language that reflects a truth in subjectivity. It is here, at the window, that the film leaves us.

Endnotes

1. Kent Robert Mackenzie, *A Description and Examination of the Production of The Exiles: A Film of the Actual Lives of Young American Indians*, A Thesis Presented to the Faculty of the Graduate School, University of Southern California, 1964, 1, in The Mackenzie Papers, included on *The Exiles* DVD, Milestone Film & Video, 2009.
2. Critics Richard Brody and John Adams agree. See Richard Brody, "L.A. States of Mind," *The New Yorker*, November 23, 2009, and John Adams, "*The Exiles*," Movie Habit website, November 17, 2009. Prior to the November 2010 release of the *Exiles* DVD, Mackenzie's thesis was unavailable to either researchers or the general public. One can hope its publication (and the release of the film itself) will initiate further study.
3. Mackenzie, 7.
4. Mackenzie, 24.
5. Some discussion of terminology is in order at the outset. At the time of this essay's initial revision in 2014, the term "Native American" remained in common usage but was no longer in a position of preference. Some suggest that the decline in acceptance of the term is traceable to a bureaucratic quality associated with census-taking (in which tribe differentiation is ignored), yet acknowledge that the term is still widely employed (Borgna Brunner, "American Indian versus Native American." http://www.infoplease.com/spot/aihmterms.html, accessed January 25, 2014). A number of contemporary artists and activists indeed seem to veer away from it, but not in one particular direction. Photographer Pamela J. Peters, who has created a series of contemporary images inspired by *The Exiles*, prefers "American Indians" and, context-dependent, "Indigenous" ("Pamela J. Peters Photography," http://www.tachiiniiphotography.com/about- me.html, accessed January 25, 2014). Contrarily, the writer and filmmaker Sherman Alexie said he prefers the term "Indian" because he views both "Native American" and "American Indian" as oxymorons (phone conversation between Sherman Alexie and Dennis Doros, fall 2007). The term "First Nations" has its advantages, but as its reference context is Canadian it has limitations as well. In essence, a diversity of terms can be noted in contemporary speech. Acknowledging the multiple forms in play, this essay primarily utilizes the "Native American" formulation. However it retains Mackenzie's original "Indians" when quoted, and also within the text body, context-dependent, to denote the specific individuals who participated in the film's production.
6. Mackenzie, 21.
7. He had previously documented the area in another short film, *Bunker Hill—1956*. Now returning to his old haunts, he concentrated particularly on the bars near Third and Main Streets.
8. John Morrill, at the Los Angeles premiere screening of *The Exiles*' restoration, in the Billy Wilder Theater of the UCLA Film & Television Archive on August 15, 2009. Morrill's comments were made in a panel with Erik Daarstad, Merle Edelman, Lawrence Silberman, and Norm Knowles, moderated by Jan-Christopher Horak (audio recording included in *The Exiles* DVD). This may in part have been based on notions of what the word "documentary" meant at the time of the film's production. I did not press Morrill for clarification on his comment, but took his use of the word documentary to refer to films such

as Leo Hurwitz's *Native Land* or any number of works by Robert Flaherty, which intermingle forms of acted scenarios with documentary footage and/or commentary. Regardless, it should be noted that this viewpoint clearly represents Morrill's point of view, and should not be understood as representing Mackenzie's.

9. In an early review of the film, Benjamin Jackson notes that "we must remember that *The Exiles* is not a "documentary" film in the ordinary sense. It is an original and personal film which defies classification." Benjamin Jackson, "*The Exiles*," *Film Quarterly*, Spring 1962, 60. In another early piece, Pauline Kael's notes on the film do not classify it but frame their discussion as if it were a narrative work. Pauline Kael, "*The Exiles*," in *Kiss Kiss Bang Bang* (Bantam, 1969), 326. These differing examples viewed together help clarify the work's unique vantage as a hybrid.
10. Mackenzie, 25.
11. Mackenzie, 26.
12. In this respect he evokes not so much Curtis, but his own contemporary, Robert Frank, whose *The Americans* was published in 1958, as *The Exiles* was shooting.
13. See Amy Taubin, "Minority Report," *Art Forum*, July 10, 2008, http://artforum.com/film/id+20717. Taubin singles out the openly sexist behavior of the men, and chides Mackenzie for portraying "drunken Indians." It's possible she would have preferred a more clearly stated viewpoint in relation to Tommy's rampant womanizing, which is presented without overt comment. In his thesis, Mackenzie acknowledged that Tommy was his best friend for several years, and one can easily imagine him perhaps turning a blind eye to the darker side of some the latter's actions, the outgoing Tommy being a perfect conduit for Mackenzie into the Indians' social scene. Those displeased with his apparent "free pass" can argue that there were other types of characters floating around Bunker Hill than those found in *The Exiles*, whose stories aren't told here. However, alcohol was undeniably an active part of the particular world Mackenzie found, and the gender roles depicted were common. Likewise, while the depiction of Tommy is affectionate, it strikes this writer and many others that his behavior is nonetheless completely unglamorized, and speaks all too clearly for itself. To openly editorialize would have flown in the face of Mackenzie's entire aesthetic and ethos.
14. The Indians' relation to their own heritage is no less ambiguous. While the film's protagonists find strength in their ancestry, the meanings are transformed. Speaking of the climactic tribal dance scene on Hill X, Mackenzie notes, "Many of these young singers knew very little about their own tribal backgrounds, and the songs were actually quite corrupted from the originals. There was one older singer at the dance, and the younger Indians were fascinated to hear him sing because it was the 'old way' and so different from theirs. The "Grass Dance" song, we were told by an amateur anthropologist, was actually a young Indian version of a phonograph record of a classical symphonic poem that had originally been derived from a true "Grass Dance" song of the Sioux." The Hill X scene culminates in a fight, and stands in contrast with the tribal song sung quietly on the reservation, which Mackenzie cites as having more authenticity in the traditional sense (Mackenzie, 104-105). Despite the bleakness of events surrounding it, the Hill X dance speaks more to the historical moment than the tribal song sung on the reservation, which is preserved in its own exile.
15. Mackenzie, 12.
16. Ibid., 13.
17. Ibid.
18. In describing the methods used to shoot this scene, cinematographer Erik Daarstad recounts, "For the exteriors the bare 40 watt bulbs on the porches were replaced with brighter bulbs and then used both as part of the scene and as the motivating source." In contemporary cinematographic language, motivated on-set light sources are called "practicals," but the *Exiles* camera team's interventions went well beyond that. Daarstad continues, "Masterlites and clip lights were hidden behind stairways and poles, etc. or placed just out of camera range." Erik Daarstad, letter to Kent Mackenzie, February 1964; excerpted in Mackenzie, 64.
19. Mackenzie, 62. John Morrill states further, "In order to photograph natural light as it appears to the eye, it is usually necessary to expand or contract the brightness range." John Morrill, letter to Kent Mackenzie, December 1963. Excerpted in Mackenzie, 63.
20. This is immediately evident in a mere glance at the chapter names of Mackenzie's account, which include "Attitudes Leading to *The Exiles*, Research and Scripting, Directing and Acting, Photography, Voice Recording, Editing, Music and Sound Effects." Mackenzie, Table of Contents.

21. Looping refers to the technical process whereby a film's dialogue is post-dubbed. Mackenzie had his production soundtrack transferred from its original ¼" audiotape to 16mm magnetic film, and cut into a circular loop. This could be played continuously for the actors to listen to through headphones as they attempted to replicate the lines (for an account of his process, see Mackenzie, 76). The only dialogue in the film which was not post-dubbed occurred in the opening supper scene, the reservation scene, and the Hill X sequence.
22. In addition to the Arriflex, the crew sometimes used an NC Mitchell and an Eclair Camerette. Mackenzie notes that a synchronous motor was occasionally used with the Arriflex to avoid speed variations and flicker, but the camera remained unblimped (Mackenzie, 60).
23. Mackenzie, 92.
24. Ibid., 74.
25. Ibid., 75.
26. Ibid.
27. Ibid., 76.
28. Ibid.
29. Ibid., 78.
30. Ibid., 79.
31. Ibid., 80.
32. Ibid.
33. Ibid., 91-92. One presumes he is discussing the narration in the gas station sequence, as the text clearly distinguishes narration from dialogue, however this is not certain.
34. Ibid., 78.
35. Mackenzie provides excerpts of the full narration transcripts and their subsequent editing in Appendix E of his thesis, 152-155.
36. In the early pages of his thesis Mackenzie denounces mainstream American/Hollywood cinema, and freely admits finding inspiration within works from the international art cinema canon, as well as documentary traditions. Independent auteur John Cassavetes is included in a short list appearing in the final pages of the manuscript, marking filmmakers "who were completely unknown, or just verbal rumors, when we began in 1958" (Mackenzie, 128). However, no mention is made of forbears Helen Levitt, Sidney Meyers, and Morris Engel, or other east coast filmmakers such as Lionel Rogosin, who were concurrently developing a cinema that bears relevance to Mackenzie's interests, which may suggest that he was unfamiliar with their work or did not consider it immediately connected.
37. Another view of Mackenzie's influences can be found in Leo Goldsmith, *The Exiles* (2009), http://www.notcoming.com/. Although similarly brief, Goldsmith's review is one of the most considered readings of *The Exiles* to date.
38. Mackenzie, 37.
39. Ibid., 84. It should be noted that echoes of conventional structure remain, even as they're tossed aside. The ghost of catharsis lingers in the drunken brawl on Hill X; it functions as a momentary release of social tension that is at best generalized and results in no practical resolution.
40. The praise of this aspect of *The Exiles* has been particularly pointed. Richard Brody notes that "the night photography alone would make the film immortal. Few directors in the history of cinema have so skillfully and deeply joined a sense of place with the subtle flux of inner life." Richard Brody, *The Exiles*, *The New Yorker*, July 7, 2008. Perhaps the most famous celebration of the film's location cinematography came from director Thom Andersen, who described it as one of the best documentations of Los Angeles in cinematic history in his classic film essay, *Los Angeles Plays Itself* (2003).
41. Mackenzie, 129–130.
42. *Primary*, by Robert Drew (along with Ricky Leacock, Albert Maysles, and D.A. Pennebaker), considered by many to be the first American "Direct Cinema" film, and the first to "successfully" use lightweight portable equipment for synchronizing sound and image, was made in 1960—but the production sync on *Primary* (which involved several technical innovations by Leacock) drifted terribly, and the film was extensively post-synchronized. Although the Nagra III sound recorder (with an electric motor) was developed in 1957, there were still problems preventing its effective use for many years. It wasn't until 1962 that the Nagra III and its accompanying technology was developed sufficiently to allow reliable sync.

43. Crew members stated that Mackenzie's method differed from De Sica in that De Sica used scripts (by Cesare Zavattini), and frequently enacted roles for his non-actors to imitate (Merle Edelman, UCLA panel discussion, op cit.). Mackenzie confirms that he avoided this technique, although there were moments of exception. Mackenzie, 44-45.
44. *The Savage Eye* was photographed primarily by Haskell Wexler, Helen Levitt, and Jack Couffer. Wexler occasionally helped out on *The Exiles*, and in fact *Exiles* cinematographer Robert Kaufman is credited as an assistant on *The Savage Eye*. Kaufman confirms that he did indeed work on Savage Eye, although in a relatively small capacity. He apparently met Wexler while working at Wexler/Churchill Film Productions, which was co-founded by Bob Churchill and Sy Wexler, the latter of whom also worked on *Savage Eye*. Kaufman had mistakenly thought that Simon (Sy) Wexler was Haskell's father, who was also named Simon, but the latter was a Chicago businessman and founder of Allied Radio. Phone conversation with Robert Kaufman, November 12, 2009.
45. Mackenzie, 29.
46. Ibid., 115.
47. Mackenzie himself noted, "I am not of Hollywood, although I work in it, and aside from the fact that I owe a lot of money to people in Hollywood, I really don't identify myself with the industry as such." Mackenzie, Kent. In "Personal Creation in Hollywood: Can it be Done?," *Film Quarterly*, Spring 1962, 33.
48. Despite the cover, Mackenzie did not have a star-studded Hollywood career. He went on to produce several short documentaries, and worked on numerous other films, including Saul Bass' *Why Man Creates*, which was photographed by Erik Daarstad. He was only to complete one other feature, *Saturday Morning* in 1971, photographed by Daarstad and Morrill. The film documents a weeklong psychological encounter session of a group of teenagers, and again shows a fascination with the relationship between truth and simulation, as shown in play-acting sessions between its subjects, which in some instances include Mackenzie himself.
49. As an example, see: Wesley Morris, "A Study of Outcasts in Their Own Land," *Boston Globe*, September 26, 2008.
50. See, for example: Andrew O' Hehir, "All–night Party in a Lost City," Salon.com, July 10 2008.
51. See, for example: Jonathan Rosenbaum, "*The Exiles*" capsule review, *The Chicago Reader*.
52. See, for example: Quintin, "*The Exiles*," *Cinema Scope* online (undated).
53. Mackenzie, 115.
54. Ibid., 121.
55. Ibid., 122.
56. Ibid.
57. Mackenzie, 81.

On Samuel Beckett's *Film*
(1965)

Samuel Beckett's *Film* was restored by UCLA Film & Television Archive in cooperation with the British Film Institute, with funding from The Film Foundation administered by the National Film Preservation Foundation. The restoration was subsequently digitally remastered by UCLA in collaboration with Milestone Films at NT Picture & Sound, and Fotokem. Laboratory services provided by Cinetech, Ascent Media, NT Picture & Sound, Dolby Laboratories, and Audio Mechanics. Restoration and remastering supervised by Ross Lipman in collaboration with colleagues including audio restorationist John Polito, the Academy Film Archive, Edward Beckett, Nicole Brenez, Les Éditions de Minuit, Evergreen Review, David Gray, Shawn Jones, Andrew Lampert, Jonathan Lee, Irène Lindon, Bruce Mazen, the Pacific Film Archive, Barney and Astrid Rosset. Distributed by Milestone.

In some ways my most academic essay, this piece takes a deep dive into film language itself, and how cinema works. While I've not been alone in questioning the use of the word "language" in describing cinematic properties, or "cinematic texts" to describe films, there is some relevance in its usage here, in light of Beckett's concept of Film *and his related work in other media forms. He is not merely repeating or illustrating George Berkeley's statement that "To be is to be perceived," but offering a cinematic response to it. Beckett's separation of subject and object in the respective forms of the camera eye and what it sees, speaks to a larger problem—addressing not just Berkeley's legacy, but the Cartesian dilemma of the alienated and divided self. I find this same theme running through the preceding essay on* The Exiles, *as well as much of my other work; most notably* Notfilm. *Why this ongoing fascination on my part? I have some thoughts, but that's a discussion for another time.*

This essay was adapted from a lecture presented at the conference 'Samuel Beckett and the Nonhuman', Vrije Universiteit, Brussels, February 2019. It was subsequently published in The Journal of Beckett Studies, Vol. 24, No. 2, 2019. *The citations retain the formatting of the JoBS edition. Special thanks to Edward Beckett, Stan Gontarski, Barney Rosset, Jean Schneider, and Pim Verhulst. Photos of production documents courtesy the Samuel Beckett Estate, the Mandeville Special Collections Library at University of California San Diego, and Milestone Films.*

Reframing Berkeley: The Form of Non-Being,

or:

Fixing *Film*

Abstract

This essay seeks to elucidate some of the many challenges faced by Beckett and his collaborators in their attempt to realize his exploration of subjective consciousness in cinema. It utilizes Beckett's unpublished production notes, correspondence, and examples from the production's original camera tests to examine the technical and formal ways that he, director Alan Schneider and cinematographer Boris Kaufman sought to make physically manifest the abstract ideas underlying the unconventional script of *Film*. In the many photochemical experiments they conducted prior to production, discovered amidst the outtakes in the course of *Film*'s restoration, one sees Beckett's unique vision struggling with not just the theoretical constructs of a new medium, but with its nuts-and-bolts construction. The interaction between the idea and its realization in turn serves as a metaphor for Beckett's larger dialogue with Bishop Berkeley, and its questions on the nature of Being, which drive *Film*.

Conception

Samuel Beckett's ambivalent relationship with Bishop Berkeley traces back to at least his mid-twenties. In 1933 we find him already writing that he found Berkeley to be "full of profound things, and at the same time of a foul (& false) intellectual canaillerie, enough to put you against reading anything more." (Beckett to MacGreevy, April 23, 1933; Beckett, 2009a, 154) Five years later, he again expressed his ambivalence in *Murphy*. (Beckett, 2009b, 154) Yet like his fascination with cinema, this paradoxical dynamic would wait decades before focused exploration.[1] When he at last dove in, the two lines of thought would unexpectedly dovetail, in *Film*.

By basing his script on Berkeley's premise *esse est percipi* ("To be is to be perceived"),[2] and in title, throwing its focus back on the mechanism of recording, he located the existential crisis of modernity in the very fabric of the movies themselves. *Film* reframes Berkeley by perversely denying being. It asks, "What is it to not be?" The answer is in the asking, and the asking is realized through the interplay of camera and actor.

For Beckett, these are but two parts of a split consciousness. Describing his project in an early letter of June 21, 1963 to *Film*'s producer Barney Rosset, he wrote:

It is [...] the old theme of split personality, except that here the split is [...] between the being that is perceived and the being that perceives. And in order that this may be shown (on a screen) the two halves are given shape [...] in the form of a fleeing object and a perceiving eye. (Beckett, 2014, 549–50)

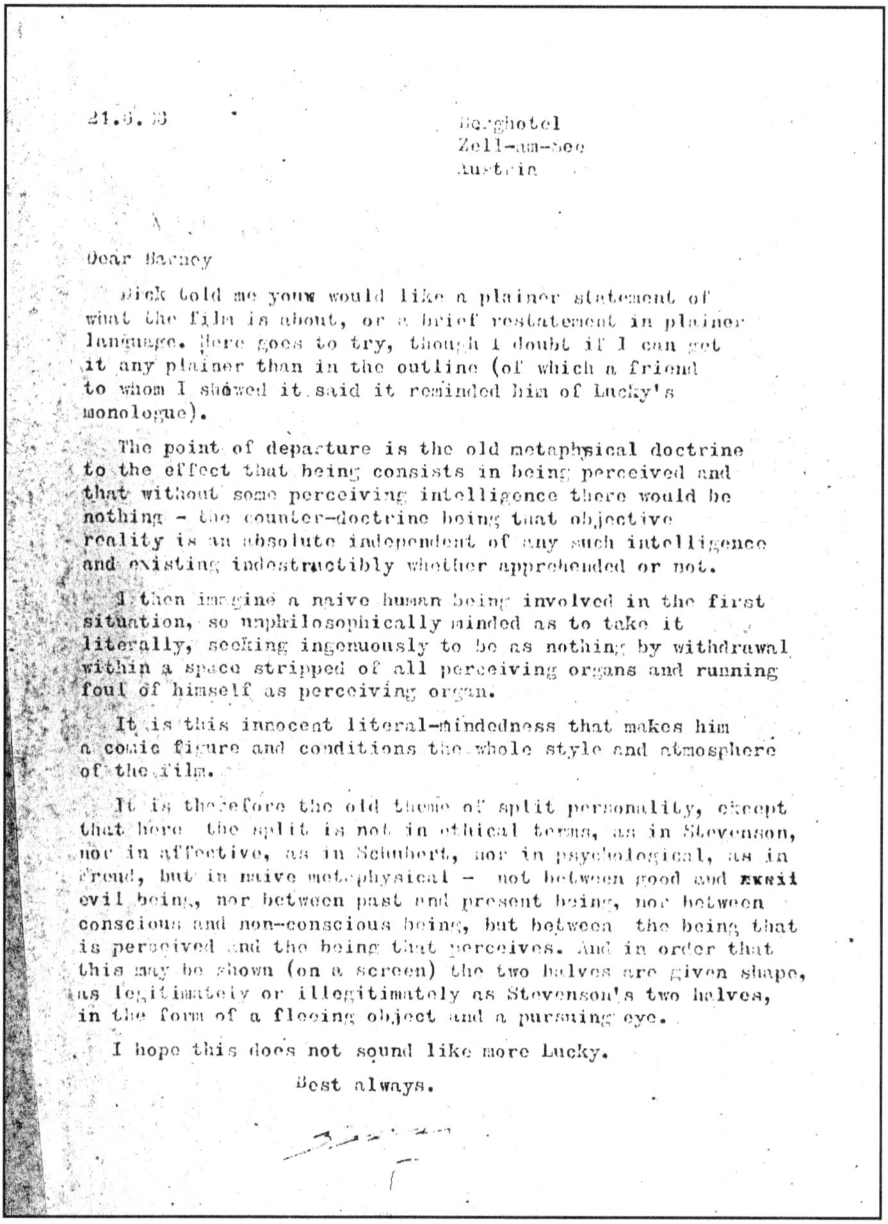

> 21.6.63
>
> Berghotel
> Zell-am-See
> Austria
>
> Dear Barney
>
> Dick told me you would like a plainer statement of what the film is about, or a brief restatement in plainer language. Here goes to try, though I doubt if I can get it any plainer than in the outline (of which a friend to whom I showed it said it reminded him of Lucky's monologue).
>
> The point of departure is the old metaphysical doctrine to the effect that being consists in being perceived and that without some perceiving intelligence there would be nothing – the counter-doctrine being that objective reality is an absolute independent of any such intelligence and existing indestructibly whether apprehended or not.
>
> I then imagine a naive human being involved in the first situation, so unphilosophically minded as to take it literally, seeking ingenuously to be as nothing by withdrawal within a space stripped of all perceiving organs and running foul of himself as perceiving organ.
>
> It is this innocent literal-mindedness that makes him a comic figure and conditions the whole style and atmosphere of the film.
>
> It is therefore the old theme of split personality, except that here the split is not in ethical terms, as in Stevenson, nor in affective, as in Schubert, nor in psychological, as in Freud, but in naive metaphysical – not between good and evil being, nor between past and present being, nor between conscious and non-conscious being, but between the being that is perceived and the being that perceives. And in order that this may be shown (on a screen) the two halves are given shape, as legitimately or illegitimately as Stevenson's two halves, in the form of a fleeing object and a pursuing eye.
>
> I hope this does not sound like more Lucky.
>
> Best always.

Figure 1. The "Lucky" letter (Samuel Beckett to Barney Rosset, June 21, 1963). Courtesy of Mandeville Special Collections Library, University of California San Diego, and Jean Schneider. © The Estate of Samuel Beckett.

Through this split consciousness, Beckett takes Berkeley's premise to its absurd conclusion. In a humorous if indifferently cruel world, the "mechanical" eye of the camera stands in for the all-seeing Eye of Self, in the act of witnessing itself. He would name the personalities E, for Eye, and O, for Object.

The twist on Berkeley lies in O's response to the perceiving Eye: terrified flight. Beckett dryly posits that Berkeley's *esse* isn't worth the pain of *percipi*. If one takes the Latin *percipere* (to perceive) as the inverse of *percipi*, the drama exists in their interplay. Beckett himself noted the distinction of these principles in *Murphy*: "Then this also faded and Murphy began to see nothing, that colourlessness which is such a rare postnatal treat, being the absence (to abuse a nice distinction) not of *percipere* but of *percipi*." (2009b, 154) Yet as shall be seen, there was another level of paradox. His cinematic response to Berkeley was initially moored in its intellectual construct, existing only on the page. To realize his premise it would need to be recorded. And this was for him, new territory. He would need to give flesh to *Film*.

Gestation

In the translation from concept to flesh, one finds flux, as the idea gestated through different forms. From the beginning, this flux was driven by Beckett's self-acknowledged unfamiliarity with the practical aspects of filmmaking. In his 1936 letter to Sergei Eisenstein in application of placement at Moscow's VGIK State School of Cinematography, he wrote:

> I have no experience of studio work and it is naturally in the scenario and editing end of the subject that I am most interested. It is because I realise that the script is a function of its means of realization that I am anxious to make contact with your mastery of these and beg you to consider me a serious *cinéaste* worthy of admission to your school. I could stay a year at least. (Beckett, 2009a, 317)

This note implicitly references Pudovkin, who wrote of the scenario in relation to the technical aspects of cinema in his book *Film Technique*, and with whom Beckett expressed interest in studying. (Beckett to MacGreevy, February 6, 1936; Beckett, 2009a, 311) But as he never heard back from Eisenstein or VGIK, his inexperience remained in place at the time *Film*'s production commenced in the summer of 1964, twenty-seven years later. He directly forefronts this dilemma in the opening notes to *Film*, saying the production "poses a problem of images which I cannot solve without technical help."[3] (Beckett, 1969, 12)

The specific stages of his search for a practical way to realize *Film*'s underlying concepts bear study. Per his thoughts of 1936, he began with the scenario. In his previously cited letter to Barney Rosset explaining *Film*'s script, he described the futility he intended to elucidate in the piece, writing of the split-personality protagonist "seeking ingenuously to be as nothing by withdrawal from a space stripped of all perceiving organs and running foul of himself as perceiving organ."[4] (Beckett, 2014, 549–50) Yet in the scenario instructions he writes, "No truth value attaches to (the reframing of Berkeley described), regarded as of merely structural and dramatic convenience."[5] (1969, 11) That structural and dramatic convenience—envisioned in the split personality of camera and object—elucidates Beckett's thoughts on the medium, but in its challenges proved far from convenient in practice.

By May 1964, just over a month before shooting, one finds him writing an extraordinarily detailed enumeration of his intentions (1964a).[6] (See figures 2a and 2a overleaf.)

The scenario depicted therein is quite different than the published edition of the script, which traces to the original 1963 manuscript. It is thus interesting to note that while the final shooting script (Beckett and Schneider, 1964b) was based on the later document, virtually none of its finer details found their way to the screen in the end.[7] What went wrong?

It's not until his actual arrival in the US and his production meetings with the technical team that one finds a grounded endeavor to physically manifest the ideas that in conception seemed inherently cinematic.[8] Here too, the explorations veer toward abstraction. The audio recordings of the meetings, illicitly made by Rosset, reveal that of all the technical concerns they faced, creating distinct cinematic interpretations of E and O's perspectives was by far the most pressing and problematic. This topic dominates the majority of the extensive meeting time, wherein Beckett struggles to convey his vision to the production team.

A full enumeration of the methods proposed to address the issue is beyond the scope of the present study, but suffice it to say that a wide variety of approaches are explored in the meetings.[9] As an example, they devote considerable time discussing how it might work if E's eyes were closed.[10] At another point Beckett defines E as the "cutter" and O as the "panner," then with some hint of exasperation, asks, "Isn't that the idea we've reached?" His asking reveals that the proposed dynamic was arrived at only then, and even so remained uncertain. E's perspective shots in *Film* indeed begin with a pan—supposedly O's domain, and pan-like movement can be found consistently throughout the work in shots from both perspectives.

This abandoned approach points to a traditional construct in film theory in which *montage* (the juxtaposition of shots) is distinguished from *mise-en-scène* (composition and movement within a single shot), creating a cinematic art in their interaction (Godard, 1972). Yet in this context, the proposed dynamic could not successfully address the E/O divide. In practice, *both* E (Eye) and O are intrinsically "seeing" perspectives, whereas "cutting" (or editing)—the technique proposed for E—requires a third consciousness apart from seeing that inherently absorbs both visions. In conventional cinema, linear construction in time dictates this for any single-channel work in which different camera perspectives are intercut. In the perception of the viewer, only one visual perspective exists at a time, as they alternate.

Beckett expressly rejected showing both perspectives in the same image, via split screen or other method, on the grounds that it would "perhaps make impossible for the spectator a clear apprehension of either." (Beckett, 1969, 58) In theory one could create a multi-channel work consisting of the two perspectives shown simultaneously on different screens or monitors, but that would again take the work beyond the confines of traditional cinema, and hence beyond *Film*.

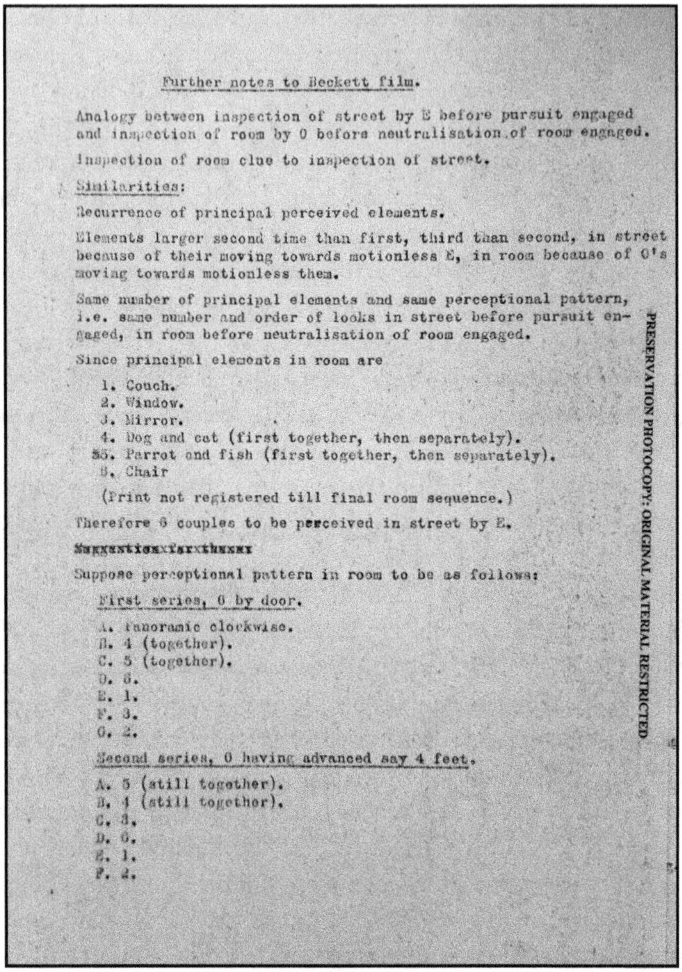

> Further notes to Beckett film.
>
> Analogy between inspection of street by E before pursuit engaged and inspection of room by O before neutralisation of room engaged.
>
> Inspection of room clue to inspection of street.
>
> Similarities:
>
> Recurrence of principal perceived elements.
>
> Elements larger second time than first, third than second, in street because of their moving towards motionless E, in room because of O's moving towards motionless them.
>
> Same number of principal elements and same perceptional pattern, i.e. same number and order of looks in street before pursuit engaged, in room before neutralisation of room engaged.
>
> Since principal elements in room are
>
> 1. Couch.
> 2. Window.
> 3. Mirror.
> 4. Dog and cat (first together, then separately).
> 5. Parrot and fish (first together, then separately).
> 6. Chair
>
> (Print not registered till final room sequence.)
>
> Therefore 6 couples to be perceived in street by E.
>
> ~~Suggestion:Isixthxxxx~~
>
> Suppose perceptional pattern in room to be as follows:
>
> First series, O by door.
>
> A. Panoramic clockwise.
> B. 4 (together).
> C. 5 (together).
> D. 6.
> E. 1.
> F. 3.
> G. 2.
>
> Second series, O having advanced say 4 feet.
>
> A. 5 (still together).
> B. 4 (still together).
> C. 3.
> D. 6.
> E. 1.
> F. 2.

Figures 2A and 2B. "Further notes to Beckett film" (c. May 1964), pp. 1-2 of 4; courtesy of Mandeville Special Collections Library, University of California San Diego, and Jean Schneider. © The Estate of Samuel Beckett.

It is worth noting that within the above construct, Beckett further described the nature of the camera movement specifically as panning, which is in fact largely what's seen from O's perspective in *Film*. The panning is brilliantly executed, but one can argue that panning in itself is an insufficient metaphor for subjective vision, in that the human eye's natural movements in sight are generally not so linear, and far more kinetic. While one might think such movements would not work cinematically, it is not necessarily that intuitive. Concurrent to the production of *Film*, avant-garde filmmakers including Stan Brakhage were exploring highly sophisticated experiments in cinematic sight, alongside highly articulated theoretical models of the same, of which the most elaborate is arguably Brakhage's *Metaphors on Vision*.

This text opens with his famous imperative to undo all previous constructs of seeing and return to the origins of sight:

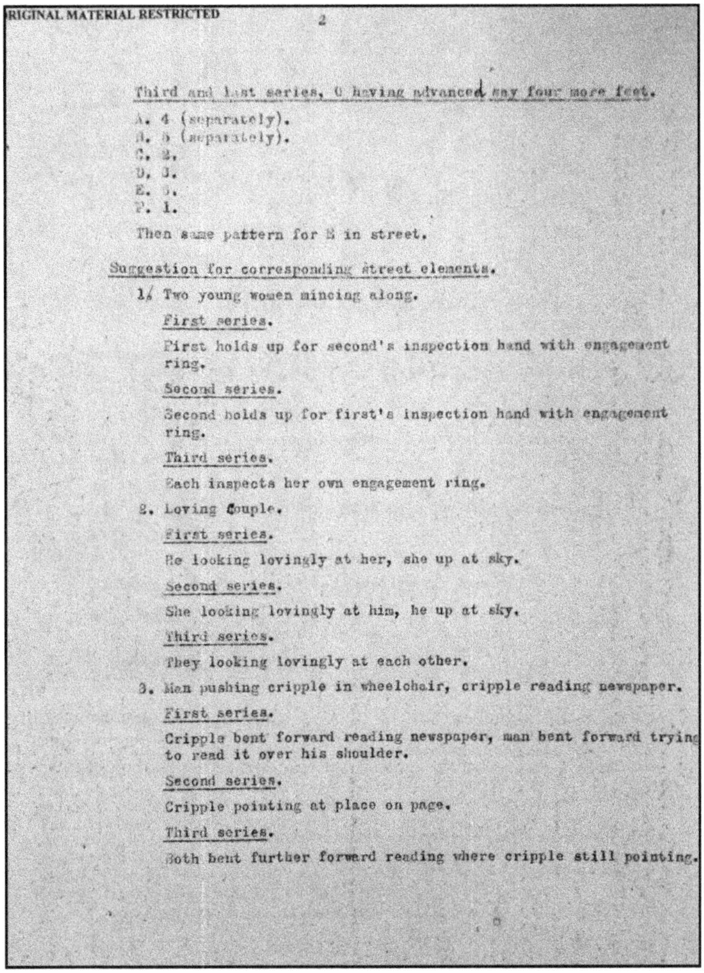

RIGINAL MATERIAL RESTRICTED

2

Third and last series, O having advanced say four more feet.

A. 4 (separately).
B. 5 (separately).
C. 2.
D. 3.
E. 6.
F. 1.

Then same pattern for B in street.

Suggestion for corresponding street elements.

1. Two young women mincing along.

First series.

First holds up for second's inspection hand with engagement ring.

Second series.

Second holds up for first's inspection hand with engagement ring.

Third series.

Each inspects her own engagement ring.

2. Loving couple.

First series.

He looking lovingly at her, she up at sky.

Second series.

She looking lovingly at him, he up at sky.

Third series.

They looking lovingly at each other.

3. Man pushing cripple in wheelchair, cripple reading newspaper.

First series.

Cripple bent forward reading newspaper, man bent forward trying to read it over his shoulder.

Second series.

Cripple pointing at place on page.

Third series.

Both bent further forward reading where cripple still pointing.

Figure 2B.

> Imagine an eye unruled by man-made laws of perspective, an eye unprejudiced by compositional logic, an eye which does not respond to the name of everything but which must know each object encountered in life through an adventure in perception. How many colors are there in a field of grass to the crawling baby unaware of 'Green'? (Brakhage, 1963)

Brakhage's clarion call posits common sight perception as a learned or socialized process, and specifically rejects classical perspective and mathematical projections of space in favor of a more sensory-induced model. Berkeley (1929a), as it happens, also proposed a sensory model of sight, but argued that our sense impressions are the very building blocks of learned constructions of visual space, in *opposition* to the same perspectival laws that Brakhage rejects.

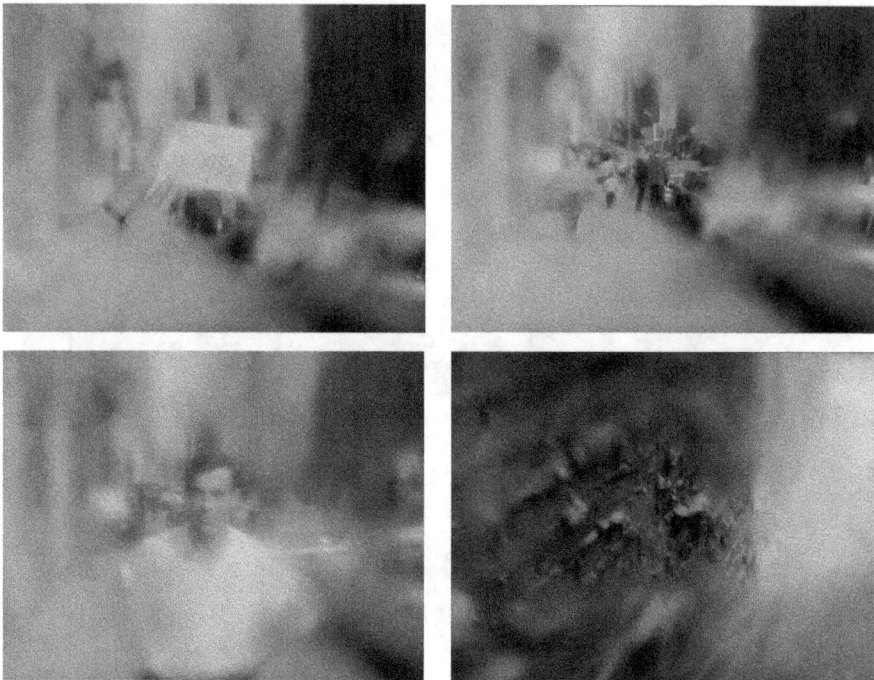

Figure 3A. Film camera tests: E's blurred vision experiments. July 15, 1964.

In this series of tests, Vaseline has been used, with less applied in the center of the frame, perhaps to invoke the appearance of an eye's iris.

Top left: Camera slate ("Vaseline on glass")
Top right: street scene
Bottom left: Grove editor Dick Seaver
Bottom right: the wall

Brakhage here varies from Berkeley, and finds in the origins of sight a chance to move beyond learned framing of percepts. In this regard, Beckett's explorations comprise a valuable parallel track that is at once retrograde and a singularly fascinating counterpoint to the 1960s experimentalists.

While the 'cutting' proposal referenced above was only discussed briefly in *Film*'s production meetings, significant time was given to the specific visual character of E's and O's perspectives. Most concisely, Beckett delineated O's vision as "slower" and "softer," whereas director Alan Schneider, on Beckett's behalf, described E's abnormal sight as "heightened." The requests for "heightened" vision distressed their highly experienced cinematographer Boris Kaufman, who rejoined that he could not cinematographically "heighten" reality, because any cinematic alteration of the image would in fact be a movement away from verisimilitude (see Gontarski, Ardoin).[11] The meetings concluded with the treatment methods largely unresolved,

Figure 3B. Film camera tests: E's blurred vision experiments. July 15, 1964.

Top left: moderate blurring
Top right: severe blurring
Bottom left: camera slate ("B" glass diffusion + "A" silk)
Bottom right: Director Alan Schneider making the "shhh" sign.

leaving Kaufman and his technical team to conduct a series of camera experiments during pre-production week.[12]

Revealingly, these tests with just one exception, copiously explored different photographic methods of creating the "soft" vision of O. In support of Kaufman's position, the single test of E's perspective involved no image manipulation at all.[13] The tests for O's perspective however, involved a number of different blurring effects. No definitive record has been found linking their eventual choice to the slated tests, but it was presumably one of them.[14]

The level of its success is another question. Speaking later of the final film, Beckett wrote:

> The problem of the double vision [...] is not really solved, but the attempt to solve it has given the film a plastic value which it would not have otherwise [...]. I described [*Film*] to Barney after the first screening as an "interesting failure." This I now see is much too severe. It does I suppose in a sense fail

with reference to a purely intellectual schema [...] but in so doing has acquired a dimension and a validity of its own that are worth far more than any merely efficient translation of intention. (Beckett, 2014, 631)

Figure 3C. Film camera tests: E's blurred vision experiments.
Different tests depicting the drawing of the Sumerian god Abu that appears in the film.

In so writing, Beckett acknowledged that Kaufman's cinematography captures an ethereal essence that transcends the initial conception.

Yet intriguingly, more experimentation seems to have occurred after production was concluded. A 16mm print of *Film* found in the collection of the Academy Film Archive in Los Angeles shows still another attempt to differentiate the visions. In this print, the work's editing is identical, but laboratory techniques have been applied to further distinguish the two perspectives. Specifically, the shots from O's perspective, while retaining the identical de-focusing of earlier prints, were here printed more darkly. No documentation of this experiment could be found in the papers of Beckett, Barney Rosset, Alan Schneider, or Boris Kaufman. For this reason its provenance is unknown, but as Rosset retained *Film*'s rights even after selling Grove Press,[15] it can be presumed to represent an effort of someone connected to the production. As it has been found in just a single print in the 16mm format with no documentation, it can be further presumed that this was a limited experiment that was deemed at best inconclusive.[16]

Figure 4A and 4B. Comparison of original approved print and experimental print of unknown origin.

Left: Grading of E's vision in an original 35mm print.

Right: Simulation of the darker grading of E's vision in the unique 16mm print found in the collection of the Academy Film Archive.

Another attempt to address the problem can be found in the 1979 BFI remake of *Film*, directed by David Rayner Clark. In some ways, this interpretation of Beckett's scenario looks back to the Grove edition of the text more faithfully than the original 1964 production, but in others varies farther from it.[17] Most notably, the remake differs from the original by adding sound and color. These factors both come into play addressing the question of E and O, wherein the film's picture cuts from E's to O's perspective are accompanied by an audio transition from on-camera diegetic location noises to the (close) off-camera sound of O's breath, alongside a switch from a sharp if somewhat muted color image to one that is grainy, defocused and primarily monochromatic.[18] Beckett found this adaptation of the scenario, which was made without his involvement, "regrettable." (letter to David Warrilow, 17 September 1984; Beckett, 2016, 644) Nonetheless, these changes arguably articulate the difference between the two perspectives more successfully than the 1964 version, in that the audio switch to O's internal breathing reinforces the subjectivity of the accompanying picture.

Figure 5A and 5B. Comparison of E's perspective in original and BFI productions.

Left: *Film* (Alan Schneider, 1964)

Right: *Film* (David Rayner Clark, 1979) (color)

 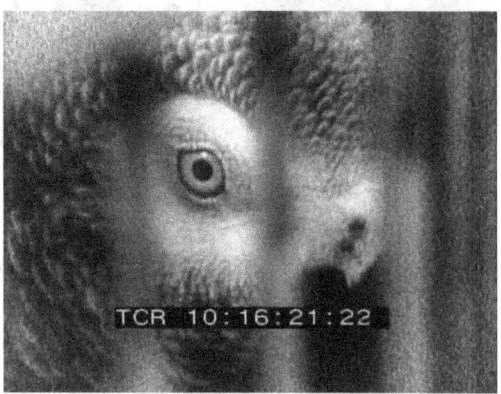

Figure 6A and 6B. Comparison of O's perspective in original and BFI productions.

Left: *Film* (Alan Schneider, 1964)

Right: *Film* (David Rayner Clark, 1979) (color)

The question of best approach still lingers. Anthony Paraskeva posits that the production team should have opted to print O's perspective in a negative image (58).[19] Further, records indicate that Beckett himself continued to deliberate some of the departure points of the 1979 interpretation not only after the original manuscript's completion, but—at least briefly—after the 1964 version's shooting had concluded.

As an example, Beckett's letters to Schneider, written after editing had commenced suggest that the question of sound remained open. In the previously cited letter of 29 September 1964, he wrote, "Now I am definitely and finally opposed to any sound whatever apart from the 'hssh.'" (Beckett, 2014, 631) Principal photography was completed on 29 July 1964, and Beckett left the US on 7 August after working with editor Sidney Meyers on the initial cut. His writing thusly a month later suggests the question remained open upon his departure.

Perhaps the most pertinent experiment of all can be found not in *Film* and its direct gestational shapes, but rather in a short experimental work shot by Boris Kaufman years beforehand. In 1951 he lensed a production entitled *The Gentleman in Room 6*. This cinematic oddity uncannily predicts *Film* in depicting a subjective camera perspective that hides the seeing face until the end of the movie, exactly as in Beckett's later work. Some of the shots in *The Gentleman in Room 6* closely resemble shots in *Film*, and it's clear that the earlier work influenced Kaufman's approach to Beckett's questions in 1964.

There is one telling difference, which Kaufman himself would well understand. On the general issue of cinematic effects, he had said:

> I reject tricks. I think when tricks start, the medium stops [...] you have to heighten certain segments of this thing, to get the feeling you're seeking—but [...] not for the sake of the visual effect—only when dramatically required. These are two different things, you know. One is justified, and I accept that, then it's not a trick anymore. (Kaufman, 1959)

In coincidental harmony, Beckett himself used nearly identical phrasing, cautioning in the production meetings against the danger of "gimmicks."[20] (Ardoin, 2014) *The Gentleman in Room 6*'s final shot dramatically reveals through a mirror that the camera's subjective view is that of a postwar Adolf Hitler, alive and in hiding in South America. While *Film*'s end "reveal" of E's face can be seen as equally shocking, its predecessor is in essence a gimmick of the exact sort that Beckett and Kaufman sought to avoid in their more nuanced reprisal of the formal trope years later.

Film takes a similar notion of the cinematic camera-eye and moves it beyond the realm of gimmick to a substantive investigation of the nature of cinematic subjectivity. In this way, *Gentleman* bears a similar place in relation to *Film* that Balzac's *Mercadet* does to *Waiting for Godot*. In both works, a light popular entertainment's conceptual construct is reconceived as an absurdly profound ontological quandary. In the case of *Mercadet*, that construct is the off-stage portent of Godeau, whose absence determines the on-stage action; yet as employed by Balzac it remains at the level of clever plot device. Beckett finds in the same scenario no less than a model for the conditions of life. *Film*'s recasting of *Gentleman*'s construct functions similarly. It is extremely unlikely that Beckett knew of *Gentleman*, which was a truly obscure work. But of course Kaufman did, and it arguably deeply influenced the way he approached the question.[21]

Kaufman's contribution is herein reified as a notable factor in Beckett's embrace of the admittedly flawed 1964 version and rejection of the BFI remake. As in the original *Film*, there is an odd beauty to *The Gentleman in Room 6* that is absent in the 1979 production, despite its superior articulation of the two visions. In both earlier cases an intangible quality arises, traceable directly to Kaufman's mastery of light—a quality so similar that upon seeing *Gentleman*, a noted Beckett scholar only half-jokingly remarked that the 1964's long-form name should be changed from *Samuel Beckett's Film* to *Boris Kaufman's Film*.[22]

Some credit must also be given to *Gentleman*'s director, Alexander Hammid. Hammid was not only an excellent cinematographer in his own right, but the former husband of legendary filmmaker Maya Deren, and her key collaborator on the classic *Meshes of the Afternoon* (1943). In the person of Hammid, and his work with Kaufman, we at last find a close if indirect linkage of Beckett and the experimental film movement whose explorations of vision parallel those in *Film*.[23]

Figure 7. *The Gentleman in Room 6* (Alexander Hammid, with cinematography by Boris Kaufman, 1951).

Birth

If Beckett's metaphor on vision lacked some of the refined technical sensibilities of his more cinematically experienced avant-garde counterparts, who were by and large focusing their formal explorations of that era in the sensory aspects of perception, he characteristically compensated in the realm of psychological depth. His camera metaphor is as much a model of the mind as of the eye. Further, his analysis of the cinematic medium can be seen as just part of a larger investigation of the potentials of different media forms for psychological/ aesthetic exploration. His work extended far beyond dramatic works for the stage and motion pictures to radio plays, teleplays, and prose. His exploration of subjective consciousness in the mechanics of each medium is again beyond the scope of the present study, but for purposes of introduction in this short examination, it can be beneficially encountered by translating notions of literary perspectives to other media forms.[24]

As a characteristic example, *Not I*, in the course of a dramatic monologue, employs an odd form of personal discourse in which the speaker relates first-person experiences through the more distant third-person voice. When Mouth says, "she could still hear the buzzing… so called… in the ears" (Beckett, 1984b, 217), the third person perspective would normally presume a distance but is in fact a case of Mouth describing *herself* in the third person, as an object, hearing the buzzing. *Not I* is one of many instances in which Beckett's theatre and literary works convey an objectification of the self through formal structures embedded in their very language.

In *Film*, a similar distance is established between the perspective of E observing O, and O's subjective vision—a distance wherein E can be interpreted as a projection of O; or rather they are one. The literary third person here transposed to the cinema is not the traditional third person, but rather a uniquely Beckettian third person expression in which a person's consciousness observes itself. In the shots from E's perspective, E can in essence be seen as the mind and O the body. At least in intent.

As acknowledged, the schema was not entirely successful, in that the two perspectives were not satisfactorily distinguished cinematographically. But it should not be viewed as a failure of Kaufman, because the unacknowledged or misconstrued factor is editing. As previously discussed, a larger consciousness that organizes the shots is implicit in the act of assembly. The organizing mind, unmentioned in Beckett's scenario, silently interacts with the "split personality" of the formal camera schema as the shots advance successively in time. This is not necessarily a conflict, but remained unresolved in *Film* and the incomplete discussion of E as a 'cutter.'

In Beckett's subsequent work, the teleplay *Eh Joe*, it is perfectly resolved through a different formal schema. A functionally split personality is expressed not through two alternating pictorial visions, but through the audio track and its relation to the picture. In this case it is a classically Beckettian second-person voice that speaks, in which the "you" addressed is in a sense also the speaker. When the Woman's Voice asks, "Anyone living love you now,

Joe?" (Beckett, 1984a, 203), she alerts the viewer to the fact that she may be dead, but also to the notion that she may be a projection of Joe's thoughts of the deceased.

The camera depicts Joe from what is apparently a third-person vantage, but its continuing zooms into close-up parallel the probing depth of the voice's interrogation of Joe. In this case the voice manifests the split personality, or if one will, its superego or guilty conscience. In turn, the visual track conveys Joe's waking response. By sending the differing perspectives to discrete sensory channels of picture and sound simultaneously, allowing their parallel development (a collision or dialectic of the senses that can arguably be seen as Eisensteinian), Beckett avoids the confusion of perspectives found in *Film*.

Different variations on these structural dynamics re-occur through Beckett's work across varying media forms. The issue of perspective is in this sense but one part of Beckett's life-project. He expressed it succinctly to composer Morton Feldman: "To and fro, between unattainable self and unattainable non-self."[25] (quoted in Knowlson, 557) In his divergent formal experiments, his works can themselves be viewed as floating between poles of being and non-being, across shifting shapes.

An investigation of the gestation of Beckett's works herein becomes integral to fully understanding them. Stan Gontarski and many excellent scholars since have demonstrated this through in-depth analyses and documentation of Beckett's creative process, explicating the transition between thought and substance.[26] The elusive balance of that transition marks Beckett's journey through his work.

In the case of *Film*, one finds a concept continually seeking a form that was not to be fully realized even in completion. "Real" film—photographic film—stands in analogy, as it requires a chemical process to transform the light to which it has been exposed into an image. The name for the chemical stage that locks the images in place is "fixative," or "fix." Yet that same photographic film is itself based upon organic cellulose, which decomposes. It is never truly "fixed." So too was Beckett's *Film* never truly "fixed."

This is not a terrible problem. In its search for resolution, it is a work that's continually alive—the flesh of thought. A body, if impermanent, is needed to convey that life: the physical body of the work as perceived by the viewer. When *Film* was on the page of Beckett's notebooks, it remained an idea. It was not until photographed by Kaufman and edited by Sidney Meyers that it could achieve its elusive *percipi*, in passing.

So too, the abstract concept could not bear conception without the body of Beckett, the author. As the poet Anne Atik wrote of him, "pure spirit needed and met a body to hail and hold it" (67). The body of the actor is similarly needed to fully realize a dramatic work. The cellulose of *Film* is one kind of body, the corpus of the artist, another.

In this manner, one can, at least temporarily, "fix" Beckett's critique of Berkeley. *Film* upends his forbear's maxim by denying being. This in turn is balanced—in both *Film*'s production and the larger context of Beckett's performative works—by a corresponding outward movement, in which the creation itself strives to leave the conceptual realm for a state of temporary embodiment.

If *percipere* is oppositional to *percipi*, one can say that Beckett's larger project entails not so much an inversion of Berkeley's premise, as a reframing of it: *To embody is to be*.

WORKS CITED

Ardoin, Paul, *Product and Process: Making and Unmaking Films with Beckett and Burroughs*, unpublished PhD dissertation, University of Antwerp, Belgium (2014).

Atik, Anne, *How it Was: a Memoir of Samuel Beckett* (Faber and Faber, 2001).

Beckett, Samuel, 'Further notes to Beckett film', in Alan Schneider archives, Mandeville Special Collections Library, University of California San Diego (1964a).

Beckett, Samuel and Alan Schneider, *Beckett Film*, July 20 shooting script, in Alan Schneider Archives, Mandeville Special Collections Library, University of California San Diego (1964b).

Beckett, Samuel, *Film* (Grove Press, 1969).

Beckett, Samuel, *Eh Joe*, in *Collected Shorter Plays* (Grove Press, 1984a) [1965].

Beckett, Samuel, *Not I*, in *Collected Shorter Plays* (Grove Press, 1984b) [1972].

Beckett, Samuel, *The Letters of Samuel Beckett, Vol. 1: 1929-1940*, eds. Martha Dow Fehsenfeld and Lois More Overbeck (Cambridge:, 2009a).

Samuel Beckett, *Murphy*, ed. J. C. C. Mays (Faber and Faber, 2009b).

Beckett, Samuel, *The Letters of Samuel Beckett, Vol. 3: 1957-1965*, eds. George Craig, Martha Dow Fehsenfeld, Dan Gunn and Lois More Overbeck (Cambridge, 2014).

Samuel Beckett, *The Letters of Samuel Beckett, Vol. 4: 1966-1989*, eds. George Craig, Martha Dow Fehsenfeld, Dan Gunn and Lois More Overbeck (Cambridge, 2016).

Berkeley, George, *An Essay Towards a New Theory of Vision*, in *Essays, Principles, Dialogues*, ed. Mary Whiton Calkins (Charles Scribner's Sons, 1929a [1709]), 1–98.

Berkeley, George, *A Treatise Concerning the Principles of Human Knowledge*, in *Essays, Principles, Dialogues*, ed. Mary Whiton Calkins (Charles Scribner's Sons, 1929b [1710]).

Brakhage, Stan *Metaphors on Vision*, special issue of *Film Culture*, No.30, Fall 1963.

Godard, Jean-Luc, 'Montage My Fine Care', in *Godard on Godard*, ed. Tom Milne (Viking Press, 1972) [1956], 39–41.

Gontarski, S. E., *The Intent of Undoing in Samuel Beckett's Dramatic Texts* (Indiana, 1985).

Katz, Daniel, *Saying I No More* (Northwestern, 1999).

Kaufman, Boris, oral history interview (transcript), Oral History Research Office, Columbia University, New York, 28/1293 (1959).

Knowlson, James, *Damned to Fame* (Simon and Schuster, 1996).

Matthews, Steven, '"The Books are in the Study as before": Samuel Beckett's Berkeley', *Sofia Philosophical Review*, 5:1, 2011 (Special Issue Beckett/Philosophy), 146–68.

Notfilm, film, Ross Lipman, Milestone Film and Video, 2017 [2015].

Paraskeva, Anthony, *Samuel Beckett and Cinema* (Bloomsbury Academic, 2017).

Tubridy, Derval, *Samuel Beckett and the Language of Subjectivity* (Cambridge, 2018).

Van Hulle, Dirk and Mark Nixon, *Samuel Beckett's Library* (Cambridge, 2013).

Endnotes

1. Beckett's lifelong engagement with Berkeley is detailed in Van Hulle and Nixon's *Samuel Beckett's Library*, and analyzed in depth in Steven Matthews' "The Books are in the Study as before: Samuel Beckett's Berkeley."
2. Berkeley specifically writes: "As to what is said of the absolute existence of unthinking things, without any relation to their being perceived, that is to me perfectly unintelligible. Their *esse* is *percipi*; nor is it possible they should have existence out of the minds or thinking things which perceive them." (1929b, 125–6)
3. Here he refers specifically to the problem of E and O's respective visions, as discussed in detail in the present essay.
4. This letter is particularly notable in that it is a rare instance of Beckett explaining his intentions quite directly. Characteristically, he mocks himself in qualifying the explanation by saying, "I doubt if I can get it any plainer than in the outline (of which a friend to whom I showed it said it reminded him of Lucky's monologue)." And then in concluding adds, "I hope this does not sound like more Lucky." (Beckett, 2014, 549–50)
5. Beckett's "General" notes accompanying the original scenario read: "All extraneous perception suppressed, human, animal, divine, self-perception remains in being. Search of non-being in flight from extraneous perception breaking down in inescapability of self-perception." (Beckett, 1969, 11) In referring to the scenario, the present essay specifically means the published edition. The publication's source was a typescript dated May 1963, in correspondence with Beckett's manuscript dated 22 May 1963 and sent to Barney Rosset on 2 June. This version was slightly modified from the original notebook draft of 5–9 April 1963.
6. The document appears in Alan Schneider's archive, and was also sent by Beckett to Barbara Bray along with a letter dated 2 June 1964.
7. The production script confirms that key aspects of the notes were initially intended for inclusion. After an ill-fated first day of shooting, the crucial opening scene was reconceived by necessity, and the footage was abandoned. A further glimpse of Beckett's original intentions can be found in a reconstruction of the day's outtakes, included as supplemental material in the DVD edition of *Notfilm*.
8. The production meetings occurred on 11 and 12 July 1964.
9. A selected transcription of Beckett's comments can be found in Gontarski (1985, 187–92), while audio files of the original recordings and a complete transcription of the meetings (compiled by Paul Ardoin, Evelyn Emile and Gina Napolitan) can be found in the Gontarski archive in Dublin. Ardoin's dissertation (2014) contains the complete transcription.
10. This conversation can be heard as a self-contained audio recording, "What if E's Eyes Were Closed?," as supplemental material in the DVD edition of *Notfilm*.
11. The dialogue on "heightening" can be found near the beginning of tape number 4 of the meeting's recordings.

12. Schneider's production calendar dates the test shooting to 16 July; their viewing and evaluation to 17 July, whereas the camera slates suggest the test shooting itself extended from 15 to 17 July.
13. One could argue that the "no alteration" test is merely a reference by which to contextualize the blurring of the other experiments, in which case no testing of E's perspective occurred. It is here cited as an example of E's vision presumptively, based on the eventual shooting of E's shots with no alteration. Either way, Kaufman's position seems validated.
14. In addition to the still images accompanying the present essay, moving image clips of the tests can be found in *Notfilm*, and the preserved complete outtake rolls can be found at the UCLA Film & Television Archive.
15. Grove Press was sold to Ann Getty and British publisher George Weidenfeld in 1985. At the time the UCLA Film & Television Archive began preservation of *Film* in 2006 (when the cited research was initially conducted), it was still owned by Rosset and soon thereafter leased to Milestone Films, who currently control international rights.
16. Although the AMPAS print is an anomaly, it cannot have been created by accident. In the print, all O perspectives were darkened, but all E's retained their original tonality. As motion picture contact printing technology of the era prohibited an alternating phenomenon like this resulting by accident, it can be confirmed as intentional, even as its authorship remains a mystery.
17. The BFI edition alludes to writings in Beckett's early notebooks that did not make their way to the published edition, such as the inclusion of Schubert's "Der Doppelgänger." Its opening scene is clearly adapted from notebooks and the published version, whereas the 1964 production had a substantially altered scene in that place, as revealed by both the shooting script text and surviving outtakes, mentioned earlier. Although Beckett chose to excise the revised opening sequence from the original after the first day of shooting, the Grove Press edition seems to have simply used the earlier draft as a practicality. It begins with a disclaimer reading, "This is the original project for *Film*. No effort has been made to bring it into line with the finished work." (Beckett, 1969, 10)
18. The specific look of the grain and defocusing suggests an intermediate printing step that may have involved video image processing, which was certainly an available tool in 1979.
19. In a photographic negative, the image's tonality is reversed, so that lights appear as darks and vice versa. As the visual difference in such an approach is quite acute and not something that occurs in waking vision save as an after-effect of staring into a bright light, it would be out of keeping with Beckett's intentions and likely distracting. To establish a difference between the perspectives, or that they are oppositional is not enough in itself. Rather, it must be the *right* difference. I nonetheless appreciate Paraskeva's desire to seek further, and as a purely academic exercise unsuccessfully attempted similar experiments myself as a side-project to the restoration of *Film*. These experiments included the emulation of silent film tints and tones, such as would have been commonly used in 1929, the year in which *Film* was set.
20. The discussion occurs in tapes 3 and 4.
21. It should be noted that *The Gentleman in Room* 6 foregoes the interchange of perspectives present in Film, so the present discussion refers only to the question of O's subjective vision.
22. Shane Weller, University of Kent. *The Gentleman in Room* 6 was screened alongside an earlier version of this paper when presented at 'Samuel Beckett and the Nonhuman', a conference at Vrije Universiteit, Brussels, February 2019.
23. *The Gentleman in Room 6* was one of several short films produced by George K. Arthur and written by Sidney Carroll, who had no connection to the parallel world of avant-garde cinema. *The Stranger Left No Card* (1952), as an example of one of the other Arthur/Carroll works, bears similarity to *Gentleman* in its use of a trick ending, but notably differs in its absence of experimental technique and its less atmospheric lighting.
24. Countless texts have discussed Beckett's use of literary perspective, but two salient examples are the cited works by Katz and Tubridy.
25. Beckett would subsequently adapt it as a text for Feldman entitled "Neither."
26. Gontarski's *The Intent of Undoing* (1985) is a seminal work in this area. Particularly notable endeavors in recent years include the Beckett Digital Manuscript Project, and the work of Mark Nixon.

On Competing Histories of American Experimental Film

This text was originally presented as an illustrated lecture included in a panel entitled "Media at the Crossroads: Surviving Canon Formation," which took place as part of the Misfits: Time-Based Media and the Museum symposium at the Carnegie Museum of Art in Pittsburgh, in October 2015. This date situates it some time after my initial screed of a draft of "A New Model" in the first section of this book, and it includes a more playful rendition of some of the material removed from that text. Part of this lighter treatment was the use of a slide lecture/PowerPoint format. To give a sense of the original live presentation, quite a few of the accompanying images have been retained. But in the end the lecture had more in mind than its source, joining its polemical aspects to a larger question of the nature of moving image canons... and hence its inclusion in the present volume's "Histories" section rather than Poetics.

It's interesting to note that in the decade since this talk was presented, time has moved irrepressibly onward, and with it, the fixity of P. Adams Sitney's canon has declined further; without a notable replacement—which raises further questions regarding our current historical epoch. I happily leave those to the reader.

Special thanks: Emily Davis, Marilyn Brakhage.
Images of Jonas Mekas and the Invisible Cinema courtesy Anthology Film Archives.

My Art is Better Than Your Art,

or:

Skill and Dilettantism in Canon Formation

Summary

This illustrated lecture investigates some different definitions of moving image art, and how those notions strategically influence both canon formation and our understanding of art history. Specifically, it finds a class structure embedded in differing relationships to moving image technology on the part of both artists and institutions; a structure that reaffirms existing values and social norms. This is at once reflected in divergent canons, and in the material manifestation of moving image works in technical presentation. The lecture ultimately encourages a deeper investigation of moving image technologies on the part of both individuals and institutions, to bridge disparate notions of artistic practice, and allow the expansion of canons across existing boundaries, or to allow respectful dialogues between them.

Here stands Jonas Mekas, in front of his greatest creation of many, Anthology Film Archives.[1] In his hands, a book on Maya Deren rests poised, while his inviting gaze is out to the camera. We're invited in, so let's begin here, and see where we land.

Anthology's mission statement reads:

> Anthology Film Archives is the first museum exclusively devoted to the film as an art.

In a discussion of moving image art canons, Anthology is the monolith one can't avoid, nor should one, even if one disputes its legacy, as some do.

One of Mekas' key collaborators in its creation was P. Adams Sitney,

who would define through his scholarship an avant-garde canon that was startlingly successful, and for that reason, controversial. His *Visionary Film*, first published in 1974, set the standard which subsequent generations have been trying to displace ever since. Though conscious efforts to overturn the Visionary canon have largely been unsuccessful, technology's relentless advance has made great inroads.

To understand this trajectory, let first look at Sitney's forebears. At the very end of *Visionary Film*'s many acknowledgements, one finds this revealing note:

> My debt to Harold Bloom must be singled out. While I was at my typewriter at least one of his books was always on my desk and in continual use.

For those of us coming from non-literary traditions, Harold Bloom is one of the foremost scholars of the last few decades. In particular, he's been interested in canonicity, as one can tell by a mere glance at his *The Western Canon*, which is very much as its title suggests. Bloom, a brilliant thinker, does take care to specify that it's a *western* Canon he's discussing. But this book wasn't published until 1994. In 1973, when Sitney was in the throes of finalizing the first draft of *Visionary Film*, Bloom published *The Anxiety of Influence*, which takes an Oedipal reading of history and canonicity. Bloom posits that each generation struggles with the influence of its forebears, and tries to define itself by killing the father, and/or similar tactics, ultimately aiming to take his place.

As Bloom himself suggests, this view is inherently patriarchal. He writes, "Battle between strong equals, fathers and sons as mighty opposites, Laius and Oedipus at the crossroads; only this is my subject here…"[2]

Thus that which ennobles can also kill: we enshrine works, giving them life, but in that life establish the seeds of rebellion and potential displacement.

Let's then, place this mission itself in context. Looking back further, one finds Bloom's own "father," Mortimer Adler, who made a career of exploring the Great Works, again in the Western tradition. His project was no doubt well intentioned, but arguably less nuanced than Bloom's.

He sought to enumerate not just the great works, but also the great thoughts.

Here we see a view of his list of the great ideas in history, arranged alphabetically.

A Syntopical Approach to The Great Books
By Category

TRANSCENDENTAL		
Beauty	Being	Good and Evil
Same and Other	Truth	

ETHICS		
Beauty	Being	Courage
Desire	Duty	Equality
Good and Evil	Happiness	Honor
Justice	Prudence	Same and Other
Sin	Temperance	Truth
Virtue and Vice	Wealth	Wisdom

POLITICS		
Aristocracy	Citizen	Constitution
Custom and Convention	Democracy	Equality
Family	Government	Justice
Labor	Liberty	Monarchy
Oligarchy	Progress	Punishment

Here they are again, broken down thematically.

His project is a classification of the abstract, and I would suggest that again we see in the canon's formation its own death foretold. Here it's death by classification; by breaking down the infinite or indivisible to defined blocks, and assigning a value to it.

It's an ultimately futile project, and while different from Sitney's, helps establish some fundamental traps one encounters when setting down such a road.

With this approach of classification in the back of our minds, I'd like to look at moving image works, and some of the division points that have been used to help define canons and their boundaries. Such distinctions can at least be useful as conversation starters, if not so well as finishers.

In a 2006 essay in *Film Comment* by Paul Schrader entitled "Canon Fodder," Schrader poses the question: "By what criteria do we determine cinema's masterworks?" He focuses primarily on a mainstream canon, including both Hollywood and international fiction films.

Schrader cites as his boundaries Pauline Kael's division of "trash" and narrative art. For Schrader, trash is trash, as distinguished from the best of Hollywood and international traditions. Hollywood and international cinema could easily be another point of division if one wished, but for Schrader they can be joined.

So, let's call this Division #1; simply "trash" and "cinema."

Schrader openly claims an elitist vantage, even while some of his preferred works may be seen as lowbrow and populist. He ultimately links the highbrow work with entertainment classics, joining them in traditional notions of "the movies."

Unlike Schrader, the Anthology canonization effort was focused on avant-garde films, and had as its core the Essential Cinema project. Their methodology is instructive. Here, a formal committee situated the avant-garde precisely in the context of Schrader's more established cinema, despite being traditionally oppositional to it. In so doing, they saw a practical way of ennobling the then-new work.

Here we see a sampling of some of the titles in the Essential Cinema list, and some of the contents of the accompanying book.

Let's call this Division #2: Schrader's "classical film" and the avant-garde, which join together in the Essential Cinema.

Here we see the Essential Cinema committee members.³ It's a great photo, but very male, and many considered the list, like its predecessors, patriarchal. So it's not surprising to note that several decades of scholars since have been rebelling against them and their list.

Most of these efforts have been unsuccessful, but we now find ourselves at a juncture where at least some of the Essential Cinema works are indeed receding from their position of prominence.

Much has been written about the seeming opposition of Anthology's tradition of the avant-garde, and today's world of Time Based Media in the galleries, which are, in the eyes of many, distinct from it.

We'll call this Division #3, and it's here that we'll linger.

Does the Art world (of museums and galleries) tend to eschew both international art cinema, and experimental film... or is it the reverse?

One of the best investigations of this question comes in a dialogue between Erika Balsam and Marilyn Brakhage, widow of Stan Brakhage.

Here we see Brakhage, perhaps looking over his shoulder at Erika's excellent essay, "Brakhage's Sour Grapes."[4] Citing letters between Brakhage and Paul Sharits, Balsam suggests the filmmakers in Sitney's canon actively disdained the worlds of museums and galleries on their own initiative. Marilyn Brakhage made a spirited response that it was the other way around.

Either way, we do see a historical split. Why? As we'll discover, the Essential Cinema's apparent estrangement from the galleries has less to do with critical discourse than technological changes.

Tacita Dean, who is in my view one of the best contemporary gallery-based moving image artists, made an interesting remark at an event at the Getty Center in Los Angeles a few years ago. An audience member asked her how she had achieved a certain visual effect. Tacita, customarily candid in discussing her work, said that she didn't know how the effect was created, because her cinematographer had shot it. She said, humorously, "I'm the *artist*. I'm a dilettante."

This joking remark is revealing, in that it presumes an artist does not personally have an expertise in technical matters.

Yet the Anthology canon, while—per their mission statement—pursuing Art with a capital A, were largely masters of their craft.

Marilyn Brakhage in fact cites a mystification of technical matters as one possible reason for the exclusion of the Anthology filmmakers from the art world's canon. She writes of film as a newer medium that… few traditional art curators (felt) comfortable assessing—easier just to assume that if an acknowledged painter made it, it had validity, perhaps.

Tacita's joke points to a long-standing tradition in the art world which has perhaps taken on a greater role in recent years. I'm speaking of Fabricator culture—in which there is a separation of labor, dividing the conceiver of works from the people who craft them.

Here we see a large clay hippo, exhibited at the Venice Biennale in 2005. In a reversal of traditional attribution, I'll tell you that the fabricators who actually made the hippo were the Barnacle Brothers.[5] I've forgotten the names of the brilliant artists who conceived it, but I'm sure they won't mind, because they're the ones who *normally* get the credit.

This separation of labor falls along a traditional a blue collar/white collar divide, and is a question of social class. The fabricators, who are often artists themselves, are rarely taken seriously in their personal work.

In referring to their status, some technical gallery workers I know refer to the British TV series *Downton Abbey*.

Can we really presume a hierarchical relationship in this equation, without addressing class issues? I think not, but prefer to return to the role of skill and craftsmanship, and their valuation.

Should the word "craft" be considered in a negative light? Who exactly would be offput by it, presuming craftsman incapable of creative insight? Perhaps the answer is simply those without that skill set. But looking further, perhaps it is those who are removed from the *physical*.

Here we see an image from one of Brakhage's many hand-painted films.[6] He was an expert craftsman who explored many formal dimensions in his work, using not just lenses, but also the film itself as his material.

In *Mothlight*, he famously mounted grasses and insects between strips of 16mm Mylar splicing tape, showing at once an intense materiality *and* conceptualization. The film brilliantly translated physical properties into cinematic experience within a framework of ideas. Brakhage was equally active as theorist and practitioner, and while critique of him is understandable, his relative absence in the high art canon is almost baffling. So further investigation is merited.

One finds his exclusion just part of a larger picture.

To understand this third divide, we need to look not just at artists, but institutions. Here again, one finds a disparity in technical concerns, and approaches to presentation.

Much has been written about the incompatibility of gallery-based viewing and moving images, on many fronts, but particularly that of noise and light pollution. The problem is usually described in terms of the "black box / white cube" split. There are many definitions and a lot of history behind this, but for conversation's sake let's describe it as a distinction between controlled and uncontrolled viewing spaces.

The moving image black box, in seeking to control or limit noise and light pollution, might be seen in its purest form as aspiring to the conditions of a movie theater, at the populist end of our earlier discussion of Schrader.

Characteristically, the Anthology project carried this even further.

Here we see the apotheosis of the black box in Anthology's "Invisible Cinema," designed by the formalist Peter Kubelka.[7]

Kubelka called for special chairs that blocked one's view from distracting neighbors.

Here we see one of the distracting neighbors.

The white cube of gallery exhibition, in contrast, has uncontrolled conditions in which ambient noise and light can often dominate the sound and image of the piece itself. In recent years, when visiting museum exhibitions with moving image works, I've taken to observing the ways in which visitors engage with them. In most instances, people walk through, stand in the back, or perhaps take a seat on a bench for a few minutes that might comprise a small portion of a work's duration. The images are often washed-out phantoms due to the reduced contrast of white-walled rooms, where light is bouncing around, often with nearby cellphone illumination pulling eyes away from the exhibit. Soundtracks are mingled with noise from adjacent galleries, and—as the human eye tracks motion—the viewers themselves divert attention as they walk in and out of the gallery.

Clearly, such conditions offer little of substance to the moving image artist who is concerned with having their work be actively *seen*.

So why would any audiovisual artist aspire to exhibition in galleries? Can we conclude that an artist's actual *aim* is to have just fragments of a work be seen, with just fragments of a viewer's attention?

Balsam writes, in contradiction to this, that

> the museum, with its official status as a repository of "high culture," presents itself as an elevation or "saving" of cinema. Its institutional frame accords an increased cultural capital to a medium traditionally allied with mass culture.[8]

So prestige is certainly a factor, and it's no accident that the operative phrase is "cultural capital," with all that the word *capital* implies. Balsam goes on to suggest that some artists enter reluctantly, in quoting German artist Matthias Müller's interview with historian Scott MacDonald,

> As Müller has put it, "After twenty years of making 'experimental films' [...] I know there will never be enough profit to secure my existence. Thus, there is no alternative *but* a gallery."[9]

As Kevin Jerome Everson, an artist who manages to straddle both worlds says, with no small amount of humor, "I'm in the art-making business."

Or, as our distracting neighbor in the Invisible Cinema said, perhaps sincerely:

> Being good in business is the most fascinating kind of art.[10]

On Competing Histories of American Experimental Film 289

There's no mystery as to why experimental filmmakers aspire to the gallery world. Money. And, what is money at its core, but precisely:

Breaking down the infinite and indivisible to defined blocks, and assigning a value to it…. à la Adler.

Mathematical equations, of which this is the simplest:

Commodity fetishism, in this instance assigning artworks a financial value, functions subconsciously as a way to tame the untamable.[11] Art becomes discussable as a quantifiable product, rather than experiential expression. This has been much discussed at the political level, but let's look at the way the transformation happens.

In works such as our mud hippo, artists seek a conceptual hook on which to hang the physical. In so doing, they reproduce and reify a white collar / blue collar class structure in which thought is divided from labor, and idea from material. Labor and material are placed on the lower side of our hierarchy.

The class dynamic is further replicated at the institutional level, wherein white cube culture, perhaps unconsciously, exhibits a disdain for black box culture through its failure to adequately respond to it. White cube presentation of moving image works occurs in institutions that frequently have financial resources to create black box environments when appropriate, but frequently they choose not to pursue it.

This is in part a prioritization of older models of museum exhibition, which were designed for other media forms such as painting and sculpture, for which a white cube is more suited.

It's also a matter of convenience. It's simply more difficult to create controlled viewing conditions. But it's well documented how to do so in other, more populist, quarters. Every local multiplex can do it. So, why not do it properly, if one has the resources, and one's very mission is to present visual art?

It's also, ultimately, a matter of moving image *medium*.

As a practical matter it's easier to install video works than film works. This is at once a factor of the ubiquity of digital technology, the relative scarcity of appropriate photochemical presentation equipment, and:

the disembodied digital signal taking cultural precedent over the embodied analog film image. We are used to watching digital video in any kind of distracted environment, and associate the focused, darkened space of the theater with the cultural history of the movies.

Hence we see the Anthology canon displaced not by Oedipal rebellion, but by technological change that favors contemporary forms, and states of distraction, as foretold by Walter Benjamin.

Contemporary artists, interestingly, tend not to challenge this structure, but adapt to it.

Here we come full circle: to how artists not only *create* their work, but design it for specific exhibition contexts.

At the same Getty symposium referenced earlier, Tacita Dean mentioned that she actively prefers white cube to black box environments, because she "has more control there." At first I was confused by this statement, until I understood her to mean that in a gallery, she creates an environment where the spectator watches in a state of disengagement! She doesn't want her viewers watching her works as totalities, with fixed attention. Rather, she hopes precisely for a more casual encounter.

This is a radical inversion of notions of "cinema" which implies engagement, as in Kubelka's Invisible Cinema, and the inversion evokes Benjamin's notions of *dis*engagement as a marker of modernity.

As a further example, many of the more successful gallery artists today create pieces that do not require sequential viewing in time. Their works are conceived so that an ambulatory viewer can enter and exit at any point. Herein, the notion of editing or montage that was often at the core of cinema artists' work, is fundamentally transformed—or from another vantage, lost.

In this sense, the phrase "Time Based Media" might even be misleading, in that time is not used as a primary formal property. The works exist in time, but are not substantially based in it. What we see in these cases are artists using their formal control precisely to abandon formal control. A valuation of concept and content dominates, while form and material craftsmanship recede.

In so doing, this dynamic replicates a "class" separation of concept freed from the body and its tactile concerns, which are of the earth.

In being above bodily concerns, this approach—or positioning—fits within Bloom's and Schrader's notions of elitism, even as it implicitly opposes those two thinkers, as patriarchal and populist, respectively.

The elitism is established by a distanciation from the body, which is seen as vulgar, unless itself commodified in concept.

We hence have a situation in which the very technology of technology-based art is separated from both artists and institutions, in a financial structure that is not doing full service to the cultural mission we all hope to support. In this scenario, canons evolve in both Bloom's Oedipal cycle, and a parallel track in which deserving artists become obsolete alongside their media forms. Many forms of genuine cinema art exist, but only some are given financial value, or "cultural capital."

As conservators, artists, & scholars, where do we stand amidst this?

I have no answers, which, in establishing themselves, would themselves become fodder for the next canon's blast.

Instead, I'll leave you with a series of questions.

To artists, in targeting of our work: Where and how would we like our work to be presented?

To curators, in selection and presentation: How can we technically present and conceptually reframe work in a way that is at once respectful to its history, but also adapts to different times?

To conservators, in embodying the works: How can we conserve both the physical properties and essence of a work amidst a context of continually shifting technologies and ways of seeing?

To scholars, in analysis: How can we improve our technical understanding of the media forms we discuss?

In all cases, I advocate a learning and valuation of craft alongside concept, because only through a breakdown of the class distinctions between white collar and blue collar, and if you will, mind and body—by embracing both—can we find a way to end the Oedipal cycle of patriarchy within the canonization process.

Endnotes

1. The accompanying photo features Jonas Mekas outside the future home of Anthology Film Archives, Second Avenue and Second Street. Photo by Hollis Melton.
2. Harold Bloom, *The Anxiety of Influence* (second edition) (Oxford, 1997), 11.
3. Depicted in photo, from left to right: Ken Kelman, James Broughton, P. Adams Sitney, Jonas Mekas, Peter Kubelka.
4. Erika Balsam, "Brakhage's Sour Grapes," *The Moving Image Review & Art Journal* (MIRAJ), January 2012.
5. 20,000 pound "Hope Hippo," 2005. Made of mud, whistle, daily newspaper, with live person. Approximately 192x72x60". Photo courtesy of the 51st Venice Biennale, Allora & Calzadilla. Made by Barnacle Brothers, LA based fabricators for Venice Biennial.
6. *Night Music*, 1986.
7. The Invisible Cinema was installed at Anthology's short-lived residency at Joseph Papp's Public Theater.
8. Balsam, op cit, p.20. She notes that Brakhage makes a distinction between museums, and home-viewing or classroom viewing. This takes the form of his choice to make his work available in those latter two contexts on DVD, with the understanding that it's not the real thing and does not represent his intended viewing experience.
9. Balsam cites Scott MacDonald's 2005 interview with Müller, which originally appeared in *Framework: The Journal of Cinema and Media*, Spring 2005. The citation appears in: Erika Balsam, "Brakhage's Sour Grapes," op cit.
10. I found the quote, and accompanying photo mounted on the wall in the hallway of the Wyndom Hotel in Pittsburgh, where I was staying when I initially presented this talk, and integrated it into the presentation.
11. The image on the left is Van Gogh's *Self-Portrait*, spring 1887.

American Neorealism

The leading text in this grouping is adapted from notes written for a two-part film exhibition series at the UCLA Film & Television Archive presented in 2020 and 2022, curated by the archive's Paul Malcolm and myself. The series grew from a realization I had when restoring Barbara Loden's Wanda *that a lot of the films on which I'd been steadily working could be seen as neorealist. This was in part by accident: Charles Burnett's* Killer of Sheep *was already on the docket for preservation when I arrived at UCLA in 1999. But in retrospect I can't help but feel that the resonance also arose by unconscious design, for many of the titles I'd worked on after* Killer of Sheep *were films I'd helped bring into the archive's collection, without considering their neorealist aspect. At any rate I eventually made the connection, and when later linking them with additional works, realized there was in fact a whole sector of American independent cinema that shared this influence. Despite — or perhaps because of — their extreme eclecticism in origin, these films are bonded in that they took the ideals of the Italian neorealists as a jumping-off point for a diversity of visions that is uniquely American.*

Following the lead text is a collection of shorter pieces on some of the individual films, culled from assorted publications and screening introductions. An additional text on David Schickele's Bushman, *which was restored after series completion, has been included in this section.*

Special thanks to: Dennis Doros, May Haduong, Amy Heller, Todd Wiener.

AMERICAN NEOREALISM: 1948—present

by Paul Malcolm and Ross Lipman

This series brings together a wide range of films that, when joined, comprise a movement that never was. Shot over a span of nearly eighty years, arising from a diversity of cultures within the vast panoply of American life, made by a range of directors who rarely or never knew each other, they cumulatively raise questions about the very nature of cinematic movements.

No manifestos were written, few alliances were made. Yet linked they are, following directly or indirectly in the wake of the pioneering vision of the Italian neorealists, with a decidedly American spin.

The profound influence of Italian neorealism on the postwar cinemas of Europe, Latin America, Africa and Asia is established film history. Roberto Rossellini (*Rome, Open City*, 1945), Vittorio De Sica (*Bicycle Thieves*, 1948), Luchino Visconti (*La Terra Trema*, 1948) and others miraculously transformed Italy's postwar deprivations into production virtues as they sought to directly represent the social reality of their time. Their use of nonprofessional actors, location shooting, and open-ended stories and visual structures formed a new cinematic language that Millicent Marcus described as *"una nuova poesia morale"*—a new moral poetry. That vision then grew and spread throughout the world, posing a rich alternative to Hollywood's classical style in the films of Satyajit Ray, Ousmane Sembène, Nelson Pereira dos Santos, the French New Wave, the Czech New Wave, Third Cinema and countless other individual artists and movements. But what of the US?

Neorealism's influence on American cinema has been equally significant but the exact definition and lineage of American neorealism—a term coined by Thom Andersen—have sparked heated debate. In 1966, the Italian critic Antonio Napolitano used language drawing on the New American Cinema group's "First Statement" to connect it with neorealism when reporting from the States for an Italian film magazine. He wrote that a new generation of "young American cineastes" had embraced the Italian movement's principles to make "rough, imperfect but living films" in contrast to the "glossy, impeccable, banal" films of the "cinema moguls." Among those neorealist-inspired works, Napolitano cited Sidney Meyer's *The Quiet One* (1948), Morris Engel's *Little Fugitive* (1953), John Cassavetes' *Shadows* (1961) and Shirley Clarke's *The Cool World* (1964). But the New American Cinema films were only one interpretation of their predecessor, and arguably not even a conscious one, for they avoided the term themselves even as they linked themselves to their counterparts around the world. For others, neorealism took root in the U.S. in the fusion of film noir and progressive politics found in the postwar films of soon-to-be blacklisted directors such as Robert Rossen (*Body and Soul*, 1947), Abraham Polonsky (*Force of Evil*, 1948) and Jules Dassin (*Thieves' Highway*, 1949), or the collaborative *Salt of the Earth* (1954) by director Herbert Biberman, producer Paul Jericho, and writer Michael Wilson.

The debate over the influence of Italian neorealism in American cinema burst into public view most prominently in 2009 during an exchange in print between *New York Times* and *New Yorker* critics A. O. Scott and Richard Brody. In an essay headlined "Neo-Neo Realism," Scott described a resurgent "cinematic ethic" in the films of Kelly Reichardt, Ramin Bahrani and So Yong Kim, which, he argued, echoed earlier neorealist-inspired works such as Charles Burnett's *Killer of Sheep* (1978) and Kent MacKenzie's *The Exiles* (1961). Brody strongly disagreed with Scott's critical assessments and historiography, and posited an alternate view of the term, citing filmmakers including Ronald Bronstein and others.

Our series does not seek to reconcile all the disparate views, but does take its primary inspiration from some commonly accepted tenets of the form, leaving the vital works of the blacklisted Hollywood artists for another time and space. The selected works, rather, were mostly shot on location, in places far off the Hollywood grid. Often starring non-actors in scenarios based on their own lives, they document the streets and landscapes of a hidden America. Almost budgetless, they compensate with a freedom and depth that shatter the myth of the American dream and life our country so broadly trumpets. Their individual voices speak to each other across the span of years, miles, and cultures.

As a practicality, the series has been broken up into two parts, spanning roughly forty years each. Part One begins with the classic, if more documentary-like *In the Street*, included here for its intrinsic connection to *The Quiet One*, made in parallel by many of the same artists (even using some of the same film footage) in 1948. The two works were produced not just alongside each other, but almost contemporaneously with the early Italian films that defined the seminal Italian movement. Whether the Americans worked in response, or common inspiration to the times remains unknown, but we'd like to think a little of both. The films in this first part of the series then trace the arc noted by Napolitano, alongside films that flew largely under the radar in their own time such as Kent Mackenzie's *The Exiles*, Joe Anderson and Franklin Miller's *Spring Night, Summer Night*, and Barbara Loden's *Wanda*. Part One culminates in the now classic works of Charles Burnett and those following in his wake in what's now known as the LA Rebellion.

As a generality, the films embrace open-ended structures and stark depictions of unpolished reality, positioning the lives of individuals and communities within larger currents of history, economics and politics. In so doing, they bypass the contrived narratives and superficial social depictions of mainstream fare in their respective eras.

Part Two, from 1984 to the present, finds these cinematic qualities not just intact, but thriving… and not surprisingly, transformed. The rise of Sundance and regional film festivals, the emergence of a vibrant if unpredictable independent film market, the advent of digital technologies and new influences from Europe (most notably the films of Luc and Jean-Pierre Dardenne) have each had their impact on the form and its practitioners, while the increasing social, racial and economic inequality of the post-9/11 era has given them new urgency. Part Two is indebted to A. O. Scott's taxonomy, as well as Richard Brody's rebuttal, while extending in scope to include subsequent developments.

One of the most prominent questions arising from these works is that of the filmmaker's role in regard to the issues they depict. While neorealist films live precisely in the burning inferno of our times, we would distinguish them from "social justice" or "social impact" filmmaking. These latter terms encompass a body of important work made both in and out of Hollywood, but if used here, risk subsuming the aesthetic and moral focus of neorealist films within their thematic concerns. Neorealist films tend to display the world in its complexity, without prescription or solution, and ascribing direct messages to them is sometimes difficult. Despite, or perhaps because of that, their immersion in specific milieus, cultural authenticity, and intense commitment to an improved life is unmistakable.

The films presented in Part Two also, in their very DNA, display the sheer diversity of contemporary life in the most organic way possible. America as a multi-faceted array of different lives is nowhere so present as in these films. Here, an interesting contrast arises with Part One. Though each part spans a period of roughly four decades, we are at a sufficient distance from Part One to see the emergence of a canon, even if it's one that wasn't previously understood in this grouping. With Part Two, as curators we were suddenly confronted with a tremendous abundance of cinematic riches from which to choose. In part due to the ready availability and affordability of digital video, more stories are being told, and the amount of truly excellent films we encountered was remarkable. As the world grows and the amount of stories grows with it, is the idea of a canon even meaningful anymore?

Another interesting distinction from Part One is the sheer number of brilliant filmmakers who cut their teeth in neorealism before going on to successful industry careers. Earlier filmmakers like Barbara Loden and Charles Burnett brushed elbows with Hollywood, and sometimes operated on its edges, but remained largely independent. Even Cassavetes usually found little institutional support for the films he directed. The fact that the industry now has room for the likes of Chloé Zhao, Jim McCay, Sean Baker, Ryan Fleck, Anna Boden, Garret Bradley and David Gordon Green is an intriguing development, and we hope that these artists are able to bring the full extent of their visions to the wider audiences available.

Ultimately the two parts of our series seek to re-examine a lineage from the Italian neorealists through their early American counterparts up to the present day, a thread underscoring the importance of cinematic form in direct portraits of a complex world. Our selection is not meant to be comprehensive or definitive in its own taxonomy of American neorealism, but rather we hope to further a conversation long under way, fuel more discoveries, and inspire more filmmaking.

The selected films were screened in the groupings below, primarily as double features.

Film titles in **bold text** have been preserved by the UCLA Film & Television Archive.

AMERICAN NEOREALISM, PART ONE: 1948—1984

Part One of the series was presented at the UCLA Film & Television Archive's Billy Wilder Theater/Hammer Museum in Los Angeles in January and February of 2020. Series guests included filmmaker Robert Young, film restorationist Peter Conheim, Barbara Loden's son Marco Joachim, filmmaker Monona Wali, actress Susan Lynch, and filmmaker Charles Burnett.

Films screened:

Little Fugitive (Morris Engel, 1953) / *In the Street* (James Agee/Helen Levitt/Janice Loeb, 1948)/*The Quiet One* (Sidney Meyers, 1948)

Shadows (John Cassavetes, 1959) / *On the Bowery* (Lionel Rogosin,1957)
The Exiles (Kent Mackenzie, 1961) / *The Savage Eye* (Ben Maddow/Sidney Meyers/Joseph Strick, 1960)

The Cool World (Shirley Clarke, 1964) / *Nothing But a Man* (Michael Roemer, 1964)

Spring Night, Summer Night (J. L. Anderson/Franklin Miller, 1967) (screened with documentary shorts on the film by Peter Conheim and Ross Lipman)

Wanda (Barbara Loden, 1970) / *The Visitors* (Elia Kazan, 1972)
Dusty and Sweets McGee (Floyd Mutrux, 1971) / *The Panic in Needle Park* (Jerry Schatzberg, 1971)

Neorealist shorts: **The Jungle** (Charlie "Brown" Davis/Jimmy "Country" Robinson / David "Bat" Williams, 1967) / **Several Friends** (Charles Burnett, 1969) / **The Pocketbook** (Billy Woodberry, 1980) / **Grey Area** (Monona Wali, 1983)

The Whole Shootin' Match (Eagle Pennell, 1978) / *Northern Lights* (Rob Nilsson, 1978)
Killer of Sheep (Charles Burnett, 1977) / **Bless Their Little Hearts** (Billy Woodberry, 1984)

AMERICAN NEOREALISM, PART TWO: 1983—the present

Part Two of the series was delayed by the pandemic and presented at the UCLA Film & Television Archive's Billy Wilder Theater/Hammer Museum in Los Angeles in June and July 2022. Series guests included: *Songs My Brothers Taught Me* actress Jashaun St. John (via Zoom), filmmaker Charles Burnett, *Sugar* actor Algenis Perez Soto, filmmaker Roberto Minervini, filmmaker Sean Baker, filmmakers Jim McKay and Bradley Rust Gray, *Never Rarely Sometimes Always* producer Sara Murphy, filmmaker Ramin Bahrani, filmmaker Dean Lent.

Films screened:

My Brother's Wedding (Charles Burnett, 1983) / *Residue* (Merawi Gerima, 2020)

Border Radio (Allison Anders/Dean Lent/Kurt Voss, 1987)

Ruby in Paradise (Victor Nunez, 1993) / *Strange Weather* (Peggy Ahwesh/Margie Strosser, 1993)

Our Song (Jim McKay, 2000) / *In Between Days* (So Yong Kim, 2006)

Man Push Cart (Ramin Bahrani, 2005) / *Chop Shop* (Ramin Bahrani, 2007)

Frownland (Ronald Bronstein, 2007) / *Wendy and Lucy* (Kelly Reichardt, 2008)

Ballast (Lance Hammer, 2008) / *George Washington* (David Gordon Green, 2000)

Sugar (Anna Boden/Ryan Fleck, 2008) / *En el Septimo Dia* (Jim McKay, 2017)

Below Dreams (Garrett Bradley, 2014) / *It's Impossible to Learn to Plow by Reading Books* (Rick Linklater, 1988)

The Other Side (Roberto Minervini, 2015) / *Tangerine* (Sean Baker, 2015)

Songs My Brothers Taught Me (Chloé Zhao, 2015) / *The Rider* (Chloé Zhao, 2017)

Never Rarely Sometimes Always (Eliza Hittman, 2020)

Short Takes: American Neorealism

The following texts offer additional information and thoughts on a selection of the films presented in the series. For expedience, the films are discussed here in roughly chronological order, although they were not presented as such in screening. I should note that not all titles discussed here are ones on which I personally worked. For clarity, restoration credits have been added for those titles to which I contributed, unless discussed elsewhere in this volume.

In the Street (1948) / The Quiet One (1948)

The following notes were prepared to introduce a joint presentation of In the Street *and* The Quiet One *on January 12, 2020, the opening weekend of the series.*

A 16mm print of In the Street *was provided for the series by the Museum of Modern Art.*

A 16mm print of The Quiet One *was provided for the series by James Goldwasser.*

In the Street

By one definition, the first Neorealist film was Luchino Visconti's *Ossessione*, in 1943. Vittorio De Sica and Roberto Rossellini would soon follow with works that would define the movement even more strongly.

Somewhat remarkably, we find American works evoking Neorealist principles as arising as early as 1948, the year of De Sica's *Bicycle Thieves* and Rossellini's *Germany, Year Zero*. These works were made by a small group of Americans who were in many ways interconnected.

We'll begin with a short work that's more in a documentary vein, made by an ensemble led by the great photographer Helen Levitt, whom Walker Evans had linked with Cartier-Bresson and himself as the only photographers with "something original to say."

Levitt had begun photographing children at play in the streets of New York in 1938, and published a book of the photographs under the title *In the Street* around the same time the film was released. Working with her on the film were writer James Agee, and painter/photographer Janice Loeb. It was shot in 16mm in Spanish Harlem, often with a hidden camera enabling the intimate vision you'll see on the screen. The print we'll present tonight is 16mm, from MoMA.

Levitt edited the film and, subsequent to its first release, added a piano soundtrack composed and performed by Arthur Kleiner. In our research to determine the best method of showing the film, it seemed however, that the film's photography and rhythms arose much more clearly when projected in its original silent form, at 18 frames per second—the rate at which most of it was photographed. It's a classic case of "less is more," and that's the way we'll be seeing it tonight.

The Quiet One

Two years prior to *In the Street*, in 1946, Loeb and Levitt had formed a production company with Sidney Meyers, a greatly underappreciated figure in American film history.

Meyers was born in New York in 1906, and was an accomplished musician as well as a film editor. In the early 1930s, he got involved with the Workers Film and Photo League, documenting social conditions for working-class audiences. But as he was also playing cello in a WPA orchestra, daytime rehearsals prevented him from going out with the film crews, and he drifted into editing.

In 1937 he joined Frontier Films, along with many of his colleagues from the Film and Photo League, where they continued their work in left-leaning social documentary, collectively, without government funding. Among his colleagues there were film historian Jay Leyda, and Ben Maddow, with whom Meyers would work again on *The Savage Eye*, showing later in this series. Elia Kazan worked briefly as their assistant.

Meyers' collaboration with Levitt and Loeb bore fruit in *The Quiet One*, released in 1948, the same year as *In the Street*. They were joined again by Agee, and by cinematographer Richard Bagley, who later shot Lionel Rogosin's *On the Bowery*, also showing later in this series. You'll also see some of the location footage from *In the Street*, repurposed in *The Quiet One*.

The film stars a youth named Donald Thompson, and tells a story largely based on Thompson's real life, and his experiences at Harlem's Wiltwyck School.

The film was nominated for an Oscar for Best Story and Screenplay, but when the Academy refused Meyers' request to have Bagley's name added to the group of writers, he declined the nomination. It went on to be named the second best film of 1949 by the National Board of Review.

Sidney Meyers died December 4, 1969, at age 63. His assistant on *The Quiet One*, Clancy Sigal, wrote that he had "never seen such playful competence. At first, it was terribly confusing to me because I never knew what was supposed to be serious and what was a joke. Later, I learned that this was Sidney's method of instruction, to break down the distinction." At Meyers memorial, Jay Leyda said, "His value as a filmmaker spread so much further than 'credits.' What did 'edited by' really mean in his case? Most of the people sitting there…knew that Sidney had helped them more than they could ever admit to themselves."

Before we start, I'd like to offer a special thanks goes to James Goldwasser who's provided us with a 16mm print that used to belong to Meyers' widow, Edna.

I hope you enjoy the films.

Figure 1. A promotional image for *The Quiet One*. Top: Donald Thompson. Bottom, from left: director Sidney Meyers, co-writer and co-cinematographer Helen Levitt, producer Janice Loeb and associate producer William Levitt. Courtesy of Helen Levitt Estate.

The Savage Eye (1959)

The following notes were prepared to introduce a double feature of The Savage Eye *and* The Exiles *on January 23, 2020.*

A discussion of The Exiles *can be found in the essay "The Savage Heart of Kent Mackenzie," presented elsewhere in this volume.*

The Academy Film Archive's restored 35mm print of The Savage Eye *was provided for the screening.*

The Savage Eye presents a very different view of late 1950s Los Angeles than *The Exiles*. In so doing, it also offers a different model of how neorealist principles were intersecting with filmed drama and documentary at that time. Loose fiction scenarios were constructed to be enacted in public spaces, and various sub-plots and framing devices were conceived to work with the largely candid footage they were shooting simultaneously. In the end, a biting script was utilized to thread the disparate scenes into a whole. Today it plays like a beat-era spin on the silent-era city symphony.

The Savage Eye's production team integrates players from a number of earlier works in our series. Not only was Sidney Meyers—of *The Quiet One*—co-director along with Ben Maddow and Joseph Strick, but *In the Street*'s Helen Levitt was among the principal cinematographers, alongside Haskell Wexler and Jack Couffer. On top of that, *Exiles* co-cinematographer Robert Kaufman worked on both films, as did Haskell Wexler and Sy Wexler (no relation to each other).

The film cost $65,000 and was produced over the course of four years, on weekends, finally being released in 1960. Like *The Quiet One* and *The Exiles*, the film features voiceover narration. This was apparently mostly penned by Maddow, who's better known as the screenwriter of *Asphalt Jungle*, *Johnny Guitar*, and many others. Co-author and director Strick also had an incredibly diverse career and is perhaps best known for his cinematic adaptations of the works of James Joyce. Strick told Judith Crist of the *New York Herald Tribune* in a 1960 interview, "Our first idea was Los Angeles as seen by Hogarth... life is not so very different. Then we realized the parallel was too stretched for a film." The Hogarth influence, although abandoned, lets us know that a harsh social critique was very much part of the goal from the outset.

Helen Levitt told critic Jonathan Rosenbaum that little of her own work was used in the final version, and mainly recollects going around with Strick and filming "everything that appealed to us," including "a lot of oil pumps and places in Venice" and the dinosaurs in the La Brea Tar Pits. Strick's son David provides a small glimpse of hope, playing tetherball near the end.

Like *The Exiles*, *The Savage Eye* represents a side road never fully explored in American film. But it differs from *The Exiles* in its opposing mode and register, offering an alternate—and perhaps harsher—sensibility and vision.

On the Bowery (1957) / Shadows (1959; 1961 release)

The following notes were prepared to introduce a double feature of On the Bowery *and* Shadows *on January 25, 2020.*

A DCP of L'Immagine Ritrovata's restoration of On the Bowery *was provided by Milestone Film & Video.*

A more detailed discussion of Shadows, *as well as its preservation credits can be found in the essay "Mingus, Cassavetes, and the Birth of a Jazz Cinema," presented elsewhere in this volume.*

I'll just offer a brief introduction tonight, which will cover both films. Following on from last Thursday's Los Angeles-themed show of *The Savage Eye* and *The Exiles*, we now swing back for a view of New York City at roughly the same time.

On the Bowery

Lionel Rogosin, director of *On the Bowery*, was an heir to the Rayon Corporation when he walked away in 1954 in pursuit of a vow to fight racism and fascism through film. He actively cited Italian neorealist director Vittorio De Sica as an influence, and, looking for a subject, became fascinated by the lives of the down-and-out on Manhattan's Bowery. Writer Mark Sufrin said they were asking, "What brutal world created these broken lives?" and said the idea "was to extract a simple story from the Bowery itself."

Rogosin eventually chose railroad worker Ray Salver as his lead, and fashioned his narrative around him. Salver's compelling performance led to offers from Hollywood, which he declined. The primary supporting role is played by a former reporter named Gorman Hendricks, who died of cirrhosis of the liver just weeks before the film opened. Rogosin helped both, and paid for Hendrick's burial.

The film was shot by Richard Bagley, who obscured his 35mm Arriflex camera under a bundle to hide it while filming bar scenes. Shooting began in July 1955 and continued for three months. Among the many problems they encountered were harassment by police, and the fact that many of the cast members, pulled from the street, would disappear or get arrested. If and when they returned, they'd often been given shaves or haircuts, making continuity difficult. In *Sight and Sound*, Suffrin said that Rogosin's direction was aimed at "defining the action but not the gesture or inflection."

Cinematographer Bagley, who had also shot Sidney Meyers' *The Quiet One*, which screened earlier in this series, was himself an alcoholic, and would pass five years later, in 1963. Rogosin became the first American director to win the Best Documentary award at the Venice Film Festival in 1956, and the film was also nominated for an Academy Award for Best

Documentary Feature in the US. From his experiences in making *On the Bowery*, he would go on to make his classic *Come Back, Africa* in 1960.

Along with Cassavetes, he was one of the founding members of the New American Cinema group, and both were seminal figures in the establishment of American independent film culture as we know it today.

Shadows

Although *Shadows* is sometimes listed as a 1961 release, it's in many ways more of a 1950s film, and its infamous first edit screened as early as 1958. One can argue whether it's "neorealist" per se. Not to conflate things, but in a 1961 interview, Cassavetes himself said, "I don't think anything related to *Shadows* was documentary" (*Films and Filming*, February 1961). One presumes from this that he considered it pure fiction. Yet New York of the era features vibrantly in its location photography, and there are aspects of its fiction that overlap with neorealist tenets. An important part of *Shadows*' making was its arising from the acting workshops Cassavetes led along with Burt Lane. While they were very much in rebellion against Stanislavski's "method acting" of the era, a key component of their approach was that the actors brought personal aspects of themselves to their roles. The scenarios depicted in the film are unconnected to the cast's lives, but the characters they play are very much extensions of themselves, and their characters' names are their own. So we in a sense do see yet another spin on neorealist principles, in which performers more or less play themselves. The four leads—Lelia Goldoni, Ben Carruthers, Hugh Hurd and Rupert Crosse—all deliver excellent performances, and Ben Carruthers and Goldoni would go on to notable careers.

I won't say much more about the film, because we'll in fact be talking a bit more about it on the final night of the series. For tonight, it's more than enough to sit back and enjoy *Shadows* on its own terms.

The Cool World (1964)

The following notes were prepared to introduce a double feature of The Cool World *and* Nothing But a Man *on January 18, 2020.*

The Library of Congress Packard Campus for National Audio-Visual Conservation's preserved 35mm print of The Cool World *was provided for the series courtesy of Zipporah Films.*

The Library of Congress Packard Campus for National Audio-Visual Conservation's 35mm restoration print of Nothing But a Man *was provided for the series courtesy of Cinema Conservancy.*

The Cool World is Shirley Clarke's second feature. For her follow up to *The Connection*, which was based on a stage play, Clarke again looked to the theater. *The Cool World* was initially a novel by Warren Miller, and then adapted for the stage by Miller and Robert Rossen, playing in Philadelphia and then Broadway's Eugene O'Neill Theater in 1960. The days when anything remotely like that could play on Broadway are long gone, but thankfully the film remains. If *The Connection* was in part a response to *cinéma vérité*, *The Cool World* is very much Clarke's dive into neorealist techniques. Filmed in the streets with actual gang members, it has a grittiness quite different from its predecessor. Clarke's partner Carl Lee appears in the film, and also helped closely in the making. The great jazz score is by Mal Waldron with the Dizzy Gillespie Quintet. It also represents the first film work of Frederick Wiseman, who produced it, four years before his own directorial debut in *Titicut Follies*.

UC Berkeley scholar and historian Albert Johnson called it "the best film ever made about American Negro life in Harlem, and almost prophetic in its implications."

Two side notes: *The Cool World* features another great look at Coney Island, ten years after Morris Engel's *Little Fugitive*, which screened earlier in our series. And look for actress Gloria Foster, who appears as Duke's mother in the film. You'll see her again in the second film tonight, *Nothing But a Man*, where she appears as the girlfriend of Ivan Dixon's father. About that film, I'll say only that it's another truly extraordinary work from 1964, and Paul Malcolm will tell you more about it after the break. If you've never seen it, I can't recommend it highly enough.

Spring Night, Summer Night (1967)

Spring Night, Summer Night was initially restored in 35mm by UCLA Film & Television Archive with funding from the Packard Humanities Institute. The film was subsequently digitally restored by ByNWR and Cinema Preservation Alliance. 35mm laboratory services provided by the Stanford Theatre Film Laboratory, Audio Mechanics, NT Picture & Sound, and Simon Daniel Sound; restoration supervised by Ross Lipman in consultation with J. L. Anderson, Franklin Miller, and Peter Conheim. Digital restoration laboratory services by Illuminate Hollywood and Cinema Preservation Alliance; supervised by Peter Conheim and Ross Lipman, in collaboration with colleagues including digital colorist Andrew Drapkin; produced by Nicolas Winding Refn. Distributed by Flicker Alley and Powerhouse Films Ltd.

ByNWR and Cinema Preservation Alliance's digital restoration of Spring Night, Summer Night, *followed UCLA's earlier photochemical restoration, was presented on January 10, 2020.*

"Lost in Appalachia" was originally published in Sight and Sound *in January 2012, prior to the film's restoration.*

Figure 2. Ted Heimerdinger and LaRue Hall in *Spring Night, Summer Night*.

Figure 3. LaRue Hall in *Spring Night, Summer Night*.

LOST IN APPALACHIA

Peter Conheim of the Guild Cinema in Albuquerque was the one who alerted me to the existence of a mysterious film called *Spring Night, Summer Night* by J. L. Anderson. Peter had seen it in the Rural Route Festival, a touring program curated by Kino International's Mike Schmidt, a former student of Franklin Miller, who served as Anderson's co-producer and, in many ways, co-author. *The Village Voice* described the film as "the missing link between *Shadows* and *The Last Picture Show*," and according to Peter it was something I simply had to see.

    For better or worse I get DVDs all the time, from colleagues I inherently trust, but rarely have time to watch them. (I'm not a critic or true historian, and am frankly delighted that there are more gems out there than I can see in my lifetime.) So it was with *Spring Night*—the disc languished in a pile with other worthy contenders for a full two years before I brought it along on vacation back in 2008. Thankfully, I found myself awake one night and, having intentionally left my work behind for once, popped it into my laptop. After a few minutes it became apparent what Peter had been trying to tell me. This wasn't just a nice obscure film that would speak to a few cinephiles like ourselves, but a compelling and beautiful drama that held its own with the very best of independent cinema.

What's more, there was suddenly a context for it. Alongside works like Charles Burnett's *Killer of Sheep*, Kent Mackenzie's *The Exiles*, Barbara Loden's *Wanda*, Billy Woodberry's *Bless Their Little Hearts*, and arguably Floyd Mutrux's *Dusty and Sweets McGee*, I had gradually been realizing the existence of an unknown and completely accidental—but surprisingly coherent—body of American neorealism. These works largely used non-actors playing themselves alongside trained or semi-trained actors, location shooting with existing light cinematography, and loose-at-best storylines to depict a gritty underbelly of American life unseen in mainstream cinema. Arguably more than even their semi-pro or underground independent counterparts, these works were a window into lost chapters of our cultural history.

Set in rural southeastern Ohio, *Spring Night, Summer Night* tells the story of a conflicted love affair with a distinctly hillbilly twist. The doomed couple might or might not be siblings. The machinations of small-town gossip blend with their own soul-searching in emotional fireworks that wind a discursive narrative through atmospheric dive bars, farms, and rolling countryside. The story becomes just one part of a landscape of Americana—a canvas in which the characters are engulfed by a larger reality from which there might be no escape, even in solitude. They're inseparable from the environment in which they live, yet to escape it is their only hope. The land is as much a character as the haunted leads and is captured in exquisitely lyric cinematography by David Prince, Brian Blauser and Art Stifel.

Anderson is more known among cineastes today for his collaboration with Donald Ritchie on the expanded edition of the latter's classic history *Japanese Film: Art and Industry*. He plucked his talented trio of cinematographers from among his students—as production began he had recently been hired to found the film production department at University of Ohio, Athens. Working in collaboration with co-writer, producer and editor Miller, Anderson originally sought to adapt a 1920s story by Wilbur Daniel Steele set in Appalachia. The rights were unavailable, something Miller cites as a fortunate break, in that it forced them (along with Douglass Rapp) to collectively author a story more suited to the times.

Unlike Burnett and Loden, they weren't themselves from the community they depicted. Yet like Mackenzie, their method was immersive: they spent two years scouting locations in the remote coal-mining hills of Ohio, picking up speech patterns and dialects, and writing the script. For the crucial lead roles of Jesse and Carl they cast Larue Hall and Ted Heimerdinger, who had backgrounds in community theater, and who illuminate the screen with all the tortured hope of youth. Unsurprisingly, the cast and crew volunteered their time against a share of future profits which never materialized.

Shooting took place in the summer of 1965, accompanied by an unexpected hail of locusts who were returning after their seventeen-year hiatus. The film's bar scenes were shot in Columbus and filled with locals who had been given $5.00 apiece in fake money. With beer going at twenty-five cents a bottle, in Miller's words, "things got loose pretty quickly." The forest scene near the film's end was filmed in an area so remote that all the heavy 35mm gear had to be hand-carried a half-mile to the site. As the scene took three days to shoot in itself, crew members camped out to safeguard the gear.

The incest theme that drives the film is simultaneously its one aspect some audience members may find troubling: the potential-siblings' haunted love culminates in a scene that fully realizes the moral issues at play. The crucial moment has an emotional ambiguity that is both disturbing and affecting, with close-ups of Hall's brilliant performance expressing alternately horror and love. If the usually-true camera occasionally lapses to a sexist male gaze, the lapses occur amidst otherwise fluid moments of exquisite beauty. Cumulatively the cinematography evokes a pastoral vision that's at times otherworldly and, in its own weight, more than balances a moral compass whose questionable nature is at the heart of the film's subject.

Post-production was completed in the spring of 1967, and it premiered at the Pesaro Film Festival. Anderson half-jokingly presented the film as part of the "New Appalachian Cinema" and I believe we're still waiting to see the rest of those films. There were no stars or starlets in Pesaro, but Anderson tells that he did get to see Susan Sontag in a bikini. Willard Van Dyke was an early proponent of the film, and it also screened at the Flaherty seminar.

Despite this reception, things soon went downhill. After a futile year spent seeking distribution, the film was scheduled to screen at the 1968 New York Film Festival, but was ironically bumped at the last minute to make way for John Cassavetes' *Faces*. *Spring Night* was eventually picked up not by the art cinema scene but by a New York exploitation distributor named Joseph Brenner. Upon seeing the success of *I Am Curious Yellow*, particularly around 42nd Street, Brenner decided the film needed to be spiced up to attract an audience. He hired none other than a young Martin Scorsese to make recommendations for a re-edit. According to legend, Scorsese told him the film was perfect as it was and should remain unchanged. Brenner ignored this and went back to Anderson requesting that he shoot some gratuitous nude scenes. Brenner's daughter subsequently discovered that the word "pregnant" had never been used in a film title, and thought it would generate controversy to include it. They released it under the awkward name *Miss Jessica is Pregnant*. Brenner's sister was right in a backwards kind of way: they couldn't run newspaper ads in the south, where the word "pregnant" was apparently taboo.

Needless to say the re-edit flopped miserably. Miller can't even bear to think of the changes. Hoping his memory had clouded his judgment, I optimistically viewed the final version. Yet he's right: though the changes are minimal, much of the magic is lost. The gratuitous nudity is just that, and completely unerotic, clouding the interesting moral ambiguity of the original even further. Nonetheless that's how many know it today: a hatchet-job trailer can be seen at http://www.archive.org/details/SadsStorefront18, sandwiched amidst *Miss Olga's Massage Parlor*, *Blaze Starr Goes Nudist* and *Michelle* aka *Sexy Gang*. Anyone watching this film for a sadistic thrill will be greatly disappointed, but the trailer does provide glimpses of the original's lyric cinematography amidst some bobbing breasts.

Both the original negative (conformed to the *Miss Jessica* version) and the sole surviving print of the director's cut are now safely housed at the UCLA Film & Television Archive, but we've no funding as yet to restore it. We await the day when funds are secured, to allow us to correct the historical record.*

---

* As noted, this text preceded the film's actual restoration.

Bushman (1971)

Bushman was restored by the Pacific Film Archive and The Film Foundation, in association with the Schickele family, with funding from the Hobson/Lucas Family Foundation and additional support by Peter Conheim. Laboratory services provided by Illuminate Hollywood, Fotokem, Audio Mechanics, and Simon Daniel Sound. Restoration supervised by Ross Lipman in collaboration with colleagues including archivists Antonella Bonfanti and Jon Shibata, audio restorationist John Polito, photochemical grader Doug Ledin, and digital colorist Andrew Drapkin. Special thanks to Dennis Doros, Amy Heller, Susan Oxtoby, and Gail and Nighttrain Schickele. Distributed by Milestone Films and Kino Lorber.

> *Although David Schickele's* Bushman *was restored after the screening series concluded and was hence not part of the original grouping, it adds another dimension to our understanding of the possibilities emerging from a neorealist approach to filmmaking in the U.S., and reiterates our curatorial view that the form's definition and emerging canon will always be changing. The following talk was initially presented at Il Cinema Ritrovato in June 2023, and again at the Pacific Film Archive in Berkeley in February 2024.*

Figure 4. Paul Okpokam in *Bushman*.

Bushman is a film that was previously lost to history. Its beginnings lay in the early 1960s, when David Schickele went to Nigeria with the Peace Corps, where he made a film called *Give Me A Riddle*. It was a *cinéma vérité* documentary featuring a young Nigerian named Paul Okpokam, and the two became friends. Filmmaker Rob Nilsson describes *Bushman* as the "reverse angle" of *Give Me a Riddle*, "shot when the tables were turned and David brought Paul to America to see his hometown" in 1968.

In *Bushman*, Schickele moves away from straight documentary to an auto-fiction loosely adapted from Paul's own life in the US. In this way the film falls into an extraordinary strand of American neorealist films, alongside now-classic works such as Charles Burnett's *Killer of Sheep*, and Barbara Loden's *Wanda*. But things took a startling turn when events in Paul's life exploded in an unexpected way at the time of the riots at San Francisco State College in 1968. I'll leave it to you to experience when you watch the film.

I will, however, leave you with this quote from the scholar and critic Albert Johnson, who wrote:

> For the first time in American cinema, an educated African elucidates in a no-nonsense manner, the bewildering inability of American society to live humanistically, with every opportunity to do this either ignored or thwarted. (The film is) a gift so timeless that one must learn from it and cherish its possession."

Bushman was honored with the Best First Feature at the Chicago International Film Festival upon its completion in 1971. Cinephiles will want to look for the small role played by a young Jack Nance, who would go on to fame in David Lynch's *Eraserhead*.

I'd like to thank the Pacific Film Archive, the Film Foundation, Milestone Films, Kino Lorber, and Cinema Preservation Alliance for undertaking and releasing the restoration, which we conducted at Illuminate Hollywood and Audio Mechanics. I'd also like to thank Antonella Bonfanti, now at Lucasfilm, for her collaboration. It's now my pleasure to present the world premiere of the restored *Bushman*.

The Visitors (1972)

The following notes were prepared to introduce a double feature of Wanda *and* The Visitors *on January 17, 2020.*

Discussions of Wanda *can be found in the essay "Defogging* Wanda*" and in the short piece on Barbara Loden, presented elsewhere in this volume.*

A 35mm print of The Visitors *was provided for the series by the Academy Film Archive.*

The Visitors is perhaps the farthest departure from classical neorealism in our series, but is presented here as a fascinating point of reference to Barbara Loden's *Wanda*, the first film in tonight's double bill. As most of you will know, *The Visitors* was helmed by noted Hollywood director Elia Kazan, Loden's husband. What's perhaps less well known is its backstory. It had been three years since completion of his last film, *The Arrangement*, which was such a flop he'd been able unable to secure funding for another. Inspired by Loden's collaboration with Nicholas Proferes on the low-budget 16mm production of *Wanda*, he for the first time abandoned his high-budget production models, and contracted Proferes as cinematographer to help him go underground. Filming took place on location at their own house, and Kazan's son Chris wrote the script. Outwardly inspired by a *New Yorker* exposé called "Casualties of War" by Daniel Lang—the same story that inspired Brian De Palma's later film of that name starring Michael J. Fox and Sean Penn—it features James Woods in his first film role as an idealistic pacifist who blew the whistle in a rape and murder court-martial case during the Vietnam war. Things go awry when Woods' court-martialed colleagues, now released after two years in a military prison, drop by for a visit. Steve Railsback delivers an utterly terrifying performance as the main perpetrator that no doubt led to his being hired to play the role of Charles Manson a few years later in *Helter Skelter*.

    The film's relevance to our series comes in through the low-budget location shooting in Kazan's home, with the *Wanda* production team, and the potential autobiographical resonances with Kazan's own life; most notably his lifelong internal conflict after his infamous naming of names in the McCarthy-era HUAC hearings. I'll save a more detailed discussion of that for another time, but will offer the idea that the film is confessional in more ways than one. In the end it's an extremely powerful and compelling work that one might call "a confused film about confused people." Its direct predecessor, *Wanda*, is now recognized as one of the masterpieces of modern cinema, and might be seen in contrast as an *un*-confused film about confused people. I'll close by mentioning that seeing the two works together can be an overwhelmingly dark experience, so be forewarned that you might want to seek a light-hearted comedy tomorrow night by way of recovery.

Neorealist Shorts (1967-1983)

All of the films were originally produced in 16mm, and restored or preserved by UCLA Film & Television Archive. Funding provided by the National Film Preservation Foundation, Milestone Film & Video, the Andy Warhol Foundation for the Visual Arts, and the Packard Humanities Institute. Laboratory services provided by the Stanford Theatre Film Laboratory, Fotokem, and Audio Mechanics. Restoration and preservation supervised by Ross Lipman in collaboration with colleagues including film restorationist Jillian Borders, film graders Sharol Olson, Josh Rushton and Doug Ledin, and optical printing technician Dave Tucker. Special thanks to Charles Burnett, Dennis Doros, Amy Heller, Jay Schwartz, Monona Wali and Billy Woodberry.

The following notes were prepared to introduce a program joining the listed films on February 8, 2020.

The Jungle (1967). 35mm, b/w, 22 mins.

Directors: Charlie "Brown" Davis, Jimmy "Country" Robinson, David "Bat" Williams.

Tonight's program joins together a wonderful group of short films, all printed or preserved by UCLA. We open with *The Jungle*, made in Philadelphia in 1967 by a group of inner city high school members of the 12th and Oxford gang, in a collective facilitated by social worker Harold Haskins. It's a particularly compelling portrait of gang life that serves as a fascinating counterpart to Shirley Clarke's *The Cool World*, seen earlier in this series, as well as in its own right. The gang members were high school students at the time, and they created everything from the credits to the soundtrack. The result is an early example of modern, independent African-American filmmaking, imbued with a raw fusion of documentary and fiction that opens a unique window into street life through the lens of gang members themselves.

It was in part sponsored by WCAU TV, but after seeing the results, they cancelled screenings at least four times, with a station executive telling *Philadelphia Magazine*, "After all, we have to consider all those normal children who might have seen it. They were waiting for *Lassie*." The film nonetheless went on to much-deserved acclaim, and the street gang—which was in fact one of the largest in Philadelphia—later professionalized as the Oxford Filmmakers Corporation. The film was named to the Library of Congress National Film Registry in 2009.

Several Friends (1969). 35mm, b/w, 21 mins.

Director/Screenwriter: Charles Burnett.
Cast: Andy Burnett, Eugene Cherry, Charles Bracy.

Following *The Jungle*, we'll move back west with Charles Burnett's extraordinary first film, *Several Friends*, from 1969, made shortly after his becoming a student at UCLA. This film was a particular pleasure to preserve, as it never even existed as a composite print before we rescued it from Charles' garage. And it's an amazing piece, in that we find Charles exploring in rough form the exact terrain which was to describe his later *Killer of Sheep*. Not only do we see many of the same faces who turn up in the later film—Charles Bracy, Eugene Cherry, Cassandra Wright, and others—but we even see similar scenarios occurring.

The film documents a group of friends navigating their daily lives in South Central LA, trying to find hope and not get caught in the mire of the ghetto. The lead is played by Charles' brother, Andy. Also look for Donna Deitch, director of *Desert Hearts*, in a small role.

Like *Killer of Sheep*, *Several Friends* is both episodic and neorealist, creating a montage of moments that seem literally cut from life—which work cumulatively to paint a portrait of a specific milieu and the very individual lives within it. While the film is a short, made by a younger Burnett, and may not have quite the depth or intensity of the later work, it nonetheless points directly to it. And its theme is slightly different—in some ways even trickier; exploring that point where one's attempts to pull a life together coalesce or drift into intangibility.

The Pocketbook (1980). 35mm, b/w, 13 mins.

Director/Screenwriter: Billy Woodberry.
Cast: Simi Nelson, Ray Cherry, David Jenkins.

Following that will be Billy Woodberry's second film, and first completed in 16mm, which adapts Langston Hughes' short story, "Thank You, Ma'am." It follows the course of a botched purse-snatching and its aftermath. As he was working on it, Billy caught the attention of Charles Burnett, and the two would later collaborate on *Bless Their Little Hearts*.

The Grey Area (1983). 16mm, b/w, 38 mins.

Director/Screenwriter: Monona Wali.
Cast: Eve Holloway, Haskell V. Anderson III, Lance Nichols.

The program concludes with Monona Wali's riveting *The Grey Area*, from 1983. Wali's UCLA thesis film examines the lives of an African-American woman television reporter and a former Black Panther, at times evoking the 1970s documentary *Scared Straight* within a fictional frame.

As I was working on my end of the archive's LA Rebellion project, this film struck me as one of the more notable discoveries of that series, and it's our hope that this screening will help bring it some of the attention it deserves.

A study guide for the film
THE JUNGLE

Subject areas: Sociology, teacher education, contemporary American problems, urban affairs, guidance

Level: C, A, Sh

Length: 22 minutes

CONTENT

THE JUNGLE is that rarity, a picture of the life of Negro ghetto youths told by Negro ghetto youths. It is their story, produced by them with a minimum of professional assistance. They were the 12th and Oxford Street gang of Philadelphia, now the 12th and Oxford Film Makers Corporation.

It is a picture of gang life in the street. The girls that appear briefly have a minor place in this world of violence and male loyalties. Gang war opens and closes the film and occupies much of the middle, interwoven with statements by the actor-gang members who tell how they feel about their lives.

"Country", as he arrives in North Philadelphia, is drawn into this world when he comes to the aid of one of the gang who is jumped by a number of rival gang members. He is absorbed into the aimless street life of boozing and fighting. The great sin of disloyalty is committed by another member who "stays with the wine" instead of joining the war. A kangaroo court sentences him to a gauntlet beating.

This fact-fiction story is fiction in that Country and other gang members aren't really shot to death in the final fight. It is fact in that it tells it the way it is.

PURPOSE

THE JUNGLE presents no solutions. Rather, it allows insights.

For the teacher planning to work in ghetto schools or the student of urban problems the film pulls the curtain aside for a privileged glance at the young Negro in the streets, his style, values and code of ethics. For students in center city high schools the film holds up a mirror which can be used to open up discussion of life values. For high school students outside the ghettos the film, if used with careful preparation, can be a bridge to an understanding of the problems confronting the Negro in the other America.

ABOUT THE 12th AND OXFORD STREET GANG

Unlike most of their peers, these young men are on their way to "making it". Having savored the sweet taste of accomplishment and recognition for a real film achievement, they have a long list of plans (made with the help of an inventive youth worker). In the Spring of 1968 they had found a sponsor (Churchill Films) for the production of a second film, WHY I DROPPED OUT OF SCHOOL. The City of Philadelphia (to its lasting credit) has turned over three occupied tenements to them to maintain and manage. They are negotiating with a major manufacturer of automatic laundry equipment and the gas company to stake them to the opening of a laundromat. A number of the young men have found the kind of employment that will help them to learn to handle the gang's finances and administration.

This dramatic change that the production and acceptance of THE JUNGLE has made in the attitudes of members of the gang should be of major interest to observers of urban problems. Its implications may perhaps overshadow the actual content of the film itself.

SPECIAL SCREENINGS

THE JUNGLE is available for special screenings accompanied by a member of the 12th and Oxford Film Makers to discuss the film and related matters. For information.

Presented by
CHURCHILL FILMS
662 North Robertson Boulevard, Los Angeles, California 90069

Figure 5. Churchill Films study guide for *The Jungle*. Courtesy Jay Schwartz.

Killer of Sheep (1977) / Bless Their Little Hearts (1984)

Bless Their Little Hearts was restored by UCLA Film & Television Archive with funding from the National Film Preservation Foundation and The Packard Humanities Institute. Laboratory services provided by the Stanford Theatre Film Laboratory, Audio Mechanics, and Simon Daniel Sound. Restoration supervised by Ross Lipman in consultation with Billy Woodberry, and in collaboration with colleagues including audio restorationist John Polito, film grader Sharol Olson, and optical printing technician Dave Tucker. Distributed by Milestone Films.

"Killer of Sheep: *An Appreciation*" was commissioned by Sight and Sound magazine on occasion of the film's selection in its 2022 poll of the Greatest Films of All Time.

The notes that follow it were prepared to introduce a double feature of Killer of Sheep and Bless Their Little Hearts *on January 19, 2020, as part of the American Neorealism series.*

As this book goes to press, Killer of Sheep *is being re-restored (or digitally remastered, depending on one's parlance) in 4K digital video as a collaborative project between UCLA Film & Television Archive, Milestone Films, and Criterion. Further discussion of the film, as well as its preservation credits can be found in the Case Studies section, and in the essay "The Gray Zone," presented in the Poetics section of this volume.*

KILLER OF SHEEP: An Appreciation

It's hard to believe there was a time when *Killer of Sheep* wasn't widely recognized as a canonical work. The operative word, however, is *widely*: it got great reviews from its moment of its premiere in 1978. So why the recognition gap? In some ways it's a story that parallels the film itself: it simply lacked the cultural benefits of more privileged contemporary productions. *Killer of Sheep* was made on shoestring while writer/director Charles Burnett was still a student at UCLA, studying under luminaries including Basil Wright and Elyseo Taylor. Despite the looming presence of Hollywood, Burnett found inspiration in the Italian neorealist films he saw in class, and defying expectations, adapted the department's resources to tell tales of a previously undocumented America: everyday lives in the black community he knew in East Los Angeles. But just as the film's subjects were in a sense ghetto-ized, so was the film.

Without funds available music rights couldn't be cleared, and the film spent several decades as highly lauded marginalia. I first saw it in a poor-quality 16mm print in the mid-1980s: the only way it could be seen at the time. The picture was soft and the dialogue muffled, leaving me with the memory of a feeling as much as anything else. It wasn't till I was fortunate to restore the film for the UCLA Film & Television Archive in the early 2000s—with improved laboratory techniques that allowed Burnett's brilliant photography and dialogue to emerge— that I realized its true genius. The visionary team at Milestone Films concurred, going through Herculean battles to clear the music rights, and launched its first international 35mm release in 2007, a full thirty years after its completion. Suddenly wide audiences throughout the world were seeing scenes that have since been etched forever in our collective memory: young children filmed from below as they leap across the gap between tenement rooftops, a hard-won car engine teetering precariously on the edge of a departing truck, the sad lonely dance of slaughterhouse worker Henry Sanders and his wife, Kaycee Moore.

Upon the restoration's premiere, I was occasionally fortunate to present the film with Charles in attendance, and would introduce him not as one of America's "great black directors" but rather as one of the "great American directors." It's true he's spent a career championing black lives in his storytelling, but I always felt the former term was not enough, and implied a privileging the work decried. Now I think it's probably time to omit the true but limiting "*American*" descriptor as well: he's simply one of the world's great directors.

KILLER OF SHEEP (screening introduction)

In re-watching the films in our series as it's unfolded, I've been simultaneously inspired, and overtaken with the direness of the many situations portrayed. Amidst neorealism's deep investment in social concerns, none of the directors expect easy answers, and all find beauty in the small moments of everyday life amidst the tales their telling. Tonight's films continue that, but bring a slightly different emphasis to the issues. In these works, those moments become the story itself, and the result is transcendent.

Killer of Sheep, Charles Burnett's first feature, was actually his thesis film at UCLA, where he was a student in the late 1960s and the '70s. As you'll see though, it's hardly a "student" film or an apprentice piece. Completed when he was already in his thirties, it's the work of a mature artist: a film with a clear and piercing view of the world; a story told from a passion for truth, rather than a drive to dazzle or shock.

It tells the story of a slaughterhouse worker in Watts, and his daily life with his family and friends. But it defies conventional expectations of narrative, acting, and filmmaking. Don't expect suspense-filled drama building to a clear resolution. Life is more complicated than that, and that's what Burnett shows us. In an interview with Jacqueline Stewart of the University of Chicago, Burnett said: "The thing was to get an inconsistent, sort of documentary look, like you just found the camera and shot something and didn't know anything about filmmaking.

I didn't want to get close to a plot or conventions, like reaction shots and things like that. I tried to make it look sort of like life."

The result is a mosaic-like structure, where scenes build in relation to each other poetically, rather than simply from one to the next. Our sense of the characters constantly changes and develops as we get to know and care about them. This basic method is also clearly present in Burnett's later works, such as *To Sleep With Anger* and *The Glass Shield*.

The film's formal aesthetics are not its only groundbreaking aspect. Shooting in South Central LA with a cast including many non-actors, Burnett sought to de-mystify the filmmaking process for the community he filmed. Members of the cast, including the children you'll see throughout, doubled as crew and took turns doing the actual sound recording. In addition to the many non-actors who appear in the film, I'd also like to single out the extraordinary performances of Henry Sanders and Kaycee Moore in the lead roles.

Killer of Sheep initially received the critics' prize at the Berlin Film Festival and the US Film Festival—or what's now known as Sundance, and became one of the very first films selected for the Library of Congress National Film Registry of the most important works in American film culture. However, it had never been released due to music rights issues, and had never even existed in a 35mm copy before the UCLA restoration. Thankfully that's now all ancient history due to the hard work of our friends at Milestone Films, who cleared the music rights and at long last brought the film to distribution in 2007, three decades after its completion.

There's one other special aspect to tonight's screening I'd like to mention. Even after seven years and spending way too much money, Milestone wasn't able to *completely* clear the music rights to *Killer of Sheep*. So when we created the release version for Milestone, we actually had to work with Charles to make a few small changes to navigate the legal situation. The result was wonderful, but it also means that the version everyone's been watching since 2007 isn't Charles Burnett's original cut. I'm pleased to announce that because our screening tonight is part of the University's educational program, we'll be able to present the only existing 35mm restored print of Charles' original cut. So this is truly a rare event.[*]

As for Charles Burnett, he was the recipient of a MacArthur Foundation "genius" grant long ago, and is now considered a national treasure. I'm delighted that he'll join us in conversation after the first screening, following which we'll present the UCLA restoration of *Killer of Sheep*'s equally powerful follow-up film, *Bless Their Little Hearts*, on which Charles collaborated with the great Billy Woodberry.

---

[*] I'm pleased to report that as this book goes to press in early 2025, we are completing a new digital restoration of *Killer of Sheep*, and this time the music rights have been successfully cleared, so general audiences will at last be able to see Charles Burnett's original vision of the film's ending.

BLESS THEIR LITTLE HEARTS

The second film in the program, *Bless Their Little Hearts*, represents the closure and pinnacle of a neorealist strand within what's now described as the LA Rebellion. That strand traces to Charles Burnett's *Several Friends* (1969), which will be showing on the final night of our series.

Bless Their Little Hearts chronicles the devastating effects of un- and underemployment on a family in the same Los Angeles subculture depicted in *Killer of Sheep*, and it pays brutal witness to the ravages of time in the short years since its predecessor. Nate Hardman and Kaycee Moore deliver gutwrenching performances as the couple whose family is torn apart by events beyond their control. If salvation still exists, it's in the sensitive depiction of everyday life, which persists through moments both quiet and painful.

The film's connection to *Killer of Sheep* can't be overstated; the linkage existing through Charles Burnett's script and cinematography, its Watts milieu, and the performance of Moore and several others (including Burnett's niece and nephew), who appear in both works. By 1978, when *Bless'* production began, Burnett, then 34, was already an older statesman and mentor to many within the UCLA film community, and it was he who encouraged Billy Woodberry to pursue a feature-length work. In an extraordinary act of trust, Burnett offered the newcomer a startlingly intimate seventy-page original scenario and also shot the film. Yet critically, he then held back further instruction, leaving it to Woodberry to develop the material, direct, and edit. As Woodberry reveals, "He would deliberately restrain himself from giving me the solution to things. And not letting them look to him for the answer, or whatever. After the first week he said, 'No, I can't interfere too much.'" But always there and always, you know, giving his talent, his eye, his feeling."[*] The first-time feature director delivered brilliantly, and the result is an ensemble work that represents the cumulative visions of Woodberry, Burnett, and their excellent cast.

Whereas Burnett's original scenario placed emphasis on the spiritual crisis of Hardman's Charles Banks, the then-married Woodberry, alongside Moore and Hardman, further developed the domestic relationships within the film and articulated the depiction of a family struggling to stay alive in a world of rapidly vanishing prospects. The events portrayed cut so close to the community's bone that Hardman left the production for nearly a year, feeling it was telling his own story, and not his character's. Yet Burnett knew nothing of that, and was writing from his own experience. In Hardman's absence, Charles produced *My Brother's Wedding* (1983), before Woodberry persuaded Hardman to return and complete the film in 1984.

The film's ending can be read as a spiritual goodbye not just for Hardman's Banks, but for Burnett, who would move away from his neorealist work with his next film, *To Sleep With Anger* (1990), for Woodberry, who moved into documentary, and for Hardman himself, who left cinema shortly after—having (with Moore and a cast of unknowns) left behind an unforgettable landmark in American film.

---

[*] Billy Woodberry interview with Ross Lipman, July 2012.

Frownland (2008)

The following notes were prepared to introduce a double feature of Frownland *and* Wendy and Lucy *on June 18, 2022.*

Ron Bronstein's 35mm print of Frownland *was provided for the screening.*

A DCP of Wendy and Lucy *was screened courtesy of Kelly Reichardt.*

Tonight's program was loosely organized on the theme of "Lost Twenties."

Our first film is Ronald Bronstein's *Frownland*. It's not quite the male counterpart to *Wendy and Lucy*, but its lead character is trying just as badly to hold everything together. Lead actor Dore Mann's performance as a stuttering door-to-door salesman is a study in desperation that's hard to forget, something like a filmic rendition of Edward Munch's *The Scream*. He and director Ronald Bronstein apparently haven't spoken since the film's production, and after seeing it, it's not hard to imagine why. Bronstein has described the film as "a rotten egg lobbed with bad aim at the silver screen." When he heard we wanted to show it, his immediate reply was, "Why?" He followed up to say that "To this day, there's an active piece of real estate in my skull that questions the sense of screening the thing. I guess I've never shed the lasting effects of its initial reception."

Nonetheless it had its early appreciators. *The New Yorker*'s Richard Brody, in his rebuttal to A.O. Scott's influential piece on "Neo-neorealism," cited *Frownland* as a counter-example that was closer to his own ideas, citing the film's "audaciously expressive images, coming through but not staying with realism." Bronstein, responding to its place in our program, didn't agree. He wrote, "Appreciate the explanation of the series. Sounds cool. Though 'realism' was never a goal, or even a criteria, when making the movie." He concluded, "Trust me, had you been on set, you'd have thought you were witnessing a very incompetent piece of Kabuki theater." Paul and I included it nonetheless, and feel that if it's a grueling experience, it's grueling in all the right ways, somehow finding a heart within its horrors.

Bronstein is of course best known for his long-time collaboration with the Safdie brothers, including playing the lead role in *Daddy Longlegs*. Despite his success, and Frownland's high regard among cinephiles, he hasn't directed a feature since making it, back in 2007. I won't say much more because, really, the film needs to be experienced. But look for Bronstein's wife Mary in the role of Laura. I can't really say, "enjoy" the film, so I'll just end with, "Welcome to *Frownland*."

The Other Side (2015)

The following notes were prepared to introduce a double feature of The Other Side *and* Tangerine *on June 17, 2022.*

A DCP of The Other Side *was screened courtesy of Roberto Minervini.*

Sean Baker's new Cinevator (direct to positive filmout from digital file) 35mm print of Tangerine *was beta-tested at the screening.*

Tonight's odd pairing was originally conceived as a program called "Divided Nation," a very general attempt to speak to the polarization currently experienced in the US. First up is a film that many, including myself, feel to be absolutely essential viewing for anyone interested in the fate of our country and our democracy. As critic Robert Koehler wrote me upon seeing our program, "*The Other Side* is one of the most important films about America in the 21st century." That's high praise, and you'll soon see why.

Born in Fermo Italy, in 1970, Roberto Minervini moved to the US in 2000, and at the age of 34, got a master's in media studies at the New School. Since then, he's been chronicling little seen aspects of American life, most notably in 2013's *Stop the Pounding Heart*, and 2018's *What You Gonna Do When the World's on Fire?*

In *The Other Side*, Minervini offers a glimpse into the frustrated dreams that ultimately fueled the storming of the capital on January 6, 2021. Filmed in Louisiana, the film alternates between a too-close-for-comfort chronicle of the lives of real life drug addicts Mark Kelley and Lisa Allen, and shocking *vérité* footage of the far-right militias on their periphery.

In its split structure, the film vividly reveals not just the militias' inner dynamics, but the dire economic conditions around them, and that in many ways led to them.

Although the parallel stories don't quite overlap, their unspoken connection is the driving force of the film: a path from disenfranchised personal lives to a divided nation barely hanging onto its soul. One leaves with a portrait of 2015 America as a fuel-drenched car wreck, waiting to be lit aflame just a few years later.

In this light, the film gives new meaning to the term "trigger warning." There's a lot of disturbing content here. But at the same time, it shows us the human conditions that lie behind the dark spectacle. Despite the advent of what's known as "White Studies" in academia, an oddly overlooked group emerges in our larger society's discussion of diversity in America: poor whites. With tonight's screening we don't aim to celebrate them by any stretch of the imagination. But the film indelibly shows why it's essential to try to understand the realities of life in what us coastal elites disparagingly call "the flyover states." In a direct challenge to politically correct mores, Minervini brought along some of his cast members to *The Other Side*'s Cannes premiere in 2015. And we're still living the film's realities today.

I'm delighted to report that Roberto Minervini will be joining us in person for a conversation after the screening, following which Sean Baker will introduce *Tangerine*. It's now my honor to present *The Other Side*.

Figure 6. Mark Kelley in *The Other Side*.

Short Takes: People

This section compiles short texts about filmmakers whose work I've been fortunate to restore, or otherwise work with in some capacity. An additional text translating and interpreting an interview with Artur Aristakisian has been included, although I've never worked with either him or his films.

While these entries are quite brief and in some cases repeat established histories, I include them here for their hopeful inclusion of some lesser known details to add to the record, or to celebrate an underappreciated artist.

01—BARBARA LODEN
02—STEPHEN LIGHTHILL
03—BARNEY ROSSET
04—TOM CHOMONT
05—SID LAVERENTS
06—BRUCE BAILLIE
07—ARTUR ARISTAKISIAN

○   ○   ○

BARBARA LODEN

The following text was adapted from notes prepared for Wanda's *restoration premiere at the New York Museum of Modern Art in October 2010, and from program notes and screening introductions presented at the UCLA Festival of Preservation and London Film Festival the following year. For a discussion of* Wanda's *restoration, see the essay "Defogging* Wanda*" in the Case Studies section of the present volume.*

Barbara Loden, at surface glance, might be the least likely candidate to have produced one of the masterpieces of American cinema. According to legend, she was "conceived in a field of daisies."[*] Born in Marion, Ohio in 1932, she had to face not only class but also gender discrimination throughout her life. Today it's harder to appreciate the struggles she had to confront, not just in her professional encounters, but within herself—for by her own admission

---
[*] Elia Kazan, *A Life* (Da Capo, 1988) (1997 edition), 571.

she had grown up in an environment wherein a woman's only chances for self-improvement were through attachment to a man. It's precisely from these struggles that *Wanda* grew.

She began her career at seventeen as a dancer at the Copacabana, and with the help of her first husband, Larry Joachim, began appearing on the Ernie Kovacs show. She soon thereafter met noted director Elia Kazan, whom she was later to marry. Kazan cast her in a small role in his excellent *Wild River* (in 1960), and, more famously, *Splendor in the Grass* (1961), alongside a young Warren Beatty. However, it wasn't until she appeared in Kazan's stage production of Arthur Miller's *After the Fall* in 1964 that she came to true public attention, for her spectacular portrayal of the character modeled after Marilyn Monroe.

Figure 1. Barbara Loden in *Wanda*.

Her celebrity was short-lived however, for it was soon after this that Kazan and Loden withdrew into a life of relative seclusion. Partially at Kazan's urging, she turned down the role of Bonnie in *Bonnie and Clyde* (1967), and her understudy in *After the Fall*, Faye Dunaway, took the role opposite Beatty.

 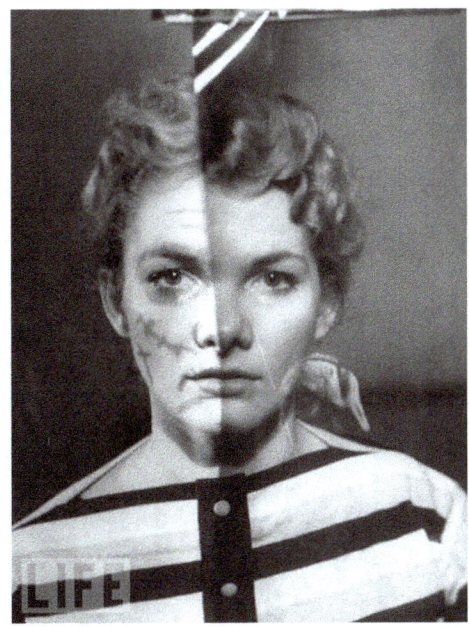

Figures 2A and 2B. The many faces of Barbara Loden.
Left: Her early career as a pinup girl. Right: On *The Ernie Kovacs Show*.

Of such details, history is made. We can be grateful in one respect. If her acting career had taken off, who knows whether we'd ever have seen *Wanda*. Loden was furious when Kazan later cast Dunaway in a role largely based on her in *The Arrangement* (1969), but she revealed that her own misgivings about *Bonnie and Clyde* lay elsewhere. She stated that the movie "was unrealistic and glamorized the characters… People like that would never get into those situations or lead that kind of life—they were too beautiful… *Wanda* is the anti-*Bonnie and Clyde*."

Loden's vision for the film was initially based on a newspaper clipping she had seen about a working-class Polish woman involved in a failed bank robbery, who upon hearing of her sentence to twenty years in prison, thanked the judge. It eventually grew into a screenplay called *The Gray World*, before settling on its final name.

It took six years to raise the $200,000 needed to complete the film. I was to later learn from documentarian D.A. Pennebaker that the film had been funded by their friend Harry Shuster as a tax write-off, and intended to lose money. However, while it was indeed a huge financial flop, its critical success—particularly in Europe—led to just enough income that it even failed as a write-off. It had in effect, failed at losing.

The connection to Pennebaker is no accident. Loden needed a creative partner in the project, and ultimately chose cinematographer Nick Proferes, who had begun his career as an editor for Pennebaker, and, crucially, emerged from the documentary tradition of *cinéma vérité*.

Figure 3. Barbara Loden as Maggie, modeled on Marilyn Monroe, in *After the Fall*.

With its location shooting, available-light cinematography, long takes, and extensive use of non-actors it functions at one level as pure documentary. Yet with the exquisitely honed performances of the two professional leads, Loden and Michael Higgins, and perhaps a trace of its Kazanian pedigree, it also functions as high-level, if intentionally laconic, drama.

The two skilled leads' brilliant performances are held in perfect balance by the non-actors who surround them and Proferes' existing-light photography. These elements combine to depict a rural Pennsylvanian housewife's lost flight to nowhere—an American landscape of decrepit factories, two-lane wastelands, and ratty motels.

Dragged seemingly by the wind into a relationship with small-time crook Michael Higgins, Loden's Wanda floats through her own life as if witness to it, a view of desperation filtered through a tinted windshield. Cumulatively, Proferes' *cinéma vérité* origins ultimately fuse with Loden's expert direction in one of the most authentic visions of middle America committed to screen.

According to Loden, Kazan was supportive, and without him, she may never have completed it. Kazan also assisted in the direction of the climactic bank robbery scene. Yet scholar Berenice Reynaud correctly notes a patronizing tone in Kazan's comments on the enterprise. He wrote that he "didn't really believe she had the equipment to be an independent filmmaker, but she and Nick were a good combination… I thought by supplementing each other they might make it. I admired her because she never stopped trying."* The comment inspires questions as to whether he thought he made his own films by himself.

Throughout Kazan's autobiography, one finds him commenting on Loden's "limitations," while simultaneously marveling at her results, and the depth in her work as both actress and director. Some even speculate a jealousy at the acclaim *Wanda* was to receive; it clearly helped as a model and/or inspiration for his own low-budget film, *The Visitors* (1972), also shot by Proferes.

In hindsight, *Wanda* serves as a key work of a largely unnoticed wellspring of American neorealism, which also includes Kent Mackenzie's *The Exiles*, Floyd Mutrux's *Dusty and Sweets McGee* (1971), Charles Burnett's *Killer of Sheep* (1977), and the virtually unknown masterpiece, *Spring Night, Summer Night*, by J. L. Anderson and Franklin Miller. As none of these films received public attention on their initial release, it's only recently that we've begun to understand there even *was* an American neorealism.

Figure 4. Original French publicity material for *Wanda*.

---

* Kazan, ibid, 794.

The film premiered at the Venice Film Festival in 1970, where it won a FIPRESCI prize. It was a critical sensation, but, as noted, a commercial flop. Although Loden was to subsequently produce two short films, and starred in the first NY production of *Come Back to the 5 & Dime, Jimmy Dean, Jimmy Dean*, she never again worked on a scale as large as *Wanda*. Today it's considered a classic, listed as one of the hundred greatest American films of all time by noted critic Jonathan Rosenbaum.*

Loden was to die tragically of cancer at the tender age of 48 in 1980, and as Kazan has described in his autobiography, she died angry at a life and brilliant career cut short. *Wanda* remains her lasting legacy.

---

* Since the writing of this piece, *Wanda* was also named one of the top 100 films of all time in *Sight and Sound*'s once-a-decade poll.

STEPHEN LIGHTHILL

The following text was initially published in Karen L. Ishizuka and Patricia Zimmerman's Mining The Home Movie: Excavations in Histories and Memories *(California Press, 2008).*

THE STEPHEN LIGHTHILL COLLECTION AT UCLA FILM & TELEVISION ARCHIVE

The UCLA Film & Television Archive's collection has historically focused on professional film productions, its core being Hollywood studio features and Hearst newsreel footage. Over the years, however, a number of excellent examples of alternative film forms have made their way into the Archive's vaults. Prominent among these is a growing collection of American independent cinema. By its very nature independent film crosses the boundaries between "professional" and "amateur" quite freely, often exhibiting characteristics of both within the same production. An illuminating instance of this dynamic is the Stephen Lighthill Collection at UCLA.

Stephen Lighthill, now a professional cinematographer, began his career in the Bay Area in the 1960s by documenting the anti-war and civil rights movements, both locally and nationally. He filmed scores of protests, demonstrations, and rallies, and also documented key cultural moments such as the first Human Be-In in Golden Gate Park in 1967. A journalism student with no professional production training, he was drawn into filmmaking through his own social activism.

His first major project was *Sons and Daughters*, a documentary centering on the anti-war movement in Berkeley, by filmmaker Jerry Stoll. Out of this experience a number of the crew's members, who, like Lighthill, were primarily activists, formed American Documentary Films, a collective devoted to radical filmmaking. Lighthill later went on to become a stringer for CBS News, but maintained his involvement with activist cinema at the same time. He helped film the Rolling Stones' 1969 Altamont concert for the Maysles brothers' *Gimme Shelter*, and contributed to such documentaries as *Seeing Red*, *The Good Fight*, and *The Day After Trinity*. Not only did he serve as DP on Mark Kitchell's *Berkeley in the Sixties*, but the film also included clips of both his activist footage and his CBS work.

The Stephen Lighthill Collection at UCLA Film & Television Archive contains all the outtakes from *Sons and Daughters*, as well as a substantial amount of footage shot by Lighthill and others from the American Documentary collective. Together it comprises a treasure trove of moments from the turbulent era it documents. While it is heavily splattered with coverage of key figures of the era, ranging from Allen Ginsberg and Jerry Rubin to Huey Newton and Bobby Seale, it also documents the unseen faces in the crowd, the untold women and men who formed a generation. Their counterparts the police are documented too, in both clinical detail and occasional intimacy. Even bystanders play a part, in their observations of the events around them. These glimpses are perhaps ultimately the most revealing, as we see in these faces a country trying to understand the drastic changes it's undergoing; in their confusion we feel both the political urgency of the times and the human sensibility behind it.

Lighthill himself admits that he was, at the time, somewhere in the gray area between professional and amateur. Technically the film's quality is that of a pro, but the proximity of the camera to the events it documents speaks of an involvement in the moment that is decidedly radical. The footage is thus both highly partisan and strangely neutral. Looking for the contemplative moment amidst the flurry of activity, Lighthill lets his viewpoint be known while ultimately allowing the images to speak for themselves.

The footage is for the most part 16mm reversal, and encompasses both color and black-and-white, and silent and sound footage. Large portions of the collection consist of Lighthill's original 400-foot camera rolls. It spans the period from the mid 1960s to the early 1970s, and Lighthill's work as both an amateur and professional. The rolls inspected thus far have not exhibited excessive deterioration, and UCLA is currently in the midst of transferring much of the footage to video to create viewing access copies. In this process, Lighthill's original footage logs, which are part of the collection, have served as an invaluable guide. Due the collections' size, there is a great quantity that remains to be inspected and no doubt many gems still to uncover.

Encompassing both professional and amateur filmmaking as it does, the Stephen Lighthill Collection is an excellent example of how independent cinema can infiltrate the mainstream and help to shape our cultural perceptions. Here at UCLA we are trying to expand notions of what comprises our national cinema. In the heart of Hollywood, the well-composed images of Stephen Lighthill help disarm conventional critiques of amateur footage. As collections like this are recognized and utilized, the path is paved for a deeper understanding of the vast "non-professional" cinema that is the greatest record of so much of our culture.

BARNEY ROSSET

This memorial piece was originally published in Evergreen Review, *#130, 2012.*

STRANGE VICTORIES

My first thoughts of Barney, as for many, are of late afternoons lapsed into evening, rum and cokes in hand raised lazily above the 4th Avenue din. The stories the drinks unleashed, of America's great culture wars, would rarely foreground Barney. His absence was striking, but his reach was long. To imagine our cultural landscape without him was to conjure an unrecognizable and barren land. Barney had invisibly enabled the present.

Moving past the stories, which others can tell far better, I think of our project together. Barney had loomed large in my pantheon since the early 1980s, when I was an undergraduate in Ann Arbor, Michigan. Ken Jordan lived in our dorm and through him our sensibilities were entirely focused through the prism of Barney's Grove Press, for whom Ken's father Fred was a senior editor. As a kid, Ken would come home from an average schoolday to greet Abbie Hoffmann, a long-term houseguest while hiding from the FBI. Ken knew him as "Barry." I half-pictured them tossing baseballs in an East Village lot. Through Ken I came to understand Grove's role as crucible for a generation.

So years later, in my role as a film restorationist at the UCLA Film & Television Archive, it was with nervous excitement that I approached Barney about preserving Samuel Beckett's *Film*. Legends abounded in archiving circles about the lost negative, gone missing around the time of Grove's sale. Barney knew nothing about the negative's whereabouts, and he was delighted to work with us. The preservation itself will be chronicled elsewhere; what I want to relate rather, is something of our struggle to *find* the movie.

Through some old receipts that turned up in one of Barney's thousands of folders, I traced the best-known surviving elements to a now-defunct New York laboratory. I'd dealt with the owner before and had difficulties. He was a man whose business had died, and he carried with him the tragedy of a lost career. Unlike Barney however, who also lost an empire, the man was destroyed and embittered. After years of begging, pleading, bribing and threatening, the lab owner still refused to release Barney's film. Through an incongruity of the law, he was able to hold Beckett's *Film* hostage, in hopes that Barney might bail him out of his entire catastrophic debt.

The levels of irony stagger. The monetary value of the film was frankly negligible, and the request to pay the larger sum was preposterous. Said the lab owner on the phone one day, "I don't give a damn about artistic importance. In our society whoever holds the gun holds the power, and I have the gun." In his younger days Barney would have taken him straight to court and shown him something about power. Now, years later, there were no resources to do so, and we had to drop the matter. The lab owner remains ruined, and the copy of *Film* collects dust in a vault in New Jersey.

The story does not end sadly, however. With funding from the Film Foundation and the National Film Preservation Foundation, UCLA has managed to restore *Film* with digital tools, and it now looks like new. The results will be released by Milestone Films in 2013. Barney's lifelong dreams of cinema, tracing back to *Strange Victory*, will at last be realized in wide distribution. Perhaps as important to me is the lesson I learned from Barney. Like the lab owner, he'd lost his empire. Yet even in that loss he held his head high, and when seeing him, I felt only his achievements. He was weakened with age, but unbeaten by circumstance, and heartwarmingly human. The rum and cokes tasted the same, empires be damned.

TOM CHOMONT

The following was adapted from a program note for a tribute to Tom Chomont, presented in UCLA Film & Television Archive's Festival of Preservation on March 11, 2011.

Selected short films by Tom Chomont were restored by UCLA Film & Television Archive as part of the Outfest UCLA Legacy Project, with funding from the National Film Preservation Foundation's Avant-Garde Masters Grant program provided by The Film Foundation.

Laboratory services by Triage and Fotokem. Restoration supervised by Ross Lipman in consultation with Tom Chomont and Jim Hubbard.

At the surprising intersection of eroticism, mysticism, and the everyday one finds Tom Chomont. Filmmaker/curator Jim Hubbard has written that "Chomont's films offer a lyric depiction of the ordinary world, but at the same time reveal an unabashedly spiritual and sexualized parallel universe. His incomparable technique of offsetting color positive and high contrast black-and-white negative creates a subtly beautiful, otherworldly aura." Hubbard observes that in this sense, "the subtitle of his film *Phases of the Moon* best characterizes all of his work: *The Parapsychology of Everyday Life*." His films lovingly depict the commonplace, while the richness of texture, layer, and observation always point to something beyond.

Infusing this dynamic is a palpably human longing for love. In Chomont's world, the boundaries that limit us are in fact gateways, be they door, window, skin, or spirit. Nowhere is this more visible than in his most famous, although outwardly least characteristic 16mm work, *Love Objects*. In *Love Objects*, explicit scenes of heterosexual and homosexual lovemaking are intercut so seamlessly that one doesn't know quite one's watching. And yet—while the rapid editing speaks to the era from which it emerged (evoking such films as Carolee Schneemann's *Fuses*)—the gentility of depiction renders it far from jarring. While its subject and content are daringly transgressive, the film reveals in its tenderness, rather, that life itself is a transgression on prurience.

Other films in the program include lyrical portraits both intimate and abstract, ranging in subject from a closeted lover encountered in Central Park (*Oblivion*), to experimental film icon Robert Beavers, in the youthful days before his departure to Greece with Gregory Markopolous (*The Mirror Garden* and *Jabbok*).

Chomont completed approximately 40 short films between 1962 and 1989. He suffered from Parkinson's during the last decades of his life, a time in which he also produced a wide range of video works. These later pieces include documents of his struggles with illness as well as his immersion in ritual S & M culture. While outwardly quite different from his earlier work, characteristically they transcend their striking subject matter and point to the spiritual aspects of our physical existence.

Ironically, the impoverished and disabled Chomont was only able to get financial assistance for his Parkinson's once he became HIV-positive, allowing at least a modicum of medical treatment in his later years. This program of newly restored titles focuses on Chomont's exquisite early 16mm work. UCLA ultimately hopes to restore more of the oeuvre of this truly underappreciated genius of experimental cinema.

SID LAVERENTS

The following notes were written in May 2012 for a proposed tribute to Sid Laverents to take place at the Academy of Motion Picture Arts & Sciences, under sponsorship of the Academy's Technical Commission. Circumstances prevented the event from ever taking place. For further information on Sid Laverents, see the notes on his masterpiece, The Sid Saga, *in the "Short Takes—Films" section of the present volume.*

Selected short films by Sid Laverents were restored by UCLA Film & Television Archive with funding from the National Film Preservation Foundation and Fotokem Film and Video. Laboratory services by Fotokem and Audio Mechanics. Restoration supervised by Ross Lipman in consultation with Sid Laverents, in collaboration with colleagues including color grader Walt Rose, audio restorationist John Polito, archivist Amy Sloper, scholars Melinda Stone and Jake Austin, collector Pea Hicks, and with Charlotte Laverents.

For many, the term "amateur cinema" may conjure blurry images of happy families waving their hands at the camera in a 1950s fairground. But for those who know better, it conjures an alternate universe of technical virtuosity and imagination that rivals the best of Hollywood cinema. When one dives into this world, one finds an entire subculture of amateur film clubs dating back decades, in all parts of the US and indeed, the world. And as one dives further in, one finds Sid Laverents.

Among these clubs were many stars, but none that shone as brightly as Laverents. Born in 1908, he began his career in the 1920s as a barnstorming Vaudevillian with a one-man band act, in which he played sixteen instruments at once. He later moved on to work ranging from Fuller Brush salesman, carpenter, sign painter, soldier, and sheet metal worker, to aeronautical engineer—he was literally everything from dishwasher to rocket scientist.

What he's known for today, however, are his films. These works included hysterical comedies, dazzling trick films, and eccentrically brilliant nature documentaries, dominated not just by his quirky sense of humor, but by a technical ingenuity that is mimicked and celebrated to this day.

For *Multiple Sidosis*—the second amateur film elected to the National Film Registry after the Zapruder film—he used complicated in-camera multiple exposures to create as many as twelve images of himself playing instruments simultaneously on the screen. To achieve this effect, he not only custom-built unique matte-boxes and hand-modified camera motors, but devised his own foil-and-light-flash based audio cuing system to maintain sync, Les Paul-style, on his Roberts ¼" tape recorder.

For his nature films, he designed and constructed large photo observation towers in his backyard, to enable macrophotography of hummingbirds—to the horror and chagrin of his more conventional suburban neighbors. For his comedy *It Sudses and Sudses and Sudses* (1962), he designed a machine that created enough soap bubbles to drown a small army—again to the chagrin of his neighbors, when the bubbles, not to mention a bubble-drenched Sid, began pouring out the window.

His greatest technical achievement, however, is no doubt *Stop Cloning Around* (1980). In this masterwork, Sid's homemade "cloning machine" goes awry and with the aid of anamorphic lenses and multiple exposures, creates a short fat Sid, a tall skinny Sid, and several odd looking "middle" Sids. The film culminates in the misfired clones singing an on-camera barbershop quartet, enabled by Sid singling all four parts in different keys at varying speeds, then replaying the recordings back at the *wrong* speed to bring them into tune and tempo with each other, ranging from deep bass to high treble, beyond the vocal range of a single human. In sync, and composited in-camera!

This evening-long tribute presents an assortment of Sid's greatest hits, including both his astounding trick films and the virtually unseen nature documentaries. The films will be accompanied by an illustrated presentation on Sid's many technical innovations, including 35mm slides he himself created to demonstrate his techniques in public lectures to film clubs around the nation, as well as images and technical illustrations from articles he published in magazines including *Movie Maker* and *The Photographic Society of America Journal*.

The evening will also be accompanied by a gallery exhibition displaying Sid's inventions, patents, Vaudeville costumes, photos, and legendary Mickey Mouse ears.

BRUCE BAILLIE

I was fortunate to work with Bruce Baillie on a number of occasions, and conducted a two-day interview with him as part of the Academy of Motion Picture Arts and Science's Oral History Program.

The following text was adapted from an essay originally published in a booklet accompanying the 2010 DVD release of his film Quick Billy, *transferred and produced by the filmmaker.*

WHITHER BRUCE BAILLIE?

> "Has he really got as far as that?" he cried. "Ah, then he is worth ten thousand of me put together... What Kao keeps in mind is the spiritual mechanism. In making sure of the essential he forgets the homely details. So clever a judge of horses is Kao, that he has it in him to judge something better than horses."
>
> — Taoist tale, as read to ten-month old baby Franny in J. D. Salinger's "Raise High the Roof Beams, Carpenters!"

Whither Bruce Baillie? From the lone transcendent biker riding the two-lane highway of nightmares in 1964's *Mass for the Dakota Sioux* to 1970's *Quick Billy*, Baillie blazed a path through nothing less than the American consciousness itself, closing the cycle with the Quixotic epigram "Ever Westward Eternal Rider!" As the admonition warns, the journey continues, and endpoints are illusory—only movement is of essence.

The new, radiant *Entr'acte* of his in-progress opus, *Memoirs of an Angel*, tips the jester's hand that Baillie can still check into our mortal world when the moment chooses. Just as his early pre-*Parsifal* films show inflammatory sparks of brilliance, his later, mostly unseen, videos burn like embers in the ash. The spiritual energy that infuses all of his creation burns throughout, in continual transformation.

Quick Billy, if one is measuring, fluidly marks the transmigration from flame to ember. In a recent e-mail, Bruce wrote me that the film's "Rider" end quote now strikes him as a kind of epitaph. If it's an epitaph, it's only so in the sense that epitaphs speak to the physical world. *Quick Billy* was Baillie's last "recognized" major work, and spoke to his own near-death experience after contracting hepatitis in 1967. The illness left him to suffer the remainder of his days on our modest planet with chronic fatigue syndrome, and forced him to parse physical energy in small doses. It simultaneously pushed him half into the realm of spirit. A Bodhisattva of crazed wisdom now walks Camano Island.

From Baillie's notebooks on the making of the film: "The difficulty in bringing a work of art to describe Death." And: "The burden of eternal movement (like mirrors, passing through—beyond—your own image)."

It's thus some epitaph that Baillie has chosen for himself. *Ever Westward Eternal Rider*. Completion of a life, or an artwork, is a mirage. Straight from his inspiration, the *Bardo Thodol*: Death is journey, not conclusion.

Allen Ginsberg once remarked that most scholars wouldn't know poetry if it jumped them on the street and buggered them in broad daylight. When viewing any work by Baillie, prepare to be buggered, in the best of senses, and with utmost affection. And may you see the experience clearly: spark, flame, ember, and smoke. They are of the same fabric. Whither Baillie? Here and onward.

ARTUR ARISTAKISIAN

The following is a bit of guerilla scholarship, if you will. I became fascinated with Artur Aristakisian's Palms (Ladoni) *after seeing it at the San Francisco Film Festival in 1994.*

Finding a third generation English translation of his interview with Galina Antoschewskaja somewhat garbled and baffling, I set out to make my own version of his remarks, which included what I understood to be a mystical interpretation of the photochemistry of film.

The interview between Artur Aristakisian and Galina Antoschewskaja appeared in abbreviated form in the Internationales Forum des Jungen Films catalog from the Berlin Film Festival, 1994. The new English text presented here was created in 1997 from a complete German transcript of the interview, which took place in St. Petersburg, in Russian. Using the German transcript (original translator unknown), my colleague Tülin Emercan produced a literal English version, which I in turn freely interpreted, taking liberties as I thought appropriate in the writing of the final text, below. This methodology, while in part derived from necessity (the lack of an original), was in no small part inspired by Tarkovsky's writings on the adaptation of literature to cinema, wherein he states that a director must be prepared to abandon their source to remain true to it. In this sense, the generational separation from the Russian freed me to adapt subjectively, and not literally. Aristakisian's original words are long lost in the following text, and what remains is the expression of a vision inspired by Aristakisian.

2010 translation by Tülin Emircan and Ross Lipman. Thanks to Ulrich Gregor and Edith Kramer.

Figure 5. Artur Aristakisian's *Palms* (*Ladoni*).

PALMS

There is a beggar in Kishinev who wanders the streets all day long, speaking aloud to his unborn son. People stop and listen to him. The child was to be born twenty years ago, but his bride aborted it. From that day on, the man's life was transformed. He lost his reasoning.

    Seven years ago, I also walked the streets of half-destroyed Kishinev, telling my son—who was not granted birth, either—about my town. In this way I got to know people, most of them beggars. They had become beggars through the experience of love.

    I shot the film between 1986 and 1990, accompanying the beggars for months on end. They were willing to open themselves before the camera. One even told me that he was ready to kill himself on camera, so that I could film his death. Sometimes shooting became a kind of game. Once I put the camera in the hands of a blind beggar, and he took two panning shots. One of them can be seen in the film.

Artur Aristakisian

EXODUS OF LOVE—an interview with Artur Aristakisian

Q: How did you come to the idea to make this film?

A: I shot the film between 1986 and 1990 in my home town of Kishinev. For two years I edited and worked on the soundtrack at the VGIK training studio in Moscow. Filming in 16mm allowed me to shoot much more footage of each individual than would working in 35mm. Then the edited material was transferred to 35mm, a process which I think brought about a particular aesthetic most appropriate to speaking of the lives of the beggars.

Had it been possible, I would have used color in the final sequence, at the Jewish cemetery. In this cemetery, no new graves are dug. The images of the dead look out at us, and dead ravens lie in the snow.

The people I filmed got used to me, in the way that one gets used to a stray dog. I could be near to them as long as was necessary. For months I went to their homes, and they told me everything.

The film material, when sharply focused, transforms all things into pictures, or artworks. The film material thus sacrifices itself to the one it features. It gives up its intrinsic light, and in so doing, transforms all events into pictures, into pure light.

Reality is arbitrary, subject to the selection of our will, or seeing. In this reality lies our salvation. But when salvation appears to us, it disappears in an instant. The film material fixes the hope for salvation. The reality and moment that are fixed, that have been taken, can be given back, as the literal development of the shared substance of the body of Man—the body of God's mother—putting us in relationship to a spiritual essence, rather than just re-presenting a moment.

Q. The title of your film is *Palms.* What does the word mean to you?

A. As a child, I would often be left alone for long periods of time. And I would often feel the touch of unknown hands. These strangers first appeared to me through their palm's touch, caressing my face and covering my eyes. This would happen again and again, when someone was trying to calm me. Palms open me to men and unite me with them in the darkness. This was the secret of that time as a child. I would wait for help, and it would come to me in the form of naked palms. As in tales, these palms held the secret of love.

The open palm at once offers mercy, and at the same time is granted it. When a baby is born, it's received by palms. The last request of the dying is the touch of a palm. Embraces are performed through palms. The crucified Love views us with palms. Our hands look into heaven with palms. And as our palms can look into heaven, so can they look into people's faces. That is how I would like my camera to see—in the way of palms. I want to touch and caress people with it.

Q. Your film is about beggars, people who have broken with society.

A. The beggars I met in the street were only the social reflection of that beggar whom I was seeking, the beggar who lives inside us. The outer beggar emerged from this spirit. The beggar's life became a form and way of love. The beggar's life begins as a vocation, and transmutes into a sphere synonymous with the lover's. Blessed are the spiritually poor. The film is my version of the first commandment of blessing.

These beggars have nothing but their love. Because of this, they are the holders of a transfigured relationship. Not of a blood relationship, but of a spiritual transformation. They are holders of a new death. Not violent death, but a redeeming death, that frees us all.

The film material, which sacrifices itself to its subject, became for me a form of this redeeming death. The beggar's life is similar. Something lives inside you, and opens your eyes and heart.

I spent days with these beggars, who became beggars because of their love. They told me their stories. About the persecutions they suffered as a result of their love. They told me of their moments of joy, of their losses and privations. We talked about how best to tell their stories. And together we decided that the life story of each individual should be the tale of their love.

The movie grew into a long documentary fresco, shot in the language of parables and religious metaphors. It is a wreath of blossoms, in which one love flows into the next. These men and women were filmed in the state of waiting for their love. They remained in that state of love, of the time of last encounters with their love.

Q.   How was the movie produced? How was it financed?

A.   Even before I enrolled at the Moscow Film Academy, I shot a lot of material in the old Kishinev. During my studies I could drive to Kishinev and shoot new material, to connect with the footage and characters filmed earlier. The film was shot as a documentary. But there is an unseen protagonist, whose sight is dissolved in the camera's, and whose disembodied voice addresses his unborn yet already killed son.

While shooting, I thought I should determine a particular genre for my film. I would call it a documentary parable, or a dramatic chronicle. The beggars are at once actors and vagrant kings. They chronicle their own exodus of love. And I would like for them to pierce the heart of the viewer.

As for the financing, I sold my books and belongings, and with the money I bought film stock. At that time it was cheap and easy to come by. When I ran out of money and film stock, some beggars gave me the change they collected. I worked on the sound and editing for two years.

Q.   The word "System" appears in your movie. What does it mean?

A.   I read in the gospel of Matthew, "Come to me, all who labor and are heavy laden, and I will give you rest." So I began to think about the System, about who controls our fortune. And how what is not part of the body of God, cannot become love.

Q.   Through your film, I for the first time encountered a penetrating belief in God. For that I thank you! Is the bible a part of your perception of the world?

A.   In this film I sought to express my perception of the Christian commandment of blessing. I didn't want to address either a social or religious theme, but rather to create visual, poetic metaphors. When we see the world, we can't perceive the metaphors that surround people. Therefore film is for me a method of changing the way we see.

Short Takes: Films

Most of the following short texts were presented as introductions to screenings of restored films. Some make only passing reference to the project's restoration process: in general, they tend to focus on the film itself. Much of their substance is common knowledge. So why include them here? While their connection to film restoration practice is limited, they nonetheless relate to the larger project underlying this book: the quality presentation of moving image works. Introductions can be an underappreciated aspect of a screening, as works are brought to new audiences. I once attended a program of films by Vietnamese filmmaker Trinh T. Minh-ha, who opened the evening by comparing her role on stage to that of a baker. She said the task was not to eat the cake in front of you, but rather to prime one to appreciate the cake on their own.

In adapting these introductions to the page, I tended to re-insert details that I excised in live presentation, where an overly long speech can harm rather than help reception of the actual film. In both the live and text versions, I try to avoid spoilers, and stick to information that might help the viewers commence their own voyage of discovery. In this way, an introducer can join in the community of people who place themselves at the service of a work.

01—*Dawn to Dawn* (1933)

02—*The Connection* (1961)

03—*Gamperaliya* (1963)

04—*Sunday* (1961) / *Point of Order!* (1964)

05—*Come Back to the 5 & Dime, Jimmy Dean, Jimmy Dean* (1982)

06—*Ornette: Made in America* (1985)

07—*Matewan* (1987)

08—*The Sid Saga* (1985/1987/1989/2003, etc.)

Dawn to Dawn (1933)

Dawn to Dawn (aka *Black Dawn*) was restored by UCLA Film & Television Archive in association with Anthology Film Archives as part of the Unseen Cinema Project, with funding from Cineric, the Eastman Kodak Company, the National Film Preservation Foundation, and NT Audio. Laboratory services provided by Cineric and NT Audio. Restoration supervised by Ross Lipman. Special thanks to Bruce Posner.

The following brief notes are extracted from a longer introduction to a program of short films presented in their restoration premieres on August 9, 2002 at the James Bridges Theater in Los Angeles, as part of UCLA's Festival of Preservation, and are presented here to call attention to a virtually unknown gem.

Tonight we'll be seeing a truly unusual work: an American "art film" from 1933. *Dawn to Dawn*, or *Black Dawn*, was directed by Josef Berne, a Russian immigrant who worked in the Yiddish cinema and later directed some "Soundies"—the precursor to the music video. Here he tells the tale of a lonely young woman who tends a farm with her domineering and possessive father.

What stands out today, as it would have then, is the lyrical eroticism of the film—something truly unusual in American cinema at the time. As *Dawn to Dawn* is nearly wordless, it would seem to have been inspired by the sensual cinema of the Czech Gustav Machaty, whose controversial *Ecstasy* with Hedy Lamarr (then Hedy Keisler) was made the year before.

Contributing to the film's strength is an excellent score by Cameron McPherson, who also produced the film. The scenario is by Seymour Stern, who later become legendary among film scholars for his polemical diatribes in *Film Culture* and other journals. I'd especially like to single out the film's star, Julie Hayden, who turns in a performance that's at once delicate and extremely powerful. She later went on to appear in Ben Hecht's *The Scoundrel* and numerous Broadway plays, taking the role of Laura in *The Glass Menagerie*.

While the other performances are a bit clunky, as is some of the technique (when viewed by professional standards), what holds the film together—and in a way links the very different films we're seeing tonight—is a kind of rough aesthetic that's somehow intimately connected with a raw vision, a quality that's all too often weeded out of more professional productions.

I'd like to thank Anthology Film Archives, Cineric, Inc., Eastman Kodak, and NT Audio for their work and contributions to this project, David Pierce for calling my attention to the film, and Bruce Posner for helping to make it happen. You can also read a bit about it in Jan Christopher Horak's book, *Lovers of Cinema*.

The Connection (1961)

The Connection was restored by UCLA Film & Television Archive in association with Lewis Allen Productions and the British Film Institute, with funding from The Film Foundation. The restoration was subsequently digitally remastered by UCLA in collaboration with Milestone Films at Modern Film and Video. Laboratory services provided by Fotokem, Audio Mechanics, DJ Audio, and YCM. Restoration and remastering supervised by Ross Lipman in collaboration with colleagues including audio restorationist John Polito, film grader Walt Rose, Sharon Fallon, and Wendy Clarke. Distributed by Milestone.

> *The following is adapted from an introduction initially presented on the occasion of the film's restoration premiere on July 21, 2004 at the James Bridges Theater in Los Angeles, as part of UCLA's Festival of Preservation.*

On September 28th, 1960, twenty-four independent filmmakers assembled at the Producer's Theater on 46th Street in New York to discuss the state of contemporary film. The following is from the document that resulted, "The First Statement of the New American Cinema Group":

> The official cinema all over the world…is morally corrupt, aesthetically obsolete, superficial, [and] boring. As in the other arts in America today, our rebellion against the old, official, corrupt, and pretentious is primarily an ethical one. We are concerned with what's happening to Man. We are not an aesthetic school that constricts the film-maker within a set of dead principles. We feel we cannot trust any classical principles in art or life.

It goes on to delineate a comprehensive restructuring of the entire model of film production and distribution.

The group's executive board consisted of Jonas Mekas, Edward Bland, Emile de Antonio, Shirley Clarke, and Lewis Allen. Lewis Allen was a stage producer who was collaborating with Clarke at that time on the production of her film. Allen passed away on December 8th, 2003, and I'd like to pay tribute to him for making this project possible. Allen worked with UCLA for many years, and donated the original negative of *The Connection* to the archive as one of his last acts before he died. So our thanks go to him and also his assistant, Sharon Fallon.

The Connection is ultimately, however, a Shirley Clarke film. Shirley Clarke is arguably one of the most underrated filmmakers to emerge from the U.S.. My belief is that this is because she worked in so many different cinematic forms over the course of her career that she is exceedingly difficult to pigeonhole, and so fits uncomfortably into established Film Studies canons.

Clarke was Russian by descent, the daughter of a wealthy New York machine parts manufacturer, and the granddaughter of the inventor of the Phillips head screw.

She began her career as a dancer, performing with numerous artists including Martha Graham. It's hence no surprise that her earliest films were dance films, starting with the experimental *Dance in the Sun* in 1953. Indeed, the influence of dance never left her work, and she soon moved on to short experimental works noted for the graceful, dancelike quality of their editing.

After her 1959 short *Skyscraper* was nominated for an Academy Award, Clarke felt that she was ready to tackle a feature. In an interview with Lauren Rabinowitz,* she said:

> My brother-in-law (the critic Kenneth Tynan) was an enormous supporter of an off-Broadway play, *The Connection*. So one rainy night I went to see it.
> I just knew it was photogenic, and got in touch with the author, Jack Gelber.
> We made a deal and proceeded to work on the screenplay for months.

The Connection's stage production was originally produced at Julian Beck and Judith Malina's Living Theatre in the late 1950s. While the play's stark, unromanticized portrayal of heroin addiction was controversial enough, its radical stage aesthetics, including breaking down the "fourth wall" of naturalist drama, made it even more groundbreaking. Its cast—junkies awaiting their heroin fix—included an on-stage writer and producer, who, in a structuring device, were paying the junkies to play themselves on stage, with the audience itself a part of the experience. An actor sat in the crowd, making occasional comments, and at intermission the actors—still in character—mingled with the audience, harassing them for money. Legend has it that when "the Connnection" arrives in the second act and the junkies shoot up, real drugs were sometimes used. The ensemble was joined onstage by noted jazz musicians who played sets as part of the show.

In a stroke of prescience when adapting it for cinema, Clarke replaced the theatrical concept by transplanting the action to a Harlem apartment, and changing the writer and producer into a two-person documentary film crew. The film consisted entirely of the footage they supposedly shot. *The Connection* thus stands as one of the earliest instances of what's now become a genre unto itself: the "mockumentary."

Ultimately, however, *The Connection*'s "project" is decidedly different than most of its contemporary peers. Clarke's film is an affectionate if pointed parody of the then-recently born *cinéma vérité*, or Direct Cinema movement, known for its hand-held cinematography with portable equipment, and its supposedly neutral "fly-on-the-wall" point-of-view. Clarke exquisitely choreographed the former, including the flies, and lambasted the latter in a scathing exam of documentary ethics. Its critique was soon aped in later works like Mitchell Block's *No Lies,* and developed further in classics like Jim McBride's *David Holzman's Diary* and Haskell

---

* *Afterimage*, December 1983.

Wexler's *Medium Cool*. Today this is all familiar ground, but Clarke was one of the trailblazers, and *The Connection* is where you can see it all happening.

The last major aesthetic component of the film I'd like to mention is its stunning jazz score, written by Freddie Redd, the pianist whose wonderful scowl you'll get to see throughout the film, and performed by Redd and other jazz greats including Jackie McLean on sax.

Given both its radical form and content, the film indeed caused a sensation—briefly.

It premiered at Cannes in 1961, winning the Critics' Prize in a 110-minute version outside the main competition, and ultimately served as the model for what would later be known as the Critic's Week (la Semaine de la Critique), which began the following year. *The Connection* was hardly a sidebar, however, given that the festival gave Clarke her own private villa, and her poet friends Alan Ginsberg, Peter Orlovsky, and Gregory Corso, along with an assortment of jazz musicians, artists, and hangers-on all came down from Paris to join her, sending the press into a frenzy over the "Beat Invasion of Cannes." Between parties and sleeping on the beach, however, the film was indeed shown, and garnered raves and praise from critics including George Sadoul.

Returning to the U.S., Clarke was alas not as triumphant. America was in another one of its puritanical moods, and *The Connection* was banned by the New York state film licensing board. The Board of Education had objected to the junkies' using the word "shit" to describe heroin, and to the brief appearance of a male "nudie" magazine. Clarke, not one to compromise easily, fought them in a legal battle that lasted a year and a half. She ultimately won the case, but the clamor had died down over the course of the battle, and the film flopped domestically.

The 110-minute version that premiered at Cannes no longer exists; what we'll be seeing today is 103 minutes, and represents Clarke's final cut. The editing took place on a flatbed table Clarke shared with Jonas Mekas, who was editing *Guns of the Trees* at the time. Despite the battles over censorship of the film itself, the edits were Clarke's and not the censors. What we have today is her preferred release version of the film, made after Cannes, and before the censorship trial.

The film was ultimately restored from the original camera negative at UCLA, with damaged sections replaced by a fine grain master positive coming from the British Film Institute's National Film and Television Archive. I'd like to thank Fotokem Film and Video, Audio Mechanics, and DJ Audio for their expert work in collaborating with me to restore *The Connection* to the form you'll see tonight, and the Film Foundation for generously funding the project.

The restoration process was unusual, however, in that its most interesting aspect for me was for once not technical: it involved the near impossibility of getting the negative to UCLA. Like many independent film producers, Lewis Allen kept his printing elements at the laboratory that made the film, in this case Guffanti Films in N.Y. And like many labs, Guffanti shut its doors over a decade ago. In their financial distress, they fell into debt to Deluxe, a third party that stored Guffanti's holdings.

So while Lewis Allen was unknowingly sending storage payments to Guffanti for years, Guffanti was unable to pay Deluxe, who locked up the entire Guffanti collection as collateral for future payments. Payments which alas never came. It took over two years of phone calls, letters, begging and threats on behalf of myself and Sharon Fallon to get *The Connection* released from this legal deep freeze. During those two years we thought, based on Sharon's inventory lists, that we were pursuing a duplicate negative, with the original lost. You can imagine my excitement when after years of pursuit the package finally arrived, and the negative in question turned out to be the original.

In an interview with Gretchen Berg, Shirley Clarke once said:

> What got me started in film was a very basic simple fact: I got tired of rehearsing for six months for one performance at the "Y" and wanted to preserve forever what everyone had worked so hard to achieve.

Well, some perseverance and luck was involved, but *The Connection* has now indeed been preserved.

Before ending, I want to say a few last words on the film itself.

It lives in an odd space between forms, with a striking tension between its stage-influenced narrative and its *cinéma vérité* grittiness. Artifice and reality swing back and forth by the instant, at times clearly, at times blending so subtly you don't even notice it. But cumulatively, as the manifesto said, this is a piercingly human film—a stark portrayal of junkies and the effects of the drug scene on people's lives.

Extending the dance between fiction and reality on screen to the actual lives of the film's makers, Clarke began a relationship with actor Carl Lee during shooting. Lee, the son of noted actor Canada Lee, gives the brilliant portrayal of Cowboy, the film's title role, and is the ultimate synthesis of the film's theatrical and *vérité* threads. As in the film itself, Lee introduced the director to heroin, as well as to a new world and life in the underbelly of Harlem's ghetto. She subsequently left her marriage and family to join him in a long, if volatile romance. They were traumatic years, but it was exactly this "connection" that led to her later masterworks, *The Cool World* and *Portrait of Jason*.

I'll now close with another passage from "The First Statement of the New American Cinema Group," back in 1960:

> Common beliefs, knowledge, anger and impatience bind us together with the new cinema movements of the rest of the world. Our colleagues in France, Italy, Russia, Poland, or England can depend on our determination. As they, we have had enough of the Big Lie... As they, we are for art, but not at the expense of life. We don't want false, polished, slick films—we prefer them rough, unpolished, but alive; we don't want rosy films—we want them the color of blood.

It's now my pleasure to present Shirley Clarke's *The Connection*.

Gamperaliya (1963)

Gamperaliya (aka *The Changing Village*) was restored by UCLA Film & Television Archive, with funding from The Stanford Theatre Foundation. Laboratory services provided by the Stanford Theatre Film Laboratory, Audio Mechanics, DJ Audio, and Titra. Restoration supervised by Jere Guldin. Translations by Chandrani Warnasuriya and Lenny Borger; English version and subtitles by Sanji Warnasuriya and Ross Lipman. Special thanks to: Lester James Peries, Pierre Rissient, Edith Kramer.

The following is adapted from an introduction presented on the occasion of the film's restoration premiere on April 17, 2009, at the Billy Wilder Theater in Los Angeles, as part of UCLA's Festival of Preservation.

Although I did not work on the film's restoration proper (which was supervised by my colleague Jere Guldin), I fell in love with the film and signed up to do the English subtitles. This helped me learn some of the nuances of this underappreciated art. Our project took a circuitous path, as we had initially inherited an English-language version created by veteran subtitler Lenny Borger. Borger is one of the best in the industry, but was handicapped in this case, in that he had to work from a French translation from the original Sinhala rather than the original itself.

Unlike my adaptation of Artur Aristakisian's interview (presented in the "Short Takes: People" section of the present volume), which was by design an act of interpretation, our translation of Gamperaliya, *being a restoration, sought to ensure that accuracy was retained. To this end we worked with Sri Lankan writer Chandrani Warnasurijya and her son Sanji. Chandrani first created a literal, verbatim translation that was faithful to the source in content, but—we fully realized—might lose the original's poetic sensibilities, and was too long to match the film's spoken pacing. From that verbatim document I freely adapted an English-language version that would be more in tune with the actual film's sensibility, but which might stray here and there in "literal" accuracy. Finally, Sanji and I then revised my free interpretation to correct any errors of interpretation that might have arisen.*

When author Martin Wickramsinghe was approached by Lester James Peries with the idea of making a film of his celebrated novel *Gamperaliya*, he was baffled. To intellectuals of his era, Sri Lankan cinema was a form of populist entertainment completely unsuited to the intricacies of a literary work of art. Luckily, he gave Peries a chance, for in the ensuing film we find the advancement of Sri Lankan cinema to an art form of its own.

Western audiences will probably mainly know of Sri Lankan cinema through *Song of Ceylon*, the classic documentary made by UCLA's own Basil Wright, for the British GPO, then led by John Grierson. Although *Song of Ceylon* was commissioned by a tea company, the film's beauty and subtlety transcended its somewhat colonial origins and stands as a landmark in the history of documentary film.

Similarly, *Gamperaliya*, while openly addressing colonial issues, shows traces of Western influence, and transcends both in the humanity of Peries' vision. While Western audience might think of *Song of Ceylon*, the average Sri Lankan—like Wickramsinghe—would think primarily of huge popular hits at the time, which might best be described as a cousin of Bollywood. Lester James Peries was to provide an alternative that not only revolutionized Sri Lankan cinema, but also brought it to the forefront of the international film world.

Peries was initially a journalist, and hence began his film career by making documentaries. This journalistic or documentary impulse is apparent throughout his later fiction films, which frequently emphasize location cinematography and serve as critical records of undocumented aspects of Sri Lankan life. In point of fact there is a direct line from the British documentary movement of the 1930s to Peries, as his mentor was none other than Ralph Keene, who worked for Grierson in the years following *Song of Ceylon*.

Peries began his career with 1954's *Conquest of the Dry Zone*, which was celebrated at the Venice film festival. He went on to make three more documentaries, but his breakthrough was not to occur until 1956 with his first fiction film, *Rekava*. *Rekava* was adapted from his own script, and was such a departure from Sri Lankan cinema of the era that he was only able to complete it with assistance from David Lean, who was in Sri Lanka at the time filming *Bridge Over the River Kwai*.

After several more original features, Peries felt ready to try his hand at an accepted masterwork. He turned to *Gamperaliya*. To quote Peries:

> *Gamperaliya* had all the qualities I was looking for—it rang so true in the depiction of characters, their relationships, their social background. It had insight, a sense of compassion, a profound humanity. Its characters leapt off the page not as romanticized caricatures, but as living beings molded by their social background. In a way, despite my Anglicized Roman Catholic isolation, I had discovered my roots through Martin Wickramsinghe.

The film was made with the direct cooperation of Wickramsinghe, and critically, shot on location. In addition to the two lead roles, brilliantly played by Henry Jayasena and Punya Heendeniya, the film also featured mainstream film star Gamini Fonseka in the role of Nanda's husband. Another critical feature of the film is the wonderful soundtrack by famed Sri Lankan musician Amaradeva.

Seen with today's eyes, *Gamperaliya* is a window into another world. Set at the turn of the twentieth century, the film portrays the fading of village life in a transitional moment, and raises complex questions about the nature of colonialism. It does so with a warmth and humanity that at once evokes Satyajit Ray and Anton Chekhov. Yet more importantly, it displays the distinctly Sri Lankan vision of Lester James Peries.

Figure 1. Punya Heendeniya and Henry Jayasena in *Gamperaliya*.

Sunday (1961) / *Point of Order!* (1964)

Sunday was restored by UCLA Film & Television Archive, with funding from The Film Foundation. Laboratory services provided by Fotokem, Audio Mechanics, and NT Audio. Restoration supervised by Ross Lipman in consultation with Dan Drasin, and in collaboration with colleagues including audio restorationist John Polito, film grader Josh Rushton, and historian Dan Streible.

Point of Order! was restored by UCLA Film & Television Archive in association with the Wisconsin Center for Film & Theater Research and New Yorker Films, with funding from The Film Foundation. Laboratory services provided by the Stanford Theatre Film Laboratory, T & T Effects Co, Audio Mechanics, and NT Audio. Restoration supervised by Ross Lipman in collaboration with colleagues including audio restorationist John Polito and film grader Ed Rarer. Special thanks to: Nancy de Antonio, Maxine Fleckner Ducey, Robert Duncan, Jose Lopez, Dan Streible, and Dan Talbot.

The following is adapted from a catalog note and screening introduction presented on the occasion of the film's restoration premiere on April 3, 2009 at the James Bridges Theater in Los Angeles as part of UCLA's Festival of Preservation, followed by a conversation with Sunday's *director Dan Drasin,* Point of Order!'s *editor Robert Duncan, and de Antonio scholar Douglass Kellner. It was subsequently presented at the New York Museum of Modern Art, followed by a conversation with Dan Talbot, and the London Film Festival.*

SUNDAY—screening introduction

Sunday, our opening short, was produced by Emile de Antonio and directed by his friend and colleague Dan Drasin, who was only 17 years old at the time. Drasin trained with legendary *Cinéma vérité* pioneers Albert Maysles, D.A. Pennebaker and Ricky Leacock. *Sunday*, his first film as a director, was shot on raw stock short ends literally carved out of Pennebaker's freezer with an ice pick. It documents the police crackdown on a group of protesters in New York's Washington Square Park in 1961, who were engaged in the subversive activity of singing folk songs. Seen today, it not only crackles with excitement, but provides a fascinating glimpse into the very early days of 1960s radicalism. Look out for the charismatic figure prominently being arrested. That's noted writer and activist HL (Harold Louis) "Doc" Humes, founder of *The Paris Review*. Now, it's my pleasure to present filmmaker Dan Drasin.

POINT OF ORDER!—screening introduction

Tonight's screening continues our ongoing collaboration with Nancy de Antonio, and the Wisconsin Center for Film and Theater Research, who holds the de Antonio archive. In particular I'd like to thank my colleague Maxine Ducey. Our restoration's other major collaborators are Dan Talbot and Jose Lopez of New Yorker Films. Dan Talbot was in fact the co-producer of the film. He and de Antonio feuded bitterly in the years after, but despite their conflict, Dan and Jose kindly offered their help at every step of the way.

This screening differs from a typical UCLA restoration in that we did little to "beautify" the film. This is in part a response to what I'd call de Antonio's "radical aesthetics." To paraphrase de Antonio:

> Hollywood produces industrial products. Like Twinkies. High production values are usually empty screens. I want to make a political filmic art with the barest of means.

and:

> The pretty is rarely art. Glorious color and great technique do not make great films. The old, worn footage I use becomes something else. It achieves the personal in the impersonal.

As a result we've chosen to leave the flaws in the original exactly as they were, in keeping with de Antonio's politics and aesthetics. Basically we've just made the best possible record of what's there in the negative, leaving the "flaws" intact as records of their original sources. Having said this, I find a strange beauty in the very roughness of the film. I hope you'll agree.

From today's vantage, it's hard to imagine that *Point of Order!* actually grew out of a need for programming at the New Yorker Theater, owned by Henry Rosenberg and run by Dan Talbot. According to de Antonio:

> One night Dan said to me (and he knew the answer, it was a rhetorical question): What was the most exciting event that ever took place on American television? I said: The Army-McCarthy hearings. He said: Absolutely. He wondered how we could get them onto the New Yorker screen.

The Army-McCarthy hearings took place as live television in 1954, and they represent the end of the era's celebrated "communist witchhunts." In the film, you'll see the fabled downfall of Joseph McCarthy. However, de Antonio, Talbot, and their collaborators were interested in more than just the famed anti-communist. At a political level, they sought to show a moral corruption that seeped through our entire social structure. And at a cultural level, as the quote I read reveals, they were particularly interested in TV.

Point of Order! is comprised virtually entirely of kinescopes—extremely rough film recordings of television broadcasts. In our new print, restored directly from de Antonio's and Talbot's original copies of the CBS "kines," you'll actually see the horizontal lines of the television raster—a physical relic of the original presentation that gives a nearly three-dimensional quality to the otherwise extremely grubby images, a vital reminder of the film's subject and very substance.

The film famously used neither expert testimony nor narration. Said the characteristically blunt de Antonio, narration is "inherently fascist and condescending." Working with editor Robert Duncan for a period of two years, de Antonio and Talbot boiled 40 days of televised footage into a sizzling 97 minutes. In the process, all sense of conventional chronology was dismembered. De Antonio described the original broadcasts as "188 formless hours ending in a whimper." The result of their work is not just a searing indictment of McCarthyism, but an exposé of the fissures in American democracy as filtered through the then-new medium of television.

While that was indeed radical in 1964, many mistook the lack of narration for objectivity, and for that reason—mistakenly—compared it to works of the Direct Cinema movement. Responding to a critic who said *Point of Order!* was "the only good example of *cinéma vérité*," de Antonio said:

> The phrase is silly if we look at the cutting-room floor. If all 188 hours (of the hearings) were the whole *vérité*, then any cut would make for less, or no *vérité*. The *vérité* as well as the prejudice, is Talbot's and mine. And there is enough material to make fifteen different movies, including one that would make Roy Cohn look like Tennyson's Galahad. Our prejudices *are* the film. Without them, it would not have existed.

Included along the way are many of the hearings' signature moments, such as Army counsel Joseph Welch's legendary June 9 rejoinder to McCarthy, "Have you no sense of decency, sir? At long last, have you left no sense of decency?" Yet perhaps ironically, much of our collective memory of the hearings today stems not so much from the broadcasts themselves as from *Point of Order!*'s reframing. Like the best of the Direct Cinema works, *Point of Order!*'s attitudes are constructed precisely in its edit: a surface-level "objectivity" that's in reality brilliantly fabricated. Its aim is no less than a death blow to 1950s American politics and to conventional notions of the interplay of television and cinema.

Come Back to the 5 & Dime, Jimmy Dean, Jimmy Dean (1982)

Come Back to the 5 & Dime, Jimmy Dean, Jimmy Dean was restored by UCLA Film & Television Archive in cooperation with Sandcastle 5 Productions and Paramount Archives, with funding from The Hollywood Foreign Press Association and The Film Foundation. Laboratory services provided by Cineric, Technicolor, NT Picture & Sound, and Audio Mechanics. Restoration and remastering supervised by Ross Lipman in collaboration with colleagues including picture restorationist Laura Thornburg, audio restorationist John Polito, and engineer Shawn Jones. Special thanks to: Barry Allen, Kathryn Altman, Ed Graczyk, Andrea Kalas and Matthew Seig.

The following is adapted from an introduction presented on the occasion of the film's restoration premiere on March 3, 2011 at the Billy Wilder Theater in Los Angeles as part of UCLA's Festival of Preservation, followed by a conversation with Karen Black and Kathryn Altman. It was subsequently presented at the Festival du Nouveau Cinéma in Montreal in October 2013, along with a posthumous tribute to Karen Black.

1. STAGE HISTORY

When watching Robert Altman's *Come Back to the 5 & Dime, Jimmy Dean, Jimmy Dean*, it's interesting to note that its author, Ed Graczyk, primarily considers himself a writer of comedy. In an interview with the *Dallas Voice*, he said:

> I don't write one-liners, I write humor. Humor comes out of sincerity. When things get serious, I get nervous and write jokes naturally.*

Comedy is certainly present, especially in the text, but it was much more apparent in the original stage versions.† The play was originally conceived for two parallel casts on stage simultaneously: one set in 1975, the other younger, in flashback twenty years earlier.

Upon the success of its initial run, Elia Kazan was approached to direct a Broadway staging. He declined, and suggested in his place his wife, Barbara Loden.

---

* Ed Graczyk, in: "Jimmy Dean playwright goes back to the Ilana estacado for new play," Arnold Wayne-Jones, *Dallas Voice*, August 27, 2010.
† The first production of *Come Back to the 5 & Dime, Jimmy Dean, Jimmy Dean* was by the Players Theatre of Columbus Ohio in September 1976, directed by the author.

Loden staged it off-Broadway at the Hudson Guild Theater in late 1979, where the lead role of Mona was to be played by Sandy Dennis, at Graczyk's direct request.

Within the first week the two brilliant actresses clashed, and Dennis left the production. Loden took over the role of Mona, and Graczyk briefly took over the direction before handing the baton to David Heefner. But the production was Loden's, and one of her last notable achievements. Within six months of the play's closing she was to die of cancer, a theme touched on in the play itself.

The Hudson Guild production's short run time of five weeks was in part due to producer Joseph Clapsaddle's wish to bring it to Broadway. At around that time, Robert Altman was rebounding from Hollywood backlash to his 1980 *Popeye*. With the studios reluctant to give the freedom he desired on larger projects, he scaled back to retain artistic control of his work, and undertook the direction of the Broadway production of *Jimmy Dean*. It was to be the first in a series of theater-originated works he helmed, and he cast it with a star-studded ensemble. Sandy Dennis would return to the role of Mona, alongside Karen Black, Cher, and a then less well-known Kathy Bates.

Figure 1. Clockwise from left: Cher, Robert Altman, Sandy Dennis and Karen Black.

Altman told *New York* magazine:

> Just those names sound interesting together—it's an interesting combination. I don't pick one actress for one part and another for another part. I chose them all together.*

Jennifer Allen, his interviewer, wrote:

> They are attempting a serious play—as anomalous on Broadway these days as a minister at an orgy.†

Altman apparently conceived the set's unique concept himself. Discarding the younger, duplicate cast, he instead doubled the set with two identical, mirrored 5 and Dimes placed one in front of the other, with the rear raked slightly upward. He initially said the set had "a sense of infinity about it that you can't get in film."

Figure 2. Karen Black, Sandy Dennis, and Cher in Robert Altman's Broadway staging of *Come Back to the 5 & Dime, Jimmy Dean, Jimmy Dean.*

Separated by a counter, which the cast freely crossed, the two areas represented the dual time frames. Altman told his ensemble, "We're going to have a lot of things going on simultaneously. We're going to really screw the audience up."

Initially concerned with choreography, he later moved onto structural changes to the play itself. Describing the work environment, Allen wrote, "When Altman breaks up a

---

* Robert Altman, in Jennifer Allen, "Cher and Altman on Broadway," *New York* magazine, February 1, 1982.
† Ibid.

speech to create time shifts, Graczyk leaves the rehearsal. "I'm going to hang myself," he says. Altman, impervious, is pleased. "I think this is going to work."

The play, which opened at the Martin Beck Theatre on February 18, 1982, was not however, universally well received by the critics. Graczyk also felt the production was problematic, complaining of Altman's dispensing of the dual cast, and in particular of the size of the theater. On at least the latter issue, he has a point. The Martin Beck had 1,300 seats, way too large for what's in essence a chamber drama.* Altman, however, still in love with the material, came up with the idea of salvaging it by making it into a movie.

2. FILM HISTORY

No screenplay was written; they simply used the stage play as a script. The set was moved to a soundstage, where it was rebuilt with some modifications, to retain the concept of the original theatrical production while adapting for cinema. The movie was shot in Super-16mm as a budget saver by Canadian cinematographer Pierre Mignot, who was to work with Altman many times over the years. The central filmic device was their ingenious use of a two-way, half-silvered mirror, which was alternately reflective and transparent, depending on complicated lighting changes manually controlled on a dimmer board. As in the play, when the cast appears behind the counter (in the mirror), it's the 1950s, in flashback. This proved problematic in filming, and confusing to some critics. While I agree it's at times disorienting, its execution was quite brilliant.

Upon release the reviews were mixed. Some dismissed it, while others simply loved it, and it won the top prize at the 1982 Chicago International Film Festival. Observed Altman, "On stage it was humorous and bawdy. On film it's more emotional."†

After the original release by Viacom, and a brief time in VHS, the film fell out of distribution and has existed only in poor VHS copies and extremely faded prints for many years prior to the print you're about to see.

3. RESTORATION

By a stroke of good fortune, concurrent with our restoration project, Paramount was remastering the film for cable broadcast, and we agreed to collaborate. Special attention was given to the film's color, which needed to be adapted for digital restoration before going out to

---

* The critics were also right in a perhaps minor respect, that the play showed echoes of many classic plays that preceded it. But strangely, I've yet to find a review that cites the influence I believe to be most vital. *Who's Afraid of Virginia Woolf?* no doubt led to Graczyk's selection of Sandy Dennis, who played the (Oscar-winning) role of Honey in the 1966 Mike Nichols film with Elizabeth Taylor, Richard Burton and George Segal.

† Robert Altman in Ina Warren, "Unorthodox film director hit of Montreal festival," *Ottawa Citizen*, August 28, 1982.

film again. The original negative varied widely from shot to shot, in part due to the two-way mirror effects, which required vastly different film exposures on set. This challenge was amplified by color breathing in the source, and further amplified by the fact that Sandy Dennis' complexion inherently drifted toward cooler tones, while Karen Black drifted warmer—a difference heightened by the color breathing to the point of being problematic rather than merely "different." In NT Picture & Sound's digital color correction suite we were able to even these issues out to what is likely a finer degree than the original film prints.

The result is something we never expected, given the film's stage origins: Pierre Mignot's cinematography is in fact stunningly atmospheric and beautiful. This was fully in keeping with Altman's observation that the filmed version highlights the story's *drama* far more than the comedy. In particular, by controlling burned out highlights in the negative, we were able to better render the computer-controlled lighting effects used in shooting, bringing out the darker exposures resulting from the on-set half-silvered mirror. In parallel to this, we worked to better articulate the sometimes confusing time-differences, which are distinguished in the original audio track by its use of reverb. The extensive sound work was conducted by John Polito of Audio Mechanics from the original 35mm stereo magnetic tracks, which we found to be superior to a ½" DME track that was surprisingly, not the source of the mag, but apparently made concurrently.

4. CONCLUSION

But I don't want to dwell overly long on the restoration. Ultimately, the film stands as a celebration of transgender identity uncommon to the era,[*] and was lauded for its all-star cast, who were tailor-made for Altman's particular skill at choreographing ensemble acting. They bring true genius to their roles. All the performers are excellent, but it's the relationship of Sandy Dennis and Karen Black that ultimately drives the movie. There's an electricity between them that literally pulses off the screen. Wrote Pauline Kael, "When Robert Altman gives a project everything he's got, his skills are such that he can make poetry. Moving in apparent freedom, the principal actresses […] go at their roles so creatively that they find *acting truth*."[†]

---

[*] Contemporary viewers might take issue with the fact that the key role of Mona was played by a woman rather than a true trans woman, but of course the times were different then. Karen Black understandably found this aspect of the role challenging to perform, and responded with a riveting interpretation.
[†] Pauline Kael, *5001 Nights at the Movies* (Macmillan, 1991), 148. In classic Kael fashion, she concludes her comment by adding, "They bring conviction to their looneytunes characters."

Ornette: Made in America (1985)

Ornette: Made in America was restored by UCLA Film & Television Archive with funding from the Packard Humanities Institute and Milestone Films. Laboratory services provided by NT Picture & Sound, Fotokem, the Stanford Theatre Film Laboratory, and Audio Mechanics. Restoration and remastering supervised by Ross Lipman in collaboration with colleagues including cinematographer Ed Lachman, producer Kathelin Hoffman Gray, audio restorationist John Polito, engineer Shawn Jones, and editor Iris Cahn. Distributed by Milestone.

The following is adapted from an introduction presented on the occasion of the film's restoration premiere on March 24, 2011, at the James Bridges Theater in Los Angeles, as part of UCLA's Festival of Preservation, which was followed by a Skype conversation with Denardo Coleman.

Figure 3. Ornette Coleman and Shirley Clarke.

Tonight's screening represents our third collaboration with Milestone Films in restoring the works of Shirley Clarke. Nearly thirty years after its premiere *Ornette: Made in America* can at last be fully appreciated on its own terms as a *film*—beyond the extraordinary interaction of the two visionary artists at its core. Upon its release in 1985, Clarke's playful experimentation with cinematic language overwhelmed viewers struggling merely to keep up with her subject. That subject was demanding enough by itself: Ornette Coleman's profound re-invention of all music.

Coleman had long been deemed a pariah, whose status as such is hard to exaggerate. He had literally been beaten up and had his saxophone smashed in his early career in Los Angeles, becoming an underground legend there, years before his famous national breakthrough at the Five Spot in New York in 1959. In the footage one sees in the film, spanning decades, one finds both evolution and consistency, through scenes with "third stream" classical compositions, collaborations with the Master Musicians of Joujouka, Morocco, and with Nigerian tribal musicians. By the 1980s, fusion and funk were further factors, but always uniquely spun through Ornette's personal filter, as heard in the work with his Prime Time ensemble.

At the time of the film's release, Clarke's and Coleman's careers were on opposing trajectories. Clarke had seen her greatest success in the 1960s with a remarkable trio of features, *The Connection*, *The Cool World*, and *Portrait of Jason*. Her subsequent career as one of the earliest experimental video pioneers was remarkable, but received far more limited acclaim. *Ornette* was to be her last major piece.

Coleman, on the other hand, was enjoying a renaissance. As critic John Rockwell notes in the film, his work "got him branded as an eccentric when he was young; it gets him branded as a genius when he's old." By 1985, Coleman was collaboratively touring with popular artists such as Pat Metheny on their *Song X* project, and getting the key to his native city of Fort Worth, Texas (as documented by Clarke), all without compromising in the slightest. He retains his completely unique vision to this day, undeterred by mainstream acceptance, and reiterating his importance as a living part of jazz history.

Clarke began filming Coleman around 1968, at the time he was recording his album *The Empty Foxhole* with bassist Charlie Haden and his son Denardo, a soon-to-be virtuoso drummer who was then all of twelve years old. Shirley became fascinated by Coleman's relationship with his son, and although she eventually had to abandon shooting, she made that a major part of the film when she finally returned to it almost twenty years later. Denardo's mother, the noted poet Jayne Cortez, also appears in the finished work.

In 1983, the town of Fort Worth was preparing to open a new arts facility called Caravan of Dreams, funded by the famous Hunt brothers and their silver fortune. The artistic director of Caravan of Dreams was Kathelin Hoffman, and when she was hunting for a suitable act for the center's opening, Rockwell suggested Coleman, who was a native of Fort Worth. This was both sensible and outrageous. Sensible, in that Coleman was and is one of the great artistic geniuses of the last century. Outrageous, in that his music was and is as avant-garde as it gets.

Hoffman reached out to Coleman, and they agreed to present multiple events for the unveiling, including a new version of his *Skies of America* symphony, two nightclub acts by his Prime Time band, and a chamber work performed in a Buckminster Fuller geodeisic dome on the roof. Clarke was brought in as the perfect director, and cinematographer Ed Lachman was hired on the basis of his recent photography of Peter Greenaway's *The Draughtsman's Contract*. Extra points are given to anyone who can find both Ed and Shirley's cameos in the film (*hint: it's not the same scene*).

The editing of the film occurred in several stages. The first, done on video, occurred in the Chelsea Hotel in Manhattan, where Shirley lived. Viva (of Andy Warhol fame) also lived there and was good friends with Shirley, which is how she got involved in the project. You'll find her pushing a baby carriage near the end of the film. Later sections were edited by Iris Cahn under Clarke's direction. Cahn relates the tale of Clarke doing a preliminary cut of the flicker sections, or "flutter cuts" as Clarke called them, by rapidly tapping her fingers on the video edit controller as if she were playing "Chopsticks" on the piano.

The finished work integrates practically every format of film and video footage available at the time, as well as practically every form, technique and strategy one could imagine, including concert footage, interviews, re-enacted memories and dreams, video game imagery, a pre-cursor-to-Skype teleconference performance, and classic early 1980s video fuzzbox effects. It also features the editing and mixing of different performances of the same song.

Clarke's formal innovation in *Ornette*, involving this integration of a myriad of techniques and formats, has often been compared to Coleman's sonic experimentation. His concept of Harmolodics, in which all the various components of music—harmony, melody, rhythm, timbre, time—carry equal weight, indeed has some corollary in Clarke's polyphonic construction of *Ornette*. But the comparison does full justice to neither, for Clarke's work is as filmic as Coleman's is musical, and each is uniquely their own. Her voice intermingles with his, even as they remain singular, the epitome of what Coleman called unisons, working in concert. The film thus represents both, but also a whole beyond either—at once dense and weightless, beyond emptiness or gravity—and a thoroughly entertaining provocation.

A key framing device for the film is the *Skies of America* performance. *Skies of America* was originally recorded by the London Symphony Orchestra with Coleman in 1972, but contractual problems prevented Coleman's ensemble from playing alongside them. For the Caravan of Dreams, Coleman re-envisioned the work to alternate between sections for orchestra and the Prime Time ensemble. Clarke brought in the idea of contrasting Ornette's world with the symphony hall by removing all the curtains from the stage, heightening the institutionality of the context. The sounds of the two sonic voices are conceptually linked, yet strikingly different in realization and effect. Interestingly, the conductor John Giordiano was also a Fort Worth native, as well as a saxophonist, and had played on occasion with Ornette when they were both young men in the early 1950s.

Despite Coleman's fame and newfound acceptance, he remains inscrutable to the present day. My friend Ken Jordan, whose father was a key figure at the legendary underground Grove Press, grew up surrounded by virtually every key counter-culture figure you can imagine—yet he tells me that Ornette is the most "outer space" person he ever met.

Editor Iris Cahn relates a charming story in this regard. During the film's sound mix, Ornette kept telling one of the technicians to "lower the church bells." There were no church bells in the score at that part, and Ornette's repeating of his request was unintendedly driving the poor technician—in fact one of New York's top mixers—into a mild state of panic. Finally, listening to the music, Iris told him, "he means the violins." To which Ornette said, "Yeah! The church bells!" He always had his own way of seeing and hearing the world. Cahn relates that Clarke always understood Coleman's thoughts as clear as day. In her, Hoffman and her Caravan of Dreams team found the perfect interpreter of his story.

Ornette: Made in America still dazzles as an experimental thunderstorm, exploding with creativity in every area. But to Clarke and Coleman, the film you're about to see was in fact a mainstream movie. The two of them would come up with some crazy ideas for it, but then say, "we'll save that for the *art* movie." To them, this was pure Hollywood, the straightest thing in the world.

Figure 4. Ornette Coleman at Caravan of Dreams.

Matewan (1987)

Matewan was restored by UCLA Film & Television Archive in association with Anarchists' Convention. The restoration was subsequently digitally remastered by UCLA in collaboration with IFC Films at Universal Studios. Laboratory services provided by Monaco Labs, Audio Mechanics and DJ Audio. Restoration and remastering supervised by Ross Lipman in consultation with John Sayles, Maggie Renzi, and Haskell Wexler, and in collaboration with colleagues including archivist Susan Ceresko, audio restorationist John Polito, film grader Skip Hansen, and engineer Scott Smerdon. Distributed by IFC.

> *The following is adapted from an introduction presented on the occasion of the film's restoration premiere on August 16, 2002, at the James Bridges Theater in Los Angeles, as part of UCLA's Festival of Preservation, which was followed by a conversation with Haskell Wexler. As will be apparent, the text version presented here includes several updates marking developments in the years that followed.*

Tonight we'll be honoring the archive's collaboration with John Sayles, in presenting our new preservation print of his classic film *Matewan*. If our recent screening of John Cassavetes' *Shadows* in many ways exemplified the birth of America's independent cinema movement, tonight's show documents the work of someone whom many consider to be its current torchbearer. Of course Sayles' films mark just one voice in an incredibly diverse independent field, but it's a powerful and essential voice. By looking at his work tonight we'll be able to see just how far the field has come since *Shadows*, and how things have changed since 1959.

Both Cassavetes and Sayles come from a theatrical background, and have orchestrated their filmmaking in an ensemble-based, almost familial environment, with many of the same cast and crew members returning from film to film. Both are considered consummate auteurs, maintaining tight control over production and editing, ensuring that the vision on the screen is uniquely theirs. And both have aimed their films, while holding true to that vision, to speak to a non-elitist general audience. They also managed to subsidize their directorial careers in part by working professionally as hired hands in Hollywood; Cassavetes as an actor, Sayles as a writer and occasional actor.

But there the similarities stop. Cassavetes' work developed primarily from his own experiences. He was most interested in the psychological and emotional worlds of his characters, allowing the sociological and political to loom importantly but subtly in the background. Sayles is the converse: actively engaged with political questions, fleshing out his characters with a good writer's skill within the sociological worlds he's exploring, which shift from film to film.

And while Sayles is considered to be a "writer's filmmaker," with strong dialogue and characters, he has nonetheless created a body of work that is highly proficient at a technical level. This in turn emblemizes a new movement of independents who aspire to industry careers and standards, even while they're currently shooting in low-budget DV. This isn't a bad thing. If Hollywood were filled with people of Sayles' talent and political commitment, the world would no doubt be a better place. Sayles himself, of course, chooses to produce his own films outside the industry.

The archive has had a unique relationship with Sayles and his partner, producer Maggie Renzi. Their company, Anarchists' Convention, approached us after being told that UCLA was "the place to go" for film preservation. A fine compliment, but we had never partnered on such a large project with a living filmmaker before. Sayles was in the process of re-acquiring the elements and rights to four of his early films: *Return of the Secaucus Seven*, *Lianna*, *Brother from Another Planet*, and *Matewan*—a convoluted process which Sayles discusses in an interview in our Festival catalogue. It's worth a look for filmmakers, because the issue of lost elements and rights controversies is a constant problem one faces in the preservation of independent works.

Fortunately for us, Anarchists' Convention saved UCLA from dealing with those issues in this case and got the elements for us. John and Maggie were extraordinary colleagues, and I'd also like to thank Suzanne Ceresko, who helped at every step along the way.

Once the materials were in hand, we were gratified to discover that the technical quality of the films was of a much higher level than I was used to encountering in independent cinema. Nonetheless, there were *always* things to work out. For example, *The Return of the Secaucus Seven* was originally shot in 16mm in the nearly square 1.37-to-one aspect ratio, but was cropped to rectangular 1.85-to-one 35mm when it surprised everyone by being an overwhelming success. We restored it to its true 1.37 image in a high-quality 35mm blow-up.

But our subject tonight is *Matewan*. The film's 35mm original negative came to us in nearly perfect condition—a true rarity in this field—in no small part because it was shot by the great Haskell Wexler, who knew a thing or two about handling film. But Scott Smerdon of Monaco Labs and I were concerned because the currently available positive stocks have a slightly higher contrast than those dating to the film's production in 1986, and thus might subtly alter the look of the original photography. Further, in looking at an old copy of the film, I realized that the original prints were struck on Fuji, rather than Kodak stock. Suzanne contacted Haskell to see if that was an artistic choice or simply a quirk of post-production. Haskell confirmed that it was indeed a conscious choice. Not that Kodak stocks had any problem (he used them all the time), but he chose Fuji in this instance because its slightly softer color palette was what he wanted for this picture.

We thus conducted a series of tests on contemporary stocks by both Kodak *and* Fuji, and screened the results for him. Indeed, the current Fuji materials, with their slightly softer quality, proved better suited to Wexler's vision for the "period" look of *Matewan*. Then began the task of re-timing, from scratch, the original negative, to achieve the best color rendition on current Fuji print film 3519.

I should add at this point that Sayles' choice of Wexler as cinematographer was no accident—there was no one better suited to shoot *Matewan* than him, on several levels. Wexler's renowned not just for his Academy Award-winning work on classic films like *Who's Afraid of Virginia Woolf?* and *Bound For Glory*, but for his commitment to social justice. In parallel to his industry work, Wexler has spent a lifetime making his own pictures that document the struggles of our times, from *Medium Cool*, *Latino*, and *Brazil: A Report on Torture*, to his recent documentary on the LA Bus Rider's Union. He also worked with Emile de Antonio on *Underground*, the classic documentary clandestinely filmed with members of the Weathermen, the militant wing of the Students for a Democratic Society, who were fugitives at the time.

After our initial consultation, Wexler got intrigued and agreed to work further with us on the restoration. That led to some extraordinary moments that I was previously honor-bound not to reveal, but sufficient time has passed, and now I safely can. The stories connect to several of the themes I've brought up, as well as those in the film, so I'm happy to at last be able to share them.

I'd met Haskell before, but to work collaboratively with him on the restoration was another story, and I wanted to bring my "A-game." We planned to meet at Universal's in-house lab on the grounds of the studio lot, where we'd view the most recent answer print and assess color with the grader. Things began well. I have a bit of a perfectionist streak, and—no doubt keen to impress someone I'd long admired—I dove into small details of color as the film went by. Haskell was lively, and approved, but I noticed he began interjecting less as we proceeded, and eventually seemed to let me run the show. Eventually the film reached the scene where the striking miners meet and rousingly sing the classic socialist anthem, "Bandiera Rosa" ("The Red Flag"). At that moment, Haskell, who was sitting in the row in front of me, turned back and said, "I'm leaving it to you." He then stood up, saluted me from the aisle, and exited the theater pumping his arm in exaltation and proudly singing the anthem along with the workers on screen:

> *Avanti popolo, alla riscossa,*
> *Bandiera rossa, Bandiera rossa.*
>
> *Forward people, toward redemption,*
> *Red Flag, Red Flag.*

Then he was gone. On the one hand I was flattered that he trusted the film to me, but on another level I was disappointed, as I'd been looking forward to working with him further.

This was a Friday, and I wondered about it over the weekend. The following Monday, back at the archive, I received a call, and it was Haskell. He told me he owed me an apology, and I asked why. He then offered a confession… and this is the part I was temporarily honor-bound not to share. "You see," he said, "I'm color blind. I can't distinguish red and green properly. A lot of your notes were in that region, and I couldn't actually see them! But I knew from your other notes that you were on track and seeing the film well. I was embarrassed, and thought it better if I called it a day.

"But I need to ask you a favor. Don't tell this to anyone! I'm still trying to work, and no one will hire a color-blind cinematographer." I was totally flabbergasted, as his work had always struck me as impeccable, and his reputation in the industry beyond reproach. He said that didn't matter, because now he was old—in his eighties!—and he had to fight to be taken seriously even under normal circumstances. I agreed to his request, wished him well, and sat on the story.

Now flash forward some years, to the release of the Haskell Wexler documentary *Tell Them Who You Are*, by his son Mark. In the film, Haskell reveals his secret. By that time he'd retired from cinematography, and so it was safe to tell the tale. In retrospect, I think now that his ability to effectively compensate for his color blindness throughout his career was all the more remarkable.

Enough. I could go on with similar tidbits, but I don't want to end with anecdotes, or discussions of technique. *Matewan,* which relates the brutal tale of a coal-mining strike in West Virginia, is more-or-less based on true events. Although adapted slightly from literal truth, the film grows out of Sayles' extensive research into labor history, compiled while writing his 1977 novel *Union Dues*. It's on this concern, with the daily lives of working people, that I'd like to end. One of the most important thrusts of independent film history, and John Sayles' work in particular, is the championing of social justice, of calling on people to recognize what's right and true in our society, and speaking out for those without a public voice. It's in solidarity with this sentiment that we offer tonight's screening.

Haskell Wexler.

The Sid Saga (1985/1987/1989/2003, etc.)

The Sid Saga (parts 1-3) was restored by UCLA Film & Television Archive with funding from the National Film Preservation Foundation and The Packard Humanities Institute. The restoration was subsequently digitally remastered by UCLA in collaboration with Turner Classic Movies at Modern Film and Video. Laboratory services provided by The Stanford Theatre Film Laboratory, Fotokem, Audio Mechanics, NT Picture & Sound. Restoration and remastering supervised by Ross Lipman in collaboration with colleagues including Sid and Charlotte Laverents, audio restorationist John Polito, optical printing technician Dave Tucker, and digital colorist Gregg Garvin. Special thanks to: Jake Austin, Pea Hicks, and Melinda Stone.

The following is adapted from an introduction presented on the occasion of the film's restoration premiere on March 21, 2011, at the Billy Wilder Theater in Los Angeles, as part of UCLA's Festival of Preservation.

Long known as a legend in the amateur filmmaking community, ex-Vaudevillian Sid Laverents burst into national attention in 2000 at age 92, when he was "re-discovered" by filmmaker/historian Melinda Stone. His short film *Multiple Sidosis*—preserved by the UCLA Film & Television Archive—was selected for inclusion in the National Film Registry, and the rest is history.

    I normally begin introductions to Sid's films with background on his amazing life, from his early days as a one-man-band act, to dishwasher, to rocket scientist. But tonight's film does that itself, in far more detail. So I'll begin with my own introduction to Sid and his work. I first encountered it through Melinda, who presented *Multiple Sidosis* on a small monitor at the 2000 edition of the Association of Moving Image Archivists conference in Los Angeles. I was immediately inspired, got Sid's contact information from her, and drove down to Bonita, near San Diego, California, to meet him. During my visit, Sid showed me parts of *The Sid Saga* on the hanging screen in his garage theater, and I realized I was watching the work an unknown genius. Now, years later, through partnerships with many wonderful colleagues including the National Film Preservation Foundation, the Packard Humanities Institute, and Turner Classic Movies, we've at last been able to restore it in 35mm and digital video.

    The Sid Saga is his magnum opus, a feature-length autobiographical work that is not only extremely entertaining, but establishes the importance of amateur cinema as a vital part of our cultural heritage. It's every bit as vibrant and dynamic as the best of mainstream cinema—all the while foregrounding its amateur production status, front and center.

    The Sid Saga is a filmed scrapbook, consisting of still photos, home movies, audio recordings, newspaper clippings, you name it. It's also a filmic collage joining the archival materials with newly shot footage and animated sequences, on practically every film stock imaginable, all cut together freely in the film's original edit—which made it extremely difficult to preserve. Some of the stocks had faded, some hadn't, and each needed to be printed differently to best render what remained.

Further complicating things was the fact that *The Sid Saga* was in one sense unfinished. While he had completed all the editorial work, he never made a final composite print. For two of the three parts all we had was a silent checkprint and the original magnetic recordings, which he would play in a dual-projector setup. For the other part we had a single print marked "NG." Between them, we only had the roughest guides for what the film should actually look like. Luckily, these preliminary checkprints were unfaded, so, while they were down a generation (or in some cases several) from their original sources, and would not provide a definitive reference for color, we could nonetheless pull shots from them when needed.

In the end we made complete 35mm A-B-C rolls, each individually calibrated for a particular type of image source, and used the workprints as a rough guide for the look of the film, which required different methods of printing. As it progresses toward its third part, you'll see much of the film burst into now obsolete but glorious Kodachrome.

The Sid Saga was originally made as a three-part feature in 16mm in the mid-1980s. In form, it's classic Laverents, beginning with the archetypal living room scene in which a suburban neighbor asks Sid about his photo album and ultimately receives much more than she bargained for. It sets Sid off on a biographical quest in which we learn he's led not just a long life, but seemingly led hundreds. Beginning with his impoverished Dutch immigrant family's many moves across the country in the early part of the century searching for work, it follows Sid through his marriages and many careers.

And that's just the beginning. The film also includes a detailed account of his work as a filmmaker, which, characteristically spanned everything from eccentric nature documentaries to mind-boggling comedies. A final part, shot in video, documents the physical and emotional struggles he faced in his eighties, after the death of his wife Adelaide. This includes graphic footage of his facelift operation, part of a successful attempt to ultimately attract a new partner as he approached his next milestone, age 90.

Throughout it all is what Laverents scholar/*Roctober* editor Jake Austin describes as a "can-do optimism," which carries Sid and his audience through everything from natural disaster to the financial woes of the Depression, to World War II, as well as through some incredible personal dramas. In typical Sid fashion, he handles all aspects of the filmmaking himself, including cinematography, writing, narration, editing, and post-production. In the telling, we learn not just about Sid, but about the supposedly ordinary, yet fantastic worlds in which he traveled. The film is the story of one life and an American century.

Sid passed away on May 6, 2009, at age 100. I'm happy to report that he was able to attend a 100th birthday party screening which we hosted for him here at the archive only months before his passing. Tonight, I'm pleased to present the restoration premiere of what may be his greatest movie, which was in turn, based on perhaps his greatest work: his own life.

Appendix 1

Teaching Resources

These somewhat technical texts were written when I was teaching in London and San Francisco in the early-mid 1990s. Half-written for myself, they served as primers for the things I felt filmmakers—and by implication, restorationists—need to know about their fundamental materials: light, film stock, and their various properties. No doubt I should have covered sound as well, but that's for another lifetime. The format of the texts is liberally borrowed from Dennis Couzin, from whom I believe I affectionately plagiarized a bit in the process. His "Notes on Optical Printing" are particularly recommended for anyone interested in the practice of moving image restoration. Such knowledge becomes increasingly important the more removed its actual details become from our everyday life and practice: the end result of an art/science divide discussed in "The Gray Zone." Hopefully my own notes retain a small hint of the vital connection between the energetic principles that underly both our physical world and the mysteries of art.

The first piece asks what color is, then proceeds to its practical application in film, and ultimately, to our perception of the works we make.

The second piece is built upon another idea discussed in "The Gray Zone"— that while a photographer's ostensible subject is the physical world, the restorationist's subject is at its core, a piece of film. The underlying spirit embodied in the film's images is thoroughly discussed in the main body of the present volume—but this appendix focuses on film as a physical thing. While contemporary restoration of film-based works is based upon a scan, an understanding of the optical principles needed to re-photograph a piece of film remains invaluable in retaining our connection to the physical world in which the images live.

Both of the texts are presented in facsimile of the original pre-digital class handouts used in my classes while serving as Visiting Faculty at the San Francisco Art Institute in 1994.

a) Some Notes on Color (ca. 1993)
b) Some Notes on Close-up Photography (ca. 1994)

SOME NOTES ON COLOR

According to conventional theory, all things in the world are
made of tiny particles, called atoms, which can cluster together
in things called molecules. When molecules move (which is usually),
the things they comprise emit radiation, which takes the form of
heat, light, etc..

These emissions make up the electromagnetic spectrum, and can be
seen as repeating waves. As such, they can be measured for their
length (called wavelength), and speed of repetition (called
frequency). Wavelength and frequency are inversely proportional:

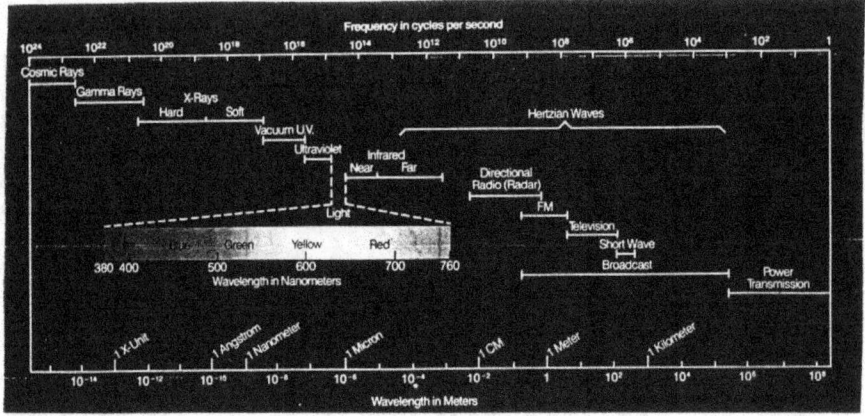

The radiant energy (electromagnetic) spectrum.

The spectrum of visible light is one portion of the electromagnetic
spectrum.

As temperature is a measure of the molecular energy of motion, we
can measure these emissions in terms of <u>degrees Kelvin</u>, or the
<u>absolute scale</u>. When something has very little molecular motion,
it is very "cold". Molecular motion stops at -273° Centigrade.
This is the zero of the Kelvin scale. As a thing heats up, its
temperature rises. The absolute scale uses the same increments
as the Centigrade scale, but transposed up 273°. Thus

$$-273° \text{ C} = 0° \text{ K}$$
$$0° \text{ C} = 273° \text{ K}$$
$$100° \text{ C} = 373° \text{ K}$$
$$\text{etc.}$$

A chart showing relative temperature scales follows:

Appendix 1 375

Thermometer scales

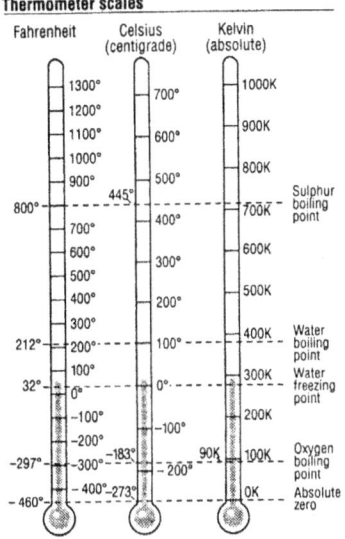

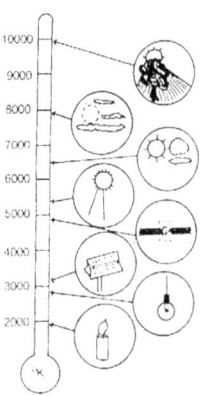

Different things radiate with
different efficiencies, and these
differences are perceived by us
as the properties of that thing.

Much further up along the scale we get towards those emissions we
call visible light, and hence, color. Again, light emissions can
can be measured for temperature, frequency, or wavelength. Now,
as a thing that radiates relatively efficiently heats up, it becomes
first red, and finally blue-violet to the human eye. Thus blue has
a higher temperature, or color temperature than red. We nonetheless
have practical psychological associations with the colors that are
apparent in our language, which contradict this. On a film set,
for example, we might say we are "warming" a scene by lighting it
with a reddish cast, or "cooling" it with blue.

As the efficient radiator heats from red to blue, its emission
frequency increases, while its wavelength decreases; a move from
"longer, slower waves" to "shorter, faster waves".*

* - Note that 1) recalling our earlier definition, speed is not a
a completely accurate description of frequency, and 2) waves are
only one metaphor for the phenomenon we know as light.

When dealing with light in this discussion, we will be primarily concerned with wavelength. Visible light is that part of the spectrum with wavelenghts of aproximately 400 millimicrons to 700 millimicrons:

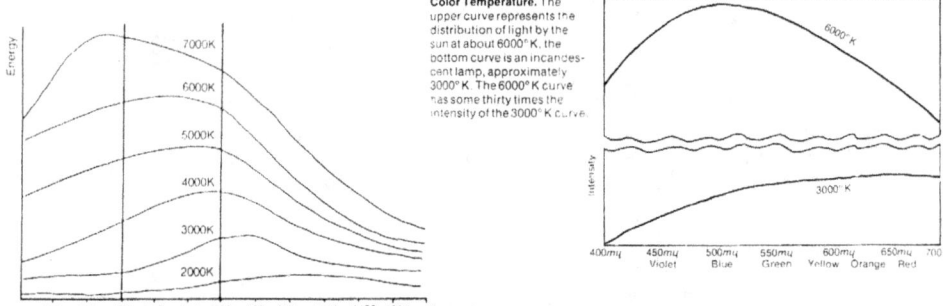

1 millimicron (mµ) = 1 nanometer = 1 millionth of a millimeter

The symbol for wavelength is λ, the Greek letter Lamda.

Now as an object is heated, it becomes first (visibly, to the human eye) Red, then Orange, Yellow, Blue, Indigo, and Violet-- the spectrum of ROYGBIV we all know and see in the rainbow. White light is comprised of all the colors in the spectrum. When it passes through a prism, it breaks down into the individual colors:

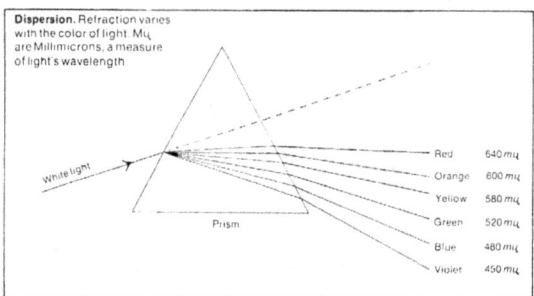

When light passes through a typical, well-made, aberration-corrected lens, it is transmitted with roughly the same color properties that it had when it entered.

Colored filters will effect light passing through them by transmitting some portions of the spectrum, but absorbing others.

PHOTOGRAPHIC FILM

Silver halide emulsion films are sensitive primarily to ultra-violet and blue light. Stocks with this sensitivity are called color blind, or blue sensitive.

By adding spectrally sensitive dyes, we can make the halides effectively sensitive to other colors. This is true for many black and white stocks, which then render the colors into a corresponding on a grey scale. Stocks with sensitivity extended into the green part of the spectrum are called orthochromatic, and stocks which see across the visible spectrum are called panchromatic.

Infra-red stocks are also available.

Films (and for that matter, light meters), are not perfectly calibrated to match the human eye:

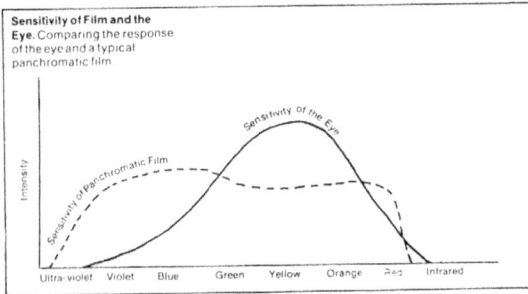
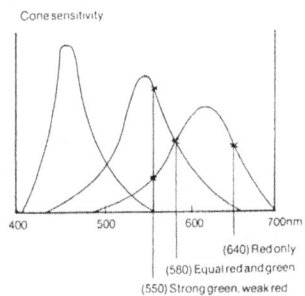

To more accurately match BW panchromatic film sensitivity to the human eye, use a Yellow #8 (K2) filter when shooting.

In general, a colored filter used with BW film renders colors similar to itself lighter, and complementary colors darker. (See following discussion).

In color film, dyes eventually replace the halides themselves.

Like the human eye, color film has three types of receiving areas for color; one for each of the additive primaries.

ADDITIVE AND SUBTRACTIVE COLOR

If you take red light, blue light, and green light, and combine them, you get white light. They are therefore called the additive primary colors. Depending on their relative quantities, you can in fact add them to make any color.

By mixing any given <u>two</u> of them, we get one of the so-called secondary colors:

    Blue + Green = Cyan

    Green + Red   = Yellow

    Red + Blue   = Magenta

Thus each secondary can be thought of as white light minus one primary:

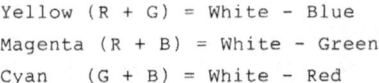

    Yellow (R + G) = White - Blue

    Magenta (R + B) = White - Green

    Cyan   (G + B) = White - Red

The secondaries, or "subtractive" colors, are also called the opposites, or complementaries, of the additive primaries.

Now, a color filter transmits itself, and absorbs its opposite. So

    a yellow filter absorbs blue, and transmits red and green

    a magenta filter absorbs green, and transmits blue and red

    a cyan filter absorbs red, and transmits blue and green

      a blue filter absorbs red and green (Y), and transmits blue

      a red filter absorbs blue and green (C), and transmits red

      a green filter absorbs blue and red (M), and transmits green

In additive color systems, primary colored lights are added to each other in varying quantities to produce new colors or white.

In subtractive color systems, secondary-colored filters are layed over a light source to remove various bits of color; producing new colors or black.

Contact printers usually use an additive system.

Optical printers normally use a subtractive system.

Sets of varying density R, G, B, C, M, & Y filters used with optical printers (as well as elsewhere) are called Color Correction, or CC filters.   .30C + .30M + .30Y = .30ND = 1 Stop

COLOR FILM

Most color film is based on integral tri-pack of three emulsion
layers. Each layer has a subtractive color dye incorporated
into the emulsion (in fact coupled to the silver halide grains).
As each color absorbs its opposite, it is therefore "sensitive"
to an additive primary. In actual fact, the dyes are transparent,
and assume their respective subtractive colors upon development.
Thus red, green, and blue light (which we recall can combine to
make any color) enters the film and stimulates cyan, magenta,
and yellow dyes. Then the developed film is projected with white
light (technically, of course the color of the light depends on
the qualities of the bulb or light source), and the subtractive
dyes act as filters to reconstitute the image.

A reversal film:

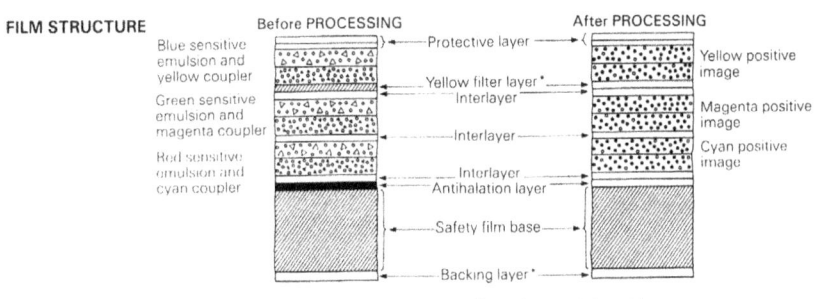

△ silver halide, ○ coupler, ● development induced dye

* These layers become colorless and transparent after processing.
** The backing layer is colorless and transparent both before and after processing.

But each color-sensitive emulsion layer is not perfectly sensitive
to just its own color. For example, some unwanted blue light might
stimulate the green sensitive layer, and stray green light might
stimulate the red layer. Thus in negative film, where the original
camera stock will usually not be seen, a special system of "orange
masking" accounts for this. The green sensitive layer also
incorporates a yellow-colored dye, and the red sensitive layer also
incorporates a magenta-colored dye, which exactly cancel out the
imperfections of the main dye-couplers. After processing, the
extra magenta and yellow combine to make the orange color common
to negative film, which in fact prevents us from seeing "true"
negative color" by being in effect slapped on top of it. Unlike
the main dyes, which only assume their color after interacting
with oxidized color developer, the orange mask dyes are already
colored:

A negative film

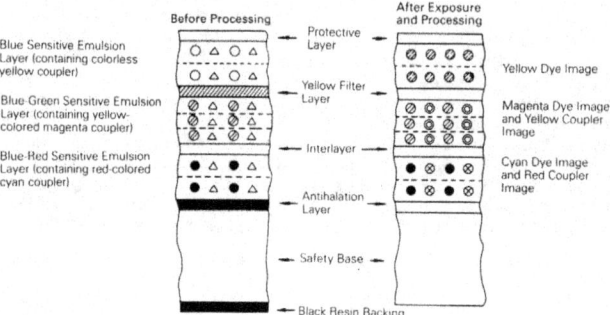

So what happens when color film "sees" light?

With reversal film:

    red light -- stimulates R-C layer, which goes light in process
              does not effect B-Y layer, leaving yellow dye
              does not effect G-M   layer, leaving magenta dye

            - - - Y + M = Red

    green light - - stimulates G-M ,   which goes light (clear)
               does not effect R-C, leaving cyan dye
               does not effect B-Y, leaving yellow dye

            - - - C + Y = Green

    blue light - - stimulates B-Y, which goes clear
              does not effect R-C, leaving cyan dye
              does not effect G-M, leaving magenta dye

            - - - C + M = Blue

With negative film, we must have two generations to achieve a positive image:

1) Negative film:

    red light - - stimulates R-C layer, leaving cyan dye w/ neg. tones
                does not effect B-Y layer, which goes clear
                does not effect G-M layer, which goes clear

            - - - cyan negative tonality, plus
                  yellow-magenta "orange mask"

    green light - - stimulates G-M, leaving magenta dye w/ neg. tones
                does not effect R-C, which goes clear
                does not effect B-Y, which goes clear

            - - - magenta negative tonality, plus
                  Y-M orange mask

    blue light - - stimulates B-Y, leaving yellow dye w/ neg. tones
                does not effect R-C, which goes clear
                does not effect G-M, which goes clear

            - - - yellow negative tonality, plus
                  Y-M orange mask

2) Positive film:

   In printing, the films described above will in effect
   act as filters:

   With an even distribution of red, green, and blue light sources:

     where there is only cyan dye on negative tones,

        red light is absorbed by <u>exposed neg</u>; so R-C sees no light
        blue light stimulates B-Y, leaving yellow dye
        green light stimulates G-M, leaving magenta dye

        - - - Y + M = R, w/ positive tonality
            (orange mask removed)

     where there is only magenta dye on negative tones,

        green light is absorbed by neg, so G-M sees no light; goes clear
        red light stimulates R-C, leaving cyan dye
        blue light stimulates B-Y, leaving yellow dye

        - - - C + Y = G, w/ positive tonality
            (orange mask removed)

     where there is only yellow dye on negative tones,

        blue light is absorbed by neg, so B-Y sees no light, goes clear
        green light stimulates G-M, leaving magenta dye
        red light stimulates R-C, leaving cyan dye

        - - - M + C = B, w/ positive tonality
            (orange mask removed)

Of course most things in the world are mixtures of colors, which stimulate all three emulsion layers in varying degrees. I'm sure the diligent student will enjoy figuring out how complex colors are finally arrived at through the various processes described.

COLOR CORRECTING

Contact Printing from Negative to Positive
(or making still photographic prints from neg):

    A hue can be reduced by
        1) adding more of itself
        2) subtracting some of its complement

Print too	Add	Subtract
B	B (M + C)	Y
G	G (Y + C)	M
R	R (Y + M)	C
Y	Y	M + C (B)
M	M	Y + C (G)
C	C	Y + M (R)

Contact Printing from Reversal onto Reversal or Negative
(or making still photographic prints or dupes from transparencies):

    A hue can be reduced by
        1) removing some of itself
        2) adding some of its complement

Print too	Add	Subtract
B	Y	M + C (B)
G	M	Y + C (G)
R	C	Y + M (R)
Y	B (M + C)	Y
M	G (Y + C)	M
C	R (Y + M)	C

Corrections can be made in the timing, and are measured in terms of printer points on a contact printer. These usually occur on a scale of 1 - 50, with 1 being dark and 50 bright to our eye, for a red, green, and blue light; which are then composited.

    .3 ND = 1 Stop = apr. 7 or 8 printer points

    so 7-8 R + 7-8 G + 7-8 B = apr. 1 Stop, for reference, and
    .15 ND = apr. 4R + 4G +4B = apr. 1/2 Stop

OPTICAL PRINTING IS USUALLY DONE FROM POSITIVE MATERIAL, AND THEREFORE USUALLY FOLLOWS THE RULES OF CONTACT PRINTING FROM REVERSAL.

ARTISTS' PRIMARIES

There is often confusion with the artists' primaries of blue, red, and yellow, and the secondaries of orange, green, and purple.

In this system,

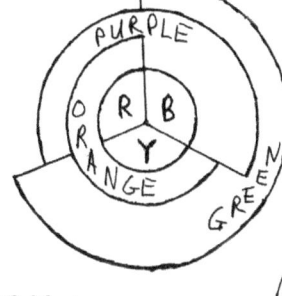

```
red + yellow = orange
blue + yellow = green
red + blue = purple
```

and

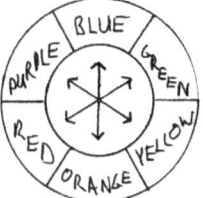

```
orange is the complement of blue
green is the complement of red
purple is the complement of yellow
```

If you stare intently at a field of one of the colors for long enough, then look away, you will see a "ghost" of the compliment.

In fact, however, there is no conflict with our previous theory of color. It is a question of naming the colors. Paints behave something like filters, and in fact

- the artists' red corresponds to the photographers' magenta
- the artists' blue corresponds to the photographers' cyan
- the artists' yellow corresponds to the photographers' yellow

or the subtractive color system. And so

- the artists' green corresponds to the photographers' green
- the artists' orange corresponds to the photographers' red
- the artists' purple corresponds to the photographers' blue

To my eye, the artists have it. How colors seem to interact with each other when perceived by the eye is a potentially vast and fascinating topic. Compare, for example, the color of the Metropolitan Line at say, Barbican and Amersham on a typical London Tube map. Studies of this type have been conducted by many people, notably the artist Josef Albers. It has been relatively underexplored in cinema, where time adds another dimension.

SOME NOTES ON CLOSE-UP PHOTOGRAPHY

for optical printing

Close-up photography refers to the photography of small subject areas, irrespective of their distance from the camera.

As you begin to film smaller and smaller things with the same medium (for example, 16mm film), their relative size to the film frame <u>decreases</u>, and hence their magnification <u>increases</u>.

One method of achieving this effect involves pushing the lens out farther from the camera than it usually goes for conventional photography. When you do this, there is a small light loss that becomes noticeable at a distance of 10 X the lens' focal length, measured from the subject to the front principle point of the lens. (With a symmetrical enlarging lens typical to J.K. optical printers, such as the El-Nikkor 50mm, this can be thought of as aproximately right in the middle). In 16mm this occurs when the rectangle you're filming has a field width of 4".

We therefore must compensate for the light loss in our exposure, if we want to attain a "normally" exposed image. Lenny Lipton, in <u>Independent Filmmaking</u>, cites the formula as follows:

$$\text{effective f\# (i.e., what your meter reads)} = \frac{\text{focal length + extension}}{\text{focal length}} \times \text{marked f\# (what you set your lens at)}$$

For example, with a 50mm lens, 50mm of extension tubes or bellows, and a meter reading of f 8,

$$8 = \frac{50 + 50}{50} \times \text{f number}$$

$$8 = 2 \times \text{f number}$$

$$\frac{8}{2} = \text{f number}$$

$$4 = \text{f number}$$

Therefore set your lens to f 4, or use some other stop with appropriate filtration, etc..

Note that $\frac{\text{focal length + extension length}}{\text{focal length}}$ yields an <u>exposure factor</u>, so you can think of this number as the number of <u>stops</u> you must change from your initial estimate. In our example, f 4 allows <u>2</u> stops more light than our reading of f 8.

It also might be more convenient to invert the equation like so:

$$\text{marked f number} = \frac{\text{focal length}}{\text{focal length + extension}} \times \text{meter reading}$$

if you are using a <u>non</u>-through-the-lens meter which is accurate for small subjects.

As in conventional photography and cinematography, we want to shoot with the lens at its sharpest aperture for best results. This is determined in tests. In a pinch shut down 1 or 2 stops from the lens' widest aperture--often around f 4 or f 5.6, and adjust your exposure with N.D. filters or some other method.

MAGNIFICATION

When optical printing, we usually want the lens to focus on a rectangle exactly the size of one frame in a film. When filming, for example, 16mm film with 16mm film, the two rectangles should ideally equal each other. This situation is called 1:1, or image magnification, and is achieved when the length of the extension is equal to the lens' normal focal length. Thus, in our earlier example, where we had a 50mm lens and a 50mm extension, we had a 1:1 set-up.

It could be argued that optical printing for most any purpose offers a simultaneous opportunity to improve on the original composition, by changing the magnification (and/or X-Y adjustment).

Now: $$\text{magnification} = \frac{\text{image size}}{\text{subject size}} \quad \text{or,} \quad \frac{\text{image distance}}{\text{subject distance}}$$

(In the latter case, again measure from principle point)

So when doing a blow-up, you can use this to determine the magnification. Then, assuming you have already decided on the best 1:1 exposure, you can calculate how much exposure change is needed:

$$\text{N.D. compensation} = 2 \times \log \left(\frac{m+1}{2}\right)$$

For example, with magnification 2, when we know our ideal exposure is f 5.6 with 1.00 N.D.,

$$\text{N.D. compensation} = 2 \times \log \left(\frac{2+1}{2}\right)$$

$$= 2 \times \log 1.5$$

$$= 2 \times .1761$$

$$= .3522$$

Therefore, removing .35 Nuetral Density from 1.00, we have an exposure of f 5.6 with .65 N.D..

Note that to blow up, you must move the lens <u>towards</u> the subject, while in a reduction you move the lens <u>away from</u> it. But to focus in any non-1:1 set-up, you always move the camera <u>away</u> from the subject. Therefore in blow-ups, the subject distance decreases, while in reductions, it increases. So from a 1:1 starting point, with blow-ups, your remove N.D., while in reductions you add it.

```
            magnification              compensation

               m = .13                 add ND .50
               m = .18                 add ND .46
               m = .25                 add ND .41
               m = .35                 add ND .34
               m = .50                 add ND .25
               m = .71                 add ND .14
               m = 1                      normal
               m = 1.4                 remove ND .16
               m = 2                   remove ND .35
               m = 2.8                 remove ND .56
               m = 4                   remove ND .80
               m = 5.7                 remove ND 1.04
               m = 8                   remove ND 1.31
```

DEPTH OF FIELD

As your magnification increases, your depth-of field decreases.
At 1:1 it is quite small, but still enough to comfortably bi-pack.

Extreme Close Up
35mm DEPTH of FIELD and EXPOSURE FACTOR
vs.
Magnification or Field of View   Circle of Confusion – 0.001"

Magnification Ratio		Field of View 1.85:1 AR	DEPTH OF FIELD (Total: front + back, in inches)											Exposure Increase Factor	T-Stop Increase
Dec.	Frac.		1/1	1/1.4	1/2	1/2.8	1/4	1/5.6	1/8	1/11	1/16	1/22	1/32		
0.100	1/10	4.46"-8.25"	0.22"	0.31"	0.44"	0.62"	0.88"	1.23"	1.76"	2.42"	3.52"	4.84"	7.04"	1.21	2/7
0.111	1/9	4.01-7.43	0.18	0.25	0.36	0.51	0.72	1.01	1.44	1.98	2.89	3.97	5.77	1.23	30
0.125	1/8	3.57-6.6	0.14	0.20	0.29	0.40	0.58	0.81	1.15	1.58	2.30	3.17	4.61	1.27	1/3
0.143	1/7	3.12-5.78	0.11	0.16	0.22	0.31	0.45	0.63	0.89	1.23	1.79	2.46	3.58	1.31	39
0.167	1/6	2.68-4.95	0.08	0.12	0.17	0.23	0.34	0.47	0.67	0.92	1.34	1.84	2.68	1.36	45
0.200	1/5	2.23-4.12	0.06	0.08	0.12	0.17	0.24	0.34	0.48	0.66	0.96	1.32	1.92	1.44	53
0.250	1/4	1.78-3.3	0.04	0.06	0.08	0.11	0.16	0.22	0.32	0.44	0.64	0.88	1.28	1.56	2/3
0.333	1/3	1.34-2.48	0.02	0.03	0.05	0.07	0.09	0.14	0.19	0.26	0.38	0.53	0.77	1.78	83
0.500	1/2	.89-1.65	0.012	0.017	0.02	0.03	0.05	0.07	0.10	0.13	0.19	0.26	0.38	2.25	1 1/4
0.667	2/3	.67-1.24	0.007	0.010	0.015	0.02	0.03	0.04	0.06	0.08	0.12	0.17	0.24	2.78	1.47
0.750	3/4	.59-1.10	0.006	0.009	0.012	0.017	0.03	0.04	0.05	0.07	0.10	0.14	0.20	3.06	1 1/2
0.875	7/8	.51-.94	0.005	0.007	0.010	0.014	0.02	0.03	0.04	0.05	0.08	0.11	0.16	3.52	1.81
1.0	1/1	.45-.83	0.004	0.006	0.008	0.011	0.016	0.03	0.03	0.04	0.06	0.09	0.13	4.0	2.0

Magni-	Field of View		DEPTH OF FIELD (Total: front + back, in inches)										Exposure	T-Stop
fication	(projected image)												Increase	Increase
Ratio	.286"×.380"	.251"×.463"	1/1	1/1.4	1/2	1/2.8	1/4	1/5.6	1/8	1/11	1/16	1/22	1/32	Factor	
Dec. Frac.	Std 16	Super 16													
0.100 1/10	2.86-3.80	2.51-4.63	0.13"	0.19"	0.26	0.37"	0.53"	0.74"	1.06"	1.45"	2.11"	2.90"	4.22"	1.21	27
0.111 1/9	2.58-3.42	2.26-4.17	0.11	0.15	0.22	0.30	0.43	0.61	0.87	1.19	1.73	2.38	3.46	1.23	30
0.125 1/8	2.29-3.04	2.01-3.70	0.09	0.12	0.17	0.24	0.35	0.48	0.69	0.95	1.38	1.90	2.76	1.27	½
0.143 1/7	2.0 -2.66	1.76-3.24	0.07	0.09	0.13	0.19	0.27	0.38	0.54	0.74	1.07	1.48	2.15	1.31	39
0.167 1/6	1.71-2.28	1.50-2.78	0.05	0.07	0.10	0.14	0.20	0.28	0.40	0.55	0.80	1.11	1.61	1.36	45
0.200 1/5	1.43-1.90	1.26-2.32	0.04	0.05	0.07	0.10	0.14	0.20	0.29	0.40	0.58	0.79	1.15	1.44	53
0.250 1/4	1.14-1.52	1.00-1.85	0.02	0.03	0.05	0.07	0.10	0.13	0.19	0.26	0.38	0.53	0.77	1.56	⅔
0.333 1/3	.859-1.14	.754-1.39	0.014	0.02	0.03	0.04	0.06	0.08	0.12	0.16	0.23	0.32	0.46	1.78	83
0.500 1/2	.572-.760	.502-.926	0.007	0.010	0.014	0.02	0.03	0.04	0.06	0.08	0.12	0.16	0.23	2.25	1½
0.667 2/3	.429-.570	.376-.694	0.004	0.006	0.009	0.013	0.018	0.03	0.04	0.05	0.07	0.10	0.14	2.78	1.47
0.750 3/4	.381-.507	.335-.617	0.004	0.005	0.007	0.010	0.015	0.02	0.03	0.04	0.06	0.08	0.12	3.06	1½
0.875 7/8	.327-.434	.286-.529	0.003	0.004	0.006	0.008	0.012	0.016	0.02	0.03	0.05	0.07	0.09	3.52	1.81
1.0 1/1	.286-.380	.251-.463	0.002	0.003	0.005	0.007	0.010	0.013	0.019	0.03	0.04	0.05	0.08	4.0	2.0

Extreme Close Up
16mm DEPTH of FIELD and EXPOSURE FACTOR
vs.
Magnification or Field of View

Circle of Confusion = 0.0006"

From the table above, 16mm 1:1 has a field of .286" X .380", which is equal to the standard aperture of a 16mm film projector.* The depth of field at f 5.6 is .013 inches. The Exposure Increase Factor is 4, meaning the film needs to see 4 times the amount of light it would see if no compensation were made. You therefore must open your lens up by 2 T Stops--or compensate by some other method, etc.....

* - Note however, that 1) most projectors are designed to slightly crop a .404" X .295" camera-recorded image to .380" X .286", and 2) the relative registration systems of the optical printer camera and projector are critical when attempting to print at exact 1:1.

w/ thanks to,
and liberal plagiarization from,

Lenny Lipton
Dennis Couzin
ACM

Appendix 2

Early Publications

These two interlinked texts preceded and later grew into the more theoretical "Technical Aesthetics in the Preservation of Film Art," which opens this collection. The two texts here are more nuanced in their discussion of the details of film printing. Some of the film stocks discussed are long obsolete, but somewhat disturbingly, the root problem described—of printing new internegatives from positive films—remains intact almost exactly as described. Some of the solutions discussed remain valid in principle as well, and those that don't serve at once as historical record, and a model for how to approach such questions.

a) "Problems of Independent Film Preservation" was originally published in the *Journal of Film Preservation*, Vol. XXV, No. 53, 1996.

b) "A Brief Note on Dye Stability" was originally published in the *Journal of Film Preservation*, Vol. XXVI, No. 54, 1997.

Problems of Independent Film Preservation

Summary

The independent artist's film—made, received, and valued in a context outside industry standards—poses a unique challenge to the archivist. While many basic principles of preservation still hold, their practical application is often so transformed as to merit only passing resemblance to conventional work. The common wisdom is often inappropriate, and unique printing methods are frequently needed. Ethical issues are similarly transfigured, to illuminating end. In preservation, as in aesthetics, the artist's film can serve as vanguard, highlighting issues of technique and philosophy that impact beyond its specialized sphere.

Introduction

When Kodak announced the discontinuation of its ECO color reversal film stock[1] in 1984, it heralded the end of an era in independent filmmaking. In so doing, it also left behind a kind of acetate standing stone for archivists. This was the death-knell for professional reversal work as well as for those artists clinging to its coattails. Reversal stocks continued to exist, but the negative/positive system was in essence canonized, leaving an effective void of printing methods for untold numbers of "direct-positive" films. Like the haunting formations at Avebury, Lewis, Stonehenge, those old images now please us while implying a logic whose order we've alas forgotten—and their preservation may be altogether more precarious.

Today's intermediate stock 7272 is ideally designed to print from ECO. Yet the simple fact is that most extant reversal images are not in fact ECO, but higher-contrast materials like Ektachrome or Kodachrome. When one prints an internegative from these films, or in fact any non-ECO positive material,[2] the contrast is boosted to the effectual quality of mud.[3] Anyone who has seen an old black and white film that seems very dark to the eye, with almost no delineation of greys, can imagine the look. So one is faced today with an industry that has on the one hand canonized the internegative system, while simultaneously leaving behind a massive body of films that are unprintable within this system.[4]

Artists' Films

Prominent among these are the works of independent artists. Independents have historically gravitated to the reversal film for reasons economic, practical, and aesthetic. There is something lovely and elegant in the camera-original that, bypassing the negative, simulates directly the tones and colors of the world as seen to the eye. No negative means less expense, and therein allows more experimentation—an attractive package for the artist/filmmaker. But while appealing to the artist, it presents a minefield for the archive preserving the work.

Not only must archivists consider the vital issue of image contrast, but they must be aware of any peculiarities in the piece itself. As often as not, the iconoclastic artist will be working at cross-purposes with industry standards. As an introductory example, one might take Larry Jordan's recent *H.D. Trilogy*. Jordan, the acclaimed animator and restorer of Joseph Cornell's films, had his black-and-white reversal originals for this work printed—via black-and-white internegative—onto Kodak's special low-contrast color television film 7385, with an amber tone added. Now one could emulate an amber tone easily enough, but without instructions to print onto 7385, the results would be horrendous. Jordan himself ran no fewer than seven entirely different printing tests before settling on this path. And rare is the case when a preservationist has access to coherent, detailed printing instructions.

To make things more difficult, the renowned "artist's temperament" can come into play as one attempts to faithfully render a meticulous vision. The Pacific Film Archive was recently involved in the preservation of Bruce Conner's CROSSROADS, a reworking of U.S. government footage of the atomic bomb tests at the Bikini Atoll. Conner, a great activist for the artist's film, periodically helped out with the project. After failing to remove a visible smudge in the original by, say, the fifth answer print, one member of the preservation team amiably noted that it might be easier to blow up the atoll again and to refilm it, than to satisfy Bruce Conner.

Color, Grain, and Format

Conservers of this work must develop a high level of resourcefulness and invention in their craft, often developing unique solutions on a film-by-film basis. For their current project preserving small-format artists' films, the San Francisco Cinematheque and New York Museum of Modern Art ran a series of tests to determine possible printing methods. Using the Canadian firm Optimage, which employs several techniques for contrast reduction,[5] we printed outtakes from the works of Joe Gibbons, Ellen Gaine, and Scott Stark. Each piece suggested a different method.[6]

Gaine's films, all Super-8, feature delicate tones and spectacular swirling grain fields. The delineations of grey were lost entirely and the granularity increased to a state of blotchiness in the first test, which consisted of a traditional blow-up to 16mm internegative and a positive print. As there is no low-con stock for B/W material, and as we have strong reservations regarding its use with color (to be discussed shortly), we requested that Optimage run a new test, in which they decreased the developing time/temperature combination, and increased exposure. This technique of over-exposing and "pull" processing is somewhat accepted with color internegatives, where it does not entirely eliminate the contrast boost, but rather gives it a good nudge in the right direction.[7] With Gaine's work, it did just the trick, adding some fine detail in the greys, while reducing the clotting of grain.

Stark's piece was made by respooling Standard-8mm Kodachrome into a 35mm still camera, and exposing still images of his garden across the film strip without regard to its perforations. Again Optimage's standard blow-up—which included a low-con 7385 print—did not do justice to the rich detail of the images. While their method did reduce contrast, the attendant decrease in saturation diminished both the color intensity of the Kodachrome and the flickering effect caused by the irregular frame line. While a conventional 16mm optical internegative would have too much contrast, we found that we could thread the needle by using the special diffusion within Optimage's printer, and striking a standard 7386 positive release print.

It is worth noting that Stark's method of making this film renders notions of a standard 24 (or 18 or 16) frames-per-second projection speed somewhat meaningless. In fact, Stark would often present the piece as a projection "performance" on a variable speed projector, varying the playback rate from 24 fps all the way down to 6 fps. While this effect could be simulated by step-printing, it should be pointed out that the perceptual effect of watching a single frame repeated is different than that of watching that same frame once[7] with an extended shutter-time. Similarly, step-printing an 18 fps original to 24 fps for 16mm viewing creates a subtle stutter every sixth second. As the only alternative is often to blow-up frame-for-frame and project at heightened speed, many small-format film artists forsake blow-up entirely.

Gibbons' *Punching Flowers* raised other considerations. Here the low-con 7385 stock's desaturation effectively rendered the muted tones in Gibbons' original work. While this stock, intended for video-transfer prints, has too little density and richness for most purposes; in this case the subject matter demanded exactly these qualities. In fact, however, this led to another question. A companion test on regular 7386 print stock, while boosting contrast, showed such an improvement in saturation that both project coordinator Steve Anker of the Cinematheque and myself agreed it in fact looked *better* than the original. The issue then became whether in fact our aim as preservationists were best served by faithfully rendering the qualities of the original work, or in fact enhancing them. Mr. Anker, a meticulously dedicated professional with an exacting eye, preferred the more saturated ("enhanced") version, while I myself found the muted 7385 more in keeping with the work's wry meditations on nature and beauty. This is not to say that I would always opt for "preservation" over enhancement, but simply that I preferred it in this case. Of course neither interpretation is right or wrong in absolute—they remain judgments. And it is just this sort of precise judgment which is demanded of the preserving archivist.

Now, *Punching Flowers*, shot in handheld Super-8, is in many ways an archetypal amateur film. The physical conditions of screening in 16mm, as well as a variety of social constructs, create more of a sense of professionalism in 16mm work than in the small-format underground or basement-screening genres. While some home movies or "actualities" footage, viewed primarily for image content, may benefit from blow-up, it is quite conceivable that other works would actually *suffer* in blow-up.[9] In fact, one quickly runs into a philosophical impasse when pondering the very preservation of works whose strengths lay in their rejection of traditional notions of the permanence of art, or else were grounded in their own physical form and/or temporality.[10] Mr. Anker, I think rightly, felt that this piece is ideally viewed in an intimate, less formal small-format projection. Yet as preservationists, we ultimately opted for the more stable medium of 16mm.[11]

Historical Considerations

Perhaps the most puzzling project of this nature I have come across recently is the preservation of Bruce Baillie's *All My Life* with the Pacific Film Archive. Mr. Baillie, an internationally recognized artist whose Castro Street has been included in the Library of Congress National Film Registry, and who along with his Canyon Cinema[12] co-founder Chick Strand, is one of the American experimental movement's great sensualists, produced a body of works in the 1960s and early '70s renowned for their visual richness and use of color. Among his most famous pieces is *All My Life*, a short (3 minute) single-shot film consisting of one elegant pan across an archetypal California country field in summer, followed by a weightlessly gentle tip skyward at the end. Ella Fitzgerald sings the title song, adding a sense of timelessness to this simple piece, which perching at a very narrow intersection of "structural" and "lyrical" film movements, has a grace and rigor beyond categories.

I got involved with this project after an internegative had been struck at W.A. Palmer Films in Belmont, California. Palmer's has long been a leading force in experimental film lab work, and their color grader, Lewis Motisher, has arguably among the best eyes in the business. Palmer's produced a second answer print with a degree of detail, softness, and color "accuracy" entirely absent in older copies of the film. There was only one problem. It looked awful. *All My Life* was originally shot on an Ansco reversal stock, described by Lenny Lipton in the first edition of his classic *Independent Filmmaking* as among "the best color films ever made available for the 16mm worker."[13] While perhaps lacking a range of values within a given hue or spectral range, the colors it does render have a striking deepness and vibrancy. Indeed, one scholar has referred to *All My Life*'s color as being something akin to the experience of a psychedelic trip on LSD. All of which is to suggest that the color for which the film is renowned is in fact heightened and *non-naturalist*; its strength lying precisely in its extraordinary saturation.

The question, then, was what was the experience of this new item, produced from the internegative? Certainly it looked more "realistic" in terms of a 1990s palette,[14] with the flat muted tones of current stocks, but it lacked the older version's dynamism. To answer the question, we sent the new answer print and an old release print to Baillie himself, who lives in seclusion on an island in Washington state. His answer, however, only deepened the nature of the dilemma.

Baillie decidedly preferred the *new* print, stating that it came much closer to the color and quality of light at Paul Tulley's home in Caspar, California, where the film was shot than did the original prints. Yet to most other eyes it was clearly inferior. We were then faced with the following questions:

> 1) Was our own dissatisfaction with the new print unfairly swayed by conceptions of what the work has historically looked like?
>
> 2) Was Baillie's judgment, while in one sense authoritative, to be taken as the last word on the topic?
>
> 3) If so, are historical notions of the film incorrect?
>
> 4) If not, can several versions be considered authoritative?

and lastly:

> 5) Are there any other printing methods that merit attention?

In consideration of the first issue I took up the highly subjective task of viewing as many different prints as I could find at hand. Upon repeated screenings of the new answer print I eventually satisfied myself that the new print was in fact unsatisfactory. A unique feature of original prints of *All My Life* is that—in no small part due to the film's conceptual structure of the linear pan—each time a new color appears on the screen, in the form of say, a flower, brush, or sky; it takes on the dramatic weight of the entrance of a new character in a narrative work.[15] In the new print, however, the slightly muted colors reduced perceived color contrast, thereby creating a more monotonous sensation of horizontal movement in a single direction, without articulation or emphasis. More "accurate," maybe, but entirely less evocative of mood and expression.

Is that not conceivably exactly what Baillie sought to achieve with the film? Perhaps. But I find it equally possible that Baillie's views now are something different than they were thirty years ago. Regardless, the older prints' historical associations have generated an authority of their own, which merits consideration. There are numerous examples in the history of art wherein works exist in multiple version, and many of the preferred versions are not the creator's final draft. To cite just one well-known example, no fewer than three editions of Wordsworth's "Prelude" are considered distinct works, with the middle draft, presented to Coleridge forty years before completion of the final draft (published posthumously) being the version of choice for many—precisely because readers find the revised draft to have diffused the earlier's most radical poetic and metaphysical statements. Perhaps an even better example comes from film history itself, with Teinosuke Kinugasa's legendary rediscovery of *A Page of Madness* in a barley barrel. No sooner had he recovered this masterwork, than he destroyed it by authorizing a vulgar modern soundtrack in what was perhaps an attempt to make it palatable to contemporary audiences.[16] The older artist's vision, while entitled in name, did not retain hold over the work's qualitative essence, which, in arising, had acquired a force of its own.

If one then took the new "authorized" answer print of *All My Life* as one version, it remained to find a way to salvage the other, older one. I had recalled seeing an unusual print through Canyon Cinema, which still distributes Baillie's work, several years previously. As part of my research, I visited Canyon to look at their copy and review printing records. I had imagined the print to be a 7399 reversal print, because my memory of it had strong saturation but a substantial difference in hue from original prints, which were likely to have been on 7388 or 7389, 7399's predecessors.[17] I was surprised to find that the print had been struck from an internegative, also made at Palmer's, and graded by Mr. Motisher! I called Palmer's to inquire as to the difference between the two internegs. Apparently, the distinction was actually just a result of grading and the different positive stock batches. Yet this difference, which gave the Canyon copy a slightly surreal cyanic cast, was enough to make this less naturalist rendition more appealing to my eye.

What was even more interesting were the facts Mr. Motisher revealed on the original prints of *All My Life*, which he himself had graded. It seems that rather than using the aforementioned gamma-1 stocks, he had opted to have the projection-contrast Anscochrome printed onto the more contrasty print stock Ektachrome 7390.[18] Thus the unique color for which *All My Life* was renowned was in fact the result of a variant printing technique which in fact boosted contrast. For the preservation internegative, however, he had chosen an entirely different strategy, seeking instead to emulate the qualities of the original. He felt he had largely succeeded, yet when pressed admitted that he too personally preferred the more deeply saturated older prints.

We were back to square one. The 7390 and 7387 stocks no longer existed, and the only major alternative involved attempting a reversal print. Copying onto Kodak's gamma-1 reversal 7399 material might potentially best preserve the tonal detail of the original, and more closely approximate the color of the old prints. Yet there are many obstacles to this approach.

It seems ironic that the 7399 stock, intended exactly for printing from projection-contrast materials, should not enter this discussion until so very near the end, but prejudices against its use in professional work are so widespread that it is very rarely employed. Such was the case here, the thinking being that *reversal stocks are not viable as a professional or archival medium*, primarily because the industry does not support them.

There are technical considerations. 7399 has a slightly higher RMS granularity than do negative stocks. More importantly, it produces a nearly unusable soundtrack.[19] It should be remembered, however, that the operating needs—and assets—of archives are qualitatively different than those of film productions. What would be in practice unthinkable for a release print might be curiously efficient for a preservation project. The printing of *All My Life*, a film known for its color, might be just the case where traditional factors became secondary, and unusual alternatives could be considered.

Regarding the audio of *All My Life*, Baillie himself has said the Fitzgerald song, which played constantly at the Tulley cottage when he was visiting, "had to have the same sound it had at Paul's with a potato sack over the speaker. It's supposed to sound a little scratchy."[20] Now, a review of Baillie's other major films of the era shows an incredible dexterity in the use of audio collage, with extreme attention paid to the flow and movement of mood. It is in part the simplicity of *All My Life*'s soundtrack, relying only on the qualities of Fitzgerald's singing, and the precise sense of listening to a beat-up record, that distinguishes the film from Baillie's other works. It is evocative, but audio fidelity is not as crucial to its success as color. In this case I find Baillie's judgment to be sound, and, further, to serve as justification for a possible reversal print.

The problem remained, however, as to just how to print the sound in a reversal scenario. Several possibilities existed, all of which were plausible only because the project's intended purpose was *preservation*, with screening always occurring within an archival context.

All of these involved a variation of double-system sound. In terms of audio fidelity, the striking of a new, separate magnetic track would actually improve quality over the best possible optical configuration,[21] while being playable on any standard interlock projector. In addition to this one might consider the production of a black-and-white optical sound master,[22] which would have all the preservation advantages of a silver-based medium.

The concept of dual-system printing opens up one final, unique method meriting mention. If one has accepted the idea of a separate physical sound strip, one is then free to conceive the absolute best possible avenue for image rendition. In terms of a deep saturation most like the old classic prints, the most appropriate stock to try might actually be Kodachrome camera stock, which normally would be unthinkable due to its higher contrast and lack of a sound process. But as *All My Life* already was known to print well in high contrast, and sound was being preserved separately, it might well prove to be an extraordinary alternative.[23]

All of these methods offer high-quality image preservation possibilities, as well as acceptable (and in some cases, superior) audio accompaniment. As in any delicate printing operation, testing would be required to determine which methods were effective and which were not. The verdict? None, as PFA had no funding with which to continue the project. Which leads into the last issue I would like to address.

Longevity

Lack of resources, a problem common to all archivists, is perhaps even more pronounced in the field of the art film. As a result, some special considerations arise regarding the physical conservation of an item. Proper storage conditions are widely acknowledged as the single most important aspect of moving image preservation, yet remarkably few facilities housing independent works come close to meeting recognized standards in this area. When funding is scarce, one must then recast the question: how can one best preserve a piece with the resources at hand? If proper storage is not feasible, emphasis should be placed on reproduction methods that build longer life into the physical materials themselves.

Reversal prints on 7399 may have one interesting, if slight, advantage over negative/positive systems in terms of long-range durability. The 7272 internegative stock has not been significantly modified in many years, while the Ektachrome line, including 7399, has undergone various changes that include improvements in dye stability. Also, it seems that the "low-fade" technology[24] introduced by Kodak in 1979 was incorporated into release print stocks, but not negatives of that era. This is because the principal agent in dye fading is usually not so much age as repeated projection under a high-intensity lamp, and negative materials are deemed to be infrequently used items which are never projected. 7399, which doubles as an intermediate and projection film, should incorporate the technique. One may therefore infer that 7399 prints will exhibit a slightly greater dye stability than 7272 internegatives, when used as preservation materials.[25]

Another consideration is the film's base material. As vinegar syndrome is now ravaging several generations of safety film, it is probably practical to start thinking of using polyester-based stocks in pre-print as well as print materials. Unfortunately, Kodak only offers polyester-based internegative film in large quantities as a special-order item, and polyester reversal materials are not available in 16mm at all.[26] It would be necessary for archives to cooperate in group purchases of stock to make this a feasible alternative. The extended life polyester stocks can offer to viewing prints and/or preservation materials[27] would then enter the field of variables considered in choosing a printing path, alongside other technical and aesthetic issues.

Conclusion

It is important, even inspiring, to note that reversal film has continued to survive as a medium. The very nature of its workings as a one-piece imaging system implies a wholly different approach to film production than does negative, and the works made with it merit serious attention both in themselves, and as historical records. While a print stock exists for it, that stock, 7399, has attendant difficulties, and is essentially an unsupported item. Because it understandably represents a small market, this reflects not so much a bias on Kodak's part, as actual industry trends. In point of fact, reversal currently functions as an "amateur" medium,[28] within which the striking of prints does not factor. But film art perseveres in disregard of standards, and the pool of positive materials is only growing.

Steps must be taken to ensure the life of these works. Several measures may be undertaken by Kodak or Fuji, and in fact some of the groundwork may already be lain. Two items would be of immediate use:

1) *a fine-grained, polyester, gamma-1 reversal print stock, with high-quality sound recording capacity*

Either an improved 7399, or a new stock would be appropriate. This would not only serve to preserve the works themselves, but also increase the viability of reversal film as a medium.

2) *a low-fade, polyester, low-contrast internegative*

A suitable material may already exist in the new 7287 and 7277 (Vision 320T) camera stocks. It is unorthodox to consider the use of production materials for preservation, but as great strides have been made in emulsions in the last ten years, either is very likely to be an improvement over the 7272 interneg. These new stocks both exhibit fine grain and strong dye stability, as well as reduced contrast. Ideally, a low-speed variation of the newer 7277, intended specifically for printing from positive, would be designed. This would ensure the preservation of many, many works, and also allow low-budget filmmakers to continue using reversal films as a front-end production medium.

Archives can contribute by lobbying for these items, pooling resources, and by working closely with laboratories. As 7399 sound printing would be a low-volume service, it seems that one or perhaps two labs dealing with archival and independent work might be encouraged to offer it on an occasional-run basis, thereby making it economically viable, with all such jobs channeled to them.

In the meantime, archivists preserving independent films are left to their own ingenuity. Even with ideal printing systems, the unusual nature of the art film presents unique considerations which arise from each individual work. When printing from positive, any method involves some kind of trade-off. An infrequently screened reversal-originated piece may be best preserved in terms of audiovisual accuracy and long-term stability with a dual-system strategy involving a reversal print and separate sound master, but frequently screened works with critical audio may demand a negative/positive scenario, which heightens image contrast. In all cases, one must delve into the specific qualities of the film at hand, and ask how best to preserve them.

Under current conditions, most restorations from positive source material are probably not so much preservations as *translations* to another medium, which vary widely in quality. A translation may be expedient, but should not be mistaken for actual preservation. If no conventional route is appropriate, then one must modify the function of existing materials to meet the situation, rather than compromise quality. Otherwise, we will be left in the position of those latter-day druids conducting rituals at Stonehenge: paying well-intentioned homage to a reminder of what we do not know.

Endnotes

1. Eastman Commercial Original 7252.
2. At one time, ECO's lower contrast was a standard system, so that in point of fact, other stocks, such as Agfa's Gevachrome 6.00, offered similar properties. A more specific term than "non-ECO" might therefore be "non-commercial film."
3. A film's contrast is measured by a "characteristic curve," which is basically a plot of the emulsion's density (the thickness, or darkness of its tones) against its exposure, using logarithmic scales. Of most relevance to this discussion is the curve's straight-line portion, or "gamma." When the slope, or gamma of a film is 1, as is ECO's, the film reproduces the tones of its subject in direct, one-to-one proportion. Gammas of less than 1 reduce contrast, while gammas greater than 1 increase it. Thus, to print a still picture, the final image should ideally have gamma 1. But with motion pictures, the cumulative conditions of projecting in a darkened room demand a higher image contrast, of gamma 1.6 to 1.8 (or 1.3 to 1.6 for black-and-white) to give the appearance of "natural" tonality. Since gammas multiply in printing, gamma 1 ECO's corresponding print films had a gamma of 1.8. It's internegative, 7272, has a gamma of .65, similar to a camera negative's. Therefore, printing ECO (gamma 1) onto 7272 (gamma .65), and then striking a positive release print (gamma 2.6 - 3), produces a gamma 1.8 image—ideal for viewing. Here then, is the crux of the problem. Current reversal materials like the Kodachrome and Ektachrome lines—and in fact any positive print intended for projection—already have a 1.8 gamma. Thus, printing them onto the 7272 material and then the 7386 print stock (or an Agfa or Fuji equivalent), results in a final image gamma of around 3, which is unsatisfactory by any standard.
4. Kodak has a gamma 1 reversal stock intended for these materials, which will be discussed later. But because "the print stock... must have extraordinary latitude to capture the range of image tones in a projection-contrast original[,] high gamma original is an irrational course, if prints are intended. Also if an internegative is intended." Dennis Couzin, "Dear Film Artists," *Experimental Film Coalition Newsletter*, Vol. 1, No. 2, June 1984, 2-3.
5. Optimage regularly utilizes the aforementioned low-contrast stock, in combination with "alterations" to their optical printer. I suspect their alterations allow the placement of a strong diffuser or opal glass near to the printer projector's film plane, while retaining a high level of illumination.
6. These tests took place in December, 1994. At the time of this writing (May, 1996), the Museum's intention is to use an East Coast laboratory; I believe John Allen's. To my knowledge all parties were

very pleased with the test results, and the change was primarily due to the attendant difficulties of a long-distance lab relationship. Clear communication channels with one's technical services are obviously of utmost importance in any non-standard printing operation.

7. Black-and-white films generally pose less of a problem in this area, for a variety of reasons. Contrasty subjects reproduce better in black-and-white than color, partially because colors suffer saturation loss in reproduction, and color print stocks are accordingly designed to work best with low contrast subjects, or "flat" lighting. See Russell Campbell, *Photographic Theory for the Motion Picture Cameraman* (Tantivy, 1974), 122. In this system, lack of inherent tonal contrast is compensated for by color contrast. But it poses another problem for the film artist who may not like the "soft light" quality favored in the mainstream film.

    Also, limitations exist within the overexposing/pulling method. There are often bottom-ends to development time on conventional lab machinery, as well as bottom-ends to ideas of accepted practice. Most labs which offer pull-processing seem unable to successfully correct the process by more than 1/4 to 1/2 stop, when the printed neg is actually measured densitometrically. Forde Labs in Seattle has apparently perfected a system along these lines which results in an ideal projection-gamma positive, but I have yet to test it. A general word of caution comes from Sam Bush, the excellent optical printing technician at Western Cine in Denver, who has printed most of the renowned artist Stan Brakhage's works. He fears that many labs would "cheat" in their pulling by merely speeding up the machine and not lowering the temperature. This would result in an insufficient bleach time. Despite these qualifications, however, overexposing and pulling remains one of the better available solutions.

    Western Cine, for their part, has developed a special process called LGN (for Low Gamma Negative). This technique, involving flashing, approaches the problem not so much by altering a film curve's straight-line portion as by modifying its toe and shoulder, giving an *impression* of lower contrast. This is more pronounced an alteration than overexposing and pulling, but may not be appropriate for many subjects which need deeper color saturation.

8. Super-8 projector shutters are cut to show a frame three times. A single frame step-printed twice would therefore flash six times upon projection.
9. From a purely visual standpoint, the crucial issues are reproduction method and projected image size. If 16mm and 8mm copies of an 8mm original are projected to the same dimensions, the 16mm will often be superior – depending on the optics of the blow-up system. When the 16mm print fills a larger screen, as is often the case, the effectively greater image dispersion can increase perceived graininess.
10. A striking case is the *Song* series by Stan Brakhage, which was made in 8mm for a variety of aesthetic, personal, and practical reasons. While 16mm copies exist, many feel the only true way to appreciate the *Songs* is in their original 8mm prints.
11. One option consisted of doing a preservation 16mm interneg, and a Super-8 reduction print for viewing. Logistics prevented us from pursuing this path further.
12. One of two major independent film distributors in the U.S. Canyon Cinema is located in San Francisco; the Film-makers' Cooperative is in New York.
13. Lenny Lipton, *Independent Filmmaking* (Straight Arrow, 1973), 82.
14. It could, and should, be argued that notions of visual verisimilitude to "reality" are not only subjective, but to a large extent also socially determined. Today's standard is often tomorrow's obsolescence, or charming artifact.
15. In conventional dramaturgy, the shift of direction when a character leaves or enters the stage is called a "French scene". The comparison seems quite relevant in the case of *All My Life*.
16. A similar example within the independent film tradition would be Harry Smith's *Early Abstractions*. Smith essentially made the ornate visual rhythms of these works unviewable when he slapped on an overpowering "needle drop" soundtrack of (otherwise excellent) Beatles recordings, in some ill-conceived alchemical strategy.
17. Other possibilities, though slightly less likely, also existed at that time, including Ansco 2470.
18. The occasional print may also have been made on Kodachrome print stock 7387.
19. Until a few years ago, inferior but just about passable silver tracks were printable on 7399. When environmental regulations made the already difficult application nearly impossible, no new techniques were pursued, and the printing of 7399 sound prints ceased. Technically, a dye track could still be made on the film, but as these silver-less tracks would pass infrared radiation, they would yield a low signal-

to-noise ratio on standard 16mm projectors, which are primarily red and infrared sensitive. Despite this impediment, this method has a few proponents in the independent sector. In such instances, boosting the gain in projection is necessary. I have not heard a dye track print, but suspect it would only be plausible for film artists working with a rough aesthetic.
20. Bruce Baillie, interviewed by Scott MacDonald, in *A Critical Cinema 2* (California, 1992), 121.
21. Mag striping would offer similar quality, but as this practice is essentially obsolete, it seems to offer no practical advantages over dual-system. Striping is also disadvantageous from a preservation standpoint, as the magnetic coating may cause earlier deterioration of the film itself.
22. One would then have the choice of whether to make a negative or reversal master. While neg is the standard procedure, here the direct positive method offers some advantages. As positive image tracks play better than do negatives, a reversal track would offer playback potential in some double-system set-ups. It also might allow more avenues for sound prints to be struck in future reversal scenarios, should either new printing stocks or optical readers become available.

There are some considerations unique to the reversal method, however. Neg/pos optical systems are effective because image spread in the variable area track of the negative is effectively cross-modulated by image spread in the positive track. In cases where a direct positive is desired, the cross-modulation occurs between the two developments of the reversal process. Tests may be required if the lab is not accustomed to processing sound stock reversal. Also, as in the striking of any optical master, one should remember to consider film wind in relation to one's overall printing needs.
23. Slight variations exist between camera stocks, which are designed to render the tonal range of the world, and printing stocks, designed to render the tonal range of a film image, so it would certainly be an experiment. But stranger things have been known to work. Also, while I have not studied the changes made to Kodachrome materials over the years, I know from many viewings that the older Kodachrome stocks exhibit a strong advantage in the area of dye stability.
24. It should be noted that this term is frequently used by archivists, but not professionally recognized by Kodak. The technique falls among those improvements in stock design too variable to cite as a standard, and hence does not feature in the company literature.
25. This argument assumes that the modifications to the dye couplers in the low-fade stock will have an effect on rarely screened or printed items. The technology is considered a trade secret, and hence information on it is rather scarce on the ground.

It is worth noting that the new EXR negatives and their intermediate 7344 are also designed with strong dye stability. While 7344 would have too much contrast for printing from positive, the EXR camera stocks may present their own advantages in this regard.
26. Direct positive 5360, a 35mm reversal stock, is available in polyester, but it is probably not the best archival choice in terms of image rendition. Kodak's new 7378 sound stock, which may be processed reversal, is available in polyester as stock number 3378E.
27. While extensive studies have not been made in all aspects of polyester use, most signs point to significant stability advantages. The disadvantages—including legends of broken projectors, etc.—seem for the most part to be exaggerated.
28. Artists and archivists will understand that this is not necessarily a pejorative term. One of the best works on the topic is by Stan Brakhage, who (at the time he was making the aforementioned *Songs*) wrote eloquently of those works which, unencumbered by professional constraints, were free to express a truly open and honest vision. (Stan Brakhage, "In Defense of Amateur," written ca. 1967; *Filmmakers Newsletter* 4 (9-10), Summer 1971, in *Brakhage Scrapbook – Collected Writings 1964–1980* (Documentext, 1982).

A Brief Note on Dye Stability

The following comments include corrections of errors in the essay "Problems of Independent Film Preservation," published in the previous issue of the Journal of Film Preservation.

Dye stability, like other issues of film longevity, will vary depending on a number of physical factors. At a broad level, these may be broken down into the concepts of dark stability and light stability. Dark keeping refers to fade resistance when a film is stored in darkness, while light keeping indicates its fade resistance to exposure to light. Different films will thus have different conditional stabilities, depending on both their physical makeup, and storage/usage. In previous research, I had been incorrectly informed that Kodak's "low-fade" stocks incorporated dye "stabilizers" which addressed a deficiency in their light-keeping ability. This mistake led me to several incorrect assumptions which I would here like to clarify.

While current print stocks, such as 53/7386 do indeed have the aforementioned stabilizers, the stabilizers are quite distinct from the "low-fade" technology. Richard Patterson observes in *American Cinematographer* that until the introduction of the LF line of print stocks in the late 1970s, print stability was not an issue, because Kodak believed most positive prints would be destroyed after use.[1] Therefore, they actually had an inferior dark stability when compared with negative stocks, which had a need for greater longevity. As issues of preservation became increasingly apparent, Kodak introduced the more stable line of "low-fade" stocks to complement their normal print stocks.[2] Beginning with 53/7384 (and also the low contrast 53/7380), these changes were adopted for all Kodak color positive materials, and the distinctive LF designation dropped.

In terms of preservation, the key issue is dark stability. While negative materials do not have the "stabilizers" present in positive films, the dangers of exposure to light are in general less significant than the inherent dark-keeping properties of the film itself, and its storage conditions.

If one then compares different stocks as potential preservation media,[3] some clear distinctions arise. Kodak's 7399 reversal material, which I had hypothesized might have better dye stability than the 7272 internegative, decidedly does not. The dark-keeping properties of the 7272 are clearly superior,[4] and its light fading risks are not critical. Current camera negatives are of a similar quality to the 7272. I have not obtained data on the higher-contrast Kodachrome, but Kodachrome films traditionally exhibit excellent longevity.

A final remark would be that dye stability itself is only one of several factors that should be considered in the selection of a printing stock—albeit a very important one. The color palette—as well as other rendering properties—of each of the stocks mentioned is quite different, and will vary further in the course of a printing path. A traditional 7272/7386 approach, without alteration, may prove inappropriate for many positive subject originals.[5] Thus, depending on the intended purpose and life of a preservation project, variations may be a preferred option if they offer aesthetic advantages. Ideally, specific printing and preservation projects will indicate their own solutions.

Endnotes

1. Richard Patterson, "The Preservation of Color Films, Part 1," *American Cinematographer*, July 1981.
2. The change consisted of a substantially improved cyan dye, which was historically the least stable of the three layers in Eastmancolor stocks.
3. This discussion is intended to be of relevance to the printing of films which exist in reversal or positive viewing copies.
4. Although such valuations are subjective, it is estimated that a trained eye will notice dye fading at 20% dye loss, an untrained eye at about 30%. Stored at 40% RH and 59 degrees F, 7399 should suffer 25% fading in only 17 years. Under the same conditions, 7272 should last about 100, based on accelerated aging tests.
5. A thorough discussion of the drawbacks of 7272 is contained in my earlier article, "Problems of Independent Film Preservation," *Journal of Film Preservation*, Vol. XXV, No. 53, 1996.

Appendix 3

Sample Preservation Histories

An often overlooked facet of a restorationist's work is creating proper documentation of the work conducted, so those following in our wake can better understand the surviving materials and their relation to a film's history. To help keep the information intelligible, I found it's usually best to begin with the source materials and work forward from there, through intermediates to viewing formats. Of course, in practice, there are parallel steps that happen and flow charts can be invaluable supplements.

The notes below are also of interest for their discussion of version issues, and of the carefully selected replacement of original music tracks with higher fidelity versions of the same recordings, as well as the decision to avoid this practice when not appropriate.

documents prepared for UCLA Film & Television Archive:

preservation histories of films by Kenneth Anger

01—*Fireworks* (ca. 1947 / 195x / 196x / 198x etc.)
02—*Rabbit's Moon* (1951 / 1971, etc.)
03—*Scorpio Rising* (1963)
04—*Kustom Kar Kommandos* (1965)

Fireworks (ca. 1947/195x/196x/198x etc.)
Kenneth Anger

original release: 16mm. restored in 35mm. 15 mins.

Preservation funded by The Film Foundation

Preserved from three original 16mm prints and Kenneth Anger's reconstructed duplicate A/B rolls. Laboratory services by Triage Motion Picture Services, Audio Mechanics, DJ Audio, NT Audio. Special thanks to: Kenneth Anger, Anthology Film Archives, Canyon Cinema, Michael Friend, The Kinsey Institute for Research in Sex, Gender, and Reproduction, Andrew Lampert.

prologue version M02967

picture restoration:

Kenneth Anger apparently made five versions of FIREWORKS:

> V1: pre-release (dating from privately held preview screenings. uncensored, but lost).
>
> V2: 1947 release version (made with no opening title sequence).
>
> V3: Anger spoken prologue version. adds main title. origin date unknown.
>
> V4: 1966. single edition hand-painted print. lost in a fire.
>
> V5: 198x. 16mm distribution version. features a new title sequence and printed with a blue color cast. All (or most) shots truncated to accommodate insertion of title sequence without altering music edit.

The original 16mm negative a/b rolls of FIREWORKS are lost. Kenneth Anger's surviving 16mm a/b rolls are in fact positive copies made in the 1970s and have been edited to conform to his final version of the film (per above), which apparently dates to the 1980s.

UCLA has preserved the original release version (no titles) and the subsequent "prologue" version in 35mm. The sources for these were three old 16mm prints belonging to respectively, the Kinsey Institute (on loan), the Creative Film Society (on deposit at UCLA), and Anthology Film Archives (on loan). Preservation lab was Triage.

These 16mm prints were blown up to 35mm and edited (for best quality) into 35mm BW preservation dupe negative M02189. This negative contains Anger's spoken prologue and the first Main Title sequence, which Anger apparently added after the film's premiere. As the prologue and MT precede the film body, this same negative also serves to preserve the original release version of the film. The 35mm dupe negative was printed alongside 35mm Dolby SR ("widerange mono") restored track negative M02188 (with no digital noise reduction) to strike print M150380, which was conformed to the original release version.

The 35mm dupe negative was also printed alongside 35mm Dolby SR ("widerange mono") restored track negative M150625 (with digital noise reduction) to strike prints M02967 and M143851 (prologue version).

As Version 2 (original release) may be seen to most accurately reflect Anger's original vision, print M150380 (original release version) is included in UCLA's KENNETH ANGER restoration compilation program M161266. It can also be used for stand-alone exhibition.

Preservation credits for the original release version are on separate 35mm preservation dupe negative roll M150620. For instructions how to make new prints of the original release version and the prologue version, see printing notes below.

To preserve Version 5, UCLA used Kenneth Anger's 16mm re-printed reversal a/b rolls (M202558) to strike 16mm preservation color internegative M150632. This can be used alongside 35/32 preservation track negative M150631 to strike new prints. 16mm color MOS print M150633 can be used as a rough color reference (to be adapted as needed), and can also be used as a workprint.

sound restoration:

The three 16mm exhibition prints used to preserve the picture (as detailed above) were first transferred to digital file. These three files were then used to create the best possible version of Version 2 (original release) and Version 3 (prologue). First, a file was created of both versions with restored audio (including pop and click removal resulting from dirt), but no automated noise reduction, to better simulate the rough quality of the original sound transfer evident in the older 16mm prints. This file was then transferred to DVD-R M150619, which was in turn used to strike 35mm preservation mag track M02174 and 35mm Dolby SR ("widerange mono") preservation track negative M02188. This track neg was then printed alongside 35mm preservation pic neg M02189 to strike viewing print M150370, conformed to Version 3. An extra DVD-R of the restored track with no noise reduction, M150617, was created with reduced bias at head during preservation credits. However for quietest overall track it would be optimal to use the version with noise reduction, as detailed immediately below.

After creating the above, the restored audio file then underwent noise reduction to create a fully restored track, while still retaining the "needledrop" quality of Kenneth Anger's original recording. This represents the best quality, and was used to make DVD-R M150626 (preservation), M150627 (access), and M150628 (extra). These were then used to strike 35mm preservation mag M150624 and 35mm Dolby SR ("widerange mono") preservation track neg M150625. From the mag, a 4th DVD-R (M150629) was made, in sync with the mag which contained the preservation credits, but downstream one analog generation from the other DVD-R's.

Simultaneous to this, Kenneth Anger's 16mm track negative M150989 was used to strike 16mm track positive M150630 at Fotokem, for the preservation of Version 5. This was transferred to digital file and restored at Audio Mechanics, and included on DVD-R's M150626, 150627, and M150628. This was then used to strike 35/32 track negative M150631.

notes for future printing and remastering:

35mm prints to be struck at gamma 2.10.

To make new copies of Version 3 (prologue version), simply use 35mm picture negative M02189 and track negative M150625.

To make new copies of Version 2 (original release), begin by using 35mm BW preservation dupe negative M02189 alongside 35mm Dolby SR ("widerange mono") restored track negative M150625) to strike a 35mm composite print. Simultaneously to this, use 35mm BW dupe negative M150620 to strike a 35mm print of the preservation credits with "blacktrack" soundtrack. Then remove the Main Title / Prologue scene from the new print, and replace it with the preservation credit sequence. If the edit point does not seem clear, exhibition print M150380 can be used as a guideprint.

To make new copies of version 5, use 16mm picture internegative M150632 alongside 35/32 track negative M150631. 16mm color MOS print M150633 can be used as a rough color reference (to be adapted as needed) in grading, and can also be used as a workprint.

Rabbit's Moon (1951/1971, etc.)
Kenneth Anger

original release: 16mm. restored in 35mm. 16 mins.

Preserved through the Avant-Garde Master's program funded by The Film Foundation and administered by the National Film Preservation Foundation

Preserved from the 35mm original nitrate picture negative, the original 16mm color A/B rolls, the original sound recordings, and three 16mm prints. Laboratory services by Triage Motion Picture Services. Fotokem Film and Video, Audio Mechanics, DJ Audio, NT Audio. Special thanks to: Kenneth Anger, Anthology Film Archives, Canyon Cinema, Michael Friend, Andrew Lampert.

UCLA print M02969

picture restoration:

RABBIT'S MOON was shot in the Films du Pantheon Studio in Paris in 1950. Shooting was never completed. Anger retrieved his unedited footage from the Cinematheque Francaise in 1970 and released a 16-minute version in 1971. A 7-minute version was released in 1979.

When the 35mm nitrate film was reduced to 16mm in 1971, the picture's original left-right orientation was reversed as an artifact of printing, resulting in a mirror-image of the original.

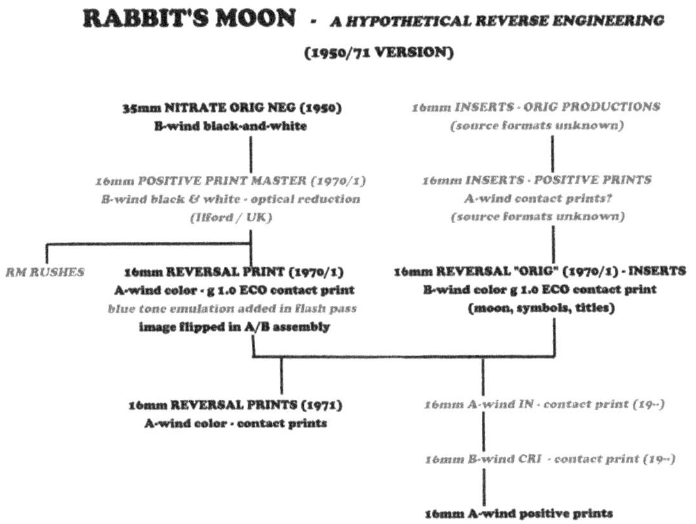

RABBIT'S MOON - *A HYPOTHETICAL REVERSE ENGINEERING*
(1950/71 VERSION)

35mm NITRATE ORIG NEG (1950)
B-wind black-and-white

16mm INSERTS - ORIG PRODUCTIONS
(source formats unknown)

16mm POSITIVE PRINT MASTER (1970/1)
B-wind black & white - optical reduction
(Ilford / UK)

16mm INSERTS - POSITIVE PRINTS
A-wind contact prints?
(source formats unknown)

RM RUSHES

16mm REVERSAL PRINT (1970/1)
A-wind color - g 1.0 ECO contact print
blue tone emulation added in flash pass
image flipped in A/B assembly

16mm REVERSAL "ORIG" (1970/1) - INSERTS
B-wind color g 1.0 ECO contact print
(moon, symbols, titles)

16mm REVERSAL PRINTS (1971)
A-wind color - contact prints

16mm A-wind IN - contact print (19--)

16mm B-wind CRI - contact print (19--)

16mm A-wind positive prints

Figure 1. A flowchart assessing the probable method by which Kenneth Anger had initially completed *Rabbit's Moon*. Missing elements and speculated methodologies are indicated by gray text.

The 35mm preservation negative ABC rolls were printed alongside track negative M102669 to strike preservation prints M02969 (intended for screening as a single title) and M03105 (as part of the combined KENNETH ANGER restoration program).

For the 16mm version, the source was Kenneth Anger's original 16mm positive a/b rolls. These were printed to 16mm color preservation internegative M150608. This should be used alongside 16mm preservation track negative M150609 when striking new 16mm prints. 16mm preservation internegative M150606 contains the preservation credits, and can be assembled into a B-roll as needed.

UCLA's preservation fine grain master M08604 was also used as the source for Fantoma's HD digital remastering of RABBIT'S MOON conducted at Post Logic Studios with Lou Levinson as colorist, under project supervision by UCLA's Ross Lipman in collaboration with the Fantoma team. After completing the remastering of the 16-minute version, Fantoma then used the same master files to re-create Anger's 7-minute version.

sound restoration:

Initially, several original 16mm prints were transferred to DA 98 tape 150362 . This was ingested for sound restoration at Audio Mechanics.

However, the sound for the long (sixteen minute) version of RABBIT'S MOON was comprised primarily of needle-drop use of the following recordings:

> The Flamingos: "I Only Have Eyes For You"
> The Dells: "Oh, What a Night"
> The Capris: "There's a Moon Out Tonight"
> Mary Wells: "Bye Bye Baby"
> Indonesian Ketjak: Ramayana Monkey Chant (ca. 1960s field recording)

The original recordings of all of the above (including the precise version of the Monkey Chant—which had been recorded multiple times, and the correct mix of the others, which had been re-mixed in the course of multiple re-releases of the songs) were tracked down and conformed to Anger's original sound edit, as found on the 16mm prints. Then, in sections where sound effects were also used, the newly conformed master was overlayed with the best of the prints for perfect sync. These were mixed together with targeted EQ and leveling applied to emulate the film's original mix levels, and ultimately preserved in restored DVD-R M150613. This was in turn used to strike 35mm preservation mag track M150611 and 35mm preservation track neg M102669. An additional 35mm preservation track neg (M150614) contains the entirety of the film, but is lacking bias track during the introductory preservation credits (to distinguish them from program content).

The remastered audio files contained in the 35mm track neg were used with the reconstructed 35mm ABC rolls to strike 35mm prints M02969 and M03105.

Simultaneously to the above, a separate sound restoration was created from the 16mm prints (without "upgrading" via track replacement), tracing to Anger's original 1971 transfer of the actual source recordings. This additional restored audio file is also contained on DVD-R M150163.

When striking new 35mm prints, it should be noted that the 35mm a and b rolls are BW, while the c-roll is color. Therefore laboratories should be careful to note trim adjustments and/or use of orange mask filter for the C-roll as noted in additional printing notes, to be found with the timing tapes in UCLA's timing tapes archive. (The rolls are intended for checkerboard, rather than sequential printing.)

notes for future printing and remastering:

If/when striking a 16mm print, preservation credits are available on a separate 16mm DPN roll (M150605). If it's desired to assemble this into conformed C-rolls, 16mm color positive MOS roll M150610 can be used as workprint for the main picture, and 16mm pos roll M150606 can be used as a workprint for the preservation credits.

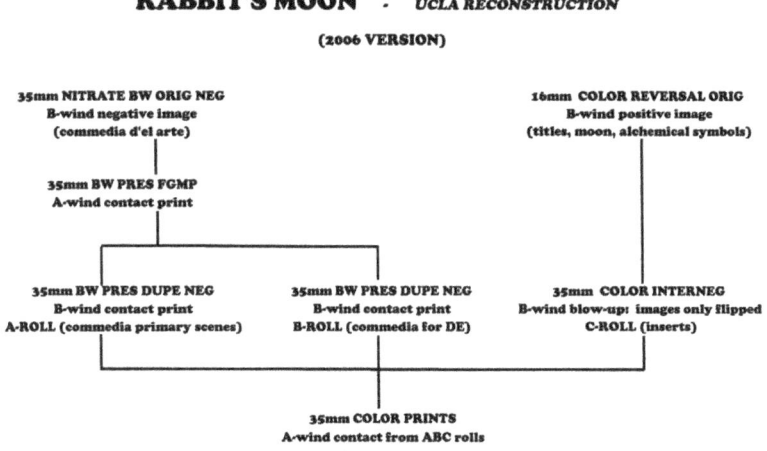

Figure 2. A flowchart documenting the workflow of UCLA's reconstruction of *Rabbit's Moon*.

Scorpio Rising (1962)
Kenneth Anger

original release: 16mm. restored in 35mm. 29 mins.

Preservation funded by The Film Foundation

Preserved from the original hand-painted 16mm Ektachrome color reversal A/B rolls and from the 16mm original magnetic track. Laboratory services by Fotokem Film and Video, Audio Mechanics, DJ Audio, NT Audio. Special thanks to: Kenneth Anger, Michael Friend, Pacific Film Archive, P. Adams Sitney.

UCLA print M02970

picture restoration:

From Kenneth Anger's original 16mm color Ektachrome reversal a/b rolls (including hand-painted sections), a 35mm color blow up internegative (M102651) was struck at Fotokem on 5212 acetate camera negative. Camera neg was chosen for superior color rendition. Stock was processed normal - NOT pulled - for appropriate contrast and tonal rendition based on material. Pickups shot as needed to address physical problems in original rolls. The new color internegative was printed along with 35mm Dolby SR preservation soundtrack negative M149594 to yield release prints M02970 and M03106.

sound restoration:

Kenneth Anger's original 16mm magnetic track was transferred at DJ Audio to DA-98 (M163668), and this sound file was used for sound restoration at Audio Mechanics. The resulting cleaned-up sound file was transferred to DA 98 (M163669), and ultimately to strike a 35mm Dolby SR preservation track negative (M149594) and 35mm mag track (M163667).

Unlike RABBIT'S MOON, where a version was created remastering from the original source music, SCORPIO was restored solely from KA's mag because of the extensive overlay of sound effects embedded in the mag master.

Kustom Kar Kommandos (1965)
Kenneth Anger

original release: 16mm. restored in 35mm. 3 min.

Preservation funded by The Film Foundation

Preserved from the 16mm original Ektachrome color reversal A/B rolls and from a 16mm positive soundtrack print. Laboratory services by Fotokem Film and Video, Audio Mechanics. DJ Audio, NT Audio. Special thanks to: Kenneth Anger, Anthology Film Archives, Michael Friend, Andrew Lampert.

UCLA print M02968

picture restoration:

From Kenneth Anger's original 16mm color Ektachrome reversal a/b rolls, a 35mm color blow up internegative (M102652) was struck at Fotokem on 5212 acetate camera negative. Camera neg was chosen for superior color rendition. As the film is so short, the entire film was initially test-printed for gamma, with one neg processed normal and the other pull-processed. Unlike SCORPIO RISING, wherein stark lighting benefitted from higher gamma, the pastel color palette of KUSTOM KAR benefitted from the reduced contrast of pulling. Thus, the normal process neg was accessioned as a backup element, M163662, and the reduced contrast neg M102652 is the primary preservation element. Pickups were shot as needed to address physical problems in the original rolls and inserted into M102652.

The new color internegative M102652 was printed along with 35mm Dolby SR preservation soundtrack negative M163663 to yield release prints M02968 and M03104. See sound notes for more information.

When shooting KUSTOM KAR KOMMANDOS, Kenneth Anger's camera had a problem resulting in on-screen jitter. This artifact has been preserved in the analog/photochemical preservation elements above. This jitter can now be corrected digitally, and was in fact improved when Fantoma created their HD master for DVD release. The Fantoma re-mastering (which was also issued by the BFI and perhaps a Japanese label) was not transferred from UCLA's restoration elements or KA's original camera rolls, but rather from an old 16mm single-roll internegative. On the film's crossfades, the jitter from original a-roll shots is hence superimposed upon the jitter from a second image in the source b-roll. Therefore the existing Fantoma/BFI HD masters retain jitter in the cross-faded shots, and subsequent improvements cannot be made from previously existing internegatives. For this reason, UCLA has created additional 16mm preservation color internegatives copies of the individual original reversal a and b rolls (M150600 and M150601). For future remastering efforts, these two rolls can be scanned individually, have the jitter removed, and then be superimposed to create a jitter-free restoration including the cross-fades. Theoretical arguments can be made that one should or shouldn't correct that problem, but if proceeding, that's likely the best way to correct the problem.

sound restoration:

A 16mm print and 16mm track positive were transferred to digital files and used for sound restoration at Audio Mechanics. The resulting cleaned-up sound file was transferred along with the original, unrestored files to DVD-R M163665 and DVD-R M163666, and ultimately to strike a 35mm Dolby SR preservation track negative (M163663) and 35mm mag track (M163664). The first prints struck revealed slightly higher bias than desired in the opening preservation credits sequence, so NT Picture & Sound re-shot the track to reduce the bias. This improved 35mm Dolby SR track (M150599) should ideally be used in conjunction with picture preservation IN M102652 when striking new prints, although soundtrack neg M163664 remains acceptable for use if needed.

Unlike RABBIT'S MOON, for which UCLA created a version tracing to the original music recordings, KUSTOM KAR KOMMANDOS was created from KA's 16mm masters, because the source music—the Paris Sisters' "Dream Lover"—had undergone a speed change in the original transfer for film. This change (3½% slowing, on average) commenced in the middle of the film, at 120'07 in 35mm and 48'07 in 16mm from a Zero at First Frame of KA's Puck logo. While this speed change could in theory be replicated or corrected in a new digital re-mastering from the original recordings, it was decided to use the original 16mm source for authenticity/sync.

notes for future printing and remastering:

When striking new prints, use improved soundtrack negative M150599 and pull-processed pic IN M102652.

In future digital remastering efforts, if one wishes to address the built-in camera jitter tracing to the original cinematography's camera problem, one should use 16mm preservation color internegatives M150600 and M150601, per notes in Picture Preservation History above.

Appendix 4

Sample Production and Migration History

To more fully understand a work's history, one ideally studies the many iterations that preceded a restoration. The following text is more detailed than is commonly practical for most projects, but offers an idea of the challenges in undertaking a full account of a work, as well as—hopefully—an idea of the potential of such studies.

Thank you to Jean Conner, Michelle Silva, and the Conner Family Trust for permission to present this document on Bruce Conner's A MOVIE.

Additional thanks to Louis Pelletier for his excellent research on Bruce Conner's source materials as documented in his essay, "Hidden in Plain Sight," Found Footage, *March 2019.*

A MOVIE
Bruce Conner

Production, Preservation and Migration History
with Printing Notes

[text in brackets is speculative and needs further verification]

1958—original production and release

Bruce Conner's A MOVIE picture content was comprised of title cards photographed in 16mm by Conner himself, and a variety of found images pulled from sources including Castle Films home exhibition releases such as *Hindenburg Explodes!*, *A Thrill a Second*, *Spills* and *Thrills*, and *Thrills on Wheels*. The film was originally conceived for projection as a gallery installation, in which the film would be rear-projected onto the walls of a small cube which the viewer would enter, accompanied by an ever-changing audio mix of recordings and live sound from radios and televisions. This presentation form never materialized.

As A MOVIE was Conner's first film, he was instructed in editing technique by filmmaker Larry Jordan, and it was initially prepared as a 16mm B-wind a-roll (only) master positive (UCLA #M83195; see UCLA inventory record for detailed condition notes).

An original optical track negative from1958 (M83160) appears to be the earliest existing sound source. No corresponding 1958 dupe negative or 16mm mag track can be found.

Track negative M83160 was used to strike A wind-track positive M83157. The track positive's date code (double circle) suggests either 1959 or 1979 manufacture, but presumably the former. Notes on its leader dating to 1974 are presumed to mark later lab work. Some mysteries remain, as a label on its can states: "one-light timed print (NG pic)....1st answer print" which suggests an early dupe negative may have once existed, used in tandem with its source track negative (M83160). Both tracks (negative and positive) are 6-band multi-bilateral.

1970-80

Several dupe neg / track neg combinations were created in the early 1970s.

> dupe pic neg M83192 (stock date: 1970) and B-wind track neg M82735
> (VA dual bilateral)
> dupe pic neg M83159 (stock date: 1970) - "Number 3" (no corresponding track)
> dupe pic neg M83196 (stock date: 1973) and B-wind track neg M83163
> [VA dual bilateral]

Of these, at least one was made at Palmer's.

The source of the track negatives is not verified, but they were presumably re-recorded from Conner's early soundtrack master positive M83157. 16mm original positive M83195 was the picture source. Note that no corresponding track neg can be found for dupe pic neg #3.

Catalog records for track pos M83157 indicated it was used as the source to strike a 16mm mag track at Palmer's in 1979, although that mag track cannot be found in the collection as of August 2020. It's possible it was included in the 1990 mag track assembly built up for the Facets video release, as detailed below.

In September 1980, Conner removed his negatives from Palmer's Labs.

One of the above pic neg / track neg pairs served as the source to strike positive print M83161 at Multichrome in October 1980.

1990 video transfer

As part of a Facets home video release of a compilation of Conner films, A MOVIE was initially transferred to 1" video at Monaco Film and Video in San Francisco on Feb. 15, 1990. The 1" tape in Conner's Sussex St. home archive was labeled as a "Protection Copy" which would suggest the creation of another master, whereabouts unknown.

The compilation was released by Facets on VHS as B.C. FILMS: I, and contained: TEN SECOND FILM, PERMIAN STRATA, MONGOLOID, AMERICA IS WAITING and A MOVIE. The source for the transfers is unknown.

As part of the compilation's workflow, a 16mm magnetic track was assembled from previously existing mag tracks. It's possible the A MOVIE mag track was the 1979 Palmer's mag.

Conner retained VHS copies of the Facets release in his Sussex St. home archive.

1998—2000, 2000 BC exhibition

One of the existing/old dupe negs and one of the tracks (from Palmer's; presumably ca. 1970-73) were used to make new prints at Forde, for the 2000 BC Walker Arts exhibition. Forde lowered their print contrast at Bruce Conner's request. The work was overseen by Timoleon Wilkins, and approximately 30 prints were created. To obscure a negative repair in the last shot, Conner had Wilkins apply by hand a small amount of marker to about three or four frames in each print. After testing about 20 markers, a Lumocolor Non-permanent marker was selected for its compatibility with the Photoguard process Conner used to protect the prints from scratches. Nonetheless Wilkins felt the marker looked worse than the repair it was attempting to cover.

One print from this era is archived: Final Answer Print M83167, created at Forde in 1998.

A 16mm dupe negative was made at Cinema Arts in 2000, presumably from the original A-roll positive. A 16mm track negative was made at the same time, but the source and laboratory are unknown. The work was overseen by Michael Friend. Since the 2000 BC exhibition premiered at Walker Arts Center in 1999, it is presumed but not verified that this work was undertaken separately, or for a later stage of the tour.

These elements were subsequently sent to California for deposit at UCLA, but no inventory numbers are currently available.

Print M217420 was made from the Cinema Arts 2000 neg.

2002-3 video transfer

On 4/1/2002, a Digibeta copy of the "BC Films: 1" compilation (including A MOVIE) was made at Monaco Film & Video. It is labeled "Monaco transfer" but it seems more likely that the source was Conner's 1990 1" Protection Master, from his Sussex St. home archive.

The 1990 1" and 16mm mag fullcoat assembly were also used as the source for A MOVIE's inclusion in an oversize Digibeta in the Sussex St. Archive labeled "BC FILMS COMPILATION"—"mag transfer—Monaco—5/8/02."

A DAT audio transfer of the 16mm fullcoat mag assembly was made in 2002 at "Annex Digital" which is believed to in fact be Music Annex.

A subsequent Digibeta clone of the Monaco Digibeta was made at Video Arts on 9/3/03. Other clones seem to have been made at Video Arts as well.

Note that at this same time, Conner released a DVD entitled "2002 BC" which contained eight films, but A MOVIE was not included.

From the above workflow, the following items were kept in the Conner Sussex St. archive:

Selects only—DIGIBETA CLONE—made at Video Arts

BC FILMS COMPILATION—DIGIBETA CLONE—made at Video Arts 9/3/2003

2015—CFT Restoration and Edition

Picture

A MOVIE's original 16mm a-roll (only) master positive (UCLA #M83195) was used as the source for a blow-up to 35mm BW duplicate negative, made at UCLA's Stanford Lab. [No inventory number noted for the duplicate negative. Believed to be at UCLA.]

This was in turn used as the source for a 4K scan at Fotokem. The files were then subjected to minimal and carefully selected digital restoration, also at Fotokem, in dialogue with the Conner Trust. Digital repairs were applied to sections of the original element that had been damaged, but in keeping with A MOVIE's construction as a work comprised of found and purchased sources, whose subject was cinema itself, printed-in dirt and damage tracing to the source elements was intentionally retained. Prior to scanning, the original A-roll of A MOVIE was damaged by another laboratory, resulting in the loss of a single frame of the number "4" appearing in one of the projection countdowns which Bruce Conner intentionally cut into the interior of the film. This frame was scanned from a 16mm positive projection print and digitally inserted into its appropriate place in the film to restore the work to its exact original frame sequence.

The original raw 4K scans were archived to hard drive and LTO 6 tape (no inventory number), and the final restored digital file was archived to hard drive and LTO 6 tape tape (no inventory number), and also output to 35mm BW dupe negative. (As of 7/28/2020, this dupe negative is vaulted at Fotokem and has no UCLA inventory number.)

The restored digital file DSM (DPX) was also used to strike an Apple ProRes 422 digital file, and a DCP, with copies owned by the Conner Trust/Kohn Gallery.

The restored 35mm digital picture negative was used alongside the restored 35mm mono track negative to make 35mm prints as follows:

> one Artist's Proof print for UCLA (no inventory number assigned yet)
> two Artist's Proof prints for CFT / Kohn Gallery, as circulation prints
> six prints as Limited Edition for sale by CFT / Kohn Gallery, per notes below

Sound

The sound source was a copy of the same original vinyl LP recording of Respighi's *Pines of Rome*, which Bruce Conner originally used to make the film. This was newly re-recorded from vinyl to digital file by Timoleon Wilkins, and the file was then digitally remastered at Audio Mechanics, using digital transfers of old 16mm prints as a reference, to evoke the qualities of Bruce Conner's original prints in high fidelity. Vinyl record noise was retained.

The remastered audio was output in multiple configurations:

1) restored 1.0 mono flat
2) restored 2.0 wide range mono (for optical recording drop 3 dB & encode SR)

3) restored 1.0 mono with Academy pre-emphasis

This was output to archival DVD-R and access DVD-R copies as listed below. The restored mono file with Academy pre-emphasis was used to create a 35mm restored mono track negative. (As of 7/28/2020, this track negative is vaulted at Fotokem and has no UCLA inventory number.)
The track negative was in turn used alongside the final restored 35mm dupe negative to strike 35mm prints per picture notes above. The restored audio file was also output alongside the restored picture to an Apple ProRes 422 file and DCP, per picture notes above.

Archival DVD-R and access DVD-R copies
M2245769—DVD-R. Unrestored: Mono Comp. Archival copy data DVD-R 23.98 fps. (multiple sources)
M2448669—DVD-R. Unrestored: Mono Comp. Access copy data DVD-R 23.98. (multiple sources)

M245771—DVD-R. Restoration: Mono Comp. Archival copy data DVD-R 23.98 fps.
M245770—DVD-R. Restoration: Mono Comp. Access copy data DVD-R 24 fps.
M248668—DVD-R. Restoration: Mono Comp. Archival copy data DVD-R 23.98.
M248667—DVD-R. Restoration: Mono Comp. Access copy data DVD-R 23.98.

Digital Archive note

Many iterations of the final digital restoration have been created, and are maintained and logged by the Conner Trust.

Limited Edition notes

CROSSROADs was restored and digitally remastered in 2013 as a limited edition of six copies, plus two artist's proofs. Each edition consists of:

>   *LTO and RAID containing:*
>   *DSM 4K Cineon log files*
>   *ProRes files*
>   *restored audio files*
>   *DCP*
>   *35mm print*

Note that purchasers of the edition receive the DSM, but not the raw scans.

The first two editions have been sold, as follows:

    Edition # 1—Museum of Modern Art, New York / SF MoMA
    Edition # 2—Glenstone Museum

FUTURE USAGE NOTES

35mm prints are timed for future printing at Fotokem, targeted for gamma 2.6

16mm prints are timed for future printing at Fotokem, targeted for gamma 2.8.

2015-16 – It's All True exhibition

Original picture positive M83195 was used by Fotokem as the primary source to make 16mm A-wind dupe neg M250942. Due to damage in the original, a print struck from the 2000 Cinema Arts 16mm neg was used as the source for the first 27 feet of the film.

The restored digital file on DVD-R M245770 (which had originated from the original 1955 vinyl LP per above) was used by Gibbs Chapman to strike A-wind optical track neg M250941.

New 16mm dupe neg M250942 and new 16mm track neg M250941 were used by Fotokem to make prints for the It's All True exhibition.

IT'S ALL TRUE PRINTS:

About [10] additional prints were made for MoMA.

[Sixteen] 16mm looper prints were also made for MoMA, and [six] each for SF MoMA and the Reina Sofia Museum. One additional 16mm print was made for each of the three venues to use for theatrical exhibition. All prints Xenon balanced.

[Old notes indicate two sets of pic/track negs were originally planned for the It's All True exhibition, but only one was completed.]

Appendix 5

A Note on Sound

This short text might more appropriately be called "Some Notes on Sound," plural, but I've left it in this form to distinguish it from the similarly-titled teaching aids in Appendix #1, which are quite different. It might, even more appropriately, be called "Some Short Notes on Sound Along with Some Very Long Footnotes" because it's quite guilty of deserving that description. It was originally intended as an introduction, but that awkwardness suggested it was better placed here, at the conclusion of the book, inviting more avenues for future inquiry.

Cinema is the interaction of light and sound, but all too often in our field, discussion of the latter takes a back seat to the former. For better or worse, the same disproportionate relationship unfolds in these pages. This does not speak to their relative value. The same principles of technique, artistry, and subjectivity hold equally true for sound, but I find them a bit harder to discuss. Why is that?

One might look first to the way restoration has historically been approached by archives, in contrast with studios and the film industry. It's a bit of an oversimplification, but not entirely untrue to say that archival expectations lean toward a more conservative approach to sound. One should not, for example, replace or add sound effects, ambience, or music recordings. One should only clean up damage to a *physical print's* sound, such as dirt particles in an optical track, or systemic hiss and noise generated in downstream lab work, but not a film's production qualities. Equalization might be applied, but it would not be considered normal procedure to adjust internal audio levels between a film's scenes. The studios and those in the industrial side of the business, in contrast, have historically taken a more aggressive approach, doing not just the above, but conducting all manner of modernizations and "upgrades."

Despite this truism, the reality is much more complex than such a rough schema would have it. In the early years, I worried about backlash from more orthodox peers if they learned how the sausage was made. For example, archival ethics might have it that one should never, under any circumstance, correct out-of-sync dialogue in an independent film if the film was always that way. In point of fact such things might on occasion be done, pending context, and it's become increasingly common over time. (Living filmmakers almost always request it.) Which is not to say it should *always* be done. Merely that it's permissible, pending context.

Conversely, the studios have learned to incorporate some archival concerns which might seem more conservative. To offer an example from the picture realm, it was previously normal for the studios to heavily "de-grain" their digital restorations, in keeping with the notion that modern audiences expected crystal clear grainless images. Luckily, due to the work of insightful studio restorationists such as Grover Crisp at Sony, the archival and aesthetic value of film grain was gradually recognized and subsequently integrated into studio work. "Grain reduction" is a term now used less frequently in lab parlance; largely replaced by "grain management."

In sound work, these types of boundaries have long been floating and easily crossed, in both directions. After UCLA's restoration of John Cassavetes' *Shadows* was released in the early 2000s, a well-known scholar noted the clarity of the audio track and attributed it to Cassavetes' pioneering use of lavalier microphones, presuming that's the only way such clarity could have been achieved. My own research, including interviews with cast members, and just a superficial dive into microphone history, made clear that no lavs had been used, but they had tried snaking mic cables up a couple of cast members pants legs in a few scenes. Pants legs aside, the real reason for the restoration's clarity of dialogue was the careful audio work we conducted with John Polito at Audio Mechanics. Our work resulted in what might be described as a recovery of lost content. The film's lead actress, Lelia Goldoni, told me it was the first time she'd actually deciphered some of the dialogue since standing on the set. On the one hand we may have exceeded archival mores of the moment; on the other we were careful to honor the film's low-budget ethos at all times, never allowing the film to sound too "clean."[1]

If anything, tasteful *non*-intervention was what that restoration became known for. In the *Shadows* restoration featurette directed by my colleague Claire Didier, I stressed our respect for the film's low-budget origins so strongly that it had unintended effects. That short doc got widely seen, and I soon discovered that a generation of archivists began thinking that no cleanup should occur with low-budget films![2]

Before concluding this short note, I'll offer one last observation. As suggested, in my experience even "archival" restorations don't take a strictly orthodox approach to sound. I've frequently been involved in projects where a film's audio levels are adjusted to small degrees here and there, subtly changing the sound mix. It's just another of those issues about sound that, like sync, seems hard to talk about, but is commonly done. As it happens, I know of a recent project where this happened to a somewhat larger degree. That same project also added sound effects in parts of the film that previously had none. I was not involved in that, but can attest it was done tastefully, with the filmmaker's consent, and it's likely no one would ever notice. I've suggested such work be called a re-mix, in parallel to the picture equivalent of "digital remastering," but some (rightly or wrongly) consider that pejorative, and this project's sound work was ultimately labeled restoration.

At any rate, the project featuring the new audio work also attached a copyright to the release. I'm no legal expert, but the extent to which a restoration can claim copyright seems to depend on making the case that it (the restoration) has enough substantial differences from the "original" to deem it a new work. In this case, one might argue that the changes made are precisely their case for copyright.

Some might find it paradoxical. As Peter Bagrov of the George Eastman Museum humorously noted, "The real question is: How unethical must a film restoration be for it to be copyrighted?" A gentler way of phrasing it might be: is it still restoration? These things all speak to a slippage, or slippery slope between "restoration" and "remastering." In my mind, neither is a bad thing, and both have their place.

One could argue that the question is ultimately one of degree, and the point of distinction may always be changing. Thus this book, despite its deep dive into the issues, may leave one with the same question with which it begins. What is restoration?

In the end, restoration—of both sound and picture—is one of those words, like "art" or "freedom," that has no fixed meaning, because it can be stretched to mean almost anything one likes. The texts presented here, while focused primarily on picture work, do contain discussions of sound, which in their brevity hopefully speak to the larger world behind this small sampling. As with picture, ideas and approaches to audio work arise—but these approaches don't aspire to be programmatic doctrine, so much as living, flexible principles, floating in the gray zone between theory and practice.

Endnotes

1. It is now common for top-level audio restorationists such as John Polito of Audio Mechanics to log all notable "alterations" (such as sync repair) conducted. At the time of our work on *Shadows*, record-keeping was not as meticulous, but the kind of thing we may have done would be to *reduce*, rather than eliminate camera noise. A conservative "archival" approach would involve leaving all such noise intact as an artifact of production. A more liberal "studio / industry" approach would be to eliminate it entirely. Our intention was to honor *Shadows*' celebrated low-budget production history in feeling, while helping dialogue intelligibility, by balancing these approaches situationally, depending on the auditory source material and historical context of the work. In absence of a detailed work log twenty-four years later, I can't recall if we did reduce camera noise in *Shadows*, but it serves as an example of the kind of thing we were doing in such instances.
2. Related misunderstandings occur among educated, well-intentioned film viewers. An example—again from the picture side—might be found on some of the excellent DVD and BRD review sites. Oftentimes a restoration might be considered shoddy if dirt remains visible in it. Shoddy work may indeed be the cause, but two key pieces of information are missing in that assumption: a project's budget, and the condition of its sources. Cleanup usually bears a direct relationship to hours of work conducted, which in turn is tied to funds available. If an archive has a limited budget, and the only existing source for a project has been beaten to smithereens, have they done bad work by leaving some dirt in? I would counsel well-intentioned reviewers to explore such factors before assuming the worst.

    Another area of well-intentioned, intelligent misunderstanding is the subjectivity of laboratories. A few years ago, an insightful web columnist wrote a widely seen piece that called out some labs for imposing a "house style" on their work, whether it was appropriate for the film at hand or not. I was quite impressed by the writer's eye and awareness of such issues, but realized they may have had limited experience with labs. If they worked with labs regularly they'd know that such mandates would be not just unlikely, but virtually impossible to implement across workflows between multiple technicians. What I suspect the writer was seeing was a *colorist*'s personal signature, which I've witnessed many times. It's far more common to see "style" enter a lab's work unconsciously, as one or more strands within their cumulative production, through the eyes and ears of individuals within it.

In the case of sound, an interesting example of this lies in the work of an excellent audio engineer named Nick Bergh of Endpoint Audio, a contractor of both industry clients and archives. Nick has argued that an audio restoration should trace its source back not just to a film's original mix, but to its original field recordings; then re-mix them. In his view, this parallels a picture restoration's aim of going back to the original negative as a source. It's an interesting proposal to say the least. I would suggest that it's not exactly apples-to-apples, because a film's production workflows differ for sound and picture. Most notably, a picture's original physical negative is the actual film that's traditionally conformed to the final edit. In sound, a traditional historical production workflow would begin with ¼" field recordings, which were then transferred to 16mm or 35mm magnetic film and edited into multiple strands. The final edited strands would then be mixed into a single magnetic element, be it in 16mm or 35mm.

Nick's absolutely correct that this represents a generational loss not present in an original picture edit. However the preceding generations, in the case of sound, do not represent the finished film's *ur* element. That claim would fall to the mixdown. I can see where it makes sense from a purely technical standpoint to go back to the multi-strand edited mag workprints, if available, and then mix those to match the completed work's original sound balance, or at least something close to it. But to go back to the original field recordings would be, in essence, to re-make the film from scratch. (A hypothetical discussion of a similar strategy for picture work can be found in the case study of *The Times of Harvey Milk* presented earlier.)

A practical impediment to Nick's approach lies in the fact that the magnetic elements preceding the single-strand mixdown frequently no longer exist. A second practical impediment lies in the fact that the labor involved in re-making a film, or even re-mixing from multiple rolls of single-strand mag, is considerable and usually prohibitive; far beyond the resources of most archives to conduct or pay for. A notable case where Nick was actually able to follow his vision fully was Les Blank's *Burden of Dreams*. Blank himself was no longer alive, so Nick worked in collaboration with Blank's partner, editor and sound recordist Maureen Gosling and Blank's son Harrod, going all the way back to the original ¼" Nagra field recordings and also replacing the music. The result is in many ways stunning, but represents a dramatic change from the original film's sound. As one example, their version is 5.1 channels as opposed to the original mono. On the occasion I heard it, the theater volume was far too loud to my ear, making it hard to assess with certainty the actual dynamics of the new mix. My impression, compromised as it was by the playback volume, was that it sounded extremely impressive, but quite unlike a 16mm independent film of the era. It seemed to have a more modern sensibility. Good or bad? Most who have heard it loved it. Archival? I leave it to readers to make their own determination.

Presuming that Nick carries this approach to other projects, and knowing that he is sole proprietor of Endpoint, one might in this case genuinely ascribe a house style to a lab. This fascinating example, and the others mentioned above highlight the fundamental subjectivity at the heart of our work, and which runs as a continuing theme through the course of this book.

Bibliography

In addition to the texts presented here, we had originally discussed including a disc containing some video essays and illustrated lecture recordings that align with the book's concerns. In the end, that proved impractical, and a number of them are already available online, so they are merely listed here. As their web availability tends to change with time, the best place to find up-to-date information as to where one can access them would be: https://www.corpusfluxus.org/Pages/Essays_Lectures.html

I. POETICS

"A School of Seeing"
(Illustrated lecture on cinematic perception, originally presented at Hirshhorn Museum, Washington DC, 2012)

II. CASE STUDIES

a. "The Restoration of John Cassavetes' *Shadows*"
(short documentary originally included in Criterion DVD set, 2004)

b. "New Directions in Independent Film Restoration"
(illustrated lecture originally presented at Il Cinema Ritrovato, 2023)

III. HISTORIES

a) "In the Middle of the Nights: From Arthouse to Grindhouse and Back Again"
(video essay on J.L. Andersen's *Spring Night, Summer Night* originally produced for Flicker Alley / Indicator Media DVD, 2020)

b) "The Cropping of the Spectacle"
(video of live documentary on Emile de Antonio's *Point of Order!*, originally presented at REDCAT, 2010)

Index

4MC 98, 99, 104

Academy of Motion Picture Arts and Sciences xvi, xxi, xxiv, 75, 80-81, 86, 96, 100, 108, 111-112, 120, 124, 127, 130, 139-141, 146, 153, 255, 265, 302, 304-305, 314, 337, 339, 344, 348, 368, 417
Accidental Genius (Fine) 222
Ackerman, Jack 192, 207, 211, 215
A Critical Cinema 2 (MacDonald) 400
Actors Studio 195
Adair, Peter 97
Adams, Ansel 17, 21-22, 33, 36-37
Adler, Mortimer 278-289
After the Fall (Miller) 326, 328
Agee, James 139, 298, 302
Agfa 398
Ah Um (Mingus) 211, 223, 225-226
Alco Film Corporation 77-78, 80, 82, 86, 92
Alexie, Sherman 251
"Alice's Wonderland" (Mingue), 211, 224
Allen, Jennifer 359
Allen, Lewis 347, 349-350
Allen, Lisa 323
Allied Radio 254
All My Life (Bailie) 392-396, 399
Alternative Projections (James) 229
Altman, Kathryn 357
Altman, Robert 357-361
Amaradeva, W. D. 352
AMERICA IS WAITING (Conner) 415
American Cinematographer 401-402
American Documentary Films 331
American Film Institute 133, 168
A Midsummer Night's Dream (Reinhardt/Dieterle) 155
Ammiano, Tom 105
A MOVIE (Conner) 162, 413-419
Anarchists' Convention 366-367
Anders, Allison 299
Andersen, Fay 65, 67
Andersen, Thom 65-74, 247, 253, 296, 425
Anderson, Joseph 299, 308-311, 329
Andre, Carl 74
Andy Warhol Foundation for the Visual Arts 315
Anger, Kenneth 153-162, 403-412
Anker, Steve 6, 7, 392
Anna Christie (Brown) 92
Anthology Film Archives 275, 277, 281-3, 286, 287, 291, 293, 346, 404, 407, 411
Antin, Eleanor 147-148, 150-151
Antinov, Yevgeny 148, 149-151

Antoschewskaja, Galina 341
Anxiety of Influence, The (Bloom) 278, 293
A Penny From Heaven (Winkler) 93
Appelbaum, Larry 225
Arbelos Films 133, 138, 168-169, 178-179
Archer, Fred 17, 21-22, 33
Ardoin, Paul 262, 267, 271-272
A Regular Bouquet (Beymer) 164
Aristakisian, Artur 325, 341-4, 351
Aristotle 244
Arnheim, Rudolf xv - xxiv
Arrangement, The (Kazan) 314, 327
Art Center School 21
Artforum 55, 62, 107
Arthur, George K. 273,
Art Institute of Chicago xvii
Asphalt Jungle, The (Huston) 304
A Star is Born (Pierson) 119
Astro Labs xvi
A Thrill a Second 413
Atik, Anne 270-271
Audio Mechanics 28-29, 65, 95, 102, 107, 117, 121, 126-127, 133, 139, 141, 153, 163, 173, 178-179, 183, 186-187, 191, 229, 255, 308, 312-313, 315, 318, 337, 347, 349, 351, 354, 357, 361-362, 366, 370, 404, 406-408, 410-412, 417, 422-423
Austin, Jake 337, 370-371
Ayler, Edith 174

Babbitt, Milton 176
Bagley, Richard 302, 305
Bagrov, Peter 423
Bahrani, Ramin 296, 299-300
Baillie, Bruce 339-340, 392-395, 400
Baker, Sean 298-300, 323-324
Baldwin, James 222
Ballast (Hammer) 300
Balsam, Erika 282-283, 288, 293
Balzac, Honoré de 267
Barnacle Brothers 284, 293
Bartok, Dennis 163, 168
Basic Photography (Langford) 35
Bass, Saul 254
Bates, Kathy 358
Beatles, The 183, 399
Beatty, Warren 326
Beavers, Robert 336
Beckett, Samuel 192, 255-273, 333
Beck, Julian 216, 348, 360
Becky Sharp (Mamoulian) 186

Belasco, David 244
Below Dreams (Bradley) 300
Belson, Jordan 24
Beneath the Underdog (Mingus) 220, 222, 225, 227
Benjamin, Walter, 3-4, 7-9, 36, 41, 55-58, 291
Berg, Gretchen 350
Bergh, Nick 185, 187, 424
Berglund, Bo 75, 82-83, 92-93
Berkeley, George (Bishop) 61, 256-273
Berkeley in the Sixties (Kitchell) 331
Berlin Film Festival 320, 341
Berne, Josef 346
Beymer, Richard 163-171
Biberman, Herbert 296
Bicycle Thieves (De Sica) 296, 301
Big As Life: An American History of 8mm Films 3, 36, 56
Birdland 195-196
black box exhibition spaces 48-55, 60, 109, 117, 119, 286-287, 291
Blackhawk Bulletin 37
Blackhawk Films 37, 87, 92
Black, Karen 357-361
Black Panther Party 316
Black Saint and the Sinner Lady, The (Mingus) 223
Blackton, J. Stuart 67
Blade Runner (Scott) 20
Blake, Larry 185, 187-188
Bland, Edward 347
Blank, Harrod 424
Blank, Les 424
Blanton, Jimmy 205
Blauser, Brian 310
Blaze Starr Goes Nudist 311
Bless Their Little Hearts (Woodberry) 299, 310, 316, 318, 320-321
Block, Mitchell 348
Bloom, Harold 278, 292-293
Bochco, Joanna – See Frank, Joanna
Boden, Anna 298, 300
Body and Soul (Rossen) 296
Bonfanti, Antonella 312-313
Bonnie and Clyde (Penn) 326-327
Border Radio (Anders et al.) 299
Borders, Jillian 173-174, 185-186, 315
Borger, Lenny 351
Boston Globe 254
Bound For Glory (Ashby) 368
Bowser, Eileen 6, 36, 119
Bradford, Bobby 226
Bradley, Garret 298-300
Bragadóttir, Bryndis Petra 133, 135
Brakhage, Marilyn 275, 282-283
Brakhage Scrapbook, The (Brakhage) 400

Brakhage, Stan 27, 42- 43, 155, 260-262, 271, 275, 282-283, 285-286, 293, 399-400
Bray, Barbara 272
Brazil: A Report on Torture (de Antonio) 368
Brecht, Bertolt 62, 192
Brenner, Joseph 311
Bridge Over the River Kwai, The (Lean) 352
Briggs, John 104
British Film Institute 75, 90, 92, 173-174, 179, 215, 221, 226, 255, 265-266, 268, 273, 347, 349, 411
Brody, Richard 251, 253, 296, 297, 322
Bronstein, Mary 322
Bronstein, Ronald 296, 300, 322
Brother from Another Planet, The (Sayles) 367
Brownlow, Kevin xviii, 36, 75, 92-93
Brown, Sheila 155
Brown, Willie 105
Brunner, Borgna 251
Buchloh, Benjamin 51-52, 55-56
Bunker Hill 1956 (Mackenzie) 251
Burden of Dreams (Blank) 424
Burnett, Charles 25-30, 37, 174, 185-188, 295-299, 310, 313, 315-316, 318-321, 329
Burns, Ken 67
Burton, Richard 360
Burwood Pictures Corporation 92
Bushman (Schickele) 295, 312-313

Cahn, Iris 362, 364-365
California Institute of the Arts 174
Caligari (journal) 57
Campbell, Russell 399
Cannes Film Festival 134, 323, 349
Canyon Cinema 153, 394, 399, 404, 407
Carlin, Lynn 121, 226
Carnegie Museum of Art 275
Carney, Ray 126, 192, 194-195, 197, 204-206, 211, 214, 221-227
Carroll, Sidney 273
Carruthers, Ben 192-193, 195-196, 202, 209, 222, 306
Case, Brian 201, 212
Cassavetes, John xxiv, 24, 121-126, 191-226, 227-228, 244-245, 248, 253, 296, 298-299, 305-306, 311, 366, 422, 425
Cassavetes on Cassavetes (Carney) 126, 222-226, 228
Castellani, Renato 246
Castle Films 413
Casualties of War (Lang) 314
Cazale, John 174
CBS 331, 356
Century of Sound xviii, xxiv
Chambers, Paul 223
Chammah, Ronald 129
Chaplin, Charles 75-92

Chapman, Gibbs 419
Charity, Tom 194, 195, 212, 216, 226-227
Charles Laughton Directs The Night of the Hunter (Gitt) xxiv
Charles Mingus Presents Charles Mingus (Mingus) 216
Chekhov, Anton 353
Cher 358, 359
Cherry, Eugene 316
Chicago International Film Festival 121, 313, 360
Chicago Reader, The 105, 254
Chicago Sun 134
Chomont, Tom 325, 335-336
Chop Shop (Bahrani) 300
Christian Science Monitor, The 134
Churchill, Bob 254, 317
Chute, David 27, 38
Cinecittà Studios 246
Cinema 16 193, 217, 221
Cinema Arts 148, 415, 419
Cinema Conservancy 307
Cinema Guild 65
Cinema Preservation Alliance 150, 308, 313
Cinema Scope 225
Cinémathèque française 65, 158
Cinematograph 3, 36, 56
Cineric 346, 357
Cine Services 123
Cinetech 107, 111, 127, 129, 255
Citizen Kane (Welles) 101
Clapsaddle, Joseph 358
Clark, David Raymer 265- 266
Clarke, Shirley 227, 296, 299, 307, 315, 347-350, 362- 365
Claxton, William 192, 195-196
Clift, Montgomery 164
Clock, The (Marclay) 56
Clown, The (Mingus) 199, 223
Cocteau, Jean 157
Cohen, Fred 192, 224
Cohen, Mike 65, 67
Cohn, Roy 356
Coleman, Ornette 216-217, 227, 345, 362-365
Collette, Buddy 222
Collins, Barry 173-174, 176
Coltrane, John 223
Columbia Records 200, 212, 223, 226-227
Come Back, Africa (Rogosin) 306
Come Back to the 5 & Dime, Jimmy Dean, Jimmy Dean (Graczyk) 330, 357-361
Come Back to the 5 & Dime, Jimmy Dean, Jimmy Dean (Altman) 357-361
Complaints of a Dutiful Daughter (Hoffman) 105
Conheim, Peter 147, 150, 298-299, 308-309, 312

Connection, The (Gelber) 216, 307, 348
Connection, The (Clarke) 227, 307, 345, 347-350, 363
Conner, Bruce 107-120, 162, 171, 390, 391, 413-419
Conner Family Trust 107, 110, 112, 120, 413
Conquest of the Dry Zone (Peries) 352
"Conservation at a Crossroads" xxi, xxiv, 62, 108
Cool World, The (Clarke) 296, 299, 307, 315, 350, 363
Coplans, John 74
Coppola, Sofia 130
Corpus Fluxus xxiii, 163, 173, 179
Corso, Gregory 349
Cortez, Jayne 363
Corvinus, L. A. 46
Couffer, Jack 254, 304
Couzin, Dennis ix, xvi-xviii, 373, 398
Creative Film Society 159, 404
Crisp, Grover 422
Crist, Judith 304
Criterion xxiv, 95-96, 105, 121, 123, 126-127, 130-131, 139, 146, 185, 191, 224, 227, 318, 425
Crosse, Rupert 306
CROSSROADS (Conner) 107-120, 390
Curtis, Edward 232-233, 250, 252
Czech New Wave 296

Daarstad, Erik 229, 236, 241, 251-252, 254
Daddy Longlegs (Safdie Brothers) 322
Dallas Voice 357
Dance in the Sun (Graham) 348
Dancer in the Dark (Von Trier) 134
Dardenne Brothers 297
Dargis, Manohla 126
Darin, Bobby 221
Dassin, Jules 296
David Holzman's Diary (McBride) 348
Davis, Carl 93
Davis, Miles 198, 220-224, 226-227
Dawn to Dawn (Berne) 345-346
Day After Trinity, The (Else) 105, 331
Dean, Tacita 50, 283-284, 291
de Antonio, Emile 347, 354-356, 368, 425
Death of Naturalistic Photography, The (Emerson) 32-33, 38
Debut Label, The (Weiler) 225
Deitch, Donna 316
de Koenigswarter, Nica 192, 201, 223
Deluxe Labs 25, 349-350
Dennis, Sandy 358-361
De Palma, Brian 314
"Der Doppelgänger" (Schubert) 273
Deren, Maya 155, 157, 162, 268, 277
Descartes, René 3, 50, 255
Desert Hearts (Deitch) 316

De Sica, Vittorio 164, 246, 254, 296, 301, 305
Dichter, Lee 102, 105
Dickson/Vasu 67
Didier, Claire 422
Dieterle, William 155
Different Fur Music 111
Dinner at Eight (Cukor) 92
Direct Cinema 245-246, 253, 348, 356
Dissent (journal) 222
Dixon, Ivan 307
DJ Audio 95, 121, 126, 153, 185, 191, 347, 349, 351, 366, 404, 407, 410-411
Dolby 95, 102, 107, 111, 117, 119-120, 255, 405-406, 410-412
Dolphy, Eric 197, 205, 222
Doros, Dennis 28-29, 38, 147, 185, 229, 251, 295, 312, 315
Dorr-Dorynek, Diane 211, 224-226
Down Beat (magazine) 200, 222-223, 226-227
Downton Abbey 284
Draper, Fred 125
Drapkin, Andrew 133, 147, 150, 163, 173, 175, 179, 185, 187, 308, 312
Drasin, Dan 354
Draughtsman's Contract, The (Greenaway) 364
Dressler, Marie 75-92
Drew, Robert 253
Driffield, Vero Charles 13-14, 16-17, 31, 33-35, 38
Ducey, Maxine 354-355
Duchamp, Marcel 56
Dukakis, Olympia 174
Dunaway, Faye 174, 326-327
Duncan, Robert 354, 356
Dusty and Sweets McGee (Mutrux) 299, 310, 329

Eadweard Muybridge, Zoopraxographer (Andersen) 65-74
Early Abstractions (Smith) 399
Eastman, George 14
Ebert, Roger 140
Ecstasy (Machatý) 346
Edelman, Merle 251, 254
Eggers, Robert 138
Eisenstein, Sergei 258, 270
Electronic News Gathering 104
Elements of a Pictorial Photograph, The (Robinson) 36
Elevator to the Gallows (Malle) 222-227
Ellington, Duke 42, 197, 205, 223-224
Else, Jon 105
Emercan, Tülin 341
Emerson, Peter Henry 31-33, 38
Emile, Evelyn 272
Emma (Brown) 92
EMP Pop Conference 191

Empty Foxhole, The (Coleman) 363
Emshwiller, Ed 173-177
Endpoint Audio 65, 185, 424
En el Septimo Dia (McKay) 300
Engel, Morris 253, 296, 298, 307
Enticknap, Leo 93
Epitaph (Mingus) 223
Epstein, Robert 95-105
Eraserhead (Lynch) 313
Erwin, Lee 147, 150
Esquire (magazine) 222
Essential Cinema 281, 282-283
Evergreen Review 255, 333
Everson, Kevin Jerome 288
Exiles, The (Mackenzie) 229-255, 296-297, 299, 304-305, 310, 329
Experimental Cinema: The Film Reader (Dixon et al.) 43
Experimental Film Coalition Newsletter 398
Experimental Media Congress 41

Faber, Carolyn 141
Fables of Faubus (Mingus) 198
Faces (Cassavetes) 24, 121-126, 195, 197, 213-215, 311
Facets Multimedia 414-415
Fallon, Sharon 347, 350
Fantasy Records 225
Fantoma 153, 160, 162, 408, 411
Farnsworth, Sam 242
Feldman, Morton 270, 273
Festival des Films des Femmes de Montreal 134
Festival du Film Maudit 157
Festival du Nouveau Cinéma 357
Fierstein, Harvey 95, 105
Film and Its Techniques (Spottiswoode) 35, 38
Film as Art (Arnheim) xv, xxiii, xxiv
Film Culture (journal) 66, 271, 346
Film Foundation 75, 121, 126-128, 131, 133, 135, 153, 191, 255, 312-313, 334-335, 347, 349, 354, 357, 404, 407, 410-411
Film History 92
Filmmakers Newsletter 400
Film Parade, The (Blackton) 67
Film Quarterly 221, 247-248, 252, 254
Films and Filming 129, 306
Films Beget Films (Leyda) 103
Film (Schneider) 255-273, 333-334
Films du Pantheon Studio 407
Film Technology Company 25, 185, 186
Fine, Marshall 199, 222
Finnish Film Archive 175
FIPRESCI 205, 330
Fireworks (Anger) 153-162, 404-406
Fisher, Morgan 67

Fitzgerald, Ella 392, 395
Five Spot (club) 217, 363
Flaherty, Robert 246, 252, 311
Fleck, Ryan 298, 300
Flicker Alley 308, 425
Fonseka, Gamini 352
Foolish Wives (von Stroheim) 244
Force of Evil (Polonsky) 296
Forde Labs 399
Fossati, Giovanna xviii, xix, xx, xxiv, 9
Foster, Gloria 43, 307
Fotokem 25, 133, 137, 229, 255, 312, 315, 335, 337, 347, 349, 354, 362, 370, 406, 407, 410-411, 416-417, 419
Fox, Michael J. 314
Frank, Robert 161, 163, 193, 226, 252
Frank, Joanna 163, 165, 169, 170
Free Cell Block F, 'Tis Nazi USA (Mingus) 198
French New Wave 248, 296
French, Philip 223
Friend, Michael 108, 153, 404, 407, 410-411, 415
From Grain To Pixel (Fossati) xviii, xx - xxi, 9
Frontier Films 302
Frownland (Bronstein) 300, 322
Fuji 120, 180, 367, 397-398
Fuller, Buckminster 337, 364
Fuses (Schneemann) 335

Gaine, Ellen 5, 391
Gamperaliya (Peries) 351-353
Ganguly, Suranjan 43
Garland, Red 223
Garvin, Gregg 65, 130, 139, 191, 229, 370
Gates, William 139, 146
Gelber, Jack 217, 348
Gemini Films 129
Gentleman in Room 6, The (Hammid) 267-268, 273
George Eastman Museum 423
George Washington (Green) 300
Gerima, Merawi 299
Germany, Year Zero (Rossellini) 301
Get Back (Jackson) 183
Getty, Ann 273, 283, 291
Gibbons, Joe 5-6, 391-392
Giddins, Gary 198, 201, 222- 224, 226-227
Gilbert, Peter 139-140
Gillespie, Dizzy 307
Gimme Shelter (Maysles et al.) 331
Ginsberg, Allen 331, 340, 349
Giordiano, John 364
Gitt, Robert ix, xviii, xxii - xxiii, xxiv, 36, 58, 75, 186, 223, 254
Give Me A Riddle (Schickele) 313
Glass Menagerie, The (Williams) 346

Glass Shield, The (Burnett) 320
Gleeson, Patrick 107-108, 111, 118-120
Glenstone Museum 418
Goffman, Erving 201, 218, 223
Going Home (Robeson) 30
Goldman, Nancy xviii
Goldoni, Lelia 193, 195-197, 211-212, 221, 225, 306, 422
Goldsmith, Leo 253
Goldstein, Susan 104
Goldwasser, James 301, 303
Gontarski, Stan 255, 262, 270-273
Good Fight, The (Sills et al.) 331
Gordon, Nat 211
Gosling, Maureen 424
Gow, Gordon 129
GPO Film Unit 352
Graczyk, Ed 357-358, 360
Graham, Martha 348
Gray, Bradley Rust 299
Gray World, The (Loden) 327
"Gray Zone, The" xx - xxii, xxiv, 9, 13-39, 55, 57, 74, 120, 188, 318, 373
Greenaway, Peter 364
Green, David Gordon 298, 300
Gregor, Ulrich 341
Grey Area (Wali) 299, 316
Grierson, John 352
Griffithiana 8, 36, 119
Grimm Brothers 134
Grinko, Nikolai 34
Grove Press 262, 265, 271, 273, 333, 365
Gucci 128, 131
Guðmundsdóttir, Björk 133-134, 138
Guffanti Films 349
Guldin, Jere 75, 351
Gully, Nora 139, 141
Gunning, Tom 55
Guns of the Trees (Mekas) 349

Haden, Charlie 363
Haden, Denardo 362-363
Hadi, Shafi 192, 202, 206-208, 212, 215, 224-226
Hall, Larue 308-311
Hammer, Lance 298-300
Hammid, Alexander 162, 268
Hampton, John 75, 81, 92
Handy, John 226
Hansen, Skip 95, 366
Hanson, Dave 74
Hardman, Nate 321
Harper's (magazine) 231
Harvard Film Archive 9
Haskins, Harold 315
Havel, Václav 42, 43

Hayden, Julie 346
H.D. Trilogy (Jordan) 390
Hecht, Ben 346
Heefner, David 358
Heendeniya, Punya 352-353
Heffernan, John 173-175
Heimerdinger, Ted 308, 310
Heller, Amy 28-29, 147, 185, 229, 295, 312, 315
Helmholtz, Hermann von 38
Helter Skelter (Gries) 314
Hemenez, Ray xvii
Hendricks, Gorman 305
Hentoff, Nat 199, 211, 217, 222, 225
Heraclitus 169
Herrmann, Bernard 101
Hicks, Pea 337, 370
Higgins, Michael 127, 131, 328
Hiller, Lejaren 173, 176-178
Hindenburg Explodes! 413
Hirschberg, Lora 95, 102
Hirshhorn Museum 425
His Favorite Pastime (Chaplin) 93
History of Photography, The (Newhall) 35
Hitchcock, Alfred 101
Hitler, Adolf 267
Hittman, Eliza 300
Hobson/Lucas Family Foundation 312
Hoffman, Kathelin 362-365
Hoffmann, Abbie 333
Hoffmann, Deborah 105, 333
Hollywood Babylon (Anger) 156
Hollywood Film and Video 128
Hollywood Foreign Press Association 121, 126, 191, 357
Home Movie, The (Ishizuka and Zimmerman) 331
Hoop Dreams (James) 139-146
Horak, Jan Christopher 192, 251, 346
Hormel Collection 105
Horne, Stephen 86
Horse in Motion, The (Muybridge) 66, 72
Hubbard, Jim 335
Hudson Guild Theater 358
Hughes, Langston 199, 225, 316
Human Figure in Motion, The (Muybridge) 73
Humes, HL (Doc) 354
Hunt Brothers 363
Huppert, Isabelle 129
Hurd, Hugh 193, 212, 306
Hurter, Ferdinand 13-14, 16-17, 31, 33-35, 38
Hurwitz, Leo 252
Hyman, Adam 192, 229

I Am Curious Yellow (Sjöman) 311
Ich Bin Wanda (Raganelli) 130
IFC Films 27, 366

Il Cinema Ritrovato 163, 173, 178, 312, 425
Illiac Suite for String Quartet (Hiller) 176, 178
Illuminate Hollywood 133, 147-150, 163, 173, 175, 179, 185, 187, 308, 312-313
Illuminations (Benjamin) 8, 55
Image Entertainment 92
Images Festival 153
Image Transform 104
Immagine Ritrovata 305
In Between Days (Kim) 299
Independent Filmmaking (Lipton) 393, 399
Indicator Media 425
Innerview, The (Beymer) 163-171, 179
Instituto Moreira Salles 96
Intent of Undoing, The (Gontarski) 271, 273
International Documentary Association 139, 140
International Federation of Film Archives 175
In the Street (Agee et al.) 297, 298, 301, 302, 304
Invisible Cinema (Kubelka) 275, 287, 288, 291, 293
Isham, Mark 95, 101, 105
It's Impossible to Learn to Plow by Reading Books (Linklater) 300
It Sudses and Sudses and Sudses (Laverents) 338

Jabbok (Chomont) 336
Jackson, Benjamin. 252
Jackson, Peter 183
Jagger, Mick 156
James C. Hormel Gay and Lesbian Center 95, 98
James, David 229
James, Steve 139-146
Japanese Film (Ritchie) 310
Jayasena, Henry 352, 353
Jazz Composer's Workshop (Mingus) 216
Jazz on the Screen (Meeker) 226
Jazz Portraits (Hentoff) 225-226
Jeffes, Simon 179, 183
Jericho, Paul 296
Joachim, Marco and Larry 127, 131, 298, 326
Johnny Guitar (Ray) 304
Johnny Staccato 221
Johnson, Albert 221, 307, 313
Jones, Jennifer 164
Jones, Philly Joe 223
Jones, Shawn 107, 112, 116, 120, 127, 209, 211, 229, 255, 357, 362
Jordan, Fred 333, 364
Jordan, Ken 333, 364
Jordan, Larry 390, 413
Jost, Jon 179-181
Journal of Beckett Studies, The 255
Journal of Cinema and Media, The 293
Journal of Early Popular Visual Culture, The 75
Journal of Film Music, The 191

Journal of Film Preservation, The 3, 37, 119, 389, 401-402
Journal of the Society of Chemical Industry, The 35
Judd, Donald 74
Juilliard 174, 201
Jungle, The (Davis et al.) 299, 304, 315-317
Jung, Robert 104
Juniper Tree, The (Keene) 133-138, 162

Kael, Pauline 252, 280, 361
Kajdanovsky, Aleksandr 34
Kartemquin Films 139-144
Kass, Peter vi, 173-176
Kaufman, Boris 256-273
Kaufman, Robert 236, 254, 304
Kazan, Elia 127, 192, 299, 302, 314, 325-330, 357
Keaton, Buster 192
Keene, Nietzchka 133-138, 352
Kelley, Mark 323-324
Kelman, Ken 293
Keystone Studios 76, 77, 78, 79, 80, 82, 83, 87, 92
Killer of Sheep (Burnett) 25-30, 185-188, 295, 296, 299, 310, 313, 316, 318-321, 329
Killiam, Paul 92
Killing of a Chinese Bookie, The (Cassavetes) 195
Killsonic 226
Kilmer, Val 174
Kim, So Yong 296, 299
Kino International 34, 309
Kinsey, Alfred 153, 156-157, 162, 404
Kirk, Rahsaan Roland 197
Kiss Kiss Bang Bang (Kael) 252
Klawans, Stuart 123-124
Knepper, Jimmy 192, 201, 222-223
Knowles, Norm 251
Kodachrome 5, 8, 25-26, 53, 128, 371, 390-391, 395, 398-401
Kodak 5, 14, 15, 21, 26, 37, 128, 129, 346, 367, 389, 390, 395, 396, 397, 398, 400, 401
Koehler, Robert 323
Köhler, Wolfgang xv
Kohn Gallery 107, 110, 118, 417
Kops and Custards (Lahue and Brewster) 92
Korean Film Archive 13
Kovacs, Ernie 326, 327
Kramer, Edith xvii, xviii, 108, 341, 351
Krauss, Rosalind 50, 108, 119
Krim, Seymour 222
Kubelka, Peter 287, 291, 293
Kuchar, George and Mike 24
Kustom Kar Kommandos (Anger) 153, 155, 403, 411

Lachman, Ed xiii, 362, 364
Ladoni (Aristakisian) 342
Lady Chatterly's Lover (Lawrence) 157

Lamarr, Hedy 346
Lampert, Andrew 255
Lane, Burt 194-195, 197, 306
Lang, Daniel 314
Langford, M.J. 35
LA Rebellion 297, 317, 321
La Terra Trema (Visconti) 296
Latino (Wexler) 368
Laurenson, Pip 52, 56, 120
Laverents, Charlotte 337, 370
Laverents, Sid 25-26, 37, 337, 370-371
Leacock, Ricky 253, 354
Lean, David 352
Lee, Carl 227, 307, 350
Lent, Dean 299
Leslie, Alfred 193
Levey, Bert 82
Levitt, Helen 253-254, 298, 302-304
Levitt, William 303
Lewis Allen Productions 347
LeWitt, Sol 74
Leyda, Jay 103, 302, 303
Lianna (Sayles) 367
Library of Congress 72, 75, 225-226, 233, 307, 315, 320, 392
Lichtenstein, Roy 74
Lichtner, Marvin 192, 202-204, 206-208, 210, 220, 225
Lightbox Film Center 163, 165, 168, 173-174, 179
Lighthill, Stephen 325, 331, 332
Linklater, Richard 300
Lipton, Lenny 393, 399
Little Fugitive (Engel) 296, 298, 307
Living Theatre 216-217, 348
Loden, Barbara 127-132, 192, 295, 297-299, 310, 313-314, 325-330, 357-358
Loeb, Janice 298, 302-303
London International Film Festival 86, 93, 325, 354
London Symphony Orchestra 364
Lopez, Jose 354-355
Lorenz, Peter 22, 37
Los Angeles Examiner 92
Los Angeles Plays Itself (Anderson) 247, 253
Los Angeles Times 165
Love Objects (Chomont) 335
Lowry, John 88, 100, 104
Lucasfilm 313
Luckily Illuminate 150
Lumière Brothers 234
Lynch, David 313
Lynch, Susan 298, 313

MacArthur Foundation 320
MacDonald, Scott 288, 400
MacKenzie, Kent 229-254, 296-297, 299, 304, 310, 329

Maddow, Ben 246, 299, 302, 304
Maddox, Richard Leach 35
Madonna 130
Mailer, Norman 196, 221-222
Malcolm, Paul 295, 307
Malina, Judith 216, 348
Malle, Louis 223-224, 227
Maltz, Andy 140
Mandeville Special Collections Library 255, 257, 260, 271
Mann, Dore 322
Man Push Cart (Bahrani) 300
Manson, Charles 314
Man Without a World, The (Antin) 147-148
Marclay, Christian 56
Marcus, Millicent 296
Mariposa Group 97, 103
Markopolous, Gregory 336
Marley, John 121, 125, 226
Marriott, David 133, 163, 168, 173, 179
Marx, Fred 139-140
Marx, Karl 139, 140, 222, 224
Mass for the Dakota Sioux (Baillie) 339
Matewan (Sayles) 345, 366-369
Matthews, Steven 272
Maysles, Albert 253, 331, 354
McBride, Jim 348
McCarthy, Joseph 314, 355-356
McCay, Jim 298
McEndree, Maurice 121, 202
McKay, Jim 299, 300
McLean, Jackie 215, 227, 349
McPherson, Cameron 346
Medium Cool (Wexler) 349, 368
medium integrity xxiii, xxiv, 41, 49, 52, 55, 69, 108, 111, 135
Meeker, David 226
Mekas, Jonas 192, 214, 221, 226, 275, 277, 293, 347, 349
Méliès, Georges 89
Melton, Ruby 129, 293
Memoirs of an Angel (Baillie) 339
Mercadet (Balzac) 267
Meshes of the Afternoon (Deren/Hammid) 162, 268
Metaphors on Vision (Brakhage) 260
Metheny, Pat 363
Meyer, Mark-Paul 9, 10-11, 296
Meyers, Sidney 246, 253, 267, 270, 298-299, 302-305
Michael Kohn Gallery 107, 109, 118
Michel, Ed 225
Michelle aka *Sexy Gang* 311
Mickey Mouse 338
Mignot, Pierre 360-361

Milestone Films 26, 28, 147, 148-150, 185-186, 188, 227, 229, 247, 251, 255, 272-273, 305, 312-313, 315, 318-320, 334, 347, 362-363
Milk, Harvey xxi, xxiv, 95-105, 424
Miller, Franklin 297, 299, 308-309, 329
Miller, Warren 307
Min and Bill (Hill) 92
Minervini, Roberto 299, 300, 323-324
Mingus, Charles 121, 191-228, 305
Mingus (Reichman) 223,
Mingus, Sue 223, 225
Minh-ha, Trinh T. 345
Mirror Garden, The (Chomont) 336
Miss Jessica is Pregnant (Anderson) 311
Miss Olga's Massage Parlor 311
Modern VideoFilm 28, 65, 130, 139, 141, 185, 187
MoMA (Museum of Modern Art) 130
Monaco Film and Video 95, 104,191, 366-367, 415-416
Monet, Claude 74
MONGOLOID (Conner) 415
Monkees, The 67
Monroe, Marilyn 326, 328
Moog, Robert 119
Mooney, Jordan 24, 179-183
Moore, Kaycee 28, 37, 185, 319, 320, 321
Morrill, John 229, 238, 251-252, 254
Morris, Wesley 254
Moscone, George 97
Moscow Film Academy 344
Mosher, Adrian 123, 125-126
Mothlight (Brakhage) 286
Motion Picture News 78, 80, 93
Motisher, Lewis 393-394
Movie Journal (Mekas) 221
Movie Maker 338
Moving Image Review & Art Journal, The 293
Moving Image Technology (Enticknap) 93
Moving Image, The 13, 41, 55, 62, 120
Moving Picture World 36
Muhl, Edward 20
Müller, Matthias 288, 293
Multiple Sidosis (Laverents) 25-26, 37, 337, 370
Munch, Edward 322
Munroe, Tony 75, 121,126
Murnau, F. W. 148
Murphy (Beckett) 256, 258, 271
Murphy, Sara 299
Museum of Modern Art 3, 5, 35, 36, 56, 130, 301-302, 325, 354, 391, 418
Mutrux, Floyd 299, 310, 329
Mutual Films 96
Muybridge, Eadweard 65-74
"My Art is Better Than Your Art" (Lipman) 47, 276-293

My Brother's Wedding (Burnett) 299, 321
Myers, Sidney 267, 270
Myself When I am Real (Santoro) 222

Naked Eye, The (Stoumen) 67
Nance, Jack 313
Naples, Ron and Suzanne 163, 173-174, 179
Napolitan, Gina 272
Napolitano, Antonio 296-297
NASA 104
National Archives and Records Administration 111, 120
National Board of Review 302
National Film Preservation Foundation xvii, 75, 163, 165, 168, 229, 255, 315, 318, 334-335, 337, 346, 370, 407
National Film Registry, 370, 392
Nation, The (journal) 123, 323
Native Land (Hurwitz) 252
Naturalistic Photography for Students of the Art (Emerson) 33, 38
Negative, The (Adams) 36-37
Negri, Sabrina xx
Nelson Pereira dos Santos 296
Nesmith, Michael 67
Never Rarely Sometimes Always (Hittman) 299-300
New American Cinema 221, 296, 306, 347, 350
Newborn Jr., Phineas 192, 202-203
Newhall, Nancy 38
New Statesman 35
Newton, Huey 331
New Yorker Films 95, 354-355
New Yorker, The (magazine) 223, 251, 253, 296, 314, 322
New York Film Festival 311
New York Herald Tribune 304
New York (magazine) 359
New York Philharmonic 223
New York Times, The 119, 126, 296
New Zone System Manual, The (White et al.) 22, 37
Nichols, Mike 316, 360
Night People (radio show) 198, 199, 200, 218
Nightshift (Rose) 179-183
Nilsson, Rob 299, 323
Nin, Anaïs 156
Nixon, Mark 273
Nobody Knows My Name (Baldwin) 222
No Lies (Block) 348
Normand, Mabel 75, 86, 91
Northeast Historic Film 163, 165, 168
Northern Lights (Nilsson) 299
Northman, The (Eggers) 138
"Nostalgia in Times Square" (Mingue), 205, 211, 224
"Notes on Optical Printing" (Couzin) 373
Notfilm (Lipman) i, 192, 255, 272-273
Nothing But a Man (Roemer) 299, 307

Not I (Beckett) 269, 271
NT Picture & Sound 65, 107, 112, 116, 121, 126-127, 153, 229, 255, 308, 346, 354, 357, 361-362, 370, 404, 407, 410-412
Nunez, Victor 299

Oblivion (Chomont) 336
O' Hehir, Andrew 254
Okpokam, Paul 312-313
Olson, Sharol 65, 75, 121, 126, 153, 191, 315, 318
On the Bowery (Rogosin) 299, 302, 305-306
Opening Night (Cassavetes) 195, 214
Optimage 5-6, 391, 398
Origin of Film Music, The (Winkler) 86, 93
Orlovsky, Peter 349
Ornette: Made in America (Clarke) , 362-365
Other Side, The (Minervini) 300, 323-324
Our Song (McKay) 299
Oxford Filmmakers Corporation 315

Pacific Film Archive xvii, 108, 111, 153, 255, 312-313, 390, 392, 396, 410
Packard Humanities Institute 65, 308, 315, 318, 362, 370
Page, Jimmy 156, 394
Paik, Nam June 43
Palmer, Charles 231
Palmer Labs 104
Palms (Aristakisian) 341-344
Panic in Needle Park, The (Schaztberg) 299
Papp, Joseph 293
Parallaxis (Andersen) 74
Paramount Archives 357
Parapsychology of Everyday Life, The (Chomont) 335
Paraskeva, Anthony 266, 272-273
Paris Theater (New York) 192, 206, 225
Parker, Charlie 200
Parlour Pictures 127, 129
Parsifal (Baillie) 339
Parthenon Pictures 231
Pasadena Art Museum 74
Patchen, Kenneth 199
Patterson, Richard 401-402
Paul, Les 337
Peanuts (Schulz) 67
Pelletier, Louis 405
Penguin Café Orchestra 183
Pennebaker, D.A. 129-130, 253, 327, 354
Pennell, Eagle 299
Penn, Sean 314
Pentagon 111
Pereira dos Santos, Nelson 296
Perfect Films 126
Peries, Lester James 352-353

PERMIAN STRATA (Conner) 415
"Persistence of Revision, The" (Lipman) xv-xxiii, 147
Pesaro Film Festival 311
Peters, Pamela J. 251
Phases of the Moon (Chomont) 335
Philadelphia Magazine 315
Phipps, Steven 92
Photographic Society of America Journal, The 338
Photographic Theory for the Motion Picture Cameraman (Campbell) 399
Phylon (journal) 222
Physiological Optics (Helmholtz) 38
Physique Pictorial (magazine) 155
Pictorial Effect in Photography (Robinson) 38
Pierce, David 36, 75, 92, 346
Pines of Rome (Respighi) 159, 417
Pires, Jesse 163, 168, 173-174, 179
Pithecanthropus Erectus (Mingus) 216
Placing Movies (Rosenbaum) 105
Playboy 157, 221
Pocketbook, The (Woodberry) 299, 316
Pogorzelski, Mike 75, 139, 141
Point of Order! (de Antonio) 345, 354-356, 425
Pokotilow, David 205, 209
Polito, John 28, 30, 65, 95, 102, 107, 117, 121, 126-127, 133, 139, 153, 163, 173, 178-179, 183, 185-188, 191, 229, 255, 312, 318, 337, 347, 354, 357, 361-362, 366, 370, 422-423
Polonsky, Abraham 296
Popeye (Altman) 358
Portrait of Jason (Clarke) 350, 363
Posner, Bruce 346
Powell, Bud 198
Prayer For Passive Resistance (Mingus) 198
Praunheim, Rosa von 105
Priestley, Brian 201, 215, 217, 223-227
Prime Time 363-364
Prince, David 155, 310
"Principles of Film Restoration" (Bowser) 6, 36, 119
"Problems of Independent Film Preservation" (Lipman) xvii, xxiv, 3, 8, 37, 119, 389-402
Proferes, Nicholas 74, 127, 129-130, 185, 187, 314, 327-329, 424
Pryce, Charlotte xiii, xvii
Public Theater (New York) 293
Pull My Daisy (Leslie/Frank) 193
Punching Flowers (Gibbons) 6, 392

Quick Billy (Baillie) 339
Quiet One, The (Meyers) 296-298, 301-305

Rabbit's Moon (Anger) 153, 155, 407- 410, 412
Rabinowitz, Lauren 348
Railsback, Steve 314

Rapp, Douglass 310
Ray, Satyajit 296, 353
Ray, Tony 197, 205-206, 212, 225
Read, Paul 9, 10-11
REDCAT 425
Redd, Freddie 227, 349
Reel Thing Technical Symposium 65, 127, 153
Reese, Lloyd 179, 200, 223
Refn, Nicolas Winding 308
Reichardt, Kelly 296, 300, 322
Reichman, Thomas 223
Reid, Francis 95, 105
Reina Sofia Museum 419
Reinhardt, Max 155
Rekava (Peries) 352
Renzi, Maggie 366-367
Residue (Gerima) 299
Respighi, Ottorino 159, 160, 417
Restoration of John Cassavetes' Shadows, The (Didier) xxiv, 425
Restoration of Motion Picture Film (Read and Meyer) 9, 10
Return of the Secaucus Seven (Sayles) 367
Rheinshagen, Herman 200, 223
Richardson, F. H. 36
Richardson, John 38
Richmond, Dannie 192, 203-204, 206, 208, 225
Rider, The (Zhao) 300, 339-340
Riley, Terry 107-108, 111, 117-120
Rissient, Pierre 351
Ritchie, Donald 310
Roadside Picnic (Strugatsky) 38
Robeson, Paul 30
Robinson, Henry Peach 18, 36, 38
Rocco, Pat 100
Rockwell, John 363
Roctober 371
Roemer, Michael 299
Rogers, Shorty 221
Rogosin, Lionel 253, 299, 302, 305
Rolling Stones, The 331
Rome, Open City (Rossellini) 246, 296
Rosborn, Magnus 173, 176
Rosenbaum, Jonathan 101, 105, 192, 204-205, 214, 224- 226, 254, 304, 330
Rosenberg, Henry 355
Rose, Robina 179-183
Rose, Walt 25, 179-181, 229, 337, 347
Rossellini, Roberto 246, 296, 301
Rossen, Robert 296, 307
Rosset, Barney 255-259, 265, 272-273, 325, 333
Rotterdam Film Festival 204
Rouge 191
Rowlands, Gena 121, 125, 195, 214, 226

Ruban, Al 121, 124-126, 192, 214
Rubin, Jerry 331
Ruby in Paradise (Nunez) 299
Ruitenbach, Jason 133, 147, 150, 163, 173, 179, 185
Ruppel, Wolfgang 140
Rural Route Festival 309
Rushton, Josh 315, 354
Russell, George 226-227
Russell, Luis 28
Rutan Jr., Paul 75, 121, 126
Ryzik, Melina 119

Sacred Physics (Corvinus) 46
Sad Lover Blues (Russell) 28-29
Safdie Brothers 322
Salinger, J. D. 339
Salt of the Earth (Biberman) 296
Salver, Ray 305
Samuel Beckett's Library (Van Hulle/Nixon) 272
Sandcastle 5 Productions 357
Sanders, Henry 28, 37, 185, 319, 320
San Francisco Cinematheque 3, 5-6, 36, 56, 391-392
San Francisco International Film Festival 341
San Francisco Museum of Modern Art 418-419
San Francisco Public Library 98, 104
Santoro, Gene 202-203, 221, 223, 225-226
Santvoord, Peggy 174
Saturday Morning (Mackenzie) 254
Savage Eye, The (Strick et al.) 246, 254, 299, 302, 304-305
Sayles, John 27, 366-369
Scared Straight (Shapiro) 316
Schatzberg, Jerry 299
Scheuchzer, J. J. 46
Schickele, David 295, 312-313
Schmiechen, Richard 95, 97, 105
Schneemann, Carolee 335
Schneider, Alan 255-273
Schrader, Paul 280-281, 286, 292
Schuller, Gunther 223
Schwan, Valerie 229
Schwartz, Jay 315, 317
Scorpio Rising (Anger) 153, 155, 403, 410-411
Scorsese, Martin 311
Scott, A. O. 296, 297, 322
Scott, Ridley 20
Scoundrel, The (Hecht) 346
Scream, The (Munch) 322
Sculpting in Time (Tarkovsky) xxiv, 39
Seale, Bobby 331
Seeing Red (Klein and Reichert) 331
Sellars, Randolph 133-138
Sembène, Ousmane 296
Sennett, Mack 75, 77, 92

Several Friends (Burnett) 299, 316, 321
Shadows (Cassavetes) xxiv, 121-124, 191-227, 245, 296, 299, 305-306, 309, 366, 422-423, 425
Shank, Bud 192, 220
Sharits, Paul 283
Shaw, Sam 192, 199
Shepard, David 37, 75, 92, 162
Shepherd, Jean 198-200, 212, 217, 227
Shuster, Harry 128, 327
Sid Saga, The (Laverents) 337, 345, 370-371
Sigal, Clancy 303
Sight and Sound 92, 305, 308, 318, 330
Silberman, Lawrence 251
Silent Movie Theater 81
Silva, Michelle 107, 112, 117-119, 413
Sims, George 121, 124
Sinatra, Frank 225
Siskel & Ebert 140
Sitney, P. Adams 157, 162, 217, 227, 275, 277-278, 280, 283, 293, 410
Situationist Internationale 51
Skies of America (Coleman) 364
Skyscraper (Clarke) 348
Skywalker Sound 95, 102
Sloper, Amy 28, 133-138, 337
Smerdon, Scott 95, 366, 367
Smith, Harry 399
Smith, Jack 24, 171
Snow, C. P. 16, 34-36
Snow, Michael 41-42
Society of Cinema and Media Studies xx
Society of Motion Picture and Television Engineers 153
Solonitsyn, Anatoli 34
Song of Ceylon (Wright) 352
Songs My Brothers Taught Me (Zhao) 299-300
Song With Orange (Mingus) 225-226
Song X (Coleman/Metheny) 363
Sons and Daughters (Lighthill) 331
Sontag, Susan 311
Sony 226, 422
Sosin, Donald 147, 150
Soto, Algenis Perez 299
Sound One 95, 102
Spielberg, Steven 170
Spills and Thrills 413
Splendor in the Grass (Kazan) 326
Spottiswoode, Raymond 35, 38
Spring Night, Summer Night (Anderson/Miller) 297, 299, 308-311, 329, 425
Stalker (Tarkovsky) 30, 33-34, 38-39
Stanbury, Patrick 93
Stanford, Leland 66, 72
Stanford Theatre Film Laboratory 65, 308, 315, 318, 351, 354, 362, 370

Stanislavski, Konstantin 195, 306
Stark, Scott 5-6, 391
Star Wars (Lucas) 102
Stauffacher, Frank 161
Steele, Wilbur Daniel 310
Stern, Seymour 346
Stevens, Leith 220
Stewart, Jacqueline 319
Stifel, Art 310
Stigma (Goffman) 224
Sting, The (Hill) 174
St. John, Jashaun 299
St. Louis Post Dispatch 134
Stoll, Jerry 331
Stone, Melinda 337, 370
Stop Cloning Around (Laverents) 338
Stop the Pounding Heart (Minervini) 323
Stoumen, Louis Clyde 67
Strand, Chick 392
Stranger Left No Card, The (Toye) 273
Strange Victory (Hurwitz) 334
Strange Weather (Ahwesh/Strosser) 299
Strasberg, Lee 195
Streible, Dan 354
Strick, Joseph 246, 299, 304
Stroheim, Erich von. 244-245
Students for a Democratic Society 368
Sufrin, Mark 305
Sugarcubes 134
Sundance 95, 99, 134, 139, 140-141, 144-145, 185, 191, 297, 320
Sunday (Drasin) 345, 354
Sunrise Foundation 147, 148
Svigals, Alicia 147, 150
Swedish Film Institute 173, 175-177
Sweet Toronto (Pennebaker) 130
Swiss Effects 95-99, 104-105

Talbot, Dan 354-356
Tangerine (Baker) 300, 323-324
Tao xviii, 46
Tarkovsky, Andrei xxii, xxiv, 33-34, 38-39, 341
Tate Modern 50, 56, 120
Taylor, Elizabeth 360
Taylor, Elyseo 318
TCM 130
Technical Aesthetics in the Preservation of Film Art (Lipman) xxiv, 3-8, 36, 56, 389
Technicolor 357
Telling Pictures 95, 104
Tell Them Who You Are (Wexler) 369
Telluride Film Festival 103
Tennyson, Alfred 356
TEN SECOND FILM (Conner) 415

Terminal Station (De Sica) 164
Theory of Film (Kracauer) 249
Thieves' Highway (Dassin) 296
This Bitter Earth (Washington) 28
Thom Andersen, Re-Zoopraxographer (Lipman) 65-74
Thomas, Kevin 165
Thompson, Donald 302, 303
Thomson Kathy 28, 29, 185
Threepenny Opera, The (Brecht and Weill) 62
Thrills on Wheels 413
Tillie's Nightmare (Sloane et al.) 86, 93
Tillie's Punctured Romance (Sennett) 75-93, 121
Time Based Media 47-48, 50, 60, 62, 120, 275, 282, 292
Time of the Heathen (Kass) 173-178
Times of Harvey Milk, The (Epstein) xxi, xxiv, 95-105, 424
Titicut Follies (Wiseman) 307
Too Late Blues (Cassavetes) 195, 220-221, 224, 227
Toronto Star 134
Touch of Evil (Welles) 20
Trachtenberg, Alan 36
Triage Motion Picture Services 75, 80, 86, 89, 121, 126, 153, 191, 335, 404, 407
Trier, Lars von 134
Troia International Film Festival 134
True Story of the Civil War, The (Stoumen) 67
Tucker, Dave 65, 75, 121, 126, 153, 191, 315, 318, 370
Turner Classic Movies 370
Twin Peaks (Lynch) 164
Two Cultures, The (Snow) 16, 35, 36
Tynan, Kenneth 348

UCLA Film & Television Archive xvii - xviii, 10-11, 13, 28, 58, 65-67, 74-75, 86, 90, 95-96, 99, 104-105, 107, 110-111, 118-121, 123, 126-129, 131, 134, 139, 141, 146, 153, 155, 159-160, 162, 173-174, 178, 185-186, 188, 191, 222, 225, 229, 247, 251, 254-255, 273, 295, 298-299, 308, 311, 315-316, 318-321, 325, 331-337, 346-347, 349, 351-355, 357, 362, 366-367, 370, 403-405, 407-413, 415-417, 422
Underground (de Antonio) 368
Unforgettable (Washington) 28-29, 188
Union Dues (Sayles) 369
Universal Studios 20, 366, 368
University of Illinois Champaign 173, 176-177
University of the Arts (Philadelphia) 163, 173-174, 179
Urtreger, René 224

Val (Scott/Poo) 174
Van de Mark, Dorothy 231
Van Dyke, Willard 311
Van Gogh, Vincent 293

Veil of Reality, The (Watts) xv
Venice Biennale 284, 293
Venice Film Festival 305, 330
Vertigo (Hitchcock) 101, 105
VGIK 258, 343
Video Arts 416
Village Voice, The 192, 221, 224, 309
Viola, Bill 50
Visconti, Luchino 296, 301
Visionary Film (Sitney) 162, 217, 227, 278
Visions of Jazz (Giddens) 222-223, 226-227
Visitors, The (Kazan) 299, 314, 329
Viva 364
Vogel, Amos 193, 221, 224
Voss, Kurt 299

Waiting for Godot (Beckett) 267
Waldron, Mal 307
Wali, Monona 298, 299, 315-316
Walker Arts Center 415
Wanda (Loden) 127-132, 295, 297, 299, 310, 313-314, 325-330
W.A. Palmer Films 393
Warhol, Andy 56, 74, 315, 364
Warnasurijya, Chandrani 351
Warnasurijya, Sanji 351
Warner Bros. 139, 141
Warrilow, David 266
Washington, Dinah 28, 188
Watts, Alan xv
WCAU TV 315
Weathermen 368
"Wednesday Night Prayer Meeting" (Mingus) 205-206, 209, 224
Weidenfeld, George 273
Weiler, Uwe 192, 225
Wein, George 200, 223
Weiss, David 163, 168
Welch, Joseph 356
Weller, Shane 273
Welles, Orson 20, 101
Wendy and Lucy (Reichardt) 300, 322
Wertheimer, Max xv
Western Canon, The (Bloom) 278
Western Cine 399
West Side Story (Spielberg) 170
West Side Story (Wise/Robbins) 164
Wexler, Haskell 254, 304, 348-349, 366-369
Wexler, Mark 369
Wexler, Simon 254
What You Gonna Do When the World's on Fire? (Minervini) 323
white cube exhibition spaces 48-54, 60, 109, 117, 134, 286-291

White, Dan 97, 99, 103
White, Minor 22, 37
White Negro, The (Mailer) 196, 219, 222
Whitney brothers 24, 95
Whole Shootin' Match, The (Pennell) 299
Who's Afraid of Virginia Woolf? (Nichols) 360, 368
Why Man Creates (Bass) 254
Wickramsinghe, Martin 351-352
Wild One, The (Benedek) 221
Wild River (Kazan) 326
Wilkins, Timoleon 415, 417
Wilson, Michael 296
Winkler, Max 86, 93
Winokur, Ken 86, 93
Wire (magazine) 201, 222, 225
Wisconsin Center for Film and Theater Research 133-135, 355
Wiseman, Frederick 307
Wizard of Oz, The (Fleming) 174
Woodberry, Billy 299, 310, 315-316, 318-321
Woods, James 314
Word Is Out: Stories of Some of Our Lives (Mariposa Group) 97, 103
Workers Film and Photo League 302
"Work of Art in the Age of Mechanical Reproduction, The" 4, 8, 36, 55
Works Progress Administration 302
Wright, Basil 318, 352
Wright, Cassandra 316

Young, Robert 298

Zakia, Richard 22, 37
Zanzibar Group, The 171
Zapruder, Abraham 337
Zavattini, Cesara 254
Zhao, Chloe 298, 300
Zipporah Films 307
Zone System (Adams) 21-23, 27

www.ingramcontent.com/pod-product-compliance
Lightning Source LLC
Chambersburg PA
CBHW081427070526
44586CB00020B/2508